MW00572864

Biographical Dictionary of
Professional Wrestling

ALSO BY HARRIS M. LENTZ, III

Obituaries in the Performing Arts, 1995:
Film, Television, Radio, Theatre, Dance,
Music, Cartoons and Pop Culture
(McFarland, 1996)

Obituaries in the Performing Arts, 1994:
Film, Television, Radio, Theatre, Dance,
Music, Cartoons and Pop Culture
(McFarland, 1996)

Western and Frontier Film and
Television Credits: 1903–1995
(2 vols., McFarland, 1996)

Heads of States and Governments: A Worldwide
Encyclopedia of Over 2,300 Leaders, 1945 through 1992
(McFarland, 1994)

Science Fiction, Horror & Fantasy Film and
Television Credits Supplement 2: Through 1993
(McFarland, 1994)

Science Fiction, Horror & Fantasy Film and
Television Credits Supplement 1: Through 1987
(McFarland, 1989)

Assassinations and Executions: An
Encyclopedia of Political Violence, 1865–1986
(McFarland, 1988)

Science Fiction, Horror & Fantasy
Film and Television Credits
(2 vols., McFarland, 1983)

BIOGRAPHICAL DICTIONARY OF PROFESSIONAL WRESTLING

Harris M. Lentz, III

McFarland & Company, Inc., Publishers
Jefferson, North Carolina, and London

Front cover: Lou Thesz.

British Library Cataloguing-in-Publication data are available

Library of Congress Cataloguing-in-Publication Data

Lentz, Harris M.
    Biographical dictionary of professional wrestling /
Harris M. Lentz, III.
      p.   cm.
    Includes index.
    ISBN 0-7864-0303-9 (case binding : 50# alkaline paper) ∞
    1. Wrestlers — Biography.   2. Wrestling — Encyclopedias.
I. Title.
    GV1196.A1L45   1997
    796.812'092'2 — dc21
[B]   96-46346
                                           CIP

Manufactured in the United States of America

Second printing, with corrections

*McFarland & Company, Inc., Publishers
Box 611, Jefferson, North Carolina 28640*

This book is dedicated to Madusa Miceli,
a great wrestler and gracious person

and to

Ron Crum, Bud Greene,
George Alsup, Doy L. Daniels, Jr.,
Fred Davis, and Mickey Alderson
for their interest and encouragement

Contents

Acknowledgments

Helene Lentz, Nikki & Jimmy Walker, Carla Clark, Madusa Miceli, Pat Tanaka, Terry Gordy, Eddie Marlin, Jerry Lawler, Robert Gibson, Bill Dundee, Jim Jamieson, Guy Coffey, Roddy Piper, Fred Davis, Bud Greene, Bill Rose, Eric Downey, the late Treach Phillips, Lance Russell, Bill Watts, Jimmy Hart, Jake Roberts, Rockin' Robin, Sputnik Monroe, Al Greene, Don Greene, Buddy Wayne, Corsica Joe, Billy Wicks, Jerry Jarrett, Wayne Farris, Bubba Rogers, Jimmy Valiant, Melinda Rentrop, Dr. W. Rentrop, Mike Harper, Bill Carlyn, Sid Cromwell, Bettye Dawson, Jeff Tackett, Steve Tackett, Rusty Tackett, Jason Bendall, Robin Greene, Tammie Caraway, Casey Jones, Mickey Alderson, Dale Warren, Ed & Mary Ann Kuespert, Louis & Vicki Berretta, Donnie Juengling, Drew Thompson, George & Leona Alsup, Mark & Nina Heffington, Anne & Monty Taylor, Doy L. Daniels, Jr., Mid-America Books, Comics and Collectibles, Memphis Comics and Records, Fred P. Gattas, Co., Memphis and Shelby County Public Library System, State Technical Institute Library, Memphis State Library and all my friends at Berretta's Spike and Rail.

Abbreviations

AWA	American Wrestling Association
CWA	Catch Wrestling Association
CWA	Continental Wrestling Association
CWUSA	Championship Wrestling USA
EMLL	Empresa Mexican de la Lucha Libre
FMW	Frontier Martial Arts
GWA	Global Wrestling Alliance
ICW	International Championship Wrestling
IWA	International Wrestling Alliance
IWE	International Wrestling Enterprise
JWA	Japan Wrestling Association
LPWA	Ladies Professional Wrestling Association
MSCW	Mid-States Championship Wrestling
MWA	Mid-Continental Wrestling Association
NEWA	New England Wrestling Association
NEWF	New England Wrestling Federation
NWA	National Wrestling Alliance
PWF	Professional Wrestling Federation
RWF	Renegade Wrestling Federation
SCW	Southwest Championship Wrestling
TWA	Tri-State Wrestling Association
UIW	Universal Independent Wrestling
USWA	United States Wrestling Association
WCCW	West Coast Championship Wrestling
WCW	World Championship Wrestling
WCWA	West Coast Wrestling Alliance
WWA	World Wrestling Association
WWC	World Wrestling Council
WWWA	World Wide Wrestling Alliance
WWWF	World Wide Wrestling Federation
WWF	World Wrestling Federation

Introduction

Wrestling is the world's oldest sport, likely dating back thousands of years to the time of the caveman. The ancient Greeks practiced a style of no-holds-barred wrestling called pancration until 900 B.C., when King Theseus of Athens tightened the rules to eliminate the more violent aspects of the competition. Following the Roman conquest, the Roman form of grappling was combined with that of the Greeks to create Greco-Roman wrestling. The basic rules of that style of grappling remain constant today in amateur bouts and Olympic competition. No holds are permitted below the waist and numerous rules dictate this particular style, which is quite different from professional wrestling. Wrestling remained a popular sport throughout Europe and the British Isles. In the 16th and 17th centuries competitions between wrestlers of various nations often took place before an audience that included kings and other royals. Wrestling has also long been popular in Japan, where a form of the sport called sumo evolved. The city of Kyoto, Japan, is a leading claimant to the title of the "birthplace of Japanese wrestling" in approximately 29 B.C. Judo and other forms of martial arts also evolved from the Japanese style of wrestling.

Wrestling's popularity spread to the United States, where the Greco-Roman style was initially practiced. A more free style of competition developed in the 19th century, largely springing from carnivals and fairs, where local men would challenge the carnival champ. Free-style wrestling proved to be a faster-paced and more entertaining sport to the general public, and the popularity of the Greco-Roman style diminished. Numerous wrestlers throughout the country were self-proclaimed world champions around the turn of the century. An early championship bout pitted ring tactician Frank Gotch against Ohio strongman Tom Jenkins in 1904. Following Gotch's victory a number of promoters around the country felt it necessary to form an alliance to designate an official champion. Gotch defeated George Hackenschmidt, another title claimant, in 1905 and was recognized as the first U.S. title holder. Wrestling's popularity remained steady through the 1920s and 1930s, with tag-team wrestling, where four competitors would pair off to grapple in the ring, being introduced in the late 1930s.

Wrestling's popularity greatly increased following World War II. Matches were promoted from large cities to small towns, with an ever growing number of competitors needed to fill the wrestling cards. The flamboyant style of wrestlers so common today was largely inspired by the ring antics of Gorgeous George Wagner in the late 1940s. Gorgeous George dyed his long hair blonde, wore gaudy robes and was accompanied by a perfume-spraying valet to the ring. He became the man America loved to hate as television added a new dimension to wrestling's growing popularity.

Five leading promoters met to form a stronger wrestling association in 1948, when they joined forces as the National Wrestling Alliance (NWA). The purpose of this alliance was to reestablish a national champion and to help insure that promoters in various wrestling territories did not engage in unfair competition. Leading contenders were parceled out to the various regions to ensure that quality wrestling was available throughout the country. The NWA expanded to represent promotions not only in the United States, but Canada, Australia, Japan and Europe as well. A schism developed in the NWA following Edouard Carpentier's defeat of Lou Thesz in a match in Chicago in June of 1957. Despite Carpentier's victory, rules prevented the title from being exchanged. A group of promoters disputed the ruling and recognized Carpentier as champion. He was defeated the following year by Verne Gagne. Gagne challenged NWA champion Pat O'Connor to a unification match in August of 1960, and when the NWA declined to accept the challenge, the American Wrestling Association (AWA) was formed with Gagne as its first champion. Another dispute developed following a match involving NWA champion Buddy Rogers and challenger Lou Thesz in January of 1963. Thesz defeated Rogers in a one-fall match and several New York promoters protested the exchange of a title belt on the basis of a single fall, as most championship bouts were best-two-out-of-three-falls at the time. The East Coast promoters formed the World Wide Wrestling Federation (WWWF), which recognized Rogers as their champion. That promotion became known as the World Wrestling Federation (WWF) in 1979. Besides a world heavyweight title, the major promotions have also recognized various other titles during their history. Tag-team titles, U.S. titles, intercontinental titles, TV titles, national titles, women's titles, midget titles, 3-man titles, brass knucks titles, and numerous other championships have been, and in some cases still are, recognized by the major promotions. A plethora of regional titles have also existed throughout wrestling's history.

Wrestling experienced another surge of popularity in the early 1980s, largely due to the efforts of the WWF's Hulk Hogan and Vince McMahon. Mainstream audiences flocked to the spectacle of rock 'n' wrestling, with media stars Mr. T and Cyndi Lauper in the ring with such wrestlers as Hogan, Wendi Richter and Roddy Piper. Cable television added another element to the public's fascination with wrestling, as major matches from throughout the country could be seen in every small town. Pay-per-view also added revenue to the coffers of the major promotions.

Various promotions have come and gone in the past several decades, with the AWA folding its tent in late 1990. The NWA largely evolved into the current World Championship Wrestling (WCW), owned by media magnate Ted Turner, in 1991. Larger regional promotions such as World Class, Global, Smoky Mountain, Calgary Stampede and Pacific Northwest have either folded or been absorbed by larger promotions. Others, such as the United States Wrestling Association (USWA) and Extreme Championship Wrestling (ECW), continue to survive into the mid-1990s.

Though professional wrestling is largely dismissed or ignored by the mainstream sports writers and magazines, its popularity is undeniable. The competitors in wrestling are undoubtedly gifted athletes and showmen, and few of its fans are overly concerned with whether pro wrestling is a legitimate sport. They are content that it is exciting and entertaining. Many of the wrestlers in this volume have excelled in athletic competition outside the squared circle. Football legends Bronco Nagurski and Joe Savoldi, boxers Tony Galento and Primo Carnera, and Olympic champions Ken Paterna and Brad Rheingans have all made their mark in the wrestling world. Many of the leading grapplers have also gone on to success in films, as the credits of Woody Strode, Mike Mazurki, Hard Boiled Haggerty, Prof. Toru Tanaka, Harold Sakata, Andre the Giant, Hulk Hogan, Jesse Ventura and Roddy Piper will attest.

The purpose of this volume is to recognize many of the thousands of men and women who have engaged in professional wrestling in the 20th century. The scope of the book leans heavily towards grapplers who have competed in the United States, though most major Japanese, Mexican and European figures are included. It would be impossible to list everyone who has ever set foot in the wrestling ring, but I have tried to include all the major competitors and title holders from most regions. I have pored through nearly a century of newspaper reports, arena cards and wrestling magazines, and picked the brains of numerous promoters and wrestlers, past and present, to compile this information. Royal Duncan and Gary Will's *Wrestling Title Histories* (7600 N. Galena Rd., Peoria IL 61615) was extremely helpful in tracking down obscure regional titles. Another very helpful source of information on current activities in the wrestling world is Wade Keller's *Pro Wrestling Torch* newsletter (P.O. Box 201844, Minneapolis MN 55420). Of the current newsstand magazines dedicated to the sport, *Pro Wrestling Illustrated* provided the most useful information.

Each wrestler is listed in alphabetical order under the name by which he was best known, with cross-references from real name, other ring names and tag team names. It is sometimes difficult to determine exactly which wrestler was competing under a mask at a given time. There have been dozens of individuals who wrestled as Assassins, Medics and Interns over the years. I have attempted to indicate the major grapplers who competed under the masks when possible. The name is followed in parentheses by the wrestler's real name, date of birth, date of death, home town, height and weight, when such information could be determined. These data are as accurate as possible, though reliable information is often difficult, if not impossible, to obtain. One must rely on the statistics given by promoters or the wrestlers themselves. Adding height and weight and subtracting years, and sometimes even decades, is not an uncommon occurrence. The wrestler's hometown listing is the area that he claimed to wrestle from, though not necessarily where he is really from. I have indicated the wrestler's place of birth, when known, in the body of the entry. I have also included information on the areas and promotions the wrestlers were most active in, their various ring names, titles held, managers, tag team partners and major bouts. I have tried to indicate when a wrestler has other members of his family involved in the sport. In some cases, where non-related wrestlers competed in the ring as "brothers," I designate the family tie in quotation marks to indicate the likelihood that they are not really related.

Major managers and promoters and other individuals who made an important contribution to the sport have also been included in the listings.

I believe this to be the first comprehensive compilation of wrestlers past and present. Undoubtedly there will be errors and omissions, which I regret, and I welcome any corrections or comments for possible future editions.

The Wrestlers

A Team, The *see* Bass, Don & Rose, Bill

Abbott, Ace (b. 1916, d. 19??; Houston, Texas; 5'8", 194 lbs.) began wrestling in the late 1930s. Despite his small size, he remained a leading mat star through the 1950s.

Abdul the Turk (Turkey; 225 lbs.) was a leading wrestling villain from the 1930s through the 1950s.

Abdullah the Butcher (Larry Shreeve; Khartoum, the Sudan; b. November 2, 1936; 6'1", 360 lbs.) began wrestling in 1958. With his huge size and penchant for using foreign objects in the ring, he quickly gained a reputation as one of the most violent competitors in wrestling. He teamed with Jerry Graham to hold the Canadian Tag Team Title in October of 1967. He held the AWA Title in Montreal, Canada, several times in 1969. He held the Stampede North American Title in Calgary, Canada, several times in 1970, and held the NWA Cleveland/Buffalo title in 1972. He wrestled in New Zealand in 1974, holding the British Empire Title there. He held the NWA U.S. Title and the NWA Georgia Title for several months in early 1975. Abdullah held the NWA TV Title in early 1977. He captured the WWC Universal Title in Puerto Rico in July of 1982. He held the Canadian International Title in Montreal in February of 1987. He was a frequent competitor in NWA/WCW in the 1980s. He recaptured the WWC Universal Title in Puerto Rico in March of 1990. He began wrestling with All-Japan in September of 1990. He also wrestled in the WCW in the early 1990s, where he engaged in a brutal feud with Cactus Jack.

Abdullah the Great teamed with Sheik Ali Hassan to briefly hold the WWA Tag Team Title in June of 1982. He again held the title, wrestling with Jerry Valiant, in 1983. He teamed with Roger Kirby as the Sheiks to capture the NWA Central States Tag Team Title in July of 1983.

Abell, Carl (Cleveland, Ohio) played football with Ohio State and was a national YMCA wrestling champion before becoming a professional wrestler. He was a leading contender in the 1940s and 1950s.

Abrams, Lou *see* Gordon, Ace

Abughdadien *see* Dien, Abbuda

Ace, Johnny (John Laurinaitis; b. July 31, 1965; San Bernardino, California; 6'3", 250 lbs.) began wrestling in 1987 as the flagbearer for the Sheepherders. He and Shane Douglas formed the Dynamic Dudes in 1989. Ace was the first champion of ICWA in Florida in December of 1991. He began wrestling with All-Japan in 1992. He is the brother of the Terminator and Road Warrior Animal.

Acelinger, Richard *see* Slinger, Richard

Aceves, Roberto *see* Bonales, Bobby

Ackles, Kenneth V. (b. 1912, d. November 5, 1986; Santa Monica, California; 5'11", 215 lbs.) was a native of Nova Scotia and raised in Boston, Massachusetts. He was a popular wrestler from the late 1930s, and was known in the ring for his use of the abdominal stretch wrestling maneuver. He retired from the ring in the 1950s to concentrate on a career as a film actor and stuntman. He appeared in several films including *Bodyhold* (1950), *Li'l Abner* (1959), *Death Wish* (1974) and *Night of the Juggler* (1980). He also appeared in the television soap operas *Edge of Night* and *Guiding Light*. He died of a stroke in a Houston, Texas, hospital on November 5, 1986.

Acocella, Gabriel *see* Britton, Jack

Adams, Bryan *see* Crush

Adams, Chris (b. February 10, 1955; Stratford, England; 6'1", 228 lbs.) began wrestling in 1978. He teamed with Tom Prichard to hold the NWA Americas Tag Team Title in Los Angeles in February of 1981. The British mat star was known as Gentleman Chris Adams in the World Class promotion in Texas in the early 1980s. He won the World Class Championship several times in 1983 and 1984 in a series of matches against Jimmy Garvin. Adams was accompanied to the ring by Sunshine, Garvin's former valet, during the matches. He again held the World Class belt in early 1985, while managed by Gary Hart. He teamed with Gino Hernandez to hold the World Class American Tag Team Title several times in 1985. He captured the WCWA World Title in July of 1986. He was sentenced to three months in prison following an assault on an airline pilot in a flight from Puerto Rico to Texas in September of 1986, and was forced to relinquish the WCWA belt. He teamed with Terry Taylor to hold the UWF Tag Team Title in Oklahoma in February of 1987. Adams was married to Jeanie Clark and Toni Adams. He feuded with Brian Christopher in the USWA in late 1993 over Toni Adams. He captured the Global North American Title several times in 1993 and 1994, competing against King Parsons and Rod Price.

Adams, Toni feuded with Jeannie Clark, the ex-wife of Chris Adams, in 1990. She appeared as Miss Simpson, Brian Christopher's valet, in the USWA from July of 1993. Her appearance set up a feud between Christopher and Chris Adams, Toni's husband.

Adessky, Bob (b. 1918; Montreal, Canada; 6'2", 219 lbs.) began wrestling in the mid-1940s. He was a rough competitor in the ring through the 1950s.

Adidas, Brian (Dallas, Texas; 6'1", 238 lbs.) began wrestling in 1979. He teamed with Buddy Rose to hold the NWA Pacific Northwest Tag Team Title in August of 1983. He held the World Class Texas Title several times in 1985 and 1986, often competing against Gino Hernandez. He teamed with Al Madril to hold the World Class Tag Team Title in December of 1986. He again held the World Class tag belts in October of 1987, teaming with Frank Lancaster. He also competed in Global in Texas in the late 1980s.

Adkisson, Chris *see* Von Erich, Chris

Adkisson, David *see* Von Erich, David

Adkisson, Jack *see* Von Erich, Fritz

Adkisson, Kerry *see* Von Erich, Kerry

Adkisson, Kevin *see* Von Erich, Kevin

Adkisson, Mike *see* Von Erich, Mike

Adnan al-Kaissie, Sheik (5'10", 245) began wrestling in 1959 as the American Indian grappler Billy White Wolf. He teamed with Neff Maivia to hold the Hawaiian Tag Team Title in June of 1961. He held the NWA Pacific Northwest Title several times in the early 1960s. He held the U.S. Title in Honolulu in November of 1962. He teamed with Shag Thomas to capture the Pacific Northwest Tag Team Title in June of 1963. He held the NWA Texas Title in September of 1963. He regained the Pacific Northwest tag belts in August of 1964, teaming with Pepper Martin. He returned to Hawaii to regain the tag belts several times in the late 1960s, teaming with Peter Maivia and Jim Hady. He wrestled in the WWWF in the mid-1970s, teaming with Chief Jay Strongbow to capture the Tag Team Title in a tournament in December of 1976. He was injured by Ken Patera in August of 1977 and was forced to relinquish the title. He adopted the name of Arabic Sheik Adnan al-Kaissie and became a leading manager in the AWA in the 1980s. He managed the champion tag team of Ken Patera and Jerry Blackwell as the Sheiks in 1983 and 1984. He entered the WWF as General Adnan to manage Sgt. Slaughter in 1990.

Adonis, Adrian (Keith Franke; b. September 15, 1953, d. July 27, 1988; New York; 5'11", 312 lbs.) began wrestling in 1974. He held the NWA Americas Title in Los Angeles in May of 1977. He held the NWA Americas Tag Team Title several times in 1977, teaming with Black Gordman and Roddy Piper. He and Jesse Ventura teamed as the East-West Connection to take the AWA Tag Team Title in July of 1980. They retained the belts until their defeat by Jim Brunzell and Greg Gagne in June of 1981. Adonis captured the SCW World Title in May of 1983. He subsequently went to the WWF where he and Dick Murdoch teamed as the North-South Connection to win the WWF Tag Team Title from Rocky Johnson and Tony Atlas in November of 1983. They lost the title to Mike Rotundo and Barry Windham in Hartford, Connecticut, on January 21, 1985. During his later career in the WWF Adonis adopted an effeminate persona in the ring. He was killed in an automobile accident in Lewisporte, Newfoundland, Canada, with Pat Kelly and David McKigney on July 27, 1988.

Adonis, Terry teamed with Moondog Moretti to hold the Canadian Tag Team Title in May of 1981.

Afa (Afa Anoia; b. November 21; 6'1", 304 lbs.) began wrestling in 1973. He teamed with his brother, Sika, as the original Samoans. They held the Calgary Stampede International Tag Team Title several times in 1973. They held the NWA Florida Tag Team Title in June of 1973, and captured the Canadian Tag Team Title in November of 1973. They held the Southern Tag Team Title in 1977. Under the management of Lou Albano, they defeated Ivan Putski and Tito Santana for the WWF Tag Team Title in April of 1980. They lost the belts to Bob Backlund and Pedro Morales in August of 1980, but reclaimed them the following month in a tournament. They were defeated by Tony Garea and Rick Martel in November of 1980. Managed by Sonny King, the Samoans held the NWA National Tag Team Title in late 1982. They returned to the WWF championship in March of 1983, defeating Chief Jay and Jules Strongbow. They lost the title to Rocky Johnson and Tony Atlas in November of 1983. The Samoans left the WWF to wrestle in Louisiana, where they were managed by Ernie Ladd. They held the Mid-South belt before they turned on Ladd and joined Gen. Scandor Akbar's stable. Afa is the father of Samu, and managed the Headshrinkers in the WWF in the early 1990s.

Afflis, Michelle *see* Maxine, Miss

Afflis, Richard *see* Dick the Bruiser

Aguayo, Francisco "Charro" was a leading Mexican wrestler in the 1930s. He captured the Mexican National Heavyweight Title in June of 1934, holding the belt during much of the late 1930s.

Aguayo, Perro (Zacatecas, Mexico; 5'10", 215 lbs.) began wrestling in 1969. He is a leading Mexican wrestler who held the Mexican Middleweight Title several times in the 1970s. He also held the UWA Light Heavyweight Title in Mexico several times in the early 1980s. His son, Perro Aguayo, Jr., also wrestled professionally.

Akbar, Skandor (Beirut, Lebanon) teamed with Ox Baker to hold the NWA Georgia Tag Team Title in September of 1972. He held the MSWA North American Title for several months in early 1975. He teamed with Choi Sun to hold the U.S. Tag Team Title in Louisiana in early 1977. He became a leading wrestling manager in the Texas area in the 1980s and continued to manage in Global in the 1990s.

Akiyama, Jun (b. October 9, 1969; 5'11", 225 lbs.) began wrestling in October of 1992. He was trained by Kenta Kobashi and is a leading Japanese star with All-Japan.

Alaskan, The *see* York, Jay

Alaskans, The *see* York, Mike & Monte, Frank

Albano, Captain Lou began wrestling in Montreal, Canada, in 1953. He teamed with Tony Altimore as the Sicilians to hold the Midwest Tag Team Title in Chicago in June of 1961. They captured the WWWF U.S. Tag Team Title from Sprios Arion and Arnold Skoaland on July of 1967. They lost the title to Arion and Bruno Sammartino later in the month. Albano became a successful manager in the WWF during the 1970s. He managed Ivan Koloff when he held the WWWF Title in early 1971. He also managed many WWWF/WWF tag team champions including Mr. Fuji and Toru Tanaka, the Valiant Brothers, Blackjack Lanza and Blackjack Mulligan, the Executioners, the Yukon Lumberjacks, the Samoans, the Moondogs, Mike Rotundo and Barry Windham, and the British Bulldogs. Albano returned to the WWF in 1994 to manage the Headshrinkers, leading them to the tag team championship.

Albright, Gary (Billings, Montana; 6'4", 350 lbs.) began wrestling in 1985. He is a native of Montana who wrestled often in Canada. He wrestled as Vokkan Singh to captured the Calgary Stampede International Tag Team Title with Makhan Singh in December of 1988.

Alexander, Al (b. 1911; Brooklyn, New York; 5'9", 207 lbs.) wrestled out of Brooklyn, New York, and was the Army's wrestling champion in Europe during World War II. He remained a popular wrestler after the war and throughout the 1950s.

Alfonso, Bill was a referee in the ECW in the mid-1990s. He was also a villainous manager in the promotion, and accompanied Taz in his matches. Alfonso is the brother of David "the Cuban Assassin" Sierra.

Ali Baba (Harry Ekizian; b. 1903, d. 19??; Fresno, California; 5'5", 200 lbs.) was billed as a native of Bitlis, Turkey, and claimed to have entered the sport by wrestling bears in European circuses. He began wrestling professionally in the late 1920s. He defeated Dick Shikat for the World Heavyweight Title in Detroit, Michigan, on April 24, 1936. He was defeated for the title by Everett Marshall in November of 1936. He retired to Fresno, California, in the late 1940s, but subsequently emerged from retirement, wrestling Antonino Rocca in a major match in 1951. He again retired later in the 1950s to manage his California orange grove.

Ali Bey (b. 1916; Constantinople, Turkey; 5'6", 220 lbs.) was famed for his handlebar mustache and the Turkish garb he wore to the ring. He was known as "the Turkish Terror" and "Scourge of the Balkans" during the 1950s and 1960s. He held the EMLL Light-Heavyweight Title in August of 1963.

Ali Pasha (Assas Batros; d. 19??) wrestled in the Mid-South during the early 1950s. He was known for his cobra hold.

Allen, Terry *see* Magnum TA

Allen, Walter *see* Gorky, Soldat

Alls, Randy *see* Rose, Randy

Altimore, Tony wrestled with Lou Albano as the Sicilians to hold the Midwest Tag Team Title in Chicago in June of 1961. They captured the WWWF U.S. Tag Team Title from Spiros Arion and Arnold Skoaland in July of 1967. They were defeated for the belt later in the month by Arion and Bruno Sammartino.

Ambulakila, Elijah Akeem *see* Brown, Bad Leroy

American Dream, The *see* Rhodes, Dusty

American Force *see* Diamond, Paul & Michaels, Shawn

American Males, The *see* Bagwell, Marcus Alexander & Riggz, Scotty

American Starship *see* Spivey, Dan & Hall, Scott

Americus (Gus Schoenlein; d. 19??) was a leading wrestler in the early part of the century. He held the World Light Heavyweight Title in 1910.

Anaya, Cyclone (Jesus Anaya; b. 1914; Venezuela; 5'11, 210 lbs.) was a leading South American wrestler in the 1940s and 1950s. He held the NWA Texas Title in late 1952. He teamed with Gory Guerrero to hold the NWA Texas Tag Team Title in December of 1952. He held the

Southern Junior Heavyweight Title for several months in mid-1957. He teamed with Ramon Torres to hold the NWA World Tag Team Title in San Francisco several times in late 1957 and early 1958. He again held the Texas tag belts in December of 1959, teaming with Leo Garibaldi.

Anderson, Arn (Marty Lunde; b. September 20, 1957; Minneapolis, Minnesota; 6', 249 lbs.) began wrestling in January of 1982. He teamed with Jerry Stubbs, under the management of Sonny King, to hold the NWA Southeastern Tag Team Title several times in 1984. He was a member of the Four Horsemen in the NWA from the mid-1980s and teamed with Ole Anderson to hold the NWA National Tag Team Title in April of 1985. Arn Anderson won the NWA TV Title in a tournament in January of 1986. He held the belt until September of 1986. Anderson captured the NWA World Tag Team Title with fellow horseman Tully Blanchard in a match against the Rock 'n' Roll Express in September of 1987. They lost the belts to Barry Windham and Lex Luger in March of 1988, but regained the title the following month. They were again defeated for the title by the Midnight Express in September of 1988. Anderson and Blanchard entered the WWF in 1989 and, wrestling as the Brainbusters and managed by Bobby Heenan, they defeated Demolition for the WWF Tag Title in July of 1989. They lost the belts in a rematch against Demolition the following October. Anderson subsequently returned to the WCW and held the NWA Title several more times in the early 1990s. He also teamed with Larry Zbyszko as the Enforcers and won a tournament final over Rick Steiner and Bill Kazmaier to be the WCW World Tag Team Champions on September 5, 1991. They lost the belts to Rick Steamboat and Dustin Rhodes in November of 1991. Anderson teamed with Bobby Eaton as part of Paul E. Dangerously's Dangerous Alliance to retake the WCW tag belts on January 16, 1992. They were defeated for the title by Rick and Scott Steiner on May 3, 1992. Anderson joined the reformed Four Horseman in 1993, and teamed with Paul Roma to capture the tag belts on August 18, 1993. They were defeated for the belts by the Nasty Boys the following month on September 19, 1993. He remained a leading competitor in the WCW, often teaming with Ric Flair, through the mid-1990s. He defeated Johnny B. Badd for the WCW TV Title on January 8, 1995. He lost the belt to the Renegade on June 18, 1995.

Anderson, Brad (Minneapolis, Minnesota; 6'1", 220 lbs.) is the son of wrestler Gene Anderson. He began competing professionally in 1989. He wrestled in the WCW and Pacific Northwest. He teamed with Ricky Santana to hold the NWA Pacific Northwest Tag Team Title in February of 1991.

Anderson, Bryan is the son of Ole Anderson. He made his professional wrestling debut in the Smoky Mountain Wrestling league in October of 1994.

Anderson, Gene (b. 1933, d. October 31, 1991) teamed with Lars Anderson to hold the NWA Southern Tag Team Title in 1966. He was subsequently a member of the Minnesota Wrecking Crew tag team with Ole Anderson. The duo held the NWA Atlantic Coast Tag Title and NWA Georgia Tag Team Title several times in the early 1970s, and held NWA World Tag Team title four times in the mid-1970s. He also managed Ray Stevens when he held the tag title with Jimmy Snuka and Ivan Koloff in 1980 and 1981. Gene and Ole Anderson last captured the title in May of 1981 from Paul Jones and the Masked Superstar, holding the belts until Gene was injured in October of 1981. He is the father of Brad Anderson. He died of a heart attack in Huntersville, North Carolina, on October 31, 1991.

Anderson, Lars (Larry Heinemi) was a leading Midwest villain in the 1960s and 1970s. He teamed with Gene Anderson to hold the NWA Southern Tag Team Title in 1966. He teamed with Paul DeMarco to hold the NWA World Tag Team Title in San Francisco for several months from May of 1972. He briefly held the NWA Florida Title in 1977. Lars and Ole Anderson briefly held the NWA Georgia Tag Team Title in March of 1978. They again captured the belts in June of 1980. He held the Polynesian Pacific Title in Honolulu several times in 1985 and 1986.

Anderson, Ole (Al Rogowski; b. September 22; Minneapolis, Minnesota; 6'1", 256 lbs.) began wrestling in 1966. Wrestling as Rock Rogowski he held the Mid-West Tag Team Title in Omaha with the Claw and Ox Baker in 1971. He teamed with Ron Garvin to briefly hold the NWA Florida Tag Team Title in July of 1971. He held the NWA Eastern States Title in 1973. He often teamed with his "brother," Gene Anderson, as the Minnesota Wrecking Crew during the 1970s. The duo held the NWA Atlantic Coast Tag Title and the NWA Georgia Tag Team Title several times in the early 1970s, and held the NWA World Tag Team title four times in the mid-1970s. Anderson also held the NWA Georgia Tag Team title numerous times in the late 1970s, teaming with Gene Anderson, Jacques Goulet, Lars Anderson, Ivan Koloff, Ernie Ladd and Jerry Brisco. He and Gene Anderson last captured the NWA World Tag Team belts in May of 1981, defeating Paul Jones and the Masked Superstar. Gene Anderson was injured in October of 1981 and the belts were declared vacant the following December. Ole Anderson teamed with Stan Hansen to win a tournament for the NWA Eastern Tag Championship in February of 1982. He held the NWA National Tag Team Title for several months in early 1985, teaming with Thunderbolt Patterson and Arn Anderson. He was a member of the Four Horseman in the WCW during the 1980s. He retired from the ring in the late 1980s, but continued his involvement with wrestling as a promoter.

Anderson, Ox teamed with Killer Kowalski to hold the Pacific Coast Tag Team Title in Vancouver, Canada, in August of 1961.

Anderson, Samuel N *see* Newt the Brute

Andersson, Frank (Gothemberg, Sweden; 6'2", 245 lbs) began wrestling professionally in 1993. The Swedish native was a bronze medal winner in the 1984 Olympic games and a three-time Greco-Roman World champion. He entered the WCW briefly in 1994, before returning to Europe, where he often competes.

Andre the Giant (Andre Rene Roussimoff; May 19, 1946, d. January 29, 1993; 7'5", 520 lbs.) was born in Mollen, France. He exhibited unusual size at an early age and was over six feet tall by the age of 12. He began wrestling in Paris in 1964 as the Butcher and toured Japan in 1968. Edouard Carpentier brought Andre to North America in 1970 where he wrestled under such names as Jean Ferre, Monster Roussimoff, Monsieur Eiffel Tower and the French Giant. He began working for the WWF in 1973, where he became a star attraction. He won the Los Angeles Battle Royal in 1975. He teamed with Dusty Rhodes to hold the U.S. Tag Team Title in Louisiana in December of 1978. He again won the Los Angeles Battle Royal in 1980. He teamed with Dusty Rhodes to hold the NWA Florida Tag Team Title in February of 1981. He wrestled as the Giant Machine in the WCW. Usually a fan favorite, Andre wrestled as a villain in 1987, engaging in a feud with Hulk Hogan, whom he defeated for the WWF Title on February 5, 1988. The title was subsequently declared vacant when Andre turned it over to Ted DiBiase. He wrestled with Haku as the Colossal Connection and, under the management of

Bobby Heenan, defeated Demolition for the WWF Tag Team Title on December 13, 1989. They lost the belts back to Demolition at Wrestlemania VI on April 1, 1990. Andre's degenerative physical condition led to rare appearances in the ring in the early 1990s, though he remained an imposing figure in the WWF. Andre also appeared on television in such series as *The Six Million Dollar Man*, *B.J. and the Bear* and *The Incredible Hulk*, and had a featured role in the film *The Princess Bride* (1987). He died in his sleep of a heart attack in a Paris hotel on January 29, 1993, while in France to attend the funeral of his father.

Andrea the Giant *see* Baby Doll

Andrews, Ray teamed with Eric Pomeroy to hold the Southern Heavyweight Tag Team Title in December of 1962.

Andrews, Tom wrestled as the Claw to hold the Mid-West Title in Omaha in June of 1971. He also teamed with Ole Anderson to hold the Mid-West Tag Team Title in 1971. He teamed with Ron Starr to hold the NWA Central States Tag Team Title in July of 1978.

Angel, The *see* Morrell, Frank

Angel, Tommy (6'3", 255 lbs.) began wrestling in 1989. He has competed in independent leagues and the WCW.

Angel of Death (Dave Sheldon; Los Angeles, California; 6'5", 310 lbs.), who brings a trumpet to the ring, began wrestling in 1985. He was brought to the UWF by the Freebirds in 1987. He won the World Class Texas Title from Kerry Von Erich in a forfeit in July of 1990. He wrestled in Global in the early 1990s as the Angel.

Anibal (Ignacio Carlos Carillo; b. 1941, d. March 9, 1994) was a leading Mexican wrestler from the 1960s. He held the Mexican Middleweight Title several times in the early 1970s.

Animal (Joseph Laurinaitis; b. January 26, 1960; Chicago, Illinois; 6'5", 310 lbs.) was born in Minneapolis, Minnesota. He made his wrestling debut as the Road Warrior in Georgia Championship Wrestling in September of 1982. He continued to wrestle in the South and Midwest over the next several months as Joe Lauren. In 1983 he joined with Hawk and returned to Georgia as the Road Warriors. They quickly became the most popular team in the organization. Managed by Paul Ellering, they held the NWA National Tag Team Title several times in 1983 and 1984. They abandoned the NWA Title and moved to the AWA in July of 1984 and, on August 25, 1984, they defeated Baron von Raschke and the Crusher in Las Vegas for the AWA World Tag Team Title. They relinquished the title to Jim Garvin and Steven Regal in September of 1985. Later in 1985 the Road Warriors went to Japan to wrestle with All-Japan Wrestling, where they were again immensely popular. They returned to the NWA in 1986 and held the 6-Man Tag Team Title several times over the next few years. They captured the tag championship from the Midnight Express in October of 1988.

They retained the title until they relinquished the belts to Mike Rotundo and Steve Williams in April of 1989. They went to the WWF as the Legion of Doom in 1990 for a brief time, and in March of 1991 they returned to Japan. They returned to the WWF in August of 1991 and defeated the Nasty Boys for the WWF World Tag Team championship at New York's Madison Square Garden on August 26, 1991. They lost the title to Money Inc. in February of 1992. Animal remained in the WWF following Hawk's departure, and briefly teamed with Crush. He soon left the WWF as well, returning to Minnesota to recover from numerous minor injuries he had suffered over the years in the ring. He and Hawk reunited as the Road Warriors in WCW in late 1995. He is the brother of wrestlers Johnny Ace and Marc "Terminator" Laurianaitis.

Anoia, Afa *see* Afa

Anoia, Lloyd wrestled as the Tahitian Warrior in Puerto Rico. He teamed with Muhammad Hussein to hold the WWC Tag Team Title in June of 1994.

Anoia, Rodney *see* Yokozuna

Anoia, Sam wrestled as the third Samoan in the WWF in 1983, replacing an injured Sika in some tag team title matches.

Anthony, Mike (Calgary, Alberta, Canada; 5'10", 205 lbs.) teamed with Jeff Gaylord to hold the USWA Tag Team Title in November of 1993.

Anthony, Scott (6'1", 235 lbs.) began wrestling in 1988. He is a three time Pacific Northwest champion formerly known as Scotty the Body.

Anthony, Tony (b. April 12; Bucksnort, Tennessee; 6'1", 235 lbs.) began wrestling in 1977. He teamed with Len Denton as the Grapplers to capture the Southern Tag Team Title in August of 1983. They also held the NWA Central States Tag Team Title in April of 1984. He wrestled as the Dirty White Boy and is managed by his valet, Dirty White Girl Kimberly. He held the Alabama Title several times in 1986. He captured the USWA Southern Title in a tournament in October of 1989. He teamed with Tom Burton to hold the USWA Tag Team Title in June of 1990. He again held the tag belts several times in late 1990, teaming with Doug Gilbert. He subsequently went to Smoky Mountain Wrestling, where he held the championship several times from 1992 through 1994.

Antol, Scott *see* Riggz, Scott

Antone, Adele (b. 1929; Dayton, Ohio; 5'7", 138 lbs.) was born in Jacksonville, Florida. The aggressive competitor was known in the ring as the Nature Girl and was a leading female wrestler in the 1950s.

Apocalypse (6'4", 265 lbs.) began wrestling in 1987. He and Destruction formed the tag team the Blackharts under the management of Luna Vachon in the UWF.

Apollo, Otis (5'11", 243 lbs.) began wrestling in 1992. He teamed with Irish Bobby Clancy as Canadian Lightning. They held the Border City Wrestling Can-Am Tag Team Title in May of 1993, and the Global Tag Team Title from July of 1993 until March of 1994. Apollo and Clancy subsequently split, and engaged in a feud.

Apollo, Phil (5'10", 229 lbs.) began wrestling in 1986. He also wrestled as Vince Apollo. He teamed with Eric Sbracchia in the ICW and held the tag title in 1989. He wrestled with the New England Wrestling Association promotion in New Bedford in the early 1990s, holding the championship in February of 1993.

Apollo, Ray wrestled in the WWF as Doink the Clown when Matt Borne left the promotion in 1993.

Apollo, Vince *see* Apollo, Phil

Apollo, Vittorio "Argentina" (Vincente Denigris; d. August 2, 1984) was an acrobatic mat star in the 1950s and early 1960s. He teamed with Don McClarity to win the WWWF U.S. Tag Team Title from Chris and John Tolos in February of 1964. They were defeated for the belts by Jerry and Luke Graham in June of 1964. He teamed with Jose Lothario to hold the NWA Florida Tag Team Title from April until September of 1970. He teamed with Dick Steinborn to hold the NWA Georgia Tag Team Title in October of 1972. He left the promotion the following month to wrestle with Ann Gunkel's All South Championship Wrestling. He died on August 2, 1984.

Arakawa, Mitsu was a leading Japanese wrestler active from the 1950s. He teamed with Kinji Shibuya to hold the NWA World Tag Team Title in Minneapolis in August of 1957. He teamed with Mr. Moto to hold the Pacific Coast Tag Team Title in Vancouver, Canada, in March of 1961. He again teamed with Kinji Shibuya to hold the NWA World Tag Team Title in San Francisco in late 1961 and 1962. He and Shibuya to hold the Canadian Tag Team Title in March of 1963. Arakawa held the WWA championship for several months in the fall of 1967. He teamed with Dr. Moto to win the AWA Tag Team Title from Pat O'Connor and Wilbur Snyder in December of 1967. They were defeated by Crusher and Dick the Bruiser in December of 1968. They also held the WWA Tag Team belts in 1967 and 1968. He teamed with Toru Tanaka as the Rising Sons to hold the WWWF International Tag Team Title from June of 1969 until they relinquished the belts to Tony Marino and Victor Rivera later in the year.

Araya, Nobutaka wrestled with Takashi Okano as the Masters of the Orient in the USWA in 1994.

Arcidi, Ted (Boston, Massachusetts; 300 lbs) was a leading competitor in the World Class promotion in Texas in the mid-1980s. He held the World Class Texas Title in August of 1987.

Ardelean, Simeon "Sam" (b. 1927, d. February 1, 1986; 5'10", 235 lbs.) served in the Merchant Marines during World War II. He played with several Indiana football teams in the 1950s before becoming a professional wrestler. He shaved his head and grew a Fu Manchu mustache for his ring persona of the Mongol. He was a leading competitor throughout the United States and Japan during the 1960s. In 1972 Ardelean joined the U.S. Treasury Department as an agent for the Bureau of Customs. He died in a Munster, Indiana, hospital on February 1, 1986.

Arena, George (b. 1908, d. July 16, 1992) was born in Chicago and raised in Racine, Wisconsin. He began wrestling in 1936, and was the first of several mat stars to use the name Gorgeous George during his career. He continued to compete as Gorgeous George, usually wrestling in the Milwaukee and Chicago areas, through the mid-1950s. He later wrestled as Baron Arena. He retired from the ring in 1970. Arena died of bone cancer in Boca Raton, Florida, on July 16, 1992.

Arion, Spyron (b. 1941; Athens, Greece; 268 lbs.) was an amateur wrestling champion who competed in the 1960 Olympics in Rome. He began his professional career as a popular scientific wrestler. He held the IWA Championship in Australia in late 1965. He teamed with Antonio Pugliese to win the WWWF U.S. Tag Team Title from Baron Mikel Scicluna and Smasher Sloan in December of 1966. He teamed with Arnold Skoaland when Pugliese left the WWWF and they lost the title to the Sicilians in July of 1967. Arion later became a vicious rulebreaker in the WWWF, where he was managed by Fred Blassie.

Armstrong, Bob "the Bullet" (Robert James, Sr.; b. October 3; Marietta, Georgia; 229 lbs.) began wrestling in 1966. The Marietta, Georgia, native is the father of wrestlers Brad, Brian, Scott and Steve Armstrong. He teamed with Dick Steinborn to hold the NWA Georgia Tag Team Title in August of 1972. He again held the title several times in 1973 and 1974, teaming with Robert Fuller. Armstrong held the NWA Southern Title in Florida in 1974, the Southern Heavyweight Title in 1975, and the Mid-America Title in 1976. He held the NWA TV Title in 1979. He teamed with his son, Brad Armstrong, to capture the NWA National Tag Team Title in November of 1981, holding the belts until the following January. They also held the NWA Southeastern Tag Team Title several times in 1981. Armstrong remained active in the ring throughout the 1980s. He was heavily involved with the Somky Mountain Wrestling organization in the 1990s and made frequent appearances as a villainous manager and wrestling official in the USWA in the mid-1990s.

Armstrong, Brad (Robert James, Jr.; b. June 15, 1961; Marietta, Georgia; 6', 226 lbs.) began wrestling in 1981. He is the oldest son of wrestler Bob Armstrong. He teamed with his father to capture the NWA National Tag Team Title in November of 1981, holding the belts until the following January. They also held the NWA Southeastern Tag Team Title several times in 1981. Brad Armstrong also teamed with Norvell Austin to briefly hold the belts in May of 1981 after his father was injured. He teamed with his brother, Scott Armstrong to hold the Southeastern belts in October of 1983. He defeated Ted DiBiase for the NWA National Title in February of 1984, holding the belt several times until July of 1984. He teamed with Tim Horner to again capture the NWA National Tag Team Title in November of 1984. He captured the MSWA North American Title in December of 1984. He again teamed with Tim Horner as the Lightning Express to capture the UWF Tag Team Title in Oklahoma in May of 1987. He wrestled as Bad Street with the Fabulous Freebirds in the WCW in the early 1990s. He defeated Scotty Flamingo for the WCW Light Heavyweight Title in July of 1992. Armstrong was injured several months later and relinquished the title. He held the Smoky Mountain Wrestling Title several times in 1995 and also competed in the USWA.

Armstrong, Brian *see* Armstrong, Jesse James

Armstrong, Jesse James (Brian James; b. May 20; Marietta, Georgia; 6'4", 240 lbs.) is the youngest son of Bob Armstrong. He began wrestling as Brian Armstrong in 1992. He entered the WWF as "the Roadie," Jeff Jarrett's corner man in 1993. He and Jarrett left the promotion in Summer of 1995. He emerged in the USWA and the Smoky Mountain area later in the year as Jesse James Armstrong. He defeated Brian Christopher for the USWA Heavyweight Title in October of 1995, but lost the belt in a rematch later in the month. Though initially competing as a villain, he became a fan favorite in the USWA in 1996.

Armstrong, Scott (Scott James; b. May 4, 1959; Marietta, Georgia; 6'1", 212 lbs.) began wrestling in 1983. He is the son of Bullet Bob Armstrong. He teamed with his brother, Brad, to hold the NWA Southeastern Tag Team Title in October of 1983. He again held the Southeastern Tag belts several times in 1984, teaming with Johnny Rich and the Tonga Kid as R.A.T. Patrol Inc. He wrestled as Dixie Dynomite in Smoky Mountain Wrestling in the early 1990s.

Armstrong, Steve (Steve James; b. March 16; Marietta, Georgia; 6'2", 224 lbs.) began wrestling in 1983. He is the son of Bob Armstrong. He teamed with Tracy Smothers as the Southern Boys to win the Florida Tag Team Title in February of 1987. They entered the WCW as the Young Pistols in the early 1990s. They teamed to defeat the Patriots for the WCW U.S. Tag Team Title in November of 1991. They were defeated for the belts by Ron Simmons and Big Josh in January of 1992. He subsequently wrestled as Lance Cassidy in the WWF in 1993 and wrestled as The Falcon in 1994.

Arnold, Jody began wrestling in the Arizona area in the late 1960s. A powerful rulebreaker, Arnold held the Arizona Title four times in the early 1970s, competing against such opponents as Tito Montez, Cowboy Bob Yuma and Johnny Kostas.

Asai, Yoshihiro (b. 1966; 5'8",

180 lbs.) began wrestling in 1989. The Japanese wrestler became a popular aerial performer in Mexico teaming with Naoki Sano. He held the UWA Middleweight Title in Mexico several times in the early 1990s. He also wrestles under the name Ultimate Dragon, and captured the Mexican Middleweight Title in November of 1994.

Asako, Satoru (b. March 2, 1971) made his debut in All-Japan wrestling in April of 1992.

Asari, Charita (4'11", 115 lbs.) made her wrestling debut in late 1992. She was a leading female mat star with All-Japan in the 1990s.

Ashenoff, Charles *see* Konnan El Barbaro

Ashford-Smith, Mark *see* Star, Mark

Aska, Lioness *see* Asuka, Lioness

Assassin, The *see* Sierra, David

Assassin #1 *see* Renesto, Tom

Assassin #2 *see* Hamilton, Jody

Assassins, The *see* Bass, Don & Smith, Roger

Asselin, Ovila (b. 1927; Quebec, Canada; 6'1", 225 lbs.) was a leading Canadian wrestler from the late 1940s. A former Mr. Canada, Asselin was known for his dropkick and Irish whip. He remained a leading competitor through the 1950s.

Assirati, Bert (Bernardo Esserati; b. 1908, d. August 31, 1990; London, England) began wrestling in Great Britain in the late 1920s. He was a leading wrestler in the 1930s and 1940s. He held the British Heavyweight Title for nearly a decade in the 1940s. He also held the British World Heavyweight Title in 1947. He reclaimed the British Heavyweight Title in 1955, holding the championship until 1960.

Asuka, Lioness was a leading wrestler with the All-Japan Women's Promotion. She teamed with Chigusa Nagayo as the Crush Girls, and they were a formidable tag team in the 1980s. They held the All-Japan WWWA Women's Tag Team Title several times from 1984 through 1989.

Atkins, Fred (Fred Atkinson; b. 1912, d. May 14, 1988; Australia; 6', 240 lbs.) was a leading wrestler in Australia, holding the Australian Title during much of the decade before coming to the United States in 1949. He held the British Empire Title in Toronto, Canada, in March of 1949. He remained a leading mat star during the 1950s. He held the Canadian Open Tag Team Title in Toronto with Lord Athol Layton in 1952. He teamed with Ray Eckert to hold the NWA World Tag Team Title in San Francisco in December of 1952. He and Eckert also held the Pacific Coast Tag Team Title several times in 1952 and 1953. He recaptured the British Empire Title in Toronto in 1959.

Atkinson, Fred *see* Atkins, Fred

Atlanta, Mr *see* Zane, Tony

Atlas, Omar wrestled as Buddy Mareno to briefly hold the NWA Pacific Northwest Tag Team Title with Nick Bockwinkel in 1964. He held the NWA Central States Title in November of 1972. He held the Stampede North American Title in Calgary, Canada, in 1973. Wrestling as Omar Negro, teamed with Ciclon Negro to hold the NWA Florida Tag Team Title in 1975.

Atlas, Tony (b. Apr. 23; Roanoke, Virginia; 6'2", 247 lbs.) began wrestling in 1977. He was a former Mr. U.S.A., and teamed with Tommy Rich to capture the NWA Georgia Tag Team Title in November of 1977. He held the belt several times in 1978, teaming with Mr. Wrestling II and Thunderbolt Patterson. Atlas captured the NWA Eastern States Title in 1978. He held the NWA Georgia Title for several months in late 1980. He also held the NWA Georgia Tag Team Title, teaming with Kevin Sullivan in April of 1980. He teamed with Rocky Johnson to win the WWF Tag Team Title from the Samoans in November of 1983. They held the belts until April of 1984, when they were beaten by Adrian Adonis and Dick Murdoch. He captured the World Class TV Title in December of 1986. He teamed with Miguelito Perez to hold the WWC North American Tag Team Title in Puerto Rico in April of 1987. He teamed with Skip Young to hold the World Class Texas Tag Team Title for several months from June of 1987. He wrestled in the ICW in New England and held that championship in 1989. Tony Rumble served as his manager. Atlas entered the WWF in 1990 and wrestled as Saba Simba. He returned to the ICW in New England in 1991 and reclaimed the championship. Atlas wrestled on various independent cards in the 1990s, holding the CWA Title in 1993.

Atom Bomb (Brian Clark; March 14; Harrisburg, Pennsylvania; 6'6", 292 lbs.) began wrestling in 1991. He initially wrestled in the Smoky Mountain promotion as the Nightstalker. He debuted in the WWF as Atom Bomb in the Spring of 1993. The huge wrestler with the glowing eyes soon became a fan favorite in the WWF, where he remained until the Fall of 1995.

Atomic Blonds *see* Valentine, Johnny & Wallich, Chet

Austeri, Jim (b. 1908; Passaic, New Jersey; 5'7", 215) was trained by Strangler Lewis and became a professional wrestler in the late 1930s. He captured the world light-heavyweight title in 1938. He held the title until the early 1950s. He teamed with Tiny Mills to hold the NWA Southern Tag Team Title in 1956. Austeri remained a leading competitor throughout the decade.

Austin, Buddy (Francis Gabor; d. August 12, 1981) began wrestling in the 1950s. He held the NWA Central States Title for several months from June of 1961. He teamed with Great Scott to capture the WWWF U.S. Tag Team Title from Johnny Barend and Buddy Rogers in March of 1963. They lost the title to Skull Murphy and Brute Bernard the following May. He teamed with El Mongol to hold the WWA Tag Team Title in Los Angeles in April of 1966. He also held the WWA Title in Los Angeles several times in 1966. He held the World

Class Texas Title in May of 1967. He teamed with Ripper Collins to hold the Hawaiian Tag Team Title in April of 1969. He teamed with Bob Orton to hold the NWA Central States Tag Team Title in June of 1971.

Austin, Chuck (b. 1957) was crippled in his debut match with the WWF against Marty Jannetty and Shawn Michaels in Tampa, Florida, on December 11, 1990. Austin won a $25 million damage suit against the WWF in April of 1994.

Austin, Norvell began wrestling professionally in the 1960s. He teamed with Sputnik Monroe to hold the Southern Tag Team Title in May of 1972, and the NWA Florida Tag Team Title in October of 1972. Austin again held the tag belts several times in 1977, wrestling with Pat Barrett and Bill Dundee. He teamed with Rufus R. Jones to briefly hold the NWA Georgia Tag Team Title in April of 1979. Wrestling as the Shadow, he teamed with Brad Armstrong to hold the NWA Southeastern Title in May of 1981. He subsequently joined with Dennis Condrey and Randy Rose as part of the Midnight Express tag team. They held the Southeastern belts numerous times in 1982 and 1983. The Midnight Express also held the Southern Tag Team Title several times in 1982. Austin teamed with Koko B. Ware as the PYT (Pretty Young Things) Express to capture the Southern Tag Team Title in February of 1984. They also held the U.S. Tag Team Title in Florida in February of 1985. They again held the Southern tag belts several times in 1985.

Austin, Steve (Steve Williams; b. December 18; Dallas, Texas; 6'2", 241 lbs.) began wrestling in 1989. He was accompanied to the ring with his valet, Lady Blossom, when he captured the NWA TV Title from Bobby Eaton in June of 1991. He soon became part of Paul E. Dangerously's Dangerous Alliance. He was defeated for the TV Belt by Barry Windham in April of 1992, but recaptured the belt the following month. He lost the TV Title again in September of 1992 in a bout against Rick Steamboat. He wrestled with Brian Pillman as the Hollywood Blondes in 1993. The duo captured the WCW World Tag Team Title from Rick Steamboat and Shane Douglas on March 3, 1993. Austin and Lord Steven Regal were defeated for the title by Arn Anderson and Paul Roma on August 18, 1993, following an injury to Pillman. Austin wrestled as Stunning Steve Austin and was managed by Colonel Parker in the WCW from late 1993. He defeated Dustin Rhodes for the U.S. Title on December 27, 1993. He was defeated for the belt by Rick Steamboat on August 24, 1994, but regained the belt the following month when Steamboat was unable to defend the title on September 18, 1994. He subsequently lost the belt to Jim Duggan on the same day. Austin entered the WWF in late 1995 as the Ringmaster, Ted DiBiase's "Million Dollar Champion." He was subsequently billed as "Stone Cold" Steve Austin. Austin is married to Jeannie Clark, who manages as Lady Blossom.

Austin, Terry (6', 240 lbs.)

began wrestling in 1991. He teamed with Austin Steele to hold the Professional Wrestling Federation Tag Team Title for several months in 1994.

Australians, The *see* O'Day, Larry & Miller, Ron

Avalanche *see* Earthquake

Avatar *see* Snow, Al

Avenger, The *see* Soto, Roberto

Awesome Kong (Duane McCullough; 6'4", 440 lbs.) began wrestling in 1989. He defeated Jerry Lawler for the USWA title in July of 1991, but Lawler regained the belt on August 12, 1991, in Memphis. He teamed with King Kong as the Colossal Kongs in the WCW in 1994.

Ax (Bill Eadie; 6'2", 303 lbs.) began wrestling in the 1970s. He wrestled as the Masked Superstar, holding the NWA Georgia Title several times in 1979. He also held the NWA Georgia Tag Title with Austin Idol in November of 1979. He teamed John Studd to hold the NWA Atlantic Coast Tag Title in early 1980. He teamed with Paul Jones to captured the NWA tag team belts from Ray Stevens and Jimmy Snuka in November of 1980. They held the belts until February of 1981, when they were defeated by Ray Stevens and Ivan Koloff. They recaptured the title in a rematch the following month, holding the belts until their defeat by Gene and Ole Anderson in May of 1981. As the Masked Superstar, he again held the NWA Georgia Title in August of 1981. He also held the World Class

Championship in Texas and the NWA National Title several times during the year. He briefly held the NWA Southern Title in Florida in July of 1986. He subsequently wrestled as the Super Machine in the Machines tag team in the WCW. He was a founding member of Demolition with Smash when wrestling in the WWF. The duo, originally managed by Mr. Fuji, defeated Rick Martel and Tito Santana for the WWF Tag Team Title at Wrestlemania IV on March 27, 1988. They were defeated by Arn Anderson and Tully Blanchard in July of 1989, but again regained the belts the following October. They lost the belts to Andre the Giant and Haku on December 13, 1989, but regained the title at Wrestlemania VI on April 1, 1990. Demolition later added Crush to the team, and he and Smash lost the belts to the Hart Foundation in August of 1990. Ax subsequently left the WWF. He wrestled on various independent cards and held the New England Wrestling Federation Title and the All-Star Can-Am Title in 1993. Ax also wrestled as Axis the Demolisher in Global.

Axis the Demolisher *see* Ax

Ayala, Hercules teamed with Jim Neidhart to hold the Calgary Stampede International Tag Team Title in 1980. He held the WWC Caribbean Title in Puerto Rico several times in the mid-1980s. He held the WWC North American Title in Puerto Rico in 1985. He held the Canadian International Title in Montreal in January of 1987. He also held the WWC Universal Title in Puerto Rico several times in 1987 and 1988, often feuding with Carlos Colon.

Azteca, Charro (b. 1916; Tamanchuchalli, Mexico; 6'2", 235 lbs.) was a leading Mexican wrestler in the late 1940s and 1950s.

Azzeri, Jose *see* Iron Sheik, The

Baba, Ali *see* Ali Baba

Baba, Shohei "Giant" (b. January 23, 1938; Niigata, Japan; 6'9", 283 lbs.) made his professional wrestling debut in September of 1960. He captured the Japanese Wrestling Association NWA International Title in November of 1965, and held the belt several more times through the early 1970s. He beat Jack Brisco for the NWA World title in Kagoshima, Japan, on December 2, 1974. Brisco regained the title on December 9, 1974, in Tokyo. Baba also won the NWA title from Harley Race on October 31, 1979, and on September 4, 1980, in Japan, relinquishing the belt to Race on both occasions after several days.

Babich, George (b. 1918; New York City; 6'4", 229 lbs.) attended Fordham University, where he played football. He also played professional football in the 1940s, and was the basketball coach at St. Peter's College in New Jersey. He entered wrestling in the late 1940s and continued to compete through the 1950s.

Baby Blimp *see* Harris, George

Baby Doll (Nickla "Jennifer" Roberts; b. February 13, 1962; Lubbock, Texas; 6'1", 180 lbs.) was the daughter of wrestlers Nick Roberts and Lorraine Johnson. She worked in her father's promotion office in Lubbock, Texas, in the early 1980s, and began her career in the ring as Andrea the Giant, Gino Hernandez's valet, in the Summer of 1984. She engaged in a feud with Sunshine in the World Class promotion later in the year. She joined Tully Blanchard as Baby Doll in the World Championship area in 1985. She became a popular mat personality the following year when she sided with Dusty Rhodes in a feud with Blanchard. She also engaged in a feud with Jim Cornette in 1986. Baby Doll went on to be a valet to such mat stars as the Warlord, Larry Zbyszko and Ric Flair. She joined her husband, Sam Houston, in Global in 1991. They have since divorced.

Backlund, Bob (b. August 14, 1950; Princeton, Minnesota; 6'1", 234 lbs.) was an amateur wrestling champion. He began wrestling professionally in the AWA in 1974. He wrestled as a scientific fan favorite and was considered one of the greatest mat technicians of his day. He teamed with Jerry Brisco to hold the NWA Georgia Tag Team Title in October of 1975. He teamed with Steve Keirn to hold the NWA Florida Tag Team Title in 1976. He held the NWA Missouri Title for several months from April of 1976. He won the Los Angeles Battle Royal in 1978. He won the WWWF Title from Superstar Billy Graham in New York's Madison Square Garden on February 20, 1978. He was defeated by Antonio Inoki in Japan on November 11, 1979, but the WWF did not recognize the title change and Inoki vacated the title on December 6, 1979. Backlund teamed with Pedro Morales to defeat the Samoans for the WWF Tag Team Title in August of 1980, but was forced to give up the belt because he already possessed the WWF Title. Backlund lost the WWF Title to the Iron Sheik in Madison Square Garden on December 26, 1983, when his manager, Arnold Skoaland, conceded the match when the Iron Sheik put the "camel clutch" hold on Backlund. He returned to the WWF in October of 1992. His later years in the WWF were as an erratically disturbed villain, who demanded to be called Mr. Backlund. He defeated Bret Hart by submission for the WWF Championship after locking on the "crossface chicken wing" hold on Hart at the Survivor Series on November 23, 1994. Backlund lost the title three days later on November 26, 1994, to Diesel at a match in Madison Square Gardens in New York that only lasted six seconds. Backlund considered himself a candidate for President of the United States in 1996.

Backlund, Jim *see* Del Rey, Jimmy

Bad Breed *see* Rotten, Axl & Ian

Bad Company *see* Hart, Bruce & Pillman, Brian

Bad Street *see* Armstrong, Brad

Badd, Johnny B. (Mark Merro; b. July 9, 1964; Macon, Georgia; 6', 235 lbs.) boxed in New York from the late 1970s, winning five state boxing titles over his seven year career in the ring. He was also a member of the USA Boxing Team in 1981. He was trained as a wrestler by Boris Malenko in Florida, and made his professional debut in Sun Coast Wrestling in Bradenton, Florida, in 1990 as Mark Merro. He soon entered the WCW, where he continued his training with Jody Hamilton. He was managed in the WCW by Teddy Long and developed a Little Richard persona for his wrestling style as Johnny B. Badd in 1991. Badd captured the WCW TV Title from Lord Steven Regal in September of 1994. He lost the TV belt to Arn Anderson on January 8, 1995. He engaged in a lengthy feud with Diamond Dallas Page over the Diamond Doll during 1995. He defeated Page for the TV Title on October 29, 1995. He left WCW to enter the WWF in March of 1996, wrestling as Madman Mark Merro. He was accompanied by his wife, who went by the name of Sable in the WWF. Merro engaged in a feud with Hunter Hearst Helmsley shortly after his arrival in the WWF.

Badd Company *see* Pat Tanaka and Paul Diamond

Bagwell, Marcus Alexander (b. January 10, 1970; Marietta, Georgia; 6'1", 240 lbs.) began wrestling in 1990. Wrestling as Fabian, he teamed with Chris Walker to capture the Georgia All-Star Tag Team Title in May of 1991. He was known as the Handsome Stranger in Global from mid-1991. He later joined the WCW, where he teamed with 2 Cold Scorpio in 1993. They defeated the Nasty Boys for the WCW Tag Team Championship on October 4, 1993, but were defeated for the belts in a rematch on October 24, 1993. He teamed with the Patriot as Stars and Stripes the following year and the duo captured the tag title from Paul Roma and Paul Orndorff in September of 1994. They lost the belts the following month in a rematch, but regained them on November 16, 1994. They were defeated by Harlem Heat on December 8, 1994. He subsequently teamed with Scotty Riggz as the American Males. They defeated Harlem Heat for the WCW Tag Team Title in September 18, 1995. They lost the belts in a rematch ten days later.

Baillargeon, Adrien (b. 1917, d. 1995; St. Maglorie, Quebec, Canada; 6'5", 233 lbs.) was a leading Canadian wrestler in the 1940s and 1950s. He and his five brothers, Paul, Antonio, Jean, Lionel and Charles, all competed in the ring. Adrien Baillargeon was considered one of the strongest men in professional wrestling. He teamed with his brother, Paul, to hold the NWA World Tag Team Title in San Francisco in February of 1957.

Baillargeon, Antonio (b. 1926; St. Maglorie, Quebec, Canada) was one of the six Baillargeon brothers that wrestled from the late 1940s. He often teamed with his brother, Adrien. He was crowned Mr. Europe after a tour of the continent in 1951. He teamed with Jos LeDuc to hold the Montreal Tag Team Title in 1971.

Baillargeon, Charles (St. Maglorie, Quebec, Canada) was one of the six Baillargeon brothers to wrestle in the 1940s and 1950s.

Baillargeon, Jean (St. Maglorie, Quebec, Canada) was one of the six Baillargeon brothers to wrestle in the 1940s and 1950s.

Baillargeon, Lionel (St. Maglorie, Quebec, Canada) was one of the six Baillargeon brothers to wrestle in the 1940s and 1950s.

Baillargeon, Paul (St. Maglorie, Quebec, Canada) was one of the six Baillargeon brothers to wrestle in the 1940s and 1950s. He teamed with Whipper Billy Watson to hold the Canadian Open Tag Team Title in Toronto in 1954. He teamed with his brother, Adrien, to capture the NWA World Tag Team Title in San Francisco in February of 1957.

Baker, Ox (Indianapolis, Indiana; 325 lbs.) began wrestling in the early 1960s. A former boxer, Baker was known for his heart punch. He held the Mid-West Tag Team Title in Omaha several times in 1971, teaming with Ole Anderson, the Claw and the Great Kusatsu. He teamed with Scandor Akbar to hold the NWA Georgia Tag Team Title in September of 1972. Baker held the NWF North American Title in 1973, and held the WWA title in Indiana in 1974 and 1975. Baker briefly held the NWA Southern Title in Florida in late 1976. He teamed with Big John Studd, then known as Chuck O'Connor, to hold the WWA Tag Team Title for several months in early 1976. He teamed with Billy Graham to hold the NWA Florida Tag Team Title in 1977. He also held the World Class Championship and the World Class Texas Title several times in 1977 and 1978.

He teamed with Enforcer Luciano to capture the NWA Americas Tag Team Title in Los Angeles in 1980. He teamed with Carl Fergie to hold the NWA Atlantic Coast Tag Title in 1981. He held the WWC Universal Title in Puerto Rico in May of 1983. Baker appeared in John Carpenter's 1981 film *Escape from New York*.

Balbo, Johnny "the Great" was a popular wrestler in the Mid-South in the early 1950s.

Bald Eagle, The *see* Rentrop, Charles A.

Bambi (b. May 24) is a Stone Mountain, Georgia, native. She made her debut in Alabama in 1986. She entered the Continental area in 1988 and teamed with Tom Prichard against the Dirty White Boy and Kimberley in 1989. She wrestled in the WCW and AWA in 1990, and also feuded with Peggy Lee Leather in the IWA in 1990. She held the IWA Women's Title and the Ladies Major League Wrestling Title on several occasions in 1990 and 1991. She subsequently entered the LPWA.

Banda, Remo *see* Volador

Banks, Jimmie *see* Kasavubu

Banner, Penny was a popular woman wrestler in the 1960s. She teamed with Lorraine Johnson to win the Ohio Women's tag team title in he mid-1950s. She held the Texas Women's Title in 1961. She held the AWA Women's Title in 1961. She is married to former wrestler Johnny Weaver and has retired to Charlotte, North Carolina.

Banos, Juan *see* Lizmark

Barbarian, The (Sionne Vailahi; 6'5", 295 lbs.) began wrestling in 1981. He was originally known as Konga the Barbarian. He teamed with the Warlord in the tag team known as the Powers of Pain in the late 1980s. The duo often feuded with the Road Warriors in several promotions. He teamed with Dick Slater to win the WCW U.S. Title from the Freebirds in June of 1992. They held the title until the following month. He joined the Headshrinkers in the WWF as Sionne in 1994, replacing Samu. Teaming with Fatu, the Headshrinkers defeated the Quebecers for the WWF Tag Team Title in Burlington, Vermont, on April 26, 1994. They were defeated for the belts by Diesel and Shawn Michaels in a match in Indianapolis, Indiana, on August 28, 1994. He left the team and the federation the following year. He reclaimed the name the Barbarian and reteamed with the Warlord to wrestle in Canada in 1995.

Barend, Johnny (b. 1926; Rochester, New York; 6', 212 lbs.) was a Navy veteran and weigh-lifting champion. He was known in the ring for his airplane spin and flying head scissors maneuvers. He teamed with Enrique Torres to hold the NWA World Tag Team Title in San Francisco in July of 1955. He teamed with Sandor Kovacs to hold the Hawaiian Tag Team Title in September of 1955. He held the Ohio Eastern States Title several times in the late 1950s. He teamed with the Magnificent Maurice to briefly hold the AWA Tag Team Title in February of 1961. He teamed with Buddy Rogers to win the WWWF U.S. Tag Team Title from Johnny Valentine and Bob Ellis in July of 1962. They were defeated for the belts by Buddy Austin and Great Scott in March of 1963. Barend and Rogers briefly feuded after their defeat. He held the Hawaiian Title and the U.S. Title in Honolulu several times between 1964 and 1970. He also held the Hawaiian Tag Team Title several times in the late 1960s and early 1970s, teaming with Jim Hady, Ripper Collins, Magnificent Maurice, Hans Mortier and Billy Robinson.

Barnes, George (Melbourne, Australia; 225 lbs.) teamed with Bobby Shane to hold the Australian Tag Team Title in Australia in 1974. He subsequently came to the United States, where he teamed with Bill Dundee in the Mid-South in the mid-1970s. He returned to the Memphis area in 1987 to hold the CWA International Title briefly in August of that year. He engaged in several battles with Dundee during his return.

Barnes, Ron *see* Garvin, Ronnie

Barr, Art (b. October 8, 1966, d. November 12, 1994; 6', 200 lbs.) was born in Portland, Oregon. He was the son of wrestling promoter Sandy Barr. He made his professional wrestling debut in Salem, Oregon, in April of 1987. He held the Pacific Northwest TV Title in November of 1987. Barr was transformed into the character Beetlejuice by Rowdy Roddy Piper in January of 1989. He teamed with Jeff Warner as the Juice Patrol to hold the NWA Pacific Northwest Tag Team Title several

times in early 1990. He entered the WCW as the Juicer in July of 1990. His career in the WCW was short-lived because of his conviction on sexual assault charges on a minor. He returned to the Pacific Northwest to recapture the tag belts with his brother, Jesse Barr, in January of 1992. He teamed with Ryuma Go to capture the Championship Wrestling USA International Tag Team Title in Japan in 1992 and 1993. He entered Mexico's AAA as the American Love Machine in mid-1993, where he often teamed with Eddy Guerrero. He was accompanied to the ring by figure skater Tonya Harding in June of 1994. He died in his sleep on November 12, 1994.

Barr, Jesse (b. January 28; Portland, Oregon; 6', 243 lbs.) is the son of wrestling promoter Sandy Barr. He began wrestling professionally in 1981. He held the NWA Florida Title for several months in late 1984. He held the U.S. Tag Team Title with Rick Rude in April of 1985. He briefly held the NWA Southern Title in Florida in January 1986. He also wrestled as Jimmy Jack Funk, claiming to be a member of the Funk family, during much of the 1980s. He briefly captured the Mid-America Title from Jeff Jarrett in November of 1987. He teamed with John Tatum to hold the World Class Texas Tag Team Title in September of 1988. He teamed with Steve Doll to capture the NWA Pacific Northwest Tag Team Title in June of 1991. He also held the tag belts with his brother, Art Barr, in January of 1992.

Barr, Sandy was a leading promoter in the Pacific Northwest area. He is the father of wrestlers Art Barr, Jesse Barr and Shawn Barr.

Barr, Shawn is the son of wrestling promoter Sandy Barry. He began wrestling professionally in the 1990s.

Barrett, Paddy teamed with Tim Geohagen to hold the Canadian Tag Team Title several times in 1965 and 1966. They also held the International Tag Team Title in Winnipeg in November of 1965.

Barrett, Pat was a leading mat villain from the 1970s. He replaced Victor Rivera as co-holder of the WWWF Tag Team Title with Dominic Denucci in June of 1975. They lost the belts to Blackjack Lanza and Blackjack Mulligan in August of 1975. Barrett won the NWA World Junior Heavyweight Title by defeating Nelson Royal in a tournament on September 28, 1976. He lost the belt to Ron Starr the following December. He teamed with Norvell Austin to hold the Southern Tag Team Title in 1977. He held the NWA Americas Title in Los Angeles in August of 1979.

Barroom Brawlers *see* Vines, Doug & Sword Jeff

Bartelli, Count *see* Condliffe, Geoff

Bashara, Ellis (b. 1908, d. 19??; Norman, Oklahoma; 5'9", 219 lbs.) began wrestling in high school. He wrestled and played football at Oklahoma University in the early 1930s, and later played professional football in Memphis and St. Louis.

He was a member of the U.S. Olympic wrestling team in 1932 and began wrestling professionally in 1936. He remained a popular mat star through the 1950s.

Basher *see* Jeffers, Mac

Bass, Bobby wrestled as the Texas Outlaw to hold the Canadian Tag Team Title several times in 1977 and 1978, teaming with Joe Palardy, the Black Avenger and the Iron Sheik.

Bass, Don (Memphis, Tennessee; 6'4", 283 lbs.) began wrestling in 1982. He competed primarily in the Mid-South area during the 1980s. He teamed with Roger Smith as the Assassins to hold the CWA Tag Team Title several times in 1983. They also competed as the Interns to captured the Southern Tag Team Title in December of 1984. Bass also teamed with Bill Rose as the Assassins and the A Team in the mid-1980s. Bass, wrestling as Fire, again teamed with Roger Smith, wrestling as Flame, to hold the tag belts in July of 1986. The duo again captured the Southern Tag Team Title in November of 1986, with Smith wrestling as Dirty Rhodes. He teamed with Gary Young to briefly hold the CWA Tag Team Title in June of 1988. He is the brother of wrestler Ron Bass.

Bass, Ron (Pampa, Texas; 6'4", 285 lbs.) began wrestling in 1975. He teamed with Ken Mantell to hold the NWA Central States Tag Team Title in November of 1975. He held the NWA Pacific Northwest Title for several months from April of 1977. He also held the Pacific

Northwest tag belts several times in 1977, teaming with John Anson and Moondog Mayne. He held the NWA Americas Tag Team Title in Los Angeles several times in 1978, teaming with Dr. Hiro Ota, Moondog Lonnie Mayne and Roddy Piper. He held the Mid-South Arkansas Title in January of 1979, and held the Southern Heavyweight Title in July of 1979. He held the NWA TV Title in late 1981. He teamed with Stan Lane to hold the Southern Tag Team Title in July of 1982. He held the NWA Southern Title in Florida several times in 1983, and teamed with the One Man Gang to hold the U.S. Tag Team Title in Florida in November of 1983. He held the NWA Mid-Atlantic Title in 1984. He teamed with Black Bart as the Long Riders and they held the U.S. Tag Team Title in Florida several times in early 1984. Under the management of James J. Dillon, they also held the NWA Atlantic Coast Tag Title in 1984. Bass held the NWA Florida Title several times in 1986, exchanging the belt with Barry Windham. The tough Texan also engaged in a lengthy feud with Brutus Beefcake in the WWF in 1988. He is the brother of wrestler Don Bass.

Bass, Sam (b. 1935, d. July 26, 1976) was a wrestler in the Memphis area who began managing Jerry Lawler in 1970. He was killed in an automobile accident near Dickson, Tennessee, while en route from Memphis on July 26, 1976, at the age of 41. Wrestlers Pepe Lopez and Frank Hester were also killed in the crash.

Bastien, Lou *see* Klein, Lou

Bastien, Red held the NWA Pacific Northwest Tag Team Title several times in the mid-1950s, teaming with Andre Drapp and Roy Heffernan. He held the NWA Texas Junior Heavyweight Title in May of 1957. He teamed with Lou Klein, wrestling as Lou Bastien, to capture the WWWF U.S. Tag Team Title from Jerry and Eddie Graham in April of 1960. They lost the belts to the Fabulous Kangaroos in August of 1960. The duo won the AWA Tag Team belts twice in 1961. He also teamed often with Billy "Red" Lyons in the 1960s. He teamed with Jim Hady to capture the Canadian Tag Team Title in March of 1965. Bastien held the NWA Florida Title and the NWA Southern Title in Florida in 1968. He teamed with Hercules Cortez to win the AWA Tag Team Title from Mad Dog and Butcher Vachon in May of 1971. He teamed with Crusher after Cortez was killed in an automobile accident, and they lost the title to Nick Bockwinkle and Ray Stevens in January of 1972. Bastien held the World Class Texas Title in March of 1972. He teamed with Tex McKenzie to hold the World Class Texas Tag Team Title in 1974. Wrestling as Texas Red, he held the NWA Americas Title in Los Angeles several times in 1977. He also held the Americas Tag Team Title in October of 1977, teaming with Victor Rivera.

Batros, Assas *see* Ali Pasha

Batten, Bart (5'10", 229 lbs.) began wrestling in 1982. He and his twin brother Brad have teamed in Texas and the WWC. They captured the NWA Central States Tag Team Title several times in 1985 and 1986. Bart Batten teamed with Rick Mc-Cord to again hold the Central States tag belts in February of 1987, and captured the title with Bobby Jaggers in June of 1987. He reunited with his brother, Brad, to hold the belts from August until November of 1987. They also held the WWC Tag Team Title in Puerto Rico several times in 1988 and 1989. They recaptured the WWC tag belts in April of 1993.

Batten, Brad (5'10", 229 lbs.) began wrestling in 1981. He and his twin brother Bart have teamed in Texas and the WWC. They captured the NWA Central States Tag Team Title several times in 1985 and 1986. They again held the Central States tag belts from August until November of 1987. They also held the WWC Tag Team Title in Puerto Rico several times in 1988 and 1989. They recaptured the WWC tag belts in April of 1993.

Batterman, Ralph *see* Dupree, Ron

Baxter, Brandon appeared in Global as a manager in late 1992. He managed in the WWA in Texas and the USWA in Tennessee in the mid-1990s.

Baxter, Laverne (b. 1916; Little Rock, Arkansas; 6'3", 230 lbs.) played professional football before becoming a wrestler. He was a leading mat villain in Canada and the Pacific Northwest during the 1940s and 1950s. He wrestled as Mr. X in Boston in the early 1950s.

Bayonne Bombshell, The *see* Gob, Steve

Beach, Sunny (b. Sept. 24; Santa Monica, California; 6'4", 270 lbs.) began wrestling in 1985. He teamed with Terminator to hold the IWA Tag Team Title in August of 1990. He teamed with Steve Ray in Global in the early 1990s.

Bearer, Paul (William Moody; b. April 10, 1954) began his career in wrestling as the Embalmer in Alabama in 1975. He became a leading manager in Florida, Japan and World Class as Percy Pringle. He managed such stars as Rick Rude, Hercules Hernandez and Eric Embry. He came to the WWF in December of 1990 as Paul Bearer, manager of the Undertaker.

Beast, The (John Yachetti; b. 1928, d. 1987) was a leading wrestler in the 1950s and 1960s.

Beast, The *see* Gullen, Mark

Beautiful Bobby *see* Harmon, Bob

Becker, Bob (John Emmerling; b. 1916, d. November 25, 1954; Brooklyn, New York; 5'11", 220 lbs.) often teamed with his older brother, George. He began wrestling in the 1940s and he and his brother were a leading tag team in the early 1950s. They teamed to hold the NWA Southern Tag Team Title in 1954. Becker sometimes wrestled under the name Ray Schwartz during singles matches. Becker died of leukemia in a Floral Park, New York, hospital on November 25, 1954.

Becker, George (b. 1914;

Brooklyn, New York; 5'10", 215 lbs.) often teamed with his brother, Bob. He began wrestling in the late 1930s and was sometimes known as the German Bomber. He held the World Title in Los Angeles in 1946. He and his brother were a leading tag team in the early 1950s. They held the NWA Southern Tag Team Title in 1954. He teamed with Jack Witzig following his brother's death in 1954, and they held the NWA tag belts several times in 1956. He also held the tag title with such partners as Sandy Scott, Dick Steinborn, Mike Clancy, Billy Two Rivers and Johnny Weaver during the late 1950s and early 1960s.

Bedlam, Bruiser (Newark, New Jersey; 5'10", 270 lbs.) began wrestling in 1984. The Canadian wrestler was known as Johnny K-9 in the WWF. He joined the Smoky Mountain Wrestling as Bruiser Bedlam in 1994. He held the TV Title there in April of 1994.

Beefcake, Brutus (Edward Leslie; b. April 21, 1957; 6'4", 273 lbs.) began wrestling in 1978. Early in his career he wrestled as Eddie Boulder, Eddie Hogan and Dizzy Golden, often wrestling as the "brother" of Hulk Hogan. He teamed with Robert Fuller to briefly hold the NWA Southeastern Tag Team Title in February of 1980. Wrestling as Dizzy Eddie Hogan, he also held the tag belts in June of 1983, teaming with Ken Lucas. He achieved fame in the WWF in the 1980s as Brutus "the Barber" Beefcake. He and Greg Valentine, wrestling as the Dream Team, won the WWF Tag Team Title from

Mike Rotundo and Barry Windham in Philadelphia, Pennsylvania, on August 24, 1985. They were defeated by the British Bulldogs for the belts at Wrestlemania II on April 7, 1986. Beefcake was seriously injured in a parasailing accident on July 4, 1990. He returned to the WWF in February of 1993. He subsequently wrestled in the WWWA in Pennsylvania, where he captured the title in April of 1994. He joined Hogan in the WCW in 1994, where he wrestled as Brother Bruti until he turned on Hogan in October of 1994 and became known as The Butcher and the Man With No Name. In 1995 he joined with Kevin Sullivan's Dungeon of Doom, wrestling as the Zodiac. Later in the year he reteamed with Hogan, wrestling as the Bootie Man.

Beell, Fred (d. August, 1933) was an early wrestling star who defeated Frank Gotch for the American Title in December of 1906. He lost the belt in a return match against Gotch several weeks later.

Belafonte, Carlos *see* Colon, Carlos

Belanger, Leslie wrestled and managed in the USWA in the early 1990s. Managed by Bert Prentice, she held the USWA Women's Title in December of 1992.

Belfast Bruiser (David Finlay) was a leading mat villain in England and Germany during the 1980s, often feuding with Tony St. Clair. He held the Catch Wrestling Association Intercontinental Title in Europe in 1993. He entered the WCW in 1996 as the Belfast Bruiser, and engaged in a feud with Lord Steven Regal.

Belkas, Christos (d. February 5, 1981) was born in Lowell, Massachusetts. He played football and wrestled during his college years at Springfield College. He served in the Army Air Corps during World War II, where he held the Army record for one-armed chin-ups and push-ups. He began wrestling professionally after the war, and was often known as the Golden Greek. He continued to compete through the 1960s. He died after a short illness in a Lynn, Massachusetts, hospital on February 5, 1981.

Bell, Carl Donald *see* Eagle, Chief Don

Bell, Kay (b. 1914, d. October 27, 1994; Seattle, Washington; 6'3", 245 lbs.) attended Washington State University, where he played football. Bell played professional football from 1937 until 1943, playing his last season with the New York Giants. He subsequently began wrestling professionally under his own name and as Samson. He held the NWA Texas Title in July of 1946. He remained a popular mat star through the 1950s. He also worked on several films as a stunt man and double. He doubled for Victor Mature in 1949's *Samson and Delilah* and appeared in the films *Everybody Does It* (1949) and *Those Redheads from Seattle* (1953). He retired from the ring in 1953 and worked for several years as a jailer in San Mateo, California. He also worked as a teacher and special education instructor in San Mateo. He died of cancer at his home in Redmond, Washington, on October 27, 1994.

Bellomo, Salvador (b. June 18; Sicily, Italy; 5'10", 240 lbs.) began wrestling in 1977. Wrestling as Salvatore Martino, he teamed with Mike Sharpe to hold the Canadian Tag Team Title in October of 1978. He also held the Canadian tag belts with Bill Cody in February of 1979. He captured the Pacific Coast Title in Vancouver, Canada, in March of 1979. He teamed with Victor Rivera to hold the NWA Americas Tag Team Title in Los Angeles in May of 1981. He wrestled as Centurian Marsella in the early 1990s. He wrestled as Wildman Sal Bellomo in ECW in 1993.

Ben-Gurion, Joshua (6'7", 303 lbs.) was born in Israel and raised in Philadelphia. He was trained by Killer Kowalski and debuted as a professional wrestler in 1980. He competed in South Africa and New Zealand and returned to the United States after a stint in the Israeli air force. He entered the UWF in the early 1990s, where he feuded with Mohammad the Butcher.

Bennett, Mars (b. 1922; Detroit, Michigan; 5'3", 140 lbs.) was a circus performer before she entered professional wrestling. Usually a rulebreaking competitor, she was known in the ring as the Girl with the Iron Jaw. She was a leading women's wrestler of the 1940s and 1950s.

Bennett, Reggie (Venice Beach, California; 5'8", 170 lbs.) was a leading female wrestler from the 1980s. She held the IWF Women's Title in California several times from

1988 through 1990. She was also active in the USWA in Memphis.

Benoit, Chris (b. May 21, 1967; Edmonton, Alberta, Canada; 5'10", 218 lbs.) was born in Montreal, Canada. He was trained by Stu Hart and made his ring debut in December of 1985 with Calgary Stampede Wrestling. He teamed with Keith Hart to hold the Stampede International Tag Team Title in May of 1986. He went to Japan to wrestle the following year, where he became a popular star. He recaptured the Calgary Stampede International tag belts in 1988 and 1989, teaming with Lance Idol and Biff Wellington. Benoit was injured in an automobile accident in Canada in July of 1989. After recovering from a knee injury he wrestled as the Pegasus Kid in Japan and Mexico. He held the UWA Light Heavyweight Title in Mexico from March of 1991 until September of 1992. He wrestled in ECW in 1994 and entered the WCW the following year. He joined with Ric Flair, Arn Anderson and Brian Pillman as the new Four Horsemen in 1995.

Berber, Adi was a leading German wrestler in the 1940s and 1950s. The hulking mat star was also a popular character actor in several German and international films from the late 1950s. His film credits include *Circus of Love* (1958), *Ben Hur* (1959), *The Return of Dr. Mabuse* (1961), *Dead Eyes of London* (1961), *The Secret Ways* (1961), *The Door with Seven Locks* (1961), *The Indian Scarf* (1963), *The Nylon Noose* (1963) and *The Strangler in the Tower* (1966).

Berg, Slammin' Sammy (b. 1926; Montreal, Canada; 6'4", 235 lbs.) was a swimming champion at McGill University. He competed on the wrestling and swimming teams in the 1948 Olympics. He was also crowned Mr. Canada in a bodybuilding tournament in the late 1940s. Berg was a popular wrestler of the 1950s and 1960s. He was signed for a film contract in the early 1960s and appeared in such films as *The Vengeance of Ursus* (1962) and *The Three Stooges Meet Hercules* (1962) under the name of Samson Burke.

Berger, Casey (Ireland) was a leading wrestler in the 1940s and 1950s.

Bergstrom, C.W. (Portland, Oregon; 5'11", 235 lbs.) began wrestling in 1989. He wrestled in CW-USA in Portland and the USWA in Tennessee in 1993 as a tough school principal. He teamed with Melvin Penrod to hold the USWA Tag Team Title in July of 1993.

Bermudez, Adolfo *see* Dudley, Dances With

Bernard, Barney (Kansas City, Missouri; 265 lbs.) was a leading wrestler in the 1950s. He was known as "the Chest" because of his 63" measurement.

Bernard, Jim "Brute" (d. July 14, 1984) was a leading wrestling villain from the 1950s. He teamed with Skull Murphy to capture the WWWF U.S. Tag Team Title in May of 1963. They held the belts until November of 1963, when they were defeated by Killer Kowalski and Gorilla Monsoon. They were also NWA World Tag Team Champions in Florida several times in 1964. He and Murphy also held the IWA Tag Team Title in Australia several times in the mid-1960s. He held the World Class Championship in Texas in 1966, and the Texas Brass Knucks Title in September of 1967. He teamed with Mike Paidousis to hold the World Class American Tag Team Title in Texas in October of 1967. He again held the World Class American tag belts in 1972, teaming with Larry "the Missouri Mauler" Hamilton. Bernard also held the NWA Atlantic Coast Tag Title several times, teaming with Hamilton in 1972 and Mike York in 1973.

Berry, Ralph *see* Berry, Wild Red

Berry, Wild Red (Ralph Berry; b. 1907, d. July 29, 1973) held the World Light Heavyweight Title six times from 1937 until his defeat by Danny McShane in September of 1947. He held the NWA Texas Title in January of 1949. He held the NWA Central States Title in 1952 and 1957. He was also a wrestling manager in the 1950s. He managed the Fabulous Kangaroos and Gorilla Monsoon in the 1960s. He retired in 1969.

Bertha Fay *see* Monster Ripper

Bertucci, Lou (b. 1920; Los Angeles, California; 5'10", 210 lbs.) was a leading mat villain from the late 1940s. The Brooklyn-born Bertucci often wrestled as the Jungle Boy or the Golden Boy.

Berzerker *see* Nord, John

Beverly, Beau *see* Bloom, Wayne

Beverly, Blake *see* Enos, Mike

Beyer, Dick was a leading wrestling villain from the 1950s, who often competed in the ring as the Destroyer. He held the WWA Title in Los Angeles from July of 1962 until May of 1963. He teamed with Art Michalik to hold the NWA Pacific Northwest Tag Team Title several times in 1963 and 1964. He held the WWA Title several more times in 1964, competing against Dick the Bruiser, Bob Ellis and others. He teamed with Hard Boiled Haggerty to hold the WWA Tag Team Title in Los Angeles from July until October of 1964. He teamed with Billy Red Lyons to hold the NWA World Tag Team Title in San Francisco in March of 1965. He teamed with the Golden Terror to capture the World Class World Tag Team Title in Texas in February of 1966. He wrestled as Dr. X when he defeated Verne Gagne for the AWA Title in July of 1968. He lost the belt back to Gagne in a rematch later in the month. He is the father of wrestler Kurt Beyer.

Bialo, Allen "the Giant" (b. 1960, d. April 24, 1991; 6'5", 550 lbs.) began wrestling in the late 1980s. He was an imposing figure in the East Coast independent promotions. Bialo appeared in the 1991 Steven Seagal action film *Out for Justice*. He died at his home in Brooklyn, New York, on April 24, 1991.

Bianci, Warren *see* Man of the '90s

Biasetton, Antonino *see* Rocca, Antonio

Big Bad John (Bholu Zaman; d. 19??) teamed with Gary Martin to hold the World Tag Team Title in Tennessee in 1971. He teamed with Tim Woods to hold the NWA Florida Tag Team Title in January of 1972. He teamed with Bill Dundee to hold the Southern Tag Team Title several times in 1976. Big Bad John also held the Mid-America Title in 1976.

Big Black Dog teamed with the Moondogs in the USWA in early 1993. He broke with the team and partnered with Brian Christopher to defeat the Moondogs for the USWA Tag Team Title in March of 1993.

Big Bossman, The (Ray Traylor; b. May 2, 1963; Cobb County, Georgia; 6'6", 310 lbs.) began wrestling in 1985 as Big Bubba Rogers. He held the Mid-America Title in October of 1986. He also held the CWA International Title for several months from October of 1986. He teamed with Jerry Lawler to captured the Southern Tag Team Title in November of 1986, but turned on Lawler shortly after winning the belts. He held the UWF Title in Oklahoma in April of 1987. He joined the WWF in 1988 as the Big Bossman. He teamed with Akeem as the Twin Towers in the early 1990s. He entered WCW using the same prison guard motif, but under the name The Boss in December of 1993. In June of 1994 he briefly wrestled as The Guardian Angel for the WCW become turning villainous. He continued to compete in the promotion under his original ring name of Big Bubba Rogers.

Big Daddy (Shirley Crabtree; b. November 14, 1930, d. December 2, 1997; Halifax; 322 lbs.) was one of Great Britain's most prominent wrestler in the 1970s and 1980s. He held the European Heavyweight Title several times in the 1950s and 1960s. Big Daddy retired in 1993 after suffering a stroke. He died of a stroke on December 2, 1997.

Big Heart, Chief held the NWA Southern Title in January of 1957. He was a leading Indian mat star in the United States and Canada. He teamed with Little Eagle to hold the NWA Texas Tag Team Title in April of 1959. He often teamed with Chief Kit Fox in the 1960s. He subsequently retired to Oklahoma.

Big Humphrey teamed with Timothy Geohagen to hold the NWA Texas Tag Team Title in May of 1951.

Big Josh *see* Borne, Matt

Big Juice *see* Storm, J.W.

Big Red (Atlanta, Georgia; 6'5", 355 lbs.) was trained by Harley Race and began wrestling professionally in the mid-1970s. He competed throughout the world during the 1970s. He was a popular wrestler in independent promotions from the 1980s. He teamed with Miguelito Perez to hold the WWC North American Tag Team Title in Puerto Rico in December of 1986. He teamed with Calypso Jim to hold the AWF Tag Team Title in Indiana in May of 1991.

Big Yukon *see* Nord, John

Bigelow, Bam Bam (Scott Bigelow; b. September 1, 1961; Mount Laurel, New Jersey; 6'3", 368 lbs.) began wrestling as Crusher

Yircov in 1985. He held the Southern Heavyweight Title in July of 1986, and the World Class TV Title in October of 1986. He became known as Bam Bam Bigelow, the Beast from the East, and wrestled in the WWF, USWA and New Japan. Bigelow was one of the most agile big men in wrestling. The imposing wrestler was distinguished by tattoos of flames lacing his bald head. He returned to the WWF in the early 1990s, where he was managed by Ted DiBiase and accompanied to the ring by Luna Vachon. He lost a bout to football star Lawrence Taylor at Wrestlemania XI in April of 1995. Bigelow subsequently became a fan favorite, and feuded against members of DiBiase's stable.

Bigliardi, Luis (Buenos Aires, Argentina) attended Henry Ford Tech, where he studied to become a machinist. The large, bearded South American became a leading wrestler in the 1940s and 1950s.

Billington, Tom *see* Dynamite Kid, The

Billion Dollar Babies, The *see* Samson, Mike & Stratus, G.Q.

Billionaire Boys Club *see* Roselli, Mike & Tyler, Randy

Billy Jack *see* Haynes, Billy Jack

Bischoff, Eric (b. 1955) was a commentator with the NWA from the mid-1980. He was named senior vice president of WCW in 1992 and was largely responsible for the creation of the WCW Monday Night Nitro television program to compete directly with WWF's Monday Night Raw in 1995. Bischoff was co-host of the new program.

Bitter, Lillian (b. 1932; Newark, New Jersey; 5'5", 135 lbs.) began wrestling professionally in the early 1950s. She was one of the leading women wrestlers during the decade.

Black, Billy (6', 237 lbs.) began wrestling in 1989. The popular aerial star held the Georgia TV championship in 1990.

Black Avenger, The *see* Morowski, Moose

Black Bart (Rick "Hangman" Harris; Pampa, Texas; 6'4", 261 lbs.) began wrestling in 1980. He teamed with Ron Bass as the Long Riders and, under the management of James J. Dillon, held the NWA Atlantic Coast Tag Title in 1984. He also held the NWA National Title for several months in mid-1985. He held the NWA Mid-Atlantic Title and the WCWA World Title in 1986. He held the CWA Title several times in the Summer of 1989, competing against Dutch Mantell. He teamed with Bill Irwin as the Wild Bunch to hold the Global World Tag Team Title in December of 1991. He regained the Global tag belts, teaming with Johnny Mantell as the Rough Riders, in October of 1992. He again held the tag title in late 1993 and early 1994, teaming with John Hawk.

Black Blood (6'3", 245 lbs.) was a masked wrestler who briefly wrestled in the WCW in 1990 under the management of Kevin Sullivan.

Black Cat (Victor Manuel Mar; b. October 7, 1954) was a Mexican wrestler who began wrestling with

New Japan in the early 1980s. He competed in Mexico as Kuroneko in 1987 and wrestled in the AAA from the mid-1990s.

Black Gordman was a leading Mexican wrestler who held the Mexican National Heavyweight Title in 1966. He captured the NWA Americas Tag Team Title in Los Angeles several times in the late 1960s, teaming with Pepper Gomez, Bull Ramos, Rocky Montero and Goliath. He and Goliath held the NWA Americas Title over a dozen times during the 1970s. He teamed with Goliath in Texas and California in the early 1970s. The duo held the World Class American Tag Team Title in Texas in 1973. Black Gordman won the Los Angeles Battle Royal in 1975. He and Goliath captured the NWA Georgia Tag Team Title in June of 1976. They also held the NWA Central States Tag Team Title in July of 1976. He and Goliath captured the NWA World Tag Team Title in San Francisco in January of 1978. He again held the NWA Americas Title in August of 1982. He held the WWC Puerto Rican Title in 1984.

Black Harts *see* Nash, Tom & Heath, Dave

Black Ninja *see* Nagasaki, Kendo

Black Ninja *see* Samoa, Coco

Black Panther, The *see* Sexton, Frank

Black Scorpion *see* Culley, Randy

Black Terror *see* Graham, Bobby

Black Tiger *see* Guerrero, Eddy

Blackjacks, The *see* Mulligan, Blackjack & Lanza, Blackjack

Blackman, Don (b. 1912, d. 1977; New Hope, Pennsylvania; 6'1", 220 lbs.) served in the U.S. Army and worked as a professional model in Europe. He also played football in Tuskegee, Alabama, and boxed. He was a leading professional wrestler in the 1940s and 1950s. Blackman held the World Negro Light Heavyweight Title in the early 1940s. He also appeared in numerous films from the early 1950s including *Two Tickets to Broadway* (1951), *Affair in Trinidad* (1952), *Bomba and the Jungle Girl* (1952), *Valley of the Headhunters* (1953), *The Egyptian* (1954), *On the Waterfront* (1954), *Black Tuesday* (1955), *The Old Man and the Sea* (1958) and *Scream Blacula Scream* (1973).

Blacktop Bully *see* Smash

Blackwell, Jerry "Crusher" (b. April 26, 1949, d. January 22, 1995; Stone Mountain, Georgia; 5'11", 474 lbs.) began his wrestling career in Georgia in 1973. He was an unusually quick competitor for a man of his size. He teamed with Buck Robley to hold the NWA Central States Tag Team Title in 1977. He teamed with Bob Orton, Jr. to briefly hold the NWA Southeastern Tag Team Title in January of 1981. He soon moved to the AWA, where he was a leading villain in the early 1980s. He held the NWA Missouri Title in April of 1983. He teamed with Ken Patera as the Sheiks and, under the management of Sheik Adnan El-Kaissey, they captured the AWA Tag Team Title from Jim Brunzell and Greg Gagne in June of

1983. They retained the title until their defeat by Crusher and Baron Von Raschke in May of 1984. Blackwell returned to Georgia in the mid-1980s to start the Southern Championship Wrestling Promotion. Blackwell was seriously injured in an automobile accident in December of 1994. He died of complications from the accident on January 22, 1995.

Blade Runners, The *see* Sting & Ultimate Warrior

Blades, Zak *see* Rotten, Ian

Blair, B. Brian (5'10", 235 lbs.) began wrestling in 1981. He teamed with Al Madril to hold the World Class American Tag Team Title in Texas in June of 1981. He briefly held the NWA Florida Title in July of 1982. He again held the Florida championship in January of 1984. He joined with Jim Brunzell to form the Killer Bees in the WWF in the late 1980s. He wrestled with the UWF in the early 1990s.

Blair, Bobby (Dallas, Texas; 6'3", 275 lbs.) began wrestling in 1989. He started his career in the Pacific Northwest.

Blanchard, Joe teamed with Lord James Blears to hold the Hawaiian Tag Team Title several times in 1958 and 1959. He held the NWA Texas Title in late 1963 and early 1964. He held the World Class Texas Title in late 1966. Blanchard was a promoter for Southwest Championship Wrestling in San Antonio from the late 1970s. He is the father of Tully Blanchard.

Blanchard, Tully (b. January 22, 1954; San Antonio, Texas; 5'10",

235 lbs.) is the son of wrestler Joe Blanchard. He was managed by Baby Doll in the mid-1980s and held the NWA TV Title several times in 1984 and 1985. He lost that belt to Dusty Rhodes in July of 1985, but captured the NWA U.S. Title from Magnum T.A. later in the month. He lost the title back to Magnum in November of 1985. Blanchard was a member of the Four Horsemen in the NWA from 1986, holding the NWA National Title from March until August of 1986. He teamed with fellow Horseman Arn Anderson to captured the NWA Tag Team Title from the Rock 'n' Roll Express in September of 1987. They lost the belts to Barry Windham and Lex Luger in March of 1988, but regained the title the following month. They lost the belts to the Midnight Express in September of 1988. Blanchard and Anderson entered the WWF in 1989 and, wrestling as the Brainbusters and managed by Bobby Heenan, they defeated Demolition for the WWF Tag Title in July of 1989. They lost the belts in a rematch against Demolition the following October. Blanchard retired from wrestling in September of 1990 to become a Christian evangelist.

Blanco, Torbellino teamed with Ciclon Negro to hold the NWA Texas Tag Team Title several times in 1960. He also held the NWA Texas Title several times in 1960.

Blassie, Freddie (Fred Blassman) wrestled in the Navy during World War II, holding the 7th Naval District championship. He began wrestling professionally after the war. He suffered a serious head injury in a match against Rudy Dusek in 1947, but recovered to remain a leading contender. He held the NWA Southern Title over a dozen times from the mid-1950s through 1960. He held the WWW Title in Los Angeles on several occasions between 1961 and 1964, competing against Edouard Carpentier, the Destroyer and Rikidozan. He teamed with Mr. Moto to hold the WWA Tag Team Title in Los Angeles in October of 1964. He held the NWA Americas Title in Los Angeles in August of 1967, retaining the championship until going to Japan in March of 1968. He returned to regain the NWA title several times in 1969 and 1970. He also held the NWA Georgia Title in 1970. Blassie was a leading manager in the WWF in the 1970s and 1980s. He managed the Iron Sheik during his title reign from late 1983, and managed the team of the Iron Sheik and Nikolai Volkoff when they won the WWF Tag Team Title in 1985.

Blayze, Alundra *see* Micelli, Madusa

Blaze, Bobby (Robert Schmedley; b. June 25; Charlotte, North Carolina; 6'1", 222 lbs.) began wrestling in 1988. He wrestled in Smoky Mountain Wrestling in 1993, holding the TV Title and Junior Heavyweight Title several times. He captured the Smoky Mountain Heavyweight Championship from Jerry Lawler in February of 1995. He relinquished the title to Buddy Landel the following April.

Blears, Lord James (Jan Blears; England; 190 lbs.) was from England and often appeared in the ring wearing a monocle. He held the British Junior Light-Heavy and Heavyweight title before coming to the United States After World War II. He held the World Light Heavyweight Title in 1946. He often wrestled with Lord Layton in the 1950s, holding the Pacific Coast Tag Team Title and the World Tag Team Title in Chicago in 1953. He held the NWA World Tag Team Title in San Francisco several times in 1955, teaming with Gene Kiniski. He held the Hawaiian Tag Team Title several times from 1958 through 1960, teaming with Joe Blanchard, Jerry Gordet and Herb Freeman. He also held the Hawaiian Title in October of 1961. He teamed with Neff Maivia to hold the Hawaiian tag belts several times from 1961 through 1964.

Bliss, Mildred *see* Burke, Mildred

Blizzard Yuki *see* Hasegawa, Sakie

Blood, Richard *see* Steamboat, Rick

Bloom, Wayne (b. March 22; 6'4", 266 lbs.) began wrestling in 1988. He teamed with Mike Enos as the Wrecking Crew to win the AWA Tag Title in a tournament in October of 1989. They lost the belts to The Trooper and D.J. Peterson in August of 1990. Bloom and Enos became known as the Beverly Brothers when they moved to the WWF in 1990. They left the promotion after several years. He resumed wrestling as Wayne Bloom and continued to team with Enos. The duo primarily wrestled in Japan in the mid-1990s.

Blossom, Lady (Jeannie Clark) is the wife of wrestler Steve Austin. She was his valet when he wrestled in the WCW in the early 1990s. She is the ex-wife of Chris Adams and feuded with Chris and wife Toni in 1990.

Blu, Eli *see* Harris, Don

Blu, Jacob *see* Harris, Ron

Blue, Crystal (b. 1971) was born in Saco, Maine. She is the sister of Misty Blue and teamed with her in the LPWA. Crystal is nicknamed the Terminator.

Blue Demon (Alejandro Cruz) was a leading masked Mexican wrestler from the 1950s through 1970s. He held the Mexican Welterweight Title in 1953, and again in 1975. He competed often in the ring against El Santo, who he also appeared with in numerous Mexican films. Blue Demon's film credits include *The Curse of the Aztec Mummy* (1959), *The Blue Demon* (1963), *Blue Demon vs. the Satanical Power* (1964) *Hellish Spiders* (1966), *Blue Demon vs. the Infernal Brains* (1967) *Blue Demon vs. the Diabolical Women* (1967), *Santo Against Blue Demon in Atlantis* (1968), *Santo and Blue Demon vs. the Monsters* (1968), *The Mummies of Guanajuato* (1972), *Santo and Blue Demon vs. Dracula and the Wolfman* (1972) and *The Champions of Justice Return* (1972). His son also wrestled as Blue Demon, Jr.

Blue Infernos, The *see* Fields, Lee & Bobby

Blue Infernos, The *see* Gypsy Joe & Martinez, Frank

Blue Meanie (Brian Heffron; 6'1", 350 lbs.) wrestled in ECW in the mid-1990s. The huge, bizarre looking competitor often accompanied Raven to the ring in the Extreme promotion.

Blue Simmes, Misty (Glens Falls, New York; 5'6", 118 lbs.) began wrestling in 1984. She held the IWCCW Women's Title in 1985. She teamed with Heidi Lee Morgan as Team America to hold the LPWA Tag Team Title in 1990. She captured the WWWA Women's Title in Pennsylvania in April of 1994. She is the sister of Crystal Blue.

Blue Yankee, The *see* Smith, Curtis

Boatcallie, Ruth (b. 1930; Bryan, Texas; 5'6", 140 lbs.) was a Roller Derby star before she began wrestling professionally in 1950. She remained a popular female wrestler throughout the decade.

Boatright, Terri *see* York, Alexandra

Bockwinkel, Nick (b. December 6, 1934; St. Louis, Missouri; 6'1", 245 lbs.) was the son of wrestler Warren Bockwinkel. He began wrestling professionally in 1954. Wrestling as Dick Warren, he teamed with Ramon Torres to hold the NWA World Tag Team Title in San Francisco several times in 1958. He held the U.S. Title in Honolulu in 1962. He teamed with Wilbur Snyder to hold the NWA World Tag Team Title in San Francisco in late 1962 and early 1963. He held the

NWA Pacific Northwest Title several times in 1963 and 1964. He also held the Pacific Northwest tag belts several times during this period, teaming with Nick Kozak and Buddy Mareno. He held the Hawaiian Title in November of 1964. He teamed with Bobby Shane to hold the Hawaiian Tag Team Title in March of 1969. He was managed by Bobby Heenan when he entered the AWA in the early 1970s. He teamed with Ray Stevens to defeat Red Bastien and Crusher for the AWA Tag Team Title in January of 1972. They lost the belts to Verne Gagne and Billy Robinson in December of 1972, but reclaimed them the following month on January 6, 1973. They remained the champions for the next year and a half, before losing the title to Robinson and Crusher in July of 1974. They came back to reclaim the belt in October of 1973. Their title reign came to an end in August of 1975, when they were defeated by Crusher and Dick the Bruiser. Bockwinkel captured the AWA Title from Verne Gagne in a match in St. Paul, Minnesota, on November 8, 1975. He retained the belt for nearly five years before his defeat by Gagne in Chicago, Illinois, on July 18, 1980. He reclaimed the title following Gagne's retirement in May of 1981. He lost the belt to Otto Wanz in August of 1982, but recaptured the title the following October. He fought several close title defenses again Jerry Lawler and Hulk Hogan in 1983. Bockwinkel was defeated for the title by Jumbo Tsuruta in February of 1984. He was again awarded the belt in June of 1986. Bockwinkel's title reign was finally ended by Curt Hennig in San Francisco, in May of 1987. He subsequently retired from the ring. He emerged in the WCW in the mid-1990s as president of the federation.

Bockwinkel, Warren (b. 1921, d. March 24, 1986) wrestled in the 1920s and 1930s. He discovered Lou Thesz in St. Louis, and helped get his career started. He was the father of NWA champion Nick Bockwinkel. He died after a long battle with Alzheimer's disease on March 24, 1986.

Bodey, Mark (d. May 12, 1994) was the founder of ACW promotions in Pennsylvania in June of 1993. He was killed in an automobile accident on May 12, 1994.

Body, The *see* Stanlee, Gene

Boesch, Paul (b. October 2, 1912, d. March 7, 1989) was born in Brooklyn, New York. He began wrestling professionally in New York in October of 1932. He was credited with popularizing the sleeper hold to render his opponents unconscious. He served in the army during World War II and was wounded in combat on three occasions. He made several world wrestling tours in the late 1940s and remained a leading mat star until suffering injuries in an automobile accident in 1947. He worked as a wrestling promoter for the NWA after he retired from the ring. He sold his interest in the NWA in 1987. He died at his home in Houston, Texas, on March 7, 1989.

Bogni, Aldo (b. 1915; Argentina; 6'3", 261 lbs.) was a champion weight-lifter when he began wrestling in Argentina in 1942. He came to the United States to compete in the early 1950s. He held the North Dakota Title in 1959 and 1960. He teamed with Bronco Lubich to hold the NWA Southern Tag Team Title in 1966. He and Lubich also teamed to hold the NWA Southern Tag Team Title in Florida from November of 1967 until February of 1968.

Bohach, Bob (b. 1921, d. August 14, 1994; 6'3", 280 lbs.) was born in Hopkins, Minnesota. He began wrestling professionally in the early 1940s. He served in the Army during the war, and competed in matches in Hawaii. He continued his wrestling career when he returned to Minneapolis, where he was known in the ring as the Bohemian Grappler and Bazooka Bohach. He retired from the ring in the late 1940s to work as a bouncer and, later, a machine shop foreman. He died in a Minneapolis hospital of lung cancer on August 14, 1994.

Bollas, George (d. 19??; Warren, Ohio; 325 lbs.) was known in the ring as "Stonewall," because of his great size. He often wrestled as the Zebra Kid. He teamed with Hans Schnabel to hold the Pacific Coast Tag Team Title in September of 1952. He held the Hawaiian Title for several months from April of 1955. He held the Texas Brass Knucks Title in June of 1959.

Bollea, Mike wrestled as the Predator in the WWF in 1993. He also wrestled as Prey of the Dead in ECW in 1995. He is a nephew of Hulk Hogan.

Bollea, Terry *see* Hogan, Hulk

Bollet, Andre teamed with Frank Valois to hold the NWA Texas Tag Team Title several times in early 1959.

Bolus, Steve teamed with Rufus R. Jones to hold the NWA Central States Tag Team Title in late 1971. He teamed with Ron Star to hold the Western States Tag Team Title in 1982.

Bomb, Adam *see* Bomb, Atom

Bonales, Bobby (Roberto Aceves; b. 1917, d. June 26, 1994) was a leading Mexican wrestler from the 1930s. He held the Mexican National Welterweight Title in March of 1939. He held the Mexican National Middleweight Title several times in the mid-1940s. He captured the Mexican Welterweight Championship in July of 1951, holding the title for over a year.

Bonecrusher (6'3", 290 lbs.) began wrestling in 1987. He teamed with Crowbar as the Barroom Brawlers. They won the USWA Tag Title from Robert Fuller and Jeff Jarrett in 1991.

Bonecrusher, The *see* Curry, Jack

Bones, Crusher teamed with Big Daddy Cyrus in the USWA in 1994.

Bonica, Dr. John (b. 1907, d. August 15, 1994) was born on the island of Filicudi, in Italy, and came to the United States in 1927. He was an amateur wrestling champion in high school and began wrestling in carnivals to pay his way through medical school in the 1930s. He wrestled as the Masked Marvel, holding several wrestling championships during the decade. He graduated from medical school in 1942, and developed regional blocks as a form of pain relief for wounded combat soldiers during World War II. He was also instrumental in the development of the epidural anesthesia. He was the founder and director of the Multidisciplinary Pain Center at the University of Washington Medical Center in Seattle in 1960. He retired in the late 1970s. Bonica died in Seattle, Washington, of a cerebral hemorrhage on August 15, 1994.

Bonsignore, Joe *see* Styles, Joey

Booger, Bastien *see* Shaw, Mike

Bookbinder, Walter (b. 1927; Brooklyn, New York) was a weightlifter and former Mr. Brooklyn when he entered professional wrestling in the late 1940s. He was a popular wrestler for the next decade.

Booker, Larry *see* Moondog Spot

Booker T (Booker Huffman; b. May 1, 1965; Harlem, New York; 5'11", 250 lbs.) began wrestling in 1990. He wrestled with his brother, Stevie Ray, as the Ebony Experience in Global in 1992. They held the Global World Tag Team Title in July of 1992. They went to the WCW in 1993 as Kole and Kane in Harlem Heat, and were managed by Sherri Martell. They captured the WCW Tag Team Championship from Marcus Alexander Bagwell and the Patriot on December 8, 1994. They were defeated by the Nasty Boys for the title at Slamboree '95 in St. Petersburg, Florida, on May 21, 1995. They held the WCW tag belts several more times in 1995, defeating the Stud Stable and the American Males.

Boone, Brady (Charlotte, North Carolina; 5'7", 209 lbs.) began wrestling in 1984. He is a cousin of Billy Jack Haynes and learned aerial moves while wrestling in Japan. He held the NWA Pacific Northwest Tag Team Title several times in 1986, teaming with Coco Samoa and Ricky Santana. He wrestled as Fire Cat in Global in the early 1990s. He teamed with Jerry Flynn to hold the Suncoast Pro Wrestling Florida Tag Team Title in November of 1991.

Boone, Daniel *see* Savage, Daniel Leo

Boone, Grizzly held the WWC TV Title in Puerto Rico in 1987. He wrestled as Cousin Grizly with Fatback Festus in the Hillbillies. They teamed to hold the Georgia All-Star Tag Team belts in June of 1990.

Bootie Man *see* Beefcake, Brutus

Borden, Steve *see* Sting

Borga, Ludvig (Tony Halme; Helsinki, Finland; b. Jan. 6; 6'3", 258 lbs.) made his debut in the WWF in July of 1993. He feuded with Lex Luger and Tatanka while in the Federation, but left after suffering an injury. He returned to Europe where he wrestled Rambo for the European CWA title in 1995.

Boric, Thomas *see* Diamond, Paul

Borne, Matt (b. March 11; Portland, Oregon; 5'10", 235 lbs.) is the son of wrestler Tony Borne. He began wrestling in the Pacific Northwest in 1978. He teamed with Buzz Sawyer to hold the NWA Atlantic Coast Tag Title for several months in 1980. He held the NWA Pacific Northwest Title in April of 1981. He left the NWA following legal difficulties in June of 1983. He teamed with Ted DiBiase as the Rat Pack to capture the MSWA Tag Team Title in October of 1982. He teamed with Jeff Jarrett to hold the World Class World Tag Team Title and the USWA Tag Team Title in 1989. He held the USWA Texas Title in May of 1990. He wrestled as Big Josh in the WCW in the early 1990s, teaming with Ron Simmons to capture the WCW U.S. Tag Team Title in January of 1992. They lost the belts the following month. Borne wrestled as the first Doink the Clown in the WWF from 1992 until he departed the promotion in 1994. He continued to wrestle as Doink on independent cards through 1995.

Borne, "Tough" Tony held the NWA Pacific Northwest Tag Team Title several times in the late 1950s, teaming with Bill Savage and Shag Thomas. The mat villain was managed by Leon Newman in Texas in the early 1960s. He held the Texas Brass Knucks Title in June of 1960. He held the NWA Pacific Northwest Title in September of 1960. He teamed with Dan Manoukian to hold the NWA Texas Tag Team Title in February of 1961. He returned to the Pacific Northwest in the mid-1960s to hold the tag team title several times, teaming with Jay York, Prof. Hiro, Mr. Fuji. He teamed with John Tolos to hold the Canadian Tag Team Title several times in 1966. He and Moondog Mayne teamed to hold the tag belts nearly a dozen times in the late 1960s and early 1970s. He is the father of Matt Borne.

Boston Bad Boy, The *see* Linnehan, George T.

Bota, the Witch Doctor (Maori Islands; 270 lbs.) held the Southern Heavyweight Title in June of 1985 and the Mid-America Title in August of 1985. He was managed by Floyd Creachman III.

Botswana Beast (Ben Peacock; b. 1964; 6', 430 lbs.) began wrestling in Georgia and the WCCW in 1987. He captured the Deep South Wrestling American Title in Georgia in March of 1987. Wrestling as Kamala II, he teamed with Kamala and wrestled in Japan from 1992.

Boucher, Bette defeated the Fabulous Moolah to briefly hold the Women's World Title in the fall of 1966.

Boulder, Eddie *see* Beefcake, Brutus

Boulder, Horace (Tampa, Florida; 6'2", 240 lbs.) began wrestling in January of 1990. He often competed in Japan and held the FMW Tag Team Title with Sabu. He is the nephew of Hulk Hogan.

Boulder, Terry *see* Hogan, Hulk

Bounty Hunters *see* Novak, David & Jerry

Bovee, Marcial was one of wrestling's most hated manager's in the Arizona area in the 1970s. His group of ring villains were known as Marcial Bovee's Walking Dead. Bovee himself held the Arizona Title briefly in early 1985. Bovee was also a manager and promoter in the Phoenix, Arizona, area in the 1980s.

Bowden, Scott (215 lbs.) was a referee in the USWA before he began managing in the early 1990s. He managed a stable of villains in the promotion, and occasionally competed in the ring.

Boy Tony *see* Falk, Tony

Boyd, Jonathan teamed with Norman Frederick Charles as the Royal Kangaroos in the Pacific Northwest in the early 1970s. They held the tag team title several times in 1971. Boyd also held the NWA Pacific Northwest Title in July of 1971. The Royal Kangaroos held the Calgary Stampede International Tag Team Title in 1977. He recaptured the Pacific Northwest belt in August of 1978. He teamed with Colosso Colosetti to hold the NWA Americas Title in Los Angeles in May of 1979. He held the NWA TV Title in September of 1979. Teaming with Luke Williams as the Sheepherders, Boyd was co-holder of the Southern Tag Team Title several times in 1983. He returned to the Mid-South in 1985, teaming with Rip Morgan as the Sheepherders. They engaged in a lengthy feud with the Fabulous Ones and reclaimed the Southern tag title several times during the year. Boyd also held the Alabama championship in January of 1988.

Boyette, Bonnie Lee *see* Galento, Mario

Bozik, Fred (b. 1921; Cleveland, Ohio; 6', 222 lbs.) was a rough competitor in the ring from the 1940s. He remained active in wrestling through the 1950s.

Braddock, Scott wrestled in the World Class promotion in Dallas in the late 1980s. He teamed with Cactus Jack to hold the World Class World Tag Team Title in August of 1989. Wrestling as Sheik Scott Braddock, he again held the USWA tag belts with Ron Starr in September of 1989.

Bradley, Bob (6'2", 240 lbs.) began wrestling in 1983. He wrestled as Cowboy Bob Bradley for the NCW promotion in Massachusetts in the mid-1980s. He held the World Class Texas Title in January of 1987. He is also known as the Cat Man in the WWF.

Bradley, Boo (John Rickner; 6'2", 310 lbs.) began wrestling in 1992. He wrestled in Smoky Mountain Wrestling in 1994, where he was managed by Tammy Fytch. He briefly held the TV Title in September of 1994. After breaking with Fytch he engaged in a feud with Chris Candido. Bradley briefly appeared in the WWF in December of 1995 as Ted DiBiase's Zanta Klaus. He also wrestled as Abudda Singh.

Bradshaw, Justin "Hawk" (John Hawk; Sweetwater, Texas; 6'7", 285 lbs.) played professional football with the Los Angeles Raiders. He wrestled as John Hawk in Global in the early 1990s. He teamed with Bobby Duncum, Jr. as the Texas Mustangs to hold the Global World Tag Team Title in November of 1992. He also wrestled as Vampiro Americano in the AAA in Mexico in 1993. He again held the Global tag belts in late 1993 and early 1994, teaming with Black Bart. He has also wrestled in Japan as Death Mask. He entered the WWF as Justin "Hawk" Bradshaw in January of 1996.

Brady, Art (b. 1919; Huntington Park, California; 6'1", 220 lbs.) played football in college and professionally for the Los Angeles Bulldogs. He wrestled professionally during the 1940s and 1950s, and was known in the ring for his use of the piledriver.

Brainbusters, The *see* Anderson, Arn & Blanchard, Tully

Brandi, Tom (6'3", 255 lbs.) began wrestling in 1985. He has wrestled in the AWA and CWA. He held the IWCCW tag belts with Prince Mike Kaluha in late 1987, and was the promotions TV champion in early 1992. Brandi was also a popular star in the East Coast independent circuit in the early 1990s. He wrestled in the ECW as Johnny Gunn, teaming with Tommy Dreamer to win the tag team belts in November of 1993. He subsequently left the promotion.

Brannigan, Crusher (b. 1948; Thousand Oaks, California; 6'2", 300 lbs.) began his wrestling career on the East Coast in the 1970s. He competed throughout the world and was a popular competitor in South Africa and Great Britain.

Brave Sky *see* Youngblood, Chris

Bravo, Dino (Adolpho Brescino; b. August 6, 1948, d. March 11, 1993; Montreal, Canada; 6'1", 256 lbs.) began wrestling professionally in Canada in 1974. He teamed with Victor Rivera to hold the NWA Americas Tag Team Title in Los Angeles in December of 1974. He held the NWA Atlantic Coast Tag Title several times in 1975, teaming with Mr. Wrestling and Tiger Conway, Jr. He held the NWA World Tag Team Title with Mr. Wrestling in May of 1976. The Canadian wrestler teamed with Domenic DeNucci to defeat Toru Tanaka and Mr. Fuji for the WWWF Tag Team Title in March of 1978. They lost the belts to the Yukon Lumberjacks in June of 1978. He held the NWA Canadian Title several times in the late 1970s. Bravo held the Canadian International Title in Montreal several times in the mid-1980s. He competed in the WWF from the late 1980s, where he was billed as the world's strongest man. He was managed in the ring by Frenchy Martin and, later, Jimmy Hart. Bravo was shot to death in his home in Laval, Quebec, Canada on March 11, 1993, during a gun battle reportedly involving cigarette black-marketeers.

Brazil, Bobo (Houston Harris; b. 1923, d. January 20, 1998; Benton Harbor, Michigan; 6'4", 265 lbs.) began wrestling in 1951, becoming wrestling's first black superstar. He teamed with Enrique Torres to capture the NWA World Tag Team Title in San Francisco in July of 1956 and in May of 1957. He held the NWA U.S. Title several times from the early 1960s until 1976. He also held the WWA Title in Los Angeles in 1966 and 1968. He captured the Japanese Wrestling Association International Title in June of 1968. He captured the NWA Americas Title in Los Angeles several times in 1968 and 1969. He teamed with Bob Geigel to hold the NWA Central States Tag Team Title in 1973. He also held the WWWF U.S. Title in 1976. He captured the U.S. Title in Toronto in February of 1977. He teamed with Dusty Rhodes to hold the NWA Florida Tag Team Title in August of 1980. Brazil held the WWA title several times in 1981. He teamed with Chris Carter to hold the WWA Tag Team Title in 1985. He was recognized as the Midwest All-Pro North American champion in 1988.

Brazil, Bobo, Jr. *see* Calypso Jim

Brescino, Adolpho *see* Bravo, Dino

Brewer, Rocky held the Mid-America Tag Team Title several times in 1980, teaming with Pat Rose and George Gulas.

Brisco, Jack (b. September 21, 1941; Blackwell, Oklahoma; 232 lbs.) began wrestling in high school. He was a leading collegiate competitor at Oklahoma State University and made his professional wrestling debut in Oklahoma City in June of 1966. He held the NWA Southern Title in Florida several times in 1969 before leaving the area to wrestle in Japan. He returned to Florida to reclaim the title in June of 1971. He also held the NWA Florida Title and the NWA Eastern States

Title several times in the early 1970s. He defeated Harley Race for the NWA Heavyweight Title in Houston, Texas, on July 20, 1973. He lost the title to Giant Baba in Kagoshima, Japan, on December 2, 1974. He regained the belt the following week in Tokyo on December 9, 1974. Brisco again lost the belt to Terry Funk in Miami, Florida, on December 10, 1975. He held the NWA Missouri Title from November of 1976 until August of the following year. He teamed with his brother, Jerry Brisco, to hold the NWA Georgia Tag Team Title in January of 1979. They again captured the title in December of 1979. He held the Missouri belt again in October of 1981. Brisco again held the NWA Southern Championship in Florida in 1981. He held the NWA Mid-Atlantic Title several times in the early 1980s. He teamed with his brother, Jerry, to capture the NWA World Tag Team Title in June of 1983, defeating Rick Steamboat and Jay Youngblood. They lost the title to Steamboat and Youngblood in October of 1983, but recaptured them in a rematch later in the month. They were again defeated by Steamboat and Youngblood in November of 1983. They returned to capture the title by defeating Wahoo McDaniel and Mark Youngblood in April of 1984. The relinquished the belts in a rematch later in the month.

Brisco, Jerry held the NWA Southern Title in Florida in 1974. He teamed with Rocky Johnson to hold the NWA Georgia Tag Team Title for several months in early 1975. Brisco again held the Georgia belts with Bob Backlund in October of 1975. He teamed with his brother, Jack Brisco, to hold the NWA Georgia Tag Team Title in January of 1979. They again held the title in December of 1979, and Jerry Brisco teamed with Ole Anderson for the championship the following year. Brisco defeated Les Thornton for the NWA World Junior Heavyweight Title on September 13, 1981. He lost the belt back to Thornton the following month. He teamed with his brother, Jack, to capture the NWA World Tag Team Title in June of 1983, defeating Rick Steamboat and Jay Youngblood. They lost the title to Steamboat and Youngblood in October of 1983, but recaptured them in a rematch later in the month. They were again defeated by Steamboat and Youngblood in November of 1983. They returned to capture the title by defeating Wahoo McDaniel and Mark Youngblood in April of 1984. The relinquished the belts in a rematch later in the month.

British Bruisers, The *see* Dynamite Kid & Smith, Johnny

British Bulldog, The *see* Smith, Davey Boy

British Bulldogs, The *see* Smith, Davey Boy and the Dynamite Kid

Brito, Gino, Jr. is the son of wrestler Gino Brito. He held the Canadian TV Title in Montreal in April of 1987.

Brito, Gino, Sr. was the son of wrestler Jack Britton. Wrestling as Louis Cerdan, he teamed with Tony Parisi to win the WWWF Tag Team Title from the Blackjacks in November of 1975. They lost the belts to Killer Kowalski and Big John Studd in May of 1976. He held the Canadian International Tag Team Title in Montreal with Rick McGraw in 1982. He also captured the International tag belts with Tony Parisi in 1983. His son, Gino Brito, Jr., also wrestled professionally.

Britton, Jack (Gabriel Acocella; b. 1916, d. February 9, 1980) was a leading wrestler in the late 1930s and 1940s. He was the father of Gino Brito, Sr.

Brody, Bruiser (Frank Donald Goodish; b. June 14, 1946, d. July 17, 1988; Albuquerque, New Mexico; 6'4", 284 lbs.) began wrestling in 1973. He teamed with Stan Hansen to hold the U.S. Tag Team Title in Louisiana for several months from October of 1974. He briefly held the NWA Florida Title in late 1975. Brody wrestled in the WWF in 1976, and made several unsuccessful attempts to defeat Bruno Sammartino for the championship. He captured the World Class Championship in Texas several times in the late 1970s, wrestling against Fritz Von Erich, the Spoiler and Ox Baker. He held the World Class Texas Title in May of 1978. Wrestling as King Kong Brody, he was managed by Rev. Tiny Hampton when he won the WWA title from Dick the Bruiser in Indianapolis in August of 1979. He relinquished the belt to Dick the Bruiser the following May. He teamed with Ernie Ladd to hold the NWA Central States Tag Team Title in February of 1980. He held the NWA Central States Title in April of 1980. He teamed with Kerry Von Erich to hold the World Class American Tag Team Title in Texas several times in the early 1980s. He left the World Class promotion in late 1983 to compete in Japan. He remained a leading competitor throughout the world though the late 1980s. He was stabbed by wrestler Jose Gonzales in Bayamon, Puerto Rico, in a dressing room prior to a wrestling match. He died of his injuries the following day on July 17, 1988. Gonzales was charged with the murder, but was acquitted following a trial.

Brody, John *see* Calhoun, Jr., Haystack

Brody, King Kong *see* Brody, Bruiser

Bronco, El teamed with Invader #1 to hold the WWC Tag Team Title in Puerto Rico several times in 1991. He also held the tag belts with Ray Gonzales in 1994.

Bronx Beast, The *see* Colombo, Rocco

Brooklyn Brawler, The *see* Lombardi, Steve

Brooks, Tim "Killer" (Waxahachie, Texas; 6', 285 lbs.) began wrestling in 1967. He held the Stampede North American Title in Calgary, Canada, in 1977. He teamed with Roddy Piper to hold the NWA Pacific Northwest Tag Team Title in late 1978 and early 1979. He held the World Class Texas Title in May of 1981. He captured the NWA National Title in March of 1983. He sold the title to Larry Zbyszko following the

match. Brooks held the World Class TV Title in June of 1985.

Broomfield, Crusher *see* One Man Gang

Brower, Dick "Bulldog" (b. 1933, d. September 15, 1997; 235 lbs.) served in the U.S. Marines and was weightlifter before he began wrestling in 1960. He was known for his maniacal ring style and often teamed with Jim "the Brute" Bernard early in his career. He teamed with Sweet Daddy Siki to hold the International Tag Team Title in Toronto in 1962. He again held the tag belts in February of 1963, teaming with Johnny Valentine. Brower held the Australian Title in Australia in September of 1972, and was the IWA North American Champion in 1975. He was managed by Captain Lou Albano in the WWF in the late 1970s. Brower died on September 15, 1997.

Brown, Bad Leroy (Leroy Rochester; b. 1950, d. September 6, 1988; 302 lbs.) held the NWA Americas Title in Los Angeles in April of 1979. He won the Los Angeles Battle Royal in 1979. He teamed with Allen Cooage to hold the NWA Americas Tag Team Title in August of 1979. He also held the NWA Southern Title in Florida in late 1979. He held the NWA TV Title in late 1982. Wrestling as Elijah Akeem Ambulakila, he teamed with Ray Candy as the Zambuie Express in the 1980s. They held the Global Tag Team Title in Florida in July of 1983 and held the Southern Tag Team Title several times in early 1984. He teamed with Bill Irwin to hold the UWF Tag Team Title in

November of 1986. He died in a Savannah, Georgia, hospital on September 6, 1988.

Brown, Bad News (Alan Cooage; 6'1", 280 lbs.) competed in the Olympics in 1976, receiving a bronze medal in judo competition. He began wrestling in 1978. He held the NWA Americas Tag Team Title in Los Angeles several times in 1979, teaming with Leroy Brown and Victor Rivera. He held the Stampede North American Title in Calgary, Canada, several times from 1982 through 1986. He wrestled in the WWF in the late 1980s. He subsequently wrestled in Japan before returning to the United States to enter Global in the early 1990s.

Brown, Bearcat was a leading black wrestler in the Memphis area from the late 1960s. He teamed with Johnny Walker to hold the World Tag Team Title in Tennesssee in July of 1969. He also held the belts with Len Rossi several times in 1971. They also held the Southern Tag Team Title in 1971. Brown teamed with Tommy Gilbert to hold the Southern belts in February of 1976.

Brown, Big Business (Chris Brown) managed in the USWA in 1993 and 1994.

Brown, "Bulldog" Bob (b. October 16, 1940, d. February 6, 1997; Winnipeg, Canada; 6', 258 lbs.) began wrestling in 1958. Known as the Bulldog, he teamed with Bob Geigel to hold the NWA Central States Tag Team Title several times between 1965 and 1968. He also held the NWA Central States Title in September of 1968. He held the Canadian Tag Team Title several times in the late 1960s and early 1970s, teaming with Dutch Savage, John Quinn and Gene Kiniski. He held the Central States belt several more times from the early 1970s through the late 1980s, wrestling against such stars as Harley Race, Mike George and Bill Dundee. He teamed with Bob Sweetan to hold the NWA Central State Tag Title in October of 1978. He also held the tag belts in 1980, teaming with Dick Murdoch and Pat O'Connor, and teamed with Terry Taylor for the title in 1981. He held the belts with Buzz Tyler several times in 1983. He teamed with Al Tomko to hold the Canadian Tag Team Title in July of 1983. He teamed with Dale Veazy as the Hunters to hold the WWC Tag Team Title in Puerto Rico in August of 1987. Brown also teamed with his son, Kerry. Brown died of a heart attack on February 6, 1997.

Brown, Bozo *see* Hickey, Frank

Brown, Brickhouse (Winter Haven, Florida; 5'10", 225 lbs.) began wrestling in 1982. He wrestled often in the USWA as both a villain and fan favorite during the 1980s and 1990s. He briefly held the Southern Heavyweight Title in July of 1987. He briefly held the CWA Title in May of 1988. He held the World Class Texas Title in February of 1989. He teamed with Sweet Daddy Falcone as the Uptown Possee to capture the USWA Tag Team Title in April of 1990. They were managed by Reggie B. Fine. Brown also wrestled as M.C. Slammer in the USWA in the early 1990s. Brown and Gorgeous George III held the USWA Tag Team Title in April of 1995.

Brown, Charlie *see* Valiant, Jimmy

Brown, D. Lo (A.C. Connor; Bronx, New York; 305 lbs.) wrestled in Smoky Mountain Wrestling in 1994.

Brown, Dave began working as a commentator in the Mid-South area in 1967. He has remained with the USWA, usually working with Lance Russell, through the 1990s. Brown is also a weatherman on Memphis television.

Brown, Denny defeated Mike Davis for the NWA World Junior Heavyweight Title on November 22, 1984. He lost the belt to Gary Royal in August of 1985, but recaptured the title the following month. He was defeated for the title by Steve Regal on August 2, 1986, but again recaptured the title in September of 1986. Brown was defeated by Lazor Tron on March 7, 1987.

Brown, Jerry teamed with Buddy Roberts as the Hollywood Blonds to hold the U.S. Tag Team Title in Oklahoma in May of 1970. They again held the U.S. belts in February of 1973. They captured the NWA Americas Tag Team Title in Los Angeles several times in 1974 and 1975. They also held the NWA Florida Tag Team Title in October of 1976. They held the Southern Tag Team Title briefly the following year. Brown teamed with Bobby Jaggers to hold the U.S. Tag Team Title in Oklahoma in May of 1978. He teamed with Hartford Love to hold the NWA Central States Tag Team Title in March of 1979. He also held the tag belts with the Turk

in July of 1979. He again held the tag title with Ron McFarlane in 1981 and with Roger Kirby in May of 1982.

Brown, Kerry (Kansas City, Missouri; 225 lbs.) is the son of Bulldog Bob Brown. He wrestled as Rick Valentine in Puerto Rico. He teamed with Duke Myers to hold the Calgary Stampede International Tag Team Title in March of 1982. He teamed with Sailor White to hold the Canadian International Tag Team Title in Montreal in October of 1984. He held the Stampede North American Title in December of 1985. He teamed with Lance Idol to hold the WWC Tag Team Title in August of 1990. He also held the WWC Caribbean Tag Team Title in September of 1990, teaming with Eric Embry.

Brown, Luke (300 lbs.) originally wrestled as Man Mountain Campbell in the early 1960s. He teamed with Grizzly Smith as the Kentuckians to capture the WWA Tag Team Title in Los Angeles in August of 1965. He teamed with Tor Kamata to hold the NWA Central States Tag Team Title in June of 1969. He also held the Central States tag belts with Danny Little Bear and the Ox in 1969. He reunited with Smith as the Kentuckians to hold the U.S. Tag Team Title in Oklahoma in April of 1971. He again held the U.S. belts in January of 1974, teamed with Klondike Bill.

Brown, Natie (b. 1907, d. June, 1991; Washington, D.C.; 6'1", 220 lbs.) played football in Southern California and was a boxer in the 1930s, sometimes sparring with Joe

Louis. He became a professional wrestler in the mid-1940s and was a leading mat villain throughout the next decade.

Brown, Orville (d. January 24, 1981) held the Kansas Title in the early 1930s. He captured the MWA Heavyweight Title in June of 1940. He held the MWA Title in Kansas City numerous times during the 1940s, often feuding with Lee Wykoff and Bobby Bruns. He was recognized as the NWA World Champion from October of 1948. He relinquished the belt in November of 1949 after suffering injuries in an automobile accident.

Browning, Jim (d. June 19, 1936) was recognized as the World Champion by the New York State Athletic Commission from February of 1933 until his defeat by Jim Londos on June 25, 1934.

Bruce, Dwayne *see* Parker, Buddy Lee

Bruckman, George (b. 1912; Washington, D.C.; 5'8", 204 lbs.) began wrestling professionally in the 1930s. He served in the Coast Guard during World War II and toured in USO shows after the war. He resumed his wrestling career in the late 1940s, often appearing in matches in California and Washington State.

Bruggers, Bob teamed with Paul Jones to hold the NWA Atlantic Coast Tag Title in 1974. He survived an airplane crash that injured Ric Flair and several other wrestler in October of 1975.

Brunetti, Guy teamed with Joe Brunetti to hold the World Tag Team Title in Chicago in February of 1956. They captured the Canadian Open Tag Team Title in Toronto several times in 1956 and 1957. They held NWA World Tag Team Title in Minneapolis several times in 1957. They held the Pacific Coast Tag Team Title in Vancouver, Canada, in March of 1961. They captured the NWA World Tag Team Title in San Francisco in June of 1961.

Brunetti, Joe (Joe Tangara) teamed with Guy Brunetti to hold the World Tag Team Title in Chicago in February of 1956. They captured the Canadian Open Tag Team Title in Toronto several times in 1956 and 1957. They held the NWA World Tag Team Title in Minneapolis several times in 1957. They held the Pacific Coast Tag Team Title in Vancouver, Canada, in March of 1961. They captured the NWA World Tag Team Title in San Francisco in June of 1961.

Brunk, Terry *see* Sabu

Bruno, Downtown *see* Wippleman, Harvey

Bruns, Bobby (b. 1915, d. January 23, 1983; Des Moines, Iowa; 6'2", 225 lbs.) was the son of German opera singer Lotta Gunther. Bruns was educated in Southern California, where he studied law. He was trained as a wrestler by Jim Londos and began wrestling professionally in the 1930s. He held the South American and South African championships. He held the MWA Title in Kansas City in early 1940. He held the Kansas City Title several more times in the late 1940s, often feuding with Orville Brown. He held the Hawaiian Tag Team Title several times in the early 1950s, teaming with Lucky Simunovich and John Paul Henning.

Brunzell, Jim (b. Aug. 13, 1949; White Bear Lake, Minnesota; 5'10", 234 lbs.) began wrestling in 1972. He teamed with Mike George to hold the NWA Central States Tag Team Title in late 1973. He teamed with Greg Gagne to form the High Flyers in the AWA, and they captured the Tag Team Title from Blackjack Lanza and Bobby Duncum in July of 1977. They retained the belts until September of 1978, when Brunzell was unable to defend the title because of an injury suffered while playing softball. He held the NWA Mid-Atlantic Title several times in 1979 and 1980. He and Gagne returned to take the AWA tag belts from Adrian Adonis and Jesse Ventura in June of 1981. They remained champions for over two years until Adonis and Ventura ended their reign in June of 1983. Brunzell later joined with B. Brian Blair to form the Killer Bees in the WWF in the late 1980s.

Brute, The *see* McGraw, Bugsy

Bulba, Ivan "the Terrible" *see* Shaw, John R.

Bulba, Taras (Outer Mongolia; 237 lbs.) held the Southern Heavyweight Title in August of 1985.

Bullet, The *see* Armstrong, Bob

Bullinski, Bull teamed with Dennis Stamp to hold the U.S. Tag Team Title in Louisiana in February of 1973.

Bundy, King Kong (Chris Palies; b. November 7, 1957; Atlantic City, New Jersey; 6'4", 446 lbs.) began wrestling in 1976. He sometimes competed under the name Chris Canyon. He held the World Class Championship in Texas several times in 1982. He held the World Class American Tag Team Title several times in 1982, teaming with Bugsy McGraw and Bill Irwin. He teamed with the Masked Superstar to hold the NWA National Tag Team Title briefly in May of 1984. He held the Southern Heavyweight Title for several months in mid-1984. He teamed with Rick Rude to capture the Southern Tag Team Title in a tournament in October of 1984. He wrestled Hulk Hogan in a cage match at Wrestlemania II in April of 1986. Bundy began an acting career in the late 1980s, appearing in the film *Moving* (1988) with Richard Pryor, and on an episode of television's *Married…With Children*. He returned to the WWF in 1994 and was managed by Ted DiBiase.

Bunkhouse Buck *see* Golden, Jimmy

Burke, Leo (Leo Cormier; 6'1", 242 lbs.) began wrestling in 1978. The New Brunswick native held the Stampede North American Title in Calgary, Canada, numerous times in the late 1970s and early 1980s. He held the WWC Universal Title in Puerto Rico in late 1989.

Burke, Mildred (Mildred Bliss; b. 1915, d. February 18, 1989; Los Angeles, California; 5'2", 130 lbs.) was born in Coffeyville, Kansas. She held the Women's World Wrestling

Championship from 1937 until 1954. She also held the All-Japan Women's Title in the 1950s. She was married to wrestling promoter Billy Wolfe. She died in a Northridge, California, hospital on February 18, 1989.

Burke, Samson *see* Berg, Sammy

Burton, Tom wrestled with Tony Anthony as the Dirty White Boys to capture the USWA Tag Team Title in June of 1990.

Bushwhacker Butch Miller (Robert Miller; b. October 21; New Zealand; 5'11", 245 lbs.) is a native of New Zealand. He began wrestling in 1973 in New Zealand. He teamed with Luke Williams as the Kiwis, calling themselves Brute Miller and Sweet Miller. They soon came to North America where they wrestled with the Calgary Stampede. Wrestling as Nick Carter and Sweet William, the Kiwis held the Calgary Stampede International Tag Team Title several times in 1974. They returned to New Zealand after their Canadian tour, but were soon in the United States. They entered the NWA as the New Zealand Sheepherders, where they quickly rose through the tag team ranks. They held the Pacific Northwest tag belts several times in 1979 and 1980. They held the Canadian Tag Team Title in February of 1980. They captured the NWA Atlantic Coast Tag Title several times in 1980 and held the NWA Southeastern Title in December of 1981. They held the WWC North American Tag Team Title in Puerto Rico several times in 1985. They also held the U.S. Tag Team Title in Florida in October of 1986.

The wrestled in the UWF in Oklahoma in 1986 and 1987, holding the tag team belts several times in the area. In the late 1980s the team went to the WWF where they wrestled as the Bushwhackers.

Bushwhacker Luke Williams (Brian Wickens; b. January 8; New Zealand; 6'1", 244 lbs.) is a native of New Zealand. He began wrestling in New Zealand in 1964. In the 1970s he teamed with Butch Miller as the Kiwis, calling themselves Brute Miller and Sweet Miller. They soon came to North America where they wrestled with the Calgary Stampede. Wrestling as Sweet William and Nick Carter, the Kiwis held the Calgary Stampede International Tag Team Title several times in 1974. They returned to New Zealand after their Canadian tour, but were soon in the United States. They entered the NWA as The New Zealand Sheepherders, where they quickly rose through the tag team ranks. They held the Pacific Northwest tag belts several times in 1979 and 1980. They held the Canadian Tag Team Title in February of 1980. They captured the NWA Atlantic Coast Tag Title several times in 1980 and held the NWA Southeastern Title in December of 1981. Williams also teamed with Jonathan Boyd as the Sheepherders, holding the Southern Tag Team Title several times in 1983. They held the WWC North American Tag Team Title in Puerto Rico several times in 1985. Williams and Miller held the U.S. Tag Team Title in Florida in October of 1986. The wrestled in the UWF in Oklahoma in 1986 and 1987, holding the tag team belts several times in the area. In the late 1980s the team went to the WWF where they wrestled as the Bushwhackers.

Busick, Big Bully (Pittsburgh, Pennsylvania; 6'1", 255 lbs.) began wrestling in 1986. Known for his heart punch, he wrestled in the Georgia All Stars in 1990, winning the title in May of 1990. He entered the WWF in the early 1990s. He was managed by Harvey Wippleman, but departed the promotion after a brief stay.

Butch *see* Bushwhacker Butch

Butcher, The *see* Beefcake, Brutus

Byers, June (b. 1925; Houston, Texas; 5'7", 150 lbs.) began wrestling professionally in the late 1940s. She was one of the top woman wrestlers for several decades. She was awarded the Women's World Championship in June of 1953. She retained the belt until her retirement in 1964. She also held the Florida Women's Title in the early 1960s.

Cactus Jack Manson (Mick Foley; b. June 7, 1965; Truth or Consequences, New Mexico; 6'4", 277 lbs.) is a native of Bloomington, Indiana. He was trained by Domenic DeNucci and made his wrestling debut in a match in Clarksburg, West Virginia in June of 1983. He wrestled on the independent circuit throughout the East Coast until joining Robert Fuller's Stud Stable in the CWA in 1988. He teamed with Gary Young to capture the CWA Tag Team Title in October of 1988. He subsequently joined Gen. Skandor Akbar's organization in Texas. He teamed with Scott Braddock to hold the World Class World Tag Team Title in August of 1989. He also wrestled in the NAW in Pittsburgh, capturing that promotions title in December of 1989. Cactus entered the WCW in 1989, teaming with Kevin Sullivan. He and Sullivan defeated the Nasty Boys for the WCW Tag Team Championship on May 22, 1994. They lost the belts to Paul Orndorff and Paul Roma on July 17, 1994. Cactus lost most of his ear in an in-ring accident against Big Van Vader in a match in Munich, Germany, in March of 1994. He left the WCW later in the year to compete on the independent circuit and in Japan. Jack teamed with Mikey Whipwreck to win the ECW Tag Team Title from Public Enemy in August of 1994. They lost the belts in a re-match in December of 1994. Cactus Jack left the ECW in early 1996 to enter the WWF, where he wrestled as Mankind the Mutilator.

Caddock, Earl (b. 1888, d. August 25, 1950) was an amateur champion in Chicago in the early 1910s. He soon began wrestling professionally. He defeated Joe Stecher for the World Heavyweight Title in April of 1917 in Omaha, Nebraska. Craddock abandoned the belt to serve in the United States army during World War I. He resumed his wrestling career in the 1920s and subsequently worked in the automobile and oil businesses in Iowa. He died at his Walnut, Iowa, home on August 25, 1950.

Caiazo, George *see* Eliminator Kronus

Cain, Frankie held the Southern Junior Heavyweight Title in mid-1963. He teamed with Mike Clancy to hold the Southern Tag Team Title in July of 1965. He subsequently wrestled with Rocky Smith as the Infernos. The duo captured the NWA World Tag Team Title in Florida in October of 1966. They held the belts several times over the next three years. They were often managed by J.C. Dykes. They also held the NWA Florida Tag Team Title in early 1971 and again in January of 1972.

Cairo, Tommy (b. Feb. 19; Philadelphia, Pennsylvania; 6'3", 257 lbs.) began wrestling in 1991. He wrestled in ECW in the early 1990s.

Caldwell, Kevin *see* Sullivan, Kevin

Caldwell, Whitey (d. October 7, 1972) was a popular wrestler in East Tennessee during the 1960s and early 1970s. He was killed in an automobile accident on October 7, 1972, en route from a match in Morristown, Tennessee.

Calhoun, Haystacks (William D. Calhoun; b. August 3, 1934, d. December 7, 1989; Morgan's Corner, Arkansas; 601 lbs.) was born in McKinney, Texas. He was a popular wrestler from the 1960s, who often used his massive size to crush an opponent in the ring. He teamed with Don Leo Jonathan to hold the Canadian Tag Team Title in July of 1966. They again held the Canadian belts in June of 1968. He wrestled in the WWWF in the early 1970s and teamed with Tony Garea to win the WWWF Tag Team Title from Toru Tanaka and Mr. Fuji in May of 1973. They lost the belts back to Tanaka and Fuji the following September. Calhoun died of complications from diabetes at a North Texas hospital on December 7, 1989.

Calhoun, Haystacks, Jr. (John Brody; 6'4", 526 lbs.) began wrestling in 1990. He wrestled and promoted in the Florida area in the 1990s. He claimed to be the son of Haystacks Calhoun. He held the Florida Wrestling Alliance Title several times in 1994.

California Connection *see* Tatum, John & Price, Rod

Callous, Mean Mark *see* Undertaker, The

Calloway, Mark *see* Undertaker, The

Calypso Jim (6'1", 277 lbs.) began wrestling in 1977. He wrestled in the WWA during the 1980s. He was co-holder of the WWA Tag Team Title several times from 1986 until 1988, teaming with Chris Carter and Denny Kass. He subsequently wrestled as Bobo Brazil, Jr., holding the UWF title in Indianapolis in early 1994.

Calza, Al (b. 1927; New York City) was a boxer and professional baseball player before becoming a wrestler in the late 1940s. He remained a leading competitor through the 1950s.

Calza, Gino teamed with Tony Calza to hold the Southern Tag Team Title in April of 1963.

Calza, Tony teamed with Gino Calza to hold the Southern Tag Team Title in April of 1963.

Cameron, Larry (b. 1952, d. December 13, 1993; 6'1", 280 lbs.) began wrestling in 1986. The former Chicagoan played football with the Denver Broncos. He wrestled in the PWA, capturing the title in September of 1987. He won the Calgary Stampede North American Title in April of 1989. He held the IWA title in Ohio in 1991 and 1992. He subsequently became a top wrestler with the CWA in Germany. He held the Catch Wrestling Association Tag Team Title in Europe several times in 1992 and 1993, teaming with Mad Bull Buster. He was defending the tag title when he died of complications from asthma after collapsing in the ring during a bout with Tony St. Clair in Germany on December 13, 1993.

Campbell, Black Angus held the Stampede North American Title in Calgary, Canada, several times in 1971. He held the NWA Central States Title in 1972. He teamed with Roger Kirby to hold the NWA Central States Tag Title in June of 1972. Wrestling as Rasputin, he held the NWA Pacific Northwest Title in August of 1974.

Campbell, Ian held the Scottish Heavyweight Title in the early 1960s. He appeared in the 1973 British supernatural film *The Wicker Man*.

Campbell, Man Mountain *see* Brown, Luke

Canadian, The *see* Piper, Roddy

Can-Am Express *see* Furnas, Doug & Kroffat, Dan

Candido, Chris (b. 1971; Carteret, New Jersey; 5'8", 226 lbs.) began wrestling in the USWA in 1990. He wrestled in the WWA in New Jersey in the early 1990s, holding the Junior Heavyweight Title in 1990 and 1992, and the tag team title with Chris Evans in 1993. He entered Smoky Mountain in April of 1993, where he teamed with Brian Lee to capture the tag team belts. Candido captured the revived NWA title in a tournament in November of 1994. He relinquished the belt to Dan Severn in February of 1995. He and his wife, Tammy Fytch, joined the WWF in 1995 as the Body Donnas, with Candido as Skip and Fytch as Sunny. Candido teamed with Zip to capture the WWF Tag Team Title in the Spring of 1996.

Candy, Ray (Raymond Canty; b. 1950, d. May 23, 1994; 6'4", 297 lbs.) began wrestling in Georgia in 1973. He held the ASWA Georgia Title in July of 1973. He teamed with Pistol Pez Whatley to hold the Mid-America Tag Team Title in 1977. He teamed with Steven Little Bear to hold the U.S. Tag Team Title in Louisiana several times in early 1978. Candy held the MSWA North American Title in November of 1978. He held the NWA TV Title several times in 1979. He wrestled during the 1980s for under the name Kareem Muhammad, teaming with Leroy Brown as the Zambuie Express. They held the U.S. Tag Team Title in Florida in September of 1983. They captured the Southern Tag Team Title several times in early

1984. He also held the WWC Puerto Rican Title in June of 1987. He wrestled as Blackstud Williams to capture the Oregon Wrestling Federation title in June of 1988. Candy's last bouts were in the WCW in 1988 when he wrestled as Commando Ray with Grizzly Boone in the Commandoes. He retired from the ring to work as a supervisor and dispatcher for a transport business in Decatur, Georgia. He died of a heart attack in a Decatur hospital on May 23, 1994.

Candyman, The *see* Fine, Reggie B.

Canek, El (Mexico City, Mexico; 5'11", 235 lbs.) began wrestling in 1972. He is a leading Mexican wrestler who held the Mexican National Light Heavyweight Title in 1978. He teamed with Dr. Wagner, Jr. to hold the EMLL Tag Team Title in March of 1993.

Cannon, George "Crybaby" (George McArthur; d. July 1, 1994) managed the Fabulous Kangaroos in the late 1960s. He held the Beat the Champ TV Title in Los Angeles in late 1968. He died on July 1, 1994.

Cannonball Grizzly *see* News, P.N.

Canterberry, Mark *see* Godwinn, Henry O.

Canyon, Chris teamed with Mark Starr as Men at Work in the WCW in the mid-1990s.

Canyon, Chris *see* Bundy, King Kong

Captain USA *see* Studd, Big John

Caras, Cien (Carmelo Reyes; 6'3", 240 lbs.) teamed with Victor Rivera to hold the NWA Americas Tag Team Title in Los Angeles in January of 1977. He also teamed with Jose Lothario to hold the World Class Texas Tag Team Title in 1977. He held the Mexican National Heavyweight Title several times in the early 1980s. He teamed with Sangre Chicana and Mascara Ano 2000 to hold the Mexican National Tag Team Title several times in the mid-1980s. He held the EMLL Light Heavyweight Title in from June of 1987 until March of 1988. He captured the EMLL Heavyweight Title from Konnan el Barbaro in October of 1991. He left the promotion in June of 1992.

Carescia, Tony (Cadiz, Ohio; 190 lbs.) served in the air force during World War II and entered professional wrestling in the late 1940s.

Carillo, Ignacio Carlos *see* Anibal

Carlisle, Jim (d. 1989) co-hosted Columbus Championship Wrestling on television with Fred Ward.

Carlson, Cowboy teamed with Herb Freeman to hold the NWA Pacific Northwest Tag Team Title in 1957.

Carlson, Tug *see* Carlton, Lord Leslie

Carlton, Lord Leslie (b. 1916, d. 19??; Ipswich, England; 6'2", 225 lbs.) claimed to be educated at Oxford University in England. He wore a monocle into the ring and was accompanied by a valet. He began wrestling professionally in the late 1930s. He was a leading mat villain through the 1940s and early 1950s, occasionally wrestling as Tug Carlson.

Carlyn, Bill wrestled under the mask as one of the Assassins in the Atlanta, Georgia, area in the 1970s.

Carnera, Primo (b. October 26, 1906, d. June 29, 1967; Los Angeles, California; 6'6", 263 lbs.) was a circus strongman in Italy before coming to the United States in the 1920s. He wrestled in carnivals during the decade and soon began a career in boxing in 1928. He was known in the ring as "the Ambling Alp." He defeated Jack Sharkey for the heavyweight boxing title in 1933, but was unseated as champion by Max Baer the following year. He returned to Italy after a ring defeat by Joe Louis in the late 1930s. Carnera returned to the United States after World War II to compete as a professional wrestler. He held over 300 consecutive wins until he was defeated by Antonio Rocca in 1949. He teamed with Sandor Szabo to hold the NWA World Tag Team Title in San Francisco in 1950. He remained on of the most popular competitors in the sport during the 1950s. Carnera also appeared in several films during his career including *Mighty Joe Young"* (1949), *Casanova's Big Night* (1954), *Prince Valaint* (1954), *A Kid for Two Farthings* (1956) and *Hercules Unchained* (1960). He died in his native village of Sequals, Italy, on June 29, 1967.

Carota, Carol (b. 1929; Cincinnati, Ohio; 5'4", 134 lbs.) was an acrobat and weight-lifter before she entered professional wrestling in the early 1950s. She remained a leading female competitor throughout the decade.

Carpentier, Edouard was a leading Canadian wrestler from the 1950s. He held the AWA Title in Montreal, Canada, in 1957. He also held the Omaha World Title from June of 1957. He held the WWA Title in Los Angeles from 1957 until 1961. He also held the AWA Title in Montreal several more times in the early 1960s. He again held the WWA belt briefly in December of 1963. He teamed with Bob Ellis to hold the WWA Tag Team Title in December of 1964. He held the NWA Americas Title in Los Angeles several times in 1974 and 1975.

Carr, Charley (d. 19??) held the Hawaiian Title in 1942.

Carson, Don held the Gulf Coast Title in Alabama in the early 1960s. He teamed with Dick Murdock, wrestling as Ron Carson, to hold the Gulf Coast Tag Team Title in May of 1967. He teamed with the Red Shadow to hold the Southern Tag Team Title in July of 1968. He held the World Tag Team Title in Tennessee with Len Rossi in March of 1969. He held the NWA Americas Title in Los Angeles in July of 1971. He teamed with Dennis Condrey to briefly hold the Southern Tag Team Title in February of 1979. He managed the Mongolian Stomper in the NWA in the early 1980s.

Carson, Ron *see* Murdoch, Dick

Carter, Chris held the WWA Tag Team Title several times in the mid-1980s, teaming with Bobo Brazil, Calypso Jim, Mohammad Saad and Don Kent.

Carter, Nick *see* Bushwhacker Butch Miller

Carter, T.C. (6'1", 230 lbs.) began wrestling in 1984. The Polynesian star wrestled in the WCW in 1990.

Casas, Negro (Jose Casas Ruiz; 5'7", 180 lbs.) began wrestling in Mexico in 1979. He wrestled in several impressive bouts against Jushin Liger in 1990. He captured the UWA Middleweight Title in Mexico in January of 1991, holding the title for over a year. He is the son of Pepe Casas and the brother of wrestlers Felino and Heavy Metal.

Casas, Pepe was a popular Mexican star. He is the father of wrestlers Negro Casas, Felino and Heavy Metal.

Casey, Ann was a leading female wrestler in the 1970s. She retired in the early 1980s.

Casey, Jack (b. 1916, d. July 26, 1990; Ireland; 6', 240 lbs.) was a leading wrestler in the 1940s and 1950s. He held the Pacific Coast Title in San Francisco in October of 1941. He held the Pacific Coast belt again in January of 1946.

Casey, Kevin "the Truth" was a television host for South Pacific Wrestling Association. He subsequently managed the Heartbreakers in Puerto Rico.

Casey, Rick *see* Cooley, Wendell

Casey, Scott (b. March 19; Amarillo, Texas; 6', 242 lbs.) began wrestling in 1972. He held the World Class Texas Title in May of 1977. He teamed with Mike George to hold the NWA Central States Tag Team Title in December of 1977. He teamed with Rick Casey to hold the MSCW Tag Team Title in South Dakota in 1984. He held the World Class TV Title in April of 1985. He wrestled for several years in the WWF in the late 1980s.

Casey, Steve "Crusher" (b. 1908, d. January 10, 1987; 6', 220 lbs.) was a native of County Kerry, Ireland. He was champion oarsman and wrestler in Ireland. He was brought to Boston by promoter Paul Bowser in 1936 to compete as a professional wrestler. He defeated Lou Thesz for the AWA World Heavyweight Title in Boston, Massachusetts, on February 11, 1938. He held the AWA belt on five other occasions through 1945, defeating Gus Sonenberg, Ed Don George, the French Angel and Frank Sexton for the title. He ultimately relinquished the belt to Frank Sexton on June 27, 1945. He retired from the ring the following year and opened Crusher Casey's, a bar in Back Bay, Massachusetts. Casey was critically wounded during an armed holdup in 1968, but recovered from his injuries. He died of cancer in a Boston hospital on January 10, 1987.

Cash, Porkchop was a leading Black wrestling from the early 1970s. He held the NWA Americas Title in Los Angeles several times in 1974. He also held the Americas tag team belt several times in 1974 and 1975, teaming with Manny Soto and S.D.

Jones. He teamed with Tom Jones to hold the NWA Georgia Tag Team Title in September of 1976. He held the U.S. Tag Team Title in Louisiana several times in late 1977, teaming with Mike George and Dr. X. Cash teamed with Jay Youngblood to hold the NWA Atlantic Coast Tag Title in 1982. He recaptured the belt later in the year with King Parsons as his partner. He teamed with Troy Graham as the Bruise Brothers to hold the Southern Tag Team Title several times in 1983. He held the NWA Southeastern Title in 1984. He teamed with Ken Timbs to hold the NWA Central States Tag Team Title in April of 1987. He again held the Central States tag belts with Rick McCord in November of 1987. Cash also held the NWA Central States Title in July of 1987.

Cassidy, Lance *see* Armstrong, Steve

Cassidy, Leaf *see* Snow, Al

Cassius, Joe (b. 1927; d. March 25, 1997; 5'5") engaged in amateur wrestling while attending Southern Methodist University in Dallas, where he also participated in martial arts and weightlifting. He began wrestling professionally after graduation in 1952, competing throughout the United States as Judo Joe. He also grappled in South America under the name El Gringo. Cassius' wrestling career financed his education at Yeshiva University in New York City, where he earned a doctorate in clinical psychology in 1959. He abandoned the ring to begin practicing psychology. He open a private practice in Memphis, Tennessee, in 1970. Casius died of a heart attack in Memphis on March 25, 1997.

Castellanos, Dionicio *see* Psicosis

Castillo, Hurricane (d. December 11, 1993) was a Puerto Rican wrestler. He died of complications from surgery on December 11, 1993. He was the father of wrestler Hurricane Castillo, Jr.

Castillo, Hurricane, Jr. is the son of wrestler Hurricane Castillo. He teamed with Miguel Perez, Jr. to hold the WCW Tag Team Title in Puerto Rico in 1989.

Centopani, Paul *see* Roma, Paul

Cerdan, Louis *see* Brito, Sr., Gino

Champion, Chris (6'1", 222 lbs.) began wrestling in 1984. He teamed with Sean Royal as the New Breed, holding the Florida Tag Team Title for several months in early 1987. He teamed with his brother, Mark Starr, as Wildside to win the CWA Tag Team Title in July of 1989. He wrestled with Todd Champion as The New Breed in the late 1980s. He wrestled as Yoshi Wan in WCW in the Spring of 1993. He entered the USWA in early 1996, wrestling as Yoshi Kwan.

Champion, Todd teamed with Dave Peterson to hold the NWA Central States Tag Team Title in November of 1986. He wrestled with Chris Champion as The New Breed in the late 1980s. He teamed with Firebreaker Chip as the Patriots in the WCW in the early 1990s. The duo captured the WCW U.S. Tag Team Title from the Fabulous Freebirds in August of 1991. They lost the belts to the Young Pistols in

November of 1991. Champion defeated Butch Reed for the USWA Unified Title in Cleveland on October 17, 1992.

Charles, Emilio (b. 1924, d. September 6, 1995) is the father of wrestler Emilio Charles, Jr.

Charles, Emilio, Jr. was the son of wrestler Emilio Charles. He was a popular wrestler in Mexico from the late 1980s, holding the Mexican Middleweight Title several times in the late 1980s and early 1990s.

Charles, Norman Frederick teamed with Jonathan Boyd as the Royal Kangaroos in the Pacific Northwest in the early 1970s. They held the tag team title several times in 1971. The Royal Kangaroos held the Calgary Stampede International Tag Team Title in 1977.

Charles, Tony was a leading British wrestler from the 1960s. He held the Southern Area Heavyweight Title in England in 1969. He subsequently competed in the United States. He teamed with Leon Rossi to hold the Mid-America Tag Team Title in April of 1972. Charles also held the Mid-American Title in June of 1972. He teamed with Les Thornton to hold the NWA Georgia Tag Team Title in December of 1975. They also held the World Class Texas Tag Team Title in 1976. Charles was also active in the Memphis area in the late 1970s.

Chavis, Chris *see* Tatanka

Chaz *see* Taylor, Chaz

Cheetah Kid *see* Rock, Flyboy Rocco

Chene, Larry (d. October, 1965) teamed with Raul Zapata to hold the NWA Texas Tag Team Title in May of 1955. He held the Pacific Coast Junior Heavyweight Title in February of 1956. He teamed with Herb Freman to hold the NWA Pacific Northwest Tag Team Title in May of 1956. He held the NWA Texas Junior Heavyweight Title several times in the mid-1950s. He again held the Texas tag belts in May of 1958, teaming with Pepper Gomez.

Chi-Town Heat *see* Stevie Ray & Booker T.

Chin Lee was a leading Japanese grappler from the 1960s. He teamed with Corsica Joe to hold the Southern Tag Team Title in November of 1966. He held the Calgary Stampede International Tag Team Title several times in the early 1970s, teaming with Sugi Sito.

Cholak, Moose held the IWA Title in Chicago in late 1962 and early 1963. He teamed with Wilbur Snyder to hold the WWA Tag Team belts from December of 1965 until March of 1966. Cholak held the North American Title in Cleveland in the late 1960s. Cholak teamed with Paul Christy to capture the WWA Tag Title in February of 1977. They held the belt for several months.

Chono, Masa (Masahiro Chono; b. Sept. 17, 1963; Tokyo, Japan; 5'11", 235 lbs.) began wrestling in October of 1984. The popular Japanese star wrestled in the CWA, Continental and WCW. He held the NWA Central States TV

Title in January of 1988. He teamed with Mike Davis to hold the CWF Tag Team Title in May of 1989. He was awarded the NWA Heavyweight Championship following his defeat of Rick Rude in a tournament in Tokyo, Japan, on August 12, 1992. He was defeated for the belt by the Great Muta in Tokyo on January 4, 1993.

Chorre, Sonny (b. 1927, d. 19??; Oklahoma; 6'2", 227 lbs.) wrestled as Chief Sunni War Cloud from the 1940s. A member of the Wassek tribe, he was managed by athlete Jim Thorpe. He wore a tribal headdress and Indian garb while entering an arena, and was known in the ring for his Indian death-lock hold. He teamed with Steven Little Bear to hold the Hawaiian Tag Team Title in June of 1971.

Choshu, Riki (Mitsuo Yoshida; b. December 3, 1951; Yamaguchi, Japan; 6', 246 lbs.) began wrestling in 1974. He represented South Korea in the 1972 Olympics and won the Mexican title from El Canek in 1982. He held the All-Japan Pacific Wrestling Federation Title from April of 1986 until he joined New Japan in March of 1987.

Chou, Chino held the NWA Americas Tag Team Title several times in 1981 and 1982, teaming with Gene LeBell and the Kiss.

Christenello, Donna was a leading female wrestler of the 1970s. She often teamed with Toni Rose. They lost a bout for the women's tag team belt to Vicki Williams and Joyce Grable in 1970.

Christian, Kevin (Kevin Lawler) appeared in the ECW as a referee and wrestler in 1993. He briefly appeared under the name Freddie Gilbert. He refereed and wrestled in the USWA in the mid-1990s, sometimes competing under a mask as the Hornet. He is the son of wrestler Jerry Lawler.

Christie, Joe held the Texas Brass Knucks Title in 1954 and again in 1959. He also held the NWA Texas Title for several months in early 1959.

Christopher, Brian (Brian Lawler; Memphis, Tennessee; 5'10", 230 lbs.) is the son of wrestler Jerry Lawler. He began wrestling in 1989. He teamed with Tony Williams as the New Kids, until he broke with his partner and wrestled as a villain for several years. He captured the USWA Southern Title in March of 1992. He held that belt over a dozen times over the next several years, wrestling against Tom Prichard, Jeff Jarrett, Buddy Landell, Doug Gilbert, Eddie Gilbert and others. He held the USWA Tag Team Title several times in 1993, teaming with Big Black Dog and Scotty Flamingo. He teamed with Jeff Jarrett to hold the USWA tag belts in October and November of 1993. Christopher again held the title in April of 1994, teaming with Eddie Gilbert. He defeated Tommy Rich for the USWA Heavyweight Title on December 31, 1994. He lost the belt to Brian Lee in April of 1995. Christopher held the belt several more times during 1995 and 1996, defeating Doug Gilbert, Billy Jack Haynes and Tex Slazenger.

Christy, Paul (Chicago, Illinois; 5'10", 220 lbs.) began wrestling in the early 1970s. He teamed with Wilbur Snyder to hold the WWA Tag Team Title briefly in August of 1971. Teaming with Moose Cholak, he again captured the tag belts for several months in 1977. A popular fan favorite for most of his career, Christy became a ring villain in 1978, under the management of Miss Bunny Love. He teamed with Roger Kirby to hold the WWA tag belts for several months in 1979.

Christy, Vic (b. 1921; Los Angeles, California; 6'2", 230 lbs.) held the AWA Title in Montreal, Canada in 1938. He held the MWA Title in Kansas City in March of 1946. His brother, Ted Christy, also wrestled professionally.

Ciassio, Rick teamed with Al Snow as the Fantastix. They held the Motor City Wrestling U.S. Tag Team Title from November of 1986 until April of 1987.

Ciclon Negro *see* Negro, Ciclon

Civil, Eddie *see* Savage, Whiskers

Clancy, Irish Bobby (5'5", 220 lbs.) began wrestling in 1992. He wrestled with Otis Apollo as Canadian Lighting. They held the Border City Wrestling Can-Am Tag Team Title in May of 1993, and the Global tag belts from July of 1993 until March of 1994. Clancy briefly held the Motor City Wrestling Midwest Tag Team belts with Scott D'Amore in May of 1994.

Clancy, Iron Mike (b. 1919, d. 1988; Boston, Massachusetts; 5'9", 218 lbs.) served in the Coast Guard during World War II. Known in the ring as "Mr. Irish," he specialized in the "Irish whip" maneuver. He sometimes wrestled as the Mighty Titan. He held the NWA World Junior Heavyweight Title in 1957. He teamed with George Becker to hold the NWA Southern Tag Team Title in 1958. He held the Southern Junior Heavyweight Title during 1960. He also held the World Tag Team Title in Tennessee with Oni Wiki Wiki in May of 1960. He teamed with Red McKim to hold the Texas World Tag Team Title in September of 1962. He teamed with Frankie Cain to hold the Southern Tag Team Title in July of 1965.

Clark, Brian *see* Bomb, Adam

Clark, Jeannie *see* Blossom, Lady

Clary, Dennis (d. 1955) held the NWA Central States Title in 1951. He teamed with Rikidozan to hold the Pacific Coast Tag Team Title in October of 1952.

Claw, The *see* Andrews, Tom

Clay, Bob (Oklahoma; 200 lbs.) was a rodeo performer who began wrestling in the late 1940s. He remained active in both sports over the next decade.

Claybourne, Jim (d. 19??; Boston, Massachusetts) was a leading Black wrestler. He began wrestling in 1943, and claimed to have not lost a match in until 1948. He held the Hawaiian Title in November of 1948. He wrestled in Europe in the early 1950s.

Clayton, Jay teamed with Danny Hodge to hold the U.S. Tag

Team Title in Louisiana in July of 1975.

Clements, Sir Dudley (d. April 21, 1976) managed the Fabulous Kangaroos in the 1960s. He managed Don and Al Greene in the Mid South in the early 1970s, and Bobby Mayne and Charlie Fulton later in the decade.

Cletus the Fetus wrestled with the Incredibly Strange Wrestling promotion in California. He competed against the Abortionist in several matches in 1995.

Clifton Cutie, The *see* Martinelli, Tony

Clones, The *see* Kelly, Pat & Mike

Coach, The *see* Tolos, John

Cobra *see* Thunder

Coffield, Jim (d. 19??) was from Kansas City, where he won the Missouri Valley amateur belt. He was a race car driver before he entered wrestling. He was trained by Joe Stecher and began his professional career in 1932. He held the NWA Central States Title in 1951.

Cohen, Sammy (300 lbs.) is the father of wrestlers Shaun Simpson, Steve Simpson and Stuart Simpson.

Cole, Keith wrestled with his brother, Kent, in the WCW in the early 1990s.

Cole, Kent wrestled with his brother, Keith, in the WCW in the early 1990s.

Coleman, Abe (b. 1910; Forest Hills, New York. 5'4", 220 lbs.) began wrestling in the early 1930s. He defeated Man Mountain Dean in a match in 1936. He was known in the ring as "the Kangaroo" for his "kangaroo dropkick" maneuver. He also worked as a promoter in the 1950s.

Coleman, Bobby (b. 1919; Los Angeles, California; 5'8", 200 lbs.) began wrestling in 1942. He won the Pacific Coast light-heavyweight title in the early 1940s and later held the Texas Junior Heavyweight title. He was also a stand-in for comic Lou Costello in the 1940s.

Collette, Jeff (6'1", 215 lbs.) began wrestling in Virginia in 1990. He teamed with Stan Lane to win the VWA Tag Team Title in 1991

Collins, Roy "Ripper" (d. November 12, 1991) held the Hawaiian Title several times from 1966 through 1971. He also held the Hawaiian Tag Team Title several times during this period, teaming with Johnny Barend, King Curtis and Buddy Austin. He teamed with Gordon Nelson to hold the NWA Americas Tag Team Title in Los Angeles in May of 1973. He returned to Hawaii to capture the tag belts in 1973, teaming with Ed Francis and Johnny Valentine. He held the NWA Pacific Northwest Title several times in 1974. He held the Calgary Stampede International Tag Team Title several times in 1976, teaming with Bobby Bass, Frenchy Martin and Larry Sharpe.

Colombo, Rocco "Rocky" (b. 1926, d. March 6, 1964; Bronx, New York; 5'7", 225 lbs.) learned to wrestle while serving in the Army.

He began his professional career in the late 1940s and was known in the ring as the Bronx Beast. He remained an active competitor through the 1950s.

Colon, Carlos (b. July 18; Bayamon, Puerto Rico; 5'10", 246 lbs.) trained at Antonio Rocca's wrestling club in New York City in 1962 and began wrestling professionally two years later. He wrestled for several years in Canada, where he captured the Canadian Heavyweight belt. In the late 1960s he returned to Puerto Rico. He returned to the United States in the early 1970s. Wrestling as Carlos Belafonte, he teamed with Gino Caruso to hold the Calgary Stampede International Tag Team Title in 1973. He teamed with Assassin #2 to capture the tag belts from the Kangaroos in Atlanta in 1974. He continued to wrestle often in Puerto Rico and the Caribbean throughout the decade. The popular Puerto Rican star was a long-time holder of the WWC Universal Title, holding the belt over a dozen times from 1982 through 1994.

Colorado Kid (Denver, Colorado; 6'3", 236 lbs.) began wrestling in 1993. He was the USWA Rookie of the Year in 1994 and held the Ozark Mountain Wrestling North American Championship in 1995.

Colosetti, Colosso was a leading wrestler from Argentina. He held titles in South America and Rome, Italy, during the 1970s. He defeated Ray Mendoza for the NWA World Light Heavyweight Title in the late 1970s. He defeated Jose Lothario for the Texas state title in 1978. He teamed with Jonathan Boyd to briefly hold the NWA Americas Title in Los Angeles in May of 1979. He feuded with Boyd after losing the belts, defeating him in a loser leave town battle.

Colossal Connection, The *see* Andre the Giant & Haku

Colt, Bobby (b. January 13), wrestling as Ron Reed, held the NWA Central States Title for the first half of 1965. He held the Hawaiian Title in January of 1966. He held the Central States belt again for several months from February of 1966. He held the WWA Title in 1983. He also teamed with Dick the Bruiser to hold the WWA Tag Team Title in 1984. His brother, Jerry Colt, also wrestled professionally.

Colt, Brett *see* Gunn, Bart

Colt, Buddy (b. 1936) held the NWA Georgia Title several times in the early 1970s. He also held the NWA Southern Title in Florida several times in 1972 and 1973, and the NWA Florida Title in 1973. He teamed with Harley Race and Roger Kirby to hold the NWA Georgia Tag Team Title in late 1974. Colt was seriously injured in the crash of a private plane near Tampa, Florida, on February 20, 1975. Wrestler Bobby Shane was killed in the crash. Colt remained involved in wrestling as a manager and referee through the 1980s.

Colt, Chris (San Francisco, California; 230 lbs.), wrestling as Jim Dillinger, joined Jack Dillinger as half of the Chain Gang tag team, following the shooting of Frank

Dillinger in September of 1969. They won the WWA tag belts two months later, holding the title until the following June. Wrestling as Chris Colt he teamed with Ron Dupree as the Comancheros to hold the WAA Tag Team Title in Phoenix in 1970. He held the Mid-America Title several times in 1979. He also held the Canadian Tag Team Title several times in 1979, teaming with Bobby Jaggers and Buddy Rose.

Comancheros, The see Colt, Chris & Dupree, Ron

Combs, Cora (b. 1926; Nashville, Tennessee; 5'5", 138 lbs.) began her wrestling career in the late 1940s. She was a top female wrestler in the 1950s and 1960s, often competing in the Mid-South area. Her daughter, Debbie Combs, also wrestled professionally.

Combs, Debbie is the daughter of wrestler Cora Combs. She held the NWA Women's Title in Kansas in April of 1987. She held the USWA Women's Title in early 1994.

Compadres, The see Madril, Al & Cruz, Manuel

Condliffe, Geoff (b. 1923, d. July 26, 1993) wrestled out of Great Britain for over 20 years as the masked villain Count Bartelli. He held the British Empire Heavyweight Title several times between 1969 and his retirement from the ring in 1986. He died of cancer on July 26, 1993.

Condrey, Dennis (February 1; 6', 256 lbs.) began wrestling in 1973. He teamed with Phil Hickerson to hold the Southern Tag Team Title several times from 1976 through 1978. They also held the NWA Southeastern Tag Team Title in November of 1978. Condrey held the Mid-America Title several times in 1979. He again held the Southeastern tag belts in November of 1979, teaming with David Shults. He and Shults also held the Southern tag belts in April of 1980. He held the NWA Georgia Title in September of 1980. He also held the NWA Southeastern Title in 1980. He was an original member of the Midnight Express with Randy Rose. They held the NWA Southeastern Tag Team Title numerous times from 1980 through 1983, with Norvell Austin and Ron Starr also competing as part of Midnight Express, Inc. The Midnight Express also held the Southern Tag Team Title several times in 1982. Condrey continued as part of the Midnight Express with Bobby Eaton as his partner. They held the MSWA Tag Team Title several times in 1984. Condrey and Eaton defeated the Rock 'n' Roll Express for the NWA World Tag Team Title in February of 1986. They held the belts until August of 1986, when they were defeated by the Rock 'n' Roll Express. Condrey was fired from the Midnight Express by manager Jimmy Cornette in April of 1987. He reteamed with Randy Rose upon entering the AWA in 1987. They captured the AWA Tag Team Title from Jerry Lawler and Bill Dundee in October of 1987. They lost the belts to the Midnight Rockers the following December. Condrey teamed with Doug Gilbert as the Lethal Weapons to capture the ICW Tag Title in December of 1989.

Conley, Jack (b. 1911; Denver, Colorado) was from Boston and began wrestling in the early 1930s. He was also a professional boxer.

Connor, A.C *see* Brown, D. Lo

Convict, The *see* Kelly, Kevin

Conway, Tiger, Jr. (Houston, Texas; 6', 229 lbs.) teamed with Paul Jones to hold the NWA Atlantic Coast Tag Title in 1975. He also held the tag belts with Dino Bravo later in the year. He teamed with Bull Ramos to hold the World Class Texas Tag Team Title in December of 1978. He teamed with Jose Lothario to capture the World Class American Tag Team Title in Texas in 1980. He teamed with Mr. Wrestling II to hold the MSWA Tag Team Title in March of 1983. He teamed with King Parsons as the Dream Team to hold the Texas All-Star USA Title several times in 1986. He later wrestled with Pez Whatley as the Jive Tones.

Cooage, Alan *see* Brown, Bad News

Cook, Bob teamed with Jerry Grey as the Mighty Yankees to hold the Florida Tag Team Title in September of 1987. He also wrestled as Superstar in Suncoast Pro Wrestling, holding the title several times in the late 1980s and early 1990s.

Cook, Carol (b. 1930; Toledo, Ohio; 5'2", 135 lbs.) began wrestling in the early 1950s. She was the daughter of a wrestler and remained a leading female competitor throughout the decade.

Cook, Charlie held the Mid-South Arkansas title in March of 1979. He briefly held the NWA Florida Title several times in late 1981.

Cooley, Wendell (Milton, Florida; 6'1", 220 lbs.) began wrestling in the South in 1981. He teamed with Scott Casey to hold the MSCW Tag Team Title in South Dakota in 1984. He teamed with Al Perez to capture the MSWA Tag Team Title in August of 1985. He wrestled as Rick Casey to capture the CWA International Title in February of 1986. He held the NWA Southeastern Title several times in 1986. He was also the Alabama champion several times in 1986 and 1987. He briefly held the CWA Title in January of 1989. He also held the Continental belt in 1989. He teamed with Frankie Lancaster as the Heartbreakers to hold the WWC Tag Team Title in Puerto Rico several times in 1991 and 1992.

Corazon de Leon *see* Jericho, Chris

Corbett, Joe (b. 1916; San Francisco, California; 5'11", 230 lbs.) played football for San Francisco University. He began wrestling in 1940. He was known in the ring for his use of the "Irish whip" and the "Oklahoma Hayride" maneuvers.

Corby, Bob (d. 19??; St. Louis, Missouri; 175 lbs.) began wrestling in the late 1930s. He was a leading light-heavyweight competitor, holding the Southern and Rocky Mountain titles. He continued to compete through the 1950s.

Cordova, Polo (b. 1917; New York City; 6'1", 220 lbs.) was a

Spaniard from Buenos Aires, Argentina, where he studied medicine. He began wrestling in 1944. He went to Europe in the late 1940s and won the Spanish championship in 1949. He wrestled in the United States from the early 1950s.

Cormier, Leo *see* Burke, Leo

Cornette, Jim (b. September 17, 1961) began his career as a wrestling manager in the Memphis area in 1982. He managed the various incarnations of the Midnight Express in the NWA in the 1980s. He founded Smoky Mountain Wrestling in early 1992, and managed the Heavenly Bodies in that promotion. He entered the WWF with the Heavenly Bodies in July of 1993. He was also the spokesman for Yokozuna. Smoky Mountain folded operations in 1995 and Cornette remained in the WWF as a manager.

Corsica Jean (Jean Roy; b. 1920, d. March 28, 1992) teamed with Corsica Joe to hold the World Tag Team Title in Tennessee several times in 1957. They also held the NWA Texas Tag Team Title in May of 1959 and the Southern Tag Team Title in Tennessee in January of 1960. They again held the Southern belts in September of 1964. He was shot and killed during a robbery at his restaurant in Tampa, Florida, on March 28, 1992.

Corsica Joe teamed with Corsica Jean to hold the World Tag Team title in Tennessee several times in 1957. He held the NWA Texas Title in June of 1959. He and Corsica Jean also held the NWA Texas Tag Team Title in May of 1959 and

the Southern Tag Team Title in Tennessee in January of 1960. They again held the Southern belts in September of 1964. Corsica Joe teamed with Chin Lee to capture the tag title in November of 1966. He married female grappler Sara Lee.

Cortez, Fidel teamed with Rip Oliver to hold the Canadian Tag Team Title in October of 1980.

Cortez, Hercules (b. 1932, d. July 24, 1971) was a Mexican wrestler who teamed with Red Bastien to defeat Mad Dog and Butcher Vachon for the AWA Tag Team Title in May of 1971. Cortez was killed in an automobile accident near St. Cloud, Minnesota, on July 24, 1971.

Cortolano, Mickey (b. 1916; Brooklyn, New York; 5'9", 202 lbs.) served in the Navy during World War II. He became a popular wrestler in the 1940s and 1950s who was known in the ring as the Mighty Mickey.

Cosenza, Tony (b. 1895, d. 19??; Flushing, New York; 5'10", 218 lbs.) was a concert pianist in addition to his wrestling career. He was known in the ring as the Flushing Flash from the 1930s through the 1950s.

Costello, Al (b. 1920) began his wrestling career in Australia in the late 1930s. He held the British Empire Title in South Africa in 1949. He held the Australian Title from 1951 until he left the country to come to the United States the following year. He subsequently wrestled with Roy Heffernan as the Fabulous Kangaroos from the late 1950s. The team was managed by

Wild Red Berry and, later, Crybaby Cannon and Sir Dudley Clements. They held the Texas World Tag Team Title in November of 1958. The Kangaroos defeated Red & Lou Bastien for the WWWF U.S. Tag Team Title in August of 1960. They briefly lost the belts to Johnny Valentine and Buddy Rogers in November of 1960, and again lost the belts to Valentine and Bob Ellis in January of 1962. They captured the WWA Tag Team Title in Los Angeles in February of 1964. He and Heffernan held the Canadian Tag Team Title in Vancouver several times in 1964 and 1965. Costello held the Southern Junior Heavyweight Title in April of 1966. He teamed with Herb Welch to hold the World Tag Team Title in Tennessee for several months in mid-1966. He teamed with Karl Von Brauner to hold the World Class World Tag Team Title in Texas later in the year. Don Kent replaced Heffernan in the Kangaroos, and he and Costello captured the WWA Tag Team Title twice in the early 1970s. He managed Phil Hickerson and Dennis Condrey in the Mid-South area in 1978. Costello later retired to Florida.

Costello, J.D. managed the MOD Squad in the Mid-South area in 1986.

Cousin Junior *see* Moondog Cujo

Cowan, Wayne *see* Mantell, Dutch

Cowboy Connection, The *see* Jaggers, Bobby & Tyler, R.T.

Cox, K.O *see* Sweetan, Bob

Cox, Steve (6'2", 240 lbs.) began wrestling in 1987. He began his career in the original UWF. He partnered with Michael Hayes in World Class in 1989, winning the World Class World Tag Team Title several times. Cox wrestled in Global in the early 1990s.

Cox, Ted wrestled as the Masked Marvel to capture the AWA Title in Montreal, Canada, in 1938. He held the NWA Texas Title several times in 1945 and 1946.

Crabtree, Shirley *see* Big Daddy

Cranium Cracker, The *see* Mitchell, Jim

Crawford, Eddie *see* Snowman, The

Creachman, Eddie (b. 1927, d. March 9, 1994) was a leading manager of villains in Canada during the 1960s and 1970s. His charges included the original Sheik. Creachman was known as "the Brain." He managed Abdullah the Butcher, Richard Charland and Chuck Simms in Montreal in 1987. He died of a heart attack in Montreal, Canada, on March 9, 1994.

Creachman, Floyd, III managed Bota, the Witch Doctor in the Memphis area in mid-1985.

Crews, Art held the NWA Central States TV Title several times in 1984 and 1985.

Crockett, Jim, Jr. is the son of promoter Jim Crockett, Sr. He was chief executive of Jim Crockett Promotions, the cornerstone of the NWA, until he sold his interests to Ted Turner in November of 1988.

Crockett, Jim, Sr. (b. 1908, d. April 1, 1973) was a leading wresting promoter. He formed Jim Crockett Promotions in 1935 and headed the NWA in the Carolinas. His son, Jim Crockett, Jr., took over the promotion following the elder Crockett's death in 1973.

Crookshanks, James *see* Ice, J.C.

Crookshanks, William *see* Dundee, Bill

Crosby, Len teamed with Gene Kiniski to hold the NWA Texas Tag Team Title in September of 1956.

Crox Alvarado (Cruz Pio del Socorro Alvarado Bolano; b. 1911, d. January 24, 1984) was born in San Jose, Costa Rica. He moved to Mexico in 1936, where he married actress Amanda del Llano. He became a popular wrestler and film actor from the 1940s. He appeared in over 100 films including *The Aztec Mummy* (1957), *The Robot vs. the Aztec Mummy* (1959), *The She-Wolf* (1965), *Island of the Dinosaurs* (1966) and *Santo vs. Capulina* (1971). He also produced and scripted several Mexican films. He died of a heart attack in a Mexico City hospital on January 24, 1984.

Crusaders, The *see* Robertson, Dewey & Lyons, Billy Red

Crush (Bryan Adams; b; Apr. 14; Kona, Hawaii; 6'4", 315 lbs.) began wrestling in 1986. He teamed with Len "the Grappler" Denton to hold the NWA Pacific Northwest Tag Team Title in December of 1989. He held the Pacific Northwest Title in February of 1990. He subsequently wrestled with Ax and Smash as the third member of Demolition in the WWF. He and Smash lost the WWF Tag Team Title to the Hart Foundation in August of 1990. He subsequently teamed with Steve Doll to win the Pacific Northwest championship in July of 1991, and again held the Pacific Northwest Title in October of 1991. Crush was terminated by the WWF following his arrest at his home in Kona, Hawaii, for possession of illegal drugs in early 1995.

Crush Girls *see* Nagayo, Chigusa & Asuka, Lioness

Crusher (Reggie Lisowski; Milwaukee, Wisconsin; 255 lbs.) wrestled from the 1950s through the 1980s, often teaming with Dick the Bruiser. He captured the World Tag Team Title in Chicago with Art Neilson in February of 1954. He teamed with Stan Lisowski to hold the belts several times in 1956 and 1957. They also held the Canadian Open Tag Team Title in Toronto in August of 1958, and the NWA World Tag Team Title in Minneapolis several times in 1958 and 1959. He held the World Title in Omaha in February of 1963. He defeated Verne Gagne for the AWA Title in July of 1963, but lost the belt back to Gagne in a rematch later in the month. He again won the AWA belt over Gagne in November of 1963, but Gagne reclaimed the belt the following month. Crusher teamed with Dick the Bruiser to capture the AWA World Tag Title from Ivan and Karol Kalmikoff in August of 1963. They were defeated for the belt by Verne Gagne and

Moose Evans in February of 1964. They reclaimed the title later in the month and held the belts until their defeat by Larry Hennig and Harley Race in January of 1965. He teamed with Verne Gagne to take the belts back from Hennig and Race in July of 1965, but they lost a rematch the following month. Crusher defeated Mad Dog Vachon for the AWA Title in August of 1965. He was defeated by Vachon for the championship in November of 1965. Crusher reteamed with Dick the Bruiser for another successful championship bid against Hennig and Race in May of 1966. They lost the belts in a rematch in January of 1967. They held the WWA Tag title several times in 1967. They were again AWA champions following their defeat of Mitsu Arakawa and Dr. Moto in December of 1968. They were defeated for the belts by Mad Dog and Butcher Vachon in August of 1969. Crusher replaced the late Hercules Cortez as Red Bastien partner in August of 1971, and they remained AWA World Tag Team champions until their defeat by Nick Bockwinkel and Ray Stevens in January of 1972. Crusher teamed with Billy Robinson in July of 1974 to beat Bockwinkel and Stevens for the title, but lost the rematch in October of 1974. Crusher again paired with Dick the Bruiser to beat Bockwinkel and Stevens in August of 1975. They held the belts until their defeat by Blackjack Lanza and Bobby Duncum in July of 1976. Crusher teamed with Tommy Rich to briefly hold the NWA Georgia Tag Team Title in September of 1979. Crusher made his final successful bid for the AWA

tag belts with Baron Von Raschke in May of 1984, defeating Jerry Blackwell and Ken Patera for the belts. They relinquished the title to the Road Warriors in August of 1984. Crusher suffered from a heart attack in September of 1991, but recovered.

Cruz, Alejandro *see* Blue Demon

Cruz, Manuel *see* Invader #1

Cruz, Motley (David Price) wrestled in the USWA in 1995.

Cruz, Roberto (Spain) was a leading wrestler from Spain before coming to the United States in the early 1950s.

Crying Greek, The *see* Zaharias, George

Cuban Assassin, The *see* Sierra, David

Cujo, Moondog *see* Moondog Cujo

Culley, Randy (b. May 4; 289 lbs.) wrestled with the Moondogs as Rex. He teamed with Moondog King to capture the WWF Tag Team Title from Tony Garea and Rick Martel in March of 1981. King was later replaced with Moondog Spot and they were defeated for the title by Garea and Martel in July of 1981. He and Spot teamed to capture the Southern Tag Team Title in April of 1983 under the management of Jimmy Hart. He captured the MSWA North American Title as the Nightmare in May of 1985. Teaming with Eddie Gilbert, he held the MSWA Tag Team Title in November of 1985. He was also known as the Black Scorpion and wrestled with the Desperadoes as Dead Eye Dick.

Cumberledge, Ron (6'2", 265 lbs.) began wrestling in 1988. He has wrestled in the WWF and WCW and was Western Ohio champion in 1991.

Curcuru, Sam *see* Garibaldi, Gino

Curly Moe (6', 555 lbs.) began wrestling in the early 1990s. He was an unusual grappler, known for his size and resemblance to Curly of the Three Stooges. His favorite maneuvers in the ring were eye gouges and nose tweaks.

Curry, Fred teamed with Fritz Von Erich to hold the World Class American Tag Team Title in Texas in March of 1969. He held the Hawaiian Title in August of 1972. He was forced to vacate the title after a ring injury in a match against Johnny Valentine.

Curry, Jack "Bull" (Fred Khoury, Sr.; b. 1916, d. March 6, 1985; Boston, Massachusetts; 5'8 1/2", 235 lbs.) was born in Hartford, Connecticut. He played football with the Chicago Bears and was a police officer before he began wrestling in 1939. He was dubbed "Bull" or "Bonecrusher" for his rough mat style. He was defeated by boxer Jack Dempsey in a match in Detroit in July of 1940. He also held the NWA Texas Title in May of 1954. He held the NWA Southern Title in 1956. He held the Texas Brass Knucks Title over a dozen times from the mid-1950s through 1966. He teamed with Lucas Pertano to hold the Texas World Tag Team Title in January of 1963.

Curry, Wild Bill wrestled in Texas in the 1950s and 1960s. His son, Fred Curry, also wrestled professionally.

Curtis, Bud (b. 1924; Indianapolis, Indiana; 5'10, 220 lbs.) played football at Arizona State University. He was a champion weightlifter and amateur wrestler before turning pro in the late 1940s. He remained a popular competitor through the 1950s.

Curtis, Bulldog held the NWA Pacific Northwest Tag Team Title several times in 1955 and 1956, teaming with Tommy Martinez and Henry Lenz.

Curtis, Don teamed with Mark Lewin in the WWFW in the late 1950s. The duo captured the WWWF U.S. Tag Team Title in 1958. They lost the belts to Jerry and Eddie Graham in May of 1959. Curtis again teamed with Lewin to hold the NWA World Tag Team Title in Florida in November of 1963. He and Abe Jacobs also briefly held the belts in May of 1964. He teamed with Jose Lothario to hold the NWA Southern Tag Team Title in Florida in March of 1967. He retired from the ring to become a promoter in Jacksonville, Florida, in the 1970s.

Curtis, George (Virginia) teamed with Jack Curtis to hold the NWA Southern Tag Team Title in 1954.

Curtis, Jack teamed with George Curtis to hold the NWA Southern Tag Team Title in 1954. He later teamed with Ray Villmer to hold the belts several times in 1960.

Curtis, King (Curtis Iaukea) captured the Hawaiian Title in August of 1961. He also held the Hawaiian Tag Team Title several times in the 1960s, teaming with Tosh Togo, Cowboy Cassidy, Mr. Fujiwara and Ripper Collins. He also held the U.S. Title in Honolulu several times in the early 1960s. He captured the NWA Pacific Northwest Tag Team Title in January of 1962, teaming with Haru Sasaki. He held the NWA Pacific Northwest Title in September of 1963. Curtis held the Hawaiian belt in 1964 and 1968. Curtis held the NWA U.S. Title in San Francisco several times in 1968 and 1969. He teamed with Baron Mikel Scicluna to defeat Karl Gotch and Rene Goulet for the WWWF Tag Team Title in February of 1972. They lost the belts to Sonny King and Chief Jay Strongbow in May of 1972. He briefly held the NWA Florida Title and the Stampede North American Title in Calgary, Canaday, in 1975. He briefly entered the WCW in 1995 an advisor to Kevin Sullivan. He is the father of wrestler Abbudah Dein.

Cybaniewicz, Stan *see* Zbyszko, Stanislaus

Cybaniewicz, Wladek *see* Zbyszko, Wladek

Cyberpunks, The *see* Ice, J.C. & Wolfie D.

Cyclone Nigro *see* Negro, Ciclon

Cyrus, Big Daddy (Memphis, Tennessee; 359 lbs.) teamed with Crusher Bones in the USWA in 1994.

Daley, Hank (b. 1918; New York City; 5'10", 210 lbs.) worked as an aviation engineer before becoming a wrestler in the late 1940s. He was known in the ring as the Grumman Grappler. He worked as college wrestling coach after retiring from the ring.

Dallas, Linda was a leading contender for the NWA U.S. Women's Championship in the mid-1980s.

Dalton, Jack *see* Fargo, Don

D'Amore, Scott (6', 260 lbs.) began wrestling in 1991. He teamed with Bobby Clancy to hold the Motor City Wrestling Tag Team Title in May of 1994. He subsequently wrestled in Border City Wrestling in Canada, where he held the championship several times in 1994.

Dane, Steven (6', 232 lbs.) began wrestling in 1987 as Steven Casey. He held the NAWA North American Title in 1991. He teamed with Gary Young as the Goodfellows to hold the Global World Tag Team Title in May of 1992. He again held the Global tag belts in September of 1993, teaming with Chaz Taylor as the Skyliners. He also competed in World Class and WCW.

Dangerously, Paul E. (Paul Heyman; b. September 11, 1965) was born in Scarsdale, New York. He became Paul E. Dangerously in January of 1987. He managed the Dangerous Alliance in the WCW in the early 1990s, managing such stars as Rick Rude, Steve Austin, Bobby Eaton and Arn Anderson. Dangerously was co-founder, with Tod Gordon, and promoter for Extreme Championship Wrestling from 1993.

Daniels, Black Jack teamed with Stan Kowalski to hold the NWA Southern Tag Team Title in Florida in February of 1967.

Daniels, Terry (5'8", 223 lbs.) began wrestling in 1984. He wrestled as a member of Sgt. Slaughter's Cobra Corps. He wrestled in the USWA and Global in the early 1990s.

Daniels, Vincent *see* Lopez, Vincent

Dannenhauser, Bill *see* Sullivan, Dave

Dante (Hans Steiner) teamed with the Great Mephisto to hold the Southern Tag Team Title in Tennessee several times in the early 1960s. They captured the World Tag Team Title in Tennessee several times in 1969. They also held the NWA Southern Tag Team Title in Florida in February of 1970.

Dante *see* Heggie, Tommy

Dantes, Alfonso held the NWA Americas Tag Team Title several times in 1969, teaming with Francisco Flores, Mil Mascaras and El Medico. He also held the EMLL Light Heavyweight Title several times during the 1970s and early 1980s.

Dark Journey was a leading wrestling valet in the 1980s. She accompanied Dick Slater to the ring in the MSWA in 1986.

Dark Patriot, The *see* Gilbert, Doug

Darling, Ace (b. June 27; 6', 221 lbs.) began wrestling in 1992 in Portland, Maine. He was light heavyweight champion in the World Wide Wrestling Association in 1995, where he often competed against Devon Storm.

Darnell, Billy (b. 1924; Philadelphia, Pennsylvania; 5'10", 228 lbs.) began wrestling in 1944, often wearing a leopard skin into the ring. He engaged in a legendary match against Buddy Rogers in 1947 and remained a popular wrestler in the 1950s and 1960s. He was known as the "Wrestling Chiropractor." He teamed with Bill Melby to hold the World Tag Team Title in Chicago in 1954. He retired to Florida in the late 1960s.

Daro, Lou (d. 1956) was a leading strongman from the 1910s. He began wrestling in the mid-1920s, and became a leading wrestling promoter on the West Coast. He was known as "Carnation" Lou Daro.

Darrell, Jim *see* Zhukov, Boris

Darrow, Sam *see* Super Maxx

Darsow, Barry *see* Smash

Davenport, Lauren (Beverly Hampton) wrestled and managed in the USWA during the early 1990s. She held the USWA Women's Title several times in 1993, often feuding with Miss Texas and the Dirty White Girl.

Davidson, John began wrestling with his brother, Ric Davidson, in November of 1975. They wrestled in Texas and Mexico before capturing the Mid-Eastern

Tag Team Title from Tojo Yamamoto and George Gulas in Tennessee. They held the NWA Americas Tag Team Title in Los Angeles several times in 1981.

Davidson, Ric began wrestling with his brother, John Davidson, in November of 1975. They wrestled in Texas and Mexico before capturing the Mid-Eastern Tag Team Title from Tojo Yamamoto and George Gulas in Tennessee. They held the NWA Americas Tag Team Title in Los Angeles several times in 1981. Ric Davidson also held the NWA Americas Title in April of 1981.

Davis, Danny (b. February 4; Nashville, Tennessee; 5'9", 218 lbs.) is a native of Nashville, Tennessee. He was trained by Buddy Fuller and began wrestling in 1977. He managed Wayne Farris and Larry Latham as the Blonde Bombers in the early 1980s. He subsequently teamed with Ken Wayne as the masked Nightmares. They captured the Southern Tag Team Title in August of 1984. They held the Southeastern Tag Team Title several times in 1985, and the Deep South Tag Team Title in 1986. Davis held the NWA Southeastern Title in November of 1987. He later split with Wayne and feuded with him. They exchanged the U.S. Junior Heavyweight Title in Alabama several times in 1988 and 1989. He held the USWA Junior Heavyweight Title several times in 1990 and 1991. Davis briefly held the Global Junior Heavyweight Title in April of 1992.

Davis, Karl "Killer" (b. 1908, d. July 4, 1977; Houston, Texas; 6'2", 240 lbs.) played football, base-ball and basketball during his college years at Ohio State in the 1920s. He played professional baseball with the St. Louis Cardinals before entering wrestling in the early 1930s. He remained a popular mat star through the 1950s. He also began appearing in films in the late 1940s. His movie credits include *The Reckless Moments* (1949), *Mask of the Dragon* (1951), *Fingerprints Don't Life* (1951), *Flesh and Fury* (1952), *Salome* (1953), *Siren of Bagdad* (1953), the 1953 serial *The Lost Planet*, *Demetrius and the Gladiators* (1954), *The Egyptian* (1954), *Creature with the Atom Brain* (1955), *Apache Warrior* (1957), *Zombies of Mora Tau* (1957) and *The Bonnie Barker Story* (1958).

Davis, Mike (b. Nov. 2; Tampa, Florida; 5'11", 235 lbs.) began wrestling in 1977. He teamed with Mike Rotundo to hold the U.S. Tag Team Title in Florida in January of 1984. He held the NWA World Junior Heavyweight Championship from October of 1984 until his defeat by Denny Brown on November 22, 1984. He was a founding member of the Rock 'n' Roll RPMS, wrestling with Tommy Lane and, later, Tom Burton during the 1980s. He and Lane held the WWC Tag Team Title in Puerto Rico in March of 1986. They also held the Southern Tag Team Title several times in 1987, and captured the CWA Tag Team Title in August of 1988. In the early 1990s he wrestled in Global as the Viper. After his unmasking in May of 1992, he wrestled as Maniac Mike Davis. He later tag teamed with his brother, Tom Davis.

Davis, Sterling "Dizzy" (Houston, Texas) attended Texas A & M, where he received a degree in electrical engineering. He was active in the Houston area, where he was known as Dizzy Davis in the ring. He held the NWA Texas Title several times in late 1948 and early 1949. He also held the Texas Junior Heavyweight Title in 1951.

Davis, Tom (5'10", 243 lbs.) began wrestling in 1983. He wrestled with his brother, Mike Davis, as The Dirty Davis Brothers.

Davis, Wee Willie was a huge grappler active in the ring in the 1930s. He held the Southwestern Title in Texas in 1938. He subsequently appeared in several films including *Shadow of the Thin Man* (1941), *Gentleman Jim* (1942), *Reap the Wild Wind* (1942), *Arabian Nights* (1942), *Johnny Come Lately* (1943) *Ali Baba and the Forty Thieves* (1944), *Ghost Catchers* (1944), *Wildfire* (1945), *Pursuit to Algiers* (1945), *A Night in Paradise* (1946), *The Foxes of Harrow* (1947), *Mighty Joe Young* (1949), *The Red Pony* (1949), *Abbott and Costello in the Foreign Legion* (1950), *Bodyhold* (1950), *Son of Paleface* (1952), *The World in His Arms* (1952) and *To Catch a Thief* (1955).

Dead Eye Dick *see* Culley, Randy

Dean, Man Mountain (Frank Leavitt; b. 1890, d. May 29, 1953; 317 lbs.) began wrestling in New York City as the Hell's Kitchen Hillbilly in 1906. He was known as Stone Mountain Leavitt in the Atlanta, Georgia, area in the 1920s before taking the name Man Mountain Dean. He also played professional football with the New York Giants in 1919. He announced his retirement from the ring in 1937, after suffering a fractured left leg during a match, though he made occasional ring appearances over the next decade. Dean began a career in films when he doubled for Charles Laughton in 1933's *Private Life of Henry VIII*. He was featured in over thirty films including *Reckless* (1935), *We're in the Money* (1935), *Big City* (1937), *The Three Legionnaires* (1937), *The Gladiator* (1938) and *Mighty Joe Young* (1949). Dean was an unsuccessful candidate for Congress in Georgia in the early 1950s. He died at his home in Norcross, Georgia, on May 29, 1953.

Dean, Man Mountain, Jr. (Ray St. Bernard, 330 lbs.) was a leading wrestling in Great Britain in the 1940s and 1950s.

Death Mask *see* Bradshaw, Justin "Hawk"

Deaton, David teamed with Joel Deaton to hold the Tri-State Tag Team Title in Oklahoma in 1981. Wrestling as the Thunderfoots, they also held the NWA Central States Tag Team Title in September of 1986.

Deaton, Joel (6'5", 285 lbs.) began wrestling in 1980. He teamed with David Deaton to hold the Tri-State Tag Team Title in Oklahoma in 1981. Wrestling as the Thunderfoots, they also held the NWA Central States Tag Team Title in September of 1986. Known as the Outlaw, the former Georgia All-Star champion wrestled in the U.S. and Japan. He teamed with Doug Somers to hold the SCW Tag Team Title in 1988.

DeBeers, Colonel (Ed Wiskoski; Cape Town, South Africa; 6'1", 248 lbs.) began wrestling in 1975. Wrestling as Ed Wiskowski, he held the NWA Central States Title during the latter half of 1975. He held the NWA Pacific Northwest Title several times in 1977 and 1978. He held the NWA World Tag Team Title in San Francisco several times in 1978 and 1979, teaming with Buddy Rose and Roddy Piper. He captured the NWA U.S. Title in San Francisco in June of 1980. Wrestling as Derek Draper, he briefly held the NWA Southern Title in Florida in July of 1982. Wrestling as Mega Maharishi, he teamed with Kendo Nagasaki to hold the NWA Pacific Northwest tag belts in April of 1985. Wrestling as Colonel DeBeers from South Africa, he engaged in a vicious feud with Jimmy Snuka in 1986. He teamed with Buddy Rose to hold the Pacific Northwest tag belts for several months in early 1989. He again held the tag team title in March of 1992, teaming with John Rambo.

DeBenedetti, Alfred *see* Verdi, Count Antonio

Deglane, Henri defeated Ed "Strangler" Lewis by disqualification for the AWA World Title in a match in Montreal, Canada, on May 4, 1931. He lost the belt to Ed Don George in Boston, Massachusetts, on February 9, 1933.

Dein, Abbudah (Rocky Iaukea; 242 lbs.) is the son of wrestler King

Curtis. He teamed with Mike Miller to hold the NWA Pacific Northwest Tag Team Title several times in 1986. He held the Pacific Northwest TV Title in December of 1987. He also held the tag belt with Len "the Grappler" Denton in October of 1988. He held the WWC Tag Team Title in Puerto Rico with Rip Rogers several times in 1989.

Del Rey, "Gigolo" Jimmy (Jimmy Richland; b. November 30; Kingsport, Tennessee; 5'11", 225 lbs.) began wrestling as Jim Backlund in 1985. He held the Florida Junior Heavyweight Title on several occasions in the late 1980s. He held the ICWA Light Heavyweight Title several times in 1991 and 1992, and was the ICWA champion in 1992. He joined with Tom Prichard as the Heavenly Bodies in May of 1993. They wrestled in Smoky Mountain and WWF and were managed by Jim Cornette. Del Rey entered the ECW in 1995.

Dellaserra, Bob, wrestling as UFO, teamed with Igor Volkofff to hold the Canadian Tag Team Title in January of 1979. Wrestling as Johnny Heffernan, he teamed with Don Kent as the Fabulous Kangaroos to hold the WWC Tag Team Title in Puerto Rico in July of 1982, and the Global Tag Team Title in Florida several times in 1983. Wrestling as Karl Steiner, he captured the NWA Pacific Northwest Title in February of 1985. He also held the Pacific Northwest tag belts in June of 1986, teaming with Mike Miller. He held the WWC North American Title in Puerto Rico in December of 1986.

DeMarco, Paul teamed with Lorenzo Parente to hold the NWA World Tag Team Title in Florida in October of 1967 and January of 1968. He also held the NWA Georgia Title several times in 1969 and 1970. He held the NWA U.S. Title in San Francisco several times in 1971. He teamed with Lars Anderson to hold the NWA World Tag Team Title in San Francisco for several months from May of 1972.

Demchuk, Johnny (d. June 16, 1962; Austria) teamed with Pepper Gomez to hold the Northwest Tag Team Title in Vancouver, Canada, several times in 1953.

Demento, Damian *see* Kleen, Mondo

Demolition *see* Ax, Smash & Crush

DeMott, William *see* Morrus, Hugh

Denigris, Vincente *see* Apollo, Vittorio "Argentina"

Denton, Len wrestled as the Grappler to capture the MSWA North American Title in September of 1980. He also held the Mid-South Mississippi Title in 1980. He teamed with Tony Anthony as the Grapplers to hold the Southern Tag Team Title in August of 1983. They also held the NWA Central States Tag Team Title in April of 1984. He held the World Class Texas Title for several months from December of 1985. He held the NWA Pacific Northwest Title several times from 1987 through 1990. He also held the Pacific Northwest tag belts several times in the late 1980s and early 1990s, teaming with the Terminator, Abbuda Dein, Brian Adams, Don Harris and Steve Doll. He also held the tag title in December of 1990, teaming with the Equalizer as the Wrecking Crew.

DeNucci, Dominic (Rome, Italy; 260 lbs.) held the NWA U.S. Title in San Francisco in January of 1964. He also held the IWA Championship in Australia several times in 1964 and 1965. He teamed with Don Leo Jonathan to hold the Canadian Tag Team Title in October of 1966. He teamed with Bruno Sammartino to briefly hold the WWWF International Tag Team Title in the Summer of 1971 during a series of bouts against the Mongols. He teamed with Tony Parisi to hold the NWA Florida Tag Team Title in January of 1975. He teamed with Victor Rivera to defeat Jimmy and Johnny Valiant for the WWWF Tag Team Title in May of 1975. He remained tag champion with Pat Barrett when Rivera left the WWWF the following month. DeNucci and Barrett were defeated for the title by Blackjack Lanza and Blackjack Mulligan in August of 1975. DeNucci teamed with Dino Bravo to capture the WWWF Tag Team Title from Toru Tanaka and Mr. Fuji in March of 1978. They were defeated by the Yukon Lumberjacks in June of 1978. DeNucci also held the WWA Tag Team Title with Wilbur Snyder for several months in 1978. DeNucci teamed with Bob White to hold the MWA Ohio Tag Team Title in 1984.

Deo, Jimmy (Reading, Pennsylvania; 6', 252 lbs.) began wrestling

1987. Known as "the Maniac," he was a member of the tag team Assault and Battery in the Professional Championship Wrestling promotion.

Dern, Wally (b. 1923; New Orleans, Louisiana; 6'2", 240 lbs.) was born in Long Island, New York. He was a leading scientific wrestler in the 1940s and 1950s, who was known as Mr. Americus in the ring.

Derringer, Bret teamed with Matt Derringer to hold the PWA Tag Team Title for several months from March of 1989.

Derringer, Matt teamed with Bret Derringer to hold the PWA Tag Team Title for several months from March of 1989. He held the PWA Light Heavyweight Title several times in early 1990.

DeSouza, Mario (b. 1924; Portugal; 6', 230 lbs.) began wrestling in 1949. He won the European title during his first year in the ring. He came to the United States in 1950, where he was a popular mat star.

Destroyer, The *see* Beyer, Dick

Destroyer #1 *see* Rose, Bill

Destroyer #2 *see* Hoerr, Larry

Destruction (6'3", 255 lbs.) began wrestling in 1988. He teamed with Apocalypse as the Blackharts tag team and were managed by Luna Vachon.

Destruction Crew, The *see* Wayne Bloom & Mike Enos

Detton, Dean (b. 1909, d. February 23, 1958) was recognized as the World Heavyweight Champion in September of 1936 following his defeat of Ed "Strangler" Lewis in Philadelphia, Pennsylvania. He retained the belt until June of 1937. He held the Hawaiian Title in January of 1939. He held the Pacific Coast Title in San Francisco for several months from March of 1939. He held the Pacific Coast belt several more times from 1943 through 1945, competing against Sandor Szabo, Pat Fraley, Vincent Lopez and Earl McCready. He again captured the Hawaiian Title in December of 1949. Detton owned and operated a tavern after his retirement from the ring.

Devil's Duo *see* Markoff, Chris & Poffo, Angelo

Devil's Duo *see* Vines, Doug & Sword, Jeff

Devine, Candy (b. January 1) won the AWA Women's Title in November of 1984. She retained the belt until her defeat by Sherri Martel in September of 1985. She exchanged the title several times with Martel over the next two years. She held the Windy City Wrestling Women's Title in Chicago several times in 1988. Devine returned to take the AWA title in December of 1989 and retained the belt until the AWA closed the following year. She was recognized as the Great Lakes Wrestling Association's woman's champion in 1992. She captured the WWWA Women's Title in Pennsylvania in March of 1993.

Diamond, Jack *see* Master Blaster, The

Diamond, Paul (Thomas

Boric; Thunder Bay, Ontario, Canada; 6'1", 230 lbs.) began wrestling in 1983. He teamed with Shawn Michaels as American Force to hold the Texas All-Star Texas Tag Team Title several times in late 1985. The Canadian former pro soccer player teamed with Jeff Jarrett to briefly hold the CWA International Tag Team Title in November of 1986. Diamond subsequently teamed with Pat Tanaka to capture the CWA belts several times in late 1986 and 1987. The duo subsequently wrestled as Badd Company in the AWA. They captured the Southern Tag Team Title in August of 1987. They won the AWA Tag Team Title from the Midnight Rockers in March of 1988. They retained the title until their defeat by Ken Patera and Brad Rheingans in March of 1989. Diamond, under a mask as Kato, replaced Akio Sato as Pat Tanaka's tag partner in the Orient Express in the WWF in 1990. He wrestled as Max Moon in the WWF in 1992 and wrestled as Haito in WCW in 1994.

Diamond, Sweet Ebony *see* Johnson, Rocky

Diamond Doll (Kimberly Falkenberg) is the wife of Diamond Dallas Page. She was his valet in the WCW until mid-1995, when she became the valet for Johnny B. Badd. She remained with Badd until his departure from the WCW in early 1996. She subsequently accompanied the Bootie Man to the ring, and was called the Bootie Girl.

Diamond Stud, The *see* Ramon, Razor

Diaz, Jorge *see* Mendoza, Rey

DiBiase, Iron Mike (b. 1924, d. July 8, 1969; Nebraska) was an amateur wrestling champion at the University of Nebraska, before turning pro in the early 1950s. He teamed with Danny Plechas to hold the World Tag Team Title in Chicago in February of 1956. They also held the NWA Texas Tag Team Title several times in late 1956. DiBiase also held the NWA World Junior Heavyweight Title in 1956. He captured the NWA Pacific Northwest Title in March of 1961. He held the NWA Central States Title in 1964. He held the NWA Americas Title in Los Angeles in June of 1967 and captured the WWA Title in Los Angeles in July of 1967. He teamed with Killer Karl Kox to hold the WWA Tag Team Title in 1967. He teamed with the Avenger to hold the Mid-West Tag Team Title in Omaha in 1968. He died of a heart attack in the ring following a wrestling match in Lubbock, Texas, on July 8, 1969. He was married to wrestler Helen Hild and was the adoptive father of Ted DiBiase.

DiBiase, Ted (b. January 18, 1954; Omaha, Nebraska; 6'3", 247 lbs.) began wrestling in 1974. He is the adopted son of Iron Mike DiBiase and women's wrestler Helen Hild. DiBiase held the MSWA North American Title in December of 1976. He held the NWA Central States Title in May of 1977 and January of 1978. He held the NWA Missouri Title in February of 1978. He again held the Missouri belt from November of 1980 until October of 1981. He teamed with Stan

Frazier to hold the NWA National Tag Team Title in January of 1981. He again captured the tag belts with Steve O in June of 1981. He teamed with Matt Borne as the Rat Pack to capture the MSWA Tag Team Title in Louisiana in October of 1982. He held the tag belts again in April of 1983, teaming with Mr. Olympia. DiBiase held the NWA National Title several times in 1984. He returned to take the MSWA Tag Team Title with Steve Williams in December of 1985. He entered the WWF in the late 1980s, where he was known as the Million Dollar Man. He attempted to purchase the WWF belt from Andre the Giant after his victory over Hulk Hogan in February of 1988, resulting in the championship being declared vacant. He was subsequently defeated by Randy Savage in a tournament final to name a new champion. He teamed with Irwin R. Schyster to form the tag team Money, Incorporated. Under the management of Jimmy Hart, they defeated the Legion of Doom for the WWF Tag Team belts in Denver, Colorado, on February 7, 1992. They lost the title to the Natural Disasters in July of 1992, but recaptured the belts the following October. They ultimately lost the title to Rick and Scott Steiner in June of 1993. DiBiase retired from wrestling in October of 1993 following a neck injury suffered during a match in Japan. He remained in the WWF as a commentator and manager of the Million Dollar Team.

Dick the Bruiser (Richard Afflis; b. 1929, d. November 10, 1991) was an offensive lineman with the Green Bay Packers in the early 1950s. He injured his larynx while playing football, which resulted in the gravelly voice he was later known for. He left the Packers after four seasons and began wrestling professionally in 1954. The crew-cut grappler held the NWA U.S. Title on three occasions in the early 1960s. He held the U.S. Title in Honolulu in July of 1963. He teamed with Crusher to defeat Ivan and Karol Kalmikoff for the AWA World Tag Team Title in August of 1963. They were defeated for the belts by Verne Gagne and Moose Evans in February of 1964, but reclaimed the title in a rematch several weeks later. Dick the Bruiser defeated football player Alex Karras in a match in Detroit in April of 1963. held the WWA Title in Los Angeles for several months from April of 1964. He formed his own wrestling promotion in Indiana in 1964, and was the WWA title holder numerous times between 1964 and 1982. Crusher and the Bruiser again claimed the AWA tag belts in a match against Larry Hennig and Harley Race in May of 1966. Dick the Bruiser also briefly interrupted Mad Dog Vachon's AWA Title reign in November of 1966. He and Crusher lost the tag belts in a rematch in January of 1967. They again won the championship in December of 1968, defeating Mitsu Arakawa and Dr. Moto. They lost the title to Mad Dog and Butcher Vachon in August of 1969. He returned to team with Crusher in August of 1975 to take the tag belts from Nick Bockwinkel and Ray Stevens. They held the title until their defeat by Blackjack Lanza and Bobby Duncum in July of 1976. He held the NWA Missouri Title several times in 1978 and 1979. He again held the Missouri belt in 1982. Dick the Bruiser ruptured a blood vessel in his esophagus while weight-lifting at his home. He from internal bleeding at a Largo, Florida, hospital on November 10, 1991.

Dieckman, Donna Marie (b. 1930; Cleveland, Ohio; 5'6", 135 lbs.) was the daughter of boxer Raymond Dieckman. She began wrestling in the early 1950s and remained a tough competitor in the ring throughout the decade.

Diesel (Kevin Nash; b. July 9, 1960; Las Vegas, Nevada; 7', 356 lbs.) was raised in Southgate, Michigan. He played college basketball at the University of Tennessee. He worked as a club bouncer before joining the WCW as Steel of the Master Blasters, teaming with Al Greene as Blade, in September of 1990. He soon began appearing as Oz, wearing a mask and green cape to the ring. He subsequently became Vinnie Vegas and was managed by Diamond Dallas Page in the Diamond Exchange. He joined the WWF as Diesel, bodyguard to Shawn Michaels, in June of 1993. He won the WWF Intercontinental Title in a match against Razor Ramon in Syracuse, New York, on April 13, 1994. He also won the WWF Tag Team belt, teaming with Shawn Michaels to defeat the Head Shrinkers in Indianapolis, Indiana, on August, 28, 1994. He lost the Intercontinental belt to Razor Ramon at SummerSlam on August 29, 1994. Diesel and Shawn Michaels relin-

quished the belt when they broke up their partnership on November 23, 1994. Diesel pinned Bob Backlund for the WWF Championship at Madison Square Gardens in New York on November 26, 1994, in a match that lasted only six seconds. Diesel lost the title to Bret Hart in Landover, Maryland, on November 19, 1995. Diesel reverted to a villainous persona after his defeat, feuding with the Undertaker and his former partner, Shawn Michaels.

Dillinger, Frank (Frank Mack) teamed with Jack Dillinger as the Chain Gang to capture the WWA Tag Team Title in June of 1969. Frank Dillinger retired from the ring after being shot in Chicago in September of 1969.

Dillinger, Jack teamed with Frank Dillinger as the Chain Gang to capture the WWA Tag Team Title in June of 1969. They relinquished the belt following the shooting of Frank Dillinger the following September. Jack Dillinger reclaimed the belts, teaming with Jim Dillinger, in November of 1969, holding the title until June of 1970.

Dillinger, Jim *see* Colt, Chris

Dillinger, Kevin (5'10", 239 lbs.) began wrestling in 1985. He was formerly known as Alan Martin. He teamed with Mike Davis in The Rock 'n' Roll RPMS and entered the USWA in 1989.

Dillon, Jack (b. 1913; Chattanooga, Tennessee; 6'3", 240 lbs.) was known as "the Tennessee Hillbilly." He was a leading wrestling villain in the 1940s and 1950s.

Dillon, James J. (b. June 26) teamed with Roger Kirby to hold the NWA Florida Tag Team Title in 1975. He managed David Von Erich, Jim Garvin, Frank Dusek and Ron Bass to championships in Florida with the NWA in the early 1980s. Dillon teamed with Buzz Tyler to hold the NWA Central States Tag Team Title in September of 1981 and briefly held the NWA Florida Title in March of 1982. He remained a leading manager in the NWA through the 1980s, managing the Long Riders and the Four Horseman

Ding Dongs *see* Starr, Billy "Fatback Festus" and Powell, Jimmy

Dink (Tiger Jackson), a midget wrestler dressed as a clown, teamed with Doink in the WWF in 1993. He previous wrestled with Randy Savage as the Macho Midget.

DiPaolo, Ilio (b. 1926, d. May 10, 1995; Indrodana, Italy) came from Italy to South America in 1949. He entered the United States in mid-1951, where he became a popular wrestling star. He wrestled throughout the United States, Canada and Japan during his career. He teamed with Tex McKenzie to hold the Canadian Tag Team Title in Edmonton in November of 1954. He teamed with Whipper Billy Watson to hold the Canadian Open Tag Team Title in Toronto in December of 1955. He held the Ohio Title in 1960. He retired from the ring in 1965, due to an ankle injury. DiPaolo had settled in Buffalo, New York, in 1958 and, after his retirement, he became well known in the area as the owner of Ilio DiPaolo's Restaurant and Ringside Lounge. DiPaolo remained an active member of the community. He died from injuries received when struck by a car in the village of Hamburg, near Buffalo, New York, on May 10, 1995.

Dirty White Boy *see* Anthony, Tony

Dirty White Girl (Kim Wolser) was the manager of Dirty White Boy Tony Anthony. She held the USWA Women's Title in April of 1992.

DiSalvo, Steve (Boston, Massachusetts; 6'2", 290 lbs.) began wrestling in 1986. He was briefly known as Billy Jack Strong when he wrestled in the AWA. He held the WWC Universal Title in Puerto Rico for several months from May of 1989, wrestling as Steve Strong. He also held the WWC Tag Team Title in March of 1989, teaming with Jason the Terrible. He also held the Stampede North American championship in the late 1980s.

Disco Inferno (Glen Gilburdy; Brooklyn, New York; 6', 238 lbs.) began wrestling as Glen Gilbernetti in November of 1991. He wrestled as Disco Inferno in the USWA and the WCW from July of 1993. He teamed with Ashley Clarke to hold the NGWA Tag Team Title in Georgia in August of 1994.

Divine, Candi (b. 1962; Nashville, Tennessee; 128 lbs.) was born in Los Angeles, California, and moved to Nashville at the age of 16. She made her professional wrestling debut two years later in 1980 in Murfreesboro, Tennessee. She remained a leading women's competitor through the 1980s.

Dixie Dynomite *see* Armstrong, Scott

Dixon, Dory held the EMLL Light Heavyweight Title in Mexico in February of 1959. He teamed with Pepper Gomez to hold the NWA Texas Tag Team Title in February of 1961. He held the NWA Texas Title for several months from July of 1961. He again held the Texas belt in January of 1962. He teamed with Nick Kozak to hold the World Class Texas Tag Team Title in July of 1966. He held the NWA Americas Tag Team Title in Los Angeles several times in 1972, teaming with Earl Maynard and Raul Matta.

Doc Zoko *see* Godoy, Pedro

Dr. D *see* Styles, Carl

Dr. Death *see* Kendall, Kenny

Dr. X (Jim Osborne) teamed with Johnny Kostas to hold the NWA Pacific Northwest Tag Team Title in August of 1967. Wrestling as Dr. X, he defeated Ramon Torres for the NWA World Junior Heavyweight Title in December of 1971. He retained the belt until his defeat by Danny Hodge in March of 1972.

Dr. X *see* Beyer, Dick

Dr. X *see* Miller, Bill

Doganiero, Dominic W. "Doc" (b. 1921, d. February 27, 1994) was born and raised in Camden, Pennsylvania. He played football and wrestled during high school. He left school at the age of 16 to take over his father's barber shop business. After World War II Doganiero played on several semi-pro football teams. He also began wrestling in the Pennsylvania area. He usually competed as a villain, wrestling under such names as Don Rico and Bamba Taboo. He continued to appear in the ring while managing a pharmacy in Camden until 1971. He subsequently relocated to Philadelphia. He died at his home in Philadelphia on February 27, 1994.

Doink the Clown *see* Borne, Matt

Doink the Clown II *see* Keirn, Steve

Doink the Clown III *see* Lombardi, Steve

Doink the Clown IV *see* Apollo, Ray

Doll, Steve (Tampa, Florida; 5'10", 237 lbs.) began wrestling in 1984. He initially teamed with Scott Peterson as the Southern Rockers. They captured the NWA Pacific Northwest Tag Team Title in November of 1987, and held the belt several times over the next two years. Rex King replaced Peterson as Doll's tag partner in the Southern Rockers and they held the tag belts several times in 1989 and 1990. Doll and King also wrestled as Simply Divine. They held the USWA Tag Team Title several times in early 1990. Doll teamed with Len "the Grappler" Denton to hold the Pacific Northwest tag belts several times in 1991 and 1992. He and King again held the USWA tag belts for several months from April of 1993. Doll became Steven Dunn and the team became known as WellDone when they joined the WWF in 1994.

Dominoes, The *see* Lopez, Pepe & Hester Frank

Don the Magnificent *see* Evans, Don

Donovan, Chick (6', 245 lbs.) began wrestling in 1980. He briefly held the Southern Heavyweight Title in 1981. He held the U.S. Junior Heavyweight Title in Alabama several times in 1983. He held the CWA International Title for several months from April of 1987. He teamed with Jack Hart to hold the Southern Tag Team Title in May of 1987. He wrestled in World Class and in Georgia during the late 1980s.

Donovan, Doug teamed with Ivan Kameroff to hold the NWA Pacific Northwest Tag Team Title several times in 1955. He again held the tag belts in 1956 and 1957, teaming with Red Donovan. He held the NWA Pacific Northwest Title in August of 1957.

Donovan, Jack teamed with the Viking to hold the NWA Central States Tag Team Title in July of 1966.

Donovan, Red teamed with Doug Donovan to hold the NWA Pacific Northwest Tag Team Title several times in 1956 and 1957.

Doom *see* Reed, Butch & Simmons, Ron

Doomsday *see* Jacobs, Glen

Dorcy, Pierre (210 lbs.; Nor-

mandy, France) came to the United States in 1951, where he became a leading mat star during the decade.

Dos Hombres *see* Steamboat, Rick & Zenk, Tom

Dotson, Dot (b. 1929; Orlando, Florida; 5'9", 155 lbs.) was driving a cab when she was discovered by a Florida wrestling promoter. She was one of the top female competitors in the 1950s.

Dougherty, Pete (5'1", 245 lbs.) began wrestling in 1977. He was called the Duke of Dorchester and was active in the ring through the 1990s.

Douglas, Andrew "Bubba" (b. 1944, d. February 13, 1986) wrestled in the 1960s and 1970s.

Douglas, Dean *see* Douglas, Shane

Douglas, Shane (Troy Martin; b. November 21; Pittsburgh, Pennsylvania; 6', 223 lbs.) began wrestling in 1986. He captured the UWF TV Title in Oklahoma in August of 1987. He won the Continental tag belts with Humongous in 1988. He also teamed with Johnny Ace as the Dynamic Dudes in the WCW before joining the WWF in 1990. Douglas returned to the WCW in 1992 and teamed with Rick Steamboat to win the WCW Tag Team Championship from Barry Windham and Dustin Rhodes on November 18, 1992. They lost the belts to Brian Pillman and Steve Austin on March 3, 1993. Douglas subsequently entered the ECW, where he was awarded the championship in September of 1993. He was defeated for the title by Sabu the following month. He again captured the title, defeating Terry Funk, in April of 1994. Douglas won the revived NWA Heavyweight Title in a tournament in August of 1994, but refused to accept the belt. He relinquished the ECW Title to the Sandman in April of 1995. Douglas entered the WWF in 1995 as Dean Douglas, and engaged in a feud with Razor Ramon. He was awarded the Intercontinental Title on October 22, 1995, when injuries prevented Shawn Michaels from defending the belt. He lost the title in a match against Ramon immediately after receiving the title. Douglas left the WWF later in the year to return to ECW.

Downey, Eric *see* Fontaine, Eric

Doyle, "Irish" Mickey (5'11", 221 lbs.) began wrestling in 1970. He was the NWA Rookie of the Year in 1971. He teamed with Mando Lopez to hold the NWA Americas Tag Team Title in December of 1975. He teamed with Al Snow as the Sensationals in Motor City Wrestling, where they held the U.S. Tag Team Title for several months in the fall of 1987. He and Snow also competed in the WWA as the Motor City Hitmen, holding the tag belts in early 1989. Doyle held the MCW Title in 1993. He captured the Border City Wrestling Can-Am Title several times in 1993 and 1994.

Dragon Master (6'2", 248 lbs.) began wrestling in 1970. The Japanese star was a member of Gary Hart's stable in the WCW in the 1980s.

Dragon Master, The (Gary

Rich) was trained in Virginia. He also wrestled as the Intimidator before joining the USWA in 1991. He briefly held the USWA Unified Title in August of 1991.

Drake, "Catalina" George (Roland Hogg; d. December 28, 1967) teamed with Rito Romero to hold the NWA Texas Tag Team Title in 1954.

Drake, D.C. (b. September 16; 6'1", 255 lbs.) began wrestling in 1984. Known as "Mad Dog," he engaged in a five year feud with Larry Winters, before the two teamed up. He held the Tri-State Championship in Philadelphia in 1990.

Draper, Derek *see* DeBeers, Colonel

Drapp, Andre (b. 1922; Luneville, France; 6', 215 lbs.) held the title of Mr. Europe before coming to the United States in the late 1940s. He was a leading competitor in the 1950s, and teamed with Red Bastien to hold the NWA Pacific Northwest Tag Team Title in September of 1956.

Dream Machine, The (Troy Graham) held the Southern Heavyweight Title several times in 1981. He teamed with Bill Dundee to also hold the Southern Tag Team Title in 1981. He also held the Southern tag belts with Jim "the Claw" Mitchell in August of 1982. He teamed with Rick McGraw as the New York Dolls in Memphis in 1982. They were managed by Jimmy Hart. The duo defeated Spike Huber and Steve Regal for the WWA Tag Team Title in Memphis in September of 1982. They held the belts until losing a rematch the following February. Wrestling as Troy Graham, he teamed with Porkchop Cash as the Bruise Brothers to hold the Southern Tag Team Title several times in 1983. Dream Machine returned the USWA in 1994, capturing the USWA Southern Title in June of 1994.

Dream Team, The *see* Parsons, King & Conway, Jr., Tiger

Dreamer, Tommy (Tom Laughlin; b. February 14; Yonkers, New York; 6'3", 245 lbs.) began wrestling in 1989. He teamed with Johnny Gunn to capture the ECW Tag Team Title in November of 1993. They lost the belts to Kevin Sullivan and the Tazmaniac the following month. Dreamer feuded with Raven in ECW in the mid-1990s.

Droese, Duke "the Dumpster" (Mike Droese; August 20; Chicago, Illinois; 6'5", 306 lbs.) began wrestling in 1987 as Rocco Gibralter. Known as the "Garbage Man," he joined the WWF as "the Dumpster" in 1994.

Droese, Mike *see* Droese, Duke "the Dumpster"

Dromo, Bill held the NWA Southern Title in Florida in August of 1973.

Dubois, Michel *see* Smirnoff, Alexis

Dubuque, Gene *see* Magnificent Maurice

Dudley, Big Dick (Alex Rizzo; 6'3", 285 lbs.) teamed with various Dudley Boys in the ECW in the mid-1990s.

Dudley, Buh Buh Ray (Mark Lomonica; 6'2", 325 lbs.) teamed with various Dudley Boys in the ECW in the mid-1990s.

Dudley, Dances with (Adolfo Bermudez) teamed with various Dudley Boys in the ECW in the mid-1990s.

Dudley, D-Von (6'1", 260 lbs.) teamed with various Dudley Boys in the ECW in the mid-1990s.

Dudley, James managed Bobo Brazil, Bearcat Wright and Sailor Art Thomas in the 1950s. He worked in the WWF office in the 1960s and 1970s.

Duggan, Crusher *see* Malenko, Boris

Duggan, "Hacksaw" Jim (James Duggan; b. January 14, 1953; Glens Falls, New York; 6'3", 280 lbs.) was a champion amateur wrestler before he began wrestling professionally in 1978. He held the Mid-South Louisiana Title in November of 1982. He teamed with Magnum T.A. to hold the MSWA Tag Team Title for several months from July of 1983. He held the MSWA North American Title in March of 1986. He teamed with Terry Taylor to hold the UWF Tag Team Title in Oklahoma in December of 1986. He subsequently wrestled in the WWF, where he was a popular star. He often carried a 2"×4" board to the ring, which he sometimes used on his opponents. He entered the WCW in 1994. He defeated Steve Austin for the WCW U.S. Title on September 18, 1994.

Dukes, Derrick (6'2", 235 lbs.)

began wrestling in 1986. He teamed with Ricky Rice as the Top Guns to hold the PWA Tag Team Title in June of 1987. Dukes lost a controversial boxing bout to former New York Jet Mark Gastineaux in Salem, West Virginia, in June of 1991. He briefly held the IWA U.S. Title in the fall of 1991.

Duncum, Bobby, Jr. (Minneapolis, Minnesota; 6'4", 265 lbs.) teamed with John Hawk as the Texas Mustangs to hold the Global World Tag Team Title in November of 1992.

Duncum, Bobby, Sr. (Austin, Texas; 6'8", 280 lbs.) was a leading wrestler in the 1970s and early 1980s. He briefly held the NWA Southern Title in Florida in October of 1971. He teamed with Dick Murdoch to hold the Florida Tag Team Title later in the month. He teamed with Stan Vachon to hold the NWA Georgia Tag Team Title in September of 1973. He was managed by the Grand Wizard in the WWF in the mid-1970s, and engaged in several unsuccessful title challenges against Bruno Sammartino. He teamed with Blackjack Lanza to capture the AWA Tag Team Title from Crusher and Dick the Bruiser in July of 1976. They held the belts for nearly a year, until their defeat by Jim Brunzell and Greg Gagne in July of 1977. He subsequently returned to the WWF, where he was managed by Captain Lou Albano in the late 1970s. Duncum retired to Austin, Texas, in the 1980s. He is the father of Bobby Duncum, Jr.

Dundee, Bill (William Crookshanks; b. October 24, 1951; Melbourne, Australia; 5'7", 214 lbs.) was born in Scotland, where he lived until his family moved to Australia in the early 1960s. He began wrestling in Australia in the early 1970s, teaming with George Barnes. The duo held the Austra-Asian Tag Team Title and the New South Wales Tag Team Championship in the early 1970s. They came to the United States in 1974 and began wrestling in the Mid-South. They had a reputation as violent rule-breakers and quickly captured the Southern Heavyweight Tag Team Title. They remained a leading tag team in the area until Barnes decided to return to Australia. Dundee soon changed his wrestling style to become one of the area's most popular competitors. He teamed with Big Bad John to hold the Southern Tag Team Title several times in 1976. He teamed with Norvell Austin for the Southern belts in December of 1977 and held the tag title several times in 1978 wrestling with Jerry Lawler. He and Lawler were in the ring together numerous times over several decades, either as partners or opponents. Dundee again held the Southern tag belts several times in 1979, teaming with Robert Gibson, Robert Fuller and Lawler. Dundee held the Southern Heavyweight Title numerous times from 1979 through the mid-1980s, wrestling against Paul Ellering, Jerry Lawler, Dutch Mantell and others. He defeated Billy Robinson for the CWA World Title in August of 1980, but lost the belt in a rematch later in the month. Dundee captured the Southern Tag Team Title with Tommy Rich in December of 1980 and February of 1981. They also held the

CWA Tag Team Title in March of 1981. He briefly held the tag title with the Dream Machine in 1981, and teamed with Steve Keirn to hold the belts several times in 1981 and 1982. He also held the Mid-America Title in 1982. He held the CWA International Title for several months from May of 1986. He held the NWA Central States Title in January of 1987. He reclaimed the CWA International Title several times in the Summer of 1987. He also held the CWA International Tag Team Title with Rocky Johnson in July of 1987. He teamed with Jerry Lawler to capture the AWA World Tag Team Belt on October 11, 1987, defeating Soldat Ustinov and Doug Somers. They lost the belt to Dennis Condrey and Randy Rose later in the month on October 30, 1987. Dundee captured the USWA Southern Title in November of 1989. He exchanged the belt several times with John Tatum through mid-1990. He again held the belt in May of 1991. He also held the USWA Texas Title several times in early 1991. Dundee entered the WCW in the Spring of 1993 as Sir William, Lord Steven Regal's valet. He returned to the USWA as a wrestler in late 1994. He defeated Jerry Lawler for the USWA Unified Title on February 25, 1995. He lost the belt to Razor Ramon on April 3, 1995. Dundee was fired from the promotion in Fall of 1995 after a locker-room altercation with Wolfie D, the tag-team partner of Dundee's son, J.C. Ice. Dundee returned to the promotion in March of 1996, usually accompanied by Samantha, and engaged in a feud with Wolfie D.

Dundee, Jamie *see* Ice, J.C.

Dunn, Dick wrestled as the Red Shadow. He teamed with Don Carson to hold the Southern Tag Team Title in July of 1968.

Dunn, Steven *see* Doll, Steve

Dupree, Ron (Ralph Batterman; d. October 17, 1975) teamed with Chris Colt as the Commancheros to hold the WAA Tag Team Title in Phoenix in 1970. Dupree retired from the ring after suffering a heart attack in the early 1970s. He died of a heart attack in a Tacoma, Washington, arena while announcing a match on October 17, 1975.

Durante, Anthony *see* Pitbull #2

Durham, Mike *see* Grunge, Johnny

Dusek, Emil (Emil Hason; b. 1905, d. July 9, 1986; Omaha, Nebraska) began wrestling in the 1920s. He wrestled with his brothers Ernie, Rudy and Joe as the Riot Squad. He remained a popular star through the 1950s, joined in the ring by his cousin, Wally. Emil and Ernie Dusek held the Canadian Open Tag Team Title in Toronto in March of 1954. They also held the NWA World Tag Team Title in San Francisco in January of 1957, and held the NWA Tag Team Title several times in 1957.

Dusek, Ernie (Ernie Hason; b. 1904; Omaha, Nebraska; 5'10", 235 lbs.) began wrestling in the 1920s. He wrestled with his brothers Rudy, Joe and Emil as the Riot Squad. He held the AWA Title in Montreal, Canada, in 1939. He remained a popular star through the 1950s, joined in the ring by his cousin, Wally. Ernie and Emil Dusek held the Canadian Open Tag Team Title in Toronto in March of 1954. They also held NWA World Tag Team Title in San Francisco in January of 1957, and held the NWA Tag Team Title several times in 1957.

Dusek, Frank teamed with Bill Irwin to hold the World Class World Tag Team Title in Texas in November of 1981. He held the NWA Southern Title in Florida in March of 1983.

Dusek, Joe (Joe Hason; b. 1911, d. October 31, 1992) was from Omaha, Nebraska, and began wrestling in the 1920s. He wrestled with his brothers Emil, Ernie and Rudy as the Riot Squad. He retired from the ring in the late 1940s to manage the family's fishery business. He wrestled occasionally in the 1950s, holding the NWA Central States Title in 1954.

Dusek, Richard (b. 1924; Omaha, Nebraska) began wrestling in the late 1940s. He wrestled as a member of the Dusek brother's riot squad.

Dusek, Rudy (Rudy Hason; b. 1901, d. October 27, 1971) was from Omaha, Nebraska, and began wrestling in the 1920s. He wrestled with his brothers Emil, Ernie and Joe as the Riot Squad. He retired in the late 1940s to concentrate on promoting wrestling.

Dusek, Wally (Charles Santon; b. 1909, d. October 29, 1991; Omaha, Nebraska; 6'1", 230) began wrestling in the mid 1930s. He wrestled as a cousin of the Dusek brothers and teamed in tag matches with Emil, Ernie and Rudy Dusek. After retiring from the ring he was a longtime NWA official. He also operated an airport in Kirksville, Missouri. He died in Charlotte, North Carolina, on October 29, 1991.

Dykes, Jimmy "J.C." (b. 1926, d. November 20, 1993) managed the Masked Infernos in the NWA in Florida in the late 1960s and worked with Crockett Promotions in the Carolinas. Wrestling as Senior X he teamed with Karl Von Brauner to briefly hold the NWA Americas Tag Team Title in Los Angeles in February of 1976. He also managed the Super Infernos in the early 1970s.

Dynamite Kid, The (Tom Billington; 5'8", 228 lbs.) began his wrestling career in Great Britain in the late 1970s. He held the Joint Promotions British Welterweight Title from January of 1991 until leaving for Canada the following year. He teamed with Kasavubu to hold the Calgary Stampede International Tag Team Title in June of 1980. He held the NWA Pacific Northwest Title in September of 1983. He teamed with the Assassin to capture the Pacific Northwest tag team belts in November of 1983. He held the Stampede North American Title in Calgary, Canada, in March of 1984. He subsequently teamed with Davey Boy Smith as the British Bulldogs. The duo were managed by Lou Albano and defeated Greg Valentine and Brutus Beefcake for the WWF

Tag Team Title at Wrestlemania II on April 7, 1986. They lost the belts to the Hart Foundation in January of 1987. Dynamite Kid later teamed with Johnny Smith in matches in Canada and Japan. They wrestled as the British Bruisers with All-Japan from 1992.

Eadie, Bill *see* Ax

Eagle, The *see* Fulton, Jackie

Eagle, Chief Don (Carl Donald Bell; b. 1925, d. March 17, 1966; Caughnawaga, Quebec, Canada; 6'1", 218 lbs.) was the son of wrestler Joseph War Eagle. The Mohawk Indian began his career as a boxer, winning a Golden Globe boxing tournament in 1945. After several years of competition he accidentally shot himself in a hunting accident and retired from the boxing ring. He subsequently began wrestling professionally. He won the AWA World Heavyweight Title on May 23, 1950. He was defeated for the belt three days later by Gorgeous George in Chicago, Illinois, on May 26, 1950. He won the AWA Ohio title in August of 1950, holding the belt until June of 1952. He remained a popular competitor throughout the decade. He committed suicide on March 17, 1966.

Eagle, Robbie *see* Gorgeous George III

Eagle Man *see* Oborsky, Colin H.

Eakins, Ike (d. October 20, 1968) teamed with Bill Longson to hold the Texas World Tag Team Title in August of 1958. He teamed with Tosh Togo to hold the NWA Southern Tag Team Title in 1960.

Earl, James (Dale Veazy) teamed with Bob Brown as the Hunters to hold the WWC Tag Team Title in Puerto Rico in August of 1987. Wrestling as James Earl, he teamed with Buddy Lee Parker as the State Patrol in the WCW in 1994.

Earthquake (John Tenta; b. June 22, 1964; Montreal, Quebec, Canada; 6'4", 502 lbs.) was a Sumo wrestler, known as Kokotenzan, in Japan until his departure in July of 1986. He wrestled as Big John Tenta in Canada the following year. He entered WWF as Earthquake in the early 1990s He teamed with Typhoon as the Natural Disasters to win the WWF Tag Team Title from Money Inc. in July of 1992. They lost the belts back to Money Inc. the following October. Earthquake joined the WCW as Avalanche in October of 1994. He joined Kevin Sullivan's Dungeon of Doom in June of 1995, wrestling as the Shark.

East-West Connection, The *see* Adonis, Adrian & Ventura, Jesse

Eaton, Bobby (b; August 15, 1958; Huntsville, Alabama; 6', 233 lbs.) was trained by Tojo Yamamoto. He made his wrestling debut in Birmingham, Alabama, in May of 1976. He teamed with Lanny Poffo to hold the Mid-America Tag Team Title in 1978. Eaton held the tag belts several times over the next few years, often teaming with George Gulas. He captured the Mid-America Title in March of 1979, holding the title numerous times over the next four years. He also held the CWA World Title in October of

1980, and the NWA TV Title in January of 1981. He wrestled in the Mid-South area, where he was managed by Jimmy Hart. He formed a tag team, New Wave, with Sweet Brown Sugar, and they held the Southern Tag Team Title several times in 1982. Eaton also held the Southern belts with Duke Myers in December of 1982. He subsequently was teamed with Dennis Condrey as the Midnight Express by manager Jimmy Cornette in late 1983. He and Condrey captured the MSWA Tag Team Title several times in 1984. They entered World Class in late 1984. They soon joined the NWA, where they feuded with the Rock 'n' Roll Express. They captured the NWA Tag Team Title from the Rock 'n' Roll Express in February of 1986. They were defeated by their rivals for the belts in August of 1986. Condrey was fired in early 1987 and was replaced by Stan Lane in April of 1987. Eaton and Lane won the NWA U.S. Tag Title during the late 1980s, often feuding with the Fantastics. They defeated Arn Anderson and Tully Blanchard for the NWA Tag Title in September of 1988. They were defeated for the belts by the Road Warriors the following month. Eaton began wrestling as a single when Cornette and Lane left the promotion in late 1990. He captured the WCW TV Title from Arn Anderson in May of 1991, and lost the belt to Steve Austin the following month. He joined Paul E. Dangerously's Dangerous Alliance in 1992 and teamed with Arn Anderson to win the WCW Tag Team Championship from Rick Steamboat and Dustin

Rhodes on January 16, 1992. They lost the belts to Rick and Scott Steiner in May of 1992. He wrestled with Steve Keirn as Bad Attitude in WCW in 1994. He joined with Steve Regal as Earl Robert Eaton to form the Blue Bloods in early 1995.

Ebony, Mr *see* Jones, Tom

Ebony Experience, The *see* Stevie Ray & Booker T.

Eckert, Ray (St. Louis, Missouri; 245 lbs.) held the Pacific Coast Title in San Francisco in January of 1948. He wrestled as Sandy O'Donne to briefly hold the NWA Texas Title in July of 1949. He reclaimed the Pacific Coast belt several times in 1949 and 1950. He held the NWA World Tag Team Title in San Francisco several times in the early 1950s, teaming with Hard Boiled Haggerty, Frederick von Schacht and Fred Atkins. He lost an NWA title bout to Lou Thesz in April of 1951. He teamed with Fred Atkins to hold the Pacific Coast Tag Team Title several times in 1952 and 1953.

Efraim, Conrad *see* Jones, S.D.

Eigen, Haruka (b. January 11, 1946) began wrestling professionally in Japan in October of 1966. He was a popular star with New Japan in the 1970s and early 1980s. He joined with All-Japan in 1987.

Ekizian, Harry *see* Ali Baba

Eklund, Clarence (d. January 4, 1981) held the World Light Heavyweight title four times from 1916, until his retirement as champion in 1930.

El Gigante *see* Giant Gonzales

El Grande Pistolero *see* Gypsy Joe

El Toro *see* McCoy, Robert "Bibber"

Eliminator Kronus (George Caiazo; 6'4", 310 lbs.) wrestled with Saturn as The Eliminators in the USWA in 1994. They entered ECW the following year.

Eliminator Saturn (Perry Satullo; 5'10", 234 lbs.) wrestled with Kronus as The Eliminators in the USWA in 1994. They entered ECW the following year.

Elizabeth, Miss (Elizabeth Hewlet) accompanied her husband, Randy Savage, to the ring in the WWF from the mid-1980s. She managed both Savage and Hulk Hogan when the duo wrestled as the Mega-Powers at Summerslam in August of 1988. She was a leading figure in the feud that subsequently developed between Savage and Hogan. She was also involved in Savage's feud with Ric Flair in 1992. Following her divorce from Savage, she retired from wrestling. She returned to the ring at the WCW in late 1995, accompanying Savage and Hulk Hogan to the ring. She subsequently turned on the pair to join Ric Flair's entourage.

Ellering, Paul was managed by Jimmy Hart in the Mid-South area in the early 1980s. He teamed with Sheik Ali Hassan to hold the Southern Tag Team Title in March of 1980. He held the Southern Heavyweight Title from April until July of 1980. Ellering managed the Iron Sheik and Jake Roberts in the NWA in 1983 and 1984. He also managed the Road Warriors in the NWA throughout the late 1980s.

Ellis, "Cowboy" Bob was a popular wrestler from Texas from the late 1950s. He held the WNA Central States Title in 1958 and 1960. He briefly held the NWA U.S. Title in June of 1960, and the NWA U.S. Title in San Francisco in November of 1960. He teamed with Johnny Valentine to capture the WWWF U.S. Tag Team Title from the Fabulous Kangaroos in January of 1962. They were defeated for the belts by Buddy Rogers and Johnny Barend in July of 1962. Ellis held the NWA Southern Title in Florida from March until June of 1964. He held the WWA Title in Los Angeles in September of 1964. He teamed with Edouard Carpentier to hold the WWA Tag Team Title in December of 1964. He teamed with the Stomper to hold the NWA Central States Tag Team Title in May of 1966. He also held the tag belts with the Viking in October of 1967. He held the Mid-West Title in Omaha several times in 1968. He teamed with Alberto Torres to hold the Mid-West Tag Title in May of 1971. He held the WWA title in Indiana in 1973. He teamed with Jim Garvin to hold the Southern Tag Team Title in July of 1977. Ellis retired to Australia in the early 1980s.

Ellison, Lillian *see* Moolah

Embry, Eric (b. 1959; Lexington, Kentucky; 5'10", 225 lbs.) began wrestling in 1976. He held the Florida TV Title in December of 1981. He teamed with Ken Timbs and, later, Dan Greer, as the Fabulous Blonds to hold the Southwest Tag Team Title several times in 1983 and 1984. He held the WWC Puerto Rican Title several times in 1985 and 1986. He teamed with Frankie Lancaster to hold the World Class World Tag Team Title in June of 1987. He held the World Class Light Heavyweight Title several times from 1987 through 1989, often competing against Jeff Jarrett. He held the World Class Texas Title and the USWA Texas Title in 1989. He teamed with Rick Valentine to hold the WWC Caribbean Tag Team Title in Puerto Rico in September of 1990. He again held the Texas belt several times in early 1991. He held the USWA Southern Title from May of 1991, exchanging the belt with Tom Prichard on several occasions. He retired following serious injuries suffered in an automobile accident in Kentucky on October 30, 1992.

Emmerling, John *see* Becker, Bob

Endo, Kokichi teamed with Rikidozan to hold the Hawaiian Tag Team Title in 1959.

Enos, Mike (b. June 11, 1962; 6'4", 252 lbs.) began wrestling in 1988 as Mean Mike Enos. He wrestled with Wayne Bloom as the Destruction Crew to win the AWA Tag Team Title in a tournament in October of 1989. They were defeated for the belts by the Trooper and D.J. Peterson in August of 1990. Enos and Bloom became known as the Beverly Brothers when they moved to the WWF in 1990, with Enos wrestling as Blake Beverly. They left the promotion after several years. He

resumed wrestling as Mike Enos and continued to team with Bloom. The duo primarily wrestled in Japan in the mid-1990s.

Equalizer, The *see* Sullivan, Dave

Equalizer Zap (5'10", 245 lbs.) began wrestling in 1989. He was originally from Lake Charles, Louisiana. He teamed with his brother, Zip, as the Equalizers. They defeated the Madison Brothers for the IWCCW tag title in February of 1991. They lost the belts in a rematch the following month. They held the MASW tag team belts in April of 1992.

Equalizer Zip (5'10", 240 lbs.) began wrestling in 1989. He was originally from Lake Charles, Louisiana. He teamed with his brother, Zap, as the Equalizers. They defeated the Madison Brothers for the IWCCW tag title in February of 1991. They lost the belts in a rematch the following month. They held the MASW tag team belts in April of 1992.

Eric, Yukon *see* Yukon Eric

Eric the Lumberjack *see* Irwin, Scott

Eric the Red (Eric Hansen; b. 1944, d. November 16, 1978) teamed with Pak Song to hold the NWA Florida Tag Team Title on October 14, 1978. They held the belt until Eric's death on November 16, 1978.

Ernst, Adolph *see* Santel, Ad

Escovedo, Javier (d. 1964) was a leading Mexican wrestler in the early 1960s. He held the Mexican

National Welterweight Title from April of 1963 until his death in an automobile accident the following year.

Esserati, Bernardo *see* Assirati, Bert

Estrada, Jerry (b. January 10, 1958; Mexico City, Mexico; 5'10", 201 lbs.) began wrestling in 1977. He was a leading Mexican wrestling star.

Estrada, Jose teamed with Julio Estrada as the Super Medics. They held the WWC Tag Team Title in Puerto Rico several times in 1990. They also wrestled in Puerto Rico as Solid Gold in 1991, holding the AWF Tag Team Title several times

Estrada, Julio teamed with Jose Estrada as the Super Medics. They held the WWC Tag Team Title in Puerto Rico several times in 1990. They also wrestled in Puerto Rico as Solid Gold in 1991, holding the AWF Tag Team Title several times.

Etchison, Ronnie (b. 1917, d. March 4, 1994; Missouri) fought in the Golden Gloves and was Missouri champion in the 1930s. He began wrestling in the early 1940s and wrestled during World War II to entertain the troops. During the 1950s he was a popular West Coast mat star, known as "Wonder Boy." He held the Pacific Coast Title in San Francisco in May of 1950. He teamed with Sandor Szabo to hold the Pacific Coast Tag Team Title in late 1951. He teamed with Ray Stern to hold the NWA World Tag Team Title in San Francisco in October of 1955. He again held the tag belts with Buddy Rogers in October of 1958. He held the NWA Central States Title in March of 1961. He teamed with Dan Miller to hold the Canadian Tag Team Title in July of 1963. He teamed with Sam Steamboat to briefly hold the NWA World Tag Team Title in Florida in October of 1965. He held the U.S. Title in Missouri in September of 1967. He teamed with Klondike Bill to hold the NWA Central States Tag Team Title in January of 1968. He held the tag title again with Sonny Myers in May of 1968. He retired in 1980. Etchison died in St. Joseph, Missouri, after a long illness on March 4, 1994.

Eudy, Sid *see* Vicious, Sid

Evans, Chris (6'1", 239 lbs.) began wrestling in 1986. He was formerly known as Chris Weider. He held the WWA heavyweight championship in 1995.

Evans, Don (b. 1917; Kingston, New York; 5'11", 227 lbs.) was a farmer from Kingston, New York, before entering wrestling in 1937. He originally wrestled as a fan favorite until his leg was broken by Bobby Managoff. He returned to the ring after 16 months as a villain, sometimes billed as Don the Magnificent. He teamed with Duke Keomuka to hold the NWA Texas Tag Team Title in August of 1954. Evans held the Texas Brass Knucks Title in March of 1956.

Evans, Giant teamed with Moose Evans to hold the World Tag Team Title in Tennessee in August of 1966.

Evans, Moose (6'8", 355 lbs.)

teamed with Verne Gagne to defeat Crusher and Dick the Bruiser for the AWA Tag Team Title in February of 1964. They lost the belts in a re-match several weeks later. He teamed with Giant Evans to hold the World Tag Team Title in Tennessee in August of 1966. He teamed with Bob Stanlee as the Mighty Yankees to hold the International Tag Team Title in Toronto in February of 1966.

Evans, Ray, wrestling as the Star Rider, teamed with Moondog Moretti to hold the Canadian Tag Team Title in 1984.

Evans, Tiny held the NWA Southern Title in late 1960.

Everhart, Jack *see* McKinley, Gordon

Evers, Lance *see* Storm, Lance

Executioner, The *see* Smith, Curtis

Executioners, The *see* Kowalski, Killer & Studd, Big John

Fabian *see* Bagwell, Marcus

Fabiano, Lou (6', 275 lbs.) began wrestling in 1985. Known as the New York Brawler, he wrestled as Sheik Fabiano in the USWA in 1990. Wrestling as Muhammad Hussein, he held the WWC Tag Team Title in Puerto Rico several times in 1992 and 1993, teaming with El Vigilante #1, Dusty Wolfe, Hurricane Castillo and the Tahitian Warrior.

Fabulous Blondes, The *see* Embry, Eric & Greer, Dan

Fabulous Blondes, The *see* Embry, Eric & Timbs, Ken.

Fabulous Kangaroos, The *see* Costello, Al & Heffernan, Roy

Faietta, Ed (Steubenville, Ohio; 235 lbs.) began wrestling in the late 1940s. He often teamed with his brother, Tony, and they were some-times known as the Gardenia Broth-ers in the ring.

Faietta, Tony (Steubenville, Ohio; 235 lbs.) began wrestling in the late 1940s. He often teamed with his brother, Ed, and they were sometimes known as the Gardenia Brothers in the ring.

Faith, Jerry wrestled with Troy Haste as the Phantoms. Managed by Fantasia, they captured the USWA Tag Team Title in October of 1994.

Falcon, The *see* Armstrong, Steve

Falcone, Sweet Daddy (Tim Roberts; Dallas, Texas; 6'4", 245 lbs.) teamed with Brickhouse Brown as the Uptown Posse to capture the USWA Tag Team Title in April of 1990. They were managed by Reggie B. Fine. Falcone wrestled as Guido Falcone as part of the Sicilian Studs in Global with Vito Mussolini in 1993. They held the Global World Tag Team Title for several months from May of 1993.

Falk, Tony (Dallas, Texas; 6'1", 240 lbs.) began wrestling in 1983. He wrestled often in Tennessee and Texas under such names as Boy Tony and Cowboy Tony. Wrestling as Boy Tony, he captured the Mid-America Title in October of 1986. He held the WWC Junior Heavyweight Title in Puerto Rico in April of 1988. In late 1991 Falk became known as Driver Tony when he accepted the position of Eric Embry's limo driver. He wrestled as the Nightstalker in the USWA in 1993, and reentered the promotion as Tony Falk in the Spring of 1996.

Fallen Angel *see* Woman

Fantasia managed the Phantoms in the USWA in 1994.

Fantasio *see* Spellbinder, The

Fantastics, The *see* Fulton, Bobby & Fulton, Jackie

Fantastics, The *see* Rogers, Tommy & Fulton, Bobby

Fantastix *see* Snow, Al & Ciassio, Rick

Far 2 Wild *see* Morton, Todd & Michaels, Chris

Fargo, Don was a popular wrestler in the South and Southwest from the mid-1950s. He teamed with his "brother" Jackie Fargo to hold the World Tag Team Title in Tennessee several times in 1957. They also held the World Tag Team Title in Chicago in November of 1958 and Southern Tag Team Title in 1959. They held the Southern belts again in May of 1964. He wrestled as Jack Dalton in the Texas area in the early 1960s, holding the NWA Texas Title in December of 1961. He held the NWA Georgia Title briefly in 1964. He teamed with Frank Dalton to hold the Gulf Coast Tag Team Title in 1968. He held the Gulf Coast Title in Alabama in 1971. He teamed with Sgt. Jacques Goulet as the Legionnaires, and held the WWA Tag Team Title in late 1974. Wrestling as Don Garfield, he held

the Mid-America Title in May of 1978. Fargo held the Southern Heavyweight Title several times in late 1978. He teamed with Robert Gibson to hold the Mid-America Tag Team Title in September of 1980.

Fargo, Jackie was a leading wrestler in Tennessee from the mid-1950s. Wrestling as Wildman Fargo, he teamed with Don Stevens in New York, losing a World Tag Team Title match against Antonino Rocca and Miguel Perez in 1957. He held the World Tag Team Title in Tennessee with Don Fargo several times in 1957. They also held the World Tag Team Title in Chicago in November of 1958 and the Southern Tag Team Title in 1959. He was also Southern Junior Heavyweight Champion in October of 1959. He teamed with Sonny Fargo to hold the World Tag Team Title in Tennessee in 1961. Fargo held the Big Time Wrestling Title in Massachusetts in the early 1960s. He teamed with Lester Welch to hold the Southern Tag Team Title several times in 1962. He also held the Southern belts with Tex Riley, Mario Milano, the Masked Rebel, Don Fargo and Len Rossi during the early 1960s. Fargo held the IWA Title in Chicago in late 1963 and early 1964. He teamed with Roughhouse Fargo to hold the Southern tag belts in 1972 and held the title with Jerry Jarrett in February of 1973. He engaged in a long-running feud with Jerry Lawler in the Memphis area in the early 1970s. Fargo held the Southern Heavyweight Title in 1975, and held the Mid-American Title in December of 1975 and again in 1977. He teamed with

Randy Fargo to capture the Southern Tag Team Title in June of 1980, shortly before his retirement to Nashville, Tennessee.

Fargo, Joe *see* Fargo, Sonny

Fargo, Randy teamed with Jackie Fargo to capture the Southern Tag Team Title in June of 1980.

Fargo, Roughhouse often teamed with his "brother," Jackie Fargo. He wrestled under the name Don Stevens in New York when he and Jackie Fargo lost a World Tag Team Title bout against Antonino Rocca and Miguel Perez in 1957. He again teamed with Jackie Fargo to hold the Southern Tag Team Title in 1972.

Fargo, Sonny (Joe Fargo) teamed with Jackie Fargo to hold the World Tag Team Title in Tennessee in 1961. Wrestling as the Masked Rebel, he again teamed with Jackie Fargo to hold the Southern Tag Team Title in March of 1964. He teamed with Tojo Yamamoto to hold the tag belts in April of 1973.

Farhat, Ed *see* Sheik, The

Farouk, Abdullah *see* Grand Wizard, The

Farris, Wayne *see* Honky Tonk Man, The

Fatback Festus *see* Starr, Billy

Fatu (Salofa Fatu; b. October 11, 1966; San Francisco, California; 6'2", 260 lbs.) began wrestling in 1985. He wrestled in Canada as Tonga Kid Alopha in 1987. He teamed with Samu as the Samoans to hold the WWC Caribbean Tag

Team Title in Puerto Rico in November of 1987. They formed the original Samoan Swat Team and held the World Class World Tag Team Title three times in 1988. They became known as the Headshrinkers when they entered the WWF in the early 1990s, and were subsequently managed by Afa and Captain Lou Albano. Fatu and Samu later added Seone to the team, and Samu withdrew. Fatu and Seone defeated the Quebecers for the WWF Tag Team Championship in Burlington, Vermont, on April 26, 1994. They were defeated for the belts by Diesel and Shawn Michaels at a match in Indianapolis, Indiana, on August 28, 1994. Fatu wrestled in single matches during 1995 and 1996.

Fergie, Carl (Memphis, Tennessee; 230 lbs.) is a cousin of Jerry Lawler and Wayne "Honky Tonk Man" Farris. He teamed with Ox Baker to hold the NWA Atlantic coast Tag Title in 1981. He briefly held the Mid-America Title in September of 1987. He wrestled in the WCW in late 1994.

Fernandez, Manny (b. July 27; El Paso, Texas; 6', 259 lbs.) began wrestling in 1978. He was known as the Raging Bull and held the NWA Florida Title in late 1979. He feuded with Bugsy McGraw in the area. He held the NWA Central States Title in late 1982 and early 1983. He was the NWA World Tag Team Champion with Dusty Rhodes when they captured the belts from Ivan Koloff and Don Kernodle in October of 1984. They held the belts until March of 1985, when they were defeated by Ivan and Nikita Koloff. Fernandez teamed with Rick Rude to defeat the Rock 'n' Roll Express for the tag belts in December of 1986. They relinquished the title in May of 1987 when Rude left the promotion. Fernandez briefly held the CWA International Title in November of 1987. He captured the WWC Caribbean Title in Puerto Rico in January of 1990. He also held the IWA championship in Ohio in 1990.

Ferrara, Tommy (5'11", 228 lbs.) began wrestling in 1984. He held the PWA Light Heavyweight Title in March of 1986. He teamed with Johnny Love to hold the PWA Tag Team Title for several months from November of 1987. Ferrara also held the PWA singles title in 1993.

Ferraro, Rick *see* Verdu, Crusher

Ferri, Arnold (b. 1924, d. June 22, 1987; Philadelphia, Pennsylvania; 5'8", 190 lbs.) was a champion amateur boxer in his youth, holding the Pacific Fleet middleweight championship while serving in the Navy during World War II. Ferri began wrestling professionally in the 1950s, and was known as the Baron Bull of Montana. He continued to wrestle through the early 1970s, often competing in the Pennsylvania area with Lou Super as his partner. He worked as a production linesman at General Electric until his retirement in 1983. Ferri died of a heart attack at his home in Drexel Hill, Philadelphia, on June 22, 1987.

Festus (5'11", 236 lbs.) began wrestling in 1986. He was known as the scufflin' hillbilly from the Georgia Blue Ridge Mountains.

Fields, Bobby teamed with Don Fields to hold the World Tag Team Title in Tennessee several times in 1959. They also held the Southern Tag Team Title several times in the early 1960s. He sometimes wrestled under the name Luke Fields. He held the Gulf Coast Title in Alabama in early 1967. He teamed with his brother, Lee, as the Blue Infernos to hold the Southern Tag Team Title in October of 1966. They captured the NWA Southern Tag Team Title in September of 1968.

Fields, Don teamed with Bobby Fields to hold the World Tag Team Title in Tennessee several times in 1959. They also held the Southern Tag Team Title several times in the early 1960s. He held the Alabama Title from June of 1963 until injuries suffered in an automobile accident forced his retirement the following August.

Fields, Lee held the Gulf Coast Title in Alabama in 1957. He teamed with his brother, Bobby, as the Blue Infernos to hold the Southern Tag Team Title in October of 1966. They captured the NWA Southern Tag Team Title in September of 1968.

Fields, Luke *see* Fields, Bobby

Fine, Reggie B. (Reginald Washington; Memphis, Tennessee; 215 lbs.) wrestled in the USWA area from the 1980s. He managed Brickhouse Brown and Sweet Daddy Falcone as the Uptown Posse in 1990.

He was briefly known as the Candyman while wrestling as a fan favorite in the early 1990s. He continued to compete in the USWA, teaming with Men on a Mission in 1996.

Finkelstein, Harry (b. 1909; Boston, Massachusetts; 5'11", 218) attended Boston University, where he studied law. He entered wrestling in 1931, and was known as the Boston Bad Boy. He remained a leading wrestler through the 1950s.

Finlay, David *see* Belfast Bruiser

Fire *see* Bass, Don

Fire Cat *see* Boone, Brady

Firebreaker Chip (Curtis Thompson; 5'11", 245 lbs.) played college football and played with the Atlanta Falcons for one year. He won the Mr. North Carolina title in 1987 before deciding on a career as a professional wrestler. He was trained by Gene Anderson and debuted as Curtis Thompson in the NWA in 1988. He soon left the promotion for Puerto Rico, where he teamed with Ricky Santana. He also wrestled in Canada, where he teamed with Larry Cameron, and Portland, Oregon. He defeated Scotty the Body for the NWA Pacific Northwest Championship in October of 1989, and reteamed with Santana as U.S. Male to win the NWA Pacific Northwest Tag Team Title in May of 1990. He subsequently joined Robert Fuller's Stud Stable, but broke with the group in the USWA. He then teamed with Chris Walker, until Walker was injured in the ring. Thompson went on to the Georgia All-Star region, then entered the WCW, where he took the name Firebreaker Chip and wrestled with Todd Champion as the Patriots. The duo captured the WCW U.S. Tag Team Title from the Fabulous Freebirds in August of 1991. They lost the belts to the Young Pistols in November of 1991. Firebreaker Chip entered the IWCCW in the early 1990s and held the promotions TV title in 1992. Chip wrestled in Smoky Mountain Wrestling in 1995.

Firpo, Pampero wrestled as Ivan the Terrible in Texas in the late 1950s and early 1960s. He held the NWA Texas Title in August of 1957. Teaming with Nikita Zolotoff he held the NWA Texas Tag Team Title in September of 1957. Known as the Wild Bull of the Pampas, he held the NWA Pacific Northwest Title in June of 1964. He held the NWA Americas Title in Los Angeles in 1967. He wrestled as the Missing Link in Hawaii in the late 1960s, holding the Hawaiian Title several times in 1969 and 1970. He also held the Hawaiian Tag Team Title several times during this period, teaming with Neff Maivia and Jim Hady. He remained a leading mat star in the 1970s, recapturing the Americas Title in 1974. He held the NWA U.S. Title several times in the early 1970s. He teamed with Jack Evans to hold the NWA Americas Tag Team Title in Los Angeles in April of 1980. He also held the WWC North American Title in Puerto Rico in 1980. He held the All-California Championship Wrestling Title in 1987.

Fisher, Doug *see* Terminator Wolf

Fishman, Hyman *see* Rasputin, Ivan

Fitzpatrick *see* Cohen, Sammy

Flair, Ric (Richard Fliehr; b. February 25, 1949; Minneapolis, Minnesota; 6'1", 243) was trained by Verne Gagne and made his professional wrestling debut on December 10, 1972. He wrestled in the AWA in 1973 and began wrestling in the Carolinas in 1974. He suffered a broken back in a plane crash in North Carolina on October 4, 1975. Despite being told he would never wrestle again, Flair recovered from his injuries. Known as the Nature Boy, Flair held the NWA U.S. Title five times between 1977 and 1980. Flair also teamed with Greg Valentine to capture the NWA World Tag Team Title twice in 1977 before the duo were stripped of the belt in November of 1977. He defeated the other "Nature Boy," Buddy Rogers, in a match in July of 1979. Flair again held the tag team belt when he teamed with Blackjack Mulligan to capture the championship from Baron Von Raschke and Paul Jones in August of 1979. They lost the belts in a rematch the following month. Flair defeated Dusty Rhodes for the NWA Heavyweight Title in a match in Kansas City, Missouri, on September 17, 1981. He retained the belt until June 10, 1983, when he lost the title to Harley Race in St. Louis, Missouri. He recaptured the belt from Race on November 24, 1983. Flair was defeated for the title by Kerry Von Erich in Dallas, Texas, on May 6, 1984, but regained the belt from Von Erich in a match in Yokosuka, Japan, several weeks later

on May 24, 1984. Flair wrestled as a member of the Four Horsemen, with Ole Anderson, Arn Anderson and Tully Blanchard, under the management of James J. Dillon during much of the late 1980s. He briefly lost the belt to Dusty Rhodes on July 26, 1986, but again recaptured the title in a rematch on August 9, 1986. Flair was defeated by Ron Garvin in Detroit, Michigan, on September 25, 1987. He defeated Garvin for another title reign on November 26, 1987, in Chicago, Illinois. Flair was defeated by Rick Steamboat in Chicago, Illinois, on February 20, 1989. Flair regained the belt from Steamboat on May 7, 1989, in a match in Nashville, Tennessee. He again lost the belt in a match against Sting in Baltimore, Maryland on July 7, 1990. He recaptured the belt from Sting in East Rutherford, New Jersey, on January 11, 1991. Flair was stripped of the NWA/WCW title when he signed with the WWF in September of 1991. He won the vacant WWF Heavyweight Title at the Royal Rumble, in New York, on January 18, 1992. He lost the belt to Randy Savage in Sarasota, Florida, on April 15, 1992. Flair defeated Randy Savage for the WWF Title in Hershey, Pennsylvania, on September 1, 1992. He lost the belt to Bret Hart the following month in Saskatoon, Saskatchewan, Canada, on October 12, 1992. Flair left the WWF to return to WCW in February of 1993. He defeated Barry Windham for the NWA Title in Biloxi, Mississippi, on July 18, 1993. Flair was recognized as the WCW International Title holder when the WCW withdrew from the NWA in September of 1993. He defeated Big Van Vader for the WCW Title at Starrcade '93 in Charlotte, North Carolina, on December 27, 1993. Flair defeated Sting at the WCW Clash of Champions on June 23, 1994, to unify the WCW Heavyweight Title and the WCW International Title. He lost the belt to Hulk Hogan in a match in Orlando, Florida, on July 17, 1994. Flair battled Antonio Inoki in a bout in North Korea in April of 1995. He reformed the Four Horsemen later in the year with Arn Anderson, Chris Benoit and Brian Pillman. Flair engaged in a series of feuds with Randy Savage and Hulk Hogan in the mid-1990s. He was often accompanied to the ring by Woman and Savage's ex-wife, Miss Elizabeth.

Flame *see* Smith, Roger

Flaming Youth (5'11", 230 lbs.) began wrestling in 1991. He is a popular wrestler with the PWF promotion, holding the Tag Team Title several times in the early 1990s, teaming with Gladiator #2, Star Rider and Cruel Connection #2.

Flamingo, Scotty *see* Raven

Flanagan, Pat (Winnett Watson; d. March 29, 1985) teamed with Whipper Billy Watson to hold the Canadian Open Tag Team Title in Toronto in 1952.

Flash, Blade Runner *see* Sting

Fletcher, Bill *see* Monroe, Bill

Fliehr, Richard *see* Flair, Ric

Flores, Francisco teamed with Alfonso Dantes to hold the NWA Americas Title in Los Angeles in April of 1969. He teamed with the Cuban Assassin to hold the Calgary Stampede International Tag Team Title in September of 1983.

Flowers, Timothy held the NWA Americas Title in Los Angeles several times in 1981 and 1982, competing against such wrestlers as El Gran Hamada and Adrian Street. He teamed with Street to hold the NWA Americas Tag Team Title several times in 1982. He teamed with Rick Patterson to hold the Canadian Tag Team Title in June of 1983.

Flying Dutchman, The *see* Tenant, O.L. "Dutch"

Flying Dutchman, The *see* Whittler, Whitey

Flying Tigers, The *see* Sanchez, Pete & Soto, Manuel

Flying Tigers, The *see* Wilson, Larry & Patrick, Carl Ben

Flynn, George (b. 1922; Ireland) was a graduate of Dublin University in Ireland. He came to the United States as a professional wrestler in 1947. He was known in the ring for his rolling leglock maneuver and remained a leading competitor through the 1950s.

Foley, J.R. (b. 1938, d. July 24, 1988) was a leading Canadian manager in the 1970s and 1980s. He managed such wrestling stars as the Dynamite Kid, Junkyard Dog and Giant Haystacks in the Calgary Stampede promotion. He died of lung cancer on July 24, 1988.

Foley, Mick *see* Cactus Jack

Fontaine, Eric (Eric Downey; 5'10", 288 lbs.) began wrestling in 1982. He competed in the USWA and Global, where he teamed with Randy Rhodes as the New Pretty Young Things. They were managed by Christopher Love. Fontaine sometimes wrestled as the Dark Patriot and the Scorpion. He also wrestled briefly in the WWF, teaming was Demolition Ax. Fontaine continued to wrestle in independent promotion in the early 1990s.

Ford, Chris *see* Storm, Devon

Ford, Joyce (b. 1930; Dallas, Texas; 5'2", 130 lbs.) was a rodeo performer and professional model before she entered wrestling in the early 1950s. She remained a leading competitor throughout the decade.

Fortune, Chad, as Travis, wrestled with Erik Watts in Tekno Team 2000 in the WWF and the USWA from May of 1995.

Fraley, Cowboy Pat (b. 1911; Blair, Nebraska; 5'10", 240 lbs.) began wrestling in the 1930s. Wrestling as the Green Panther, he captured the Pacific Coast Title in San Francisco from Dean Detton in January of 1944. He lost the belt in a rematch two months later. He remained a leading wrestler through the early 1950s.

Francis, Edmund (b. 1925; Chicago, Illinois; 5'11", 210 lbs.) began wrestling in the late 1940s. He was a popular competitor in the Midwest in the early 1950s. He held the NWA Texas Title in June of 1954. He held the NWA Pacific Northwest Tag Team Title several times in the late 1950s, teaming with Henry Lenz, Bill Savage, Tony Borne, Herb Freeman, Ed Sullivan and Luther Lindsay. He also held the NWA Pacific Northwest Title several times in the late 1950s. He held the Hawaiian Title in May of 1959. He teamed with Pedro Morales to hold the Hawaiian Tag Team Title several times in 1969. He again held the Hawaiian Title in 1971 and 1973, and reclaimed the tag belts in July of 1973, wrestling with Ripper Collins. He was also a promoter in Hawaii during the 1960s and 1970s. He is the father of wrestlers Bill Francis and Russ Francis.

Franke, Keith *see* Adonis, Adrian

Fraser, Bob (b. 1926; South Braintree, Massachusetts; 5'9", 160 lbs.) served in the army and the merchant marines. He was a leading middleweight wrestler in the 1950s.

Frasier, Nelson *see* Mabel

Frazier, Stan "Plowboy" (b. 1938, d. June 30, 1992; Philadelphia, Mississippi; 406 lbs.) wrestled in Los Angeles as the Giant Convict in the late 1960s. He often wrestled in the Memphis area under such names a Playboy Frazier, the Lone Ranger, and Kamala II. He teamed with Dennis Hall to hold the Southern Tag Team Title in 1971. He again held the tag belts in April of 1976, wrestling with Jerry Lawler. He teamed with Ted DiBiase to hold the NWA National Tag Team Title in January of 1981. He entered the WWF in the mid-1980s as Hillbilly Jim's Uncle Elmer. He again teamed with Jerry Lawler to hold the Southern Tag Team Title in June of 1986.

Teaming with Cousin Junior, he reclaimed the belt the following August. Uncle Elmer married Joyce Staszko on NBC's Saturday Night Main Event in October of 1987. Soon after her returned to the Memphis area, where he continued to wrestle. Frazier died of kidney failure caused by complications from diabetes at a Biloxi, Mississippi, hospital on June 30, 1992.

Frederik, Paul *see* Jones, Paul

Freebirds, The *see* Hayes, Michael & Gordy, Terry & Roberts, Buddy

Freebirds, The *see* Hayes, Michael & Garvin, Jimmy

Freeman, Herb (Herb Schiff; d. 1966; New York City; 260 lbs.) began wrestling in 1934. He was a leading mat villain in the 1930s and 1940s. In the late 1940s he wrestled on the West Coast as Pierre Lassartes of the French underground. He remained active through the 1950s, teaming with Ray Gunkel to hold the NWA Texas Tag Team Title in September of 1956. He held the NWA Pacific Northwest Tag Team Title several times in the late 1950s, teaming with Larry Chene, Pepper Gomez, Luigi Macera, Cowboy Carlson, Henry Lenz, Nick Kozak and Seymour Freeman. He teamed with Lord James Blears to hold the Hawaiian Tag Team Title in March of 1960. He held the NWA Pacific Northwest Title several times in the early 1960s.

Freeman, Seymour teamed with Herb Freeman to hold the NWA Pacific Northwest Tag Team Title in November of 1958. They recaptured the tag belts in October of 1961.

Freeman, Zoltan "Ace" (b. 1914; New York City; 5'8", 200 lbs.) was born in Hungary and came to the United States while in his early teens. He settled in New York City and entered wrestling in 1932. He remained active in the ring through the 1950s.

Freer, Mark (6', 220 lbs.) began wrestling in 1989. He briefly wrestled as Home Boy, teaming with New Jack to hold the USWA Tag Team Title in June of 1993.

French, Valerie *see* Sunshine

French Angel, The (Maurice Tillet; d. August 4, 1954; France) was a lawyer in France before a glandular disorder distorted his features. He subsequently became a professional wrestler and was one of the most feared mat stars for three decades. He defeated Steve Casey for the AWA Heavyweight Title in Boston, Massachusetts, on May 13, 1940. He lost the belt to Casey on May 14, 1942, but recaptured the title from Casey on August 1, 1944. He again lost the belt to Casey in a rematch several weeks later on August 15, 1944. Tillet remained a wrestling headliner throughout the world until his death on August 4, 1954.

Friar Ferguson *see* Shaw, Mike

Friedrich, Robert *see* Lewis, Ed "Strangler"

Froelich, Eric teamed with Rueben Juarez to hold the NWA

Americas Tag Team Title in Los Angeles in August of 1972. He teamed with Guy Mitchell to hold the Canadian Tag Team Title in August of 1977.

Fuchi, Masanobu (b. January 24, 1954; 5'10", 215 lbs.) studied under Jumbo Tsuruta and began wrestling professionally in 1974. He teamed with Mr. Onita to hold the Southern Tag Team Title in March of 1981. He is a longtime holder of the PWF Junior Heavyweight belt and a popular star with All-Japan.

Fuji, Mr. (Harry Fujiwara; b. May 4; Japan; 5'11", 265 lbs.) began wrestling in 1959. He teamed with King Curtis to capture the Hawaiian Tag Team Title in January of 1965. He captured the NWA Pacific Northwest Title in August of 1970. He teamed with Prof. Toru Tanaka in the 1970s and they captured the WWWF Tag Team Title from Sonny King and Chief Jay Strongbow in June of 1972. They were defeated by Tony Garea and Haystacks Calhoun in May of 1973, but recaptured the title the following September. They again lost the belts in November of 1973 to Garea and Dean Ho. Fuji captured the NWA U.S. Title in San Francisco in February of 1976. He retained the title until he left the area in February of 1977. He and Tanaka again teamed to win the WWWF Tag Team Title in September of 1977, holding the belts until March of 1978, when they were defeated by Dominic Denucci and Dino Bravo. He and Tanaka held the Southern Tag Team Title in May of 1979, and the NWA Southeastern Tag Team Title in July of

1979. He teamed with Tenryu to hold the NWA Atlantic Coast Tag Title for several months in early 1981. He held the NWA Canadian Title in Toronto in July of 1981. Fuji teamed with Mr. Saito to regain the WWF Tag Team Title in October of 1981, defeating Tony Garea and Rick Martel. They lost the belts to Chief Jay and Jules Strongbow in June of 1982, but regained them the following month. They were again defeated by the Strongbows in October of 1982. He was managed by the Grand Wizard, Fred Blassie and Lou Albano during his wrestling career. Fuji managed in the WWF during the 1980s and 1990s. He led Demolition to the tag team championship in March of 1988, and managed Yokozuna in the 1990s

Fuji, Ysau teamed with Chati Yokouchi to hold the Canadian Tag Team Title in October of 1970. They also held the NWA Central States Tag Team Title in February of 1972. He and Yokouchi also held the Calgary Stampede International Tag Team Title several times in 1973. Fuji again held the Central States tag belts in March of 1975, teaming with Oki Shikina. He teamed with Kim Duk to reclaim the Central States tag title in March of 1983.

Fujinami, Tatsumi (b. December 23, 1953; Oita, Japan; 6'1", 238 lbs.) began wrestling in 1971. He is a popular Japanese wrestler who held the NWA International Junior Heavyweight Title several times in 1980. He competed in the WWF in the mid-1980s. He held the NWA Pacific Northwest Title in October of 1988. Fujinami defeated Kerry

Von Erich by countout for the WCWA World Title in Tokyo, Japan, in December of 1988, but returned the title to Von Erich. He held the Catch Wrestling Association Intercontinental Title in Europe in 1992.

Fujiwara, Harry *see* Fuji, Mr.

Fujiwara, Yoshiaki (b. April 27, 1949; Iwate, Japan; 6', 220 lbs.) began wrestling in November of 1972. He competed often in New Japan.

Fuller, Buddy is the son of promoter Roy Welch and the father of wrestlers Robert and Ron Fuller. He teamed with Lester Welch to hold the Southern Tag Team Title in October of 1962. Wrestling as George Valentine, he held the IWA Title in Chicago in 1963. He held the Southern Tag Team Title with Jesse James in 1965. He also held the NWA Georgia Title several times in 1965. He teamed with Ray Gunkel to hold the Atlanta World Tag Team Title several times in the late 1960s. He again teamed with Lester Welch to hold the NWA Southern Tag Team Title in Florida from April of 1967 until the following November.

Fuller, Robert (Robert Welch; b. 1951; Dyresburg, Tennessee; 6'5", 257 lbs.) is the son of wrestler Buddy Fuller. He began wrestling in 1970. He teamed with Bob Armstrong to hold the NWA Georgia Tag Team Title several times in 1973 and 1974. He also held the title with Mr. Wrestling II in May of 1974. He briefly held the Southern Tag Team Title with Bill Dundee in May of 1979. He also held the Southern

Heavyweight Title several times in 1979. He teamed with his brother, Ron Fuller, to hold the NWA Southeastern Tag Team Title several times in 1979 and 1980. Known as the Tennessee Stud, he formed the Stud Stable of rulebreakers in the Memphis area in the late 1980s. He teamed with Jimmy Golden and Brian Lee to hold the CWA Tag Team Title and the World Class World Tag Team Title several times in 1988 and 1989. He also held the USWA Tag Team Title several times in 1990, teaming with Brian Lee. Becoming a fan favorite, he teamed with Jeff Jarrett to win the USWA tag team belts in the early 1990s. He went to the WCW in 1993, where he was known as Colonel Parker, the manager of the Stud Stable.

Fuller, Ron is the son of wrestler Buddy Fuller. He teamed with his cousin, Jimmy Golden, to hold the NWA Florida Tag Team Title in September of 1972. He held the NWA Southern Title in Florida in April of 1973. He also held the NWA Georgia Title in December of 1973, and the NWA Florida Title in March of 1974. He held the Southern Heavyweight Title in January of 1979. He teamed with his brother, Robert Fuller, to hold the NWA Southeastern Tag Team Title several times in 1980 and 1981.

Fullington, Jim *see* Sandman, The

Fulton, Bobby (b. October 4; Columbus, Ohio; 5'10", 220 lbs.) began wrestling in 1979. He formed the tag team the Fantastics with Tommy Rogers and they captured the World Class American Tag Team

Title several times in 1984 and 1985. They also captured the Southern Tag Team Title in January of 1986. They also held the UWF Tag Team Title in Oklahoma several times in 1986, and the World Class World Tag Team Title in 1987. They captured the PWA Tag Team Title in August of 1987, holding the belts until the following November. The duo captured the WCW U.S. Tag Team Title from the Midnight Express several times in 1988. In 1990 he wrestled with his brother, Jackie Fulton, as the Fantastics. He reteamed with Rogers and entered the WCW in October of 1994.

Fulton, Charlie teamed with Bobby Mayne to hold the Southern Tag Team Title in June of 1974. They were managed by Sir Dudley Clements.

Fulton, Jackie (George Hines; b. 1968; 5'11", 225 lbs.) began wrestling in 1988. He teamed with his older brother, Bobby Fulton, as the Fantastics in the early 1990s. He wrestled as the Eagle in All-Japan from 1992.

Funk, Dory, Jr. (b. February 19, 1941; Amarillo, Texas; 6'2", 250 lbs.) began wrestling in 1964. He was the son of Dory Funk, Sr. He defeated Gene Kiniski for the NWA Heavyweight Title in Tampa, Florida, on February 12, 1969. He retained the title until his defeat by Harley Race in a match in Kansas City, Missouri, on May 24, 1973. He subsequently held the NWA Missouri Title from May of 1974 until February of 1975. He held the NWA Americas Title in Los Angeles in January of 1977. He teamed with his brother, Terry Funk, to hold the NWA Georgia Tag Team Title in December of 1978. He held the NWA Florida Title several times in 1980 and 1981. Funk captured the NWA Mid-Atlantic Title in January of 1983, holding the belt until the following August. He recaptured the title for a month in May of 1984, wrestling as the Masked Outlaw. He held the WWC Universal Title in Puerto Rico in February of 1985. He was active in the ECW in the mid-1990s.

Funk, Dory, Sr. (b. 1919, d. June 3, 1973) is the father of Dory Funk, Jr. and Terry Funk. He held the NWA World Junior Heavyweight Title in June of 1958. He held the Pacific Coast Tag Team Title in Vancouver, Canada, several times in 1961, teaming with Lou Thesz and Pancho Pico. He died at his home in Amarillo, Texas, on June 3, 1973.

Funk, Jimmy Jack *see* Barr, Jesse

Funk, Terry (b. June 30, 1944; Amarillo, Texas; 6'1", 247 lbs.) began wrestling in 1966. He is the son of Dory Funk, Sr. Funk captured the NWA Southern Title in 1971. Wrestling as the masked Texan, he held the Florida TV Title in March of 1971. He held the NWA Missouri Title in February of 1973. He held the NWA U.S. Title in November of 1975. He beat Jack Brisco for the NWA Heavyweight Title in Miami, Florida, on December 10, 1975. He lost the belt to Harley Race in Toronto, Canada, on February 6, 1977. He teamed with his brother, Dory Funk, Jr., to hold the NWA Georgia Tag Team Title in December of 1978. He also held the NWA

Southern Title in Florida in December of 1978 and was the NWA Florida champion in September of 1979. Funk held the NWA TV Title in October of 1980. Funk briefly held the USWA Unified Title for several months in late 1990 and early 1991. He entered the ECW in 1993, winning the title from Sabu in December of 1993. He was defeated for the belt by Shane Douglas in March of 1994. Funk also made occasional appearances in films and television shows. He appeared with Sylvester Stallone in the 1978 film *Paradise Alley* and starring as Prometheus Jones in the short-lived 1985 television series *Wildside*. He also appeared in the tele-film *Timestalkers* (1987) and episodes of *Swamp Thing, Quantum Leap, Adventures of Brisco County, Jr.* and *Thunder in Paradise.*

Furnas, Doug (b. 1961; Commerce, Oklahoma; 5'11", 243 lbs.) began wrestling in 1986. He held the USA Tennessee Title in Knoxville in late 1987 and early 1988. He teamed with Dan Kroffat as the Can-Am Express in Japan and Mexico.

Fury *see* Green, Al

Fuyuki, Samson teamed with Toshiaki Kawada as Footloose. They held the All-Japan All-Asian Tag Team Title several times in the late 1980s.

Fytch, Tammy (Tamara Sytch) was a manager in Smoky Mountain Wrestling from April of 1993, managing Brian Lee. She and her husband, Chris Candido, joined the WWF in 1995 as the Body Donnas, with Candido as Skip and Fytch as

Sunny. They were later joined by Tom Prichard as Bodydonna Zip, and Fytch led the team to the WWF Tag Team Championship in the Spring of 1996.

G-Men, The *see* Goelz, Billy & Gilbert, Johnny

Gabor, Francis *see* Austin, Buddy

Gadaski, George "Scrap Iron" (John Kosti; b. 1930, d. December 6, 1982) was a leading wrestler in the 1950s and 1960s.

Gagne, Don *see* Martin, Frenchy

Gagne, Greg (b. July 27, 1948; Robbinsdale, Minnesota; 6'1", 220 lbs.) is the son of wrestler Verne Gagne. He began wrestling in 1973. He wrestled with Jim Brunzell as The High Flyers in the AWA. They captured the AWA Tag Team Title from Blackjack Lanza and Bobby Duncum in July of 1977. They retained the belts until September of 1978, when Brunzell was unable to defend the title because of an injury suffered while playing softball. They returned to take the belts from Adrian Adonis and Jesse Ventura in June of 1981. They remained champions for over two years until Adonis and Ventura ended their reign in June of 1983.

Gagne, Verne (b. May 10, 1923; Robbinsdale, Minnesota; 5'11", 215 lbs.) served in the Marines during World War II. He attended the University of Minnesota after the war, where he played football and competed in amateur wrestling. He began wrestling professionally in May of 1948. He held the NWA

Texas Title in December of 1949 and September of 1950. He won the NWA World Junior Heavyweight Title in a tournament in November of 1950. He lost the title later in the month to Danny McShane. He captured the AWA Title in Montreal, Canada, in February of 1953. He teamed with Bronko Nagurski to hold the NWA World Tag Team Title in Minneapolis for several months from December of 1957. He held the NWA tag belts again with Leo Nomellini in May of 1958. He held the World Title in Nebraska in August of 1958. He held the title several more times over the next five years. He again held the NWA tag belts, teaming with Butch Levy in April of 1959. He again teamed with Leo Nomellini to capture the NWA World Tag Team Title from Tiny Mills and Killer Kowalski in July of 1960. They lost the belts in a rematch the following month. Gagne was also a ten-time AWA Title holder. He was awarded the AWA Title in August of 1960. He lost the belt to Gene Kiniski in July of 1961, but reclaimed the title in a rematch the following month. He was defeated by Mister M for the title in January of 1962, but again won the belt in August of 1962. He exchanged the title several times against such mat stars as Fritz Von Erich, Crusher, and Mad Dog Vachon during the mid-1960s. Gagne also held the AWA Tag Team Title several times in the mid-1960s, teaming with Moose Evans and Crusher. He lost the AWA Title to Dr. X in July of 1968, but reclaimed it later in the month. He also held the AWA Tag Title again for a brief

time with Billy Robinson, interrupting Nick Bockwinkel and Ray Stevens title reign in December of 1972. Gagne's reign as AWA champion was ended by Nick Bockwinkel in November of 1975. Gagne returned to the ring to team with Mad Dog Vachon and again captured the tag team belts from Pat Patterson and Ray Stevens in June of 1979. They held the belts until July of 1980, when Gagne forfeited a match to Adrian Adonis and Jesse Ventura. Gagne defeated Bockwinkel for the AWA Title in July of 1980. He retired from the ring the following year to concentrate on heading the AWA until the promotion ended in 1991. He is the father of wrestler Greg Gagne.

Gaiser, George briefly held the NWA Southern Title in Florida in October of 1971.

Galento, Al "Spider" (b. 1921; San Francisco, California; 6', 210 lbs.) wrestled for the San Francisco Olympic Club. Galento held the Pacific Coast Championship for three years. He held the Southern Junior Heavyweight Title for several months in late 1952. He wrestled in the Mid-South area in the early 1960s.

Galento, Mario (Bonnie Lee Boyette; b. 1915) began wrestling in the early 1950s, often attired in cowboy boots and a black string tie. He held the Gulf Coast Title in 1957. He wrestled in the Memphis area during much of the 1950s and early 1960s. He also wrestled in New York in the early 1960s as the Wild Rebel. Galento held the NWA Georgia Title several times in 1964 and 1965.

He teamed with Bobby Shane to hold the Southern Tag Team Title in 1966. Galento also appeared in several films including *Frontier Woman* (1956) and *Natchez Trace* (1960).

Galento, Tony (Anthony Galento, b. March 12, 1910, d. July 22, 1979; Orange, New Jersey; 5'9", 245 lbs.) began boxing professionally in January of 1929. He was a leading boxer in the 1930s and early 1940s, competing in over one hundred bouts during his career. Known in the ring as "Two-Ton Tony," Galento lost a championship match to Joe Louis in 1939. He left boxing in 1944, and began wrestling professionally in 1947. He wrestled in many novelty matches including boxing matches with a kangaroo, wrestling an octopus, and touring with Teddy, the wrestling bear. He attempted a career in films in the 1950s, appearing in several movies including *On the Waterfront* (1954), *Guys and Dolls* (1955), *The Best Things in Life Are Free* (1956) and *Wind Across the Everglades* (1958). Galento died of a heart attack at a Livingston, New Jersey, hospital on July 22, 1979.

Gallagher, Doc teamed with Ivan Kameroff to hold the Northwest Tag Team Title in Vancouver, Canada, in October of 1953. He also teamed with Mike Gallagher to hold the Northwest tag belts in December of 1953. He and Mike Gallagher also held the NWA World Tag Team Title in Minneapolis several times in 1958, and the Canadian Open Tag Team Title in Toronto in 1960.

Gallagher, George *see* Gallagher, Mike

Gallagher, Mike also wrestled as George Gallagher. He teamed with Doc Gallagher to hold the Northwest Tag Team Title in Vancouver, Canada, in December of 1953. They also held the NWA World Tag Team Title in Minneapolis several times in 1958, and the Canadian Open Tag Team Title in Toronto in 1960.

Gama (India) was from a prominent wrestling family in India. The Hindu mat star came to England to wrestle in 1910. He defeated numerous leading wrestlers during the 1910s and 1920s. His brother, Imam Bhuks, and nephew, Aram Pehlwan, were also leading Indian wrestlers. Gama was considered one of the greatest grapplers in wrestling history.

Gangstas, The *see* Mustafa & New Jack

Gantner, Ed "the Bull" (d. December 31, 1990; Tampa, Florida; 269 lbs.) was a wrestler in the Florida area. He briefly held the NWA Florida Title in February of 1987. He committed suicide at his parents' home in Tampa, Florida, on December 31, 1990, after a bout of severe depression reportedly resulting for steroid abuse.

Gantner, Rick *see* Pain, Bull

Garcia, Lee *see* Hernandez, Luis

Gardenia, Eddie *see* Faietta, Ed

Gardenia, Tony *see* Faietta, Tony

Gardini, Benito (b. 1921; Chicago, Illinois; 5'4", 230 lbs.) began wrestling in the early 1940s.

The Maryland native was known in the ring as "the Little Flower."

Garea, Tony (Auckland, New Zealand; 240 lbs.) was a popular wrestler from New Zealand. He made his professional debut in 1971, and came to the United States the following year. He made his U.S. debut in Florida in March of 1972. He teamed with Haystacks Calhoun to take the WWWF Tag Team Title from Toru Tanaka & Mr. Fuji in May of 1975. They lost the belts back to Tanaka and Fuji the following September. Garea then teamed with Dean Ho to recapture the belts in November of 1973. They were defeated for the title by Jimmy and Johnny Valiant in May of 1974. He teamed with Pat Patterson to hold the NWA World Tag Team Title in San Francisco in May of 1976. Garea teamed with Larry Zbyszko to reclaim the championship in November of 1978, ending the Yukon Lumberjacks title reign. They lost the belts to Johnny and Jerry Valiant in March of 1979. Garea teamed with Rick Martel to defeat the Samoans for the WWF Tag Title in November of 1980. They were defeated for the belts by the Moondogs in March of 1981. They reclaimed the title from the Moondogs in July of 1981, but were defeated by Mr. Fuji and Mr. Saito in October of 1981. Garea remained involved in wrestling through the 1990s as an executive in the WWF.

Garfield, Don *see* Fargo, Don

Garibaldi, Chick (b. 1917, d. February 18, 1961; Lindenhurst, New York; 6', 210 lbs.) was the younger brother of Gino Garibaldi, who trained him for the ring. He held the World Light Heavyweight Title in July of 1948. He often teamed with his brother, and remained a leading mat star through the 1950s.

Garibaldi, Gino (Sam Curcuru; b. 1904, d. December 10, 1984; Los Angeles, California; 5'11", 215 lbs.) was an Illinois coal miner before he began wrestling in the mid-1920s. He was a leading mat star for over three decades and the patriarch of a wrestling family that included his brother, Chick, and his son, Leo. He held the AWA Title in Montreal, Canada, in May of 1943. He held the Pacific Coast Title in San Francisco several times in 1949 and 1950, competing against Lee Henning, Sandor Szabo and Frederick von Schacht. He and his son, Leo, teamed to hold the Pacific Coast Tag Team Title in 1951, and the NWA Southern Tag Team Title in 1956.

Garibaldi, Leo (b. 1927; Los Angeles, California; 6'1", 210 lbs.) was a popular wrestler in California in the early 1950s, often teaming with his father, Gino Garibaldi. They held the Pacific Coast Tag Team Title in 1951, and the NWA Southern Tag Team Title in 1956. He teamed with Cyclone Anaya to hold the NWA Texas Tag Team Title in December of 1959.

Garrett, Billy teamed with Jim Starr as the Medics to hold the NWA Florida Tag Team Title several times in 1968 and 1969. The masked duo were managed by Dr. Ken Ramey.

Garvin, Jim (James Williams;

b. September 25, 1957; Charlotte, North Carolina; 5'10½", 231 lbs.) began wrestling in 1969. He is the stepson of wrestler Ron Garvin. He teamed with Bob Ellis to hold the Southern Tag Team Title in July of 1977. He held the NWA Southern Title in Florida in 1978. He held the Florida title again in August of 1982 under the management of J.J. Dillon. With his valet, Sunshine, he captured the World Class Championship in Texas in July of 1983. He also held the World Class Texas Title several times later in 1983, often competing against David Von Erich. He subsequently replaced Sunshine with Precious as his ring valet and battled with Chris Adams in a series of bouts over the next two years. He teamed with Steve Regal to win the AWA Tag Team Title from the Road Warriors in September of 1985. They relinquished the belts in January of 1986 when Regal left the AWA. Garvin joined Michael Hayes in the Freebirds in the late 1980s. He and Hayes won the NWA World Tag Team Title in June of 1989. They retained the belts until their defeat by Rick and Scott Steiner in November of 1989. Garvin and Hayes again briefly held the belts in February of 1991 before once again losing to the Steiner Brothers. Garvin and Hayes also held the WCW U.S. Tag Team Title from May until August of 1991. Garvin teamed with Terry Gordy as the Freebirds in Global in 1994. They held the Global World Tag Team Title from June of 1994 until the promotion closed three months later. Garvin continued to be accompanied to the ring by his wife and valet, Precious.

Garvin, Ron (Ron Barnes; b. March 30; Montreal, Quebec, Canada; 6'2", 231 lbs.) began wrestling in 1965. He teamed with Terry Garvin to hold the NWA World Tag Team Title in late 1967. He teamed with Ole Anderson to briefly hold the NWA Florida Tag Team Title in July of 1971. He and Terry Garvin reteamed to hold the Southern Tag Team Title in 1971 and 1973, and the NWA Georgia Tag Team Title several times in 1974. He captured the NWA TV Title five times between 1983 and 1985. Garvin teamed with Jerry Oates to hold the NWA National Tag Team Title in July of 1984. Garvin also held the NWA National Title from October of 1984 until June of 1985. Garvin held the NWA Mid-Atlantic Title several months in late 1986. He teamed with Barry Windham to capture the NWA U.S. Tag Title in December of 1986, holding the belts until the following March. Garvin was known as the Man with the Hands of Stone, and he defeated Ric Flair in Detroit, Michigan, on September 25, 1987, for the NWA World Heavyweight Title. He lost the title to Flair several months later in Chicago, Illinois, on November 26, 1987. Garvin captured the WWC Universal Title in Puerto Rico in November of 1988. He again held the WWC belt in February of 1992. He is the stepfather of wrestler Jimmy Garvin.

Garvin, Terrence (San Francisco, California; 5'10", 220 lbs.) began wrestling in 1988. He teamed with Mark Gullen as Beauty and the Beast, with Garvin wearing feather boas and rouge and wrestling as an effeminate mat star. The duo wrestled in Alabama, Tennessee and World Class, where the held the Texas Tag Team Title in March of 1989. Gullen left the team in 1990. Garvin changed his image in mid-1991 and became a fan favorite in World Class. He also changed his name to Terry Simms, teaming with Scott Putski to hold the Global World Tag Team Title in March of 1992. He captured the Global Junior Heavyweight Title in May of 1992.

Garvin, Terry teamed with Ron Garvin to hold the NWA World Tag Team Title in Florida for several months in late 1967. He teamed with Duke Myers to capture the U.S. Tag Team Title in Louisiana in August of 1972. Terry and Ron Garvin also held the Southern Tag Team Title in 1971 and 1973, and the NWA Georgia Tag Team Title several times in 1974.

Garza, Barbara *see* Perkins, Ponytail

Gattoni, Baron Ricardo (Guiseppe Ricardo Jose Gattoni; b. 1921, d. April 30, 1982; Argentina; 6', 265 lbs.) was born in Italy, but spent many years in Argentina, where he was a weight-lifting champion. He turned to professional wrestling in the mid-1940s. He subsequently came to the United States, where he was a leading competitor for several decades. The bearded mat artist teamed with Karol Kalmikoff to hold the NWA World Tag Team Title in Minneapolis in April of 1959.

Gaylord, Jeff (b. October 15, 1958; St. Louis, Missouri; 6'3", 280 lbs.), known as the Missouri Tiger, began wrestling in 1985. He teamed with Jeff Jarrett to hold the USWA Tag Team Title in September of 1990. He again held the tag belts in November of 1993, teaming with Mike Anthony. Gylord was also a professional football player.

Geralds, Elmer *see* Oklahoma Kid, The

Geigel, Bob held the NWA Central States Title in October of 1958. He held the North Dakota Title in November of 1960. He partnered with Hard Boiled Haggerty to hold the AWA World Tag Team Title in September of 1961. They were defeated for the belts by Dale Lewis and Pat Kennedy in November of 1961. Geigel teamed with Otto Von Krupp to reclaim the belts later in the month. They relinquished the title when Krupp was injured in January of 1962. Geigel teamed with Killer Kowalski to defeat Larry Hennig and Duke Hoffman for the tag championship in February of 1962. They relinquished the belts to Art and Stan Neilson in April of 1962. He teamed with Bob Brown to hold the NWA Central States Tag Team Title several times from 1965 through 1968. He again held the NWA Central States Title in January of 1966 and 1967. Geigel teamed with the Viking to hold the Central States tag belts in December of 1968 and the Mid-West Tag Team Title in Omaha in March of 1969. He recaptured the Central States belt in 1971. He held the Central States tag belts several more times in the early 1970s, teaming with the Mongolian Stomper,

Rufus R. Jones, Bobo Brazil, Pat O'Connor and Akio Sato. Geigel was subsequently a leading promoter with the NWA through the 1980s.

Geohagan, Timmy (Ireland) was educated at the University of Dublin. He came to the United States in the 1940s as a circus strongman. He began wrestling in the Pacific Northwest in the late 1940s. He teamed with Big Humphrey to hold the NWA Texas Tag Team Title in May of 1951. He teamed with Paddy Barrett to hold the Canadian Tag Team Title several times in 1965 and 1966. They also held the International Tag Team Title in Winnipeg in November of 1965.

George, Ed Don held the World Heavyweight Title for several months in late 1930 and early 1931. He defeated Henri Deglane for the AWA World Title in Boston, Massachusetts, on February 9, 1933. He retained the championship until his defeat by Danno O'Mahoney in Boston on July 30, 1935. George defeated Steve Casey for the AWA Heavyweight Title in a match in Boston on April 18, 1939. He lost the belt to Casey in a rematch on November 3, 1939.

George, Mike (6'2", 265 lbs.) began wrestling in 1969. He teamed with Jim Brunzell to hold the NWA Central States Tag Team Title in late 1973. He held the NWA Central States Title in 1974 and 1976. He held the NWA Southern Title in Florida in 1975. He again held the Central States tag belts several times in 1976 and 1977, teaming with Super Intern and Scott Casey. He teamed with Porkchop Cash to hold

the U.S. Tag Team Title in Louisiana in August of 1977. He again held the U.S. belts with Randy Tyler in November of 1978. Know as the Timekeeper, he is also a former WWA champion who wrestled in the AWA and Kansas City area. He held the MSWA North American Title for several months in late 1979. He also held the Mid-South Mississippi Title in 1979. He again held the NWA Central States Title in September of 1980. He teamed with Bob Sweetan to hold the Central States tag belts in October of 1980. He again held the tag title in July of 1982, teaming with Mark Romero. He teamed with Rufus R. Jones to again hold the Central States belts in June of 1986. George held the Missouri Wrestling Federation Title from July until November of 1992.

George, P.L. "Pinkie" (b. 1904, d. November 1, 1993) was a boxing and wrestling promoter in Des Moines, Iowa. He was the first president of the National Wrestling Alliance, from its formation in Waterloo, Iowa, in July of 1948.

German Bomber, The *see* Becker, George

Giant, The (Paul Wight; b. 1971) was raised in South Carolina. He entered the WCW in August of 1995 and challenged Hulk Hogan in a series of matches. He was managed by Jimmy Hart in the WCW.

Giant Gonzales (Jorge Gonzales; b. January 31; Buenos Aires, Argentina; 7'7", 435 lbs.) began wrestling in 1990. He was previously a center on Argentina's national basketball team. He entered WCW as El Gigante in 1990, and joined the WWF several years later as the Giant Gonzalez. He engaged in several bouts with the Undertaker, before withdrawing from the ring and returning to Argentina for several years. Giant Gonzalez appeared on television in episodes of *Thunder in Paradise*, *Swamp Thing* and *Murder, She Wrote*. He briefly reemerged in the WCW as the Yetti, a member of Kevin Sullivan's Dungeon of Doom, in October of 1995.

Giant Haystacks (Luke Mc-Masters; b. 1941) is a popular British wrestler in Europe. He held the British Heavyweight Title for several months from November of 1978. He also held the Catch Wrestling Association European Heavyweight Title in 1990 and the CWA World Title in 1991. He entered the WCW in early 1996 as Loch Ness.

Giant Hillbilly Elmer *see* Frazier, Plowboy

Gibralter, Rocco *see* Droese, Duke

Gibson, Rick held the NWA Central States Title in October of 1976. He wrestled with his brother, Robert, from the late 1970s. They teamed to capture the NWA Americas Tag Team Title in Los Angeles in June of 1979. They also held the Southern Tag Team Title several times in 1979 and 1980. He held the U.S. Junior Heavyweight Title in Alabama in September of 1983. He retired after being seriously injured in an automobile accident.

Gibson, Robert (Ruben Kane;

b. July 19, 1958; Pensacola, Florida; 5'11", 225 lbs.) began wrestling in 1977. He originally tagged with his older brother, Rick Gibson, and the duo captured the NWA Americas Tag Team Title in Los Angeles in May of 1979. They also held the Southeastern and Mid-Southern tag championships in 1979 and 1980. He held the Mid-America Title in June of 1980, and teamed with Don Fargo to capture the Mid-America Tag Team Title in September of 1980. He formed the Rock 'n' Roll Express with Ricky Morton in Tennessee in 1983, capturing the Southern Tag Team Title in November of 1983. They won the NWA tag championship from Ivan Koloff and Krusher Khrushchev in Shelby, North Carolina, on July 9, 1985. They were defeated for the title in October of 1985 by Ivan and Nikita Koloff, but recaptured the belts the following month. They lost the belts to the Midnight Express in February of 1986, but returned as champions in August of 1986. They were again defeated for the belts by Manny Fernandez and Rick Rude in December of 1986. They returned as tag champions in May of 1987, holding the title until their defeat by Arn Anderson and Tully Blanchard in September of 1987. Gibson suffered a serious knee injury and the team broke up in September of 1990. The following year Gibson returned to the ring and feuded with Morton in the WCW. He reunited with Morton to capture the Smoky Mountain Tag Team Title in November of 1992. They held the belts several times over the next few years, often feuding with the Heavenly Bodies.

They also captured the USWA Tag Team Title in January of 1994. They wrestled as villains in the USWA and again held the tag belts in July of 1995.

Gibson, Ron wrestled with Stan Pulaski as the Infernos to hold the Southern Tag Team Title in April of 1974.

Gibson, Stu teamed with Hard Boiled Haggerty to hold the NWA Texas Tag Team Title in June of 1955. He held the Texas Brass Knucks Title in July of 1958.

Gigante, El *see* Giant Gonzales

Gilbernetti, Glen *see* Disco Inferno

Gilbert, Buddy (York, Pennsylvania) was a weigh-lighting champion before he entered professional wrestling in the 1940s. Known for his muscular build, Gilbert remained a popular competitor in the 1950s.

Gilbert, Doug teamed with Dick Steinborn as Mr. High and Mr. Low to defeat Art and Stan Neilson for the AWA Tag Team Title in December of 1962. They lost the belts to Ivan and Karol Kalmikoff in January of 1963. Wrestling as the Professional, Gilbert held the NWA Georgia Title several times in 1968 and 1969. He teamed with El Mongol to hold the NWA Georgia Tag Team Title in June of 1969. He and Bobby Shane teamed to recapture the belts several times in 1970. He won the Los Angeles Battle Royal in 1971. He teamed with Mike Webster to hold the NWA Florida Title in May of 1972. Gilbert subsequently wrestled with Don Smith as the Super Infernos. Managed by J.C. Dykes, they held the NWA Georgia Tag Team Title several times in 1973. He held the NWA Central States Title in August of 1978.

Gilbert, Doug (Lexington, Tennessee; 6'2", 241 lbs.) began wrestling in 1988. He is the son of wrestler Tommy Gilbert. He teamed with Dennis Condrey as the Lethal Weapons and held the ICW tag belts in 1989. He teamed with Tony Anthony to capture the USWA Tag Team Title several times in late 1990. Gilbert wrestled as the Dark Patriot in Global from December of 1991. He held the Global Title several times, often competing against the Patriot and his older brother, Eddie Gilbert. He also wrestled in ECW, where he teamed with Eddie Gilbert to capture the tag team belts in August of 1993. They left the promotion several months later to return to the USWA, where Doug Gilbert held the USWA Southern Title several times, exchanging the belt with Brian Christopher. He teamed with Tommy Rich to hold the USWA Tag Team Title several times in early 1995. He again held the USWA Heavyweight Title in May of 1995, defeating Brian Lee for the belt. He lost the title to Brian Christopher later in the month.

Gilbert, Eddie (b. August 14, 1961, d. February 18, 1995; Lexington, Tennessee; 5'10", 222 lbs.) was the son of wrestler Tommy Gilbert. He made his wrestling debut in the Memphis promotion in 1977. He teamed with his father to hold the Tri-State Tag Team Title in Oklahoma in March of 1980 and the Southern Tag Team Title in August of 1980. He again held the Southern belts with Ricky Morton as his partner in 1981. He teamed with Ricky Romero to hold the NWA Central States Tag Team Title in January of 1982. He entered the WWF in October of 1982 but, in May of the following year, he was seriously injured in an automobile accident. He returned to Memphis in early 1984, where he teamed with Tommy Rich as Jackie Fargo's new Fabulous Ones, capturing the Southern Tag Team Title in March of 1984. After the team broke up Gilbert wrestled as a villain and began a long-standing feud against Jerry Lawler. Under the management of Jimmy Hart, he defeated Tommy Rich for the CWA International Title in August of 1984. He captured the Southern Heavyweight Title from Lawler in January of 1985. He lost the belt back to Lawler the following month. He became known as Hot Stuff. He subsequently joined Bill Watt's Mid-South promotions where he formed Hot Stuff, Inc., managing a group of villains. He held the UWF Tag Team Title in Oklahoma with Sting in July of 1986. Gilbert was often accompanied to the ring by his wife, Missy Hyatt, who he later divorced. He was also briefly married to wrestler Madusa Miceli. He left the promotion shortly after a merger with the NWA. He then joined CWF in Alabama in 1988, where he worked with Paul E. Dangerously. He then returned to the WCW, where he headed the First Family. He and Rick Steiner captured the WCW U.S. Tag Title in February of 1989, but he departed the promotion later in the year. He soon returned to the USWA in Memphis, where he captured the Southern Title in October of 1990. After another feud with Lawler he again left in January of 1991. He wrestled on the independent circuit until August of 1991 when he joined Global. He won the Global North American Heavyweight Title from his younger brother, Doug Gilbert, who was wrestling as the Dark Patriot, on March 27, 1992. Several months later he again returned to the USWA, where he captured the USWA Unified Title in June of 1992. He subsequently wrestled in Japan and the ECW, where he teamed with his brother, Doug, to capture the ECW Tag Team Title in August of 1993. They left the promotion several month later to join the USWA again. He exchanged the Unified Title with Jerry Lawler several times in early 1994, and held the USWA Southern Title on several occasions. He teamed with Brian Christopher to hold the USWA Tag Team Title in May of 1994. He went to Puerto Rico to work as a wrestler and promoter in late 1994. He was found dead of a heart attack in his hotel room in Puerto Rico on February 18, 1995.

Gilbert, Freddie *see* Christian, Kevin

Gilbert, Johnny (Gilbert Sanchez; d. December 4, 1990) teamed with Billy Goelz as the G-Men. They held the Midwest Tag Team Title in Chicago several times from 1956 through 1961.

Gilbert, Tommy (b. 1935) is the son of Arlie Gilbert and the father of Eddie and Doug Gilbert. He teamed with Eddie Marlin in the Memphis area in the early 1970s. The duo held the Southern Tag Team Title several times in 1973. Gilbert also held the Southern Heavyweight Title several times in 1973. He also teamed with Bearcat Brown to hold the Southern belts in February of 1976. He held the North American Title in Nova Scotia several times in 1976. He teamed with his son, Eddie, to hold the Tri-State Tag Team Title in Oklahoma in March of 1980 and the Southern Tag Team Title in August of 1980. He held the WWC Caribbean Title in Puerto Rico in 1981. He held the U.S. Junior Heavyweight Title in Alabama in May of 1984. Gilbert remained active in the ring through the early 1990s, often in the USWA.

Gilburdy, Glen *see* Disco Inferno

Giovanni, Don *see* Strongbow, Jr., Jay

Giroux, Lionel *see* Little Beaver

Gladiator, The *see* Hunter, Rock

Glamour Girls, The *see* Kai, Leilani & Martin, Judy

Go, Ryuma teamed with Black Gordman to hold the NWA Americas Tag Team Title in Los Angeles in August of 1978. He teamed with Jesse Barr to hold the CWUSA International Tag Team Title in 1992 and 1993.

Gob, Steve (b. 1917; Bayonne, New Jersey; 5'9", 210 lbs.) was a member of the 1940 Olympic weight-lifting team and the holder of three world records. He served in the Navy during World war II and began wrestling in the mid-1940s. He was known in the ring as the Bayonne Bombshell.

Godoy, Pedro (b. 1918; Cuba; 6', 230 lbs.) attended college in Washington, D.C. He began wrestling professionally in the late 1930s, and served in the Navy during World War II. Usually a villain, Godoy sometimes wrestled as Doc Zoko and the Masked Terror.

Godwinn, Henry (Mark Canterberry; b. March 16; Biggers, Arkansas; 6'6", 275 lbs.) began wrestling as Mean Mark Canterberry in 1991. He wrestled as Shanghai Pearce, teaming with Tex Slazenger in the WCW and USWA in 1992. He entered the WWF as hog farmer Henry O. Godwinn in November of 1994. Slazenger joined him in the ring as Phinnius Godwinn in early 1996, and the duo were managed by Hillbilly Jim. They engaged in a feud with the Bodydonnas in the Spring of 1996.

Godwinn, Phinnius (Dennis Knight) wrestled as Tex Sallinger and teamed with Billy Mack as the Lone Riders in Florida in late 1991. He subsequently teamed with the Master Blaster in the USWA. He entered WCW as Tex Slazinger in the early 1990s. He teamed with Shanghai Pierce in the WCW and USWA. Slazinger wrestled in the USWA in 1995, defeating Brian Christopher for the USWA Heavyweight Title in December of 1995. He left the USWA in January of 1996 to enter the WWF. He reteamed with Pierce, now wrestling as Henry O. Godwinn, and wrestled as his brother, Phinnius Godwinn. They were managed by Hillbilly Jim and engaged in a feud with the Bodydonnas in the Spring of 1996.

Goelz, Billy (b. 1918; Milwaukee, Wisconsin; 5'8 1/2", 190 lbs.) was a professional football player before he began wrestling in the late 1930s. He remained a popular mat star through the 1950s and early 1960s. He teamed with Johnny Gilbert as the G-Men to hold the Midwest Tag Team Title in Chicago several times from 1956 through 1961.

Gold, Mickey (b. 1922; Chicago, Illinois; 6', 230 lbs.) began wrestling in the 1940s, competing primarily in California and Canada.

Golddust *see* Rhodes, Dustin

Golden, Dizzy *see* Beefcake, Brutus

Golden, Eddie (5'11", 225 lbs.) began wrestling in 1988. He is the nephew of Jimmy Golden, and often tagged with Stan Lee in Southern promotions.

Golden, Jimmy (b. August 1; Montgomery, Alabama; 6'4", 239 lbs.) was the son of wrestler Billy Golden and the grandson of promoter Roy Welch. He began wrestling in 1970. He teamed with Dennis Hall to hold the World Tag Team Title in Tennessee in 1971. He teamed with his cousin, Ron Fuller, to hold the NWA Florida Tag Team Title in September of 1972. He teamed with Austin Idol to capture

the Australasian Tag Team Title in Australia in December of 1972. He held the NWA Southeastern Title in 1981. He also held the NWA Southeastern Tag Team Title several times from 1981 through 1984, teaming with the Mongolian Stomper, Randy Rose and Robert Fuller. He teamed with Robert Fuller to hold the CWA Tag Team Title and the World Class World Tag Team Title several times in late 1988 and early 1989. He joined the WCW as Bunkhouse Buck in February of 1994, wrestling under the management of Robert "Col. Parker" Fuller. Teaming with Dick Slater as the Stud Stable, they captured the WCW Tag Team Title from Harlem Heat on June 21, 1995. They lost the title in a rematch with Harlem Heat on September 17, 1995. Golden left the WCW in early 1996.

Golden, Sterling *see* Hogan, Hulk

Golden Adonis, The *see* Hawk, Rip

Golden Apollo, The *see* Stanlee, Gene

Golden Boy, The *see* Bertucci, Lou

Golden Boy, The *see* Skoaland, Arnold

Golden Greek, The *see* Belkas, Christos

Golden Knight, The *see* Oborsky, Colin H.

Golden Superman, The *see* Podolak, Walter

Golden Terror, The (Bobby

Stewart; b. 1913; Alabama; 6'3", 270 lbs.) began wrestling in the early 1930s. A leading mat villain, he held the NWA Southern Title in 1951.

Golden Terror, The *see* Jares, Brother Frank

Golden Terror, The *see* Stevens, Clyde

Goldust *see* Rhodes, Dustin

Goliath was a leading Mexican wrestler who held the Mexican National Heavyweight Title in December of 1967. He often teamed with Black Gordman in Texas and California in the early 1970s. They held the NWA Americas Tag Team Title over a dozen times in the 1970. The duo held the World Class American Tag Team Title in Texas in 1973 and captured the NWA Georgia Tag Team Title in June of 1976. They also held the NWA Central States Tag Team Title in July of 1976. He and Black Gordman captured the NWA World Tag Team Title in San Francisco in January of 1978.

Goliath *see* Strode, Woody

Gomez, Joe *see* Iron Eagle, Alan

Gomez, Pepper held the Northwest Tag Team Title in Vancouver, Canada, several times in 1953, teaming with John Demchuck and Ivan Kameroff. He held the NWA Texas Title over a dozen times from 1955 until 1963. He also held the NWA Texas Tag Team Title several times in the 1950s and 1960s, teaming with Rito Romero, Luigi Macera, El Medico, Larry Chene, Hogan Wharton and Dory Dixon. He held the NWA U.S. Title in San Francisco in late 1962 and early 1963. He teamed with Jose Lothario to capture the NWA World Tag Team Title in San Francisco in September of 1963. He again held the belts with Pedro Morales several times in 1967 and 1968, and teamed with Ray Stevens to hold the title in October of 1969. He relinquished the title the following month when he was injured in a battle royal. He again held the belts in September of 1971, teaming with Rocky Johnson. He held the World Class Texas Title in February of 1971. He teamed with Wilbur Snyder to hold the WWA Tag Team Title for several months in mid-1974. He was the NWA Southern Champion in Florida in 1975. He also held the WWA championship from November of 1975 until May of 1976. Gomez and Snyder again captured the tag belts in December of 1978, retaining the title until the following April.

Gonsalves, Jimmy (Hawaii) began wrestling in Hawaii during World War II, becoming the island's champion in 1945. He remained a leading wrestling star through the 1950s.

Gonzales, Jose (Jose Huertas Gonzalez; b. 1946; 5'10", 227 lbs.) began wrestling in 1969. Wrestling as Manuel Cruz, he teamed with Al Madril as the Compadres to hold the NWA Pacific Northwest Tag Team Title in July of 1973. He wrestled as Jose Gonzales before donning a silver mask as one of the Invaders in the WWF. He later wrestled in the WWC in Puerto Rico. Gonzales stabbed wrestler Bruiser Brody to death in a dressing room prior to a wrestling match in Puerto Rico in July of 1988. He was acquitted on charges of first-degree murder and continued his career as a professional wrestler. He teamed with El Bronco I to hold the tag belts several times in 1991. He also held the WWC Universal Title in August of 1992.

Gonzales, Oscar *see* Rey Misterio, Jr.

Gonzales, Pepe held the NWA Texas Title in November of 1961.

Gonzales, Ray (6', 230 lbs.) began wrestling in 1990. He is a popular high-flying Caribbean wrestling star. He held the WWC Tag Team Title in Puerto Rico several times from 1992 through 1994, teaming with Rex King, Ricky Santana and El Bronco. He held the WWC Universal Title in Puerto Rico in April of 1994.

Gonzales, Tony teamed with Donald Lortie as the Medics. They held the Southern Heavyweight Tag Team Title several times in 1962 and 1963. He and Pierre DesPlaines also wrestled as the Medics in 1963. They were forced unmask after losing a match in Memphis, Tennessee, in March of 1963 and they wrestled without masks as the Ex-Medics for the next several months.

Goodall, Luther *see* Lindsay, Luther

Goodfellows, The *see* Young, Gary & Dane, Steve

Goodish, Frank *see* Brodie, Bruiser

Gordienko, George (b. 1927; Minneapolis, Minnesota) was trained by Tony Stecher and began wrestling in the late 1940s. He remained a leading ring contender for the next several decades. He held the British Empire Title in New Zealand several times in the late 1960s. He teamed with Super Hawk to hold the Calgary Stampede International Tag Team Title in December of 1972. He wrestled as Flash Gordon to hold the Canadian Tag Team Title with Leo Madril in January of 1974. He also held the Pacific Coast Title in Vancouver, Canada, in February of 1974.

Gordman, Black *see* Black Gordman

Gordon, Flash *see* Gordienko, George

Gordon, Ray held the NWA Central States Title in February of 1962.

Gordy, Terry "Bam Bam" (Terry Ray Gordy; b. April 23, 1961; Ft. Oglethorpe, Georgia; 6'4", 275 lbs.) began wrestling in 1976. Gordy sometimes wrestled as Terry Minke early in his career. He teamed with Michael Hayes as the original Freebirds. Gordy was also a very popular star in Japan, where he often partnered with Steve Williams. He and Hayes held the Mid-America Tag Team Title for several months in early 1979. The Freebirds, consisting of Gordy, Hayes and Buddy Roberts, captured the NWA Georgia Tag Team Title in October of 1980. They also held the NWA National Tag Team Title several times from November of 1980 until January of 1981. Gordy also teamed with Jimmy Snuka to hold the tag belt in July of

1981. He held the NWA Southeastern Title in 1982, and the World Class Championship in Texas in early 1983. He and Hayes reunited as the Freebirds to capture the World Class American Tag Team Title in early 1983. He held the UWF Title in Oklahoma from May of 1986 until he was forced to give up the belt after suffering injuries in an automobile accident in November of 1986. Gordy temporarily retired from the ring in the late 1980s due to a serious illness, but returned to wrestle in Texas and Japan in the early 1990s. He and Steve Williams defeated Rick and Scott Steiner for the WCW Tag Team belt in Atlanta, Georgia, on July 5, 1992. They lost the belts to Barry Windham and Dustin Rhodes the following September. He teamed with Jimmy Garvin as the Freebirds in Global in 1994. They held the Global World Tag Team Title from June of 1994 until the promotion closed three months later. He subsequently entered Smoky Mountain Wrestling, where he held the championship in October of 1995. Gordy also wrestled in the USWA in 1995.

Gorgeous George (George Raymond Wagner; b. 1915, d. December 26, 1963; Seward, Nebraska; 5'9", 210 lbs.) was born in Nebraska and raised in Houston, Texas. He began wrestling at the age of 14 and began to attract attention when he grew his hair long, dyed it blonde and curled it in the early 1940s. The flamboyant mat star was known for his showmanship, which included a valet who sprayed perfume in the ring before his entry. His fame increased with the advent of television, as people throughout the country became aware of his ring antics. Gorgeous George remained one of wrestling's leading villains for two decades. He legally changed his name to Gorgeous George in 1950 and announced as a candidate for President of the United States in 1952. He defeated Don Eagle for the AWA Heavyweight Title in Chicago, Illinois, on May 26, 1950. He lost the belt to Lou Thesz on July 27, 1950. He held the NWA Southern Title in March of 1953. Gorgeous George lost a hair vs. mask match to the Destroyer in Los Angeles in November of 1962. He died on December 26, 1963.

Gorgeous George, Jr. (Eddie Valentino) held the Gulf Coast Title in Alabama in 1973. He teamed with Bobby Shane to hold the NWA Georgia Tag Team Title in December of 1973. He wrestled and managed in the Memphis promotion in the late 1970s and early 1980s. He held the Southern Heavyweight Title in 1976. He teamed with Luke Graham to hold the WWC North American Tag Team Title in Puerto Rico in 1980. He held the Global Wrestling Alliance Title in 1982.

Gorgeous George III (Robbie Eagle; Charlotte, North Carolina; 5'10", 225 lbs.) began wrestling in 1991. He wrestled in the USWA from January of 1995. He teamed with Brickhouse Brown to hold the USWA Tag Team Title in April of 1995.

Gorky, Ivan teamed with Soldat Gorky to capture the NWA Pacific Northwest Tag Team Title in January of 1954.

Gorky, Soldat (Walter Allen; b. 1922, d. June 4, 1991) teamed with Ivan Gorky to capture the NWA Pacific Northwest Tag Team Title in January of 1954. He held the tag belts several more times in the early 1960s, teaming with Kurt Von Poppenheim and Ivan Kameroff.

Gossett, Eddie *see* Graham, Eddie

Gossett, Ronnie P. managed in the USWA from 1989 through the early 1990s.

Gotch, Frank (b. April 27, 1878, d. December 17, 1917; 6', 205 lbs.) was born in Humboldt, Iowa. He was a protégé of Farmer Burns and made his wrestling debut in his hometown in 1899. He became one of the most successful wrestlers in the early part of the century. He was the holder of the American Title on three occasions from 1904 through 1906, defeating such mat stars as Tom Jenkins and Fred Beell. Gotch was awarded the World Heavyweight Title in a unification match against George Hackenschmidt in Chicago, Illinois, on April 3, 1908. Gotch retained the title until his retirement in 1913. He died of uremic poisoning on December 17, 1917.

Gotch, Karl *see* Kalmikoff, Karol

Goto, Tarzan (Tatsutoshi Gotho; b. May 25, 1956) began wrestling in February of 1983. He teamed with Akio Sato to hold the CWA International Tag Team Title several times in 1986 and 1987. They were managed by Tojo Yamamoto. He was a frequent competitor in All-Japan during the 1980s and 1990s.

Gouldie, Archie *see* Mongolian Stomper, The

Goulet, Jacques teamed with Don Fargo as the Legionnaires to capture the WWA Tag Team Title in September of 1974. Goulet retained the title the following year with Zarinoff LeBeouf as his partner. He also held the NWA Southern Title in Florida in April of 1981.

Goulet, Rene was a popular Canadian mat star in the 1960s and 1970s. He held the NWA Pacific Northwest Tag Team Title several times in 1966, teaming with Pepper Martin and Shag Thomas. He also wrestled in Georgia and Florida. He held the NWA Southern Title in Florida several times in late 1970 and early 1971. He teamed with Karl Gotch to defeat Luke Graham and Tarzan Tyler for the WWWF Tag Team Title in December of 1971. They were defeated for the belts by Baron Scicluna and King Curtis in February of 1972. After his retirement he worked in the WWF as a security official.

Grable, Joyce (b. November 9, 1952) was born in Georgia. She was trained by Judy Grable and made her wrestling debut in 1971 in Cleveland. Known as the Golden Goddess, she held several Women's World Tag Team Titles in the 1970s and early 1980s, wrestling with Vicki Williams and Wendi Richter. She and Richter competed as the Texas Cowgirls. She also held the Deep South Women's Title in Georgia in 1987.

Grable, Judy lost the Women's World Title to Moolah in Baltimore, Maryland, on September 18, 1956.

Grable, Lee (Los Angeles, California) was known in the ring as the Professor. He held the Hawaiian Title in 1947.

Graham, Billy "Superstar" (b. September 10, 1943; Paradise Valley, Arizona; 6'3", 265 lbs.) was a champion weight-lifter and a former Mr. Teenage America. He made his professional wrestling debut as the "brother" of Dr. Jerry Graham in a tag team match in 1969. He teamed with Pat Patterson to hold the NWA World Tag Team Title in San Francisco in January of 1971. He held the Hawaiian Title in January of 1974. He teamed with Ox Baker to hold the NWA Florida Tag Team Title in 1977. He held the NWA Southern Title in Florida in 1977. He lost the WWF World Heavyweight Title to Bob Backlund at New York's Madison Square Garden on February 20, 1978. Graham held the CWA World Title from October of 1979, until his defeat by Jerry Lawler the following month. Graham was managed by Sir Oliver Humperdink in Florida in 1984, where he held the NWA Florida Title for several months. Graham made a brief comeback in 1987, but was forced to retire due to continuing physical problems. Graham was an outspoken critic of steroid abuse in the early 1990s, claiming that his use of the drugs contributed to his physical disabilities.

Graham, Bobby wrestled as Pat Kennedy and teamed with Dale Lewis to defeat Hard Boiled Haggerty and Bob Geigel for the AWA Tag Team Title in November of 1961. They lost the belts later in the month to Geigel and Otto Von Krupp. Wrestling as the Black Terror, he teamed with John Tolos to hold the Canadian Tag Team Title in January of 1966.

Graham, "Crazy" Luke (Atlanta, Georgia; 6'3", 291 lbs.) began wrestling professionally in the mid-1950s. He teamed with his "brother," Dr. Jerry Graham, to win the WWWF U.S. Tag Team Title in June of 1964. They lost the belts later in the year. He held the WWA Title in Los Angeles for several months from July of 1965. He teamed with Karl Von Brauner to briefly hold the World Tag Team Title in Tennessee in August of 1966. He held the Hawaiian Title in October of 1968. He teamed with Ripper Collins to hold the Hawaiian Tag Team Title in November of 1968. He teamed with Tarzan Tyler to capture the WWWF Tag Team Title in June of 1971 and they defeated the Mongols to unify the belt with the WWWF International Tag Team Title in November of 1971. They lost the belts to Karl Gotch and Rene Goulet in December of 1971. He teamed with Gorgeous George, Jr. to hold the WWC North American Tag Team Title in Puerto Rico in 1980. He held the NWA Central States Title in April of 1984.

Graham, Eddie (Eddie Gossett; b. 1930, d. January 21, 1985) wrestling as Rip Rogers, teamed with Johnny Valentine to hold the NWA Texas Tag Team Title in April of 1958. He often teamed with his "brother," Dr. Jerry Graham. They held the WWWF U.S. Tag Team Title on several occasions in the late

1950s and early 1960s, defeating such teams as Mark Lewin and Don Curtis, and Red and Lou Bastien. Grahan also held the NWA Southern Title in Florida several times in 1962 and 1963. He teamed with Sam Steamboat to hold the NWA World Tag Team Title in Florida several times in 1964. He and Steamboat also held the World Tag Team Title in Tennessee in 1965. He also held the belts with Bob Orton and Jose Lothario several times in 1966. He held the NWA Southern Tag Team Title in February of 1968, teaming with Lester Welch. He teamed with his son, Mike Graham, to hold the NWA Georgia Tag Team Title for several months in early 1973. They also held the NWA Florida Tag Team Title in 1976. Graham died of a self-inflicted gunshot wound at his home in Beach Park Florida, on January 21, 1985.

Graham, Dr. Jerry (b. 1922; d. January 24, 1997; Phoenix, Arizona) held the NWA Southern Title in 1956. He often teamed with his "brother," Eddie Graham. They held the WWWF U.S. Tag Team Title on several occasions in the late 1950s and early 1960s, defeating such teams as Mark Lewin and Don Curtis, and Red and Lou Bastien. He also held the tag title with Luke Graham in mid-1964. He teamed with Abdullah the Butcher to hold the Canadian Tag Team Title in October of 1967. Graham died of a stroke on January 24, 1997.

Graham, Jerry, Jr. (Jerry Jaffee) teamed with Don Kent to hold the MWA tag team title in Ohio in 1983. He and Kent also held the WWA Tag Team Title in 1984. Graham managed Greg Wojokowski in the WWA in 1985.

Graham, Mike (Tampa, Florida; 5'8", 232 lbs.) is the son of wrestler Eddie Graham. He began wrestling in 1972. He teamed with his father to hold the NWA Georgia Tag Team Title for several months in early 1973. He teamed with Kevin Sullivan to hold the NWA Florida Tag Team Title several times in 1973. He and Eddie Graham also held the NWA Florida Tag Team Title in 1976. He teamed with Steve Keirn to hold the belts several times in 1977, and captured the title with Ray Stevens in 1979. He briefly held the NWA Florida Title in January of 1981. He also held the AWA Light Heavyweight Championship in 1981. He wrestled in the WCW in the early 1990s.

Graham, Troy *see* Dream Machine, The

Gran Apollo, El held the Florida TV Title in August of 1981. He teamed with King Tonga to hold the WWC North American Tag Team Title in Puerto Rico several times in 1983 and 1984.

Gran Markus, El was managed by the Masked Baron. He held the Mexican National Heavyweight Title several times in the late 1970s. He teamed with Gino Hernandez to hold the World Class American Tag Team Title several times in 1979. He also held the World Class Caribbean Title in July of 1979.

Gran Tapio, El teamed with Alex Perez to hold the U.S. Tag Team Title in Louisiana in July of 1973.

Grand Wizard, The (Ernie

Roth; b. June 7, 1929, d. October 14, 1983) was born in Canton, Ohio. As Abdullah Farouk, the Grand Wizard often managed the Sheik during the 1970s. He was also a leading manager in the WWWF in the 1970s. He managed Stan Stasiak during his brief reign as WWWF champion in December of 1973. He also managed Billy Graham while he held the WWWF title in 1977. The Grand Wizard also managed Ken Patera and Don Muraco during their WWF Intercontinental championship reigns in the early 1980s. He died at his home in Fort Lauderdale, Florida, of a heart attack on October 14, 1983.

Grande Pistolero, El *see* Gypsy Joe

Grappler, The (5'11", 280 lbs.) began wrestling in 1978. He originally wrestled under a mask, but later switched to war paint. He is a seven-time Pacific Northwest Champion.

Grappler, The *see* Walker, Johnny

Grapplers, The *see* Denton, Len & Anthony, Tony

Gray, George *see* One Man Gang

Great Antonio, The was popular mat star in the 1960s. He also made several movie appearances.

Great Atlas, The *see* Shapiro, Morris

Great Bolo, The *see* Lovelock, Al

Great Higami, The *see* Higami, The Great

Great Husein Arab *see* Iron Sheik, The

Great Karadagian, The *see* Karadagian, Martin

Great Mephisto, The *see* Mephisto, The Great

Great Moto, The *see* Mr. Moto

Great Scott, The *see* Scott, George

Great Togo, The *see* Togo

Green, Al wrestled as Steel with Kevin Nash as Deisel in the Master Blasters tag team in the WCW in late 1990. He teamed with Marc Laurinaitis as the Terminators in 1991, holding the ICWA Florida/ U.S. Tag Team Title. He wrestled as Fury and teamed with Rage as the Wrecking Crew in WCW in 1993.

Green, Robin *see* Woman

Green Hornet, The *see* Henry, Jim

Green Panther, The *see* Fraley, Pat

Green Terror, The *see* Singer, Jack

Greene, Al teamed with his brother, Don Greene, in the Memphis area in the 1960s and 1970s. They held the World Tag Team Title in Tennessee several times in 1959 and 1960. The mat villains held the Southern Tag Team Title in 1971. He engaged in a lengthy feud with Jackie Fargo in the Memphis area in the late 1960s and early 1970s. He teamed with Phil Hickerson to hold the tag belts in September of 1974.

Greene, Don teamed with his brother, Al Greene, to hold the World Tag Team Title in Tennessee several times in 1959 and 1960. He also held the Southern Junior Heavyweight Title for several months in late 1961. He and his brother remained leading mat villains in the Tennessee area throughout the decade, and held the Southern Tag Team Title in 1971.

Greer, Dan replaced Ken Timbs as Eric Embry's partner in the Fabulous Blonds. They held the Southwest Tag Team Title several times in 1984.

Grey, Jerry (5'11", 238 lbs.) began wrestling in 1980. He teamed with Tom Prichard to hold the NWA Pacific Northwest Tag Team Title in September of 1984. He held the Bahamas Title in March of 1986. He teamed with Bob Cook as the Mighty Yankees to hold the Florida Tag Team Title in September of 1987. He was a popular wrestler in Florida, where he was the SWF champion in 1990.

Griffin, Bob teamed with Dale Lewis as the Medics to capture the Australasian Tag Team Title in Australia in March of 1973.

Grizzly, Cousin *see* Boone, Grizzly

Grondin, Murray *see* Martin, Bull

Grumman Grappler, The *see* Daley, Hank

Grundy, Jed teamed with Scott Steiner to hold the CWA Tag Team Title in February of 1989.

Grundy, Solomon (6'2, 465 lbs.) began wrestling in World Class in 1987. He also competed in Puerto Rico and the WCW in the early 1990s.

Grunge, Johnny (Mike Durham; b. July 10; Compton, California; 6'3", 263 lbs.) wrestled with Flyboy Rocco Rock as Public Enemy in ECW from 1993, where they won the tag team belts in March of 1994. They lost the belts to Cactus Jack and Mikey Whipwreck in August of 1994, but reclaimed them in a rematch the following November. Grunge also wrested as Johnny Rotten in Europe during 1994. Public Enemy again held the ECW Tag Team Title for several months from April of 1995. They entered the WCW in late 1995.

Guardian Angel, The *see* Big Boss Man

Guay, Neil *see* Hangman, The

Guerrera, Fuerza (5'7", 175 lbs.) began wrestling in 1978. The Mexican star in a former bodybuilder. He teamed with his son, Juventud Guerrera, to capture the Mexican National Tag Team Title in December of 1994.

Guerrera, Juventud (b. 1977; 5'5", 165 lbs.) is the son of wrestler Fuerza Guerrera. He began wrestling in 1992. He is a former lightweight champion in Mexico. He teamed with his father to capture the Mexican National Tag Team Title in December of 1994.

Guerrero, Chavo (b. January 7, 1953; El Paso, Texas; 5'8", 220 lbs.) began wrestling in 1973. He was the son of Gory Guerrero and the oldest of the Guerrero brothers. He held the NWA Americas Title in Los Angeles over a dozen times from 1975 through 1979. He also held the Americas tag belt several times from 1975 through 1979, teaming with Raul Matta, John Tolos, Victor Rivera, Roddy Piper, El Halcon, Black Gordman, Al Madril and his father, Gory Gorrero. He held the NWA International Junior Heavyweight Title several times in 1980 and 1981. He teamed with his brother, Hector, to hold the U.S. Tag Team Title in Florida for several months in mid-1984. He again teamed with Al Madril to hold the Texas All-Star Tag Team Title in July of 1985. He and Madril broke soon after and engaged in a feud in matches in San Antonio. He held the All-California Championship Wrestling Title several times in 1988. Guerrero appeared in several films in the late 1970s, including *The One and Only* (1978) with Henry Winkler, *Paradise Alley* (1978) with Sylvester Stallone, and *Alligator II: The Mutation* (1991). His son, Chavito Guerrero, is also a wrestler.

Guerrero, Eddy (Eduardo Guerrero; b. 1968; Los Angeles, California; 5'8", 231 lbs.) is the youngest son of Gory Guerrero. He began wrestling in Mexico in 1987. He wrestled as Mascara Magica in EMLL and AAA in 1992 and 1993, where he teamed with El Hijo del Santo as the Atomic Pair. He also wrestled as the Black Tiger in New Japan in 1993. During 1995 he wrestled with New Japan and ECW, where he engaged in a feud with Dean Malenko. He entered WCW in 1995.

Guerrero, Gory (Salvador Guerrero; d. April 18, 1990) was a leading Mexican wrestler and a former Junior Heavyweight Champion of the World. He held the Mexican National Middleweight Title in 1945. He teamed with Cyclone Anaya to hold the NWA Texas Tag Team Title in December of 1952. He teamed with El Santo as the Pareja Atomica (Atomic Couple) in numerous bouts in the 1950s. He teamed with Luigi Macera to hold the NWA Pacific Northwest Tag Team Title in July of 1955. He held the EMLL Light Heavyweight Title in Mexico several times in the early 1960s. His four sons, Chavo, Eddy, Hector and Mando, also wrestled. He teamed with Chavo to capture the NWA Americas Title in Los Angeles in February of 1976. He died in El Paso, Texas, on April 18, 1990.

Guerrero, Hector (b. October 1, 1958; Mexico City, Mexico; 6', 232 lbs.) is the son of wrestler Gory Guerrero. He began wrestling in 1977. He held the NWA Americas Title in Los Angeles several times in 1978. He also won the Los Angeles Battle Royal in 1978. He teamed with Steve Regal to hold the Southern Tag Team Title in November of 1979. He teamed with Ron Sexton to hold the Tri-State Tag Team Title in Oklahoma in 1980. He was awarded the NWA World Junior Heavyweight Championship in July of 1984. He relinquished the belt the following October. He also held the U.S. Tag Team Title in Florida for several months in mid-1984 with his brother, Chavo. He held the NWA Florida Title in April of 1985. He wrestled as Lazor Tron to again win the title from Denny Brown on March 7, 1987. He left the promotion later in the year.

Guerrero, Mando (b. 1955; Mexico City, Mexico; 5'8", 225 lbs.) is the son of wrestler Gory Guerrero. He began wrestling in 1974. He held the NWA Americas Title in Los Angeles in May of 1977. He teamed with Tom Jones to hold the NWA Americas Tag Team Title several times in 1977. He held the Hawaiian Title in November of 1978. He again held the Americas tag belts several times in 1979, teaming with his brother, Hector, Al Madril and Carlos Matta. He and Hector again captured the belts in 1982. He wrestled in the AAA/IWC in 1994. Guerrero also worked as a stuntman in several films including *Eve of Destruction* (1991).

Gulas, George teamed with Tojo Yamamoto to hold the Mid-America Tag Team Title from August of 1977 until he was forced to abandon the belts due to injury the following December. He and Yamamoto reclaimed the belts in April of 1978, holding the title until the team broke up in August of 1978. Gulas teamed with Bobby Eaton to hold the tag belts in December of 1978. They held the title several times over the next two years. Gulas also teamed with Rocky Brewer to hold the belts in early 1980. Gulas held the MSWA Tennessee Title in April of 1992.

Gulas, Nick (d. January 21, 1991) was a leading promoter in the Tennessee area from the 1940s. He headed the Mid-South Wrestling Association, based in Nashville. He died on January 21, 1991.

Gullen, Mark wrestled as the Beast in the team of Beauty and the Beast with Terry Garvin from 1989 until 1990. They held the World Class Texas Tag Team Title in March of 1989.

Gunkel, Ann (d. 19??) was the promoter for the All South Wrestling Alliance from 1972 until 1974.

Gunkel, Dick *see* Steinborn, Dick

Gunkel, Ray (d. August 1, 1972; Terre Haute, Indiana) was educated at Purdue University, where he engaged in amateur athletics. He made his professional wrestling debut in 1951. Gunkel held the NWA Southern Title several times in the late 1950s. He also held the NWA Texas Title in September of 1951. He held the belt several more times over the next few years. He held the NWA Texas Tag Team Title several times in the early 1950s, teaming with Miguel Guzman, Ricki Starr, Wilbur Snyder and Herb Freeman. He teamed with Buddy Fuller to hold the Atlanta World Tag Team belts several times in the late 1960s. He held the NWA Georgia Title several times in the early 1970s. He also held the NWA Georgia Title during that period, teaming with El Mongol and Buddy Fuller.

Gunn, Bart (Mike Plotchek; b. December 27; Austin, Texas; 6'5", 260 lbs.) wrestled as Brett Colt in the Long Riders team in Florida in the early 1990s. The Long Riders entered the WWF as the Smoking Guns in April of 1993, with Sopt wrestling as Bart Gunn. They defeated Bob Holly and the 1-2-3 Kid for the WWF Tag Team Title on January 23, 1995. They were defeated for the belts by Owen Hart and Yokozuna on April 2, 1995.

Gunn, Billy (Monty "Kip" Sopt; Austin, Texas; b. November 11; 6'3", 256 lbs.) began wrestling in 1992. He wrestled as Kip Winchester in the Long Riders team in Florida in the early 1990s. The Long Riders entered the WWF as the Smoking Guns in April of 1993, with Poltchek wrestling as Billy Gunn. They defeated Bob Holly and the 1-2-3 Kid for the WWF Tag Team Title on January 23, 1995. They were defeated for the belts by Owen Hart and Yokozuna on April 2, 1995.

Gunn, Johnny *see* Brandi, Tom

Gunther, Joe (Birmingham, Alabama) began wrestling in the mid-1940s. He was a leading light-heavyweight contender during the 1950s and a holder of the Hawaiian championship.

Guzman, Enrique held the NWA Texas Title in May of 1954.

Guzman, Jorge *see* Santo, El Hijo del

Guzman, Miguel "Blackie" (d. 19??; Mexico) was a leading Mexican wrestler from the early 1940s. He was the holder of the Mexican Junior Heavyweight Title and competed often in Texas, where he held the NWA Texas Tag Team Title with Rito Romero in the late 1940s. He also held the NWA Texas Title several times in the late 1940s and early 1950s. He again held the Texas tag belts several times in 1951 and 1952, teaming with Ray Gunkel and again with Rito Romero.

Gypsy Joe (5'10", 225 lbs.) began wrestling in 1955. He teamed with Louis Tillet to hold the NWA Southern Tag Team Title in 1960. He teamed with Frank Martinez as the Blue Infernos in the Mid-South area in the mid-1960s. He held the Big Time Wrestling Heavyweight Title in Massachusetts in the late 1960s. Gypsy Joe held the Mid-American Tag Team Title several times in 1978 and 1979, teaming with Dutch Mantell, Buzz Tyler, Tojo Yamamoto and Tom Renesto, Jr. He was co-holder of the Southern Tag Team Title in May of 1980. Gypsy Joe also held the Central States TV Title in Kansas in September of 1984. He teamed with Mr. Pogo to hold the NWA Central States Tag Team Title in October of 1984. Gypsy Joe, wrestling as El Grande Pistolero, captured the USWA Junior Heavyweight Title in March of 1991.

Hackenschmidt, Georges (b. July 20, 1878, d. February 19, 1968) was born in Dorpat, Russia, of a Swedish mother and German father. Known as "the Russian Lion," he made his wrestling debut in September of 1896. He defeated French Heavyweight Champion Paul Pons in 1898 and captured the Russian Championship from Herr von Schmelling later in the year. He was recognized as the World Heavyweight Title holder after winning a tournament in Vienna, Austria, in November of 1901. He retained the belt until April 3, 1908, when he lost a decision to Frank Gotch in Chicago, Illinois. He authored the book *How to Wrestle* in 1909 and was a popular writer and lecturer for the next several decades. Hackenschmidt moved to London in 1946 where he spent an active retirement until his death on February 19, 1968.

Hady, Jim (b. 1929, d. January 12, 1968) held the Canadian Tag Team Title several times in 1965, teaming with Red Bastien and Don Leo Jonathan. He held the Hawaiian Title in 1967. He also held the Hawaiian Tag Team Title several times in the late 1960s, teaming with Johnny Barend, Peter Maivia, Pampero Firpo and Billy White Wolf. He held the U.S. Title in Honolulu several times in 1968.

Hagen, Jack (Edward Prodhomme; New Orleans, Louisiana; 190 lbs.) began wrestling in the mid-1930s. He held the NWA Light-Heavyweight Title and the Louisiana and Pacific Coast middleweight belts in the late 1930s. He captured the World Light-Heavyweight Title from Bill Weidner in 1939. He subsequently lost the belt in a match against Dory Detton.

Hagen, Thor (d. December 14, 1982) held the NWA Central States Title several times in 1960.

Haggerty, Hard Boiled (b. 1925) teamed with Ray Eckert to hold the NWA World Tag Team Title in San Francisco in April of 1950. He teamed with Tom Rice to hold the Pacific Coast Tag Team Title in September of 1951. He teamed with Stu Gibson to hold the NWA Texas Tag Team Title in June of 1955. He teamed with Dick Hutton to hold the Canadian Open Tag Team Title in Toronto in September of 1956. He teamed with Kinji Shibuya to hold the NWA World Tag Team Title in Minneapolis in April of 1958. He held the Hawaiian Tag Team Title several times in early 1960, teaming with Bill Savage and Butcher Vachon. He teamed with Len Montana to capture the AWA World Tag Team Title from Tiny Mills and Killer Kowalski in October of 1960. Haggerty continued to hold the belt with Gene Kiniski after Montana was injured. They lost the title to Wilbur Snyder and Leo Nomellini in May of 1961, but regained the title two months later in a rematch. Haggerty and Kiniski split as a team in August of 1961, and he defeated his former partner in a singles match the following month. He chose Bob Geigel as his new partner and held the tag title until their defeat by Dale Lewis and Pat Kennedy in November of 1961. He again teamed with Gene Kiniski to hold the Pacific Coast Tag Team Title in Vancouver, Canada, several times in 1962. He held the Hawaiian Title in February of 1964. He teamed with Dick "the Destroyer" Beyer to hold the WWA Tag Team Title in Los Angeles several times in 1964. He held the U.S. Title in Honolulu in early 1965. He again held the WWA tag belts in 1966, teaming with El Shereef. He later retired from the ring to work as an actor, appearing in numerous films including *P.J.* (1968), *Paint Your Wagon* (1969), *The Resurrection of Zachary Wheeler* (1971), *Dirty Harry* (1971), *The Wrestler* (1973), *Earth-*

quake (1974), *Foxy Brown* (1974), *Stunts* (1977), *Walking Tall — The Final Chapter* (1977), *Deathsport* (1978), *The One and Only* (1978), *Buck Rogers in the 25th Century* (1979) and *The Big Brawl* (1980). He was also active on television in the tele-films *The Cable Car Murder* (1971), *Mad Bull* (1977), *Curse of the Black Widow* (1977) and *Return of the Rebels* (1981), and in episodes of *Get Smart, Buck Rogers, The Incredible Hulk, Nichols* and *Fantasy Island.*

Haines, Clark *see* Thunder

Haku (Uliuli Fifita; b. February 10, 1959; Samoa; 6', 294 lbs.) began wrestling in 1978. He originally wrestled as King Tonga in the WWC in Puerto Rico, where he teamed with El Gran Apollo to hold the North American Tag Team Title several times in 1983 and 1984. He held the Canadian International Title in Montreal in October of 1984. He entered the WWF as Haku in 1987, where he was managed by Bobby Heenan. He was anointed as King Haku following Harley Race's injury in June of 1988. He teamed with Andre the Giant as the Colossal Connection and, under the management of Bobby Heenan, defeated Demolition for the WWF Tag Team Title on December 13, 1989. They lost the title back to Demolition at Wrestlemania VI on April 1, 1990. He left the WWF to wrestle in Japan in the early 1990s. He entered the WCW as Meng, Col. Parker's bodyguard, in May of 1994.

Hakushi (Kensuke Shinzaki; b. December 2, 1967; Tokyo, Japan; 5'11", 231 lbs.) made his professional debut in June of 1993 in Michinoku

Pro in Japan as Jinsei Shinzaki. He wrestled on the WWF cards when the promotion toured Japan and entered the WWF in early 1995, where he was initially managed by Akio Sato. He was known as Hakushi, the "Modern-Day Kamikaze." He became a fan favorite later in the year, teaming with Barry Horowitz and Bret Hart.

Halcon, El teamed with Chavo Guerrero to hold the NWA Americas Title in Los Angeles in February of 1978. He teamed with Jose Lothario to hold the World Class American Tag Team Title several times in 1979. He also held the World Class Championship in Texas in August of 1979. He held the Mexican National Light Heavyweight Title in the early 1980s.

Hales, Randy (b. 1961) worked in the USWA as an assistant to promoter Eddie Marlin from the 1980s. He took over the duties of booking for the promotion in 1995. Hales was also involved in several confrontations in the ring against manager Brandon Baxter and wrestlers from the Smoky Mountain Wrestling organization.

Hall, Dennis teamed with Jimmy Golden to hold the World Tag Team Title in Tennessee in 1971. He also teamed with Stan Frazier to hold the Southern Tag Team Title in 1971. Wrestling as Taurus, he teamed with Bob Orton, as the Zodiac, to hold the NWA Florida Tag Team Title in June of 1972.

Hall, Scott *see* Ramon, Razor

Hallick, Mike *see* Mantaur, The

Halme, Tony *see* Borga, Ludvig

Hamada, El Gran (Haraoki Hamada; Tokyo, Japan; b. November 27, 1950) began wrestling in 1972. He was a popular Japanese mat star during the 1980s and 1990s. He held the NWA Americas Title in Los Angeles in November of 1981. He held the UWA Light Heavyweight Title in Mexico several times in the early 1980s.

Hamaguchi, Animal *see* Hamaguchi, Higo

Hamaguchi, Higo (b. August 31, 1947; Shimane, Japan; 5'7", 205 lbs.) began wrestling in 1969. He teamed with Kenji Shibuya to hold the Calgary Stampede International Tag Team Title in 1976. He also wrestled as Animal Hamaguchi. He held the IWE IWA Tag Team Title several times in the late 1970s, teaming with the Great Kusatsu and the Mighty Inoue.

Hamilton, Jody wrestled with Tom Renesto as the Assassins and held the Atlanta World Tag Team Title for several months in early 1969. The Assassins held the NWA Georgia Tag Title numerous times until September of 1972, when Renesto retired from wrestling. Hamilton, as Assassin #2, captured the ASWA Georgia Title in December of 1972. He teamed with Toru Tanaka to reclaim the Georgia Tag Title in March of 1975. He held the NWA Central States Title in January of 1980. He was the promoter for Deep South Wrestling from 1986 until 1988. He is the father of referee Nick Patrick.

Hamilton, Larry (Tampa, Florida, 232 lbs.) teamed with the Great Bolo to hold the NWA Southern Tag Team Title in 1960. Known as the Missouri Mauler, he held the NWA Southern Title in Florida several times from 1966 though 1970. He teamed with Hiro Matsuda to hold the NWA Florida Tag Team Title several times in 1969. He again held the Florida belts, teaming with Dale Lewis, in March of 1970. He held the NWA Eastern States Title several times in the early 1970s. He also teamed with Brute Bernard to hold the NWA Atlantic Coast Tag Title and the World Class American Tag Team Title in 1972. He held the World Class Championship in Texas for several months from March of 1973. He held the ASWA Georgia Title in September of 1973.

Hammer teamed with Sledge as the Punishers in the PWA. They held the PWA Tag Team Title several times in 1991 and 1992.

Hammer, Van (Mark Hildreth; b. 1959; New York; 6'8", 320 lbs.) began wrestling in Georgia in 1990. He entered the WCW in the early 1990s. Hammer was arrested for illegal possession of drugs in January of 1995.

Hampton, Beverly *see* Davenport, Lauren

Hampton, Rev. Tiny was a leading manager in the WWA in the 1970s, managing such stars as Bruiser Brody, Ernie Ladd, Johnny Valiant and Blackjack Mulligan.

Hangman, The (Rick Guay) held the NWA Americas Title in Los

Angeles in September of 1976. He teamed with Roddy Piper to hold the NWA Americas Tag Team Title in late 1976. He again held the Americas belt in March of 1977, defeating Toru Tanaka for the title.

Hansen, Eric *see* Eric the Red

Hansen, Stan (John Stanley Hansen; b. October 12, 1949; Canyon, Texas; 6'3", 322 lbs.) began wrestling in November of 1974. He teamed with Bruiser Brody to hold the U.S. Tag Team Title for several months from October of 1974. Hansen broke Bruno Sammartino's neck using the "Texas lariat" maneuver in a bout in April of 1976. He held the MSWA North American Title in May of 1977. He teamed with Tommy Rich to hold the NWA Georgia Tag Team Title for several months in late 1977. He held the NWA Georgia Title in early 1978. Hansen was also a leading American wrestler in Japan during the 1980s and 1990s. He held the CWA International Title in September of 1983. He was the AWA World Heavyweight Champion from his defeat of Rick Martel on December 29, 1985, until he left the promotion in a dispute with the management on June 29, 1986. Hansen defeated Lex Luger for the NWA U.S. Title on October 27, 1990. He lost the belt back to Luger on December 16, 1990. He remained a leading competitor in Japan through the mid-1990s.

Hanson, Billy captured the Pacific Coast Title in San Francisco in a tournament victory over Nick Lutze in November of 1936. He lost the belt to Sandor Szabo the follow-ing January. Hanson again held the Pacific Coast belt several times in 1945 and 1946.

Hanson, Swede began wrestling professionally in 1960. He teamed with Rip Hawk to capture the NWA World Tag Team Title in Florida in August of 1965. They also held the NWA Atlantic Coast Tag Title several times in the late 1960s. He was managed by Fred Blassie in the WWF in the late 1970s. He teamed with the Hangman to hold the Canadian International Tag Team Title in Montreal in 1981.

Harben, Charles (b. 1918; Atlanta, Georgia; 6', 230 lbs.) began wrestling in the late 1930s. He was a popular wrestler in the South, where he often teamed with his older brother, George Harben.

Harben, George (b. 1909; d. 19??; Stone Mountain, Georgia; 6'1", 235 lbs.) began wrestling professionally in Texas in the early 1930s. The popular mat star competed throughout the United States and New Zealand before his retirement in the 1950s.

Harding, Tonya (b. 1971) was a leading U.S. female figure skater and a competitor in the Winter Olympics in 1994. Her skating career ended when she was implicated in a crippling attack on fellow figure skater Nancy Kerrigan. Harding turned down a lucrative offer to wrestle with a Japanese promotion. She did become involved with professional wrestling as the manager of the Great American Love Machine and Eddy Guerrero in an AAA Lucha Libra event in Portland, Oregon, in June of 1994.

Hargrove, Rex (Memphis, Tennessee; 235 lbs.) wrestled in the Mid-South area in the 1990s. He teamed with Koko B. Ware to briefly hold the USWA Tag Team Title in November of 1993.

Harlem Heat *see* Stevie Ray & Booker T.

Harmon, Bob, who wrestled as Beautiful Bobby, was managed by the Grand Wizard in the early 1970s. He later retired from the ring to be a promoter in Florida.

Harris, Brian *see* Lee, Brian

Harris, Don (b. 1961; 6'4", 260 lbs.) began wrestling in 1984. He teamed with his twin brother, Ron, as the Bruise Brothers in 1987. They captured the CWA Tag Team Title in February of 1988. Don Harris teamed with Brian Lee to capture the USWA Tag Team Title in August of 1990. He reteamed with his brother to hold the NWA Pacific Northwest Tag Team Title several times in 1991 and 1992. They also held USWA tag belts in December of 1992 and January of 1993. They also held the Smoky Mountain Tag Team Title in the Summer of 1993. They entered the WCW in October of 1994. They entered the WWF as Eli and Jacob Blu in early 1995, where they were managed by Dutch Mantell as Uncle Zebediah. Later in the year they left the WWF to wrestled with ECW.

Harris, George (301 lbs.) was a leading wrestler in the Memphis, Tennessee, area in the 1960s. He was known in the ring as "Baby Blimp" because of his huge size. He also wrestled in the Mid-Atlantic region in the 1960s as George "Two Ton" Harris.

Harris, Rick "Hangman" *see* Black Bart

Harris, Ron (b. 1961; 6'5", 270 lbs.) began wrestling in 1984. He teamed with his twin brother, Don, as the Bruise Brothers in 1987. They captured the CWA Tag Team Title in February of 1988. They also held the NWA Pacific Northwest Tag Team Title several times in 1991 and 1992. Ron Harris also captured the NWA Pacific Northwest Title several times in 1992. He and his brother also held the USWA Tag Team Title in December of 1992 and January of 1993. They also held the Smoky Mountain Tag Team Title in the Summer of 1993. They entered the WCW in October of 1994. They entered the WWF as Eli and Jacob Blu in early 1995, where they were managed by Dutch Mantell as Uncle Zebediah. Later in the year they left the WWF to wrestled with ECW.

Harris, Sugarbear *see* Kamala

Harrison, Mike *see* Marino, Mike

Hart, Bobby teamed with Lorenzo Parente to hold the World Tag Team Title in Tennessee in 1971. Wrestling as the Continental Warriors, they also held the U.S. Tag Team Title in Louisiana for several months from March of 1972.

Hart, Bret (b. July 2, 1957; Calgary, Canada; 5'11", 235 lbs.) is the son of wrestler and promoter Stu Hart. He began wrestling in 1976. He teamed with his brother, Keith, to hold the Calgary Stampede International Tag Team Title several times in 1979 and 1980. He also held the Stampede North American Title several times in the early 1980s. Hart wrestled with his brother-in-law, Jim Neidhart, as the Hart Foundation and, under the management of Jimmy Hart, defeated the British Bulldogs for the WWF Tag Team Title in January of 1987. They lost the belts to Rick Martel and Tito Santana in October of 1987. They returned to win the title from Demolition in August of 1990. They retained the title until their defeat by the Nasty Boys in March of 1991. Hart defeated Mr. Perfect for the WWF Intercontinental Title on August 26, 1991. He lost the belt to the Mountie in Springfield, Missouri, on January 17, 1992. He again captured the Intercontinental belt by defeating Roddy Piper in April of 1992. He was defeated for the belt by Davey Boy Smith in London, England, on August 29, 1992. Hart defeated Ric Flair for the WWF Title in Saskatoon, Saskatchewan, Canada, on October 12, 1992. He lost the belt to Yokozuna in Las Vegas on April 3, 1993. Hart defeated Bam Bam Bigelow to win the WWF's King of the Ring Tournament in Dayton, Ohio, on June 13, 1993. The match also began a longstanding feud with Jerry "the King" Lawler. He again won the WWF Championship when he defeated Yokozuna at Wrestlemania X on March 20, 1994. He lost the belt in a submission match against Bob Backlund at the Survivor Series on November 23, 1994. Hart recaptured the WWF title in a match against Diesel in Landover, Maryland, on November 19, 1995. He was defeated for the title by Shawn Michaels in a sixty minute iron-man match at Wrestlemania XII on March 31, 1996. Hart also pursued a career in acting, appearing regularly in the *Lonesome Dove* television series in 1995 and 1996.

Hart, Bruce (Calgary, Canada; 5'9", 211 lbs.) is the son of Stu Hart. He began wrestling in January of 1974. He teamed with his brother, Keith, to hold the Pacific Tag Team Title in Honolulu in 1980. He teamed with Davey Boy Smith to hold the Calgary Stampede International Tag Team Title several times in 1982. He teamed with Brian Pillman as Bad Company to hold the Stampede International tag belts several times in 1987.

Hart, Gary (Garry Williams) teamed with Don "the Spoiler" Jardine to hold the World Class American Tag Team Title in Texas in October of 1967. He subsequently managed Jardine and Smasher Sloan as the Spoilers to the championship belt in 1968. When Sloan left the promotion later in the year, Hart reteamed with Jardine to again hold the title. Hart suffered injuries in the crash of a private plane near Tampa, Florida, on February 20, 1975. Wrestler Bobby Shane was killed in the crash. He was Gino Hernandez's manager in the Texas area in the late 1970s. He managed Don Kernodle and Bob Orton, Jr. while they held the NWA World Tag Team Title in early 1984. Hart also managed the Great Muta in the NWA in the late 1980s.

Hart, Jack *see* Horowitz, Barry

Hart, Jimmy (b. January 1, 1941) was a singer and songwriter in the 1960s, performing with the rock group The Gentries. He entered wrestling as Jerry Lawler's manager in the Mid-South in 1979. He broke with Lawler soon afterwards though he continued to manage in the area. He led such wrestlers as Paul Ellering, Jimmy Valiant, Bobby Eaton, Jesse Ventura, The Assassins, Jos LeDuc and the Moondogs to championships. He left the area in February of 1985, after Eddie Gilbert lost the Southern Heavyweight Title to Lawler. He subsequently went to the WWF and managed the Hart Foundation, with Bret Hart and Jim Neidhart, during most of their tag team championship. He broke with the Hart Foundation in 1991 and managed the Nasty Boys in their capture of the belt. Hart also managed Money Inc., with Ted DiBiase and Irwin R. Schyster, during their title reign. Hart split with Money Inc. and joined Hulk Hogan and Brutus Beefcake in their feud with the team. Hart accompanied Hogan to the WCW where he continued to manage the champion. Hart also appeared regularly on Hogan's television series *Thunder in Paradise*. Hart broke with Hogan in October of 1995, joining with Kevin Sullivan's Dungeon of Doom to betray Hogan in a championship match against the Giant.

Hart, Keith (Calgary, Canada; 5'10", 209 lbs.) is the son of Stu Hart. He began wrestling in 1976. He teamed with Leo Burke to hold the Calgary Stampede International Tag Team Title in 1977. He held the Stampede International belts several times in the late 1970s and early 1980s, teaming with Hubert Gallant and his brother, Bret Hart. He teamed with his brother, Bruce, to hold the Pacific Tag Team Title in Honolulu in 1980. He again held the Stampede International Tag Team Title in May of 1986, teaming with Chris Benoit.

Hart, Owen (b. May 7, 1965; Calgary, Canada; 5'10", 227 lbs.) is the son of Stu Hart. He began wrestling in June of 1986. He wrestled in Calgary, Canada, as the Avenger in 1987. He captured the Stampede North American Title in Calgary several times in 1987. He entered the WWF the following year, appearing under a mask as the Blue Blazer. He subsequently teamed with Koko B. Ware in the High Energy tag team. He briefly held the USWA Unified Title in June of 1993. He teamed with his brother, Bret, in 1994, before breaking with his family and wrestling as a villain. Owen Hart defeated Razor Ramon in the WWF King of the Ring tournament on June 19, 1994, and wrestled as the King of Hearts. He teamed with Yokozuna to defeat the Smoking Guns for the WWF Tag Team Title on April 2, 1995. They lost the belts in a rematch with the Smoking Guns on September 25, 1995. Hart broke with Yokozuna in 1996 and formed a team with his brother-in-law, the British Bulldog.

Hart, Stu (b. 1916; Edmonton, Canada; 5'11", 225 lbs.) served in the Canadian Navy during World War II. He left the navy in 1946 and entered the pro wrestling circuit in the Atlantic region. He returned to Canada in 1948, settling in Calgary. He invested in a wrestling promotion out of Montana, where he wrestled and promoted. He teamed with Pat Meehan to hold the Northwest Tag Team Title in Vancouver, Canada, in September of 1956. He continued to purchase wrestling promotions and controlled most of Western Canada by the 1950s. He formed Stampede Wrestling in 1962. Shortly thereafter Hart quit wrestling completely to concentrate on the promotion and the training of younger wrestlers. He is the father of wrestlers Brett, Owen, Bruce, Dean, Keith, Ross, Smith and Wayne Hart. He is also the father-in-law of wrestlers Jim Neidhart and Davey Boy Smith.

Hart, Wayne (Calgary, Canada; 6'1", 215 lbs.) is the son of Stu Hart. He began wrestling in 1972.

Hase, Hiroshi (b. May 5, 1961; Tokyo, Japan; 5'11", 225 lbs.) began wrestling in February of 1986. The Japanese wrestler competed in the IWGP and New Japan. He teamed with Fumihiro Niikura as the Viet Cong Express in Canada, where they held the Calgary Stampede International Tag Team Title in October of 1986. He subsequently joined New Japan, where he became a leading mat star. He briefly captured the WCW International World Title from Rick Rude in March of 1994. Hase was elected to the Japanese House of Councilors in July of 1995.

Hasegawa, Sakie (5'9", 154 lbs.) began wrestling in 1990. She was a popular Japanese mat star who sometimes wrestled as Blizzard Yuki. She and Debbie Malenko made a formidable tag team in 1992.

Hashif Khan *see* Hashimoto, Shinya

Hashimoto, Shinya (b. July 3, 1965; Gisu, Japan; 5'11", 285 lbs.) began wrestling in September of 1984, competing often with New Japan. He briefly wrestled as Hashif Khan in Canada in 1987. Hashimoto held the IWGP Heavyweight Title in 1994 and 1995. He also captured the IWGP International Tag Team Title in July of 1995, teaming with Junji Hirata.

Haskins, David (Memphis, Tennessee; 235 lbs.) wrestled in the USWA from the 1980s. He also made appearances in the ring in the WCW and the WWF. He remained active through the mid-1990s.

Hassan, Sheik Abdullah Ali (Jack Kruger; d. 19??) teamed with Paul Ellering to hold the Southern Tag Team Title in March of 1980. He teamed with Abdullah the Great to briefly hold the WWA Tag Team Title in June of 1982. He held the NWA Pacific Northwest Title for several months from December of 1982.

Haste, Troy teamed with Jerry Faith as the Phantoms. Managed by Fantasia, the captured the USWA Tag Team Title in October of 1994.

Hatchet Man, The *see* Terry, Jack

Haviland, Donald *see* Myers, Hack

Hawk (Michael Hegstrand; b.

September 12, 1957; Chicago, Illinois; 6'3", 277 lbs.) was born in Minnesota. He trained at Professor Eddie Sharkey's wrestling school there and entered professional wrestling in Vancouver, British Columbia, as Crusher von Haig in 1982. He joined with Animal in Georgia to form the Road Warriors and entered the NWA in 1983. They quickly became the most popular team in the organization. Managed by Paul Ellering, they held the NWA National Tag Team Title several times in 1983 and 1984. They abandoned the NWA title and moved to the AWA in July of 1984 and, on August 25, 1984, they defeated Baron von Raschke and the Crusher in Las Vegas for the AWA World Tag Team Title. They lost the title to Jim Garvin and Steve Regal in September of 1985. Later in 1985 the Road Warriors went to Japan to wrestle with All-Japan Wrestling, where they were again immensely popular. They returned to the NWA in 1986 and held the 6-Man Tag Team Title several times over the next few years. They captured the tag championship from the Midnight Express in October of 1988. They retained the title until the relinquished the belts to Mike Rotundo and Steve Williams in April of 1989. They went to the WWF as the Legion of Doom in 1990 for a brief time, and in March of 1991 they returned to Japan. The returned to the WWF in August of 1991 and defeated the Nasty Boys for the WWF World Tag Team championship at New York's Madison Square Garden on August 26, 1991. They eventually lost the title to Money Inc. in February of 1992.

Hawk left the WWF and signed with New Japan Promotions. He formed the new Road Warriors with Kensuke Sasaki in November of 1992, and subsequently changed the name of the team to the Hell Raisers. The duo won the IWGP tag title on December 14, 1992. The following week on December 19, 1992, Hawk defeated Luc Porier for the CWA World Heavyweight Championship in Bremen, Germany. Hawk and Animal reunited as the Road Warriors in the WCW in late 1995.

Hawk, John *see* Bradshaw, Justin Hawk

Hawk, Rip (b. 1921; Toledo, Ohio; 5'9", 200 lbs.) was a muscular blonde grappler who was known in the ring as the Hawk and Golden Adonis. He held the NWA Texas Title in January of 1963. He teamed with Rock Hunter to hold the Texas World Tag Team Title in February of 1963. He teamed with Swede Hanson to hold the NWA World Tag Team Title in Florida in August of 1965. They also held the NWA Atlantic Coast Tag Title several times in the late 1960s. He held the NWA Eastern States Title in 1972. He again held the NWA Atlantic Coast belts, teaming with Ric Flair in 1974. He teamed with Roger Kirby to hold the NWA Florida Tag Team Title in February of 1976.

Hawk, Steve *see* Bradshaw, Justin Hawk

Hawkins, Betty Jo (b. 1930, d. December 4, 1987; Louisville, Kentucky; 5'5", 140 lbs.) suffered from polio in her teens. She recovered from her illness through strenuous exercise. She became involved in weightlifting and entered the ring as a professional wrestler in the early 1950s. She remained one of the leading female competitors throughout the decade.

Hayes, Lord Alfred (Windermere, England; 235 lbs.) was known for his quickness and his London Bridge hold. He held the British Wrestling Association Heavyweight Title in the late 1950s. He also held the Southern Area Heavyweight Title in England several times between 1967 and 1970. He subsequently came to the United States. He teamed with Roger Kirby to hold the NWA Central States Tag Team Title in January of 1974. He again held the Central States tag belts in February of 1974, teaming with Bob Brown. He retired from the ring to become a manager in the early 1980s. He managed Bobby Jaggers, Nikolai Volkoff and Chris Markoff in the NWA in the early 1980s. He was a commentator with the WWF from the mid-1980s through the mid-1990s.

Hayes, Chester (b. 1913; Texas) was born in Spring Valley, Illinois. He moved to Houston, Texas, at an early age and participated in various sports in high school and at Rice University. He began wrestling professionally in the 1930s and went to California to further his career. He competed often in the Southwest and California, where he held the light-heavyweight title. He continued wrestling in Hawaii near the start of World War II. After the war Hayes became a movie stuntman, appearing in small roles in such films as *Julius Caesar* (1953), *Daddy Long Legs* (1955), *From Hell It Came* (1957) and *Valley of the Dragons* (1961). He also appeared on television in episodes of *Gunsmoke*, *Bonanza* and *Wagon Train*.

Hayes, Michael P.S. (Michael Seitz; b. March 29, 1959; Atlanta, Georgia; 6'1", 255 lbs.) began wrestling in 1977. He was a founding member of the Freebirds with Terry Gordy. He and Gordy held the Mid-America Tag Team Title for several months in early 1979. The Freebirds, consisting of Hayes, Gordy and Buddy Roberts, captured the NWA Georgia Tag Team Title in October of 1980. He and Gordy also held the World Class American Tag Team Title in Texas in early 1983. He teamed with Steve Cox to hold the World Class World Tag Team Title several times in 1988. He defeated Lex Luger for the NWA U.S. Title on May 7, 1989, but lost the belt back to Luger several weeks later. Hayes also reformed the Freebirds with Jimmy Garvin. The duo won the NWA World Tag Team Title in June of 1989. They retained the belts until their defeat by Rick and Scott Steiner in November of 1989. They briefly regained the championship in February of 1991 before again losing them to the Steiner Brothers. They also held the WCW U.S. Tag Title from May until August of 1991. They were managed in the WCW by Diamond Dallas Page and their road manager, Big Daddy Dink in the early 1990s. Hayes managed Gordy and Garvin as the Freebirds in Global in 1994. He joined the WWF as an on-air commentator in 1995 under the name Doc Hendrix.

Haynes, Billy Jack (b. July 10, 1953; Portland, Oregon; 6'3", 245 lbs.) began wrestling in Oregon in October of 1982. He held the NWA Pacific Northwest Title several times in 1983 and 1984. He also held the Pacific Northwest tag belts several times in the mid-1980s, teaming with Stan Stasiak and Ricky Vaughn. He won the Florida title in March of 1984 and the World Class TV Title in January of 1985. He teamed with Wahoo McDaniel to hold the U.S. Tag Team Title in Florida in July of 1985. He held the Oregon Wrestling Federation Title in May of 1988. He reclaimed the Pacific Northwest belt in August of 1991. Haynes wrestled in the USWA in 1995, holding the USWA Heavyweight Title in August of 1995.

Hays, Theresa *see* McGillicutty, Beulah

Hazzard, Rick wrestled as the Terminator in the Pacific Northwest. He teamed with Len "the Grappler" Denton to hold the NWA Pacific Northwest Tag Team Title in July of 1988.

Head Hunter #1 (Manny Santiago; 5'11", 440 lbs.) began wrestling in 1992. He teamed with his brother as the Head Hunters in the ECW in 1995.

Head Hunter #2 (Victor Santiago; 5'11", 390 lbs.) began wrestling in 1992. He teamed with his brother as the Head Hunters in the ECW in 1995.

Headbanger Mosh (Chaz Warrington; 6', 243 lbs.) began wrestling in 1991. He teamed with Thrasher in the Headbanger tag team. They competed in the Smoky Mountain area in 1995 and entered the USWA in 1996.

Headbanger Thrasher (Glen Ruth; 6'2", 245 lbs.) began wrestling in 1991. He teamed with Mosh in the Headbanger tag team. They competed in the Smoky Mountain area in 1995 and entered the USWA in 1996.

Headshrinkers *see* Fatu, Samu & Seone

Heartbreakers, The *see* Cooley, Wendell & Lancaster, Frankie

Heath, Dave *see* Vampire Warrior, The

Heavy Metal (Erick Casas Ruiz; 5'7", 180 lbs.) began wrestling in 1988. He is the son of Pepe Casas and the younger brother of Negro Casas. He held the Mexican National Heavyweight Title in 1993. He teamed with the Latin Lover to capture the Mexican National Tag Team Title in September of 1994.

Heenan, Bobby (Raymond Heenan; b. November 1; 6', 245 lbs.) began wrestling as Pretty Boy Bobby Heenan in 1966. He teamed with Jimmy Valiant to hold the WWA Canadian Tag Team Title in 1973. Heenan subsequently became one of wrestling's leading managers. He managed AWA champion Nick Bockwinkel during the late 1970s. He managed a stable of rule breakers in Atlanta in 1979 that included Killer Karl Kox, Masked Superstar and Blackjack Lanza. He managed numerous villains in the WWF during the late 1980s and early 1990s, and also served as a commentator on the WWF television shows. He left the WWF and joined the WCW as a commentator in December of 1993.

Hefer, Johan was a leading South African grappler in the 1940s. He came to the United States in 1950, and remained a leading competitor through the decade.

Heffernan, Johnny *see* Dellaserra, Bob

Heffernan, Roy (b. 1925, d. September 24, 1992) was a native of Australia. He teamed with Red Bastien to hold the NWA Pacific Northwest Tag Team Title in 1956. He wrestled with Al Costello as the Fabulous Kangaroos in the late 1950s and early 1960s. They held the Texas World Tag Team Title in November of 1958. The Kangaroos defeated Red & Lou Bastien for the WWWF U.S. Tag Team Title in August of 1960. They briefly lost the belts to Johnny Valentine and Buddy Rogers in November of 1960, and again lost the belts to Valentine and Bob Ellis in January of 1962. They held the WWA Tag Team Title in Los Angeles in February of 1964. He and Costello also held the Canadian Tag Team Title in Vancouver several times in 1964 and 1965. Heffernan left the team in the mid-1960s. He died of a heart attack in Sydney, Australia, on September 24, 1992.

Heffron, Brian *see* Blue Meanie

Heggie, Tommy, wrestling as Dante, teamed with Romeo Rodriguez, as Mephisto, to hold the USWA Tag Team Title in August of 1994.

Hegstrand, Michael *see* Hawk

Heinemi, Larry *see* Anderson, Lars

Hellwig, Jim *see* Ultimate Warrior, The

Helmsley, Hunter Hearst (Paul Michael Levesque; b. July 27; Greenwich, Connecticut; 6'5", 279 lbs.) was raised in Nassau, New Hampshire. He was trained by Killer Kowalski and wrestled as Terra Rizing in the IWF in Massachusetts from 1991 before joining the WCW as Jean Paul Levesque in the Summer of 1994. He joined the WWF as Hunter Hearst Helmsley in 1995. He engaged in a feud was Wildman Mark Merro in the Spring of 1996.

Hendrix, Doc *see* Hayes, Michael P.S.

Hennig, Curt (b. March 28; Minneapolis, Minnesota; 6'3", 235 lbs.) began wrestling in 1980. He is the son of Larry "the Ax" Hennig. He teamed with his father to capture the NWA Pacific Northwest Tag Team Title in April of 1982. He also held the NWA Pacific Northwest Title for several months from May of 1983. He held the Pacific Northwest tag belts several times in 1983, teaming with Buddy Rose and Pat McGhee. He teamed with Scott Hall to take the AWA Tag Team Title in January of 1986. They were defeated for the belts by Buddy Rose and Doug Somers in May of 1986. Hennig captured the AWA Title from Nick Bockwinkel in May of 1987. He retained the belt until his defeat by Jerry Lawler in Memphis, Tennessee, on May 9, 1988. Hennig entered the WWF as Mr. Perfect and was managed by Bobby Heenan and Coach John Tolos. He won a tournament for the vacant Intercontinental Title in April of 1990. He lost the belt to Kerry Von Erich in August of 1990, but recaptured the title the following November. His title reign was ended by Bret Hart in August of 1991. Hennig left the ring in the early 1990s due to various injuries. He remained active in the WWF as a commentator.

Hennig, Jesse (Minneapolis, Minnesota; 6'2", 210 lbs.) is the son of Larry Hennig. He began wrestling in 1993 in the PWA.

Hennig, Larry "the Axe" teamed with Duke Hoffman to win a tournament for the AWA Tag Team Title in January of 1962. They lost the belts to Bob Geigel and Killer Kowalski the following month. Hennig teamed with Harley Race to defeat Crusher and Dick the Bruiser for the tag team belts in January of 1965. They lost the title to Crusher and Verne Gagne in July of 1965, but reclaimed them in a rematch the following month. They were again defeated for the belts by Crusher and Dick the Bruiser in May of 1966, but recaptured them in January of 1967. Hennig departed the team in October of 1967 when his leg was broken in a match against Verne Gagne. Hennig teamed with his son, Curt, to capture the NWA Pacific Northwest Tag Team Title in April of 1982.

Henning, John Paul teamed with Bobby Bruns to hold the Hawaiian Tag Team Title in 1954.

Henning, Lee (d. October 11, 1977; Boone, Idaho) also wrestled as Joe Palooka. He held the Pacific Coast Title in San Francisco in 1939. He held the Pacific Coast belt several more times in the late 1940s. He teamed with Danny Plechas to hold the Pacific Coast Tag Team Title in 1952. He held the NWA Central States Title several times in 1960 and 1961.

Henry, Jim (b. 1916; Tulsa, Oklahoma; 6'4", 265 lbs.) played football at Tulsa University before becoming a professional wrestler in the 1940s. He sometimes competed in the ring as the Green Hornet.

Hercules (Ray Hernandez; b. May 7; Tampa, Florida; 6'2", 255 lbs.) began wrestling in 1980. He teamed with Dewey Robertson to hold the NWA Central States Tag Team Title in September of 1982. He captured the NWA Southern Title in Florida in May of 1985. He held the belt for several months before leaving the promotion to enter the WWF. He was managed by Bobby Heenan until he broke with him in 1990. He tagged with Paul Roma as Power & Glory in the WWF in the early 1990s until he left the promotion. Hercules held the All-Star Can-Am Title in 1992. He also teamed with Scott Norton as Jurrasic Powers in New Japan in the 1990s.

Hermann, Hans (Robert Hans Hermann; b. 1920, d. June 9, 1980; Boston, Massachusetts; 6'3", 265 lbs.) was born in Hanover, Germany, and came to the United States as a child. He engaged in track and field competition as Tufts College in Massachusetts. He served in the U.S. air force during World War II and was stationed in India. He was trained by the Great Gama before becoming a professional wrestler in the mid-1940s. He teamed with Kiler Kowalski to hold the Pacific Coast Tag Team Title in 1951. He teamed with Lord Athol Layton to hold the Canadian Open Tag Team Title in Toronto in 1952. He teamed with Art Neilson to hold the NWA World Tag Team Title in San Francisco in February of 1958. He teamed with Fritz Von Erich to hold the NWA World Tag Team Title in Minneapolis in July of 1958. He retired from the ring in the late 1950s to work as a consulting engineer for a real estate development firm in Massachusetts. Hermann died of a heart attack at his home in Hampton Falls, New Hampshire, on June 9, 1980.

Hernandez, Gino (Charles Wolfe; b. 1956, d. January 30, 1986; Highland Park, Texas; 6'; 224 lbs.) was the son of wrestler Luis Hernandez. He began wrestling in Houston, Texas, in August of 1975. He held the NWA U.S. Title for several months in early 1977. He captured the World Class Texas Title in October of 1978. He was a popular wrestler early in his career, but later turned to rulebreaking under the management of Gary Hart. He feuded with Jose Lothario in the late 1970s. He teamed with El Gran Markus to hold the World Class American Tag Team Title several times in 1979, and teamed with Gary Young to reclaim the belts in October of 1980. He held the World

Class Championship in Texas in 1980, and again in 1984. He also held the World Class Texas Title several more times in the early 1980s. He again held the World Class American Tag Team belts in 1985, teaming with Chris Adams. He died of a drug overdose at his home in North Dallas, Texas, on January 30, 1986.

Hernandez, Hercules *see* Hercules

Hernandez, Javier *see* Oro

Hernandez, Juan (b. 1918; Mexico) was a leading Mexican wrestler from the late 1930s. He began wrestling in the Chicago area in the late 1940s.

Hernandez, Luis (Lee Garcia; d. May 23, 1972) sometimes wrestled under a mask as El Medico. He held the NWA Texas Title in May of 1959. He teamed with Pedro Moreales to hold the WWA Tag Team Title in Los Angeles for several months from June of 1966. He was the father of Gino Hernandez.

Hernandez, Ray *see* Hercules

Hessel, Gordon (b. 1913; Milwaukee, Wisconsin; 5'1", 200 lbs.) began wrestling as an amateur in his early teens. He began wrestling professionally in the early 1930s, holding the light-heavyweight championship on the Pacific Coast.

Hester, Frank (d. July 26, 1976) wrestled with Pepe Lopez as the masked tag team, The Dominoes. They wrestled in the Memphis area for six months before being killed in an automobile accident near Dickson, Tennessee, on July 26, 1976. They were en route from Memphis, where they had been defeated in a tag team bout against Don Kernodle and Don Anderson.

Hewitt, Frank "Tarzan" (b. 1918, d. 19??; Toronto, Canada; 6'1", 245 lbs.) attended Toronto University, where he studied engineering. He played professional hockey before turning to wrestling in the late 1930s. He was a leading mat villain over the next several decades, except for time spent in the Canadian army during World War II. Hewitt was such a hated competitor he was stabbed by fans after matches in San Antonio, Texas, and Charlotte, North Carolina. He remained a leading wrestling villain through the 1950s.

Hey, Dale *see* Roberts, Buddy

Heyman, Paul *see* Dangerously, Paul E.

Hiatt, Melissa *see* Hyatt, Missy

Hickenbottom, Michael *see* Michaels, Shawn

Hickerson, Phil (Jackson, Tennessee; 230 lbs.) was a popular wrestler in the Mid-South area. He teamed with Al Greene to hold the Southern Tag Team Title in September of 1974. He teamed with Dennis Condrey to hold the Southern belts several times from 1976 through 1978. They also held the NWA Southeastern Tag Team Title in November of 1978. He teamed with Frank Morrell to again hold the Southern Tag Team Title in June of 1984. Hickerson held the CWA International Title several times in the

Summer of 1985. He also held the CWA Title for several months from July of 1988. In the mid-1980s he wrestled as P.Y. Chu Hi and was managed by Tojo Yamamoto. He held the World Class Texas Title in July of 1989. Hickerson, though semi-retired from wrestling, made occasional appearances in the ring in the early 1990s.

Hickey, Frank "Spaceman" (d. 1993) also wrestled as Bozo Brown. He held the World Title in Ohio in 1950.

Higami, Tetsuo "the Great" held the Hawaiian Title in 1940. He teamed with Tojo Yamamoto to hold the Southern Tag Team Title in June of 1966.

Higgins, Hacksaw teamed with J.R. Hogg to hold the NWA Central States Tag Team Title in May of 1986.

High, Maury *see* Monroe, Rocket

High Energy *see* Hart, Owen & Ware, Koko B.

High Flyers, The *see* Brunzell, Jim & Gagne, Greg

Higuchi, Dean *see* Ho, Dean

Hijo del Santo, El *see* Santo, El Hijo del

Hild, Helen (d. 19??) was a leading female wrestler from the 1940s. She was married to wrestler Iron Mike DiBiase and the mother of Ted DiBiase.

Hildreth, Mark *see* Hammer, Van

Hill, Frank *see* Strongbow, Jules

Hillbillies, The *see* Starr, Billy "Fatback Festus" & Boone, Grizzly "Cousin Grizzly"

Hillbilly Jim was a popular wrestler in the WWF during the 1980s. He was often accompanied to the ring with Uncle Elmer, and was a close ally of Hulk Hogan. He left the promotion for several years before returning in 1996 as the manager of the Godwinn brothers.

Hillbilly Spunky (Kentucky) was a giant mat star during the 1940s and 1950s, who was often accompanied to the ring by the pig-tailed Daisy Mae.

Hines, Jimmy (d. May 21, 1983) wrestled as Bad Boy Hines in Texas in the late 1950s. He teamed with Danny McShain to hold the NWA Texas Tag Team Title in late 1959.

Hirai, Mitsu teamed with Tojo Yamamoto to hold the Southern Tag Team Title in December of 1964.

Hito, Mr *see* Shibuya, Kenji

Ho, Dean teamed with Johnny Kostas to hold the Pacific Northwest Tag Team Title in September of 1967. Wrestling as Dean Higuchi, he teamed with Earl Maynard to capture the Canadian Tag Team Title in May of 1969. He also held the Canadian belts with Steve Bolus in December of 1969. He teamed with Fritz Von Erich to hold the World Class American Tag Team Title in Texas in January of 1972. He teamed with Tony Garea to capture the WWWF Tag Team Title from Toru Tanaka and Mr. Fuji in November

of 1973. They held the belts until May of 1974, when they were defeated by Jimmy and Johnny Valiant. Ho and Ken Mantell briefly held the NWA Georgia Tag Team Title in July of 1976. He held the NWA U.S. Title in San Francisco several times in 1977 and 1978. He teamed with Moondog Mayne to hold the NWA World Tag Team Title in San Francisco in February of 1978. He again held the San Francisco tag belts in September of 1978, teaming with Ron Starr. He again held the Canadian tag belts in November of 1981, teaming with Mike "Klondike Mike" Shaw.

Hoag, Harold *see* Ice Train

Hodge, Danny won the NWA World Junior Heavyweight Title in July of 1960. He also held the U.S. Tag Team Title in Tennessee in May of 1962, partnered with Lester Welch. He teamed with Shag Thomas to hold the NWA Pacific Northwest Tag Team Title in 1963. He lost the Junior Heavyweight belt to Hiro Matsuda in November of 1964, but held the title on six more occasions until he was forced to retire from the ring following an automobile accident in March of 1976. Hodge also held the U.S. Tag Team Title in Louisiana with Jay Clayton in July of 1975.

Hodgson, Alfred *see* Wentworth, Jack

Hoerr, Larry teamed with Bill Rose as the Destroyers in the Atlanta area in the mid-1980s.

Hoffman, Duke (Bob Leipler) teamed with Larry Hennig to win the AWA Tag Team Title in a tournament in January of 1962. They lost the belts to Bob Geigel and Killer Kowalski the following month.

Hogan, Eddie *see* Beefcake, Brutus

Hogan, Hulk (Terry Bollea; b. August 11, 1953; Venice Beach, California; 6'8", 275 lbs.) began wrestling as Terry "the Hulk" Boulder in Florida and Tennessee in 1978. Wrestling as Sterling Golden, he held the NWA Southeastern Title in December of 1979. He captured the WWF Title from the Iron Sheik in New York on January 23, 1984. Hogan and Mr. T wrestled against Paul Orndorff and Roddy Piper in the main event at Wrestlemania I in March of 1985. He fought against King Kong Bundy in a cage match at Wrestlemania II in April of 1986 and defeated Andre the Giant at Wrestlemania III in March of 1987. He remained WWF Champion until his defeat by Andre the Giant in Indianapolis, Indiana, on February 5, 1988. He defeated Randy Savage for the WWF Title at Wrestlemania V on April 2, 1989. He lost the belt to the Ultimate Warrior at Wrestlemania VI in Toronto, Canada, on April 1, 1990. He returned to capture the title from Sergeant Slaughter in Los Angeles on March 24, 1991. He was defeated by the Undertaker in a title match on November 27, 1991, but reclaimed the belt in a rematch on December 3, 1991. The title was subsequently held up over the controversial nature of Hogan's matches with the Undertaker. Hogan regained the championship by defeat-

ing Yokozuna in Las Vegas, Nevada, on April 4, 1993, the same day Yokozuna had won the belt from Bret Hart. Hogan lost the title to Yokozuna in a rematch at the King of the Ring tournament in Dayton, Ohio, on June 13, 1993. Hulk entered the WCW in 1994 and defeated Ric Flair for the World Championship in Orlando, Florida, on July 1, 1994. He engaged in a feud with the Giant which culminated at Halloween Havoc in October of 1995. Hogan was subsequently stripped of the WCW title. He remained the leading figure in the WCW, teaming with Randy Savage and the Bootie Man in a feud against Flair, Arn Anderson, and Kevin Sullivan's Dungeon of Doom. Hogan appeared in the films *Rocky III* (1982), *No Holds Barred* (1989), *Suburban Commando* (1991) and *Mr. Nanny* (1993), and starred on television in *Thunder in Paradise* in the 1993 season.

Hogg, J.R. (6', 386 lbs.) teamed with King Harley Hogg as the Wild Hoggs to hold the WWA Tag Team Title in 1984. They also held the MWA tag belts in Kentucky in 1985. He teamed with Hacksaw Higgins to capture the NWA Central States Tag Team Title in May of 1986.

Hogg, King Harley *see* Moondog Cujo

Hogg, Roland *see* Drake, George

Hokuto, Akira began wrestling in the mid-1980s as Hisako Uno. She teamed with Yumiko Hotta to hold the All-Japan WWWA Women's Tag Team Title in 1987. Hisako Uno suffered a broken neck early in her career and wrestled as Akira Hokuto when she returned to the ring. She is married to wrestler Kensuke Sasaki.

Holbrook, Vic (b. 1920, d. 19??; Los Angeles, California; 6'4", 240 lbs.) attended the University of California, where he played football and basketball and competed in amateur wrestling. He began wrestling professionally in the early 1940s, and continued competing after service during World War II.

Holly, Bob (William Robert Howard; b. January 29, 1962; Talladega, Alabama; 6'1", 231 lbs.) is a native of Talladega, Alabama. He began wrestling in Smoky Mountain Wrestling as Hollywood Bob Holly. He entered the WWF as Thurman "Sparky" Plugg in January of 1994. He wrestled as Bob "Spark Plugg" Holly with the WWF from September of 1994. He teamed with the 1-2-3 Kid to capture the WWF Tag Team Title in a tournament on January 22, 1995. They lost the belts to the Smoking Guns the following day.

Hollywood Blondes, The *see* Rogers, Ric & Oates, Ted

Hollywood Blonds, The *see* Brown, Jerry & Roberts, Buddy

Holmbeck, Eric *see* Yukon Eric

Hombre Montana held the Pacific Coast Title in San Francisco several times in the early 1950s. He also held the NWA World Tag Team Title in San Francisco in February of 1952, teaming with Leo Nomellini. He teamed with Whipper Billy Watson to hold the Cana-dian Open Tag Team Title in Toronto in January of 1954. He teamed with Tiny Mills to reclaim the tag belts in June of 1958.

Home Boy *see* Freer, Mark

Honaga, Norio (Nobuo Honaga; August 11, 1955; Tokyo, Japan; 6', 211 lbs.) began wrestling in Japan in August of 1980. He was a popular mat star, competing with All-Japan and New Japan.

Honky Tonk Man, The (Wayne Farris; b. January 25; Memphis, Tennessee; 6'1", 255 lbs.) is the cousin of wrestler Jerry Lawler. He was trained at Herb Welch's wrestling school and began wrestling as Wayne Farris in Malden, Missouri, in 1979. He soon came to the Memphis area, where he teamed with Jimmy Valiant for several matches. He subsequently teamed with Larry Latham as the Blonde Bombers in the Mid-South. Under the management of Danny Davis, they held the Southern Tag Team Title several times in 1979. They also held the Mid-America Tag Team Title in late 1979 and early 1980. He again held the Southern tag belts with Tojo Yamamoto in 1981. He wrestled as Punk Rock Wayne Farris in the Southeastern Championship Wrestling promotion in 1982. He teamed with King Moon-dog and was managed by Louis Tillet while initially in the area. He wrestled with Ron Starr as Devastation Inc., holding the NWA Southeastern Tag Team Title in November of 1983. He held the NWA Southeastern Title briefly in February of 1984. He teamed with Ron Starr to hold the Calgary Stampede International Tag Team Title several times in 1985 and 1986. He also held the Stampede North American Title in June of 1986. He subsequently wrestled as the Elvis-impersonating Honky Tonk Man and joined the WWF. He was managed by Jimmy Hart and captured the WWF Intercontinental Title in June of 1987. He was the longest holder of belt before his defeat by the Ultimate Warrior in August of 1988. He subsequently teamed with Greg Valentine as Rhythm and Blues in the WWF. He soon left the promotion and wrestled primarily on the independent circuit in the 1990s.

Hood, The *see* Mantell, Johnny

Hood, The *see* Santana, Ricky

Horne, Bobby *see* Mo

Horner, Tim (b. August 19; Morristown, Tennessee; 5'10", 235 lbs.) began wrestling in 1983. He won the U.S. Junior Heavyweight Title in Alabama in October of 1983. He held the title several times over the next three years. He teamed with Brad Armstrong to win the NWA National Tag Team Title in November of 1984. They were forced to relinquish the belts when Horner was injured later in the month. Horner again teamed with Brad Armstrong as the Lightning Express, and captured the UWF Tag Team Title in Oklahoma in May of 1987. Horner entered Smoky Mountain Wrestling in 1993, capturing the TV Title. He held the TV Title several times over the next year.

Hornet, The *see* Christian, Kevin

Hornet, The *see* Keys, Brian

Horowitz, Barry (b. 1960; St. Petersburg, Florida; 5'10", 227 lbs.) began wrestling in 1979. Wrestling as Jack Hart, he held the NWA Florida Title in July of 1985. He teamed with Chick Donovan to hold the Southern Tag Team Title in May of 1987. He held the Global Junior Heavyweight Title in February of 1992. He entered the WWF in the early 1990s as Barry Horowitz. He also wrestled as Jerry Lawler's Red Knight in the WWF in November of 1993. Horowitz scored several victories over Bodydonna Skip and Hakushi in 1995. He later teamed with Hakushi in numerous matches.

Hoss (6'4", 399 lbs.) began wrestling in 1989. The Texan was trained at Larry Sharpe's Monster Factory and teamed with Chief Thunder Mountain.

Hot Body, Johnny (Philadelphia, Pennsylvania; 5'10", 230 lbs.) began wrestling in 1988. He held the WWA Junior Heavyweight Title in 1990. He was also active in the ECW, defeating Jimmy Snuka for the championship in April of 1992. He lost a rematch to Snuka the following July. Hot Body teamed with Chris Michaels to capture the ECW tag belts in April of 1993. They relinquished the belts several months later. Hot Body reclaimed the title, teaming with Tony Stetson, in October of 1993. They lost the belts the following month.

Houston, Sam (b. October 11; Waco, Texas; 6'2", 222 lbs.) is the son of Aurelian "Grizzly" Smith, and is the brother of Jake "the Snake" Roberts and Rockin' Robin. He began wrestling in 1983. He held the NWA Mid-Atlantic Title in 1986. He also held the NWA Central States Title in late 1986 and early 1987. He teamed with Charlie Norris to hold the PWA Tag Team Title in August of 1994. He was married to former valet Baby Doll.

Howard, William Robert *see* Holly, Bob

Hrera, Kenny *see* Mussolini, Vito

Huber, Spike (235 lbs.) began his career as a wrestler in February of 1975. He was co-holder of the WWA Tag Team Title several times from 1979 until 1982, teaming with Dick the Bruiser, Wilbur Snyder and Steve Regal. Huber held the WWA championship in 1983. He left the promotion following his divorce from Dick the Bruiser's daughter the following year. Huber remained active on the independent circuit and wrestled in the Memphis area in the early 1990s.

Huffman, Booker *see* Booker T.

Huffman, Lane *see* Stevie Ray

Hughes, Mr. (Curtis Hughes; b. December 7, 1964; Kansas City, Kansas; 6'5", 308 lbs.) began wrestling in 1987. He was originally known in the ring as Big Cat. He was bodyguard for WCW champion Lex Luger in 1990. He also wrestled in the USWA in the early 1990s, often teaming with Jeff Gaylord.

Humberto, Juan (Mexico) was a light-heavyweight boxing champion in Mexico before becoming a professional wrestler. He was a leading contender during the 1950s, known in the ring for his speed and guile.

Humongous *see* Master Blaster, The

Humongous *see* Stark, Mike

Humongous, Lord *see* Lewis, Randy

Humongous, Lord *see* Van Kamp, Jeff

Humongous, Lord *see* Vicious, Sid

Humperdink, Sir Oliver was a leading manager from the 1970s. He managed Billy Graham, Jos LeDuc, Paul Jones and Greg Valentine in the NWA in the early 1980s. He also led a stable of rulebreakers in the Florida area in the early 1980s that included Mr. Pogo, Kabuki and the Masked Assassin. He briefly held the NWA Florida Title himself in February of 1987, before giving the belt to Ed Gantner.

Hunt, Tim wrestled as Hunter and teamed with J.W. Storm as Maximum Overdrive in the PWA. They held the tag team title for several months from June of 1989.

Hunter *see* Hunt, Tim

Hunter, Rock teamed with Rip Hawk to hold the Texas World Tag Team Title in February of 1963. He also held the NWA Central States Title in 1963. Wrestling as the Gladiator, he held the NWA Florida Title several times in late 1968 through early 1970. He teamed with Assassin

#2 to hold the ASWA Georgia Tag Team Title in 1973. He held the NWA Florida Tag Team Title with Lester Welch in April of 1969. He teamed with Roger Kirby to hold the NWA Central States Tag Team Title in early 1971. He managed Ivan Koloff and Alexi Smirnoff for the NWA Georgia Tag Team championship in the early 1980s.

Hunters, The *see* Veazy, Dale & Brown, Bob

Hussein, Muhammad *see* Fabiano, Lou

Hutton, Dick was a champion collegiate wrestler. He began wrestling professionally in the 1950s. He teamed with Hard Boiled Haggerty to capture the Canadian Open Tag Team Title in Toronto in September of 1956. He won the NWA Heavyweight Title from Lou Thesz in Toronto, Canada, on November 14, 1957. He retained the belt until January 9, 1959, when he was defeated by Pat O'Connor in Chicago, Illinois. He held the Hawaiian Title in January of 1961. He teamed with Sam Steamboat to hold the NWA Texas Tag Team Title in September of 1961.

Hyatt, Missy (Melissa Hiatt; b. 1967) made her debut in World Class in September of 1985 as a valet for Hollywood John Tatum. She managed Tatum and Eddie Gilbert in the UWF, later abandoning Tatum. She and Gilbert subsequently married, and she continued to act as his valet until their divorce. She entered WCW as a commentator in the early 1990s and engaged in feuds with Paul E. Dangerously and Madusa Miceli. She was fired from the promotion in February of 1994, and filed a sexual harassment suit against the WCW several months later. Hyatt entered the Extreme promotion in late 1995, replacing Woman as the Sandman's valet.

Iaukea, Curtis *see* Curtis, King

Iaukea, Rocky *see* Dein, Abbuda

Ice, J.C. (James Crookshanks; Memphis, Tennessee; 5'8", 221 lbs.) began wrestling in 1991. He is the son of Bill Dundee. He originally wrestled as Jamie Dundee. He teamed with Wolfie D as PG-13 in the USWA. They captured the USWA Tag Team Title in November of 1993. They held the title numerous times in the mid-1990s, often feuding with Tommy Rich and Doug Gilbert. He and Wolfie D wrestled as the Cyberpunks in the USWA after they lost a loser-leave-town match in the Spring of 1996.

Ice Train (Harold Hoag; Detroit, Michigan; 6'2", 250 lbs.) wrestled in the WCW in the 1990s. He was a powerful ring competitor who teamed with Scott Norton as the Fire and Ice tag team in 1996.

Iceman, The *see* Santana, Ricky

Idol, Austin (Dennis McCord; b. October 26, 1949; Las Vegas, Nevada; 6', 240 lbs.) began wrestling in 1972. He teamed with Jimmy Golden to hold the Australasian Tag Team Title in Australia in December of 1972. Idol was injured in a private plane crash near Tampa, Florida, on February 20, 1975, that killed wrestler Bobby

Shane. Idol recovered from his injured and returned to the ring to capture the Southern Heavyweight Title from Jerry Lawler in December of 1978. Idol teamed with the Masked Superstar to capture the NWA Georgia Tag Title in November of 1979. Idol held the NWA Georgia Title from March until June of 1980, and held the Alabama Title several times in the early 1980s. He held the CWA Tag Team Title with Dutch Mantell in 1980 and captured the CWA World Title in October of 1980. Idol held the CWA International Title several times in 1983 and 1984. He teamed with Lawler to hold the CWA Tag Team Title briefly in August of 1983. He held the NWA Southeastern Title several times in 1984 and 1985. Idol held the Southern Heavyweight Title several times in 1987, winning a hair vs. hair match with Jerry Lawler in April of 1987. Lawler defeated Idol for the title the following June. Idol remained active in the ring in the Memphis area, wrestling sporadically in the 1990s.

Idol, Lance (Steve Schumann; b. 1959, d. September 26, 1991) teamed with Rick Valentine to hold the WWC Tag Team Title in Puerto Rico in August of 1990.

Iizuka, Takayuki (b. August 2, 1965; Hakkaido, Japan; 5'10", 220 lbs.) began wrestling with New Japan in November of 1986. The Japanese wrestler achieved prominence in the early 1990s.

Infernos, The *see* Cain, Frankie & Smith, Rocky

Infernos, The *see* Gibson, Ron & Pulaski, Stan

Inoki, Antonio (b. February 20, 1943; Tokyo, Japan; 6'4", 240 lbs.) was the son of a Japanese father and Brazilian mother. He made his wrestling debut with the Japan Wrestling Association as Kanji Inoki in September of 1960. He made his United States debut in Honolulu in March of 1964. He wrestled as Tokyo Tom to capture the NWA Texas Title in June of 1964. He wrestled as Kenji Inoki, teaming with Hiro Matsuda, in 1965. They held the World Tag Team Title in Tennessee in January of 1966. He left the promotion in 1966 to form the Tokyo Pro Wrestling Promotion with Masa Saito and Hiro Matsuda. The organization folded in 1968 and Inoki returned to the JWA, where he held the Asian Tag Team Title with Michiaki Yoshimura and Kintaro Oki. He again left in March of 1972 to form New Japan Pro Wrestling, where he remained a leading performer through the 1980s. He wrestled boxer Muhammad Ali in 1976. Inoki defeated Bob Backlund for the WWF title in Japan on November 30, 1979, but vacated the title on December 6, 1979. He was elected to the upper house of Japan's Diet (Congress) in 1989, and reduced his wrestling appearances to only several a year. Inoki battled Ric Flair in a bout in North Korea in April of 1995.

Inoki, Kenji *see* Inoki, Antonio

Inoue, Masao (b. March 6, 1970; 5'8", 170 lbs.) made her wrestling debut in 1988. She was a leading Japanese wrestler in the 1990s. She captured the All-Japan WWWA Women's Tag Team Title in October of 1994, teaming with Takako Inoue.

Inoue, Sueo (b. April 12, 1949) began wrestling with the IWE in Japan as the Mighty Inoue in July of 1967. He held the IWE Tag Team Title several times from 1973 through 1981, teaming with the Great Kusatsu, Animal Hamaguchi and Ashura Hara. He entered All-Japan in 1981, where he often wrestled with Ashura Hara as the Japanese High Flyers.

Interns, The were a masked tag team managed by Dr. Ken Ramey. They held the Southern Tag Team Title several times in the early 1970s. They also held the NWA World Tag Team Title in San Francisco in August of 1973.

Interns, The *see* Bass, Don & Smith, Roger

Intimidator, The *see* Dragon Master, The

Invader 1 *see* Gonzales, Jose

Invaders, The were managed by Gerhardt Kaiser in the NWA in San Francisco in 1975. The held the NWA World Tag Team Title in San Francisco several times in 1975.

Iron Eagle, Alan (Joe Gomez) teamed with Lou Perez to hold the ICWA Florida Tag Team Title in 1992. He wrestled in the WCW in 1995.

Iron Sheik, The (Jose Azzeri; b. March 15; Teheran, Iran; 6', 262 lbs.) began wrestling in 1973. He wrestled under the names Great Husein Arab, Hossein Khosrow Vasiri and Ali Vaziri. He teamed with the

Texas Outlaw to hold the Canadian Tag Team Title in July of 1978. He held the NWA Eastern State Title in 1980. He captured the NWA Canadian Title in Toronto in May of 1980. He was managed by Paul Ellering when he held the NWA TV Title in May of 1983. The Iron Sheik was managed by Fred Blassie when he entered the WWF in the early 1980s. He was known for his submission hold, "the camel clutch," and used it to defeat Bob Backlund for the WWF Title in New York on December 26, 1983. He lost the belt to Hulk Hogan the following month in New York on January 23, 1984. He and Nikolai Volkoff defeated Mike Rotunda and Barry Windham to win the WWF Tag Team Title at Wrestlemania I on March 31, 1985. They were defeated for the belts in a return match with Rotundo and Windham on June 17, 1985. He held the All-California Championship Wrestling Title several times in 1988. The former WWF champion reentered the WWF as Col. Mustafa, an aide to Sgt. Slaughter, in 1990.

Irwin, Scott (b. 1950, d. September 5, 1987; Duluth, Minnesota; 250 lbs.) wrestled as Eric the Lumberjack in the WWWF. Teaming with Pierre as the Yukon Lumberjacks, they were managed by Lou Albano. They captured the WWWF Tag Team Title from Dominic Denucci and Dino Bravo in June of 1978. They were defeated by Tony Garea and Larry Zbyszko in November of 1978. Wrestling as Thor the Viking, he captured the NWA Southern Title in Florida in January of 1979. He also held the NWA Florida Tag Team Title with Bugsy

McGraw in 1979. Wrestling as the Super Destroyer, he held the NWA National Tag Team Title from January until July of 1982, teaming with the Masked Superstar and John Studd. Irwin also held the NWA National Title in August of 1982. He teamed with his brother, Bill Irwin, as the Super Destroyers to capture the World Class American Tag Team Title in October of 1983. Managed by Scandor Akbar, they held the belts several times over the next year. They were unmasked in a match against King Parsons and Buck Zumhofe in May of 1984 and subsequently held the title as the Long Riders. They captured the NWA National Tag Team Title in November of 1984 and the Canadian International Tag Team Title in Montreal in March of 1986. He was diagnosed with an inoperable brain tumor in May of 1986. Irwin died of his illness at a Duluth, Minnesota, hospital on September 5, 1987.

Irwin, Wild Bill (Duluth, Minnesota; 6'1", 250 lbs.) began wrestling in 1973. He teamed with Bryan St. John to hold the NWA Central States Tag Team Title in May of 1979. He held the Southern Heavyweight Title in August of 1980. He teamed with Larry Latham to hold the Southern Tag Team Title in October of 1980. He held the World Class World Tag Team Title in Texas several times in 1981 and 1982, teaming with Frank Dusek and Bugsy McGraw. He held the World Class Texas Title in August of 1982. He and King Kong Bundy teamed to capture the World Class American Tag Team Title in late 1982. He teamed with his brother,

Scott Irwin, as the Super Destroyers to capture the World Class American Tag Team Title in October of 1983. Managed by Scandor Akbar, they held the belts several times over the next year. They were unmasked in a match against King Parsons and Buck Zumhofe in May of 1984 and subsequently held the title as the Long Riders. They captured the NWA National Tag Team Title in November of 1984 and the Canadian International Tag Team Title in Montreal in March of 1986. He teamed with Leroy Brown to capture the UWF Tag Team Title in Oklahoma in November of 1986. He teamed with Black Bart as the Wild Bunch to hold the Global World Tag Team Title in December of 1991. Irwin again wrestled as the Super Destroyer in Global in 1993.

Ishikawa, Yuki (b. February 8, 1967) began wrestling in April of 1992. He joined New Japan the following year.

Ishizawa, Tokimisu (b. September 5, 1968) began wrestling with New Japan in September of 1992.

Isley, David wrestled as Thunderfoot #1 in the IWA. He held the IWA Title in 1991.

Italian Stallion (Gary Sabaugh; Naples, Italy; 6'3", 260 lbs.) began wrestling in 1983. He held the PWF Title several times in the early 1990s. He was also the tag team champion several times, teaming with Ron Garvin, Star Rider and George South.

Ito, Masao was managed by

Jimmy Hart in the Memphis area. He captured the CWA International Title in June of 1984.

Ito, Mr. (Umanosuke Ueda) teamed with Tojo Yamamoto to hold the World Tag Team Title in Tennessee in October of 1966. He teamed with Chati Yokouchi to hold the NWA Georgia Tag Team Title in July of 1969. He held the NWA Americas Tag Team Title in Los Angeles in June of 1978, teaming with Pak Choo.

Ivan the Terrible *see* Firpo, Pampera

Ivan the Terrible *see* Mikaloff, Ivan

Iwamoto, Charles *see* Moto, Mr.

Izumida, Ryuma (b. October 28, 1965) began wrestling professionally with All-Japan in May of 1992.

Jaago, Jaan (d. August, 1949) was a leading Estonia grappler. He held the World Greco-Roman Heavyweight Championship in Europe several times from 1914 through 1930.

Jackson, Action (Perry Jackson; Dallas, Texas; 6'2", 300 lbs.) began wrestling in 1984. He held the CWA Tag Team Title with Billy Joe Travis in June of 1989. He held the NAWA North American Title in Texas in August of 1991. He wrestled with Iceman Parsons as the Blackbirds in World Class in 1993.

Jackson, Mike (5'10", 222 lbs.) began wrestling in 1978. He was the longtime Alabama junior heavyweight champion.

Jackson, Tiger *see* Dink

Jacobs, Abe teamed with Don Curtis to hold the NWA World Tag Team Title in Florida in May of 1964.

Jacobs, Glen (Knoxville, Tennessee; 6'7", 345 lbs.) wrestled as Jim Powers in Florida. He wrestled as Doomsday in the USWA in the early 1990s. He wrestled as Jerry Lawler's Black Knight in the WWF Survivors Series in 1993. Jacobs wrestled as Unabom in Smoky Mountain Wrestling in 1995, often teaming with Al Snow. They captured the Smoky Mountain Tag Team Title from the Rock 'n' Roll Express in April of 1995. They lost the belts to Tony Anthony and Tracey Smothers the following July. He joined the WWF as Dr. Isaac Yankem, the wrestling dentist, in July of 1995. He sided with Jerry Lawler in his feud against Bret Hart.

Jacques *see* Rougeau, Jacques

Jaffee, Jerry *see* Graham, Jr., Jerry

Jaggers, Bobby (Dunlap, Kansas; 255 lbs.) teamed with Jerry Brown to hold the U.S. Tag Team Title in Oklahoma in May of 1978. He teamed with Chris Colt to hold the Canadian Tag Team Title in July of 1979. He held the NWA Florida Title in October of 1980. He also held the NWA Southern Title in Florida in August of 1981. He teamed with R.T. Tyler as the Cowboy Connection to hold the NWA Florida Tag Team Title several times in early 1981. He held the WWC North American Title in Puerto

Rico in early 1982. He teamed with Dutch Mantell as the Kansas Jayhawks in the NWA in the mid-1980s. He held the NWA Pacific Northwest Title several times in 1984 and 1985. He held the Pacific Northwest tag belts several times in 1986, teaming with Rip Oliver and the Assassin. He teamed with Moondog Moretti to hold the NWA Central States Tag Team Title in June of 1986. He reclaimed the tag belts, teaming with Brad Batten, in June of 1987. Jaggers briefly held the Southern Heavyweight Title in October of 1987.

Jalisco, Apollo *see* Medico, El

James, Brian *see* Armstrong, Brian

James, Jesse (Chris Pappas; b. 1917; Washington, D.C.; 5'9", 220 lbs.) was the son of wrestling promoter Tony Pappas. He trained to be a wrestler at an early age, studying with Jim Londos. He began wrestling professionally in Los Angeles in the late 1930s. He held the Southern Junior Heavyweight Title in 1953, 1956 and 1959.

James, Robert, Jr, *see* Armstrong, Brad

James, Robert, Sr. *see* Armstrong, Bob

James, Scott *see* Armstrong, Scott

James, Steve *see* Armstrong, Steve

Jamison (John Di Giacomo) made comic appearances on the WWF TV shows during the early 1990s. He also accompanied the Bushwhackers to the ring on several occasions.

Jamison, Jim (Jim Jamieson; December 18, 1952) began wrestling professionally in the Memphis area in 1973. He wrestled against numerous competitors that came through the area in the 1970s and 1980s, including Jesse Ventura and King Kong Bundy. He retired from the ring in 1987. Jamison was a candidate for State Representative in Tennessee in 1996.

Jammer, Tommy (5'11", 245 lbs.) began wrestling in 1988. Known as the California Kid, he wrestled in the PWA and AWA.

Jannetty, Marty (Marty Oates; b. February 20, 1962; Columbia, Georgia; 5'11", 230 lbs.) was born in Columbus, Georgia. He wrestled in college and turned pro in 1983 in the Central States promotion. He teamed with Tommy Rogers as the Uptown Boys early in his career. They captured the NWA Central States Tag Team Title several times in 1984. He formed the Midnight Rockers with Shawn Michaels and they captured the NWA Central States tag belts in May of 1985. Jannetty also captured the NWA Central States Title in September of 1985. The Midnight Rockers entered the AWA in 1986 and the duo defeated Buddy Rose and Doug Somers for the AWA Tag Team Title on January 27, 1987. They lost the belts to Boris Zhukov and Soldat Ustinov at a match in Lake Tahoe, Nevada, on May 25, 1987. They held the Southern Tag Team Title several times in late 1987, feuding with the Rock 'n' Roll RPMS. They subsequently regained the AWA title in a match against Dennis Condrey and Randy Rose. Jannetty and Michaels finally lost the belts to Pat Tanaka and Paul Diamond on March 19, 1988. They joined the WWF the following year where they became known as the Rockers. They feuded with the Hart Foundation, and nearly captured the WWF tag title. He and Michaels later split and Jannetty left the WWF in the Fall of 1992. He returned to win the Intercontinental Title from Michaels in a TV match on May 17, 1993. Michaels recaptured the title on June 6, 1993. Jannetty teamed with the 1-2-3 Kid to defeat the Quebecers for the WWF Tag Team title on Monday Night Raw on January 10, 1994. The duo lost the belts in a return match with the Quebecers on January 17, 1994, in New York City. Jannetty left the WWF in March of 1994. He returned to the WWF in 1996, teaming with Leaf Cassidy as the New Rockers.

Janos, James *see* Ventura, Jesse

Jardine, Don, who wrestled as the Spoiler, was one of the leading mat villains from the 1960s through the 1980s. He was known for his iron claw hold. He teamed with Dutch Savage to capture the Canadian Tag Team Title in September of 1966. He teamed with Gary Hart to hold the World Class American Tag Team Title in Texas in late 1967. He again held the tag belts, teaming with Smasher Sloan as the Spoilers and managed by Hart, in 1968. He held the World Class Championship in Texas in April of 1968. He held the MSWA North American Title in 1969. He teamed with Buddy Wolfe

as the Spoilers to hold the U.S. Tag Team Title in Oklahoma in 1971. He again held the World Class title in early 1972. Managed by Gary Hart, he held the NWA Georgia title several times in 1975 and 1976. He held the NWA Florida Title and the NWA Southern Title in Florida in 1978. He also held the NWA Florida Tag Team Title, teaming with Bobby Duncum as the Spoilers. He returned to Texas to reclaim the World Class title in mid-1979. The Spoiler captured the NWA National Title several times in 1984 before leaving for the WWF. He held the WWF National Title in 1984.

Jares, Brother Frank (b. 1913, d. July 24, 1990; Provo, Utah; 5'10", 225 lbs.) was a champion weightlifter before he began wrestling professionally in the 1940s. Jares, who wrestled as the Mormon Mauler from Provo, Utah, was really lapsed Catholic from Pittsburgh, Pennsylvania. He remained a popular competitor through the 1950s, and held the Southern Junior Heavyweight Title several times in 1955 and 1956. He also competed under the names Brother Russell, the masked Golden Terror in Hawaii, and the villainous Thing, known for his bright orange hair and beard, in Illinois. He retired from the ring in the early 1960s. He died in a Los Angeles hospital on July 24, 1990.

Jarque, Gregory (b. 1921; Barcelona, Spain; 6', 225 lbs.) began wrestling in the early 1940s in Spain, where he held the championship. He came to the United States in mid-1951, where he continued to be a leading competitor.

Jarrett, Jeff (b. July 14, 1967; Hendersonville, Tennessee; 5'10", 230 lbs.) is the son of wrestler and promoter Jerry Jarrett and worked as a referee in Memphis before making his wrestling debut in April of 1986. He teamed with Billy Travis and Pat Tanaka early in his career, winning the Southern Tag Team Title and the CWA International Tag Team Title several times with each in 1986 and 1987. Jarrett also held the Mid-America Title several times in 1987, competing against Moondog Spot and Jimmy Jack Funk. He also competed in World Class from 1988, where he held the Light Heavyweight Title and often feuded with Eric Embry. Jarrett held the CWA Title for several months from March of 1989. He held the World Class World Tag Team Title with Kerry Von Erich for several months from March of 1989. He also held the World Class tag belts with Mil Mascaras and Matt Borne in 1989. He teamed with Matt Borne to hold the USWA Tag Team Title in August and September of 1989. He again claimed the USWA tag belts in September of 1990 with Jeff Gaylord as his partner, and in November of 1990, teamed with Cody Michaels. Jarrett also held the USWA Southern Title in October of 1990. He held the Southern belt six more times over the next several years. He captured the tag belts with Jerry Lawler in February of 1991, and held the title several times with Robert Fuller during the year. He teamed with Jerry Lawler in numerous matches in 1992, holding the USWA tag belts on several occasions. He held the USWA Tag Team Title sev-eral times with Brian Christopher in the Fall of 1993 before entering the WWF as country singer Double J in October of 1993. He briefly held the USWA Unified Title in November of 1993. He defeated Razor Ramon for the WWF Intercontinental Title on January 22, 1995. He lost the title in a rematch with Ramon on May 19, 1995, but regained the belt two days later. He was defeated for the Intercontinental belt by Shawn Michaels in Nashville, Tennessee, on July 23, 1995. Jarrett subsequently left the WWF in a contract dispute. He resumed wrestling in the USWA later in the year, capturing the USWA Unified Title from Ahmed Johnson in December of 1995. He relinquished the title soon after, when injuries prevented his return to the ring. Jarrett resumed wrestling in April of 1996 in the USWA and the WWF.

Jarrett, Jerry (b. September 4, 1942) is a Nashville native who teamed with Tojo Yamamoto in the Mid-South area from the early 1970s. They held the Southern Tag Team Title in May of 1971 and in January of 1973. He also held the tag belts with Jackie Fargo in February of 1973. He was a promoter and half-owner of the USWA from the mid-1970s. He again teamed with Yamamoto to hold the CWA Tag Team Title in July of 1980. Jarrett is the father of wrestler Jeff Jarrett.

Jason (Ronald Jason Knight; Philadelphia, Pennsylvania; 216 lbs.) wrestled in ECW from 1994, where he held the TV Title for several months.

Jason the Terrible (6'7", 302 lbs.) began wrestling in 1984. He wrestled under a hockey mask in Canada and Puerto Rico, where he held the WWC Caribbean Title in November of 1988. He also held the WWC Tag Team Title with Steve Strong in March of 1989. He was injured in an automobile accident in Canada with Davey Boy Smith in July of 1989. He suffered a broken leg. Jason recovered from his injuries and returned to the ring in the 1990s.

Jean, Corsica *see* Corsica Jean

Jeffers, Jim, wrestling as Spike, teamed with his brother, Mac Jeffers as Basher, to form the MOD Squad. Managed by J.D. Costello, they held the Southern Tag Team Title in March of 1986. The MOD Squad also held the NWA Central States Tag Team Title in January of 1987.

Jeffers, Mac, wrestling as Basher, teamed with his brother, Jim Jeffers as Spike, to form the MOD Squad. Managed by J.D. Costello, they held the Southern Tag Team Title in March of 1986. The MOD Squad also held the NWA Central States Tag Team Title in January of 1987.

Jenkins, Tom (b. 1873, d. 1957) was a leading wrestler in the early part of the century and a three-time holder of the American Title between 1901 and 1905. He defeated such early wrestling stars as Ernest Roeber, Dan McLeod and Frank Gotch.

Jennings, Sun was a Cherokee Indian. He attended Carlisle College, where he was on the football and track teams. He became a leading wrestler in the 1930s. He wrestled for several decade before retiring to Oklahoma.

Jericho, Chris (Vancouver, British Columbia; 5'10", 225 lbs.) wrestled as Corazon de Leon in Mexico, capturing the Mexican Middleweight Title in December of 1993. He wrestled with Lance Storm as the Thrillseekers in Smoky Mountain Wrestling in 1994.

Johnny K-9 *see* Bedlam, Bruiser

Johnson, Ahmed (Tony Norris; Pearl River, Mississippi; 6'4", 255 lbs.) wrestled as vicious rulebreaker Moadib in General Skandor Akbar's stable in Global in 1993 and 1994. He entered the WWF in October of 1995 as Ahmed Johnson. He held the USWA Unified Title in Memphis in November of 1995. He feuded with Jeff Jarrett in the USWA and the WWF in 1996.

Johnson, David wrestled with Tom Nash as the Blackhearts in the NWA in 1994.

Johnson, Kenneth *see* Slick

Johnson, Lois (b. 1929; 5'5", 145 lbs.) was a leading female wrestler in the 1950s.

Johnson, Lorraine was a leading women's wrestler in the 1950s and 1960s. She was married to wrestler Nick Roberts and is the mother of wrestling valet Baby Doll.

Johnson, Ricky teamed with his father, Rocky Johnson, to hold the Pacific Tag Team Title in Honolulu several times in 1985.

Johnson, Rocky (Washington, D.C.; 6'2", 244 lbs.) began wrestling in 1964. Know as the Soul Man, he has competed in many area. He teamed with Don Leo Jonathan to hold the Canadian Tag Team Title in April of 1967. He held the NWA Americas Title in Los Angeles in January of 1970. He won the Los Angeles Battle Royal in 1970. He teamed with Pepper Gomez to hold the NWA World Tag Team Title in San Francisco in September of 1971. He held the NWA U.S. Title in San Francisco in November of 1971. He teamed with Jerry Brisco to hold the NWA Georgia Tag Team Title in January of 1975. He also held the NWA Georgia Title for several months in early 1975, and held the NWA Florida Title in December of 1975. He held the World Class Texas Title several times in 1976. He teamed with Pedro Morales to hold the NWA Florida Tag Team Title in 1977. He again captured the NWA Florida Title in March of 1978. He also held the Southern Heavyweight Title in 1978. He teamed with Jimmy Valiant to briefly hold the Southern Tag Team Title in May of 1980. Johnson also held the Mid-America Title in May of 1980. Wrestling as Sweet Ebony Diamond, he held the NWA TV Title in 1981. He held the NWA Pacific Northwest Tag Team Title several times in the early 1980s, teaming with Iceman Parsons and Brett Sawyer. He teamed with Tony Atlas to capture the WWF Tag Team Title from the Samoans in November of 1983. They lost the belts to Dick Murdoch and Adrian Adonis in April of 1984. He teamed with his son, Ricky Johnson, to hold the Pacific Tag Team Title in Honolulu several times in 1985. He teamed with Soul Train Jones to hold the Southern Tag Team Title in April of 1987. He also held the CWA International Tag Team Title with Bill Dundee in July of 1987.

Johnson, Tor (b. 1903, d. May 12, 1971; Stockholm Sweden; 6'4", 365 lbs.) wrestled as the Swedish Angel and the Super-Swedish Angel. He held championships in Europe and the Far East before coming to the United States. He was a leading wrestling villain, and later a Hollywood character actor. He portrayed hulking brutes in numerous films including *The Ghost Catchers* (1944), *State of the Union* (1948), *Alias the Champ* (1949), *Abbott and Costello in the Foreign Legion* (1950), *The Reformer and the Redhead* (1950), *The Lemon Drop Kid* (1951), *The San Francisco Story* (1952), *The Lady in the Iron Mask* (1952), *Houdini* (1953), *Carousel* (1956), *The Black Sleep* (1956), *The Unearthly* (1957) and *The Beast of Yucca Flats* (1961). He was best known for being a member of cult film director Ed Wood's stock company, appearing in Wood's films *Bride of the Monster* (1955), *Plan 9 from Outer Space* (1956) and *Night of the Ghouls* (1959). He died of a heart attack in San Fernando, California, on May 12, 1971. Johnson was portrayed by wrestler George "the Animal" Steele in the 1994 film biography of Wood, *Ed Wood*.

Johnson, Walter held the NWA Americas Title in Los Angeles for several months from May of 1980.

Jonathan, Don Leo (b. 1928; Hurricane, Utah; 6'5", 240 lbs.) was the son of a professional wrestler. The Mormon grappler began his ring career in the late 1940s and quickly captured the Rocky Mountain Championship. The huge mat star also held the AWA Title in Montreal, Canada, in 1955. He held the NWA Texas Title for several months from April of 1957. He also held the Texas Brass Knucks Title in 1957. He teamed with Gene Kiniski to hold the Canadian Open Tag Team Title in Toronto in 1959. He again held the Texas belt in July of 1960. He held the World Title in Omaha several times in 1961. He held the AWA Ohio Title in 1962. He teamed with Kinji Shibuya to hold the Canadian Tag Team Title in January of 1964. He held the Canadian tag belts numerous times throughout the 1960s and early 1970s, teaming with Roy McClarty, Gene Kiniski, Jim Hady, Haystack Calhoun, Dominic DeNucci, Grizzly Smith, Johnny Kostas, John Tolos and Steven Little Bear. He also held the Pacific Coast Title in Vancover, Canada, several times in the early 1970s. Jonathan was the Catch Wrestling Association Heavyweight Champion in Europe in 1978.

Jones, Farmer (Paul Jones; d. 19??) was a leading wrestler in the 1940s and 1950s who often came to the ring carrying his pet pig.

Jones, Gervais *see* Ruffen, Jackie

Jones, Marvin "Wildcat" (d. 19??; 235 lbs.) was a leading wrestling villain from the 1930s through the 1950s. He was a holder of title belts in Texas and Florida.

Jones, Mike *see* Virgil

Jones, Paul (Paul Frederik; Port Arthur, Texas; 230 lbs.) captured the NWA Pacific Coast Title for the first of several times in March of 1966. He also held the Pacific Coast tag belts, teaming with Pepper Martin, in January of 1967. He teamed with Nelson Royal to hold the NWA Americas Tag Team Title in Los Angeles in January of 1969, and the NWA Atlantic Coast Tag Title in 1970. He also held the title several times in the mid-1970s, teaming with Bob Bruggers and Tiger Conway, Jr. Jones held the NWA Florida Title several times in 1972 and 1973. He briefly held the NWA Southern Title in Florida in March of 1973. He also held the NWA Georgia Title, the NWA Mid-Atlantic Title and U.S. Title several times from 1974 until 1976. He teamed with Rick Steamboat to capture the NWA World Tag Team Title in a tournament in April of 1978. They held the belts for several months. He was again tag team champion in April of 1979, teaming with Baron Von Raschke. They were defeated for the belt by Ric Flair and Blackjack Mulligan in August of 1979, but recaptured the title the following month. They lost the belts to Rick Steamboat and Jay Youngblood in October of 1979. Jones was again co-holder of the tag team belts from November of 1980, when he teamed with the Masked Superstar to take the tag title from Ray Stevens and Jimmy Snuka. They held the belts until February of 1981, when Stevens returned with Ivan Koloff to recapture the title. Jones and the Masked Superstar won a rematch the following month, remaining champions until May of 1981, when Gene and Ole Anderson took the belts. Jones held the NWA Mid-Atlantic Title several times in 1982. He became a top manager in the NWA in the 1980s. He was known as Number One Paul Jones and managed the tag champions Ivan Koloff and Dick Murdoch, and Manny Fernandez and Rick Rude in 1986 and 1987.

Jones, Paul *see* Jones, Farmer

Jones, Rocky (5'11", 234 lbs.) began wrestling in 1983. He was the first champion for the ECPW promotion in New Jersey in 1993.

Jones, Roosevelt *see* Jones, S.D.

Jones, Rufus R. (Carey Lloyd; b. 1932, d. November 13, 1992; Boston, Massachusetts; 5'10", 238 lbs.) began wrestling in 1969. Known as "the Freight Train," he teamed with Steve Bolus to hold the NWA Central States Tag Team Title in late 1971. He held the Central States belts several more times in the early 1970s, teaming with the Mongolian Stomper and Bob Geigel. He briefly held the NWA World Tag Team Title with Wahoo McDaniel in March of 1976. He teamed with Norvell Austin to briefly hold the NWA Georgia Tag Team Title in April of 1979. He teamed with Dewey Robertson to again hold the NWA Central States Tag Team Title in October of 1981. He held the NWA Mid-Atlantic Title for several months in late 1983. He also held the NWA Atlantic Coast Tag belts with Bugsy McGraw in 1983. He teamed with Mike George to hold the NWA Central States Tag Team Title in June of 1986. He held the NWA Central States Title several times in 1987. He died of a heart attack near his home in Kansas City, Missouri, on November 13, 1992.

Jones, S.D. "Special Delivery" (Conrad Efraim; b. March 30; Philadelphia, Pennsylvania; 6'1, 240 lbs.) began wrestling in 1961. He was a popular wrestler with the fans and was known for his head butt, which often knocked out his opponents. He teamed with Porkchop Cash to hold the NWA Americas Title in Los Angeles in January of 1975. He also wrestled as Roosevelt Jones.

Jones, Ski Hi *see* Smith, Grizzly

Jones, Soul Train *see* Virgil

Jones, Tom (d. August 30, 1978) teamed with Billy Red Lyons to hold the U.S. Tag Team Title in Louisiana in May of 1971. He again held the belts with Ken Mantell in August of 1972. He teamed with Porkchop Cash to hold the NWA Georgia Tag Team Title in September of 1976. He teamed with Mando Guerrero to hold the NWA Americas Tag Team Title in Los Angeles in April of 1977. Wrestling as Mr. Ebony, he teamed with Mike Miller to hold the NWA Pacific Northwest Tag Team Title several times in 1984.

Juarez, Rueben teamed with Eric Froelich to hold the NWA Americas Tag Team Title in Los Angeles in August of 1972. He again held the NWA Americas tag belt in

August of 1973, teaming with Raul Reyes.

Judge Dread (6'6", 334 lbs.) began wrestling in 1990. He has wrestled in Michigan and the USWA.

Judo Joe *see* Cassius, Joe

Juice Patrol *see* Barr, Art "Beetlejuice" & Warner, Jeff "Big Juice"

Jumping Bomb Angels, The *see* Yamazaki, Itsuki & Tateno, Noriyo

Jungle Boy, The *see* Bertucci, Lou

Junkyard Dog (Sylvester Ritter; b. December 13; Charlotte, North Carolina; 6'3", 305 lbs.) began wrestling in 1978. Wrestling as Big Daddy Ritter, he held the Stampede North American Title in Calgary, Canada, several times in 1978 and 1979. He was a popular performer in the WWF and WCW. He held the MSWA North American Title in Louisiana several times in 1982 and 1983. He held the USWA Unified Title in September of 1992.

Jurrasic Powers *see* Norton, Scott & Hercules

Kabuki, The Great (Akihisa Mera; b. September 8, 1948; Singapore; 6', 252 lbs.) began wrestling in October of 1964. He competed in Japan as Akihisa Takachiho during the 1960s and 1970s. Wrestling as Takachiho, and managed by Scandor Akbar, he teamed with Pak Song to hold the NWA Central States Tag Team Title in April of 1980. He reclaimed the tag belts in June of 1980, teaming with Killer Karl Kox. He

also wrestled as Mr. Sato and Akio Moto in 1970s and early 1980s. He entered the NWA as the Great Kabuki in the early 1980s. Managed by Gary Hart, he held the World Class Championship in Texas in September of 1981, the Mid-South Louisiana Title in October of 1981 and the NWA TV Title in 1983. He held the Mid-America Title in November of 1986. He returned to wrestle with New Japan in early 1993.

Kace, Johnny (John Kakacek; b. 1926, d. September 9, 1992) began his wrestling career in the early 1950s. He wrestled primarily in the Chicago area and his career lasted through the mid 1970s.

Kai, Leilani is the daugther of wrestler Hans Schroeder. She was managed by the Fabulous Moolah when she defeated Wendy Richter for the WWF Women's Title in New York's Madison Square Garden on February 18, 1985. Richter won the title back from Kai six weeks later at Wrestlemania I on March 31, 1985. Kai teamed with Judy Martin to hold the WWF Women's Tag Team belt in August of 1985. They were known as the Glamour Girls and were often managed by Jimmy Hart and Christopher Love. They lost the belts to the Japanese team, the Jumping Bomb Angels, in January of 1988, but returned to capture the title the following June. They left the WWF the following year. They defeated Team America for the LPWA Tag Team Title in February of 1991.

Kaiser, Jack (b. 1910, d. May 17, 1991) was a prominent wrestler in the Portland area known for his "skin the cat" finishing maneuver.

Kaissie, Adnon *see* Adnan al-Kaissie, Sheik

Kakacez, John *see* Kace, Johnny

Kalmikoff, Ivan teamed with Duke Keomuka to hold the NWA Texas Tag Team Title in January of 1952. He teamed with Karol Kalmikoff to regain the Texas tag belts in May of 1954. They captured the Canadian Open Tag Team Title in Toronto in March of 1955. They also held the NWA World Tag Team Title in Minneapolis in January of 1957. They held the title several more times over the next three years. They also held the Pacific Coast Tag Team Title in Vancouver, Canada, in October of 1961. They captured the AWA World Tag Team Title from Doug Gilbert and Dick Steinborn in January of 1963. They held the belts until August of 1963 when they were defeated by Crusher and Dick the Bruiser. Kalmikoff managed the Mighty Igor in the mid-1970s.

Kalmikoff, Karol (Karol Piwoworcyk; d. September, 1964), wrestling as Karol Krauser, was a popular star in the Mid-South in the early 1950s. He teamed with Ivan Kalmikoff to capture the NWA Texas Tag Team Title in May of 1954. They captured the Canadian Open Tag Team Title in Toronto in March of 1955. They also held the NWA World Tag Team Title in Minneapolis in January of 1957. They held the title several more times over the next three years. They also held the Pacific Coast Tag Team

Title in Vancouver, Canada, in October of 1961. They captured the AWA World Tag Team Title from Doug Gilbert and Dick Steinborn in January of 1963. They held the belts until August of 1963 when they were defeated by Crusher and Dick the Bruiser. Wrestling as Karl Gotch, he held the AWA Ohio Title in the early 1960s. As Gotch, he teamed with Mike DiBiase to hold the WWA Tag Team Title in Los Angeles in 1967. He teamed with Rene Goulet to defeat Luke Graham and Tarzan Tyler for the WWWF Tag Team Title in December of 1971. They were defeated for the belts by Baron Scicluna and King Curtis in February of 1972.

Kaluha, King (5'10", 237 lbs.) began wrestling on the East Coast in 1984. The Hawaiian star has wrestled in the NWF, IWCCW and AWA. He held the WWCA Light Heavyweight Title in New Jersey in 1990.

Kama *see* Soultaker, The

Kamaka, King *see* Kamata, Tor

Kamala (b. May 28, 1950; Uganda; 6'7", 345 lbs.) began wrestling in 1974. He originally wrestled as Sugarbear Harris, teaming with Oki Shikina to hold the Tri-State U.S. Tag Team Title in Oklahoma in October of 1979. He became known as Kamala, the Ugandan Giant, when he entered the Mid-South region in 1982. He was managed by J.J. Dillon and captured the Southern Heavyweight Title in June of 1982. He held the USWA Unified Title several times in late 1991 and early 1992. Kamala also wrestled in the WWF in the early 1990s, where he was managed by Kim Chee. Kamala entered the WCW in May of 1995, where he was managed by Kevin "the Taskmaster" Sullivan. He left the federation soon afterwards to take some time off. He returned to wrestling later in the year, wrestling on independent cards and in the USWA.

Kamala II *see* Botswana Beast

Kamata, Tor teamed with Tojo Yamamoto to hold the Southern Tag Team Title in October of 1965. He wrestled as Dr. Moto in the AWA and teamed with Mitsu Arakawa to hold the WWA Tag Team belts in October of 1967. They captured the AWA Tag Team Title from Pat O'-Connor and Wilbur Snyder in December of 1967. They lost the belts to Crusher and Dick the Bruiser in December of 1968. He teamed with Luke Brown to hold the NWA Central States Tag Team Title in June of 1969. He held the Stampede North American Title in Calgary, Canada, several times in 1972. Kamata remained a leading mat villain through the 1970s and early 1980s in the WWF, where he was managed by Fred Blassie. He captured the British Empire Title in New Zealand in 1982, wrestling as King Kamaka. He also held the Australasian Tag Team Title in New Zealand with Ox Baker in 1982. He subsequently retired to Hawaii.

Kameroff, Ivan (b. 1918, d. 19??; New Haven, Connecticut; 6'1", 230 lbs.) was known as the Russian Strongman and the Caribou. He was a leading body builder and weight lifter, and was Mr. New York in 1940. He teamed with Doc Gallagher to hold the Northwest Tag Team Title in Vancouver, Canada, in October of 1953. He held the Northwest belts several more times in the mid-1950s, teaming with Pepper Gomez, Boris Kameroff and Red Vagnone. He teamed with Doug Donovan to hold the NWA Pacific Northwest Tag Team Title several times in 1955. He again held the Pacific Northwest tag belts in July of 1963, teaming with Soldat Gorky. He teamed with Art Neilson to hold the Canadian Tag Team Title in September of 1965. He is the brother of Walter and Joe Kameroff.

Kameroff, Joe (New Haven, Connecticut) is the oldest of the three Kameroff brothers. Joe Kameroff was known for his rough mat style that often resulted in disqualification.

Kameroff, Walter (b. 1922; New Haven, Connecticut; 5'10", 205 lbs.) was the youngest of the wrestling Kameroff brothers. He began wrestling in the late 1940s and often teamed with his brothers, Joe and Ivan, in the ring during the 1950s.

Kampfer, Hans (b. 1911, d. 19??; Breslau, Germany; 5'11", 230 lbs.) held the European championship in the 1920s before coming to the United States. He was a leading mat star through the 1950s.

Kane *see* Stevie Ray

Kane, Ruben *see* Gibson, Robert

Kanemoto, Koji (b. October 31, 1966; Tokyo, Japan; 5'10", 205 lbs.) began wrestling in November of 1990. The Japanese mat star wrestled as the third Tiger Mask in New Japan and Mexico until he was unmasked in 1993. He continued to compete as Koji Kanemoto. He defeated Sabu for the IWGP Junior Heavyweight Title in June of 1995.

Kangaroo, The *see* Coleman, Abe

Kangaroos, The Fabulous *see* Costello, Al & Heffernan, Roy

Kansas Jayhawks, The *see* Mantell, Dutch & Jaggers, Bobby

Kapitanopolis, Art "Kappy" (b. 1923; Macedonia, Greece) came to the United States from Greece at the age of 11. He attended Miami University, where he played football. He began wrestling professionally in the mid-1940s and was a leading contender in the 1950s.

Karadagian, Martin (b. 1916, d. August 27, 1991; Argentina; 5'7", 210 lbs.) wrestled as the Mighty Karadagian. He was also known as the Argentine Bull. The thick bearded Karadagian was of Armenian ancestry. He began wrestling in the United States in the late 1930s. He remained a leading star in North and South America through the 1950s.

Karas, Steve (b. 1920; Lynn, Massachusetts; 5'9", 200 lbs.) played semi-pro baseball before becoming a professional wrestler in the late 1940s. He remained a popular competitor through the 1950s.

Karbo, Wally (b. 1916, d. March 25, 1993) was a leading wrestling promoter with the AWA in Min-

nesota from the 1950s. He died of a heart attack at his home in Bloomington, Minnesota, on March 25, 1993.

Kasavubu (Jimmie Banks; b. 1956, d. July 27, 1982) held the Stampede North American Title in Calgary, Canada, in September of 1978. He teamed with the Dynamite Kid to hold the Calgary Stampede International Tag Team Title in June of 1980.

Kashey, Abe "King Kong" (b. November 28, 1903, d. September 24, 1965; Compton, California) was born in Syria. He began wrestling professionally in the United States in 1920s. He held the Hawaiian Title in the 1940s. The hairy mat villain remained a popular star through the 1950s. Kashey was also an actor and stuntman in several films and serials in the 1940s including *King of the Mounties* (1942), *That Nazty Nuisance* (1943), *Crime Doctor's Courage* (1945) and *Tarzan and the Leopard Woman* (1945). Kashey died of congestive heart failure in Lynwood, California, on September 24, 1965.

Kashey, Al held the EMLL Light Heavyweight Title from November of 1957. He teamed with Nick Kozak to hold the NWA Pacific Northwest Tag Team Title in March of 1959.

Katan, John (d. 19??) held the British Empire Title in New Zealand and Canada several times in the early 1940s. He also held the AWA Title in Montreal, Canada, in April of 1943.

Kato *see* Diamond, Paul

Kato, Oyama (d. January 9, 1961) held the NWA Texas Junior Heavyweight Title in April of 1958. He teamed with Karl von Schober to hold the NWA World Tag Team Title in San Francisco in December of 1957.

Kaufman, Andy (b. 1949, d. May 16, 1984) was a popular comedian who frequently appeared on *Saturday Night Live* and starred in the television series *Taxi*. He began challenging females to a wrestling match as part of his comedy routine in the early 1980s. Billing himself as the inter-gender champion, he came to the Mid-South area where he engaged in a feud with Jerry Lawler in 1981. Lawler injured Kaufman in the ring with a series of pile-drivers during one of their matches. Kaufman subsequently managed a succession of mat villains in an attempt to get revenge on Lawler. The duo also sparred on *The David Letterman Show* on television in July of 1982. Kaufman died of cancer on May 16, 1984.

Kawada, Toshiaki (b. December 8, 1963; Tizhigi, Japan; 5'10", 230 lbs.) is a leading Japanese mat star who began wrestling with All-Japan in October of 1982. He often teamed with Samson Fuyuki as Footloose. They held the All-Japan All-Asian Tag Team Title several times in the late 1980s. He captured the All-Japan Triple Crown Title in October of 1994.

Kay, Rudy (b. 1916; Chicago, Illinois; 5'11", 220 lbs.) was a popular mat star in the Midwest from the late 1930s through the 1970s. He held the North American Title in Nova Scotia in 1975.

Kealoha, Jimmy *see* Snuka, Jimmy

Kean, Lanny *see* Moondog Cujo

Keirn, Steve (b. September 10; Tampa, Florida; 6', 235 lbs.) began wrestling in 1973. He teamed with Bob Backlund to hold the NWA Florida Tag Team Title in 1976. He captured the NWA Southern Title in Florida in November of 1976. He again held the belt briefly the following year. He recaptured the Florida tag belts in 1977, teaming with Mike Graham. He captured the NWA International Junior Heavyweight Title in December of 1979. He held the NWA Georgia Title in August of 1980. He teamed with Mr. Wrestling for the NWA Georgia Tag Team Title in July of 1980. He also held the NWA TV Title several times in 1980 and 1981, and was the Mid-American champion in August of 1981. He teamed with Bill Dundee to capture the Southern Tag Team Title in December of 1981. They again held the belts the following year. Keirn joined with Stan Lane to form The Fabulous Ones in late 1982, becoming an extremely popular tag team. Sometimes managed by Jackie Fargo, they held the Southern Tag Team Title numerous times in 1982 and 1983. They also captured the CWA Tag Team Title several times in late 1983. They held the U.S. Tag Team Title in Florida several times in late 1986. He teamed with Mark Starr to hold the CWA International Tag Team Title in March of 1987. He and Lane captured the USWA Tag Team Title in

January of 1991. He entered WWF in the early 1990s as Skinner. Keirn also wrestled as Doink the Clown II in 1993. He wrestled with Bobby Eaton as Bad Attitude in the WCW in 1994.

Kelly, Gene *see* Kiniski, Gene

Kelly, Irish Jack (b. 1919; St. Louis, Missouri; 5'11", 225 lbs.) played football at the University of Illinois before entering professional wrestling in the late 1930s.

Kelly, Kevin (Kevin Patrick Wacholz; b. April 17; Oakland, California; 6'5", 271 lbs.) began wrestling in 1985. He was managed by Sherri Martel in the AWA in the late 1980s. He briefly held the Oregon Wrestling Federation Title in 1988. He wrestled as Nailz in the WWF until he was fired in December of 1992. He captured the WWWA Title in Pennsylvania in March of 1993, holding the belt for less than a month. He entered the WCW as the Prisoner in the Spring of 1993 and later wrestled as the Convict.

Kelly, Mike teamed with Pat Kelly as the Kelly Twins, holding the International Tag Team Title in Toronto in June of 1975, and the Canadian Tag Team Title in November of 1975. They also held Gulf Coast Tag Team Title in November of 1977. They teamed to hold NWA Central States Tag Team Title in January of 1981. They also held the WWA Tag Team Title from June of 1981, until they left the promotion in February of the following year. The Kellys wrestled as the Clones to hold the Southern Tag Team Title in July

of 1987. Mike Kelly was injured in an automobile accident in Canada that killed his brother, Pat, and two other wrestlers on July 27, 1988. Mike Kelly teamed with Al Snow to form the Wild Bunch in the early 1990s. They held the Motor City Wrestling U.S. Tag Team Title several times in 1991 and 1992.

Kelly, Pat (d. July 27, 1988) teamed with Mike Kelly as the Kelly Twins, holding the International Tag Team Title in Toronto in June of 1975, and the Canadian Tag Team Title in November of 1975. They also held the Gulf Coast Tag Team Title in November of 1977. They teamed to hold NWA Central States Tag Team Title in January of 1981. They also held WWA Tag Team Title from June of 1981, until they left the promotion in February of the following year. The Kellys wrestled as the Clones to hold the Southern Tag Team Title in July of 1987. Pat Kelly was killed in an automobile accident in Lewisporte, Newfoundland, Canada, with Adrian Adonis and David McKigney on July 27, 1988.

Kendall, Kenny wrestled as Dr. Death in the USWA. He captured the USWA Southern Title in March of 1992.

Kendo the Samurai *see* Riggz, Scotty

Kennedy, Ashley was manager of LPWA champion Lady X in the early 1990s.

Kennedy, Pat *see* Graham, Bobby

Kenneth, Ken (d. 1994; 240

lbs.; New Zealand) held the British Empire Title in Toronto, Canada, in June of 1947. He teamed with Tex McKenzie to hold the Northwest Tag Team Title in Vancouver, Canada, in November of 1955.

Kenny the Stinger *see* Mussolini, Vito

Kent, Bulldog Don (b. 1933, d. June 7, 1993) held the NWA Central States Title in January of 1969. He replaced Roy Heffernan in the Fabulous Kangaroos in the mid-1960s, wrestling with Al Costello. Managed by George Cannon, they captured in NWA Tag Team Title several times in the early 1970s. He held the NWA U.S. Title twice in the mid-1970s and captured the Mid-America Title in 1977. He teamed with Johnny Heffernan (A.K.A. Bob Dellaserra) as the Fabulous Kangaroos to hold the WWC Tag Team Title in Puerto Rico in July of 1982, and the Global Tag Team Title in Florida several times in 1983. Kent teamed with Jerry Graham, Jr. to hold the MWA Tag Team Title in Ohio in 1983. He and Graham also held the WWA Tag Team Title in 1984. Kent also held the WWC North American Title in Puerto Rico in 1984. He and Chris Carter briefly held the tag belts in December of 1987. He died of leukemia on June 7, 1993.

Kentuckians, The *see* Smith, Grizzly & Brown, Luke

Keomuka, Duke (Martin Tanaka; b. 1921, d. June 30, 1991) was an Hawaiian mat star who competed in the 1950s and 1960s. He teamed with Danny Savich to hold the NWA Texas Tag Team Title several times in 1951. He also held the tag belts in 1952, teaming with Ivan Kalmikoff and Mr. Moto. He also held the NWA Texas Title several times in 1951 and 1952. He again held the Texas Title in 1956. He held the Texas tag belts several more times in the 1950s, teaming with Don Evans, Tiny Mills, Tony Martin, Tokyo Joe and John Tolos. He teamed with Sato Keomuka to hold the U.S. Tag Team Title in Cleveland, Ohio, in 1961. He teamed with Mr. Moto to hold the NWA Southern Tag Team Title several times in 1958 and 1959. He teamed with Hiro Matusuda to hold the NWA World Tag Team belts in Florida several times in 1964 and 1965. He held the World Class World Tag Team Title in Texas several times in 1966, teaming with Antonio Inoki and Fritz Von Erich. He was a promoter for the NWA in Florida in the 1980s. He died of heart failure in Las Vegas, Nevada, on June 30, 1991. His son, Pat Tanaka, was also a popular wrestler.

Keomuka, Sato *see* Shibuya, Kenji

Kernodle, Don teamed with Private Jim Nelson to hold the NWA Atlantic Coast Tag Title several times in 1982. Kernodle teamed with Sergeant Slaughter to become NWA World Tag Team Champions in a tournament in September of 1982. They held the title until March of 1983, when they were defeated by Rick Steamboat and Jay Youngblood. Kernodle held the NWA Canadian TV Title in Toronto in October of 1983. Kernodle again became NWA tag champion when he teamed with Bob Orton, Jr. to win a tournament in January of 1984. The duo held the belts until March 4, 1984, when they were defeated by Wahoo McDaniel and Mark Youngblood. Kernodle and Ivan Koloff became tag champions in May of 1984, holding the belts until October of 1984, when they were defeated by Dusty Rhodes and Manny Fernandez.

Kess, Denny (5'11", 239 lbs.) began wrestling in 1980. He teamed with Calypso Jim to hold the WWA Tag Team Title in 1986. The Australian-native wrestled with Al Snow as the New Fabulous Kangaroos in 1994, holding the Global Tag Team Title.

Ketonen, Paavo (Finland) was a leading Finnish wrestler before coming to the United States in 1950. He remained an active competitor for most of the decade.

Keys, Brian (Brian Logan) wrestled as the Hornet in the USWA in 1994.

Khadafy, Abdul *see* Miller, Danny

Khan, Killer (b. March 6) was a leading mat villain in the 1970s and 1980s. He was reviled for breaking Andre the Giant's leg in a match in 1981, an action that led to a lengthy feud with Andre. Khan held the Mid-South Mississippi Title in 1982. He captured the Mid-South Louisiana Title in July of 1982. He was managed by Fred Blassie in the WWF in the early 1980s. He captured the Stampede North Ameri-

can Title in Calgary, Canada, in January of 1984. He held the World Class TV Title in Texas in May of 1984.

Khan, Teijho (Singapore; 6'4", 265 lbs.) began wrestling in 1986. He was active in the Florida area during the mid-1980s. He wrestled with the PWA in the early 1990s, capturing the title in October of 1991.

Khoury, Fred, Sr. *see* Curry, Bull

Khrushchev, Krusher *see* Smash

Kid, The (Sean Waltman; b. July 13, 1972; 6'2", 212 lbs.) was raised in Tampa, Florida. He was trained at Boris Malenko's wrestling school in Florida. He began wrestling with Suncoast Wrestling in Florida in 1989. He was originally known as the Lightning Kid in Global, where he captured the Junior Heavyweight Title in 1991. He engaged in a feud with Chaz while in Global. He held the PWA Light Heavyweight Title in 1990 and 1991. He teamed with Jerry Lynn to hold the PWA Tag Team Title in March of 1993. He debuted in the WWF in April of 1993. He was initially billed as the Cannonball Kid and the Kamikaze Kid before he became known as the 1-2-3 Kid when he defeated Razor Ramon and Irwin R. Schyster in his early matches. He teamed with Marty Janetty to defeat the Quebecers for the WWF Tag Team title on Monday Night Raw on January 10, 1994. The duo lost the title in a return match with the Quebecers on January 17, 1994, in New York City. He reclaimed the title in a tournament on January 22, 1995, teaming with Bob Holly. They lost the tag belts to the Smoking Guns in a match the following day. The Kid subsequently teamed with Razor Ramon, until the duo split and the Kid joined Ted DiBiase's Million Dollar Corporation in late 1995.

Kid Koby *see* Kobayashi, Kuniaki

Kidd, Colin *see* Oborsky, Colin H.

Kido, Osmau (b. February 2, 1950; Kanagawa, Japan; 5'11", 242 lbs.) began wrestling in February of 1969. He wrestled with New Japan from 1972 until 1984, when he entered the UWF. He returned to New Japan in 1992.

Kikuchi, Tsuyoshi (b. November 2, 1964) began wrestling in February of 1988. He competed with All-Japan in the late 1980s and 1990s.

Killer (6', 255 lbs.) began wrestling in 1985. He teamed with Psycho as the Texas Hangmen. They won the WWC and USWA tag championships in 1990.

Kim, Il (Kintaro Oki) held the WWA Title in Los Angeles in May of 1967. He teamed with Mr. Moto to hold the WWA Tag Team Title in 1967. Wrestling as Kintaro Oki, he held the Japanese Wrestling Association International Title in December of 1972.

Kim Duk also wrestled as Tiger Toguchi and Tiger Cheung Lee. He teamed with Stan Kowalski to hold the U.S. Tag Team Title in

Louisiana in September of 1973. He teamed with Yasu Fuji to hold the NWA Central States Tag Team Title in March of 1983. He held the WWC Caribbean Title in Puerto Rico in September of 1990.

Kimala *see* Kamala

Kimchee *see* Lombardi, Steve

Kimura, Masao *see* Kimura, Rusher

Kimura, Rusher (Masao Kimura; b. June 30, 1941) began wrestling in April of 1965. He wrestled as Crusher Kimura in IWE and Canada during the 1970s and early 1980s. He briefly wrestled as Mr. Sun in Los Angeles in 1982. He entered All-Japan wrestling as Rusher Kimura in November of 1984.

King, Moondog *see* White, Sailor

King, Rex (Mark Smith; Dallas, Texas; 5'11", 240 lbs.) began wrestling in 1987. He captured the NWA Pacific Northwest Title in October of 1989. He joined Steve Doll in the Southern Rockers tag team, replacing Scott Peterson in the Summer of 1989. King and Doll held the Pacific Northwest Tag Team Title several times in 1989 and 1990. They subsequently became known as Simply Divine. They held the USWA Tag Team Title several times in early 1990. King also held the tag title with Joey Maggs in June of 1990. King teamed with Ricky Santana to hold the WWC Tag Team Title in Puerto Rico several times in 1991. King and Doll recaptured the USWA belts in April of 1993. They wrestled as Timothy Well and Steve

Dunn in the team known as Well-Done in the WWF in 1994. They left the WWF the following year.

King, Sonny teamed with Chief Jay Strongbow to capture the WWWF Tag Team Title from Baron Scicluna and King Curtis in May of 1972. They lost the belts the following month to Mr. Fuji and Toru Tanaka. He teamed with Frank Morrell to hold the Southern Tag Team Title in September of 1980. King was seriously injured in a stabbing incident outside of the Charlotte Coliseum in North Carolina in early 1982. He recovered from his injuries and returned to the ring in Memphis later in the year. King managed the Samoans in the NWA in late 1982. He managed Arn Anderson and Jerry Stubbs to the NWA Southeastern Tag Championship in 1984.

King Cobra (Memphis, Tennessee; 6', 240 lbs.) began wrestling in 1980. He held the Mid-America Title in 1982. He wrestled often in the USWA, briefly capturing the Unified Title from Jerry Lawler in 1989.

King Kong (Scott Thompson) teamed with Awesome Kong as the Colossal Kongs in the WCW in 1994.

Kiniski, Gene (b. 1925, 6'5", 285 lbs.) was a pro football player with Edmonton in the Canadian League. He teamed with Lord James Blears to hold the NWA World Tag Team Title in San Francisco several times in 1955. He wrestled in the mid-1950s as Gene Kelly, holding the NWA Texas Title in August of 1956. He teamed with Len Crosby to hold the NWA Texas Tag Team Title in September of 1956. He teamed with Fritz Von Erich to hold the Canadian Open Tag Team Title in Toronto in October of 1957. He held the British Empire Title in Toronto, Canada, several times in the late 1950s. He teamed with Dick the Bruiser to briefly hold the NWA Tag Team Title in Indiana in 1960. Kiniski replaced Len Montana as Hard Boiled Haggerty's partner and holder of the AWA World Tag Team Title in March of 1961. They lost the belts to Wilbur Snyder and Leo Nomellini in May of 1961. Kiniski defeated Verne Gagne for the AWA Title in July of 1961. He lost the belt back to Gagne in a rematch the following month. He also reclaimed the tag team belts with Haggerty in a rematch with Snyder and Nomellini on July 19, 1961. In August of 1961 he split with Haggerty, and lost a singles bout against his former partner the following month. He held the Pacific Coast Tag Team Title in Vancouver, Canada, several times in 1962, teaming with Killer Kowalski and Hard Boiled Haggerty. He teamed with Frank "Mr. X" Townsend to hold the Canadian Tag Team Title in February of 1963. Kiniski teamed with Waldo Von Erich to hold the WWWF U.S. Tag Team Title in 1964. He held the Hawaiian Title in July of 1964. He teamed with Don Leo Jonathan to again hold the Canadian Tag Team Title in January of 1965. He held the WWA Title for several months in late 1965. Kiniski defeated Lou Thesz for the NWA Heavyweight Title in St. Louis on January 7, 1966.

He lost the title to Dory Funk, Jr. in Tampa, Florida, on February 12, 1969. He subsequently held the North American Title in Honolulu. He held the Pacific Coast Title in Vancouver, Canada, several times in the early 1970s. He regained the Hawaiian Title in February of 1972. He held the NWA Missouri Title from March until October of 1973. He subsequently retired to Vancouver, British Columbia. He is the father of wrestlers Kelly and Nick Kiniski.

Kiniski, Kelly (6'3", 260 lbs.) is the son of Gene Kiniski. He played football at West Texas State in the late 1970s. He began his professional career in Calgary, Canada, in August of 1980. He was managed by Madusa Miceli in the early 1980s in the AWA. He teamed with One Man Gang to hold the NWA Atlantic Coast Tag Title in 1983. He held the World Class TV Title in February of 1984.

Kirby, Roger "Rip" teamed with the Viking to hold the NWA Central States Tag Team Title in July of 1968. He held the NWA Pacific Northwest Title several times in 1969. He teamed with Beauregard to hold the Pacific Northwest tag belts in December of 1969. He again held the tag belts with Rock Hunter in early 1971. He held the NWA Central States Title in 1971. He defeated Danny Hodge for the NWA World Junior Heavyweight Title in May of 1971. He lost the belt to Ramon Torres the following September. He again held the Central States belt in 1972 and 1974. He also reclaimed the Central States tag belts in 1972

and 1974, teaming with Black Angus Campbell, Harley Race and Lord Alfred Hayes. He teamed with Buddy Colt to hold the NWA Georgia Tag Team Title in December of 1974. He teamed with Harley Race to hold the NWA Florida Tag Team Title in April of 1975. He held the belts several times during the year, teaming with J.J. Dillon and Rip Hawk. Kirby held the Mid-America Title in June of 1976. He was co-holder of the WWA Tag Team Title several times in 1979 and 1980, teaming with Igor Volkoff, Paul Christy and Jerry Valiant. He and Valiant also held the Southern Tag Team Title in November of 1980 and the NWA Central States Tag Team Title in March of 1982. He again held the Central States belts with Jerry Brown in May of 1982. He teamed with Abdullah the Great as the Sheiks to recapture the Central States title in July of 1983. Kirby retired to Kansas City in the mid 1980s.

Kirchner, Corporal (Ft. Bragg, North Carolina; 6'1", 260 lbs.) began wrestling in the WWF in 1984.

Kirk, Malcolm "King Kong" (d. August 24, 1987) was a British wrestler during the 1980s. He was killed during a match with Shirley "Big Daddy" Crabtree in Great Yarmouth, England on August 24, 1987.

Kirkpatrick, Red (b. 1922; Brooklyn, New York; 5'10", 210 lbs.) played football at Tusculum College before becoming a professional wrestling in the mid-1940s. He was known as the Kiropractic Killer in the ring and was a leading wrestler in the 1950s.

Kiropractic Killer, The *see* Kirkpatrick, Red

Kiser, Jacob "Jack" (b. March 8, 1910, d. May 19, 1991) was born in Blodgett, Washington. He began wrestling professionally in 1936. He competed in the ring, primarily in the Pacific Northwest, for the next thirty years. He held the Pacific Coast Light Heavyweight Title in 1943 and again in 1954. He teamed with Jim Laroc to hold the Northwest Tag Team Title in Vancouver, Canada, in 1954. He retired in 1965 to work as a security guard. He died in a Portland, Oregon, hospital on May 19, 1991.

Kit Fox, Chief teamed with Chief Big Heart during the 1970s. His wrestling career ended when he was seriously injured in an automobile accident in the early 1970s.

Kiwis, The *see* Bushwhacker Butch Miller & Bushwhacker Luke Williams

Klaus, Zanta *see* Bradley, Boo

Kleen, Mr. teamed with Whipper Billy Watson to hold the Pacific Coast Tag Team Title in Vancouver, Canada, in March of 1962. He held the NWA Southern Title in Florida in February of 1973.

Kleen, Mondo (6'3", 270 lbs.) began wrestling in 1987. He is Chinese native. He held the IWF championship in Florida in 1991. He wrestled as Damian Demento in the WWF in 1992.

Klein, Lou (d. October 11, 1979) wrestled as Lou Bastien in the WWWF in the early 1960s. He teamed with Red Bastien to capture the WWWF U.S. Tag Team Title from Jerry and Eddie Graham in April of 1960. They lost the belts to the Fabulous Kangaroos in August of 1960. The duo won the AWA tag belts twice in 1961.

Klondike Bill teamed with Ronnie Etchison to hold the NWA Central States Tag Team Title in January of 1968. He teamed with Skull Murphy to hold the JWA Asian Tag Team Title in July of 1968. He held the Hawaiian Title in August of 1968. He teamed with Luke Brown to hold the U.S. Tag Team Title in Louisiana in January of 1974.

Klondike Mike *see* Shaw, Mike

Knapp, Charles (5'9", 226 lbs.) began wrestling in 1991. He held the Global Junior Heavyweight Title several times in 1993 and 1994.

Knight, Dennis *see* Godwinn, Phinnius

Knighton, Brian *see* Rotten, Axl

Knobs, Brian (Brian Yandrisovitz; b. May 6, 1964; Allentown, Pennsylvania; 6'1", 295 lbs.) trained under Verne Gagne and began wrestling with Jerry Sags in the AWA in October of 1985. They became the Nasty Boys and won the Southern Tag Team Title in Memphis in August of 1987. They held the belts several times during the year. They subsequently wrestled in Florida until 1990 when they entered the WCW. They joined the WWF later in the year, where they were managed by Jimmy Hart. They defeated the Hart Foundation for the WWF tag belts at Wrestlemania VII on March 24, 1991, and lost the belts to the Legion of Doom at Summer-Slam '91 on August 26, 1991. The duo broke with Hart in October of 1992 and began a feud with Money, Inc. They subsequently wrestled in the WCW. They won the WCW Tag Team Championship in a match against Arn Anderson and Paul Roma on September 19, 1993. They lost the title the following month to Marcus Alexander Bagwell and Too Cold Scorpio on October 4, 1993. They regained the title from Bagwell and Scorpio several weeks later on October 24, 1993, and held the belts until their defeat by Cactus Jack and Kevin Sullivan on May 22, 1994. They defeated Harlem Heat for the WCW Tag Team Title at Slamboree '95 in St. Petersburg, Florida, on May 21, 1995. They lost the title in a rematch the same month.

Kobashi, Kenta (b. March 27, 1967; Tokyo, Japan; 6'2", 260 lbs.) began wrestling in with All-Japan in February of 1988. A popular Japanese wrestler, Kobashi often teamed with Mitsuharu Misawa.

Kobayashi, Kuniaki (b. January 11, 1956; Nagano, Japan; 5'10", 211 lbs.) began wrestling in December of 1973, competing with New Japan. He wrestled as Kid Koby in Los Angeles and Mexico in the early 1980s, capturing the NWA Americas Title in Los Angeles in July of 1982. He subsequently wrestled with All-Japan before returning to New Japan in 1987.

Kohen, Sam (b. 1911; Paterson, New Jersey; 5'8", 200 lbs.) began his career as a boxer before turning to professional wrestling. He was a popular mat star for several decades, through the 1950s.

Kohler, Fred (b. 1903, d. August 24, 1969) was an amateur wrestler from 1916. He was involved in wrestling as a manager and promoter. He was the leading promoter in Chicago during the 1940s and 1950s.

Kojika, Shinya teamed with Motoshi Okuma to hold the World Tag Team Title in Tennessee in 1967. Wrestling as the Great Kojika, he teamed with Don Carson to hold the NWA Americas Tag Team Title in Los Angeles in October of 1969. He also held the NWA Americas Title in December of 1969.

Kojima, Satoshi (b. September 14, 1970) began wrestling with New Japan in July of 1991.

Kokina *see* Yokozuna

Kole *see* Booker T.

Kollins, Mike (b. 1914; Boston, Massachusetts; 5'11", 220 lbs.) was often billed as the Grappling Greek. He began wrestling in the early 1930s and remained a popular mat star through the 1950s.

Koloff, Ivan (Jim Perris; b. August 25; Moscow, Russia; 5'11", 249 lbs.) began wrestling professionally in 1961. He wrestled as Red McNulty early in his career. He was managed by Lou Albano in the WWWF in the early 1970s. He defeated Bruno Sammartino for the

WWWF Title in New York on January 18, 1971. He was defeated for the belt the following month by Pedro Morales on February 8, 1971. He teamed with Pat Patterson to hold the NWA Florida Tag Team Title in July of 1977. Koloff held the belt several more times during the year, teaming with Mr. Saito. He held the NWA Southern Title in Florida in 1977. He captured the WWA title from Dick the Bruiser in June of 1977, losing a rematch the following December. Koloff and Ole Anderson captured the NWA Georgia Tag Team Title several times in 1978 and 1979. He also held the Georgia belts with Alexi Smirnoff several times in early 1980. Koloff teamed with Ray Stevens to capture the NWA World Tag Team Title from Paul Jones and the Masked Superstar in February of 1981. They lost the belts in a rematch the following month. Koloff held the NWA Eastern State Title from April until October of 1981. He also held the NWA Mid-Atlantic Title several times in 1984. He held the NWA Canadian Title in Toronto in April of 1984. Koloff teamed with Don Kernodle to hold the tag title from May until October of 1984. He teamed with Nikita Koloff as the Russians and captured the tag title in March of 1985. They added Krusher Khrushchev to create a three-man team, until losing the belts to the Rock 'n' Roll Express in July of 1985. Ivan and Nikita Koloff returned to take the belts in October of 1985, but were again defeated by the Rock 'n' Roll Express the following month. Koloff and Khrushchev held the NWA U.S. Tag Title from Sep-

tember of 1986 until the following December. Managed by Paul Jones, Koloff teamed with Dick Murdoch to recapture the U.S. Tag Title in March of 1987. They held the belts until the following month, when Murdoch was suspended. Koloff held the UWF TV Title in Oklahoma in November of 1987.

Koloff, Nikita (Scott Simpson; b. March 9; Moscow, Russia; 6'2", 275 lbs.) began wrestling in June of 1984. He was billed as the "nephew" of Ivan Koloff. He teamed with Ivan in the NWA, defeating Dusty Rhodes and Manny Fernandez for the tag title in Fayetteville, North Carolina, on March 18, 1985. They lost the belts to the Rock 'n' Roll Express in July of 1985 and exchanged the title several times before losing to the Rock 'n' Roll Express in November of 1985. Nikita Koloff defeated Magnum T.A. for the U.S. belt in Charlotte, North Carolina, on August 17, 1986. He unified the National and U.S. Titles in a match with Wahoo McDaniel on September 28, 1986. He lost the title to Lex Luger in Greensboro, North Carolina, on July 11, 1987. He captured the NWA TV Title from Tully Blanchard in July of 1987, losing the belt to Mike Rotunda the following January. He left wrestling in the late 1980s to care for his wife, Mandi, who was suffering from Hodgkin's disease. He returned to the ring after his wife's death, competing on the independent circuit and the AWA. He returned to the WCW in 1991, where he feuded with Lex Luger and Sting.

Koloff, Vladimir (Carl Brantley; Moscow, Russia; 6'4", 265 lbs.), born in North Wilkesboro, N.C., began wrestling in 1990. He often teamed with Ivan Koloff, who was billed as his "uncle." He gained the IWA Title in Ohio by winning a battle royal in October of 1992 but lost title the following March.

Kong, Aja (5'8", 220 lbs.) is of Japanese and African-American descent. She was a leading wrestler in Japan from the early 1990s. She captured the All-Japan WWWA Women's Title in October of 1992.

Konnan el Barbaro (Charles Ashenoff; Mexico City, Mexico; b. 1965; 5'10", 237 lbs.) began wrestling in 1987. He is a popular mat performer in Mexico, holding the EMLL Heavyweight Title in June of 1991. He wrestled with AAA Lucha libre from May of 1992. He held the IWC championship in 1995 and also entered WCW during the year.

Konnan 2000 *see* Putski, Scott

Kopa, Tito teamed with Bill Savage to hold the NWA Pacific Northwest Tag Team Title for several months from February of 1961.

Korchenko, Korstia held the Mid-America Title in November of 1984.

Koshinaka, Shiro (b. September 4, 1958; Tokyo, Japan; 6'1", 217 lbs.) began wrestling with All-Japan in March of 1979. He competed in Mexico as Samurai Shiro from 1982 until 1984. He subsequently returned to Japan, where he wrestled with New Japan.

Kostas, Johnny held the NWA Pacific Northwest Tag Team Title several times in 1967, teaming with Jim Osborne and Dean Ho. He teamed with Don Leo Jonathan to hold the Canadian Tag Team Title in September of 1968.

Kosti, John *see* Gadaski, George

Kostolias, Ionias (b. 1925; Messinas, Greece; 6'1", 228 lbs.) was born in Greece, but lived most of his life in South America. He held the Argentine championship several times in 1947 and 1948. He subsequently competed in the United States, and remained a popular competitor during the 1950s.

Kovac, Karl teamed with the Warlord to hold the NWA Central States Tag Team Title in June of 1987. He relinquished the belt later in the month when he left the NWA. He teamed with Mr. Wrestling #2 to hold the Missouri Wrestling Federation Tag Team Title several times in 1992 and 1993.

Kovacs, Sandor (b. 1921; Columbus, Ohio; 6'; 215 lbs.) came to the United States from Hungary in the mid-1930s. He trained with Canadian champion Cliff Chilcott before becoming a professional wrestler in the early 1940s. He was a popular scientific wrestler through the 1950s. He teamed with Johnny Barend to hold the Hawaiian Tag Team Title in September of 1955. He teamed with Dan Miller to hold the Canadian Tag Team Title in November of 1962. Kovacs was also promoter of the NWA's affiliate in Vancouver, Canada.

Koverly, George held the Pacific Coast Title in San Francisco several times in 1944 and 1945.

Kowalski, Walter "Killer" (Wladek Kowalski; b. October 13, 1926; Detroit, Michigan; 6'7", 275 lbs.) was born in Windsor, Canada, of Polish parentage. He began wrestling professionally in 1947. He held the NWA Texas Title in August of 1950. He teamed with Hans Hermann to hold the Pacific Coast Tag Team Title in 1951. He also held the NWA Central States Title in 1951. He held the AWA Title in Montreal, Canada, several times in the early 1950s. He held the Pacific Coast Title in San Francisco in May of 1958. He also held the Big Time Wrestling Title in Massachusetts in 1958. He teamed with Ox Anderson to hold the Pacific Coast Tag Team Title in Vancouver, Canada, in August of 1961. He also held the tag belts with Gene Kiniski in January of 1962. Kowalski teamed with Bob Geigel to beat Larry Hennig and Duke Hoffman for the AWA tag championship in February of 1962. They lost the belts to Art and Stan Neilson in March of 1962. Kowalski teamed with Gorilla Monsoon to win the win the WWWF U.S. Tag Team Title from Skull Murphy and Brute Bernard in November of 1963. He held the IWA Championship in Australia several times in the early 1960s. They lost the belts the following month to Chris and John Tolos. Kowalski held the U.S. Title in Honolulu in late 1965. He held the NWA Americas Title in Los Angeles in January of 1972. Kowalski remained an active competitor through the 1970s, teaming with John Studd as the Executioners to win the WWWF Tag Team Title from Tony Parisi and Louis Cerdan in May of 1976. They were stripped of the title in October of 1976 and lost the belts to Chief Jay Strongbow and Billy White Wolf in a tournament the following December. Kowalski wrestled and promoted in the IWF in Massachusetts in the early 1980s. He retired to run a wrestling school in Reading, Massachusetts.

Kowalski, Stan teamed with Tiny Mills as Murder Inc. and were awarded the AWA Tag Team Title in 1959. They exchanged the belts with Butch Levy and Frank Townsend, and Verne Gagne and Leo Nomellini before their reign ended finally in October of 1960, when they were defeated by Hard Boiled Haggerty and Len Montana. He and Tiny Mills also captured the Canadian Open Tag Team Title in Toronto in December of 1960. He teamed with Kim Duk to hold the U.S. Tag Team Title in Louisiana in September of 1973. Wrestling as the Masked Destroyer, he held the NWA Southern Title in Florida in October of 1975. He teamed with Black Jack Daniels to hold the NWA Southern Tag Team Title in Florida in February of 1967.

Kox, K.O *see* Sweetan, Bob

Kox, Killer Karl (Amarillo, Texas; 250 lbs.) held the Texas Brass Knucks Title several times in 1964. He held the MSWA North American Title in October of 1975. He also held the U.S. Tag Team Title in Louisiana with Dick Murdoch in October of 1975. He held the U.S.

Tag Team Title in Louisiana several times in 1976, teaming with Bob Sweetan and Ken Patera. He held the NWA Florida Title in February of 1978. He was managed by Bobby Heenan when he held the NWA Georgia Title in September of 1979. He teamed with Takachiho (A.K.A. The Great Kabuki) to hold the NWA Central States Tag Team Title in June of 1980. He held the NWA Central States Title in July of 1980. He held the Mid-South Mississippi Title in November of 1980. He held the NWA Southeastern Title several times in the early 1980s.

Kozak, Jerry teamed with Nick Kozak to hold the NWA Texas Tag Team Title in September of 1959. They also held the Hawaiian Tag Team Title in May of 1960. He held the NWA Texas Junior Heavyweight Title in June of 1962. He and Nick Kozak held the Texas World Tag Team Title for several months from March of 1963.

Kozak, Nick held the NWA Pacific Northwest Title in January of 1958. He teamed with Al Kashey to capture the NWA Pacific Northwest Tag Team Title in March of 1959. He teamed with Jerry Kozak to hold the NWA Texas Tag Team Title in September of 1959. He also held the NWA Texas Title in December of 1959. He and Jerry Kozak held the Hawaiian Tag Team Title in May of 1960. He held the Texas World Tag Team Title for several months from March of 1963. He held the U.S. Title in Honolulu in January of 1966. He teamed with Dory Dixon to hold the World Class Texas Tag Team Title in July of

1966. He held the NWA Georgia Title in 1967. He also held the NWA Florida Title in September of 1968.

Kozak, Steve (b. 1919; Montreal, Canada; 5'6", 250 lbs.) was a leading amateur wrestler in Canada for over a decade before turning pro in the late 1940s. He remained a popular mat star during the 1950s.

Krauser, Karl *see* Kalmikoff, Karol

Kroffat, Dan (Phil Lafond; b. 1960; 5'11", 235 lbs.) began wrestling in Canada in 1983 as Phil Lafleur. He soon became known in the ring as Dan Kroffat. He held the Canadian International Tag Team Title in Montreal several times in the mid-1980s, teaming with Tom Zenk and Armand Rougeau. He teamed with Tama the Islander to hold the WWC Tag Team Title in Puerto Rico in January of 1989. He became a leading star with All-Japan in 1992, teaming with Doug Furnas as Can-Am Connection to hold the New Japan Asian tag title on three occasions.

Kronus *see* Eliminator Kronus

Kruger, Jack *see* Hassan, Sheik Ali

Krupp, Killer Karl (d. 1995; Mannheim, Germany; 256 lbs.) held the NWF North American Title in 1973. He teamed with Kurt Von Steiger to hold the NWA Pacific Northwest Tag Team Title in February of 1974. He was the NWA Southern Champion in Florida several times in 1975. Known for his claw holds, he was a leading villain in the Texas area in the late 1970s.

He teamed with El Mongol to hold the Southern Tag Team Title in July of 1980.

Kruskamp, Hardy (b. 1910, d. November 12, 1994; Los Angeles, California; 6', 225 lbs.) played football at Ohio State before he began wrestling in the early 1930s. He remained a popular mat star through the 1950s.

Kudo, Kiman (b. 1907; Honolulu, Hawaii; 5'5", 190 lbs.) was a native of Japan. He began wrestling in the late 1930s, and was known for his small size and judo moves. He held the Hawaiian Title in 1940.

Kulkovich, Henry (Henry Kulky; August 11, 1911, d. February 12, 1965; Warsaw, Poland; 5'11", 210 lbs.) was born in Hastings-on-the-Hudson, New York. He claimed to be an amateur wrestling champion in Poland. He was discovered by Stanislaus Zbyszko, who trained him and took him to South America to compete. Kulkovich was successful in Argentina, and came to the United States in the late 1940s. He was known in the ring as Bomber Kulkovich and the Polish Wildman. He also began a career in films in the late 1940s, appearing in numerous features including *A Likely Story* (1947), *A Foreign Affair* (1948) *Alias a Gentleman* (1948) *Call Northside 777* (1948), *Alias the Champ* (1949), *The Red Danube* (1949), *Tarzan's Magic Fountain* (1949), *Bandits of El Dorado* (1949), *Mighty Joe Young* (1949), *Wabash Avenue* (1940), *South Sea Sinner* (1950), *Bodyhold* (1950), *Jiggs and Maggie Out West* (1950), *You Never Can Tell* (1951), *The Guy Who Came Back* (1951), *The Kid from Amarillo* (1951), *The World in His Arms* (1952), *Gobs and Gals* (1952), *No Holds Barred* (1952), *Target Hong Kong* (1952), *What Price Glory?* (1952), *Red Skies of Montana* (1952), *The 5,000 Fingers of Dr. T.* (1953), *Powder River* (1953), *The Robe* (1953), *Down Among the Sheltering Palms* (1953), *The Charge at Feather River* (1953), *A Star Is Born* (1954), *Tobor the Great* (1954), *Fireman Save My Child* (1954), *Yukon Vengeance* (1954), *Hell and High Water* (1954), *The Steel Cage* (1954), *To Hell and Back* (1955), *Jail Busters* (1955), *Love Me or Leave Me* (1955), *The Girl in the Red Velvet Swing* (1955), *Prince of Players* (1955), *New York Confidential* (1955), *Abbott and Costello Meet the Keystone Kops* (1955), *Illegal* (1955), *Sierra Stranger* (1957), *Compulsion* (1959), *Up Periscope* (1959), *The Gunfight at Dodge City* (1959), *Guns of the Timberland* (1960) and *A Global Affair* (1964). He was also a popular television actor, appearing regularly in such series as *The Life of Riley*, *Hennesey* and *Voyage to the Bottom of the Sea*. Kulky died of a heart attack in Oceanside, California, on February 12, 1965.

Kulky, Henry *see* Kulkovich, Henry

Kurgis, Sonny (b. 1924; Columbus, Ohio) began wrestling in the mid-1940s. He remained an active competitor during the 1950s.

Kuroneko *see* Black Cat

Kurosawa (Manabu Nakanishi; b. January 22, 1967; 6'1", 250 lbs.) began wrestling in Japan as Manabu Nakanishi in October of 1992. He entered the WCW in July 1995 as

Kurosawa,♠ a member of Col. Parker's Stud Stable. He broke Road Warrior Hawk's arm after a bout at Clash of the Champions in 1995.

Kwan, Yoshi *see* Champion, Chris

Kwang *see* Vega, Savio

Kwango, Johnny (b. April 20, 1920, d. January 19, 1994) was born in London. He began wrestling in the 1940s and competed in matches throughout the world. He was one of Great Britain's leading mat stars in the 1950s and 1960s, known for his flying head butt and jaw hold. Kwango retired from the ring in the late 1960s, but remained active in the sport as a referee and trainer.

Kwariani, Kola (b. 1900, d. 19??) was a large bald-headed Russian grappler who wrestled in matches throughout the world from the 1920s through the early 1950s.

Kyle, Mark "Killer" (Atlanta, Georgia; 6'2", 303 lbs.) wrestled in Smoky Mountain Wrestling from 1993, where he feuded with Boo Bradley. Kyle was managed by Jim Cornette in the region.

Ladd, Ernie (Houston, Texas; 6'9", 315 lbs.) played with the San Diego Chargers, Houston Oilers and Kansas City Chief in the National Football League in the 1960s before becoming a professional wrestler. Known as the Big Cat, he held the NWA Americas Title in Los Angeles for several months from July of 1972, and again in July of 1974. He teamed with Baron Von Raschke to hold the WWA Tag Team Title for several months in 1973. Ladd

held the NWF North American Title in 1974. He held the NWA Florida Title in July of 1977 and held the NWA Southern Title in Florida in 1978. He also held the MSWA North American Title several times in 1978. He teamed with the Assassin to hold the U.S. Tag Team Title in Louisiana in April of 1978. He teamed with Ole Anderson to capture the NWA Georgia Tag Team Title in October of 1979. He teamed with Bruiser Brody to hold the NWA Central States Tag Team Title in February of 1980. He briefly held the WWA Title in November of 1980 and the World Class Championship in Texas in May of 1981. A leading rulebreaker, Ladd was often managed by the Grand Wizard and engaged in a vicious feud with Andre the Giant.

Lady X *see* Leather, Peggy Lee

LaFitte, Jean Pierre (Carl Joseph Yvon Ouellet; b. December 30; Montreal, Quebec, Canada; 5'11", 255 lbs.) began wrestling in 1992. Known as Pierre, he teamed with Jacques Rougeau as the Quebecers in July of 1993. They defeated the Steiner Brothers for the WWF Tag Team title in September of 1993. They lost the belt to Marty Jannetty and the 1-2-3 Kid on Monday Night Raw on January 10, 1994. They regained the title in a rematch the following week on January 17, 1994. They again lost the belts on March 29, 1994, in a match in London, England, to Men on a Mission. They regained the belts once more two days later in Sheffield, England, when they defeated Men on a Mission on March 31, 1994. The Quebecers lost the belts again on April 26, 1994, in a match with the Head Shrinkers in Burlington, Vermont. Pierre returned to the WWF in May of 1995, wrestling as the pirate, Jean Pierre LaFitte.

Lafleur, Phil *see* Kroffat, Dan

Lafond, Phil *see* Kroffat, Dan

Lagarde, Karloff was a leading Mexican wrestler from the 1950s. He held the Mexican National Welterweight Title several times in the late 1950s and early 1960s. He again held the welterweight championship in late 1972.

Laine, Frankie teamed with Moondog Mayne to hold the NWA Pacific Northwest Tag Team Title in March of 1970. He also held the tag belts with Bobby Nichols and Jimmy Snuka in 1971. He held the Hawaiian Title in February of 1971. He held the NWA Americas Title in Los Angeles in December of 1971. He held the Stampede North American Title in Calgary, Canada, in 1975. He also held the Stampede International Tag Team Title in 1975, teaming with Les Thornton. He held the Mid-America Title in July of 1983.

Lancaster, Frank (6'1", 239 lbs.) began wrestling in 1982. Known as the Thumper, he held the World Class World Tag Team Title with Eric Embry in June of 1986, and with Brian Adias in October of 1987. He also wrestled as one of the Dirty White Boys. Lancaster teamed with Wendell Cooley as the Heartbreakers to hold the WWC Tag Team Title in Puerto Rico several times in 1991 and 1992.

Lancaster, Jim (6'1", 360 lbs.) began wrestling in the WWF in 1972. He was also known as Man Mountain Lancaster.

Landell, Buddy (William Landel; b. August 17, 1961; Los Angeles, California; 6', 236 lbs.) began wrestling in 1980. Known as the Nature Boy, he has wrestled in WCW, Global, Tri-State and USWA. He held the WWC North American Title in Puerto Rico in 1983. He held the Mid-America Title several times in 1983 and 1985. Landell held the NWA National Title from October of 1985 until leaving the promotion the following month. He held the Southern Heavyweight Title several times in mid-1986. He held the Tri-State Title in New Jersey in 1991. Landel wrestled with Smoky Mountain Wrestling, holding the title from April until August of 1995. He also appeared in the USWA during the mid-1990s.

Lane, Bobby held the NWA Americas Title in Los Angeles in January of 1982. He teamed with Killer Kim to hold the NWA Americas Tag Team Title in April of 1982.

Lane, Stan (b. August 5, 1954; Myrtle Beach, California; 6'1", 225 lbs.) was born in Greensboro, North Carolina. He began wrestling in 1978. He teamed with Bryan St. John to hold the NWA Florida Tag Team Title several times in late 1979. Managed by Jimmy Hart, he teamed with Koko Ware to hold the Southern Tag Team Title in September of 1981. He also held the tag belts with Ron Bass in July of 1982. He teamed with Steve Keirn as the Fabulous

Ones in the early 1980s. Sometimes managed by Jackie Fargo, they captured the CWA Tag Team Title several times in late 1983. They teamed to win the U.S. Tag Team Title several times in late 1986. He joined the Midnight Express with Bobby Eaton in the NWA in April of 1987. Lane and Eaton captured the NWA World Tag Title from Arn Anderson and Tully Blanchard in September of 1988. They lost the belts to the Road Warriors the following month. He and Steve Keirn reunited as the Fabulous Ones to capture the USWA Tag Team Title in January of 1991. He teamed with Tom Prichard as the Heavenly Bodies in Smoky Mountain Wrestling to hold the Tag Team Title several times in 1992 and 1993. Lane left Smoky Mountain Wrestling in 1993 and subsequently entered the WWF as a commentator.

Lane, Tommy teamed with Mike Davis as the Rock 'n' Roll RPMS in the mid-1980s. They held the WWC Tag Team Title in Puerto Rico in March of 1986, and the Southern Tag Team Title several times in 1987. They captured the CWA Tag Team Title in August of 1988.

Lanza, Blackjack was managed by Bobby Heenan in the WWA when he won the championship in December of 1967. He later teamed with Blackjack Mulligan in the early 1970s, capturing the WWA Tag Team Title in December of 1971. Managed by Bobby Heenan, they held the belts until the following December. They also held the World Class American Tag Team Title in 1973. Lanza briefly captured the World Class Championship in Texas from Fritz Von Erich in December of 1974. He and Mulligan defeated Dominic Denucci and Pat Barrett for the WWWF World Tag Team belts in August of 1975. They were managed by Lou Albano in the WWWF, and dropped the belts to Tony Parisi and Louis Cerdan the following November. He subsequently went to the AWA where he teamed with Bobby Duncum to defeat Crusher and Dick the Bruiser for the AWA Tag Team Title in July of 1976. They held the belts for nearly a year before being dethroned by Jim Brunzell and Greg Gagne in July of 1977.

LaRance, Jacques (b. 1909; Copper City, Utah; 5'11", 234 lbs.) began wrestling in the mid-1930s. He often teamed with his brother, Jules. They remained a popular ring duo through the 1950s.

LaRance, Jules (b. 1910; d. 19??; Copper City, Utah; 5'10", 230 lbs.) began wrestling in the mid-1930s. He often teamed with his brother, Jack. They remained a popular ring duo through the 1950s.

LaSalle, Pierre teamed with Maurice Vachon to hold the NWA Texas Tag Team Title in early 1955.

Lassartes, Pierre *see* Freeman, Herb

Latham, Larry *see* Moondog Spot

Latin Connection, The *see* Santana, Ricky & Madril, Al

Latin Lover (Victor Resindez)

teamed with Heavy Metal to hold the Mexican National Tag Team Title in September of 1994.

Lauer, David *see* Wippleman, Harvey

Laughlin, Tom *see* Dreamer, Tommy

Lauper, Cyndi (b. 1953) was a popular singer in the early 1980s. She served as Wendi Richter's manager at her WWF Women's Title defense at Wrestlemania I in March of 1985.

Laurinaitis, John *see* Ace, Johnny

Laurinaitis, Joseph *see* Animal

Laurinaitis, Marc *see* Terminator, The

Lawler, Brian *see* Christopher, Brian

Lawler, Jerry (b. November 12, 1949; Memphis, Tennessee; 6', 234 lbs.) was an artist and radio disk jockey when he first wrestled professionally in West Memphis, Arkansas, in 1970. He was initially unsuccessful as a competitor, but soon began to win matches and fans. Managed by Sam Bass, Lawler teamed with Jim White to hold the Southern Tag Team Title several times in 1973. They also held the U.S. Tag Team Title in Louisiana in September of 1974. Lawler first captured the Southern Heavyweight Title in 1974. He held the title nearly forty times over the next thirteen years, competing against such wrestlers as Jackie Fargo, Bob Armstrong, Jack Brisco, Jimmy Valiant, Bill Dundee, Dutch Mantell, Ka-mala, Nick Bockwinkel, Man Mountain Link, Jesse Ventura, King Kong Bundy, Eddie Gilbert, Randy Savage, Bam Bam Bigelow, Austin Idol and Brickhouse Brown. Lawler again held the tag belts in April of 1976, teaming with Plowboy Frazier. Lawler was injured by Jos LeDuc in a match in Memphis in 1978 when he was thrown from the ring and severed his right thigh muscle on the announcer's table. Lawler defeated Billy Graham for the CWA World Title in November of 1979. Lawler brought musician Jimmy Hart into wrestling as his manager in late 1979. He subsequently broke with Hart while recuperating from a broken leg. In 1981 Lawler was attacked by Jimmy Valiant during a bout with Harley Race. Valiant smashed a beer bottle over Lawler's head and stabbed him with the broken glass. Lawler wrestled comedian and self-proclaimed Inter-Gender Wrestling Champion Andy Kaufman in 1981. Lawler used the pile-driver on the comedian and injured his neck. The two appeared on several television shows including *Late Night with David Letterman*. Lawler teamed with Austin Idol to briefly hold the CWA Tag Team Title in August of 1983. He held the CWA International Title several times in 1984, defeating Austin Idol and Ken Patera. Lawler engaged in a feud with Eddie Gilbert in early 1985. He defeated Gilbert in a match in February of 1985 that resulted in Gilbert's manager, Jimmy Hart, being forced to leave the area. Lawler teamed with his ring foe, Jos LeDuc, to capture the Southern Tag Team Title from the Zambuie Express in March of 1984. The team broke apart the following week. Lawler held the Mid-America Title several times in 1984 and 1985. Lawler again held the Southern tag team belts with Austin Idol as his partner in December of 1985. He engaged in a feud with Bill Dundee for several months in mid-1985, and left the promotion for two months after a loser-leave-town match with Dundee in December of 1985. He captured the Polynesian Pacific Title in Honolulu in January of 1986. He returned to Mid-South to recapture the Southern Heavyweight Title the following April. He teamed with Plowboy Frazier to hold the belts in June of 1986, and partnered with Big Bubba in November of 1986. Lawler was again injured in January of 1987 when he was posted by Austin idol and Tommy Rich. He recovered to reclaim the Southern belt in April of 1987, though he lost the belt and his hair in a match against Idol later in the month. He again defeated Idol for the title in June of 1987. Lawler held the CWA Title for several months in early 1988. He defeated Curt Hennig for the AWA Title in Memphis, Tennessee, on May 9, 1988. Lawler also claimed the AWA Tag Title when he teamed with Bill Dundee to defeat Soldat Ustinov and Doug Somers on October 11, 1987. They were defeated by Dennis Condrey and Randy Rose on October 30, 1987. He also captured the World Class Title from Kerry Von Erich in a unification match in Chicago on December 13, 1988. Lawler was stripped of the AWA Title on January 20, 1989, and banned from the promotion for failure to defend the belt in the federation. Lawler continued to claim the USWA Unified Title until his defeat by the Master of Pain in April of 1989. He reclaimed the belt and held the title numerous times over the next several years. Lawler was run down in a television studio parking lot by Eddie Gilbert in 1990. In 1991 Lawler quit wrestling for several months to recuperate from various injuries he had suffered over the years. Lawler was charged with statutory rape in November of 1993 and was suspended from the WWF, where he worked as a broadcaster and wrestler. The accusation was recanted and all charges against Lawler were dismissed in February of 1994. Lawler continued to hold the USWA Unified Title often through the mid-1990s. In the WWF he engaged in feuds with Bret Hart and Roddy Piper, while continuing his duties as a commentator. He is the father of wrestler Brian Christopher and referee Kevin Christian.

Lawler, Kevin *see* Christian, Kevin

Lawler, Steve (6'1", 256 lbs.) began wrestling in 1978. He teamed with Seigfried Stanke to hold the Tri-State U.S. Tag Team Title in Oklahoma in December of 1979. He was known as the Brawler, and often teamed with Nick Busick. He is a former GAW champion and co-holder of the SCW Tag Team Title in Georgia with Dino Minelli in 1988.

Lawson, Buck wrestled as the Yellow Scorpion to hold the World Junior Heavyweight Title in Nashville several times in 1944.

Layton, Lord Athol (Allan Layton; d. January 18, 1984) held the British Empire Title in Toronto, Canada, in October of 1951. He held the Canadian Open Tag Team Title in Toronto with Fred Atkins and Hans Hermann in 1952. He often teamed with Lord James Blears in the 1950s. They held the Pacific Coast Tag Team Title and the World Tag Team Title in Chicago in 1953. He teamed with Tom Rice to hold the Hawaiian Tag Team Title in April of 1957. He held the NWA U.S. Title in 1962 and 1963.

Lazor Tron *see* Guerrero, Hector

Leather, Peggy Lee held the IWA Woman's Title in the early 1990s. She wrestled as Lady X to capture the LPWA Title in January of 1991. Managed by Ashley Kennedy, she held the title until February of 1992, when she was defeated by Terri Power.

Leatherface (6'6", 322 lbs.) began wrestling in 1990. The masked wrestler was a foe of Jerry Lawler in the USWA.

LeBell, Gene held the Hawaiian Title in February of 1963. He was a promoter with the NWA in Los Angeles during the 1970s. He teamed with Chino Chou to briefly hold the NWA Americas Tag Team Title in July of 1981. LeBell also worked as an actor and stuntman in numerous films and television shows including *Childish Things* (1966), *The Split* (1968), *Hammer* (1972), *Slaughter's Big Rip-Off* (1973), *Walking Tall* (1973), *At Long Last Love* (1975), *I Wanna Hold Your Hand* (1978), *Every Which Way But Loose* (1978) and *Dead Men Don't Wear Plaid* (1982).

LeBelle, Lawrence *see* Ali Baba

LeBeouf, Zarinoff *see* Pierre the Lumberjack

LeDuc, Carl was the son of Paul LeDuc. He wrestled in Canada's Northern Championship Wrestling in 1995.

LeDuc, Jos (Godbout, Quebec, Canada; 280 lbs.) worked as a lumberjack in Quebec Province at an early age. He began wrestling as an amateur at the age of 16, winning an amateur championship in Canada. He made his professional debut in 1967. Wrestling as a Canadian lumberjack, LeDuc was one of the ring's most violent and unpredictable competitors. He held the AWA Title in Montreal, Canada, in 1971. He held the NWA Southern Title in Florida several times in 1973 and 1974. He also teamed with his brother, Paul LeDuc, to hold the NWA Florida Tag Team Title in December of 1973. He teamed with Jean Louie to hold the Southern Tag Team Title in May of 1978, engaging in a feud with Jerry Lawler and Bill Dundee. He took the Southern Heavyweight Title from Lawler in August of 1978. He held the NWA Florida Title in late 1978. He held the NWA Southeastern Title several times in the early 1980s. He also held the NWA Southeastern Tag Team Title several times in 1981, teaming with Robert Fuller. He was managed by Sir Oliver Humperdink in the NWA in the early 1980s, where he held the TV Title in 1982.

He again held the Florida belt several times in 1983. LeDuc returned to the Memphis area in 1984 under the management of Jimmy Hart. He teamed with his ring foe, Jerry Lawler, to capture the Southern Tag Team Title from the Zambuie Express on March 12, 1984. He abandoned Lawler and the belt the following week. He held the WWC North American Title in Puerto Rico several times in 1986. He remained an active competitor through the mid-1990s, though his ring appearances became more infrequent.

LeDuc, Paul wrestled with his brother, Jos LeDuc. They teamed to hold the NWA Florida Tag Team Title in December of 1973. His son, Carl LeDuc, also wrestled.

Lee, Bing Ki teamed with Luther Lindsay to hold the NWA Pacific Northwest Tag Team Title in June of 1961. He teamed with Pedro Morales to hold the Hawaiian Tag Team Title for several months from March of 1970.

Lee, Brian (Brian Harris; Los Angeles, California; 6'2", 251 lbs.) began wrestling in 1988. He held the CWA Title in November of 1988. He teamed with Robert Fuller in the Memphis area and they captured the CWA Tag Team Title in May of 1989. He and Fuller also held the World Class World Tag Team Title and the USWA Tag Team Title several times in late 1989 and early 1990. He teamed with Don Harris to hold the tag belts in August of 1990. Lee subsequently went to Smoky Mountain Wrestling, where he held the championship several times in 1992 and 1993. He also held the Smoky Mountain tag belts with Chris Candido in April of 1994. He wrestled as the 2nd Undertaker managed by Ted DiBiase in the WWF in the Summer of 1994. He returned to the USWA in 1995 and defeated Brian Christopher for the USWA Heavyweight Title on April 3, 1995. He lost the belt to Doug Gilbert in May of 1995. Lee entered ECW in 1996.

Lee, Chin *see* Chin Lee

Lee, Don "Rocky" (d. 1965) teamed with Tom Rice to hold the Pacific Coast Tag Team Title in 1953. He held the NWA Central States Title in June of 1960.

Lee, Eddie (b. 1911; Toronto, Canada; 5'10", 172 lbs.) was trained by Gus Kallio and began wrestling in the late 1930s. He held the middleweight championship in Canada several times.

Lee, Eva (b. 1923; Houston, Texas; 5'5", 138 lbs.) began wrestling in the late 1940s. The blonde, blue-eyed grappler was known for her grace in the ring and her scientific wrestling style. She remained a popular competitor through the 1950s.

Lee, Jimmy (b. 1918; Dubuque, Iowa; 6', 200 lbs.) was a popular wrestler in the 1940s and 1950s. He was known for his flying tackle maneuver.

Lee, Sara was a leading female wrestler in the Mid-South area in the 1960s. She is married to wrestler Corsica Joe.

Lee, Sky Hi (b. 1914, d. 19??; Toronto, Canada; 6'9", 240 lbs.) was a popular mat star from Canada from the late 1940s. He was one of the largest competitors in the ring during the 1950s. Lee was also a restaurateur in Toronto.

Lee, Stagger *see* Ware, Koko B.

Lee, Stan (6'1", 235 lbs.) began wrestling in 1989. Known as "Pretty Boy," he teamed with Eddie Golden in various Southern promotions.

Lee, Tiger Cheung *see* Kim Duk

Lefebvre, Pierre "Mad Dog" (d. December 20, 1985) held the Canadian International Title in Montreal in 1980. He also held the Canadian International Tag Team Title several times in the early 1980s, teaming with Pat Patterson, French Martin and Billy Robinson.

Legion of Doom, The *see* Hawk and Animal

Lehmer, Beverly (b. 1930; Council Bluffs, Iowa; 5'5", 148 lbs.) began wrestling in 1951. She was a leading contender for the women's championship during the 1950s.

Leipler, Bob *see* Hoffman, Duke

Lenz, Henry held the NWA Pacific Northwest Tag Team Title several times from 1955 through 1958, teaming with Kurt Von Poppenheim, Bulldog Curtis, Ed Francis, Herb Freeman and Eric Pederson.

Leo the Lion *see* Newman, Leo

Leon, Relampago *see* Running Bear, Don

Leone, Baron Michele (Mike Morelli; b. 1917, d. 19??; Italy; 5'11", 225 lbs.) was born in Abruzzi, Italy. The stocky Italian began wrestling in Rome in the late 1930s. He soon came to the United States, where he became one of the most popular wrestling stars of the 1940s and 1950s. He held the Pacific Coast Title in Los Angeles in early 1953. He defeated Danny McShane for the World Junior Heavyweight Title in August of 1953. He held the title until 1956.

Leone, Jesse *see* Ortega, Jesse

Leroux, Kat was a leading contender for the NWA U.S. Women's Championship in the mid-1980s.

Leslie, Edward *see* Beefcake, Brutus

Lethal Weapons, The *see* Gilbert, Doug & Condrey, Dennis

Lever, Dick (b. 1911; Nashville, Tennessee; 5'10", 220 lbs.) was a middleweight boxer in the mid-1930s before entering professional wrestling. He remained a popular competitor through the 1950s.

Levesque, Jean Paul *see* Helmsley, Hunter Hearst

Levin, Dave was born in Jamaica, Long Island, New York. He went to California be wrestle professionally in the early 1930s. He held the World Heavyweight Title in California in August of 1936. He held the MWA Title in Kansas City in May of 1944. He held the NWA Texas Title several times in the mid-1940s. He became a promoter in California in the late 1940s, making occasional ring appearances over the next decade.

Levy, Leonard "Butch" (245 lbs.) played football with the University of Minnesota and the Cleveland Rams before becoming a professional wrestler in the late 1940s. He teamed with Verne Gagne to hold the NWA World Tag Team Title in Minneapolis in April of 1959. He also held the NWA tag belts with Leo Nomellini in July of 1959.

Levy, Scott *see* Raven

Lewin, Don (b. 1925; Buffalo, New York; 6'1", 218 lbs.) served in the Marines during World War II and was the recipient of three Purple Hearts. He began wrestling professionally after the war, and remained a popular grappler through the 1950s.

Lewin, Mark (b. February 26) teamed with Don Curtis to captured the WWWF U.S. Tag Team Title in 1958. They were defeated for the belts by Jerry and Eddie Graham in April of 1959. He held the NWA Texas Title in June of 1963. He again teamed with Don Curtis to hold the NWA World Tag Team Title in Florida in November of 1963. He held the WWA Title in Los Angeles from October of 1966 until May of 1967. He also held the WWA Tag Team Title in December of 1966, teaming with Pedro Morales. He held the NWA Americas Title in Los Angeles in July of 1967. He held the Pacific Coast Title in Vancouver, Canada, in February of 1970. He teamed with Steven Little Bear to hold the Canadian Tag Team Title

in November of 1971. He held the NWA Southern Title in Florida in 1973. He held the NWA U.S. Title twice in 1975. He teamed with Dick Steinborn to hold the World Class Texas Tag Team Title in October of 1978. He held the World Class Texas Belt several times in 1979 and 1980. Lewin teamed with the Spoiler to hold the World Class American Tag Team Title several times in 1979 and 1980.

Lewis, Dale teamed with Pat Kennedy to defeat Hard Boiled Haggerty and Bob Geigel for the AWA Tag Team Title in November of 1961. They lost the belts later in the month to Geigel and Otto Von Krupp. He held the NWA Florida Title from August until December of 1969. Lewis held the NWA Georgia Title for several months in early 1969. He teamed with the Missouri Mauler to hold the NWA Florida Tag Team Title in March of 1970. He also held the NWA United National Title in Los Angeles in October of 1970, and the NWA Southern Title in Florida in July of 1972. He teamed with Bob Griffin as the Medics to capture the Australasian Tag Team Title in Australia in March of 1973. He held the NWA Pacific Northwest Title in November of 1974. He teamed with Gene Kiniski to hold the Canadian Tag Team Title in May of 1975. He also held the Canadian tag belts several times with Siegfried Steinke in 1975.

Lewis, Ed "Strangler" (Robert H. Friedrich; b. 1890, d. August 7, 1966) was born in Nukoosa, Wisconsin. He attended Kentucky University, but was forced to leave college in his junior year when he was discovered playing professional baseball. He began his wrestling career soon after, and was a four-time World Heavyweight Title holder from December of 1920 through 1931, defeating such mat stars as Joe Stecher, Wladek Zbyszko and Dr. Benjamin Roller. He was recognized as World Champion by the New York State Athletic Commission from October of 1932 until February of 1933. He held the MWA Title in Kansas City in late 1942 and early 1943. He was named wrestling's first commissioner in the late 1940s. He also appeared in several films during his career including *The Nazty Nuisance* (1943) and *Bodyhold* (1950). Lewis died at his home in Muskogee, Oklahoma, on August 7, 1966.

Lewis, Gene held the Central States TV Title in Kansas in 1981 and 1982. He was managed by Sir Oliver Humperdink in the early 1980s. Wrestling as the Mongol, he held the World Class TV Title in Texas in May of 1983.

Lewis, Jim (b. 1919; Lancaster, Ohio; 6', 220 lbs.) was a champion amateur wrestler at the University of Utah. He was trained as a professional wrestler by Chief War Eagle and made his ring debut in the late 1940s. He captured the Minnesota State championship in 1950.

Lewis, Marshall (Montreal, Canada) served in the Royal Canadian Air Force during World War II. He began wrestling professionally in the late 1940s, capturing the Light Heavyweight Title in Canada. He remained a leading competitor through the 1950s.

Lewis, Randy wrestled as Lord Humongous in the USWA in the early 1990s. He briefly held the USWA Texas Title in August of 1991.

Liger, Jushin (Keiji Yamada; b. November 10, 1964; Hiroshima, Japan; 5'6", 200 lbs.) was a leading masked Japanese wrestler. He began wrestling in 1984 in New Japan. He captured the World Middleweight Title in Great Britain in 1987, wrestling as Fuji Yamada. He came to the United States in the early 1990s to wrestle in the WCW. Liger captured the WCW Light Heavyweight Title from Brian Pillman in December of 1991. He lost the belt back to Pillman in February of 1992. He subsequently returned to Japan, where he continued to wrestle with New Japan.

Lightfoot, Joe, wrestling as Joe Ventura, teamed with Bobby Bass to hold the Canadian Tag Team Title in April of 1979. He teamed with Billy Two Eagles to hold the NWA Central States Tag Team Title in July of 1986.

Lightning Express, The *see* Horner, Tim & Armstrong, Brad

Lightning Kid, The *see* Kid, The

Ligon, Gene (5'11", 241 lbs.) began wrestling in 1978. He competed in the WCW, and wrestled as Thunderfoot #2 in the IWA in Ohio, where he held the title in 1993.

Lindsay, Luther (Luther Goodall; b. 1924, d. February 21, 1972) captured the NWA Pacific

Northwest Title in May of 1961. He also held the Pacific Northwest tag belts several times in 1961, teaming with Bink Ki Lee and Herb Freeman. He held the U.S. Title in Honolulu in June of 1964. He also held the Hawaiian Title in late 1965. He teamed with Bearcat Wright to capture the Hawaiian Tag Team Title in July of 1965. He recaptured the Pacific Northwest belt in June of 1967 and, again, in November of 1968.

Link, Man Mountain (Rick Link) captured the Southern Heavyweight Title from Jerry Lawler in June of 1983. He relinquished the belt to Lawler the following month. Link held the Mid-America Title in July of 1985.

Link, Rick *see* Link, Man Mountain

Linnehan, Cy *see* Linnehan, George T.

Linnehan, George T. (b. 1902, d. December 13, 1981; Wayland, Massachusetts; 6', 230 lbs.) was born in Wayland, Massachusetts, and began wrestling in the early 1930s. He competed primarily in the Boston area, sometimes under the names Cy Linnehan and the Boston Bad Boy. He remained active in the ring through the 1950s. He died of a heart attack at his home in West Barnstable, Massachusetts, on December 13, 1981.

Lisowski, Reggie *see* Crusher

Lisowski, Stan teamed with Crusher to hold the World Tag Team Title in Chicago several times in 1956 and 1957. They also held the Canadian Open Tag Team Title in Toronto in August of 1958, and the NWA World Tag Team Title in Minneapolis several times in 1958 and 1959.

Lister, Tiny (Tom Lister, Jr.; 6'10, 343 lbs.) was a stuntman and character actor in numerous films from the mid-1980s. His film credits include *Prison* (1988), *Midnight* (1989), *Universal Soldier* (1992), *Posse* (1993), *Immortal Combat* (1994) with Roddy Piper and *Barb Wire* (1996). He portrayed the character Zeus in the 1989 film *No Holds Barred* with Hulk Hogan. Lister entered the WWF as Zeus to compete in the ring against Hogan for several months. He returned to his film roles, but continued to wrestle occasionally in independent promotions. He reemerged in the ring in early 1996 as Ze Gangsta, to again challenge Hogan in a match.

Little Bear, Danny (d. 19??) began his professional wrestling career in Louisiana in the early 1950s. The Chiricahua Apache star teamed with Luke Brown to hold the NWA Central States Tag Team Title in June of 1969. He also held the Central States tag belts, teaming with Stan Pulaski, the Viking, Omar Atlas and the Stomper over the next several years. Little Bear held the NWA Central States Title in February of 1972 and April of 1973. He held the Stampede North American Title in Calgary, Canada, in 1974. He teamed with Chief Thundercloud to hold the Southern Tag Team Title in November of 1976. His sister also wrestled as Princess Little Cloud.

Little Bear, Steven teamed with Don Leo Jonathan to hold the Canadian Tag Team Title in November of 1970. He held the Canadian tag belts several more times in the early 1970s, teaming with Mark Lewin, Dutch Savage and Dean Ho. He teamed with Chief Sunni War Cloud to hold the Hawaiian Tag Team Title in June of 1971. He held the NWA Pacific Northwest Title in November of 1972. He teamed with Dutch Savage to hold the Pacific Northwest tag belts for several months from January of 1973. He teamed with Ray Candy to hold the U.S. Tag Team Title in Louisiana several times in early 1978.

Little Beaver (Lionel Giroux; b. 1934, d. December 4, 1995) was a leading midget wrestler from the 1960s through the 1980s. He appeared in a mixed tag match at Wrestlemania III in 1987, against King Kong Bundy. He retired the following year. He died of emphysema at his home in St. Jerome, Quebec, Canada, on December 4, 1995.

Little Eagle (d. 19??) teamed with Chief Big Heart to hold the NWA Texas Tag Team Title in April of 1959.

Little Flower, The *see* Gardini, Benito

Little Fox, Chief (b. 1923; Vancouver, British Columbia, Canada; 6'1", 240 lbs.) was a Nez Pierce Indian trained by Chief Thunderbird. He was a popular wrestling star in the 1950s and 1960s.

Little Louie (Scarboro, Maine; 4'6", 110 lbs.) was a leading midget wrestler from 1974 through the 1980s. He engaged in a feud with the Irish Leprechaun in the early 1980s.

Little Tokyo began his wrestling career in Japan before coming to the United States. He became one of wrestling's leading midget stars in the 1970s, holding the World Championship for several years.

Little Wolf, Chief (Benny Tenario; b. 1919, d. 197?; 6', 240 lbs.) was a Navajo Indian from New Mexico. He began wrestling professionally in 1934 in circus sideshows. He introduced the Indian Death Lock hold to professional wrestling. He remained a popular mat star until a crippling illness forced his retirement in 1957. He died in the late 1970s.

Littlebrook, Lord was a popular midget wrestler. He held the Midget World Title in Los Angeles in 1972.

Littlejohn, Stanley (b. 1952, d. May 16, 1993) was a midget wrestler who wrestled as "Little Coco" in the 1970s and 1980s.

Lizmark (Juan Banos; Acapulco, Mexico; 5'6", 190 lbs.) began wrestling in 1975. He captured the Mexican National Welterweight Title in April of 1979, holding the belt for almost a year. He held the EMLL Light Heavyweight and Welterweight Title several times in the late 1980s and early 1990s. His son, Lizmark, Jr., is also a popular Mexican wrestling star.

Lloyd, Carey *see* Jones, Rufus R.

Loch Ness *see* Giant Haystacks

Logan, Brian *see* Keys, Brian

Lograsso, Vito *see* Von Crush, Skull

Lolotai, Al held the Hawaiian Title several times from 1955 through 1959. He also held the Hawaiian Tag Team Title in 1957, teaming with Luck Simunovich.

Lombardi, Steve (b. April 18; Brooklyn, New York; 6', 233 lbs.) began wrestling in 1985. He wrestled as Steve Lombardi in the WWF until he was briefly managed by Bobby Heenan and became the Brooklyn Brawler. He also appeared as Kim Chee, Kamala's handler, in the early 1990s. Lombardi also wrestled in the WWF as the MVP and Doink III during 1993, and appeared in the ring as Abe "Knuckleball" Schwartz in 1994.

Lomonica, Mark *see* Dudley, Buh Buh Ray

Londos, Jim (Chris Theophelos; b. January 2, 1897, d. August 19, 1975; Los Angeles, California; 5'8", 215 lbs.) was born in Argos, Greece, and came to the United States at the age of 13. He held various odd jobs, including a stint as a vaudeville strongman, before beginning a career as a professional wrestler in 1920. He defeated numerous challengers throughout the decade including Earl Craddock and Joe Stecher. He defeated Dick Shikat for the NWA Heavyweight Title in Philadelphia, Pennsylvania, on June 6, 1930. He lost a match to Joe Savoldi in April of 1933, but was still recognized as NWA champion. He vacated the title after winning the New York Title in June of 1934. He held that title until June of 1935. He held the World Heavyweight Title in California in late 1938. He was semi-retired during World War II, wrestling in only occasional matches. He was known for his philanthropic contributions to Greek war orphans during the war. He officially retired from the ring in 1946. He emerged from retirement for a match against Primo Carnera in Chicago in 1950. He died of a heart attack in a Escondido, California, hospital on August 19, 1975.

Lone Eagle, Chief (J.D. Vazques; b. 1907, d. August 15, 1995) was a wrestler in the Mid-South area in the 1950s and 1960s. He was often accompanied to the ring by his wife, Bonita. He retired in the late 1960s and died of a heart attack in Memphis, Tennessee, on August 15, 1995.

Long, Johnny (Billy Strong; d. 19??; Charlotte, North Carolina) was both a boxer and a wrestler during the 1950s. He remained an active ring competitor for several decades. He teamed with Tojo Yamamoto to hold the World Tag Team Title in Tennessee in November of 1968. He teamed with Pepe Lopez to hold the tag belts in 1971.

Long, Teddy was a referee and manager in the WCW in the 1980s. He managed Johnny B. Badd in the early 1990s. He returned to the WCW in 1996 to manage Sgt. Craig Pittman.

Long Riders, The *see* Bass, Ross & Black Bart

Long Riders, The *see* Gunn, Billy & Bart

Long Riders, The *see* Irwin, Scott & Irwin, Bill

Longson, Bill (d. December 10, 1982; Salt Lake City, Utah) began wrestling in amateur bouts in Salt Lake City. He sometimes wrestled as the Purple Shadow in California in the 1930s. He held the Pacific Coast Title in San Francisco briefly in 1938. He held the belt several more times in 1941, competing against Frank Sexton and Bobby Managoff. He defeated Sandor Szabo for the NWA Heavyweight Title in St. Louis, Missouri, on February 19, 1942. He lost the belt to Yvon Robert in a match in Montreal, Canada, on October 7, 1942. Longson regained the title by defeating Bobby Managoff in St. Louis, Missouri, on February 19, 1943. He retained the belt until February 21, 1947, when he was defeated by Whipper Billy Watson. He again regained the title several months later when he defeated Lou Thesz on November 21, 1947. He lost the belt to Thesz in Indianapolis, Indiana, on July 20, 1948. He held the NWA Central States Title in 1950. He held the Texas Brass Knucks Title in August of 1958. He captured the Texas World Tag Team Title in August of 1958, teaming with Ike Eakins.

Lopez, Mando teamed with Micky Doyle to hold the NWA Americas Tag Team Title in Los Angeles in December of 1975.

Lopez, Miguel *see* Rey Misterio

Lopez, Pepe (Reuben Rodriguez; b. 1937, d. July 26, 1976) teamed with El Medico to hold the NWA Americas Tag Team Title in Los Angeles in December of 1969. He teamed with Johnny Long to hold the World Tag Team Title in Tennessee in 1971. He wrestled with Frank Hester as the masked tag team, the Dominoes, in the Mid-South in 1976. They wrestled in the Memphis area for six months before being killed in an automobile accident near Dickson, Tennessee, on July 26, 1976. They were en route from Memphis, where they had been defeated in a tag team bout by Don Kernodle and Don Anderson.

Lopez, Vincent (Vincent Daniels; d. 19??) held the World Heavyweight Title in California in 1935 and 1936. He captured the Pacific Coast Title in June of 1937, holding the title for several months before losing a rematch with Sandor Szabo. He again held the Pacific Coast belt several times from 1945 through 1948.

Lordi, Michael (b. 1918; Flushing, New York; 5'10", 210 lbs.) attended New York University, where he played football and engaged in amateur wrestling bouts. He was a popular scientific wrestler in the late 1940s and early 1950s.

Lortie, Bob (b. 1915, d. 19??; Quebec, Canada; 6', 205 lbs.) began wrestling in the 1940s. He teamed with his brother, Paul, as one of the top tag-teams in the 1950s.

Lortie, Donald teamed with Tony Gonzales as the Medics. They held the Southern Tag Team Title several times in 1962 and 1963.

Lortie, Paul (b. 1909, d. 19??; Montreal, Quebec, Canada; 5'11", 218 lbs.) began wrestling in the mid-1930s. He won the Canadian Junior Heavyweight Title in 1940. He competed throughout the world and began teaming with his brother, Bob, in the late 1940s. They were a top tag team in the 1950s.

Lothario, Jose was a popular Mexican wrestler from the early 1960s. He was known for his abdominal stretch. teamed with Pepper Gomez to capture the NWA World Tag Team Title in San Francisco in September of 1963. He teamed held the NWA World Tag Team Title in Florida several times in 1966 and 1967, teaming with Wahoo McDaniel, Eddie Graham and Sam Steamboat. He also held the NWA Southern Tag Team Title several times in 1967 and 1968, teaming with Don Curtis and Jay Strongbow. He held the World Class Texas Title several times in the late 1960s and early 1970s. He teamed with Argentina Apollo to hold the NWA Florida Tag Team Title from April until September of 1970. He recaptured the title in December of 1970, teaming with Danny Miller. He held the World Class American Tag Team Title several times in 1973, teaming with Ivan Puski and Mil Mascaras. He held the Mid-South Louisiana Title in September of 1978. He again held the World Class American tag belts in 1979 and 1980, teaming with El Halcon and Tiger Conway Jr. Lothario entered the WWF in 1996 to manage champion Shawn Michaels.

Louie, Jean teamed with Jos

LeDuc to hold the Southern Tag Team Title in May of 1978. They engaged in a vicious feud with Jerry Lawler and Bill Dundee in the Memphis area.

Louis, Joe (Joseph Louis Barrow; b. May 13, 1914, d. April 12, 1981; Lafayette, Alabama; 6'1 1/2", 197 lbs.) was one of the greatest boxers in the 20th Century. He defeated James J. Braddock for the World Heavyweight Title in June of 1937, and retired undefeated in 1949. He tried to stage a comeback the following year and was defeated by Ezzard Charles. He retired again following his defeat by Rocky Marciano in 1951. Louis was beset my financial problems and difficulties with the IRS after his retirement. Louis entered professional wrestling later in the decade as a referee and occasional wrestler. He died of cardiac arrest in Las Vegas, Nevada, on April 12, 1981.

Love, Brother *see* Prichard, Bruce

Love, Miss Bunny (Hollywood, California; 5'1", 130 lbs.) became involved with professional wrestling in the late 1970s. She was the manager of Paul Christy in the WWA and was a leading female wrestler in the promotion.

Love, Christopher *see* Prentice, Bert

Love, Hartford teamed with Reginald Love to hold the International Tag Team Title in Toronto several times in 1974. He teamed with Jerry Brown to hold the NWA Central States Tag Team Title in March of 1979.

Love, Johnny held the PWA Light Heavyweight Title for several months in late 1989. He teamed with Tommy Ferrara to hold the PWA Tag Team Title for several months from November of 1987.

Love, Reginald teamed with Hartford Love to hold the International Tag Team Title in Toronto several times in 1974.

Lovemark, Al wrestled as the Great Bolo. He teamed with Larry Hamilton to hold the NWA Southern Tag Team Title in 1960.

Lubich, Bronco was a wrestler and manager during the 1950s. He teamed with Angelo Poffo to hold the Midwest Tag Team Title in Chicago in August of 1956. They also held the NWA Texas Tag Team Title in May of 1961. He teamed with Aldo Bogni to hold the NWA Southern Tag Team Title in 1966. He and Bogni also held the NWA Southern Tag Team in Florida from November of 1967 until February of 1968. He teamed with Chris Markoff to hold the NWA Florida Tag Team Title for several months in late 1969 and early 1970. He and Markoff also held the World Class American Tag Team Title in Texas several times in the early 1970s. After retiring from the ring he became a longtime referee in World Class and USWA.

Lucas, Ken teamed with Johnny Walker to hold the Southern Tag Team Title in March of 1969. He teamed with Bob Kelly to hold the Gulf Coast Tag Team Title in 1972. He teamed with Mike Graham to hold the NWA Florida Tag Team Title briefly in 1976. Lucas held the Mid-America Title in January of 1977. He held the NWA Central States Title in February of 1978. He teamed with Kevin Sullivan to hold the NWA Central States Tag Team Title in April of 1978. He teamed with Dutch Mantell to hold the Mid-America Tag Team Title in August of 1978. He teamed with Kevin Sullivan to briefly hold the NWA Southeastern Tag Team Title in December of 1978. He again held the Southeastern belt, teaming with Bob Armstrong in February of 1979. He teamed with Billy Robinson to hold the Southern Tag Team Title several times in 1980. He also held the Southern tag belts with Ricky Morton several times in 1980. He held the NWA Southeastern Title several times from 1981 through 1983.

Lucenti, Nick "Alvino" (b. 1913; Brooklyn, New York; 5'9", 197 lbs.) began his wrestling career in the late 1940s. He continued to compete in the ring through the 1950s.

Luger, Lex (Larry Pfohl; b. June 2, 1958; Chicago, Illinois; 6'5", 265 lbs.) played football in the Canadian Football League. He joined Florida's Orlando Bulls in the U.S. Football League in 1985. He soon began wrestling on Florida cards, holding the NWA Southern Title several times from late 1985 through mid-1986. He was known as "the Total Package" in the NWA, and joined with the Four Horsemen. He subsequently broke with the Horsemen and engaged in a feud with his former allies. He defeated Nikita Koloff for the U.S. Title on July 11, 1987. Luger also briefly held the NWA

World Tag Team Title with Barry Windham in March and April of 1988, interrupting Arn Anderson and Tully Blanchard's title reigns. Luger lost the U.S. Title to Dusty Rhodes on November 26, 1987. He regained the belt on February 20, 1989, defeating Barry Windham. He briefly lost the title to Michael Hayes in May of 1989. He again lost the title to Stan Hansen in October of 1990, but recaptured it on December 15, 1990. Luger defeated Barry Windham for the vacant WCW Heavyweight Title in Baltimore, Maryland, on July 14, 1991. He lost the title to Sting in Milwaukee, Wisconsin, on February 29, 1992. He left the WCW in early 1992 to enter Vince McMahon's World Bodybuilding Federation, but suffered a crushed elbow in a motorcycle accident in Atlanta in June of 1992 and was unable to compete. He subsequently recovered from his injuries and entered the WWF as the Narcissist in 1993. Luger teamed with the British Bulldog as the Allied Powers in the WWF in early 1995, but soon turned on the Bulldog. He left the promotion later in the year to reenter the WCW. He was managed by Jimmy Hart and teamed with Sting to hold the WCW Tag Team Title in 1996.

Luke *see* Bushwhacker Luke

Lunde, Marty *see* Anderson, Arn

Luttrell, Clarence "Cowboy" (b. 1906, d. March 11, 1980) was a former wrestler and promoter for the NWA in Florida during the 1970s.

Lynn, Jerry (5'10", 230 lbs.) began wrestling in 1988. He was a popular star in the Pacific Northwest, holding the PWA Light Heavyweight Title in January of 1990, and the PWA Title in August of 1990. He captured the Global Junior Heavyweight Title in December of 1991. He teamed with the Lightning Kid to hold the PWA Tag Team title in March of 1993. He wrestled with the WCW from 1995.

Lyons, Billy Red often teamed with Red Bastien in the 1960s. He teamed with Dick "the Destroyer" Beyer to hold the NWA World Tag Team Title in San Francisco in March of 1965. He teamed with Fritz Von Erich to hold the World Class American Tag Team Title in Texas in 1968. He teamed with Bill Watts to hold the U.S. Tag Team Title in Oklahoma in January of 1971. He again held the belts, teamed with Tom Jones, in May of 1971. He held the World Class Championship in Texas in June of 1972. He teamed with Dewey Robertson as the Crusaders to hold the International Tag Team Title in Toronto several times in 1974.

M, Mister *see* Miller, Bill

Mabel (Nelson Frasier; b. February 14; Harlem, New York; 6'10", 503 lbs.) began wrestling in 1991. He teamed with Mo as the Harlem Knights in the USWA before joining the WWF as Men on a Mission. They defeated the Quebecers for the WWF Tag Team Championship at a match in London, England, on March 29, 1994. They lost the belts two days later in Sheffield, England, in a rematch with the Quebecers on March 31, 1994. Men on a Mission began wrestling as villains later in the year. Mabel defeated Savio Vega in the WWF King of the Ring tournament in June of 1995. HE also wrestled in the USWA in the mid-1990s.

McArthur, George *see* Cannon, George

McClarity, Don wrestled with Argentina Apollo to win the WWWF U.S. Tag Team Title from Chris and John Tolos in February of 1964. They were defeated for the belts by Jerry and Luke Graham in June of 1964.

McClarty, Roy teamed with Whipper Billy Watson to hold the Pacific Coast Tag Team Title in Vancouver, Canada, in November of 1961. He teamed with Don Leo Jonathan to hold the Canadian Tag Team Title in September of 1964.

McCord, Dennis *see* Idol, Austin

McCord, Rick held the Texas All-Star USA Junior Heavyweight Title in May of 1985. He teamed with Bart Batten to hold the NWA Central States Tag Team Title in February of 1987. He again held the Central States tag belts, teaming with Porkchop Cash, in November of 1987.

McCoy, Robert "Bibber" (b. 1903, d. March 6, 1977; Cambridge, Massachusetts; 5'10", 235 lbs.) played football at Holy Cross. He was signed to play baseball with the Detroit Tigers, but an arm injury ended his baseball career. He subsequently became a professional wrestler, and was a leading competitor from the 1930s, known for his quickness in the ring. He wrestled as El Toro in the 1950s. He held the NWA Central States Title in 1954.

McCready, Earl (d. November, 1983) held the British Empire Title in New Zealand in the late 1930s. He also held the British Empire Title in Toronto, Canada, several times in the early 1940s. He held the Pacific Coast Title in San Francisco in April of 1945.

McCreary, Benny *see* McGuire, Benny

McCreary, Billy *see* McGuire, Billy

McCullough, Duane *see* Awesome Kong

McDaniel, Wahoo (Ed McDaniel; b. June 19; McAlester, Oklahoma; 5'11", 280 lbs.) began wrestling in 1951. He played professional football with the Miami Dolphins during the 1960s. McDaniel teamed with Jose Lothario to hold the NWA World Tag Team Title in Florida in June of 1966. He briefly held the NWA Florida Title in May of 1967. He teamed with Thunderbolt Patterson to hold the World Class American Tag Team Title in Texas in 1969. He held the World Class Championship in Texas in March of 1971. He again held the World Class American tag belts several times in 1971, teaming with Johnny Valentine. He held the NWA Eastern States Title several times from 1975 until 1978. The Native American star held the NWA World Tag Team Title briefly with Rufus R. Jones in early 1976. He held the NWA Southern Title in

Florida in 1978. He and Tommy Rich held the NWA Georgia Tag Team Title in May of 1979. He also held the World Class Championship in Texas in May of 1979. McDaniel also held the NWA Georgia Title for several months in mid-1979. He captured the NWA U.S. Title from Roddy Piper in August of 1981, but was forced to give up the belt the following month when he was injured by Abdullah the Butcher. He held the U.S. Title four more times through 1984, defeating such mat stars as Sergeant Slaughter and Manny Fernandez. He was again co-holder of the tag title with Mark Youngblood, defeating Don Kernodle and Bob Orton, Jr. in March of 1984. They held the belts until the following month. McDaniel held the NWA National in August of 1986. He announced his retirement in 1989.

McDonald, Jack "Sockeye" (d. 19??) was a leading competitor in the 1950s. He held the NWA Southern Title in 1952. He engaged in a series of bouts with Wilbur Snyder in the late 1950s.

Macera, Luigi held the Pacific Coast Junior Heavyweight Title in November of 1954. He held the NWA Pacific Coast Tag Team Title several times in 1955, teaming with Gory Guerrero and Dick Torio. He teamed with Pepper Gomez to hold the NWA Texas Tag Team Title in February of 1956. He also held the Texas Junior Heavyweight Title in 1956. He reclaimed the Pacific Coast Junior Heavyweight belt in February of 1957. He teamed with Herb Freeman to recapture the Pacific Coast

tag belts in May of 1957. He held the Hawaiian Title in April of 1961.

McGhee, Pat *see* McGhee, Scott

McGhee, Scott (Shipley, England; 220 lbs.) wrestled in Florida in the early 1980s, teaming with Barry Windham to hold the NWA Florida Tag Team Title in October of 1980. He teamed with Terry Allen to hold the Global Tag Team Title in Florida in January of 1983. He also held the NWA Florida Title several times in 1983 and 1984. Wrestling as Pat McGhee, he teamed with Curt Hennig to hold the NWA Pacific Northwest Tag Team Title in December of 1983. He subsequently moved to the WWF. He was forced to retire in 1987 after suffering a crippling stroke.

McGillicutty, Beaulah (Theresa Hays) wrestled in ECW in 1995, often feuding with Francine. She was initially Raven's valet, but left him for Tommy Dreamer in early 1996.

McGinnis, Pat briefly held the CWA World Title in October of 1979.

McGinnis, Terry (Ohio) began wrestling in the early 1930s. He was a leading competitor on the Pacific Coast, where he held the championship for four years. He remained a popular mat star through the 1950s.

McGraw, Herman E. "Bugsy" (New York; 6'3", 280 lbs.) began wrestling in 1967. He was a popular mat star in Florida. He also wrestled in the WWF in the early 1970s. Wrestling as the Brute, he captured the Pacific Coast Title in Vancouver, Canada, in March of 1973. He also held the Canadian Tag Team Title several times in 1973 and 1974, teaming with Gene Kiniski, Mike Webster and Guy "Mr. X" Mitchell. He held the NWA U.S. Title in San Francisco in early 1975. He teamed with Thor the Viking to hold the NWA Florida Tag Team Title in 1979. He also held the NWA Florida Title for several months from August of 1980. He held the Mid-America Title in Tennessee in 1981. He teamed with Bill Irwin to hold the World Class World Tag Team Title in April of 1982. He also held the World Class American Tag Team Title in April of 1982, teaming with King Kong Bundy. He also held the World Class Championship in Texas in early 1982. He teamed with Rufus R. Jones to hold the NWA Atlantic Coast Tag Title in 1983.

McGraw, "Quick Draw" Rick (b. 1957, d. November 1, 1985) teamed with the Dream Machine as the New York Dolls in Memphis in 1982. They were managed by Jimmy Hart. The duo defeated Spike Huber and Steve Regal for the WWA Tag Team Title in Memphis in September of 1982. They held the belts until losing a rematch the following February. McGraw died in New Haven, Connecticut, on November 1, 1985.

McGuire, Benny (Benny Mc-Creary; b. 1947; Hendersonville, North Carolina; 5'9", 727 lbs.) appeared at circuses and country fairs before becoming a professional wrestler. He and his twin brother, Billy, made their wrestling debut in El Paso, Texas, in the early 1970s. They were the largest tag team in wrestling history, and often entered the arena while riding a motorized mini-bike.

McGuire, Billy (Billy Mc-Creary; b. 1947, d. July 14, 1979; Hendersonville, North Carolina; 5'9", 747 lbs.) appeared at circuses and country fairs before becoming a professional wrestler. He and his twin brother, Benny, made their wrestling debut in El Paso, Texas, in the early 1970s. They were the largest tag team in wrestling history, and often entered the arena while riding a motorized mini-bike. Billy was injured in a motorcycle accident while appearing at the Ripley Museum at the Niagara Falls, in Ontario, Canada. He died of his injuries several days later on July 14, 1979.

McGuirk, LeRoy (b. 1910, d. September 9, 1988) held the World Light Heavyweight Title from March of 1934 through most of the late 1930s. He vacated the belt in 1939. He held the NWA World Junior Heavyweight title during most of the 1940s until he was seriously injured and blinded in an automobile accident in 1950. McGuirk remained in wrestling as a promoter, heading up the NWA's operations out of Tulsa, Oklahoma. He died at his home in Claremore, Oklahoma, on September 9, 1988.

McIntyre, Don (b. 1916, d. November 20, 1989; Cedalia, Missouri; 5'10", 225 lbs.) was known in the ring for his defensive skills. The curly-haired McIntyre held the NWA Southern Title several times in the early 1950s.

McIntyre, Red held the NWA Southern Title in 1957.

McIntyre, Velvet is a native of British Columbia. She was a leading female wrestler in the WWF in the 1980s. She defeated the Fabulous Moolah for the WWF Women's Title in Brisbane, Australia, in July of 1986, but lost the belt in a rematch the following week. She held the Canadian Wrestling Alliance Women's Title in late 1993.

Mack, Frank *see* Dillinger, Frank

McKeever, Scotty (b'1", 220 lbs.) began wrestling in 1992. He teamed with Scotty Hot Body to hold the ICW tag team belts in 1994. He captured the ICW Mid-Atlantic Title in a tournament in March of 1994. He lost the belt to Dark Star two months later. He again held the Mid-Atlantic belt from March until May of 1995.

McKenzie, Tex teamed with Whipper Billy Watson to hold the Canadian Open Tag Team Title in Toronto in June of 1954. He teamed with Ilio DiPaolo to hold the Canadian Tag Team Title in Edmonton in November of 1954. He teamed with Ken Kenneth to hold the Northwest Tag Team Title in Vancouver, Canada, in November of 1955. He teamed with Ramon Torres to hold the NWA World Tag Team Title in San Francisco in September of 1957. He was a popular mat star in Texas in the 1960s and feuded with the Sheik. He teamed with Red Bastien to hold the World Class Texas Tag Team Title in 1974. He worked as an announcer with the IWA from the mid 1970s. He retired to Seattle, Washington.

McKigney, David (d. July 27, 1988) wrestled as the Wildman. He was killed in an automobile accident in Lewisporte, Newfoundland, Canada, with Adrian Adonis and Pat Kelly on July 27, 1988.

McKim, Red teamed with Mike Clancy to hold the Texas World Tag Team Title in September of 1962.

McKnight, Paul *see* Moondog Rover

McLeod, Dan (d. 19??) was a leading wrestler around the turn of the century. He was the holder of the American title on several occasions between 1897 and 1902.

McMahon, Vince, Jr. (b. August 24, 1945) formed Titan Sports in 1980. He bought out his father's Capitol Wrestling Corporation in June of 1982. He was largely responsible for the upsurge in wrestling's popular in the mid-1980s when Hulk Hogan was the WWF's champion. McMahon remained a leading figure in professional wrestling through the 1990s and was often a commentator on the WWF television programs. He was acquitted on charges of steroid distribution in the WWF in July of 1994.

McMahon, Vince, Sr. (d. May 27, 1984) was the son of boxing promoter Jess McMahon. He promoted his first wrestling card in 1935. He was a founder of the WWWF promotion in 1963 and was a leading wrestling promoter in the New York area for the next several decades. His son, Vince McMahon, Jr., bought out his interest in Capitol Wrestling Corporation in June of 1982.

McManus, Paul *see* Morgan, Tank

McMasters, Luke *see* Giant Haystacks

McNulty, Red *see* Koloff, Ivan

McPherson, Jim (5'10", 229 lbs.) began wrestling in 1988. Known as "Jungle" Jim, he wrestled in the WWF and WWA.

Macricostas, George (b. 1914; Reading, Pennsylvania; 5'8", 215 lbs.) wrestled for Greece in the 1936 Olympics. He subsequently began wrestling professionally, holding the light-heavyweight championship in London. He came to South America, and then the United States, in the late 1930s. He remained a leading competitor in the 1940s and 1950s, known for his agility and his airplane spin closing move.

McShain, Casey teamed with Danny McShain to hold the NWA Texas Tag Team Title in January of 1958.

McShain, Irish Danny (b. 1912, d. July 16, 1991; Los Angeles, California; 6'1", 215 lbs.) began wrestling in the 1930s in Texas and the Southwest. He captured the World Light Heavyweight Title in December of 1940, and held the title on four occasions through September of 1947. He held the NWA Texas Title several times in 1948 and 1949. He defeated Verne Gagne for the NWA World Junior Heavyweight Title on November 19, 1951, in Memphis, Tennessee. He held the

title until his defeat by Baron Leone in August of 1953. He again held the NWA Texas Title on several occasions in the late 1950s and early 1960s. He teamed with Casey McShain to hold the NWA Texas Tag Team Title in January of 1958, and with Bad Boy Hines to hold the belts in late 1959. He again held the Texas tag belts in late 1960, teaming with Sputnik Monroe. He continued to be involved in the wrestling business as a referee and promoter through the late 1970s. He died of pneumonia in Alvin, Texas, on July 16, 1991.

Madd Maxx (John Richmond; 6'1", 240 lbs.) began wrestling in 1984. He wrestled with Super Maxx as the World Warriors in the AWA. The duo was managed by Saul Creachman and Miss Maxine and held the WWA Tag Team Title in 1984. They also held the Pacific Tag Team Title in Honolulu several times in 1986. He primarily wrestled in Chicago in the 1990s.

Madd Maxxine (5'9", 190 lbs.) began wrestling in the PWF in 1994. She defeated several male wrestlers in the area, where she also managed the Russian Assassin.

Madison, G.Q. (6'2", 239 lbs.) began wrestling in 1988. He teamed with his brother T.D., to win the IWCCW Tag Title several times in 1990 and 1991. They often feuded with the Billion Dollar Babies.

Madison, T.D. (6'1", 242 lbs.) began wrestling in 1989. He teamed with his brother, G.Q., to win the IWCCW Tag Title several times in 1990 and 1991. They often feuded with the Billion Dollar Babies.

Madonna's Boyfriend *see* Louie Spicolli

Madril, Al (Los Angeles, California; 6'1", 231 lbs.) began wrestling in 1972. He was a leading mat villain for the next two decades. He teamed with Manuel Cruz as the Compadres to hold the NWA Pacific Northwest Tag Team Title in July of 1973. He held the World Class Texas Title several times in 1975. He teamed with Pepper Gomez to hold the NWA World Tag Team Title in San Francisco in June of 1977. He was forced to relinquish the title later in the month due to an injury. He held the NWA Americas Title in Los Angeles in June of 1979. He also held the NWA Americas tag belts several times in 1979 and 1980, teaming with Chavo Guerrero, Mando Guerrero and Tom Prichard. He teamed with Kerry Von Erich to hold the World Class World Tag Team Title in Texas several times in 1981 and 1982. He also held the World Class American Tag Team Title in 1981, teaming with Brian Blair. He teamed with Chavo Guerrero to hold the Texas All-Star Texas Tag Team Title in July of 1985. He also held the tag team belts in 1986, teaming with the Magnificent Zulu and Mike Golden. He teamed with Brian Adias to hold the World Class World Tag Team Title in December of 1986. He held the Pacific Northwest TV Title in October of 1988. He also held the TV Title in October of 1989 and January of 1990. He teamed with Ricky Santana as the Latin Connection to hold the Pacific Northwest Tag Team Title in August of 1990. He retired from the Pacific Northwest in the early 1990s.

Madusa *see* Miceli, Madusa

Maeda, Akira (b. January 24, 1959; Osaka, Japan; 6'2", 223 lbs.) began wrestling in August of 1978. He left the New Japan organization in 1987 to form the UWF.

Maggs, Joey (6', 233 lbs.) began wrestling in 1987. He teamed with Rex King to hold the USWA Tag Team Title in June of 1990. He briefly changed his name to Joey Magliano when he wrestled with Eddie Gilbert's Memphis Mafia in the UCWA in 1990. He captured the USWA Junior Heavyweight Title in December of 1990.

Magliano, Joey *see* Maggs, Joey

Magnificent Maurice (Gene Dubuque; b. 1925, d. January 1974; Brooklyn, New York; 5'10", 205 lbs.) was a veteran of the U.S. Navy who attended Springfield College in Massachusetts. He held the body-building title of Mr. New York in 1948 before turning to professional wrestling. He held the NWA World Tag Team Title in San Francisco several times in 1958, teaming with Mike Valentino and Fritz von Goehring. He held the Pacific Coast Title in San Francisco in 1961. He teamed with Johnny Barend to briefly hold the AWA Tag Team Title in Indiana in February of 1962. He teamed with Johnny Barend to hold the Hawaiian Tag Team Title in July of 1968.

Magnificent Zulu, The (Ron Pope) held the ASWA Georgia Title in 1974. He teamed with Al Madril to hold the Texas All-Star Tag Team Title in January of 1986. He was released from the promotion the following April.

Magnum T.A. (Terry Allen; b. June 11; Chesapeake, Virginia; 6'1", 245 lbs.) began wrestling in 1980. He teamed with Scott McGhee to hold the Global Tag Team Title in Florida in January of 1983. He teamed with Jim Duggan to hold the MSWA Tag Team Title for several months from July of 1983. He held the MSWA North American Title for several months from May of 1984. He defeated Wahoo McDaniel for the NWA U.S. Title on April 23, 1985. He was defeated by Tully Blanchard in July of 1985, but recaptured the belt on November 28, 1985. He was stripped of the belt in May of 1986, after attacking promoter Bob Geigel. Magnum's wrestling career ended following a serious automobile accident on October 14, 1986. He was a booker with WCW from 1990 until 1992.

Maivia, Neff held the Hawaiian Title several times in the early 1960s. He also held the Hawaiian Tag Team Title several times from 1961 through 1966, teaming with Billy White Wolf, Lord James Blears and Pampero Firpo.

Maivia, Peter (b. 1937, d. June 13, 1982; Samoa; 270 lbs.) was born in Samoa and raised in New Zealand, where he made his professional wrestling debut. He held the Australasian Title in New Zealand several times in the mid-1960s. He subsequently trained and competed in England for several years. White there, he was cast in a fight scene against Sean Connery in the 1967 James Bond film *You Only Live Twice*. Maivia then went to Hawaii, where he both wrestled and promoted matches. He held the Hawaiian Tag Team Title several times in 1968, teaming with Jim Hady and Billy White Wolf. He teamed with Ray Stevens to hold the NWA World Tag Team Title in San Francisco in November of 1969. He also held the San Francisco belts in June of 1974, teaming with Pat Patterson. He held the NWA U.S. Title in San Francisco in October of 1974. He was a popular competitor when he teamed with Bob Backlund for a tag team title bout. During the bout Maivia turned on Backlund and joined with rulebreakers Spiros Arion and Victor Rivera in battering his former partner. Maivia subsequently wrestled as a vicious rulebreaker under the management of Fred Blassie. He defeated Harley Race by disqualification in a match for the NWA Heavyweight Title in New Zealand in February of 1979, but Maivia refused the title. He held the NWA Americas Title in Los Angeles in May of 1981. The Samoan wrestler died of cancer in Honolulu, Hawaii, on June 13, 1982.

Majors, Terry (b. 1929; Cincinnati, Ohio; 5'4", 130 lbs.) began wrestling in the late 1940s. The brown-haired athlete was one of the roughest female grapplers in the 1950s.

Malcewicz, Joe (b. 1898, d. April 20, 1962) was born in Utica, New York. He worked as a promoter for the NWA in San Francisco in the 1950s.

Malenko, Professor Boris (Larry Simon; b. 1933, d. September

1, 1994) wrestled as Crusher Duggan to hold the NWA Texas Title in November of 1957. He wrestled extensively in the Southeast during the 1960s and 1970s, sometimes under the name Otto von Krupp. He teamed with Bob Geigel to defeat Dale Lewis and Pat Kennedy for the AWA World Tag Team Title in November of 1961. They relinquished the belts when Malenko was injured the following January. Malenko held the NWA Southern Title in Florida for several months in late 1962. He also held the NWA Florida Title from May until August of 1967. He teamed with Johnny Valentine to briefly hold the NWA Southern Tag Team Title in Florida in August of 1968. He held the World Class Championship in Texas in May of 1970. He teamed with Bob Roop to briefly hold the Florida Tag Team Title in May of 1972. He again held the Florida belts with Johnny Walker the following month. He retired from the ring in 1975 to train wrestlers in Florida. He is the father of Dean and Joe Malenko. He died of cancer on September 1, 1994.

Malenko, Dean (Dean Simon; b. August 4, 1960; Tampa, Florida; 5'9", 216 lbs.) is the son of Boris Malenko. He began wrestling in 1982. He wrestled often in Japan in the late 1980s and 1990s, sometimes teaming with his older brother, Joe. He wrestled with Ted Petty as the Kimoto Dragons in WWN in 1993. Malenko entered ECW in 1994, where he captured the TV title in November. He entered the WCW in 1995, where he often competed against Eddy Guerrero.

Malenko, Debbie was a leading female wrestler in the early 1990s. She appeared often in the ring in Japan, sometimes teaming with Sakie Hasegawa.

Malenko, Joe (Joe Simon; b. June 4, 1956; Tampa, Florida; 5'10", 220 lbs.) began wrestling in 1977. He is the son of Boris Malenko, and often teamed with his younger brother, Dean, in Japan.

Man Mountain Mike (625 lbs.) was a massive wrestler popular in the 1970s. He often teamed with Haystacks Calhoun.

Man Mountain Rock *see* Payne, Maxx

Man of the '90s (Warren Bianci) wrestled in the USWA in the early 1990s. He was managed by Lauren Davenport.

Managoff, Bobby (b. 1914; Los Angeles, California; 6', 238 lbs.) is the son of wrestler Ivan Managoff. He held the Pacific Coast Title in San Francisco several times in 1940 and 1941. He held the NWA Heavyweight Title from November 27, 1942, until his defeat by Bill Longson in St. Louis, Missouri, on February 19, 1943. He held the NWA Texas Title in 1945. He held the AWA Title in Montreal, Canada, several times in the late 1940s. He held the Hawaiian Title in 1949. He underwent eye surgery in 1950 and was sidelined from the ring for over a year. He returned to capture the Hawaiian Title again in 1953. He held the Midwest Title in Chicago in 1957.

Managoff, Pete (d. 19??) held

the NWA Texas Title in January of 1960.

Manchurians, The *see* Tio & Tapu

Mankind *see* Cactus Jack

Manlapig, Pantaleon held the Pacific Coast Title in San Francisco several times in 1940.

Manley, James *see* Powers, Jim

Manoukian, Dan teamed with Kurt Von Poppenheim to hold the NWA Pacific Northwest Tag Team Title in May of 1959. He held the NWA Texas Title in January of 1961. He teamed with Tony Borne to hold the NWA Texas Tag Team Title in February of 1961. He held the NWA Pacific Northwest Title in August of 1964. He teamed with Ray Stevens to capture the NWA World Tag Team Title in San Francisco in November of 1964.

Manriquez, Cesar *see* Medico, El

Mansfield, Eddie (Beverly Hills, California; 230 lbs.) was a leading wrestler in the 1970s and early 1980s. He held the Florida TV Title in 1981.

Manson, Cactus Jack *see* Cactus Jack Manson

Mantaur, The (Mike Hallick; 6'1", 401 lbs.) entered the WWF as the Mantaur in December of 1994. He left the promotion the following year, and entered ECW as Bruiser Mestino in early 1996.

Mantel, Dirty Dutch (Wayne Cowan; Oil Trough, Texas; 5'11", 224 lbs.) began wrestling in 1973. He often carried a whip, called "shoo-baby," to the ring. Wrestling as Wayne Cowan, he held the ASWA Georgia Junior Heavyweight Title in April of 1974. He wrestled often in the Mid-South area, where he teamed with David Shults to hold the Southern Tag Team Title in 1976. He held the Mid-America Tag Team Title several times in 1978, teaming with Gypsy Joe and Ken Lucas. Mantel also held the Mid-America Title several times from 1978 through 1983. He teamed with Jerry Stubbs to hold the NWA Southeastern Tag Team Title in 1980, and teamed with Austin Idol to hold the CWA Tag Team Title during the year. Mantell held the Southern Heavyweight Title several times in 1981 and 1982. He also held the Southeastern tag belts with Koko Ware in September of 1983, and with Tommy Rich in September of 1984. He held the CWA International Title several times in 1984 and 1985. He recaptured the Southern Tag Team Title with Bill Dundee as his partner in November of 1985. He teamed with Bobby Jaggers as the Kansas Jayhawks in the NWA in the mid-1980s. He held the NWA Southeastern Title for several months in mid-1987. He held the CWA Title several times in 1989, sometimes wrestling under the name Texas Dirt. He briefly wrestled with the Desperadoes in the WCW in 1990. He held the WWC Universal Title in Puerto Rico in June of 1994. Mantel managed the Blu Brothers as Uncle Zebadiah in the WWF in 1995.

Mantell, Johnny (Dallas, Texas; 6'1", 233 lbs.) wrestled as the

Hood to capture the NWA Americas Title in Los Angeles in 1980. He held the World Class TV Title in October of 1983. He teamed with Black Bart as the Rough Riders to capture the Global World Tag Team Title in October of 1992.

Mantell, Ken teamed with Tom Jones to hold the U.S. Tag Team Title in Louisiana in August of 1972. Wrestling as Clay Spencer, he teamed with Bull Ramos to hold the NWA Pacific Northwest Tag Team Title in June of 1973. Mantell defeated Danny Hodge of the NWA World Junior Heavyweight Title in December of 1973. He retained the belt until June of 1975, when he lost the belt to Hiro Matsuda. He teamed with Ron Bass to hold the NWA Central States Tag Team Title in November of 1975. Mantell teamed with Dean Ho to briefly hold the NWA Georgia Tag Team Title in July of 1976. He held the NWA Americas Title in Los Angeles in October of 1976. He held the Mid-South Louisiana Title in July of 1980.

Maoris, The (Tudui & Wakahi) *see* Tapu, Chief & Tio, The Great

Mar, Victor Manuel *see* Black Cat

Marella, Joey (b. 1964, d. July 4, 1994) was the son of wrestler and commentator Gorilla Monsoon. He was a referee in the WWF and was killed in an automobile accident in Burlington, North Carolina, on July 4, 1994.

Mareno, Buddy *see* Atlas, Omar

Mariko, Plum (b. 1968, d. August 16, 1997) was a leading female wrestler in Japan from the mid-1980s. She originally wrestled as Mariko Umeda. Mariko died on August 16, 1997, of brain damage from head trauma after

collapsing in the wrestling ring in Japan the previous night.

Marino, Mike (Mike Harrison; d. August 24, 1981) was a leading British wrestler from the late 1950s. He held the British World Mid-Heavyweight Title several times from 1957 through the late 1960s.

Marino, Tony teamed with Stan Stasiak to capture the NWA Pacific Northwest Tag Team Title in July of 1969. He teamed with Victor Rivera to capture the WWWF International Tag Team Title in December of 1969. They were defeated for the belts by the Mongols in June of 1970.

Mario *see* Super Mario

Markoff, Chris teamed with Angelo Poffo as the Devil's Duo to hold the WWA Tag Team belts in 1966 and 1967. Markoff teamed with Harley Race in October of 1967 after Larry Hennig's leg was broken. He and Race were defeated for the AWA Tag Team Title by Pat O'Connor and Wilbur Snyder in November of 1967. He teamed with Bronko Lubich to hold the NWA Florida Tag Team Title in late 1969 and early 1970. He and Lubich also held the World Class American Tag Team Title in Texas several times in the early 1970s. He also held the Florida belts with Bobby Shane in December of 1972. He teamed with Nikolai Volkoff to hold the NWA Atlantic Coast Tag Title in 1981.

Marlena *see* York, Alexandra

Marlin, Eddie (b. 1931) often teamed with Tommy Gilbert in the Memphis area in the early 1970s. They held the Southern Tag Team Title several times in 1973. He remained a leading grappler in the area for the next decade. He subsequently worked with the USWA as a promoter and spokesman. He occasionally wrestled through the 1990s, sometimes teamed with his grandson, Jeff Jarrett.

Marsh, Tiger Joe (Joe Marusich; b. 1911, d. May 9, 1989; Chicago, Illinois; 6'1", 222 lbs.) began wrestling in the late 1920s. He held the world championship in 1937. He wrestled throughout the world and held the All-Service Heavyweight Title in the Philippines while in the Navy during World War II. The bald and burly Marsh remained a popular competitor through the mid-1950s, when he retired from the ring to pursue a full-time acting career. Marsh appeared in the play *Teahouse of the August Moon* for two years on the stage in Chicago. appeared as a character actor in numerous films including *Pinky* (1949), *Panic in the Streets* (1950), *Viva Zapata?* (1952), *The Joe Louis Story* (1953), *On the Waterfront* (1954), *The Egyptian* (1954), *The Rebel Set* (1954), *Vengeance* (1964), *Kitty Can't Help It* (1974), *Escape to Witch Mountain* (1975), *The Cat from Outer Space* (1978) and *Love at First Bite* (1979). He died of heart failure in Chicago on May 9, 1989.

Marshall, Everett (d. 1972) held the MWA Heavyweight Title from July of 1935 until December of 1937. He defeated Ali Baba for the World Heavyweight Title in Chicago, Illinois on November 20, 1936. He also held the title through 1937. He was awarded the NWA Heavyweight Title in September of 1938 and retained the belt until his defeat by Lou Thesz in February of 1939.

Martel, Michel (d. June 30, 1978) teamed with Danny Babich to hold the Calgary Stampede International Tag Team Title several times in 1972 and 1973. He briefly held the Stampede North American Title in early 1978.

Martel, Pierre *see* Martin, Frenchy

Martel, Rick (Richard Vignault; b. March 18; Quebec, Canada; 6', 236 lbs.) began wrestling in June of 1972. He teamed with Don Muraco to hold the Hawaiian Tag Team Title in November of 1978. He held the NWA Pacific Northwest Title for several months from March of 1980. He also held the Pacific Northwest Tag Title several times in 1980, teaming with Roddy Piper. He and Piper also held the Canadian Tag Team Title in May of 1980. He teamed with Tony Garea to capture the WWF Tag Team Title from the Samoans in November of 1980. They were defeated by the Moondogs in March of 1981. They reclaimed the belts from the Moondogs in July of 1981, but were defeated for the title by Mr. Fuji and Mr. Saito in October of 1981. Martel entered the AWA in 1984 and defeated Jumbo Tsuruta for the AWA Title in May of 1984. He was defeated for the belt by Stan Hansen in December of 1985. He subsequently rejoined the WWF and wrestled with Tito Santana as Strike Force. They defeated the Hart Foundation for the WWF Tag Team Title in October of 1987. They lost the title to Demolition at Wrestlemania IV on March 27, 1988. He became known as "the Model" while wrestling in the WWF in 1989.

Martel, Sherri (Sherri Russell; b. February 8, 1954; New Orleans, Louisiana; 5'7", 132 lbs.) was born in New Orleans. She made her debut in wrestling in Memphis, Tennessee, in 1980. She competed for nearly a year and subsequently trained with Donna Christentello, and the Fabulous Moolah in South Carolina. She left wrestling in 1982, but returned to the ring in June of 1985. She became known as Sensational Sherry, and won the AWA Women's Title from Candi Devine in September of 1985. She also managed tag team champions Buddy Rose and Doug Somers in the AWA in 1986. She also managed Kevin Kelly in 1987. She exchanged the women's title several times with Candy Devine until July of 1987, when she left the AWA and entered the WWF. She defeated the Fabulous Moolah for the WWF Women's Title in July of 1987. She lost the title to Rockin' Robin in October of 1988, in a match in Paris, France. Martel left the WWF in July of 1993 and subsequently joined the WCW, where she managed Ric Flair in June of 1994. She subsequently managed the tag team Harlem Heat as Sister Sherri, leading them to several tag team championships in 1994 and 1995.

Martin, Frenchy (Pierre Martel), wrestling as Don Gagne, teamed with Ripper Collins to hold the Calgary Stampede International Tag Team Title in 1976. He also held the Stampede North American Title in 1977. Wrestling as Mad Dog Martin, he held the British Empire Title in New Zealand in 1979. He held the WWC North American Title in Puerto Rico in late 1980. He teamed with Pierre Lefebfvre to hold the Canadian International Tag Team Title in Montreal in February of 1984. He managed Dino Bravo in the WWF in the late 1980s. He is the brother of wrestler Rick Martel.

Martin, Gary teamed with Big Bad John to hold the World Tag Team Title in Tennessee in 1971.

Martin, Judy held the World Class Women's American Title in 1982. She teamed with Leilani Kai to hold the WWF Women's Tag Team belts in August of 1985. They were known as the Glamour Girls and were often managed by Jimmy Hart and Christopher Love. They lost the belts to the Japanese team, the Jumping Bomb Angels, in January of 1988, but returned to capture the title the following June. They left the WWF the following year. They defeated Team America for the LPWA Tag Team Title in February of 1991.

Martin, Pepper held the NWA Pacific Northwest Title several times in the mid-1960s. He also held the Pacific Northwest tag belts in the mid-1960s, teaming with Shag Thomas, Rene Goulet, Paul Jones, Luther Lindsay and Billy White Wolf.

Martin, Terry teamed with Tommy Martin to hold the NWA Central States Tag Team Title in October of 1968. He held the NWA Central States Title in December of 1974.

Martin, Tommy teamed with Terry Martin to hold the NWA Central States Tag Team Title in October of 1968.

Martin, Tony teamed with Duke Keomuka to hold the NWA Texas Tag Team Title in July of 1956.

Martin, Troy *see* Douglas, Shane

Martinelli, Angelo (Stan Wiggins; d. 19??; Boston, Massachusetts) began wrestling in the mid-1930s. He was active in the South and Mid-West during the 1940s. Martinelli held the NWA Southern Title in 1952.

Martinelli, Tony (b. 1911; Clifton, New Jersey; 5'11", 220 lbs.) played football at Fordham before becoming a professional wrestler in the late 1930s. He was known in the ring as the Clifton Cutie, and wrestled in California as world champion during the 1940s. He remained a popular mat star through the 1950s and was known for his great strength in the ring.

Martinez, Frank teamed with Gypsy Joe as the Blue Infernos in the Mid-South area in the mid-1960s.

Martinez, Luis "Arriba" teamed with Seymour Koenig to hold the Midwest Tag Team Title in Chicago in December of 1956. He teamed with Wilbur Snyder to capture the WWA Tag Team Title from the Assassins in July of 1966. They lost the belts two months later to Angelo Poffo and Chris Markoff.

Martino, Salvatore *see* Bellomo, Salvatore

Martinson, Yvar (d. July 22, 1975) was a leading British wrestler during the 1940s. He held the British World Heavyweight Title in 1947.

Marusich, Joe *see* Marsh, Tiger Joe

Mascara Magica *see* Guerrero, Eddy

Mascaro Ano 2000 (Jesus Reyes) was a popular Mexican wrestler from the early 1980s. He captured the EMLL Light Heavyweight Title in April of 1982. He teamed with Cien Caras to hold the Mexican National Tag Team Title in 1986.

Masked Bat, The *see* O'Shocker, Bob

Masked Black Secret, The *see* Shadow, The

Masked Destroyer, The *see* Kowalski, Killer

Masked Hoods, The *see* Santana, Ricky & Torres, Tony

Masked Infernos, The *see* Cain, Frankie & Smith, Rocky

Masked Marvel *see* Bonica, John J.

Masked Marvel *see* Cox, Ted

Masked Outlaw, The *see* Funk, Dory, Jr.

Masked Rebel, The *see* Fargo, Sonny

Masked Strangler, The *see* Valiant, Jerry

Masked Superstar *see* Ax

Masked Terror *see* York, Jay

Mason, Roger *see* Smith, Roger

Massey, Al (Charlotte, North Carolina) held the NWA Southern Title in 1952.

Master Blaster, The (Jack Diamond) teamed with Tex Sallinger in the USWA in the early 1990s. He also wrestled as Humongous in the USWA.

Master of Pain, The *see* Undertaker, The

Masters, Doug (Tulsa, Oklahoma; 6'1", 230 lbs.) began wrestling in 1990. He often tagged with Bart Sawyer in the early 1990s. They captured the USWA Tag Team Title briefly in November of 1991. He teamed with Ron Starr to hold the WWC Tag Team Title in Puerto Rico several times in 1992.

Masters, Mike held the NWA Americas Title in Los Angeles in March of 1981.

Matador, The *see* Stubbs, Jerry

Matador, The *see* Santana, Tito

Mathews, Darren *see* Regal, Steven

Matsuda, Hiro held the NWA Southern Title in Florida from February of 1963 until August of 1963. Matsuda held the NWA World Junior Heavyweight Title in late 1964. He teamed with Duke Keomuka to hold the NWA World Tag Team Title in Florida several times in 1964 and 1965. He also held the belts with Dick Steinborn in November of 1965. He teamed with Antonio Inoki to hold the World Tag Team Title in Tennessee in January of 1966. He teamed with the Missouri Mauler to hold the NWA Florida Tag Team Title several times in 1969. He held the NWA Southern Title in Florida several times in 1970 and 1971. He again held the NWA Junior Heavyweight belt from June of 1975, until his defeat by Danny Hodge in March of 1976. Matsuda was a manager in the NWA in the late 1980s, managing Michael Hayes and the Four Horsemen. Matsuda later retired to Florida where was a promoter for the NWA. He also ran a judo and wrestling school.

Matsuda, Osamu (b. September 19, 1966) began wrestling with New Japan in July of 1986. He also competed in Japan and Mexico as El Samurai in the early 1990s. He captured the UWA Middleweight Title in Mexico in May of 1993.

Matsumoto, Dump was a leading Japanese woman wrestler from the 1980s. She held the All-Japan WWWA Women's Tag Team Title several times in the 1980s, teaming with Crane Yu and Bull Nakano.

Matta, Carlos teamed with Raul Matta to hold the NWA Americas Tag Team Title in Los Angeles in September of 1976. He again held the Americas tag belts in August of 1979, teaming with Mando Guerrero.

Matta, Raul held the NWA Americas Tag Team Title in Los Angeles several times in 1972 and 1973, teaming with Dory Dixon, Ray Mendoza and David Morgan. He also held the Americas tag belts several times in 1975 and 1976, teaming with Chavo Guerrero and Carlos Matta. He teamed with Billy White Cloud to capture the World Class Texas Tag Team Title in January of 1981. They left the World Class promotion in August of 1981.

Maximum Overdrive *see* Storm, J.W. & Hunt, Tim

Maxine, Miss (Michelle Afflis) was the daughter of Dick the Bruiser. She was married to wrestler Spike Huber in the early 1980s and married to Scott Romer from 1984. She and Romer managed the tag team champions, the World Warriors, in the WWA in 1984.

May, Ida (b. 1929; Norwich, Connecticut; 5'2", 126 lbs.) began wrestling in 1951. She was known for her small stature and long brunette hair. She remained a top female grappler throughout the decade.

Maynard, Earl teamed with Dean Ho to hold the Canadian Tag Team Title in May of 1969. He held the NWA Americas Tag Team Title in Los Angeles several times in the early 1970s, teaming with Rocky Johnson and Dory Dixon.

Mayne, Bobby teamed with Charlie Fulton to hold the Southern Tag Team Title in June of 1974. They were managed by Sir Dudley Clements.

Mayne, Lonnie "Moondog" (Ronald Mayne; d. August 13, 1978) began wrestling in the late 1960s. He held the NWA Pacific Northwest Title nearly a dozen times between 1967 and 1970. He teamed with Tony Borne to hold the Pacific Northwest tag belts numerous times

in the late 1960s and early 1970s. He held the Hawaiian Title in February of 1971. He also held the Hawaiian tag belts several times in 1971, teaming with Ripper Collins and Sweet Daddy Siki. He wrestled in the Pacific Northwest in the early 1970s, often teaming with Tony Borne. He left wrestling in 1972. He returned the following year as Moondog Mayne, and captured the NWA U.S. Title in San Francisco in December of 1973. He teamed with Pat Patterson to hold the NWA World Tag Team Title in San Francisco in August of 1975. He captured the World Class Texas Title in March of 1977. He again held the San Francisco tag belts in February of 1978, teaming with Dean Ho. He held the NWA U.S. Title several more times in 1978. He teamed with Ron Bass to hold the NWA Americas Tag Team Title in March of 1978. Mayne defeated Hector Guerrero for the NWA Americas Title in Los Angeles on August 11, 1978. He was killed in an automobile accident two days later on August 13, 1978.

Mazurki, Mike (Mikhail Mazurwski; b. 1909, d. December 9, 1990; Glendale, California; 6'6", 240 lbs.) was born in the Ukraine and came to the United States as a child. His family settled in Cohoes, New York, and he played football at Manhattan College. He began wrestling in the late 1920s. He remained a popular competitor throughout the next two decades. He was known in the ring for his figure four scissors hold. Mazurki was also a popular character actor, appearing in nearly one hundred films. He often played villainous characters in such films as *Belle of the Nineties* (1934), *Black Fury* (1935), *Mr. Moto's Gamble* (1938), *The Shanghai Gesture* (1941), *Gentleman Jim* (1942), *Flying Tigers* (1942), *Henry Aldrich Haunts a House* (1943), *Mission to Moscow* (1943), *The Missing Juror* (1944), *The Canterville Ghost* (1944), *The Thin Man Comes Home* (1944), *Shine On, Harvest Moon* (1944), *Murder, My Sweet* (1945), *Dick Tracy* (1945), *Nob Hill* (1945), *The Horn Blows at Midnight* (1945), *Mysterious Intruder* (1946), *Sinbad the Sailor* (1947), *Nightmare Alley* (1947), *Unconquered* (1947), *I Walk Alone* (1948), *The Noose Hangs High* (1948), *Rope of Sand* (1949), *Samson and Delilah* (1949), *Come to the Stable* (1949), *The Devil's Henchman* (1949), *Neptune's Daughter* (1949), *Night and the City* (1950), *Ten Tall Men* (1951), *My Favorite Spy* (1951), *The Egyptian* (1954), *Blood Alley* (1955), *Kismet* (1955), *Davy Crockett— King of the Wild Frontier* (1955), *New York Confidential* (1955), *New Orleans Uncensored* (1955), *The Man from Laramie* (1955), *Comanche* (1956), *Around the World in Eighty Days* (1956), *The Buccaneer* (1958), *The Man Who Died Twice* (1958), *Some Like It Hot* (1959), *Alias Jesse James* (1959), *Pocketful of Miracles* (1961), *The Errand Boy* (1961), *Five Weeks in a Balloon* (1962), *Zotz!* (1962), *Four for Texas* (1963), *Donovan's Reef* (1963), *It's a Mad Mad Mad Mad World* (1963), *Cheyenne Autumn* (1964), *Requiem for a Gunfighter* (1965), *Seven Women* (1966), *The Adventures of Bullwhip Griffin* (1967), *Which Way to the Front?* (1970), *Challenge to Be Free* (1972), *The Centerfold Girls*

(1974), *The Wild McCullochs* (1975), *Won Ton Ton, the Dog Who Saved Hollywood* (1976), *The Magic of Lassie* (1978), *Gas Pump Girls* (1979), *The Man with Bogart's Face* (1979), *Alligator* (1980) *...All the Marbles* (1981) and *Dick Tracy* (1990). He was also a regular performer on the television series *It's About Time* in 1966 and *The Chicago Teddybears* in 1971. Mazurki died after a long illness at a Glendale, California, hospital on December 9, 1990.

Mazurwski, Mikhail *see* Mazurki, Mike

Medico, El (Apollo Jalisco) held the NWA Americas Tag Team Title several times in 1969, teaming with Alfonso Dantes and Pepe Lopez. He held the NWA Americas Title in 1980.

Medico, El (Cesar Manriquez; d. June 16, 1960) held the Texas Brass Knucks Title in November of 1956. He teamed with Pepper Gomez to hold the NWA Texas Tag Team Title in June of 1957. He also held the NWA Texas Title several times in 1957 and 1958.

Medico, El *see* Hernandez, Luis

Medico Asasino, El was a popular Mexican wrestler in the 1950s. He held the Mexican National Heavyweight Title in 1956. He initially wore a silver mask in the ring, but later changed his mask to all white to distinquish him from Mexican wrestler El Santo. Medico Asasino appeared in several Mexican films in the 1950s including *El Enmascarado de Plata* (1952).

Medics, The *see* Gonzales, Tony & Lortie, Donald

Medics, The *see* Lewi, Dale & Griffin, Bob

Medics, The *see* Starr, Jim & Garrett, Billy

Meeker, Roland (b. 1916; Shreveport, Louisiana; 6', 223 lbs.) was born in North Dakota. He began wrestling in the late 1930s. He was known in the ring for his flying bulldog headlock.

Mega Maharishi *see* DeBeers, Colonel

Melby, Bill held the NWA Texas Title in late 1957 and early 1958. He teamed with Pepper Gomez to hold the NWA Texas Tag Team Title in November of 1957.

Melson, Frank "the Tank" (6'2", 355 lbs.) began wrestling in 1986. He was a popular Chicago wrestler who held the Windy City Wrestling Title several times in 1989 and 1990.

Men at Work *see* Canyon, Chris & Starr, Mark

Men on a Mission *see* Mabel & Mo

Menacker, Frank "Slammin' Sam" (b. 1914, d. January 7, 1994) began wrestling in the mid-1930s. He served in the army during World War II, rising to the rank of major. He continued to wrestle during the 1940s and early 1950s and was later a promoter and announcer in El Paso, Texas, and St. Louis, Missouri. He appeared in several films including *Mighty Joe Young* (1949), *Alias the Champ* (1949), *Abbott and Costello in the Foreign Legion* (1950), *Bodyhold* (1950), *Sounder* (1972) and *The Wrestler* (1974) with Verne Gagne. He died in Auburn, Illinois, on January 7, 1994.

Mendeblis, Benny was a native a Tucson, Arizona. He made his wrestling debut in the early 1970s. He often teamed with Moses Morales in his feuds against such competitors as Johnny Ringer, Jody Arnold and Freddie Gomez. Mendeblis was a two-time winner of the Arizona Junior Heavyweight Title in the mid-1970s.

Mendietta, Pepe teamed with Rito Romero to hold the NWA Texas Tag Team Title in November of 1954.

Mendoza, Rey (Jorge Diaz) captured the EMLL Light Heavyweight Title in Mexico in September of 1959. He held the EMLL belt several times during the 1960s and early 1970s. He held the NWA Americas Tag Team Title in Los Angeles several times in 1973 and 1974, teaming with Raul Matta and Raul Reyes. He captured the UWA Light Heavyweight Title in Mexico in November of 1975. He held the title several more times in the late 1970s.

Meng *see* Haku

Mephisto *see* Rodriguez, Romeo

Mephisto, The Great (Louis Papineau) teamed with Dante to hold the Southern Tag Team Title several times in the early 1960s. They captured the World Tag Team Title in Tennessee several times in 1969. Mephisto held the NWA Southern Title in Florida several times in 1970. He also teamed with Dante to hold the NWA Southern

Tag Title in Florida in early 1970. He held the NWA U.S. Title in San Francisco in February of 1973. He teamed with Kinji Shibuya to hold the NWA World Tag Team Title in San Francisco in April of 1973. He managed the Manchurians in the late 1970s and early 1980s.

Mera, Akihisa *see* Kabuki, The Great

Mercenaries, The *see* Sierra, David "Cuban Assassin" & Starr, Ron

Mercer, Marvin "Atomic" (b. 1919; Reading, Pennsylvania; 5'10", 198 lbs.) began wrestling in the mid-1940s. He was known in the ring for his flying dropkick, which he called the "atomic thrust." He is a former junior heavyweight champion and remained an active competitor through the 1950s.

Mercy, Waylon *see* Spivey, Dan

Merro, Mark *see* Badd, Johnny B.

Merro, Tony *see* Vendetta, Tony

Mestino, Bruiser *see* Mantaur, The

Miami Vice Defenders *see* Savannah Jack & Roberts, Ed

Miceli, Madusa (Debra Ann Micelli; b. February 9, 1963; Milan, Italy; 5'9 1/2", 150 lbs.) was born in Milan, Italy, and raised in Minnesota. She excelled in gymnastics and track while in high school. She entered wrestling as Medusa Miceli in the AWA in 1987. She defeated Candy Devine for the AWA Women's Title in a tournament on

December 27, 1987. She retained the title until November 26, 1988, when she was defeated by Wendi Richter. She was also a manager in the AWA, guiding Kevin Kelly, Curt Hennig and Nick Kiniski in the ring. She left the promotion in the late 1980s and joined with All-Japan Women's Pro Wrestling. She captured the IWA World Title in Japan and also became a top competitor in kick boxing. She also appeared in films and recorded songs while in Japan. She entered the WCW in January of 1992, joining Paul E. Dangerously's Dangerous Alliance. She also managed Rick Rude while in the WCW. She broke with Dangerously later in the year and challenged him in the ring in several matches. She became known as Alundra Blayze when she entered the WWF in October of 1993. She won the revived WWF Women's Title by defeating Heidi Lee Morgan in a tournament final in Poughkeepsie, New York, on December 13, 1993. She lost the belt to Bull Nakano at the Tokyo Dome in Tokyo, Japan on November 20, 1994. She reclaimed the WWF title in a rematch with Nakano on April 3, 1995. She lost the belt to Bertha Faye at a match in Pittsburgh, Pennsylvania, in August of 1995. She reclaimed the belt from Bertha Faye two months later. She left the WWF and returned to WCW in December of 1995, resuming the name Madusa.

Micelli, Debbie *see* Miceli Madusa

Michaels, Chris (Oakdale, New York; 5'9", 223 lbs.) teamed with Johnny Hot Body to win the ECW

Tag Team Title in May of 1993. He entered the USWA several months later where he wrestled with Todd Morton as Far 2 Wild. They held the USWA Tag Team Title in December of 1993.

Michaels, Cody teamed with Jeff Jarrett to hold the USWA Tag Team Title in November of 1990.

Michaels, Jon (5'11", 240 lbs.) began wrestling in 1985. He wrestled in the Georgia All-Stars and was known as the Bug Man.

Michaels, Shawn (Michael Hickenbottom; b. July 22, 1965; San Antonio, Texas; 6', 230 lbs.) began wrestling in 1984. He teamed with Paul Diamond as American Force to hold the Texas All-Star Texas Tag Team Title several times in late 1985. He entered the AWA in 1986 and formed the Midnight Rockers with Marty Jannetty. They captured the NWA Central States Tag Team Title in May of 1986. The duo defeated Buddy Rose and Doug Somers for the AWA Tag Team Title on January 27, 1987. They lost the belts to Boris Zhukov and Soldat Ustinov at a match in Lake Tahoe, Nevada, on May 25, 1987. They also held the Southern Tag Team Title several times in late 1987, where they feuded with the Rock 'n' Roll RPMS. They regained the AWA title in a match against Dennis Condrey and Randy Rose in October of 1987. Jannetty and Michaels finally lost the belts to Pat Tanaka and Paul Diamond on March 19, 1988. They joined the WWF the following year where they became known as the Rockers. They feuded with the Hart Foundation, and nearly captured the WWF tag title. He and Michaels later split and battled in a series of matches until Jannetty left the WWF in the Fall of 1992. Jannetty returned to defeat Michaels for the Intercontinental Title in a TV match on May 17, 1993. Michaels recaptured the title on June 6, 1993. Michaels vacated the Intercontinental Title when he briefly left the WWF in September of 1993. Michaels feuded with Razor Ramon in 1994 in a series of bouts that culminated in several memorable ladder matches. He teamed with Diesel to defeat the Head Shrinkers for the WWF Tag Team belt in Indianapolis, Indiana, on August 28, 1994. The duo disbanded their partnership and gave up the belts on November 23, 1994. Michaels defeated Jeff Jarrett for the WWF Intercontinental Title at SummerSlam in Nashville, Tennessee, on July 23, 1995. Michaels was beaten by several assailants in a parking lot in Syracuse, New York, on October 13, 1995. He was forced to relinquish the Intercontinental belt to Dean Douglas when he was unable to defend the title later in the month. Michaels recovered from his injuries and returned to the ring. He defeated Bret Hart for the WWF Heavyweight Title in a sixty minute iron-man match at Wrestlemania XII on March 31, 1996.

Michalik, Art teamed with the Destroyer to hold the NWA Pacific Northwest Tag Team Title several time in 1963 and 1964.

Midnight Express, The *see* Condrey, Dennis & Eaton, Bobby

Midnight Express, The *see* Condrey, Dennis; Rose, Randy; Austin, Norvell & Starr, Ron

Midnight Express, The *see* Eaton, Bobby & Lane, Stan

Midnight Rockers, The *see* Michaels, Shawn & Jannetty, Marty

Mighty Atlas *see* Shapiro, Morris

Mighty Igor, The (Igor Vodic) was a popular wrestler in the Midwest during the late 1960s and 1970s. He held the Mid-West Title in Omaha in 1967. He engaged in feuds with such mat stars as Bulldog Brower and the Sheik. He briefly held the AWA Title, interrupting Mad Dog Vachon's title reign in May of 1965. He was managed by Ivan Kalmikoff in the mid-1970s. He also held the NWA U.S. Title briefly in the late 1970s. He held the WWC Puerto Rican Title in January of 1987.

Mighty Karadajian *see* Karadagian, Martin

Mighty Mickey *see* Cortolano, Mickey

Mighty Titan, The *see* Clancy, Mike

Mighty Yankees, The *see* Cook, Bob & Grey Jerry

Mighty Yankees, The *see* Evans, Moose & Bob Stanlee

Mighty Yankees, The *see* Sullivan, Eddie & Morrell, Frank

Mikaloff, Ivan (d. 19??; 6', 260 lbs.) wrestled as Ivan the Terrible in the 1940s and 1950s.

Mil Mascaras (Mexico City, Mexico; 5'11", 245 lbs.) began wrestling in 1964. The popular masked Mexican star's name means "Man of 1,000 Masks." He held the Mexican National Light Heavyweight Championship several times in 1967 and 1968. He held the NWA Americas Title in Los Angeles in June of 1968. He held the title several more times in the late 1960s and early 1970s. Mil Mascaras often teamed with his two brothers, Dos Caras and El Sicodelico, in tag matches in Mexico. He became the first wrestler allowed to wear a mask in the state of New York by the State Athletic Commission in December of 1972. He teamed with Jose Lothario to hold the World Class American Tag Team Title in Texas in 1973. He made several unsuccessful bids for the NWA Title against Dory Funk, Jr. and Jack Brisco in the mid-1970s. He teamed with Jeff Jarrett to hold the World Class World Tag Team Title in June of 1989. Mil Mascaras was also a popular Mexican film star in the 1960s and 1970s, appearing in such movies as *The Vampires* (1968), *Secret of Death* (1968), *The Scoundrels* (1969), *The Champions of Justice Return* (1972), *The Mummies of Guanajuato* (1972) and *The Castle of the Mummies of Guanajuato* (1972).

Milano, Mario held the Southern Heavyweight Tag Team Title with Jackie Fargo in November of 1963. Milano often teamed with Len Rossi during the 1960s, and they held the Southern tag belts several times from 1964 through 1966. He again teamed with Fargo to hold the World Tag Team Title in Tennessee in March of 1965. Milano held the IWA Championship in Australia several times between 1967 and 1969.

Miller, Dr. Bill (b. 1928; d. March 24, 1997; Fremont, Ohio; 6'4", 250 lbs.) was a leading collegiate athlete at Ohio State. He made his professional wrestling debut in the early 1950s. He held the AWA Ohio Title in 1952. He teamed with Ed Miller to hold the Canadian Open Tag Team Title in Toronto in February of 1957. Wrestling as Dr. X, he held the World Title in Omaha several times from 1959 through 1961. He wrestled as Mister M when he defeated Verne Gagne for the AWA Title in January of 1962. He lost a rematch with Gagne for the championship in August of 1962. He teamed with Dan Miller to win the WWWF U.S. Tag Team Title from Gorilla Monsoon and Bill Watts in July of 1965. They lost the title to Antonio Pugliese and Johnny Valentine in February of 1966. Miller retired from wrestling in 1974 to become a veternarian. He died of a heart attack on March 24, 1997.

Miller, Butch *see* Bushwhacker Butch

Miller, Dan held the Canadian Tag Team Title several times in 1963, teaming with Sandor Kovacs, Ron Etchison and Whipper Billy Watson. He teamed with Dr. Bill Miller to win the WWWF U.S. Tag Team Title from Gorilla Monsoon and Bill Watts in July of 1965. They lost the title to Antonio Pugliese and Johnny Valentine in February of 1966. He held the World Class Texas Title in December of 1969. He teamed with Fritz Von Erich to hold the World Class American Tag Team Title in early 1969. He teamed with Jose Lothario to briefly hold the NWA Florida Tag Team Title in late 1970.

Miller held the NWA Southern Title in Florida briefly in January of 1970.

Miller, Danny wrestled as Abdul Khadafy to briefly hold the CWA International Title in March of 1986.

Miller, Mike (New Orleans, Louisiana; 6'3", 265 lbs.) began wrestling in 1980. He wrestled extensively in the Pacific Northwest. He held the NWA Pacific Northwest Title several times in the mid-1980s. He also held the Pacific Northwest tag belts several times during this period, teaming with Mr. Ebony, Moondog Moretti, Karl Steiner and Abbuda Dein. He held the Oregon Professional Wrestling Federation Title in July of 1994.

Miller, Pete *see* Mongolian Mauler

Miller, Ron wrestled with Larry O'Day as the Australians to capture the NWA Florida Tag Team Title in August of 1971. They held the belts several times over the next year.

Millich, Joe (Walter J. Millich; b. 1917, d. June 14, 1990; 5'10") began wrestling in the 1930s. He was known for his ability to contort his body in the ring. He was sometimes known as the Human Turtle and the Rubber Man. Millich held the Rocky Mountain Title in Colorado in 1947. He continued to compete through the 1950s. He won the $6 million lottery jackpot in Missouri in 1985. Millich died of a heart attack while exercising at the Missouri Athletic Club in St. Louis on June 14, 1990.

Mills, Al (d. 19??; Missoula, Montana) was the younger brother of Tiny Mills. He began wrestling in the mid-1940s, often teaming with his brother. They held the Canadian Open Tag Team Title in Toronto several times in the early 1950s, and the Canadian Tag Team Title in Edmonton several times in 1954.

Mills, Tiny (b. 1916, d. 19??; Missoula, Montana; 6'3", 258 lbs.) began wrestling in the mid-1940s. A rancher from Montana, Mills often teamed with his younger brother, Al Mills, early in his career. They held the Canadian Open Tag Team Title in Toronto several times in the early 1950s, and Canadian Tag Team Title in Edmonton several times in 1954. He teamed with Duke Keomuka to hold the NWA Texas Tag Team Title in December of 1955. He teamed with Jim Austeri to hold the NWA Southern Tag Team Title in 1956. He teamed with Hombre Montana to hold the NWA World Tag Team Title in San Francisco in June of 1958. Mills teamed with Killer Kowalski as Murder Inc., and they were awarded the AWA Tag Team Title in 1959. They exchanged the belts with Butch Levy and Frank Townsend, and Verne Gagne and Leo Nomellini before their reign ended finally in October of 1960, when they were defeated by Hard Boiled Haggerty and Len Montana. He and Kowalski also captured the Canadian Open Tag Team Title in Toronto in December of 1960. Mills subsequently held the North Dakota Title for several months.

Minelli, Dino teamed with Steve Lawler to hold the SCW Tag Team Title in Georgia in 1988.

Minke, Terry *see* Gordy, Terry

Minton, John *see* Studd, Big John

Miquet, Francois (b. 1918; Paris, France; 5'9", 220 lbs.) was an amateur boxer before becoming a professional wrestler in the late 1930s. He held the French championship before coming to the United States in the late 1940s.

Misawa, Mitsuharu (b. June 18, 1962; Saitama, Japan; 5'11", 228 lbs.) began wrestling in August of 1981. He was a leading contender in All-Japan, where he wrestled as Tiger Mask from 1984 until 1990. He continued to wrestle with All-Japan in the 1990s as Mitsuharu Misawa, holding the Triple Crown Title from August of 1992 until July of 1994.

Miser, The *see* Poffo, Angelo

Miss Texas (Jaque Moore; 5'6", 130 lbs.) began wrestling in 1986. She was a popular women's wrestler in the USWA, where she was the first female wrestler to earn a ranking in the men's division. She wrestled male and female wrestlers in the promotion and sometimes managed PG-13 and the Moondogs. She held the USWA Women's Title several times in 1992 and 1993.

Missing Link, The was a leading wrestling villain in the Florida and Texas areas in the 1970s and early 1980s. He briefly wrestled in the WWF under the management of Bobby Heenan in the 1980s before returning to Texas.

Missing Link, The *see* Firpo, Pampero

Missouri Mauler, The *see* Hamilton, Larry

Mr. America *see* Stanlee, Gene

Mr. Americus *see* Dern, Wally

Mr. Atlanta *see* Zane, Tony

Mr. Brooklyn *see* Bookbinder, Walter

Mr. Canada *see* Berg, Jr., Sammy

Mr. Clyde wrestled in the USWA in the early 1990s. He also wrestled as the Iranian Assassin.

Mr. Ebony *see* Jones, Tom

Mr. Europe *see* Baillargeon, Antonio

Mr. High & Mr. Low *see* Gilbert, Doug & Steinborn, Dick

Mr. Irish *see* Clancy, Mike

Mr. Moto *see* Moto, Mr.

Mr. New York *see* Magnificent Maurice

Mr. Olympia *see* Stubbs, Jerry

Mr. Perfect *see* Hennig, Curt

Mr. Sun *see* Kimura, Rusher

Mr. Uganda *see* Cyclone Nigro

Mr. Wrestling *see* Woods, Tim

Mr. Wrestling II (Johnny Walker; Atlanta, Georgia; 6', 247 lbs.) began wrestling as Johnny Walker in 1955. He teamed with the Amazing Zuma to hold the NWA Texas Tag Team Title in 1959. He teamed with Len Rossi to hold the World Tag Team Title in Tennessee several times in 1968 and 1969. He teamed with Ken Lucas to hold the Southern Tag Team Title in March of 1969. Wrestling as the Grappler, he held the NWA Southern Title in Florida in 1971. He teamed with Boris Malenko to briefly hold the NWA Florida Tag Team Title in June of 1972. He began wrestling as Mr. Wrestling II in the early 1970s at the request of Tim Woods, the original Mr. Wrestling. He teamed with Bob Orton, Jr. to hold the NWA Georgia Tag Team Title in mid-1973, and teamed with Tim "Mr. Wrestling" Woods to capture the belt in August of 1974. The duo again held the title in January of 1977. Teaming with Tony Atlas, Mr. Wrestling II again held the Georgia tag championship in February of 1978. He also held the NWA Georgia Title several times from 1973 through 1980. He held the MSWA North American Title for several months from February of 1979. He held the NWA Florida Title several times in 1981 and 1982. He teamed with Tiger Conway, Jr. to hold the MSWA Tag Team Title in March of 1983. He again held the MSWA belt in March of 1984. He teamed with Willie Kovac to hold the Missouri Wrestling Federation Tag Team Title several times in 1992 and 1993.

Mr. X *see* Mitchell, Guy

Mr. X *see* Townsend, Frank

Mitchell, Guy *see* Valiant, Jerry

Mitchell, Jim (b. 1908, d. 19??; Toledo, Ohio; 5'9", 200 lbs.) was born in Louisville, Kentucky. Known as the Cranium Cracker, Mitchell was a boxing trainer in Chicago before he turned to professional wrestling. He became one of the first Black mat stars in the 1940s.

Mitchell, Jim "the Claw" teamed with the Dream Machien to hold the Southern Tag Team Title in August of 1982.

Mitchell, Mike teamed with Robert Fuller to hold the USWA Tag Team Title briefly in November of 1991.

Mo (Bobby Horne; b. April 13; Harlem, New York; 6'1", 260 lbs.) began wrestling in 1991. He teamed with Mabel as the Harlem Knights in the USWA before they entered WWF as Men on a Mission. They defeated the Quebecers for the WWF Tag Team Championship at a match in London, England, on March 29, 1994. They lost the belts two days later in Sheffield, England, in a rematch with the Quebecers on March 31, 1994. Men on a Mission began wrestling as villains later in the year. Mabel proclaimed Mo as Sir Mo after his success in the King of the Ring tournament in 1995.

Moadib *see* Johnson, Ahmed

MOD Squad, The *see* Jeffers, Mac "Basher" & Jeffers, Jim "Spike"

Mohammed the Butcher *see* Muhammad the Butcher

Momota, Mitsuhiro *see* Rikidozan

Momota, Mitsuo (b. September 21, 1948) was the son of legendary Japanese wrestler Rikidozan. He began wrestling professionally in Japan in November of 1970. He entered All-Japan two years later, where he remained a major star.

Mondt, Joseph "Toots" (d. June 11, 1976) was a wrestler from the 1920s. Mondt later became a leading wrestling promoter in the New York area, heading the Manhattan booking office. He was a founder of the World Wide Wrestling Federation with Vincent McMahon, Sr., in 1963.

Money, Incorporated *see* Schyster, Irwin R. & DiBiase, Ted

Mongol, The *see* Ardelean, Simeon

Mongol, The *see* Lewis, Gene

Mongol, Bepo *see* Volkoff, Nikolai

Mongol, Bolo joined Geto and Bepo in the tag team, the Mongols, in the 1970s.

Mongol, El teamed with Gorilla Monsoon to hold the WWA Tag Team Title in Los Angeles in January of 1966. He also held the WWA tag belts in April of 1966, teaming with Buddy Austin. He held the Western States Title in California in 1966. He captured the NWA Georgia Title five times from 1967 through 1972. He held the NWA Americas Title in Los Angeles in September of 1968. He also held the NWA Georgia Tag Team Title with the Professional in June of 1969. He teamed with Killer Karl Krupp to hold the Southern Tag Team Title in July of 1980.

Mongol, Geto (Newton Tattrie) entered wrestling in 1970, teaming with Bepo Mongol. They were originally managed by Tony Angelo before signing with Lou Albano. They captured the WWWF International Tag Team Title from Tony Marino and Victor Rivera in June of 1970. They exchanged the belts with Bruno Sammartino and Dominic Denucci in the Summer of 1971, and eventually lost the title to Luke Graham and Tarzan Tyler in November of 1971.

Mongolian Mauler, The (Pete Miller; b. September 2; Mongolia; 6'2", 303 lbs.) entered wrestling in 1984. He was trained by Killer Kowalski and wrestled in Europe and Canada. He toured England and South Africa in the late 1980s, and wrestled in Germany in the early 1990s. He wrestled in the WCW in 1993.

Mongolian Stomper, The (Archie Gouldie; b. November 2; Mongolia; 6'2", 239 lbs.) began wrestling in 1963. Wrestling as the Stomper, he held the NWA Central States Title in June of 1965. He teamed with Bob Ellis to hold the Central States tag belts in May of 1966. He teamed with Ciclon Negro to hold the NWA World Tag Team Title in San Francisco in December of 1966. He held the Stampede North American Title in Calgary, Canada, several times in 1968. He again held the Central States belts in the early 1970s, teaming with Bob Geigel, Danny Little Bear and Rufus R. Jones. He held the NWA Southern Title in Florida in 1974. He held the Southern Heavyweight Title in October of 1975. He also held the NWA Southeastern Title several times from 1976 through 1979. He was managed by Gorgeous George Jr. in the Memphis area in the late 1970s, and held the Southern Heavyweight Title in April of 1979.

Managed by Don Carson, he held the NWA National Title from December of 1980 until May of 1981. He teamed with Jimmy Golden to hold the NWA Southeastern Tag Team Title in October of 1981. He briefly held the CWA International Title in Memphis in September of 1985.

Mongols, The *see* Mongol, Geeto; Volkoff, Nikolai & Mongol, Bolo

Monroe, Bill (Bill Fletcher) held the Southern Junior Heavyweight Title briefly in December of 1960.

Monroe, Rocket (Maury High) teamed with Sputnik Monroe to hold the NWA Texas Tag Team Title in February of 1961. They also held the NWA World Tag Team Title in Florida in April of 1967. They held the NWA Southern Tag Team Title in Florida in Spring of 1967. He also wrestled as Rocky Montez. Monroe teamed with Flash Monroe to hold the Gulf Coast Tag Team Title in April of 1969. They also held the U.S. Tag Team Title in Mobile, Alabama, in November of 1973.

Monroe, Sputnik was a leading wrestler in the Memphis area from the late 1950s. He exchanged the Tennessee State Title in Memphis with Billy Wicks several times in 1959 and 1960. He teamed with Danny McShain to hold the NWA Texas Tag Team Title in late 1960. He again held the Texas tag belts in February of 1961, teaming with Rocket Monroe. He held the NWA Texas Title in October of 1961. He defeated Dick the Bruiser for the

NWA Georgia Title in 1964. He again teamed with Rocket Monroe to hold the NWA World Tag Team Title in Florida in April of 1967. They also held the NWA Southern Tag Team Title in Florida in Spring of 1967. He defeated Danny Hodge for the NWA World Junior Heavyweight Title in July of 1970. He lost the belt to Hodge in a rematch soon afterwards. He held the Southern Junior Heavyweight Title in 1971. Monroe teamed with Norvell Austin to hold the Southern Tag Team Title in May of 1972, and the NWA Florida Tag Team Title in October of 1972.

Monsoon, Gorilla (b. June 4; Rochester, New York; 6'7", 401 lbs.) was a leading amateur grappler before he began his wrestling career as a vicious villain managed by Wild Red Berry in the early 1960s. He teamed with Killer Kowalski to win the WWWF U.S. Tag Team Title from Skull Murphy and Brute Bernard in November of 1963. They lost the belts the following month to Chris and John Tolos. Monsoon and El Mongol held the WWA Tag Team Title in Los Angeles in January of 1966. Monsoon teamed with Bill Watts to again capture the WWWF U.S. Tag Team Title in April of 1965, losing the belts to Dr. Bill and Dan Miller in July of 1965. Monsoon later changed his ring attitude, becoming a popular fan favorite in the early 1970s. He held the WWC North American Title in Puerto Rico in early 1978. He retired from the ring in the 1980s, but remained with the WWF as commentator. He became president of the WWF in early 1996. He was the father of WWF referee Joey Morella.

Monster, The *see* Rodriguez, Tony

Monster Ripper (Rhonda Singh) is a huge woman wrestler popular in Japan, Mexico and Puerto Rico. She held the All-Japan Women's Title several times in 1979 and 1980. She held the Calgary Stampede Women's World Title in December of 1987. She held the WWC Women's Title in Puerto Rico several times in the late 1980s and early 1990s. She also held the WWA Women's Title in Mexico in late 1991. She entered the WWF as Bertha Faye in mid-1995. She was managed by Harvey Wippelman while in WWF, and defeated Alundra Blayze for the Women's World Championship on August 27, 1995. She lost the title in a rematch with Blayze on October 23, 1995. She subsequently left the WWF to return to Japan.

Montagna, Luigi *see* Montana, Bull

Montana, Bull (Luigi Montagna; b. May 16, 1887, d. January 24, 1950) was born in Vogliera, Italy, and came to the United States as a professional wrestler in the early part of the century. He was a leading mat star for several decades. Montana also began appearing in films during the silent era. His brutish appearance and cauliflower ears made him a popular screen villain in numerous films. His credits include *Down to Earth* (1917), *In Again-Out Again* (1917), *Wild and Woolly* (1917), *In for Thirty Days* (1919), *Treasure Island* (1920), *The Four Horsemen of the Apocalypse* (1921), *Crazy to Marry* (1921), *One Wild*

Week (1921), *Bashful Buccaneer* (1925), *Dick Turpin* (1925), *The Lost World* (1925), *Son of the Sheik* (1926), *Tiger Rose* (1930), *Desert Guns* (1936), *Big City* (1937) and *When's Your Birthday?* (1937). His last film appearance was in 1943's *Good Morning, Judge*. He died of a coronary thrombosis in Los Angeles, California, on January 24, 1950.

Montana, Joe (b. 1914; Camden, New Jersey; 6', 215 lbs.) began wrestling in the mid-1930s and was a holder of the light heavyweight championship. He retired from the ring in the mid-1940s to run a gym. He returned to the ring in 1948, and continued to compete through the 1950s.

Montana, Lenny "Bull" (Lenny Passofaro; d. May 30, 1992) was a leading wrestler from the early 1950s. He held the NWA Central States Title in late 1953. He held the Pacific Coast Junior Heavyweight Title in May of 1956. He teamed with Hard Boiled Haggerty to defeat Tiny Mills and Killer Kowalski for the AWA World Tag Team Title in October of 1961. Montana's leg was broken in March of 1961 and he was replaced by Gene Kiniski as the title holder. Montana held the New England Title in 1966. He appeared in several films from the early 1970s, including *The Godfather* (1971), *Patty* (1975), *Fingers* (1978), *Matilda* (1978), *Seven* (1979), *The Jerk* (1979), *Defiance* (1980), *...All the Marbles* (1981), *Evilspeak* (1981), *Pandemonium* (1982) and *Blood Song* (1982).

Monte, Frank teamed Mike York as the Alaskans to hold the NWA Florida Title in December of 1971. He held the NWA Americas Tag Team Title several times in 1976, teaming with Crusher Verdu and Porkchop Cash.

Montez, Rocky *see* Monroe, Rocky

Montez, Tito began wrestling in the early 1960s. He held the Arizona Title in Phoenix numerous times in the 1960s and 1970s, often feuding with Bearcat Wright and Kurt Von Steiger. He also held the WAA Tag Team Title in Phoenix in 1969, teaming with Armond Hussein. Montez captured the Western States Wrestling Alliance U.S. Title in Arizona in 1977.

Montoya, Aldo (P.J. Walker; b. October 16, 1973; Lisbon, Portugal; 6', 225 lbs.) began wrestling as P.J. Walker in 1992. He wrestled in the RWF in Connecticut, winning the title in 1993. Montoya entered the WWF as the masked Portuguese Man O'War in October of 1994. He remained with the promotion as Aldo Montoyo for the next several years.

Moody, William *see* Bearer, Paul

Moolah, The Fabulous (Lillian Ellison; b. July 22; Columbia, South Carolina; 5'5", 138 lbs.) began wrestling in 1945. Wrestling as Slave Girl Moolah, she was the valet for the Elephant Boy in the early 1950s. She defeated Judy Grable for the Woman's World Title in Baltimore, Maryland, on September 18, 1956. She retained the belt with few interruptions until July 23, 1984, when she lost a match to

Wendi Richter in New York's Madison Square Garden. She regained the title from Richter, wrestling under a mask as the Spider Lady, in a match in New York on November 11, 1985. She briefly lost the belt to Velvet McIntyre in July of 1986. She was defeated for the title by Sherri Martel in July of 1987.

Moon, Max *see* Diamond, Paul

Moonbeam *see* Precious

Moondog Cujo (Larry Kean; 6'4", 354 lbs.), wrestling as King Harley Hogg, teamed with J.R. Hogg to hold the WWA Tag Team Title in 1984. They also held the MWA tag belts in Kentucky in 1985. Kean wrestled as Cousin Junior to hold the Southern Tag Team Title with Plowboy Frazier, wrestling as Giant Hillbilly Elmer, in August of 1986. Kean joined the Moondogs in the USWA in the early 1990s, wrestling as Moondog Cujo. He held the USWA Tag Team Title several times in 1993 with Moondog Spike.

Moondog Fifi accompanied the Moondogs to the ring in the USWA in the early 1990s. She held the USWA Women's Title in September of 1992.

Moondog King *see* White, Sailor

Moondog Mayne *see* Mayne, Lonnie

Moondog Rex joined with the Moondogs in the USWA in late 1993. He and Moondog Spot held the USWA Tag Team Title several times in 1994.

Moondog Rex *see* Culley, Randy

Moondog Rover (Paul McKnight) wrestled on independent cards in Tennessee as Crazy Paul Patton. He entered the USWA as Moondog Rover in the Spring of 1996.

Moondog Spike *see* Smithson, Bill

Moondog Splat (Bubba White; 6'2, 344 lbs.) began wrestling in 1989. He formerly wrestled as the Mighty Goliath. He wrestled with the Moondogs in the USWA in the early 1990s. He teamed with Spot to hold the USWA Tag Team Title several times in 1993.

Moondog Spot (Larry Booker; b. June 6; 6'2", 298 lbs.) began wrestling in 1977 as Larry Latham. He teamed with Wayne Farris as the Blonde Bombers in the Mid-South. They teamed to hold the Southern Tag Team Title several times in 1979. They also held the Mid-America Tag Team Title in late 1979 and early 1980. He teamed with Bill Irwin to hold the Southern tag belts in October of 1980. He replaced King as a member of the Moondogs in the WWF in May of 1981. He teamed with Rex to defend the WWF Tag Team Title, before losing the belts to Tony Garea and Rick Martel in July of 1981. He and Rex teamed to capture the Southern Tag Team Title in April of 1983 under the management of Jimmy Hart. He teamed with Moondog Spike to hold the ICW tag belts in 1987. He also held the Mid-America Title several times in 1987. Spot and Spike held the USWA Tag Team Title several times from November of 1991.

Spot also held the tag belts with Moondogs Cujo and Splat in 1992 and 1993. He again held the belts with a new Moondog Rex several times in 1994.

Moore, Jaque *see* Miss Texas

Moore, Mike *see* Motor City Madman

Moquin, Larry (b. 1921, d. 19??; Montreal, Canada; 5'11", 210 lbs.) began wrestling in the late 1930s. The French-Canadian was a former hockey player. He was a leading competitor in the 1940s and 1950s.

Morales, Pedro (b. November 3, 1942; Culebra, Puerto Rico; 5'11 1/2", 240 lbs.) began wrestling in 1958. He held the WWA Title in Los Angeles several times in 1965. He teamed with Luis Hernandez to hold the WWA Tag Team Title in June of 1966. He held the tag belts several more times in 1966 and 1967, teaming with Mark Lewin, Ricky Romero and Victor Rivera. He teamed with Pepper Gomez to hold the NWA World Tag Team Title in San Francisco in April of 1967. He teamed with Ed Francis to hold the Hawaiian Tag Team Title several times in 1969. He also held the Hawaiian tag belts with Bing Ki Lee for several months from March of 1970. He defeated Ivan Koloff for the WWWF Title in New York on February 8, 1971. He retained the title until his defeat by Stan Stasiak in Philadelphia on December 1, 1973. He teamed with Pat Patterson to reclaim the NWA World Tag Team Title in San Francisco in October of 1975. He teamed with Rocky Johnson to hold the NWA

Florida Tag Team Title in 1977. Morales held the NWA Southern Title in Florida in 1977. He teamed with Bob Backlund to defeat the Samoans for the WWF Tag Team Title in August of 1980, but were forced to give up the belts when it was ruled Backlund could not hold two titles simultaneously. Morales defeated Ken Patera for the WWF Intercontinental Title in December of 1980. He was defeated by Don Muraco in June of 1981, but recaptured the belt in November of 1981. He retained the title until he was again defeated by Muraco in January of 1983. Morales held the WWC North American Title in Puerto Rico several times in 1983 and 1984.

Morelli, Mike *see* Leone, Baron Michele

Morelli, Tony "Madman" (b. 1909, d. 19??; Wilmington, California; 5'8", 210 lbs.) began his wrestling career in New York in the early 1930s, often appearing at carnivals and in burlesque houses. He held the Florida State championship during the 1930s and captured the Hawaiian Title in 1941.

Moreno, Buddy held the World Class Texas Title in August of 1967.

Moreno, Carlos teamed with Rito Romero to hold the NWA Texas Tag Team Title in the early 1950s.

Moretti, Moondog teamed with Terry Adonis to hold the Canadian Tag Team Title in June of 1981. He also held the Canadian tag belts in 1984, teaming with Ray "Star Rider" Evans. Moretti teamed with

Mike Miller to hold the NWA Pacific Northwest Tag Team Title in October of 1985. He teamed with Bobby Jaggers to hold the NWA Central States Tag Team Title in June of 1986. He held the WCCW Title in Vancouver, Canada, several times in 1991 and 1992. He held the Oregon Professional Wrestling Federation Title in May of 1994.

Morgan, Big Ben (b. 1914; Chattanooga, Tennessee; 6'5", 295 lbs.) began wrestling in the late 1930s. The bearded wrestler was known for his backbreaker hold during the 1940s and 1950s.

Morgan, David held the NWA Americas Tag Team Title several times in 1973, teaming with Raul Matta and Tony Rocco.

Morgan, Heidi Lee (b. June 29) teamed with Misty Blue Simmes as Team America to hold the LPWA Tag Team Title in 1990. She also held the WWWA Women's Title in Pennsylvania in the Fall of 1992.

Morgan, Rip (6'4 1/2", 270 lbs.) began wrestling in 1983. The New Zealander was a former flagbearer for the Sheepherders. He teamed with Jonathan Boyd as the Sheepherders to hold the Southern Tag Team Title several times in 1985. In the early 1990s he teamed with Jacko Victory as the Royal Family.

Morowski, Moose wrestled as the Black Avenger to hold the Canadian Tag Team Title several times in 1977 and 1978, teaming with the Texas Outlaw, Mike Sharpe and Don Wayt.

Morrell, Frank teamed with Eddie Sullivan as the Mighty Yankees to hold the World Tag Team Title in Tennessee in July of 1968. They also held the Southern Tag Team Title several times in 1969. Wrestling as the Angel, Morrell teamed with Sonny King to again hold the Southern Tag Team Title in September of 1980. Wrestling as the Spoiler, Morrell teamed with Phil Hickerson to captured the Southern tag belts in June of 1984. Morrell became a referee with the USWA in the late 1980s. He remained active in the ring as a referee and occasional wrestler in the Memphis area through the mid-1990s.

Morrow, Don *see* Muraco, Don

Morrow, Jerry (5'10", 235 lbs.) began wrestling in 1971. He is from the French West Indies island of Martinique and is a former Stampede North American champion. He teamed with Eddie Morrow to hold the Canadian Tag Team Title in July of 1977. He teamed with the Cuban Assassin to hold the Calgary Stampede International Tag Team Title in July of 1988, and the WWC Caribbean Tag Team Title in Puerto Rico in October of 1989.

Morse, Bob *see* Viking, The

Mortier, Hans teamed with Johnny Barend to hold the Hawaiian Tag Team Title in February of 1967. He held the NWA Florida Title several times in early 1969. Wrestling as Tarzan Zorra, he held the AWA Title in Montreal, Canada, in 1971.

Morton, Rick (b. September 21,

1956; Memphis, Tennessee; 5'11", 228 lbs.) was born in Nashville, Tennessee. His father, Paul Morton, was a referee with the Mid-South promotions. He began wrestling in 1979. He teamed with Steve Regal during his first year of wrestling and was managed by Sonny King. He also teamed with Eddie Gilbert, Sonny King and Ken Lucas. He captured the Mid-South tag belts and the Southern belts with Ken Lucas in the early 1980s. He and Lucas also held the Mid-America Tag Team Title in October of 1980. He also held the Southern Tag Team Title briefly with Eddie Gilbert in 1981. He formed the Rock 'n' Roll Express with Robert Gibson in Tennessee in February of 1983. They captured the Southern Tag Team Title in November of 1983. They won the NWA tag championship from Ivan Koloff and Krusher Khrushchev in Shelby, North Carolina, on July 9, 1985. They were defeated for the title in October of 1985 by Ivan and Nikita Koloff, but recaptured the belts the following month. They lost the belts to the Midnight Express in February of 1986, but returned as champions in August of 1986. They were again defeated for the belts by Manny Fernandez and Rick Rude in December of 1986. They returned as tag champions in May of 1987, holding the title until their defeat by Arn Anderson and Tully Blanchard in September of 1987. They also teamed to capture CWA Tag Team Title in September of 1989. Morton also held the CWA tag belts with his cousin, Todd Morton, in December of 1989. Morton and Gibson split following a knee injury to Gibson in

September of 1990. Morton joined the York Foundation in the WCW in June of 1991. He was managed by Alexandra York and teamed with Tommy Rich and Terry Taylor to hold the WCW 6-Man Tag Title in late 1991. He returned to the Memphis area to capture the USWA Unified Title in July of 1992. He reunited with Gibson to capture the Smoky Mountain Tag Title in November of 1993. They held the belts on several occasions, often feuding with the Heavenly Bodies. They also captured the USWA Tag Team Title in January of 1994. They wrestled as villains in the USWA and again held the tag belts in July of 1995.

Morton, Todd (Todd Stratten; 5'9", 223 lbs.) began wrestling in 1988. He teamed with his cousin, Rick Morton, to capture the CWA Tag Team Title in December of 1989. He teamed with Chris Michaels as Far 2 Wild in the USWA in 1993. They held the USWA Tag Team Title in December of 1993.

Mosca, Angelo, Jr. is the son of wrestler Angelo Mosca, Sr. He held the NWA Mid-Atlantic Title several times in 1984. He also held the NWA Canadian Title in Toronto in June of 1984.

Mosca, Angelo, Sr. (Caledou, Ontario, Canada; 315 lbs.) was known in the ring as King Kong Mosca. He held the NWA U.S. Title in San Francisco in July of 1975. He held the NWA TV Title in 1976 and the NWA Georgia Title for several months in mid-1978. He held the NWA Canadian Title in Toronto several times from 1980 through

1984. He held the WWC Caribbean Title in Puerto Rico in early 1982. He also held the NWA Southern Title in Florida for several months in mid-1984. He is the father of Angelo Mosca, Jr.

Mosca, King Kong *see* Mosca, Sr., Angelo

Moser, David *see* Thunder Mountain, Chief

Moto, Akio *see* Kabuki, The Great

Moto, Mr. (Charles Iwamoto; b. 1921, d. July 6, 1992; California) began wrestling in Japan at an early age. Also called the Great Moto, the bearded giant came to the United States in the 1940s. He wrestled as a Japanese villain during the 1950s and 1960s. He teamed with Duke Keomuka to hold the NWA Texas Tag Team Title in early 1952. He also held the NWA Texas Title in July of 1955. He teamed with Kinji Shibuya to hold the NWA Southern Tag Team Title several times in the mid 1950s. He also teamed with Duke Keomuka to hold the title on several occasions in 1957 and 1958. He held the World Tag Team Title in Tennessee with Tor Yamata several times in 1960. He teamed with Mitsu Arakawa to hold the Pacific Coast Tag Team Title in Vancouver, Canada, in March of 1961. He teamed with Nikita Mulkovich to hold the Hawaiian Tag Team Title in July of 1964. He teamed with Fred Blassie to hold the WWA Tag Team Title in Los Angeles in October of 1964. He held the Western States Title in Long Beach, California, in 1966. He again held the

WWA tag belts in 1967, teaming with Ill Kim. Moto died in Los Angeles on July 6, 1992.

Motor City Hitmen *see* Snow, Al & Doyle, Mickey

Motor City Madman (Mike Moore; 6'4", 320 lbs.) began wrestling in 1986. He was brought to the WWF by Paul E. Dangerously. He wrestled in the WCW and WWC in the early 1990s. He later retired to Detroit.

Mountie, The *see* Rougeau, Jacques

Mucciolo, Louis *see* Spicolli, Louie

Muhammad, Kareem *see* Candy, Ray

Muhammad the Butcher (d. 1994; 6'2", 290 lbs.) began wrestling in 1987. He competed often in the AWC, where his vicious wrestling style was similar to Abdullah the Butcher.

Muir, Ian (Scotland; 308 lbs.) was a leading wrestler in Great Britain in the 1970s and 1980s. He teamed with the Giant Haystacks in the early 1980s. Muir appeared as the Giant in the 1981 fantasy film *Time Bandits*.

Muldoon, Pat (b. 1915; Brookline, Massachusetts; 5'10", 218 lbs.) was born in Massachusetts, and spent his childhood in Ireland. He held the Irish heavyweight championship and was a wrestling finalist for Ireland in the 1936 Olympics. He served in the air force during World War II and competed in the ring in the United States after the war. He remained a leading competitor through the 1950s.

Muldoon, William (b. May 25, 1845, d. 1933) was born in Belfast, New York. He defeated Christol for the Greco-Roman Championship in February of 1877. He faced boxer John L. Sullivan in a match in Gloucester, Massachusetts, in 1897. Muldoon retired from wrestling to enter boxing as a trainer and official.

Mulkovich, Nikita teamed with Mr. Moto to hold the Hawaiian Tag Team Title in July of 1964.

Mulligan, Blackjack (Bob Windham; b. November 26; Sweetwater, Texas; 6'7", 310 lbs.) began wrestling in 1969. He wrestled with Blackjack Lanza as the Blackjacks in the WWWF in the early 1970s. Managed by Bobby Heenan, they held the WWA Tag Team Title from December of 1971 until December of 1972. They also held the World Class American Tag Team Title in 1973. Mulligan held the World Class Texas Title in May of 1973. He wrestled under a mask as the Texan while suspended, and captured the World Class Championship under the mask in March of 1974. Under the management of Lou Albano, they captured the WWWF Tag Team Title from Dominic Denucci and Pat Barrett in August of 1975. They lost the belts to Tony Parisi and Louis Cerdan in November of 1975. Mulligan held the NWA U.S. Title several times from 1976 until 1978. He teamed with Ric Flair to capture the NWA World Tag Team Title from Baron Von Raschke and Paul Jones in August of 1979. They relinquished the title to Von Raschke and

Jones in a rematch the following month. Mulligan briefly held the WWA title in October of 1981. He teamed with Dusty Rhodes to hold the U.S. Tag Team Title in Florida in November of 1983. He also wrestled as the Big Machine in the Machines tag team in the WCW. He is the father of wrestlers Barry and Kendall Windham.

Mummy, The (Benji Ramirez) wrestled in Texas in the early 1960s. He held the NWA Texas Title in May of 1962.

Munn, Wayne (d. 19??; 6'6", 260 lbs.) held the World Heavyweight Title from January of 1925 until his defeat by Stanislaus Zbyszko in April of 1925. Munn continued to be recognized as champion in Michigan and Illinois until his defeat by Ed "Strangler" Lewis the following month.

Muraco, Don (Don Morrow; b. September 10; Sunset Beach, Hawaii; 6'4", 274 lbs.) began wrestling in 1970. He held the NWA Americas Title in Los Angeles in May of 1975. He teamed with Invader #1 to hold the NWA World Tag Team Title in San Francisco in March of 1976. He held the NWA U.S. Title in San Francisco in April of 1978. He teamed with Rick Martel to hold the Hawaiian Tag Team Title in November of 1978. He held the NWA Florida Title for several months in early 1980. He was managed by the Grand Wizard and, later, Lou Albano, when he wrestled in the WWF in the early 1980s. He defeated Pedro Morales for the WWF Intercontinental Title in June of 1981. He lost the belt to Morales in a rematch in November of 1981. Muraco returned to take the championship from Morales in January of 1983. He held the belt until his defeat by Tito Santana in February of 1984. Muraco won the first WWF King of the Ring tournament in July of 1985. He captured the Stampede North American Title in Calgary, Canada, in December of 1988. He held the All-California Championship Wrestling Title in June of 1989. Muraco defeated Jimmy Snuka for the ECW Championship in September of 1992. He lost the belt to the Sandman in November of 1992.

Murder, Inc *see* Mills, Tiny & Kowalski, Killer

Murdoch, Dick (b. August 16, 1947, d. June 14, 1996; Waxahachie, Texas; 6'4", 280 lbs.) was the son of wrestler Frankie Murdoch. He began wrestling in 1967. He teamed with Dusty Rhodes as the Outlaws to hold the NWA Central States Tag Team Title in November of 1968 and the NWA Florida Tag Team Title in late 1970. He also held the Central States tag belts with K.O. Kox in May of 1969, and the Florida tag belts with Bobby Duncum in October of 1971. He captured the NWA Southern Title in Florida in 1971. He held the MSWA North American Title for several months from June of 1975. He teamed with Killer Karl Kox to hold the U.S. Tag Team Title in Louisiana in October of 1975. He held the MSWA belt again in March of 1977. He held the NWA Central States Title in December of 1978. He teamed with Bob Brown to reclaim the NWA

Central States Tag Team Title in March of 1980. He teamed with Adrian Adonis to win the WWF World Tag Team Title from Rocky Johnson and Tony Atlas on April 17, 1984. The duo lost the title to Mike Rotundo and Barry Windham in Hartford, Connecticut, on January 21, 1985. Murdoch subsequently left the WWF and teamed with Ivan Koloff to win the NWA U.S. Tag Team Title in March of 1987. He was suspended the following month and stripped of the title. He wrestled with Dick Slater as the Hardliners in the early 1990s. He held the WWC Universal Title in Puerto Rico in October of 1992. He died of a heart attack at his Amarillo, Texas, home on June 14, 1996.

Murphy, John "Skull" (d. March 23, 1970) teamed with Brute Bernard in the early 1960s. They captured the WWWF U.S. Tag Team Title in May of 1963. They held the belts until November of 1963, when they were defeated by Killer Kowalski and Gorilla Monsoon. They were also NWA World Tag Team Champions in Florida several times in 1964. Murphy and Bernard also held the IWA Tag Team Title in Australia several times in the mid-1960s. Murphy teamed with Klondike Bill to hold the JWA Asian Tag Team Title in July of 1968.

Mussolini, Vito (Shawn Stevens; 5'10", 212 lbs.) began wrestling in 1989. He wrestled as Kenny the Stinger, winning the NAWA North American Title several times in 1990 and 1991. He also held the NAWA Tag Team Title in July of 1990, teaming with Ron Sutton. He teamed with Guido Falcone as the Sicilian Studs in Global in 1993. They held the Global World Tag Team Title for several months from May of 1993.

Mustafa, Colonel *see* Iron Sheik, The

Mustafa Saed, Sheik Jamal (Atlanta, Georgia; 6'1", 244 lbs.) wrestled with New Jack as the Gangstas in Smoky Mountain Wrestling from July of 1994. They captured the tag team belts from the Rock 'n' Roll Express the following October. They lost the tag title in a rematch in December of 1994. The Gangstas entered the ECW the following year, where the engaged in a feud with Public Enemy and the Eliminators.

Muta, The Great (Keiji Muto; b. December 23, 1962; Tokyo, Japan; 6'1", 245 lbs.) began wrestling professionally in Japan in October of 1984. Wrestling as the White Ninja he briefly held the NWA Florida Title in May of 1986. He wrestled as the Super Black Ninja to hold the WWC TV Title in Puerto Rico in 1987 and the WWC Puerto Rican Title in 1988. During the late 1980s and 1990s he wrestled as an Oriental villain under face-paint. He sometimes teamed with Kendo Nagasaki as the Rising Suns. He was managed in the NWA by Gary Hart and defeated Sting for the NWA TV Title in September of 1989. He held the belt until the following January. He defeated Masahiro Chono for the NWA Heavyweight Title in Tokyo, Japan, on January 4, 1993. He lost the belt to Barry Windham in Asheville, North Carolina, on February 21, 1993. He began wrestling with WAR in Japan as Keiji Muto in January of 1994.

Muto, Keiji *see* Muta, The Great

MVP, The *see* Lombardi, Steve

Myaki, Taro teamed with Duke Keomuka to hold the Texas World Tag Team Title several times in 1962.

Myers, Duke teamed with Terry Garvin to hold the U.S. Tag Team Title in Louisiana in August of 1972. He held the Calgary Stampede International Tag Team Title several times in the early 1980s, teaming with Bobby Bass, Mike Sharpe, David Shults, Kerry Brown and the Dynamite Kid. He teamed with Bobby Eaton to hold the Southern Tag Team Title in December of 1982.

Myers, Hack (Donald Haviland; Baltimore, Maryland; 6'2", 269 lbs.) was trained by Axl Rotten and wrested with independent promotions in the Mid-Atlantic region. He entered ECW in 1994, where he was known for his vicious ring style.

Myers, Jim *see* Steele, George "The Animal"

Myers, Sonny (St. Joseph, Missouri; 220 lbs.) was a former Mr. Texas who began wrestling professionally in the late 1940s. He held the NWA Texas Title several times in 1949 and 1950. He held the NWA Central States Title several times during the early 1950s. He held the Southern Junior Heavyweight Title for several months in early 1955. He teamed with Ronnie Etchison to hold the NWA Central States Tag Team Title in May of 1968. Myers served as Sheriff of Buchanan County, Missouri, in the early 1970s.

Nabors, Sidney *see* Dusek, Danny

Nagasaki, Kendo (b. September 26, 1948; Singapore; 6', 248 lbs.) began wrestling in 1971. He held the Southern Heavyweight Title in 1982. Wrestling as the Black Ninja, he held the WWC North American Title in Puerto Rico in 1983. He held the NWA Florida Title for several months in early 1984. He teamed with Mega Maharishi to hold the NWA Pacific Northwest Tag Team Title in April of 1985. He subsequently teamed with the Great Muta as Rising Suns. He teamed with Mr. Pogo to hold the WWC Tag Team Title in Puerto Rico several times in 1987 and 1988. He remained a leading competitor in Japan through the mid-1990s.

Nagata, Yuji (b. April 24, 1968) began wrestling with New Japan in September of 1992.

Nagayo, Chigusa was a leading wrestler with the All-Japan Women's Promotion. She teamed with Lioness Asuka as the Crush Girls in the late 1980s. They held the All-Japan WWWA Women's Tag Team Title several times from 1984 through 1989.

Nagurski, Bronko (Bronislau Nagurski; b. 1908, d. January 7, 1990; Minnesota) was born in Rainy River, Ontario, Canada, and raised in International Falls, Minnesota. He was a leading collegiate football player with the University of Minnesota in the late 1920s, and was signed by the Chicago Bears in 1930. He remained with the Bears throughout most of the decade, and was voted All-Pro three times during his football career. He left the gridiron in 1937 in a salary dispute with Bears' owner George Halas. He subsequently began a career as a professional wrestler. He was recognized as the World Heavyweight Champion from June of 1937 until November of 1938. He defeated Lou Thesz for the NWA Heavyweight Title in Houston, Texas, on June 23, 1939. He lost the belt to Ray Steele in St. Louis, Missouri, on March 7, 1940. Nagurski regained the belt when he defeated Steele in a rematch in Minneapolis, Minnesota, on March 11, 1941. Nagurski lost the belt to Sandor Szabo in St. Louis, Missouri, on June 5, 1941. Nagurski returned to the Chicago Bears for the 1943 season as a defensive tackle. He returned to the ring to hold the Pacific Coast Title in San Francisco in 1946 and 1948. He held the World Title in Minneapolis in 1948. He teamed with Verne Gagne to hold the NWA World Tag Team Title in Minneapolis for several months from December of 1957. Nagurski retired from the ring in 1960. Injuries that he had suffered on the football field and in the wrestling ring made physical movement difficult for Nagurski after his retirement and he lived his later years as a virtual recluse. He died in an International Falls, Minnesota, hospital after a short illness on January 7, 1990.

Nailz *see* Kelly, Kevin

Nakanishi, Manabu *see* Kurosawa

Nakano, Bull (b. January 8) held the All-Japan WWWA Tag Team Title several times in the mid-1980s, teaming with Dump Matsumoto and Condor Saito. She held the All-Japan Women's Title from January of 1990 until November of 1992. She also captured the EMLL Women's Title in Mexico in June of 1992. She won the WWF Women's Title by defeating Alundra Blayze at the All-Japan Women's tournament in Tokyo, Japan, on November 20, 1994. She lost the belt in a rematch with Blayze in April of 1995.

Nash, Kevin *see* Diesel

Nash, Tom teamed with Dave Heath as the Black Harts to hold the Calgary Stampede International Tag Team Title in September of 1989. He wrestled with David Johnson as the Blackhearts in the NWA in 1994.

Nasty Boys, The *see* Knobs, Brian & Sags, Jerry

Natale, Ernest "Slugger" (b. 1923; Union City, New Jersey; 6', 215 lbs.) served in the Marines during World War II and competed as a boxer before turning to professional wrestling in the late 1940s. He remained a popular competitor through the 1950s.

Natural Disasters, The *see* Earthquake & Typhoon

Nature Boy, The *see* Flair, Ric

Nature Boy, The *see* Rogers, Buddy

Nead, Wilbur (b. 1918; Boston, Massachusetts; 5'11", 240 lbs.) was a leading collegiate athlete at Iowa State College. He entered professional wrestling in the mid-1940s. He suffered a broken leg in a match with Antonio Rocca in the late 1940s, but recovered to remain a popular competitor through the 1950s.

Negra, Pantera held the Mexican National Heavyweight Title in 1966. He teamed with Tony Rocco to hold the NWA Americas Tag Team Title in Los Angeles several times in 1970. He held the NWA United National Title in Los Angeles in November of 1970.

Negro, Ciclon (Venezuela; 6'3", 260 lbs.) came to the United States in 1960. He initially wrestled under a mask in the Texas area. He teamed with Torbellino Blanco to hold the NWA Texas Tag Team Title several times in 1960. He also held the NWA Texas Title in November of 1960. He teamed with Oscar Salazar to hold the Texas World Tag Team Title in November of 1962. He teamed with the Masked Terror to briefly hold the AWA Tag Team belts in December of 1963. He teamed with the Mongolian Stomper to hold the NWA World Tag Team Title in San Francisco in December of 1966. He also held the NWA Florida Title from April until August of 1969. He teamed with Sam Steamboat to hold the NWA Florida Tag Team Title in September of 1969. He again held the Florida tag belts in 1975, teaming with Omar Atlas. He teamed with Dr. X to hold the U.S. Tag Team Title in

Louisiana in September of 1977. Wrestling as Mr. Uganda, and managed by Sonny King, he again held the Florida championship in December of 1978. He held the NWA Americas Title in Los Angeles in November of 1982.

Negro, Omar *see* Atlas, Omar

Neidhart, Jim "the Anvil" (b. February 8, 1956; Tampa, Florida; 6'1", 275 lbs.) began wrestling in 1979. He teamed with Hercules Ayala to hold the Calgary Stampede International Tag Team Title in 1980. He teamed with Butch Reed to hold the MSWA Tag Team Title in October of 1983. He captured the NWA Southern Title in Florida in July of 1984. He teamed with Krusher Khrushchev to hold the U.S. Tag Team Title in Florida in late 1984. He teamed with his brother-in-law, Bret Hart, as the Hart Foundation and, under the management of Jimmy Hart, defeated the British Bulldogs for the WWF Tag Team Title in January of 1987. They held the belts until October of 1987, when they were beaten by Rick Martel and Tito Santana. They returned to win the title from Demolition in August of 1990. They retained the title until their defeat by the Nasty Boys in March of 1991. He returned to the WWF to team with another brother-in-law, Owen Hart, in June of 1994. He left the WWF in January of 1995.

Neilson, Art (Art Nelson; d. October 20, 1983) held the NWA Southern Title several times in the early 1950s. He teamed with Crusher to capture the World Tag Team Title in Chicago in February of 1954. He teamed with Hans Hermann to capture the NWA World Tag Team Title in San Francisco in February of 1958. He teamed with Ray Shire to win the AWA Tag Team belts in 1961. He subsequently teamed with Stan Neilson to capture the AWA World Tag Team Title in April of 1962. They lost the belts to Doug Gilbert and Dick Steinborn in December of 1962. He and Stan Neilson held the NWA World Tag Team Title in San Francisco for several months from March of 1963. He teamed with Ivan Kameroff to hold the Canadian Tag Team Title in September of 1965. He teamed with Johnny Weaver to hold the NWA Atlantic Coast Tag Title in 1972.

Neilson, Stan teamed with Art Neilson to capture the AWA World Tag Team Title in April of 1962. They lost the belts to Doug Gilbert and Dick Steinborn in December of 1962. The Neilsons held the NWA World Tag Team Title in San Francisco for several months from March of 1963.

Nelson, Bobby (Lincoln, Nebraska) was a professional football player before he began wrestling in the mid-1930s. He wrestled often in Hawaii, where he held the championship. He was known there as the Clipper Boy, because he was one of the first wrestlers to come to Hawaii by air to compete.

Nelson, Gordon teamed with Ripper Collins to hold the NWA Americas Tag Team Title in Los Angeles in May of 1973. He teamed with Higo Hamaguchi to hold the WWC North American Tag Team Title in Puerto Rico in 1976.

Nelson, Private Jim see Zhukov, Boris

Nelson, Rikki (5'10", 231 lbs.) began wrestling in 1988. He competed in the WCW and IWA.

Neu, Paul *see* News, P.N.

Neutron *see* Ruvinski, Wolf

New Breed, The *see* Royal, Sean & Champion, Chris

New Jack (Jerome Young; Atlanta, Georgia; 6', 225 lbs.) began wrestling in 1992. He teamed with Mark Freer to hold the USWA Tag Team Title in June of 1993. He wrestled with Sheik Mustafa as the Gangstas in Smoky Mountain Wrestling from July of 1994. They captured the tag team belts from the Rock 'n' Roll Express the following October. They lost the tag title in a rematch in December of 1994. The Gangstas entered the ECW the following year, where the engaged in a feud with Public Enemy and the Eliminators.

New Rockers, The *see* Jannetty, Marty & Cassidy, Leaf

New Wave *see* Eaton, Bobby & Ware, Koko B.

Newman, Leo (b. 1908, d. August 5, 1992; Kimmswick, Missouri; 200 lbs.) began wrestling in the 1930s. He was known in the ring as Leo the Lion. He held the World Title in Colorado in July of 1947. He held the NWA Texas Title in November of 1949. He held the NWA Southern Title in 1952. He was forced to retire from wrestling in the early 1960s due to injuries suffered in an automobile accident. He died at his home in Imperial, Missouri, on August 5, 1992.

Newman, Shoulders held the Hawaiian Tag Team Title several times in 1960 and 1961, teaming with Hans Schnabel, Tom Rice and Ted Travis.

News, P.N. (Paul Neu; 6'3", 402 lbs.) began wrestling in 1988. He originally wrestled as Paul "the Avalanche" Neu. He teamed with Mike Golden to hold the NWA Pacific Northwest Tag Team Title in March of 1988. He also held the tag belt with Buddy Rose in September of 1988. He was a popular performer in the WCW as P.N. News in the early 1990s with his rap routine. He wrestled with the CWA in Europe as Cannonball Grizzly in 1994.

Newt the Brute (Samuel N. Anderson; b. October 25, 1953; 6'2", 250 lbs.) began wrestling in the Knoxville area in the late 1970s. He was a colorful villain in the Southeast, whose wild ring antics often resulted in disqualifications. He also wrestled in Japan before retiring from the ring in the late 1980s.

Nightmare, The *see* Culley, Randy

Nightmares *see* Wayne, Ken & Davis, Danny

Nightstalker, The *see* Bomb, Adam

Niikura, Fujihiro was a Japanese wrestler in the 1980s. He teamed with Hiroshi Hase as Viet Cong Express in Canada, where they held the Calgary Stampede International Tag Team Title in October of 1986

Nikona *see* Youngblood, Mark

911 (Al Poling; 6'7" 310 lbs.) entered ECW in 1994 and Paul E. Dangerously's bodyguard. He was known in the ring for his choke-slam maneuver, and often fought several wrestlers at once in handicap matches.

Nishimura, Osamu (b. September 23, 1971; Tokyo, Japan; 6'2", 225 lbs.) began wrestling in New Japan in April 1991.

Nobbs, Brian *see* Knobs, Brian

Nogami, Akira (b. March 13, 1966; Oita, Japan; 5'9", 216 lbs.) began wrestling in Japan in October of 1987. He defeated Jushin Liger for the IWGP Junior Heavyweight Title in 1990.

Nomellini, Leo "the Lion" (Minnesota) played college football with the University of Minnesota. He entered professional wrestling in 1950. Nomellini teamed with Hombre Montana to hold the NWA World Tag Team Title in San Francisco in February of 1952. He held the tag belts several more times in the early 1950s, teaming with Enrique Torres and Rocky Brown. He teamed with Verne Gagne to hold the NWA World Tag Team Title in Minneapolis in May of 1958. They captured the NWA World Tag Team belts from Tiny Mills and Killer Kowalski in July of 1960. They lost the belts in a rematch the following month. He captured the AWA Tag Team Title with Wilbur Snyder in a match against Hard Boiled Haggerty and Gene Kiniski in May of 1961. They held the belts for several months until Haggerty and Kiniski won a rematch in July of 1961. Nomellini was a leading wrestling promoter in the San Francisco area during the 1970s and 1980s.

Nord, John (b. October 18, 1959; Bozeman, Montana; 6'6", 316 lbs.) began wrestling in January of 1985 as Big John Nord in the AWA. He subsequently wrestled as Nord the Barbarian and Big Yukon. Wrestling as Yukon John Nord, he teamed with Scott Norton as the Lumberjacks in the AWA in the early 1990s. He entered the WWF as the Viking in 1991, but took the name Berzerker in April of 1991. He left the WWF in 1993. The following year he began competing with All-Japan as John Nord.

Nord the Barbarian *see* Nord, John

Norman the Lunatic *see* Shaw, Mike

Norris, Charlie (b. October 21, 1965; Red Lake, Minnesota; 6'7", 285 lbs.) began wrestling in December of 1989. The Chippewa Indian star was trained by Eddie Sharkey. He won the PWA Title in November of 1989 and held the title several more times over the next three years. He teamed with Sam Houston to hold the PWA Tag Team Title in August of 1994.

Norris, Tony *see* Johnson, Ahmed

North-South Connection, The *see* Adonis, Adrian & Murdoch, Dick

Norton, Scott (b. 1962; Minneapolis, Minnesota; 6'3", 360 lbs.) was trained by Verne Gagne and began wrestling in 1989. He was a former arm-wrestling champion who wrestled in the Pacific Northwest. He held the NWA Pacific Northwest Title briefly in May of 1990. He teamed with Yukon John Nord as the Lumberjacks in the AWA, and teamed with Hercules as the Jurrasic Powers in New Japan. He held the Oregon Professional Wrestling Federation Title in April of 1994. He entered the WCW in 1995 and was soon teaming with Ice Train as the Fire and Ice tag team.

Novak, David, wrestling as the Bounty Hunters with Jerry Novak, held the Southern Tag Team Title in February of 1973. They captured the WWA Tag Team Title in August of 1976. They retained the belts until February of the following year.

Novak, Jerry, wrestling as the Bounty Hunters with David Novak, held the Southern Tag Team Title in February of 1973. They captured the WWA Tag Team Title in August of 1976. They retained the belts until February of the following year.

O, Barry (Barry Orton; 6'2, 230 lbs.) is the son of Bob Orton, Sr., and the younger brother of Cowboy Bob Orton. He began wrestling in 1979. He teamed with Hector Guerrero to hold the NWA Americas Title in Los Angeles in May of 1979. He wrestled in the WWF during the 1980s. He is the son of Bob Orton Sr. and the brother of Cowboy Bob Orton.

O, Danny *see* Petty, Dan

O, Steve (Steve Olsonoski; 6'1", 233 lbs.) began wrestling in 1978. He held the NWA National Title and NWA TV Title several times in early 1981. Steve O teamed with Ted DiBiase to hold the NWA National Tag Team Title in June of 1981. He wrestled primarily in the AWA in the 1980s.

O, The Big *see* Valentine, Johnny

Oates, Jerry (Columbus, Georgia; 245 lbs.) held the NWA Central States Title in early 1975. He held the NWA Central States Tag Team Title several times in 1975, teaming with Mike George, Ted Oates and Danny Little Bear. He again teamed with Ted Oates to hold the NWA Georgia Tag Team Title in May of 1976. He captured the MSWA North American Title in August of 1977. He held the NWA Pacific Northwest Title in May of 1978. He teamed with Jesse Ventura to hold the Pacific Northwest tag belts in March of 1978. He and Ted Oates again held the NWA Central States Tag Team Title in April of 1984. He held the NWA National Tag Team Title with Ron Garvin in July of 1984.

Oates, Marty *see* Jannetty, Marty

Oates, Ted (Columbus, Georgia; 245 lbs.) teamed with Jerry Oates to hold the NWA Central States Tag Team Title in May of 1975. They also held the NWA Georgia Tag Team Title in May of 1976. He held the NWA Central States Title in February of 1977. He held the U.S. Junior Heavyweight Title in Alabama in 1982. He and Jerry Oates again held the NWA

Central States Tag Team Title in April of 1984. He again held the Central States belt in June of 1984. He held the NWA National Tag Team Title with Rip Rogers, as the Hollywood Blondes, in September of 1984.

Oborsky, Colin H. (b. 1965, d. October 25, 1995) was born in California, and raised in Revere, Massachusetts. He briefly competed as a light-heavyweight boxer after graduating high school in 1983. He began training as a wrestler in 1985 and made his debut the following year as Colin Kidd, a surfer from Venice Beach. The tan and blonde Oborsky was active in promotions in Las Vegas and Florida. He appeared as the Golden Knight in the WWF, and occasionally wrestled as the villainous Eagle Man. Oborsky died of pneumonia in an Everett, Massachusetts, hospital on October 25, 1995.

O'Brien, Jack (d. September 14, 1982) was a leading wrestler in the 1930s and 1940s. He captured the EMLL National Lightweight Title in June of 1934. He held the Mexican Welterweight Title several times during the 1940s.

O'Connor, Chuck *see* Studd, Big John

O'Connor, Pat (b. 1924, d. August 15, 1990) began wrestling in the early 1950s. He held the AWA Title in Montreal, Canada, several times in 1953 and 1954. He teamed with Roy McClarty to hold the World Tag Team Title in Chicago in March of 1955. He held the British Empire Title in Toronto, Canada, in March

of 1956. He teamed with Whipper Billy Watson to hold the Canadian Open Tag Team Title in Toronto in May of 1957. He defeated Dick Hutton for the NWA Heavyweight Title in St. Louis, Missouri, on January 9, 1959. He retained the belt until June 30, 1961, when he lost the title to Buddy Rogers in a match in Chicago, Illinois. O'Connor teamed with Wilbur Snyder to defeat Harley Race and Chris Markoff for the AWA World Tag Team Title in November of 1967. They lost the belts the following month to Mitsu Arakawa and Dr. Moto. He and Snyder briefly held the WWA Tag Team belts in September of 1968. He teamed with Bob Geigel to hold the NWA Central States Tag Team Title in July of 1974. He held the NWA tag belts again in August of 1974, teaming with Omar Atlas. He again held the Central States tag belts in June of 1980, teaming with Bob Brown. He was also a leading promoter in the Kansas City and St. Louis area. O'Connor died of cancer at his home in St. Louis, Missouri, on August 15, 1990.

Octagon (5'6", 170 lbs.) began wrestling in 1988. The Mexican masked star has wrestled in Europe and Japan.

O'Day, Larry wrestled with Ron Miller as the Australians to capture the NWA Florida Tag Team Title in August of 1971. They held the belts several times over the next year.

O'Donne, Sandy *see* Eckert, Ray

Odyssey, Ray (b. January 31; San Diego, California; 5'10", 205 lbs.) began wrestling in 1988. He often brings a surfboard to the ring. Odyssey held the IWCW Light Heavyweight Title in 1988. He was the WWW Junior Heavyweight Champion in 1992 and 1993. He also held the CWA Light Heavyweight Title in 1993 and teamed with Vic Steamboat to hold the CWA Tag Team Title in 1994.

Ogawa, Yoshinari (b. November 2, 1966; 5'8", 180 lbs.) began wrestling in Japan in September of 1985. He entered All-Japan in early 1992.

O'Hara, Doran (b. 1921; Houston, Texas; 5'10", 215 lbs.) was born in Dublin, Ireland, and came to the United States as a child. He played football at West Texas State and the University of Oregon. He entered professional wrestling in the late 1940s, and remained a leading contender during the 1950s.

Ohara, Michiyoshi (b. November 15, 1967) began wrestling with New Japan in June of 1990.

Oinada, Juan teamed with Kurt Von Himmler to hold the NWA Pacific Northwest Tag Team Title in October of 1957.

Okano, Takashi wrestled with Nobutaka Araya as the Masters of the Orient in the USWA in 1990.

Okerlund, Gene (b. December 19) made his debut as a wrestling announcer with the AWA in the late 1970s. He was a popular announcer for the WWF during the 1980s. He went to the WCW in the early 1990s.

Oki, Kintaro *see* Kim, Ill

Okuma, Motoshi (b. 1941, d. December 27, 1992) teamed with Shinya Kojika to hold the World Tag Team Title in Tennessee in 1967.

Olafsson, Phil (d. 19??) wrestled as the Swedish Angel. Known in the ring for his bald head and distorted facial features, Olafsson was a fearsome mat competitor. He held the MWA Title in Kansas City briefly in December of 1943.

Oliver, Larry (6'2", 260 lbs.) began wrestling in 1990. He is the son of Rip Oliver and teamed with his father to win the NWA Pacific Northwest Tag Team Title in September of 1990.

Oliver, Rip (Tampa, Florida; 6', 245 lbs.) began wrestling in 1976. He held the Canadian Tag Team Title several times in 1980 and 1981, teaming with Fidel Cortez and Buddy Rose. He held the NWA Pacific Northwest Tag Team Title several times in the early 1980s, teaming with the Destroyer, Buddy Rose, Matt Borne and the Assassin. He captured the NWA Pacific Northwest Title for the first of several times in April of 1982. He held the World Class Title in Texas in February of 1985. He again held the Pacific Northwest tag belts several times in the late 1980s, teaming with Bobby Jaggers, Mike Miller and Super Ninja. He held the Oregon Wrestling Federation Title in June of 1988. He became a fan favorite in 1989 and teamed with his son, Larry Oliver, to regain the tag belts in September of 1990.

Olsen, Ellen (b. 1928; Philadelphia, Pennsylvania; 5'4", 135 lbs.) was a former nightclub dancer who began wrestling in the late 1940s. She was known in the ring as the Sizzling Swede, and was a leading contender during the 1950s. She was formerly married to wrestler Buddy Rogers.

Olsen, Erniar (b. 1919; Wisconsin; 5'10", 168 lbs.) was a leading middleweight competitor in the United States and Canada in the 1940s and 1950s.

Olson, Cliff (Minneapolis, Minnesota) began wrestling in the mid-1930s. The Swedish-American mat star remained a popular competitor through the 1950s.

Olson, Ole (260 lbs.) teamed with Randy Rich to hold the Canadian Tag Team Title in June of 1984. He held the WCCW Title in Vancouver, Canada, several times in 1992.

Olsonoski, Steve *see* O, Steve

Olympian, The *see* Stubbs, Jerry

O'Mahoney, Danno (b. 1913, d. November 4, 1950) was originally from Ireland. He was a leading wrestler from the early 1930s, and was known in the ring for his "Irish whip" maneuver. He was recognized as the World Heavyweight Title holder from July of 1935 until March of 1936. He was killed in an automobile accident when he crashed his car into a parked truck near Port Laighaise, Ireland, on November 4, 1950.

Omoti, Takao (b. October 16, 1969) began wrestling with All-Japan in October of 1992.

One Man Gang (George Gray; b. February 12, 1960; 6'7", 468 lbs.) began wrestling in 1977. He wrestled as Crusher Broomfield in the ICW in the late 1970s. He began wrestling as One Man Gang in 1981. He teamed with Kelly Kiniski to hold the NWA Atlantic Coast Tag Title in 1983. He teamed with Ron Bass to hold the U.S. Tag Team Title in November of 1983. He held the UWF Title in Oklahoma in November of 1986. He was managed by Slick and wrestled as Akeem, the African Dream, in the WWF from 1988 until 1991. He teamed with the Big Bossman as the Twin Towers in the early 1990s. He entered the WCW in 1995 and was managed by Kevin Sullivan. He captured the WCW U.S. Heavyweight Title from Kensuke Sasaki on December 27, 1995.

1-2-3 Kid, The *see* Kid, The

Onita, Mr. (Atsushi Onita) teamed with Masanobu Fuchi to hold the Southern Tag Team Title in March of 1981. He held the NWA International Junior Heavyweight Title several times in 1982.

Orndorff, Paul (b. October 29, 1949; Brandon, Florida; 5'11", 252 lbs.) is a former pro football player. He made his wrestling debut in 1976. He held the Southern Heavyweight Title in June of 1977. He held the MSWA North American Title in May and June of 1978. He teamed with Jimmy Snuka to win the NWA World Tag Team Title in December of 1978. The duo retained the belt until April of 1979. He entered the Mid-South area in 1981 and feuded with Ted DiBiase. He held the NWA National Title several times in 1982. He became known as Mr. Wonderful and entered the WWF in 1984. He was managed by Bobby Heenan and challenged Hulk Hogan for the World Title. Orndorff teamed with Roddy Piper in the main event against Hulk Hogan and Mr. T at Wrestlemania I in March of 1985. He renewed his feud with Hogan in 1986. Orndorff left wrestling for some time in 1987. He returned to the ring in November of 1989 and entered the WCW the following year. He subsequently wrestled in the UWF where he feuded with Steve "Dr. Death" Williams and Col. DeBeers. He entered the WCW and captured the TV Title in a tournament in March of 1993. He lost the belt to Rick Steamboat in August of 1993. He subsequently formed the team of Pretty Wonderful with Paul Roma. They won the tag title from Cactus Jack and Kevin Sullivan on July 17, 1994. The lost the belts to Marcus Alexander Bagwell and the Patriot on September 25, 1994, but regained the title in a rematch the following month on October 23, 1994. They were again defeated by Bagwell and the Patriot on November 16, 1994. Orndorff was involved in a locker room dispute with Big Van Vader in 1995 that resulted in Vader leaving the WCW. Orndorff was sidelined from the ring during late 1995 and early 1996.

Oro (Javier Hernandez; b. 1971, d. October 26, 1993) was a popular Mexican wrestler in the early 1990s. He held the Mexican Middleweight Championship in May of 1993. He was killed in the ring when he suffered a brain aneurysm in a EMLL match at the Arena Colisseo on October 26, 1993.

Ortega, Pedro (b. 1924; Cuba; 5'11", 210 lbs.) was a professional acrobat and bodybuilder. He held the Mr. Cuba title in 1945 before entering professional wrestling. He was injured in an automobile accident in 1950, but recovered from his injuries and returned to the ring. He remained an active competitor through the 1950s.

Orton, Barry *see* O, Barry

Orton, Cowboy Bob, Jr. (b. November 10; Kansas City, Kansas; 6'1", 245 lbs.) began wrestling in 1972. He teamed with Mr. Wrestling II to hold the NWA Georgia Tag Team Title in mid 1973. Orton and Dick Slater claimed the belts in June of 1975 and captured the U.S. Tag Title two months later. He teamed with his father, Bob Orton, Sr., to capture the NWA Florida Tag Team Title in April of 1976. Orton also held the Florida tag belts with Bob Roop. Wrestling as the Invader, he teamed with Jerry Blackwell to capture the NWA Southeastern Tag Team Title in January of 1979. He again held the title the following month, teaming with Bob Roop. He held the ICW TV Title for several months in 1980 and 1981, where he often feuded with Roop. He teamed with Don Kernodle to capture the NWA World Tag Team Title in a tournament on January 8, 1984. They held the belts until the following March, when they were defeated by Wahoo McDaniel and Mark Youngblood.

Orton, Bob, Sr. wrestled in the 1950s and 1960s. He was known as the Big O. He held the NWA Central States Title in 1951 and 1954. Orton held the NWA Southern Title in Florida several times from December of 1963 until February of 1966. He subsequently teamed with Eddie Graham to hold the NWA World Tag Team Title in Florida for several months in 1966. He captured the title again in March of 1970. He teamed with Buddy Austin to hold the NWA Central States Tag Team Title in June of 1971. Wrestling as the Zodiac, he again held the Florida title several times in 1972. He teamed with Dennis Hall, wrestling as Taurus, to hold the NWA Florida Tag Team Title in June of 1972. He teamed with his son, Bob, Jr., to again hold the Florida tag belts in April of 1976. He subsequently retired to Las Vegas. He is the father of wrestlers Cowboy Bob Orton, Jr. and Barry O.

Osborne, Jim *see* Dr. X.

Osborne, Matthew *see* Borne, Matt

Osbourne, Glenn (6'2", 265 lbs.) began wrestling in 1989. He wrestled in the NWA as half of the Natural Born Killers tag team.

Oses, Fernando was a leading Mexican wrestler in the 1950s and 1960s. He appeared in numerous Mexican films including *Santo Attacks the Witches* (1964), *The Diabolical Hatchet* (1964), *Santo vs.* *Baron Brakola* (1965), *Shadow of the Bat* (1966) and *Santo Against the Black Magic* (1972).

O'Shocker, Bob wrestled as the Masked Bat to briefly hold the Southern Junior Heavyweight Title in May of 1956.

O'Shocker, Danno was a Canadian wrestler in the 1940s. He later was a wrestling teacher whose students include Wahoo McDaniel.

Ota, Dr. Hiro held the NWA Americas Title in Los Angeles in November of 1976. He teamed with Toru Tanaka to hold the NWA Americas Tag Team Title in February of 1977. He again held the Americas tag belts in February of 1978, teaming with Ron Bass.

Otani, Shinjiro (b. July 21, 1972) began wrestling professionally in June of 1992. He entered New Japan the following year.

Ottman, Fred *see* Typhoon

Ouellet, Carl Jose Yvon *see* LaFitte, Jean-Pierre

Outlaw, The *see* Funk, Dory

Outlaws, The *see* Murdoch, Dick & Rhodes, Dusty

Oz *see* Diesel

Ozaki, Mayumi (b. 1967; 5', 125 lbs.) was a leading Japanese wrestler from the mid-1980s. She teamed with Dynamite Kansai to capture the All-Japan WWWA Women's Tag Team Title in April of 1993.

Page, Diamond Dallas (Page Falkenberg; b. April 5; Tampa,

Florida; 6'5", 260 lbs.) managed the Freebirds and Badd Company in the AWA before entering the ring as a wrestler in 1991. He teamed with Vinnie Vegas as the Vegas Connection in the WCW in 1992. He was often accompanied to the ring by his wife, Diamond Doll Kimberley. He engaged in lengthy feuds with Dave Sullivan and Johnny B. Badd in the WCW in 1995. He defeated the Renegade for the WCW TV Championship on September 17, 1995. He lost the belt to Johnny B. Badd on October 29, 1995. Badd also won the Diamond Doll from Page, and they continued their feud until Badd left the WCW in March of 1996. Page subsequently lost a retirement match against the Bootie Man.

Paidousis, Mike (b. 1921; Knoxville, Tennessee; 6', 228 lbs.) played football at the University of Tennessee. He was also a Golden Gloves boxing champion. He began wrestling in the early 1950s, and quickly became a leading mat star. He remained active in the ring for the next two decades. Paidousis held the NWA Central States Title in September of 1960. He teamed with Brute Bernard to hold the World Class American Tag Team Title in Texas in October of 1967.

Pain, Bull (Rick Gantner; Columbia, South Carolina; 6'2", 277 lbs.) began wrestling in 1990. He competed in the USWA and Global, often accompanied by his valet and wife, Samantha.

Pain, Max *see* Payne, Maxx

Pak Choo held the NWA Americas Tag Team Title several times in 1978, teaming with Mr. Ito and Roddy Piper.

Palazola, Vince *see* Palmer, Vince

Palies, Chris *see* Bundy, King Kong

Palmer, Max (b. 1928, d. May 7, 1994; 8'2", 457 lbs.; Vance, Missouri) was a huge actor in Hollywood in the early 1950s, appearing in such films as *The Sniper* (1952), *Invaders from Mars* (1953), *Killer Ape* (1953) and *The Big Bluff* (1955). Palmer was also a professional wrestler in the late 1950s and 1960s, competing throughout the United States and Canada, sometimes as Paul Bunyon. Alcoholism and drug addiction ended Palmer's wrestling and acting careers. He beat his addiction and dedicated the remainder of his life to religion. He died of congestive heart disease in a St. Louis, Missouri, hospital on May 7, 1994.

Palmer, Vince (Vince Palazola) wrestled in the Mid-South from the late 1950s through the early 1970s.

Palmer, Walter (b. 1913; Des Plaines, Illinois; 6'1", 212 lbs.) was an amateur wrestler before turning pro in the late 1930s.

Palooka, Joe *see* Henning, Lee

Papineau, Louis *see* Mephisto, The Great

Pappas, Chris *see* James, Jesse

Pappas, Gus (Constantinos Pappaniou; b. 1881, d. January 21, 1963) was born in Greece. He immigrated to the United States in

1905. He defeated Lonney Ajax for the middleweight championship in 1916. He held the title until 1922, when he was defeated by Ira Durn. Pappas retired from the ring in 1946 and subsequently worked as a truck driver. He died in a Los Angeles sanitarium on January 21, 1963.

Paradise, Johnny (6'1", 237 lbs.) began wrestling in 1990. He held the Motor City Northern States Title in 1992. He teamed with Scott Summers to form the tag team, Hot Paradise. They held the Motor City Wrestling Midwest tag belts in June of 1994.

Parente, Lorenzo held the NWA World Junior Heavyweight Title briefly in 1965 and 1966. He teamed with Paul DeMarco to hold the NWA World Tag Team Title in Florida in October of 1967 and January of 1968. He teamed with Bobby Hart to hold the World Tag Team Title in Tennessee in 1971. Wrestling as the Continental Warriors, they also held the U.S. Tag Team Title in Louisiana for several months from March of 1972. Parente again held the world belts with Randy Curtis in 1973.

Parisi, Tony *see* Pugliese, Antonio

Parker, Buddy Lee (Dwayne Bruce; 5'10", 242 lbs.) began wrestling in 1989. He teamed with James Earl as the State Patrol in the WCW in 1994.

Parker, Colonel Robert *see* Fuller, Robert

Parsons, Iceman King (St. Louis, Missouri; 5'10", 245 lbs.) began wrestling in 1979. The St. Louis native teamed with Rocky Johnson to hold the NWA Pacific Northwest Tag Team Title in November of 1981. He teamed with Porkchop Cash to hold the NWA Atlantic Coast Tag Title in 1982. He teamed with Buck Zumhofe as Rock 'n' Soul to hold the World Class American Tag Team Title several times in 1984, often competing against Scott and Bill Irwin. Parsons defeated Chris Adams for the World Class Championship in Texas in July of 1985. He teamed with Tiger Conway, Jr. as the Dream Team to hold the Texas All-Star USA Title several times in 1986. Parsons defeated Kerry Von Erich for the WCWA title in March of 1988. He teamed with Terry Taylor to hold the World Class World Tag Team Title in 1988. He held the World Class Texas Title in August of 1988. He teamed with Action Jackson as the Blackbirds in World Class in 1993.

Passofaro, Lenny *see* Montana, Lenny "Bull"

Patera, Ken (b. November 6; Portland, Oregon; 6'1", 256 lbs.) excelled in collegiate athletics at Brigham Young University in the late 1960s. He won the weightlifting competition at the Pan American games from 1968 through 1971. He won the bronze medal in weightlifting at the 1972 Olympic Games in Munich, Germany. He began wrestling professionally in the AWA the following year. He subsequently engaged in a brutal feud with Superstar Billy Graham in Texas. Patera was frustrated by a lack of title opportunities and soon became a vicious rulebreaker under the management of Captain Lou Albano. He teamed with Killer Karl Kox to hold the U.S. Tag Team Title in Louisiana in October of 1976. He held the NWA Eastern States Title several times in 1978. Patera was managed by the Grand Wizard when he captured the WWF Intercontinental Title from Pat Patterson in April of 1980. He lost the belt to Pedro Morales in December of 1980. He also held the NWA Missouri Title from April until November of 1980. Patera held the NWA Georgia Title in June of 1981. He also held the World Class Title in Texas in 1981. He defeated Jerry Lawler for the CWA International Title in Memphis in May of 1983. He teamed with Crusher Blackwell as the Sheiks and, under the management of Sheik Adnan El-Kaissey, they captured the AWA Tag Team Title from Jim Brunzell and Greg Gagne in June of 1983. They retained the title until their defeat by Crusher and Baron Von Raschke in May of 1984. In April of 1984 Patera and Mr. Saito were arrested for throwing a large rock through a window at a McDonald's in Waukesha, Wisconsin. They injured several police officers in a brawl at the Holiday Inn they were staying at. They were convicted of assault and battery and sentenced to two years in prison in June of 1985. After his release he teamed with Brad Rheingans to form the Olympians. They captured the AWA Tag Team Title from Paul Diamond and Pat Tanaka in March of 1989. They held the belts until the following September, when Patera was injured in the ring.

He teamed with Baron Von Raschke and held the PWA Tag Team Title several times in late 1991 and early 1992.

Patrick, Carl Ben teamed with Larry Wilson as the Flying Tigers in the mid-1980s. They held the Motor City Wrestling U.S. Team Title several times in 1986 and 1987.

Patriot, The (Del Wilkes; Columbia, South Carolina; 6'4", 251 lbs.) began wrestling in 1988. He was known as the Trooper in the AWA when he teamed with D.J. Peterson to capture the AWA Tag Team Title from Wayne Bloom and Mike Enos in August of 1990. They retained the title until the promotion ended the following year. The masked wrestler became a popular star with Global as the Patriot in the early 1990s. He held the Global Title several times in 1991 and 1992, often competing against the Dark Patriot. He teamed with Marcus Alexander Bagwell as Stars and Stripes the following year, and the duo captured the tag title from Paul Roma and Paul Orndorff in September of 1994. They lost the belts the following month in a rematch, but regained them on November 16, 1994. They were defeated by Harlem Heat on December 8, 1994. He subsequently departed the WCW and competed often in Japan in 1995.

Patriots, The *see* Champion, Todd & Firebreaker Chip

Patterson, Pat (b. January 19; Los Angeles, California; 240 lbs.) captured the NWA Pacific Coast Title for the first of several times in October of 1964. He teamed with

Tony Borne and the Hangman to hold the Pacific Coast tag belts in 1964. He held the NWA World Tag Team Title in San Francisco several times from 1965 through 1977, teaming with Ray Stevens, Billy Graham, Rocky Johnson, Peter Maivia, Moondog Mayne, Pedro Morales, Pepper Gomez and Tony Garea. Patterson held the NWA U.S. Title in San Francisco in August of 1969. He regained the title in February of 1972, under the management of Dr. Ken Ramey. He held the belt several more times through 1977. He teamed with Ivan Koloff to hold the NWA Florida Tag Team Title in July of 1977. He and Ray Stevens were awarded the AWA Tag Team Title in September of 1978. They retained the belts until their defeat by Verne Gagne and Mad Dog Vachon in June of 1979. He held the NWA Americas Title in Los Angeles in the fall of 1979. Patterson subsequently moved to the WWF where he was managed by the Grand Wizard. He was one of the leading mat villains in the area and was awarded the WWF Intercontinental Title in September of 1979. He was defeated for the belt by Ken Patera in April of 1980. He was subsequently managed by Lou Albano. He broke with Albano in 1980 and wrestled as a fan favorite. He held the Canadian International Tag Team Title in Montreal several times in the early 1980s, teaming with Pierre Lefebvre and Raymond Rougeau. Patterson retired from the ring in the mid-1980s and became an official with the WWF until his retirement in 1995.

Patterson, Rick teamed with Timothy Flowers to hold the Canadian Tag Team Title in June of 1983.

Patterson, Thunderbolt (225 lbs.) teamed with Alberto Torres to hold the WWA Tag Team Title in Los Angeles in February of 1966. He teamed with Wahoo McDaniel to hold the World Class American Tag Team Title in Texas in 1969. He again held the World Class American tag belts in 1971 and 1972, teaming with Toru Tanaka and Johnny Valentine. He teamed with Jerry Brisco to hold the NWA Atlantic Coast Tag Title in 1973. He briefly held the NWA Florida Title in March of 1976. He captured the U.S. Title in Toronto in November of 1976. He teamed with Mr. Wrestling to hold the NWA Georgia Tag Team Title in April of 1977. Patterson held the tag belts several times in 1978, teaming with Tommy Rich and Tony Atlas. He also held the NWA TV Title several times in 1978 and 1979. Patterson held the CWA World Title in the Spring of 1979. He teamed with Ole Anderson to hold the NWA National Tag Team Title for several months in early 1985.

Patton, Crazy Paul *see* Moondog Rover

Patton, Tank held the NWA Central States Tag Team Title with Super Intern in June of 1976. He teamed with Jesse Ventura to reclaim the Central States tag belts in September of 1978.

Paul, John teamed with Tracy Smothers to hold the CWA Tag Team Title in March of 1989.

Payne, Maxx (Daryll Peterson; b. October 3, 1961; Iowa City, Iowa; 6'6", 350 lbs.) attended Iowa State, where he was an amateur wrestler. He began wrestling in 1987. He captured the CWA Title for Jerry Lawler in February of 1988. He held the title several times during the year. Payne also held the CWA Tag Team Title several times in early 1988, teaming with Gary Young. He wrestled in Europe as Buffalo Peterson, capturing the Catch Wrestling Association Intercontinental Title in 1992. He teamed with Cactus Jack in the WCW until he was released by the promotion in the Summer of 1994. He wrestled as Man Mountain Rock in the WWF in 1994 and 1995.

Pazandak, Joe (b. 1921, d. 1984; Minneapolis, Minnesota; 6', 236 lbs.) was a leading competitor in the 1950s. He teamed with Mr. Moto in a series of bouts.

Peacock, Ben *see* Botswana Beast

Pegasus Kid, The *see* Benoit, Chris

Pendleton, Nat (b. 1895, d. October 11, 1967) was a silver medal winner at the 1920 Olympics, and competed as a professional wrestler in the 1920s and 1930s. He was also a leading character actor in Hollywood, best known as ambulance driver Joe Wayman in eight films in the *Dr. Kildare* series and as William Powell's friend, Detective Guild, in *The Thin Man* (1934) and *After the Thin Man* (1939). His numerous film credits also include *The Hoosier Schoolmaster* (1924), *Let's Get Married* (1926), *The Laughing Lady* (1929), *Fair Warning* (1930), *Last of*

the Duanes (1930), *The Sea Wolf* (1930), *Liliom* (1930), *The Seas Beneath* (1931), *Spirit of Notre Dame* (1931), *Cauliflower Alley* (1931), *The Sign of the Cross* (1932), *Attorney for the Defense* (1932), *You Said a Mouthful* (1932), *Horse Feathers* (1932), *Deception* (1933) as a wrestler, *Whistling in the Dark* (1933), *I'm No Angel* (1933), *Fugitive Lovers* (1934), *The Cat's Paw* (1934), *Lazy River* (1934), *Manhattan Melodrama* (1934), *Times Square Lady* (1935), *Murder in the Fleet* (1935), *The Garden Murder Case* (1936), *The Great Ziegfeld* (1936), *Two in a Crowd* (1936), *Life Begins in College* (1937), *Meet the Mayor* (1938), *Arsene Lupin Returns* (1938), *The Crowd Roars* (1938), *It's a Wonderful World* (1939), *On Borrowed Time* (1939), *At the Circus* (1939), *The Ghost Comes Home* (1940), *Phantom Raiders* (1940), *Northwest Passage* (1940), *Buck Privates* (1941), *The Mad Doctor of Market Street* (1941), *Jail House Blues* (1942), *Buck Privates Come Home* (1947) and *Scared to Death* (1947). He retired from the screen after his appearance in *Death Valley* in 1949. Pendleton died of a heart attack in San Diego, California, on October 11, 1967.

Penrod, Melvin, Jr. (6'1", 351 lbs.) teamed with C.W. Bergstrom in the USWA in 1993. They held the USWA Tag Team Title in July of 1993.

Perez, Al (b. July 23; Tampa, Florida; 6'1', 238 lbs.) began wrestling in 1981. He was trained by Boris Malenko and Karl Gotch and wrestled in Texas and Florida. He was known as the "Latin Heartthrob" and held the MSWA Tag Team Title with Wendell Cooley in August of 1985. He held the WWC North American Title in Puerto Rico in early 1986. He held the World Class Texas Title and the WCWA World Title for several months in late 1987. He has also wrestled in the WWF. He is the brother of Lou Perez.

Perez, Alex teamed with Tojo Yamamoto to hold the Southern Tag Team Title several times in 1964. They also held the World Tag Team Title in Tennessee in August of 1964. He held the Southern Junior Heavyweight Title for several months in early 1966. Perez teamed with El Gran Tapio to hold the U.S. Tag Team Title in Louisiana in July of 1973.

Perez, Eduardo (b. 1928, d. September 7, 1989) was a leading South American wrestler in the 1950s and 1960s. He died at his home in Tampa, Florida, on September 7, 1989.

Perez, Lou (6', 223 lbs.) is the younger brother of Al Perez. He began wrestling in 1986. He is a former holder of the PWF Light Heavyweight Title. He teamed with Allan Iron Eagle to hold the ICWA Florida Tag Team Title in 1992.

Perez, Miguel, Jr. (Carolina, Puerto Rico; 6'1", 232 lbs.) is the son of wrestler Miguel Perez. He began wrestling in 1986. He held the WWC North American Title in Puerto Rico several times in 1987. He teamed with Hurricane Castillo, Jr. to hold the WCW Tag Team Title in Puerto Rico several times in 1989. He defeated Kim Duk to win the WWC Caribbean title on February 16, 1990.

Perez, Miguel, Sr. teamed with Antonino Rocca in the late 1950s. He and Rocca won the World Tag Team Title in March of 1957. He is the father of Miguel Perez, Jr.

Perfect, Mr *see* Hennig, Curt

Perkins, Ponytail (Barbara Garza; b. 1927, d. November 30, 1987) was born in Joplin, Missouri. She competed as a wrestler in the New England area under the name Ponytail Perkins during the 1950s. She subsequently retired from the ring to pursue an acting career on the Boston stage as Barbara Lee. She died in a Brighton, Massachusetts, hospital after a long illness on November 30, 1987.

Perris, Jim *see* Koloff, Ivan

Perschman, Paul *see* Rose, Buddy

Pertano, Lucas teamed with Bull Curry to hold the Texas World Tag Team Title in January of 1963.

Peruzovic, Josip *see* Volkoff, Nikolai

Pesek, Jack (b. 1922, d. late 1980s; Ravenna, Nebraska; 6'3" 225 lbs.) was the son of wrestler John Pesek. He attended the University of Nebraska, where he was a collegiate football star. He began wrestling in the late 1940s, and remained a leading contender through the 1950s.

Pesek, John (b. 1894, d. March 12, 1978) held the American Legion

Heavyweight Title in Los Angeles in 1931. He was recognized as the Midwest Wrestling Association champion from March of 1931 until the following year. He was recognized as the NWA Heavyweight Champion from September of 1937 until August of 1938. He again held the MWA Heavyweight Title from August of 1938 until June of 1940. Pesek was a leading dog breeder and operator of a greyhound stable after his retirement from the ring.

Peterson, Buffalo *see* Payne, Maxx

Peterson, Curtis "Spike" (d. May, 1951) was a professional wrestler during the 1940s. He suffered a fractured neck in a match against Sam Abraham in Richland Center, Wisconsin, in May of 1951, and died of his injuries.

Peterson, Darryl *see* Payne, Maxx

Peterson, Dave "D.J." (b. 1960, d. May 25, 1993; St. Joseph, Missouri; 6'4", 245 lbs.) began wrestling in 1985. He held the World Class TV Title in December of 1985. He teamed with Todd Champion to hold the NWA Central States Tag Team Title in November of 1986. He also held the NWA Central States Title in December of 1987. He teamed with the Trooper to capture the AWA Tag Team Title from the Destruction Crew in August of 1990. They retained the belts until the promotion closed the following year.

Peterson, Scott (b. 1965, d. July 25, 1994) teamed with Steve Doll as the Southern Rockers to capture the

NWA Pacific Northwest Tag Team Title in November of 1987. They held the title numerous times over the next two years. Peterson left the team in the summer of 1989 and was replaced by Rex King.

Petty, Dan, wrestling as Danny O, teamed with Mike "Klondike Mike" Shaw to hold the Canadian Tag Team Title in June of 1981.

Petty, Ted *see* Rock, Flyboy Rocco

Pfohl, Larry *see* Luger, Lex

Phantoms, The *see* Faith, Jerry & Haste, Troy

Phillips, Treach (Henry William Phillips; b. 1929, d. September 30, 1995) was a leading mat villain in the Mid-South area during the 1950s and 1960s. He retired from wrestling and worked as a corrections officer in Shelby County, Tennessee. He died of heart failure in Memphis, Tennessee, on September 30, 1995.

Pico, Pancho teamed with Dory "the Outlaw" Funk to hold the Pacific Coast Tag Team Title in Vancouver, Canada, in February of 1961.

Pierce, Shanghai *see* Godwinn, Henry O.

Pierre the Lumberjack wrestled as Soldier Zarinoff LeBeouff with Sgt. Jacques Goulet as the Legionnaires. They held the WWA Tag Team Title for several months in 1975. Pierre teamed with Scott Irwin, as Eric the Lumberjack, in the WWWF to capture the Tag Team Title from Dominic Denucci and Dino Bravo in June of 1978.

They were defeated for the belts by Tony Garea and Larry Zbyszko in November of 1978.

Pierre the Quebecer *see* LaFitte, Jean-Pierre

Piers, Henry (b. 1905; Haarlem, the Netherlands) attended the Royal Dutch Naval Academy and served in the merchant marines. He came to the United States in the early 1920s, settling in Detroit. He was an amateur wrestling champion in Michigan and returned to the Netherlands to represent his country in the 1928 Olympics. He subsequently returned to the United States and began wrestling professionally in 1933. He remained active in the ring for the next several decades.

Pillman, Flyin' Brian (b. May 22, 1962, d. October 5, 1997; Cincinnati, Ohio; 6', 226 lbs.) began wrestling in November of 1986. He teamed with Bruce Hart as Bad Company to hold the Calgary Stampede International Tag Team Title several times in 1987. He teamed with Tom Zenk to capture the WCW U.S. Tag Team Title in a tournament in February of 1990. They were defeated for the belts by the Midnight Express in May of 1990. Pillman wrestled as the Yellow Dog in the WCW later in 1990. He defeated Rick Morton in a tournament for the WCW Light Heavyweight title in Chattanooga, Tennessee, on October 27, 1991. He was defeated by Jushin Liger for the title in December of 1991, but won a rematch in February of 1992. He lost the belt to Scotty Flamingo in June of 1992. Pillman wrestled with Steve Austin as the Hollywood Blondes in 1993, and the duo captured the WCW Tag Team Championship from Rick Steamboat and Shane Douglas on March 3, 1993. Pillman was injured later in the year and the title was relinquished to Paul Roma and Arn Anderson in August of 1993. Pillman joined with Ric Flair, Arn Anderson and Chris Benoit as the new Four Horsemen in 1995. He was considered the "loose cannon" of the group, and was known for his manic style in and out of the ring. Pillman entered the WWF in 1996, but was seriously injured in an automobile accident soon after. Pillman recovered from his injuries and returned to the ring. He was found dead of a heart attack in a Bloomington, Minnesota, hotel room on October 5, 1997.

Piper, Rowdy Roddy (Roderick Tombes; b. April 17, 1951; Glasgow, Scotland; 6'2 1/2", 231 lbs.) began wrestling in 1973. He usually entered the ring wearing kilts and playing the bagpipes. He held the NWA Americas Title in Los Angeles in March of 1976. He won the Los Angeles Battle Royal in 1976. He held the Americas title several more times in 1977, sometimes wrestling as the Canadian. He also held the NWA Americas Tag Team Title several times from 1976 through 1978, teaming with Crusher Verdu, the Hangman, Chavo Guerrero, Adrian Adonis, Ron Bass and Pak Choo. He also held the NWA U.S. Title in San Francisco in June of 1978. He teamed with Ed Wiskowski to hold the NWA World Tag Team Title in San Francisco in February of 1979. He held the NWA Pacific Northwest Title several times in 1979 and 1980. He also held the Pacific Northwest tag belts several times during this period, teaming with Killer Brooks, Rick Martel and Mike

Popovich. He teamed with Rick Martel to hold the Canadian Tag Team Title in May of 1980. He defeated Ric Flair for the NWA U.S. Title in January of 1981. He held the belt until relinquishing it to Wahoo McDaniel in August of 1981. He captured the NWA Mid-Atlantic Title from Rick Steamboat in November of 1981. He held the title until May of the following year. He briefly held the U.S. Title again in April of 1983, interrupting Greg Valentine's title reign. Piper primarily wrestled in the WWF during the remainder of the 1980s. Piper teamed with Paul Orndorff against Hulk Hogan and Mr. T in the main event at Wrestlemania I in March of 1985. Piper began appearing in films in the mid-1980s, starring in *Body Slam* (1987), *Hell Comes to Frogtown* (1987), the 1987 tele-film *The Highwayman*, *They Live* (1988) and *Immortal Combat* (1994). He also appeared on television the unsuccessful pilot film *Tag Team*, with Jesse "the Body" Ventura, in 1991, and in episodes of *Superboy*, *Highlander* and *RoboCop: The Series*. Piper returned to the ring to defeat the Mountie for the Intercontinental Title at the Royal Rumble in New York on January 18, 1992. He lost the belt to Bret Hart in April of 1992. Piper made occasional appearances in the ring in the mid-1990s, engaging in notable battles with Jerry Lawler and Goldust. He was briefly interim president of the WWF in early 1996.

Piret, Ray captured the Southern Junior Heavyweight Title in March of 1954. He held the belt until early 1955.

Pit Bull #1 (Gary Smith; 6'3", 243) began wrestling in 1990. He wrestled with Pit Bull #2 in ECW from 1994. They captured the ECW Tag Team Title from Steve Richards and Raven in September of 1995. They lost the belts in a rematch the following month.

Pit Bull #2 (Anthony Durante; 6'2", 231 lbs.) began wrestling in 1990. He wrestled with Pit Bull #1 in ECW from 1994. They captured the ECW Tag Team Title from Steve Richards and Raven in September of 1995. They lost the belts in a rematch the following month.

Pittman, Sgt. Craig (Parris Island, South Carolina; 6'2", 270 lbs.) began wrestling in February of 1994. He entered the WCW in 1995 and was managed by Teddy Long the following year.

Piwoworczyk, Karol *see* Kalmikoff, Karol

Pleasant, Tommy Lee *see* Smith, Pleasant

Plechas, Danny (b. 1921, d. February 1984; South Omaha, Nebraska; 6'2", 250 lbs.) served in the Marines during World War II. He was a professional boxer before he turned to wrestling. He was trained by John Pesek and was a leading contender during the 1950s. He teamed with Lee Henning to hold the Pacific Coast Tag Team Title in 1952. He teamed with Mike DiBiase to hold the World Tag Team Title in Chicago in February of 1956. They also held the NWA Texas Tag Team Title several times later in 1956.

Plotchek, Mike *see* Gunn, Bart

Plowboy Wilbur (Jim Ryder) wrestled in Global in the early 1990s.

Plugg, Thurman "Sparky" *see* Holly, Bob

Plummer, Lou (b. 1908, d. 19??; New Waverly, Texas; 6'1", 255 lbs.) played football at Notre Dame under Knute Rockne. He began wrestling professionally in the late 1930s, and held the Southwestern Title in Texas in 1938. He briefly held the Pacific Coast Title in San Francisco in February of 1939. He teamed with Dick Raines to hold the Canadian Open Tag Team Title in Toronto in December of 1952. Plummer also traveled throughout the country in the late 1940s and early 1950s as a Baptist preacher.

Poddubny, Ivan Maximovich (b. 1871, d. August 8, 1949) was a leading Russian wrestler at the turn of the century. Known in the ring as Ivan the Terrible, he captured the World Title in Paris in 1905. He wrestled extensively in the United States from the mid-1920s. He was defeated in the ring by Joe Stecher in February of 1925, which was said to be the first defeat he had suffered in twenty-five years of competition. He continued to compete in the United States through the mid-1930s. Poddubny died in Moscow, Russia, on August 8, 1949.

Podolak, Walter (b. 1915; Hollywood, California; 5'9", 220 lbs.) was born in Syracuse, New York. He began wrestling in the late 1930s. Known as the Golden Superman, Podolak was a popular scientific wrestler for several decades.

Poffo, Angelo (b. 1925; 200 lbs.) teamed with Bronco Lubich to hold the Midwest Tag Team Title in Chicago in August of 1956. He held the NWA U.S. Title in the late 1950s. He teamed with Bronco Lubich to hold the NWA Texas Tag Team Title in May of 1961. He teamed with Nicolai Volkoff to capture the WWA Tag Team Title in July of 1964, relinquishing the belts to Wilbur Snyder and Dick the Bruiser two months later. He teamed with Chris Markoff as the Devil's Duo to capture the WWA Tag belts in 1966 and 1967. He was the promoter for the ICW in the late 1970s and early 1980s. He occasionally wrestled in ICW as the Miser. He is the father of Lanny Poffo and Randy Savage.

Poffo, Lanny (b. December 28; Sarasota, Florida; 6', 228 lbs.) is the son of wrestler Angelo Poffo. He began wrestling in 1974. He teamed with his brother, Randy Savage, to hold the Gulf Coast Tag Team Title in February of 1976. They held the NWA Southeastern Tag Team Title the following year. Lanny Poffo held the Mid-America Title in 1977. He teamed with Bobby Eaton to hold the Mid-America Tag Team Title in 1978. He wrestled as Leaping Lanny in the ICW in the late 1970s and early 1980, exchanging the title belt several times with his brother, Randy Savage. He also held the ICW U.S. Tag Title several times during this period, teaming with George Weingeroff. He subsequently wrestled and managed in the WWF and the USWA as the Genius.

Poffo, Randy *see* Savage, Randy

Poggi, Ernest "Gorilla" (d. 19??; Buenos Aires, Argentina) competed throughout the world. Known in the ring as Gorilla Poggi, he remained a leading competitor through the 1950s.

Pogo, Mr. (5'10", 210 lbs.) began wrestling in 1971. The Japanese mat star often wrestled in a devious style. He held the NWA Tri-State Title in Oklahoma in 1981. He teamed with Gypsy Joe to hold the NWA Central States Tag Team Title in October of 1984. He held the NWA Central States Title in early 1985. He held the WWC Tag Team Title in Puerto Rico several times in 1987 and 1988, teaming with TNT and Kendo Nagasaki.

Poirier, Luc *see* Rambo, John

Poling, Al *see* 911

Polish Wildman, The *see* Kulky, Henry

Polo, Johnny *see* Raven

Polynesian Wildman teamed with Prince Mama Muhammad to hold the WWA Tag Team Title in 1986. He also teamed with the Golden Lion in the WWA

Pomeroy, Eric *see* Pulaski, Stan

Pondo, Mad Man (6', 237 lbs) wrestled with Doug Vines as the Bar Room Brawlers in the USWA in 1994.

Pope, Ron *see* Magnificent Zulu, The

Popescu, Samuel *see* Papp, Zoltan

Porteau, Alex (Dallas, Texas; 6'1", 235 lbs.) began wrestling in 1988. He wrestled with Tony Anthony as the Dirty White Boys in the USWA. He held the Texas All-Pro Wrestling Title in October of 1991. He wrestled as the Beach Boy in Global in the early 1990s. He captured the Global Junior Heavyweight Title several times in 1992 and 1993.

Potts, Bill *see* Watson, Whipper Billy

Powell, Jimmy (6'2 1/2", 245 lbs.) began wrestling in 1984. He wrestled as one of several Dirty White Boys in Georgia. He teamed with Fatback Festus as the masked Ding Dongs to hold the Georgia All-Star Tag Team Title in November of 1990.

Power, David (b. 1962; 6'2", 300 lbs.) was born in Brooklyn, New York. He was trained by Dr. D. David Shults and Bobby Bold Eagle and began wrestling in 1986. He and his twin brother, Larry, formed the Power Twins and wrestled in the ICW in Kansas City, the USWA in Memphis, the Calgary Stampede and UWF in New Jersey.

Power, Larry (b. 1962; 6'2", 300 lbs.) was born in Brooklyn, New York. He was trained by Dr. D. David Shults and Bobby Bold Eagle and began wrestling in 1986. He and his twin brother, David, formed the Power Twins and wrestled in the ICW in Kansas City, the USWA in Memphis, the Calgary Stampede and UWF in New Jersey.

Power, Terri was a leading female wrestler in the 1990s. She defeated Lady X for the LPWA title in February of 1992.

Powers, Jim (James Manley; b. January 4; 6'1", 230 lbs.) began wrestling in 1986. He wrestled in the

WWF, where he teamed with Paul Roma the Young Stallions.

Powers, Johnny was a popular Canadian wrestler in the 1960s and 1970s. He held the Cleveland North American Title in the late 1960s. He also wrestled in the NWF and Japan. Powers retired in the late 1980s.

Precious (Patty Williams) joined Jimmy Garvin as his valet in the World Class Promotion in 1983. Originally called Moonbeam, she replaced Sunshine as Garvin's valet in the fall of 1983. She remained with Garvin during his feud against Chris Adams and Sunshine in 1983 and 1984. She is married to Garvin.

Predator, The *see* Bollea, Mike

Prentice, Bert, wrestling as Christopher Henderson, held the WSWA Southern Title in Phoenix in May of 1982. He was a manager in Texas and Tennessee in the 1980s and 1990s, sometimes under the name Christopher Love.

Pretty Wonderful *see* Roma, Paul & Orndorff, Paul

Price, David *see* Cruz, Motley

Price, Rod (Los Angeles, California; 6', 285 lbs.) began wrestling in 1989. He wrestled as the California Stud and teamed with Steve Austin in 1991. He teamed with John Tatum as the California Connection to hold the Global World Tag Team Title several times in 1991. He held the Global North American Title several times in 1993 and 1994.

Prichard, Bruce (b. 1962) is a wrestling manager and commentator who went by the name Brother Love in the WWF. He was the host of a regular interview skit on the WWF's television programs in the late 1980s and early 1990s. He was also the first manager of the Undertaker when he entered the WWF in 1990. Prichard subsequently went to Global, where he was initially a commentator and, later, the manager of the Dark Patriot in 1992. Prichard returned to the WWF in the mid-1990s, where he worked behind the scenes as a booker. He is the brother of wrestler Tom Prichard.

Prichard, Dr. Tom (b. August 18, 1959; Houston, Texas; 5'10", 220 lbs.) began wrestling in 1978. He teamed with Al Madril and Chris Adams to hold the NWA Americas Tag Team Title in Los Angeles several times in 1980. He teamed with Brett Sawyer to hold the NWA Pacific Northwest Tag Team Title several times in 1984. He held the U.S. Junior Heavyweight Title in Alabama several times in 1986 and 1987, and was the Alabama champion in 1987 and 1988. He was a leading contender in the USWA in the late 1980s and early 1990s, hold the USWA Southern Title several times in 1991 and 1992. He teamed with Stan Lane as the Heavenly Bodies in Smoky Mountain Wrestling, and they held the tag belts several times in 1992 and 1993. He teamed with Jimmy Del Rey from May of 1993 when Lane retired from the ring. The duo wrestled in the Smoky Mountain region and WWF. Prichard reentered the WWF in December of 1995, teaming with Body Donna Skip, as Zip. They were managed by Sunny, and captured the WWF tag belts in the Spring of 1996.

Pride, Tyree (Haiti; 5'8", 231 lbs.) began wrestling in 1983. A native of Haiti, he held the Junior Heavyweight Title in the PWF and the WWC.

Pringle, Percy *see* Bearer, Paul

Prisoner, The *see* Kelly, Kevin

Prodhomme,   Edward   *see* Hagen, Jack

Professional, The *see* Gilbert, Doug

Professor, The *see* Grable, Lee

Prossner,   Fred *see* Sweetan, Freddie

Psicosis (Dionicio Castellanos; Tiajuana, Mexico; 5'10", 200 lbs.) began wrestling in 1991. He was a leading Mexican star in the AAA and the WWA, capturing the Mexican Welterweight Title in February of 1994.

Psycho (6'1", 263) began wrestling in 1984. He and Killer wrestled as the Texas Hangmen and held the USWA tag championship in 1990.

Psycho Sid *see* Vicious, Sid

Public   Enemy *see* Grunge, Johnny & Rock, Flyboy Rocco

Pugliese, Antonio (Tony Parisi) teamed with Johnny Valentine to defeat Dr. Bill and Dan Miller for the WWWF U.S. Tag Team Title in February of 1966. They lost the title to Baron Mikel Scicluna and Smasher Sloan when Valentine be-

trayed Pugliese in the ring. Pugliese returned to the championship when he teamed with Spiros Arion to defeat Scicluna and Sloan in December of 1966. Pugliese vacated the belt and departed the WWWF in June of 1967. Wrestling as Tony Parisi, he teamed with Dominic Denucci to hold the NWA Florida Tag Team Title in January of 1975. He returned to the WWWF to win the Tag Team Title with Louis Cerdan from the Blackjacks in November of 1975. They lost the belts to Killer Kowalski and Big John Studd in May of 1976. Wrestling as Tony Parisi, he held the Canadian International Tag Team Title several times in the early 1980s, teaming with Gino Brito and Dino Bravo.

Pulaski, Stan (Eric Pomeroy) held the Southern Tag Team Title with Ray Andrews in December of 1962. He wrestled as Stan Vachon and teamed with Butcher Vachon to hold the NWA Georgia Tag Team Title and the World Tag Team Title in Atlanta in 1968. He held the Mid-West Title in Omaha in February of 1969. He teamed with Danny Little Bear to hold the NWA Central States Tag Team Title in September of 1969. Pulaski teamed with Bobby Duncum to hold the NWA Georgia Tag Team Title again in September of 1973. He wrestled with Ron Gibson as the Infernos to hold the Southern Tag Team Title in April of 1974.

Punisher, The *see* Undertaker, The

Punishers, The *see* Sledge & Hammer

Purejara, Raymond *see* Williams, Frankie

Purple Shadow, The *see* Longson, Bill

Putski, Ivan (b. January 21; Krakow, Poland; 5'10", 242 lbs.) played professional football with the Detroit Lions in the 1960s. An injury forced his retirement from football and he entered professional wrestling in 1968. The proponent of "Polish Power" teamed with Jose Lothario to hold the World Class American Tag Team Title in 1973. He won the WWF Tag Team Title with Tito Santana in October of 1979, defeating Johnny and Jerry Valiant. They lost the belts to the Samoans in April of 1980. He is the father of Scott Putski.

Putski, Scott (Austin, Texas; 6', 235 lbs.) is the son of Ivan Putski. He was a fullback on the Texas Christian University football team. He began wrestling in 1986. Putski teamed with Steve Simpson in Global in 1991. He also teamed with Terry Simms to hold Global World Tag Team Title in March of 1992. He held the Global North American Title from May of 1992 until he left the promotion the following August. Putski wrestled as Konnan 2000 in the NWA in 1995.

Quebecers, The *see* Rougeau, Jacques & Pierre

Quinn, John held the Stampede North American Title in Calgary, Canada, in 1971. He also held the Canadian Tag Team Title several times in the early 1970s, teaming with Bob Brown, Dutch Savage and Gerry Romano. He again held the Stampede North American Title several times in 1974 and 1975.

Race, Harley (b. April 11, 1943; Kansas City, Missouri; 6'1", 268 lbs.) was trained by promoter Gus Karras in St. Joe, Missouri. He began his professional career in October of 1959. Race teamed with Larry Hennig to beat Crusher and Dick the Bruiser for the AWA World Tag Team Title in January of 1965. They lost the title to Crusher and Verne Gagne in July of 1965, but reclaimed them the following month in a rematch. They were again defeated by Crusher and Dick the Bruiser in May of 1966. The returned to claim the championship in January of 1967. Race teamed with Chris Markoff when Hennig incapacitated due to a broken leg, and they lost the tag title to Pat O'-Connor and Wilbur Snyder in November of 1967. He held the NWA Missouri Title several times in 1972 and 1973. He teamed with Roger Kirby to hold the NWA Central States Tag Team Title in late 1972. Race is also a 7-time NWA World Champion. He first won the belt from Dory Funk, Jr., in Kansas City, Missouri, on May 24, 1973. He was defeated by Jack Brisco several months later in Houston, Texas, on July 20, 1973. He held the Stampede North American Title in Calgary, Canada, in 1974. Race teamed with Buddy Colt to hold the NWA Georgia Tag Team Title in October of 1974. He held the NWA Florida Tag Team Title several times in 1975, teaming with Roger Kirby and Bob Roop. Race again captured the NWA title belt, defeating Terry

Funk in Toronto, Canada, on February 6, 1977. He lost the title to Dusty Rhodes on August 21, 1979, but regained the belt from Rhodes several days later on August 26, 1979. He lost and recaptured the title from Giant Baba in Japan in 1979 and 1980, and briefly relinquished the title to Tommy Rich in April of 1981, regaining it several days later. He was again defeated for the belt by Dusty Rhodes in Atlanta, Georgia, on June 21, 1981. Race again held the belt following his defeat of Ric Flair on June 10, 1983, in St. Louis, Missouri. He lost the belt to Flair in a rematch in Greensboro, North Carolina, on November 24, 1983. He captured the Mid-America Title in Memphis in October of 1985. Race entered the WWF in the mid-1980s, where he was managed by Bobby Heenan. He won the King of the Ring tournament in July of 1986 and was coronated as King of the WWF the following month. He retired from the ring in early 1988 after suffering an injury. He entered the WCW in the early 1990s, and managed Big Van Vader until he was seriously injured in an automobile accident on January 25, 1995.

Radford, Rad *see* Spicolli, Louie

Rage *see* Laurinatis, Marc

Raines, Dick (Charles Raines; b. 1911, d. October 18, 1979; Texas; 240 lbs.) began wrestling in the late 1930s. He held the Hawaiian Title in February of 1939. He was known in the ring as "Dirty Dick," and was considered a vicious mat opponent. He suffered a major back injury in the late 1940s that kept him out of the ring for over a year. He returned

to competition in the early 1950s. He teamed with Lou Plummer to hold the Canadian Open Tag Team Title in Toronto in December of 1952.

Rambo, John (Luc Poirier; Charlotte, North Carolina; 6'2", 260 lbs.) began wrestling in 1987. He held the AWF Title in Pennsylvania in 1990, and captured the National Wrestling League Title in Guam in October of 1990. He wrestled in the Pacific Northwest in early 1990s, teaming with Colonel DeBeers to hold the tag team belts in March of 1992. He also held the Catch Wrestling Association Heavyweight Title in Europe several times in the early 1990s.

Ramey, Dr. Ken managed the masked wrestling duo, the Medics, during the 1960s. He also managed the Interns in the early 1970s. He managed Pat Patterson in the NWA in San Francisco in 1972.

Ramirez, Benji *see* Mummy, The

Ramirez, Huracan was a popular Mexican wrestler in the 1950s and 1960s He held the Mexican Welterweight Title in August of 1965. He captured the Mexican National Welterweight Title several times in the late 1960s and early 1970s. Ramirez also appeared in numerous Mexican films.

Ramon, Razor (Scott Hall; b. October 20, 1959; Miami, Florida; 6'8", 287 lbs.) played basketball at St. Mary's University in Maryland. He began wrestling in October of 1984. He wrestled as Starship Coyote with Dan Spivey in the American Starship tag team in 1984. He entered the AWA as Scott Hall the following year. He teamed with Curt Hennig to take the AWA World Tag Team Title in January of 1986. They were defeated for the belts by Buddy Rose and Doug Somers in a controversial decision in May of 1986. He subsequently engaged in a feud with Colonel De-Beers. Hall entered the WCW and wrestled as the Diamond Studd in Dallas Page's Diamond Exchange. He became known as Razor Ramon when he entered the WWF in May of 1992. He won the Intercontinental Title in a tournament over Rick Martell on September 27, 1993. He lost the WWF Intercontinental belt to Diesel at a match in Syracuse, New York, on April 13, 1994. He regained the belt by pinning Diesel at SummerSlam on August 29, 1994. He lost the belt to Jeff Jarrett in Tampa, Florida, on January 22, 1995. He regained the belt on May 19, 1995, but lost the title in a rematch two days later. Ramon reclaimed the Intercontinental Title on October 22, 1995, defeating Sean Douglas. He lost the title to Goldust at the Royal Rumble on January 21, 1996. Ramon left the WWF in Spring of 1996 to enter the WCW.

Ramos, Bull (5'10", 355 lbs.) began wrestling in 1956. He held the NWA Pacific Northwest Title several times in 1972. He held the Pacific Northwest tag belts several times in 1973, teaming with Ken Mantell and Ripper Collins. Known as the Apache, he held the MSWA North American Title for several months from April of 1974. He again held the Pacific Northwest tag belts in the mid-1970s, teaming with Jesse Ventura and the Iron Sheik. He teamed with John Studd to hold the World Class Texas Tag Team Title in 1977. He again held the Texas tag belts with Tiger Conway, Jr. in December of 1978. He held the NWA Americas Title in Los Angeles in June of 1979. He held the Mid-South Mississippi Title in April of 1980. Ramos retired in 1983, but reemerged in the Pacific Northwest territory in 1990.

Ramos, Gorilla (d. 19??) was a leading Mexican mat star in the 1930s and 1940s. He briefly held the World Light Heavyweight Title in 1941. He also held the Mexican National Light Heavyweight Title in 1944.

Ranger Ross (6', 225 lbs.) began wrestling in 1986. He was a former Army Ranger involved in the U.S. invasion of Grenada in 1983. He wrestled in Georgia and the WCW, holding the Alabama Title in January of 1988. He held the Peach State Wrestling U.S. Title in early 1992.

Raper, Ken wrestled in the Memphis area during the 1980s, often on television matches. He teamed with Robert Reed to score an upset win against the Assassins, capturing the CWA Tag Team Title in October of 1983. The Assassins regained the belts in a rematch several days later.

Raschke, James *see* Von Raschke, Baron

Rasputin *see* Campbell, Black Angus

Rasputin, Ivan (Hyman Fishman; d. 19??; Russia) was known in the ring as "The Mad Russian," the hairy massive wrestler was known for his bear hug. He primarily competed in the California area during the 1930s and 1940s. He captured the Pacific Coast Title in San Francisco in February of 1938. He relinquished the title several months later when he left the area. He again briefly held the title in January of 1941, competing against Bobby Managoff. He came East in 1946, but his ring activities were halted for several years due to a serious back injury. He returned to competition in the 1950s.

Rat Pack, The *see* DiBiase, Ted & Borne, Matt

R.A.T. Patrol Inc. *see* (Rich, Johnny; Armstrong, Scott & Tonga Kid)

Raven (Scott Levy; b. August 8; Short Hills, New Jersey; 6'1", 235 lbs.) began wrestling in 1987, as Scotty Flamingo. He held the NWA Pacific Northwest Title several times in 1989 and 1990, wrestling as Scotty the Body. He teamed with Top Gun to hold the NWA Pacific Northwest Tag Team Title in July of 1989. They split the team the following month and Scotty held the title with Len "the Grappler" Denton in August of 1989. He won the WCW Light Heavyweight Title from Brian Pillman in June of 1992. He lost the belt to Brad Armstrong the following month. He teamed with Brian Christopher to hold the USWA Tag Team Title in March of 1993. He managed the Quebecers and occa-

sionally wrestled in the WWF in 1994 until his resignation in August of 1994. Polo entered the ECW in early 1995 as Raven. He teamed with Stevie Richards to hold the ECW Tag Team Title several times in 1995, competing against the Pit Bulls and Public Enemy. He also held the ECW Heavyweight Title in early 1996. He was initially accompanied to the ring by Beulah McGillicutty, but she left him for Tommy Dreamer in the midst of a violent feud. Raven replaced her with Kimona Wanaleia as his ring valet, but she also abandoned him in the Spring of 1996. Stevie Richards and the Blue Meanie continued to accompany Raven during his matches.

Ray, Steve (6'3", 255 lbs.) began wrestling in 1987. He was trained by Sonny Myers. Know as the Wild Thing, he often teamed with Sunny Beach.

Ray, Stevie *see* Stevie Ray

Rayo De Jalisco, El was a leading Mexican masked wrestler in the 1950s and 1960s. He held the Mexican Middleweight Title several times in the early 1960s. He teamed with El Santo to hold the Mexican National Tag Team Title several times in the mid-1960s. He was also a popular Mexican actor in the 1950s, appearing in nine films including *Lo Sombra Vengadora* (1954). His son, Ray De Jalisco, Jr., was also a leading Mexican star.

Rayo De Jalisco, Jr. was the son of masked Mexican wrestler, El Rayo de Jalisco, and took over his father mask and mantle in the ring.

He held the Mexican Light Heavyweight Title in the mid-1980s. and the Mexican National Heavyweight Championship in the early 1990s.

Rechsteiner, Robert *see* Steiner, Rick

Rechsteiner, Scott *see* Steiner, Scott

Red Cloud, Billy (d. October 1981) was a Chippewa Indian from Minnesota. He began his career in the early 1960s. He held the WWA title for several months in 1972. He retired from the ring in the late 1970s due to poor health.

Red Hangman, The *see* Rice, Tommy

Red Phantom, The *see* Rice, Tommy

Red Rooster, The *see* Taylor, Terry

Red Shadow, The *see* Dunn, Dick

Reed, Bruce *see* Reed, Butch

Reed, Butch (b. July 11, 1954; Kansas City, Missouri; 6'2", 265 lbs.) began wrestling in 1978. Wrestling as Bruce Reed, he teamed with Jerry Roberts to hold the NWA Central States Tag Team Title in 1980. He also teamed with Skip Young to hold the North American Tag Team Title in Florida in April of 1982. He held the MSWA North American Title in July of 1983. He held the MSWA belt again in October of 1985. He also teamed with Jim Neidhart to hold the MSWA Tag Team Title in October of 1983. He wrestled with Ron Simmons as

Doom in the WCW. Managed by Woman, they won the WCW World Tag Team Title from Rick and Scott Steiner in May of 1990. They lost the belts to the Freebirds in February of 1991. The duo later split up and feuded. Reed won the USWA Unified Title on October 12, 1992. He relinquished the title to Todd Champion the following week. Reed held the Missouri Wrestling Federation Title in late 1993.

Reed, Robert wrestled in the Memphis area during the 1980s, often on television matches. He teamed with Ken Raper to score an upset win against the Assassins, capturing the CWA Tag Team Title in October of 1983. The Assassins regained the belt several days later.

Reed, Ron *see* Colt, Buddy

Regal, Lord Steven (Darren Mathews; b. May 10, 1968; Blackpool, England; 6'4", 247 lbs.) began wrestling in 1984. He wrestled as Lord Steven Regal in the WCW in the 1990s. He was managed by Sir William Dundee, and captured the WCW TV Title from Rick Steamboat in September of 1993. He lost the belt to Larry Zbyszko in May of 1994, but recaptured the title the following June. He again lost the title to Johnny B. Badd in September of 1994. Regal teamed with Bobby Eaton as the Blue Bloods from early 1995.

Regal, Steve (b. September 15; 6', 205 lbs.) began wrestling in 1977. He teamed with Hector Guerrero to hold the Southern Tag Team Title in November of 1979. He teamed with Matt Borne to hold the NWA

Pacific Northwest Tag Team Title in July of 1981. He also held the NWA Pacific Northwest Title several times in 1981. He teamed with Dewey Robertson to hold the NWA Central States Tag Team Title in March of 1982. He teamed with Spike Huber to hold the WWA Tag Team Title several times in 1982 and 1983. Known as "Mr. Electricity," Regal defeated Buck Zumhofe for the AWA Light Heavyweight Title in March of 1984. He lost the title back to Zumhofe in November of 1984. Regal teamed with Jim Garvin to take the AWA Tag Team Title from the Road Warriors in September of 1985. They relinquished the belts in January of 1986 when Regal left the AWA to enter the NWA. Regal captured the NWA World Junior Heavyweight Title from Denny Brown in August of 1986. He relinquished the title to Brown the following month.

Reiher, James *see* Snuka, Jimmy

Reis, Ron (b. November 18; San Jose, California; 7'2", 360 lbs.) began wrestling in March of 1994.

Remus, Bob *see* Slaughter, Sgt.

Renegade, The (Rick Williams; 5'10", 256 lbs.) was trained by Killer Kowalski. He wrestled as Reo, Lord of the Jungle, before debuting in the WCW as the Renegade in March of 1995. He was initially managed by Jimmy Hart, and teamed with Hulk Hogan and Randy Savage. He defeated Arn Anderson for the WCW TV Title on June 18, 1995. He lost the belt to Diamond Dallas Page on September 17, 1995.

Renegade Warriors *see* Youngblood, Mark & Chris

Renesto, Tom wrestled with Jody Hamilton as the Assassins and held the Atlanta World Tag Team Title for several months in early 1969. He held the NWA Georgia Title briefly in March of 1970. The Assassins held the NWA Georgia Tag Title numerous times until September of 1972, when Renesto unmasked and retired from wrestling. He returned to the ring as the Mongolian Stomper's manager in the Memphis area in September of 1985.

Rentrop, Charles A. (d. 196?; 5'11", 155 lbs.) was born in Germany and competed in the Olympics in Stockholm, Sweden, in 1912. He came to the United States after World War I and wrestled professionally in the early 1920s. Known as the Bald Eagle, he defeated Clarence Eklund for the World Light Heavyweight Title in January of 1923. He relinquished the belt to Eklund several weeks later. He retired from the ring the following year due to trachoma, an eye disease peculiar to wrestlers. Despite limited vision, he remained involved in wrestling as a major promoter, an occasional wrestler, in the South in through the 1950s.

Reo, Lord of the Jungle *see* Renegade

Repoman *see* Smash

Resindez, Victor *see* Latin Lover

Rex, Moondog *see* Culley, Randy

Rey Misterio (Miguel Lopez) was a leading masked Mexican wrestler in the 1950s and 1960s. He is the uncle of Rey Misterio, Jr.

Rey Misterio, Jr. (Oscar Gonzales; San Diego, California; 5'3", 140 lbs.) began wrestling in 1991. He is the nephew of the original Rey Misterio. The masked Mexican athlete wrestled out of San Diego, California, and was considered one of the sports greatest aerial stars.

Reyes, Carmelo *see* Cien Caras

Reyes, Jesus *see* Mascara Ano 2000

Reyes, Raul held the Mexican National Heavyweight Title several times in the late 1960s and early 1970s. He held the NWA Americas Tag Team Title in Los Angeles several times in 1973, teaming with Ray Mendoza, Victor Rivera and Reuben Juarez.

Rheingans, Brad (b. December 13, 1953; Appleton, Minnesota; 6', 248 lbs.) attended North Dakota State University. He was a leading amateur wrestler and competed in the 1976 Olympics. He was trained as a professional wrestler by Verne Gagne and made his debut in January of 1981. He teamed with Ken Patera to form the Olympians in the late 1980s. They captured the AWA Tag Team Title from Paul Diamond and Pat Tanaka in March of 1989. They held the belts until the following September, when Patera was injured in the ring.

Rhodes, Dirty *see* Smith, Roger

Rhodes, Dustin (Dustin Runnels; b. April 11, 1966; Austin, Texas; 6'5", 254 lbs.) began wrestling in 1988. Known as the Natural, he is the son of Dusty Rhodes. He teamed with Rick Steamboat to win the WCW World Tag Team Title from Arn Anderson and Larry Zbyszko on November 19, 1991. They were defeated for the belts several months later by Anderson and Bobby Eaton in January of 1992. Rhodes teamed with Barry Windham to take the tag title from Steve Williams and Terry Gordy on September 21, 1992. They lost the belts to Rick Steamboat and Shane Douglas in November of 1992 and he and Windham split up as a team. Rhodes won the WCW U.S. Title in a tournament in January of 1993. He emerged victorious in a battle for the title with Rick Rude during the summer of 1993. He also married Alexandra York on July 25, 1993. He lost the U.S. Title to Steve Austin on December 27, 1993. Rhodes left the WCW in March of 1995. He entered the WWF in October of 1995 as Golddust, sporting a long blonde wig, gold costume and makeup. His androgynous persona caused controversy in the WWF, as he engaged in feuds with Razor Raman and Roddy Piper. His wife accompanied him to the ring as his director, Marlena. Goldust defeated Ramon for the WWF Intercontinental Title at the Royal Rumble on January 21, 1996.

Rhodes, Dusty (Virgil Riley Runnels, Jr.; b. October 12, 1945; Austin, Texas; 6'1", 302 lbs.) made his professional wrestling debut in Toronto, Canada, in November of 1969. He teamed with Dick Murdoch as the Outlaws to hold the NWA Central States Tag Team Title and the NWA Florida Tag Team Title in 1970. He held the MSWA North America Title in Louisiana for several months from May of 1971. He held the NWA Southern Title in Florida and the NWA Florida Title several times from 1973 through 1980. He teamed with Andre the Giant to hold the U.S. Tag Team Title in Louisiana in December of 1978. Known as the American Dream, he defeated Harley Race for the NWA Heavyweight Title in a match in Tampa, Florida, on August 21, 1979. He lost the belt back to Race in a rematch in Orlando, Florida, several days later on August 26, 1979. He held the NWA U.S. Title in San Francisco in November of 1980. He again defeated Race for the title in Atlanta, Georgia, on June 21, 1981. He held the title until September 17, 1981, when he lost the belt to Ric Flair in Kansas City, Missouri. He teamed with Andre the Giant to hold the NWA Florida Tag Team Title in February of 1981. Rhodes also wrestled in the NWA as the masked Midnight Rider, defeating Ric Flair in a championship match February of 1983, but was denied the belt when he refused to unmask. Rhodes teamed with Manny Fernandez to capture the NWA World Tag Team Title from Ivan Koloff and Don Kernodle in October of 1984. They were defeated for the belts by Ivan and Nikita Koloff in March of 1985. Rhodes held the NWA National Title for several months in early 1986. Rhodes also held the NWA TV Title several times in the mid-1980s, and again held the NWA Heavyweight Title briefly following his defeat of Flair

in Greensboro, North Carolina, on July 26, 1986. He again relinquished the belt to Flair in a rematch in St. Louis, Missouri, on August 9, 1986. Rhodes defeated Lex Luger for the NWA U.S. Title in November of 1987. He was stripped of the belt in April of 1988 following his attack on promoter Jim Crockett. He subsequently entered the WWF, costumed in a polka-dot ring outfit, and engaged in a feud with Ted DiBiase. He was often accompanied to the ring by his valet, Sapphire. Rhodes went to the WCW in the early 1990s, where he was a booker and commentator. He remained as announcer for the WCW's television programs through the mid-1990s.

Rhodes, Randy (6'1", 321 lbs.) began wrestling in 1986. He teamed with Eric Fontaine as the New Pretty Young Things in Global under the management of Christopher Love in 1990.

Rice, Ricky (6'1", 230 lbs.) began wrestling in 1987. He teamed with Derrick Dukes as the Top Guns to hold he PWA Tag Team Title in June of 1987. He was a popular star in the AWA in the late 1980s. He captured the PWA Title in March of 1986. He held the title several more times in 1989 and 1990. He held the PWA Light Heavyweight Title several times in 1991.

Rice, Tommy (San Francisco, California) was a former football player who was known in the ring as the Red Phantom and the Red Hangman. He teamed with Frederick von Schacht to hold the NWA World Tag Team Title in San Francisco in July of 1950. He teamed with Hard Boiled Haggerty to hold the Pacific Coast Tag Team Title in September of 1951. He again held the tag belts in 1953, teaming with Don Lee. He held the Hawaiian Title in October of 1956. He teamed with Lord Athol Layton to hold the Hawaiian Tag Team Title in April of 1957. He held the Pacific Coast Title in San Francisco in January of 1959. He also reclaimed the NWA tag belts in January of 1959, teaming with Ben Sharpe. He teamed with Shoulders Newman to hold the Hawaiian Tag Team Title in November of 1960.

Rich, Gary *see* Dragon Master, The

Rich, Johnny (6', 235 lbs.) began wrestling in 1976. He teamed with Scott Armstrong and the Tonga Kid as R.A.T. Patrol Inc. to hold the Southeastern Tag Team Title several times in 1984 and 1985. He also teamed with his cousin, Tommy Rich to hold the Southeastern tag belts in February of 1986. He wrestled in the WCW in the early 1990s.

Rich, Randy held the Canadian Tag Team Title several times in 1983 and 1984, teaming with Rick Patterson and Ole Olson.

Rich, Tommy (Thomas Richardson; b. July 26; Hendersonville, Tennessee; 6', 248 lbs.) began wrestling in 1976. He held the Mid-America Title in September of 1976, and held the Southern Heavyweight Title later in the year. He teamed with Tony Atlas to capture the NWA Georgia Tag Team Title in November of 1977. Rich held the tag belts several times over the next few years,

teaming with Stan Hansen, Thunderbolt Patterson, Wahoo McDaniel and Crusher. He held the NWA Georgia Title from October until December of 1979. Rich held the Southern Heavyweight title again several times in 1980. He defeated Harley Race for the NWA Heavyweight Title in Augusta, Georgia, on April 27, 1981. He lost the belt back to Race several days later in a match in Gainesville, Georgia, on May 1, 1981. He held the NWA Georgia Title several more times in 1981, until losing the belt to the Masked Superstar in August of 1981. He teamed with Bill Dundee to hold the Southern Tag Team Title several times in late 1980 and early 1981. He wrestled against Buzz Sawyer in Atlanta in the mid-1980s. Rich teamed with Eddie Gilbert as Jackie Fargo's new Fabulous Ones in early 1984, capturing the Southern Tag Team Title in March of 1984. He and Gilbert broke later in the year and engaged in a feud. Rich briefly held the CWA International Title in July of 1984. Rich again held the tag belts with Dutch Mantel in September of 1984. He held the NWA Southeastern Tag Team Title several times in 1986, teaming with his cousin, Johnny Rich, and Steve Armstrong. He joined the York Foundation as Thomas Rich in the early 1990s. He was managed by Alexandra York and teamed with Rick Morton and Terry Taylor to hold the WCW 6-Man Tag Title in late 1991. He wrestled in the USWA during the mid-1990s, capturing the USWA Southern Title in September of 1993. He again held the belt from October of 1994, until his defeat by Brian Christopher on

December 31, 1994. He teamed with Doug Gilbert to hold the USWA Tag Team Title several times in early 1995. Tommy Rich defeated Brad Armstrong for the Smoky Mountain Wrestling Title in November of 1995, becoming the last champion of the defunct organization.

Richards, Steve (b. October 9, 1971; Philadelphia, Pennsylvania; 6'2", 225 lbs.) began wrestling in February of 1992. He teamed with Raven in the ECW in 1995 to hold the tag team title several times during the year. Richards and Blue Meanie often accompanied Raven to the ring in the mid-1990s.

Richardson, Thomas *see* Rich, Tommy

Richland, Jimmy *see* Del Rey, Jimmy

Richmond, John *see* Mad Maxx

Richter, Wendi (b. September 6; Dallas, Texas; 5'8", 142 lbs.) began wrestling in 1977. She teamed with Joyce Grable as the Texas Cowgirls in the early 1980s, to hold the Women's World Tag Team Title. She won the WWF's Women's Title from the Magnificent Moolah in New York's Madison Square Garden on July 23, 1984. She lost the title to Leilani Kai in New York on February 18, 1985, but regained the title at Wrestlemania I on March 31, 1985. Richter was managed by singer Cyndi Lauper at the event. Richter lost the belt to Moolah on November 11, 1985, in New York. She held the WWC Women's Title in Puerto Rico several times in 1987. Richter entered the AWA to capture the

Women's Title from Madusa Miceli in November of 1988. She vacated the title when she left the promotion the following year.

Rickner, John *see* Bradley, Boo

Rico, Don *see* Doganiero, Dominic W.

Riggins, Reno wrestled in the USWA in the early 1990s. He briefly held the USWA Southern Title in August of 1992.

Riggz, Scott (Scott Antol; Atlanta, Georgia; 6', 224 lbs.) wrestled as Scott Studd in WCW and Smoky Mountain Wrestling in the early 1990s. He wrestled as Kendo the Samurai in Smoky Mountain in 1994. He entered WCW as Scotty Riggz in August of 1995. He teamed with Marcus Bagwell as the American Males. They defeated Harlem Heat for the WCW Tag Team Title in September 18, 1995. They lost the belts in a rematch ten days later.

Rignati, Dan *see* Terminator Rigs

Rikidozan (Mitsuhiro Momota; d. December 17, 1963) was born in Korea. He was a leading figure in Japanese wrestling, holding the Japanese Wrestling Association Title in December of 1954. He also wrestled in the United States in the early 1950s. He teamed with Dennis Clary to hold the Pacific Coast Tag Team Title in October of 1952. He founded the Japan Wrestling Association in 1953. He captured the JWA NWA International Title in August of 1958. He teamed with Kokichi Endo to hold the Hawaiian Tag Team Title in 1959. Rikidozan defeated Fred Blassie for the WWA

Title in Los Angeles in March of 1962, relinquishing the belt in a rematch the following July. Gambling debts led to his stabbing murder by the Japanese underworld on December 17, 1963. His sons, Mitsuo Momota and Yoshihiru Momota, were also professional wrestlers.

Riley, Tex (d. 1916, d. 1964) held the World Light Heavyweight Title in Alabama and Tennessee several times from 1946 through 1948. He teamed with Herb Welch to hold the Southern Tag Team Title in Tennessee in November of 1948. He held the Southern Junior Heavyweight Title in early 1953. He teamed with Len Rossi to hold the World Tag Team Title in Tennessee in January of 1960. He held the Southern belts several times in the early 1960s, teaming with Len Rossi and Jackie Fargo.

Ringer, John (230 lbs.) began wrestling in the Arizona area in the late 1970s. The bearded villain held the Arizona Junior Heavyweight Title several times in the late 1970s and early 1980s, often feuding against Benny Mendeblis. Ringer also captured the Arizona Title in Phoenix several times in 1981.

Ringmaster, The *see* Austin, Steve

Rios, Del *see* Spellbinder, The

Rising Suns, The *see* Tanaka, Toru & Arakawa, Mitsu

Ritchie, Ron (New York; 238 lbs.) teamed with George Wells to hold the NWA Central States Tag Team Title in August of 1983. He teamed with Leo Burke to hold the

Calgary Stampede International Tag Team Title in February of 1986. He held the Stampede North American Title in May of 1986.

Ritter, Sylvester "Big Daddy" *see* Junkyard Dog

Rivera, Jose Luis (6'2", 248 lbs.) began wrestling in 1979. He appeared often in the WWF.

Rivera, Juan *see* Vega, Savio

Rivera, Victor (Puerto Rico; 253 lbs.) was raised in New York City and began wrestling professionally at the age of 17. He teamed with Pedro Morales to hold the WWA Tag Team Title in Los Angeles in 1967. He was a popular wrestler before engaging Fred Blassie as manager and becoming a leading villain. He teamed with Tony Marino to capture the WWWF International Tag Team Title in December of 1969. They were defeated for the belts by the Mongols in June of 1970. He held the NWF title in Cleveland in 1972. He held the NWA Americas Title in Los Angeles several times in 1972 and 1973. He won the Los Angeles Battle Royal in 1973. He held the NWA Americas tag belt several times in 1973 and 1974, teaming with Raul Reyes, Raul Matta and Dino Bravo. He shared the WWWF Tag Team Title with Dominic Denucci after their defeat of Jimmy and Johnny Valiant in May of 1975. Rivera vacated the title the following month when he left the WWWF. He returned to Los Angeles, where he again held the NWA Americas tag belts several times in 1977, teaming with Cien Caras, Terry Sawyer,

Chavo Guerrero and Texas Red. He returned to the WWWF in 1978 as a vicious rulebreaker under the management of Freddie Blassie. He was a frequent tag team partner of Spiros Arion in the late 1970s. He teamed with Salvatore Bellomo to recapture the Americas Tag Title in May of 1981. He held the All-California Championship Wrestling Title several times in 1987 and 1988.

Rizzo, Alex *see* Dudley, Big Dick

Roach, Pat was a leading British wrestler in the 1960s and 1970s. He retired from the ring in the late 1970s to become a stuntman and actor. He returned to the ring in April of 1986 to capture the British Heavyweight Title. He also held the CWA European Heavyweight Title in early 1990. He appeared in such films as *Raiders of the Lost Ark* (1981), *Clash of the Titans* (1981), *Never Say Never Again* (1983), *Indiana Jones and the Temple of Doom* (1984), *Conan the Destroyer* (1984) and *Robin Hood: Prince of Thieves* (1991).

Road Warriors, The *see* Hawk & Animal

Roadie, The *see* Armstrong, Jesse James

Robert, Yvon (b. 1915, d. July 12, 1971; Montreal, Canada; 6'1", 210 lbs.) was a leading French Canadian wrestler. He defeated Danno O'Mahoney for the AWA World Title in a match in Montreal, Canada, on July 13, 1936. He retained the belt until January of 1938, when the title was awarded to Lou Thesz. He held the AWA Title in Montreal, several times in the late 1930s and early 1940s. He defeated Bill Longson for the NWA Heavyweight Championship in Montreal, Canada, on October 7, 1942. He lost the belt to Bobby Managoff the following month in Houston, Texas, on November 27, 1942. He wrestled Gorgeous George in a historic match in Montreal in 1949. Robert teamed with Whipper Billy Watson to hold the Canadian Open Tag Team Title in Toronto in January of 1953. He teamed with Billy Wicks to hold the World Tag Team Title in Tennessee in 1957, and held the Southern Junior Heavyweight Title in 1958.

Roberts, Bobby was a collegiate football star at he University of Dayton in Ohio. He began wrestling in Cleveland in 1946, and remained a popular scientific grappler for the next decade.

Roberts, Buddy (Dale Hey; Del City, Oklahoma; 5'10", 247 lbs.) began wrestling in 1965. He also wrestled as Dale Roberts. He teamed with Jerry Brown as the Hollywood Blonds to hold the U.S. Tag Team Title in Oklahoma in May of 1970. They again held the U.S. belts in February of 1973. They captured the NWA American Tag Team Title in Los Angeles several times in 1974 and 1975. They also held the NWA Florida Tag Team Title in October of 1976. They held the Southern Tag Team Title briefly the following year. Wrestling as Dale Valentine, he held the World Class Texas Title in March of 1978. He wrestled during the 1980s as the third Freebird with Terry Gordy and Michael Hayes. They captured the NWA Georgia Tag Team Title in

October of 1980. He held the World Class TV Title in January of 1986. He captured the UWF TV Title in Oklahoma in September of 1986. He retired in the early 1990s.

Roberts, Dale *see* Roberts, Buddy

Roberts, Ed teamed with Savannah Jack as the Miami Vice Defenders to hold the PWA Tag Team Title for several months from April of 1985.

Roberts, Jake "the Snake" (Aurelian Smith, Jr.; b. May 30; Stone Mountain, Georgia; 6'5", 246 lbs.) is the son of Aurelian "Grizzly" Smith and the older brother of wrestlers Sam Houston and Rockin' Robin. He began wrestling professionally in Louisiana in May of 1975. He held the Stampede North American Title in Calgary, Canada, in April of 1979. He teamed with Jay Youngblood to hold the NWA Atlantic Coast Tag Title in 1981. He entered the Florida area in 1982 and was managed by Kevin Sullivan. He captured the MSWA North American Title in June of 1981. He subsequently moved to the Mid-Atlantic region, where he was managed by Paul Jones. He entered Georgia in late 1983, wrestling with Paul Ellering's Legion of Doom. He left Georgia for World Class in the mid-1980s, where he held the TV Title in August of 1984. He also competed in the Mid-South area, holding the TV Title in Oklahoma in January of 1986. He subsequently joined the WWF, where he began entering the ring with his snake, Damian. He engaged in a feud with Rick Rude during the late 1980s. Damian was

crushed by Earthquake during a match and was subsequently replaced by Lucifer. Roberts wrestled in AAA Lucha Libra and Smoky Mountain Wrestling in 1994 before retiring from the ring. He returned to the ring in early 1996 to compete in the WWF.

Roberts, Jennifer *see* Baby Doll

Roberts, Jerry teamed with Butch Reed to hold the NWA Central States Tag Team Title in 1980.

Roberts, Nick (b. 1926; Little Rock, Arkansas; 6'2", 235 lbs.) was born in Atlanta, Georgia, and was a carnival acrobat before entering professional wrestling in the late 1940s. He was a leading wrestler in the Texas area in the 1950s. He was married to wrestler Lorraine Johnson and is the father of valet Nickla "Baby Doll" Roberts.

Roberts, Nickla *see* Baby Doll

Roberts, Red held the Southern Junior Heavyweight Title in 1954. He teamed with Mike Chacoma to hold the Southern Tag Team Title in Tennessee in June of 1966.

Roberts, Tim *see* Falcone, Sweet Daddy

Robertson, Dewey teamed with Dennis Stamp to hold the U.S. Tag Team Title in Oklahoma in May of 1973. He teamed with Billy Red Lyons as the Crusaders to hold the International Tag Team Title in Toronto several times in 1974. He held the NWA Canadian Title in Toronto in September of 1979. He teamed with George Wells to hold the NWA Atlantic Coast Tag Title in

1980. Robertson again held the tag belts the following year, partnered with Johnny Weaver. He teamed with Rufus R. Jones to hold the NWA Central States Tag Team Title in October of 1981. He again held the tag belts with Steve Regal in March of 1982, and with Hercules Hernandez in September of 1982. He held the NWA Central States Title several times in 1983.

Robinson, Billy (Manchester, England; 250 lbs.) was a leading British wrestler from the mid-1960s. He was the holder of the British Heavyweight Title from January of 1967 until he abandoned the belt to come to North America in February of 1970. He held the Stampede North American Title in Calgary, Canada, several times in 1970. He held the Hawaiian Tag Team Title for several months in 1970, teaming with Johnny Barend and Ed Francis. He also held the North American Title in Honolulu several times in the early 1970s. He teamed with Verne Gagne to dethrone Nick Bockwinkel and Ray Stevens as AWA Tag Team champions in December of 1972. They lost the belts in a rematch in January of 1973. Robinson then teamed with Crusher to defeat Bockwinkle and Stevens in July of 1974. They held the belts until October of 1974, when the former champs reclaimed them. Robinson held the NWA Southern Championship in Florida in December of 1975. He teamed with Bill Watts to hold the U.S. Tag Team Title in Louisiana in late 1976. He teamed with Ken Lucas to hold the Southern Tag Team Title several times in 1980. Robinson also held the CWA World Title in Tennessee for several months in mid-1980.

Robley, Buck teamed with Crusher Blackwell to hold the NWA Central States Tag Team Title in 1977. He held the Central States tag belts again in 1978, teaming with the Blue Yankee. He held the NWA Central States Title in October of 1978. He held the NWA Central States TV Title in Kansas in 1984.

Rocca, Antonio (Antonino Biasetton; b. 1928, d. March 15, 1977; Argentina; 6', 226 lbs.) was born in Italy and came to Argentina as a young boy. He was a leading wrestling in Buenos Aires in the 1940s and came to the United States later in the decade. He held the NWA Texas Title for several months from August of 1948. He became one of the nation's leading wrestling competitors in the early 1950s. The bare-footed mat star defeated Primo Carnera in a memorable match in 1950. He held the AWA Ohio title briefly in March of 1953. He teamed with Miguel Perez to win the World Tag Team Title in New York in April of 1957. Rocca was depicted in a match against super-hero Superman in August 1962 comic book. He had a small part in the 1976 horror film *Alice, Sweet, Alice.* He died on March 15, 1977.

Rocco, Mark (5'8", 195 lbs.) is the son of wrestler Mike Hussey. He began wrestling in 1971. He is known as Rollerball and is a popular British junior heavyweight.

Rocco, Tony teamed with Pantera Negra to hold the NWA Americas Tag Team Title in Los Angeles several times in 1970. He also held the Americas tag belt with David Morgan in April of 1973. He teamed with Bob Sweetan to hold the U.S. Tag Team Title in Louisiana in March of 1977.

Rochester, Leroy *see* Brown, Bad Leroy

Rochester Roadblock (6'8", 375 lbs.) began wrestling in 1989. He was trained at Larry Sharpe's Monster Factory and wrestled in IWCCW and Japan.

Rock, Blade Runner *see* Ultimate Warrior

Rock, Flyboy Rocco (Ted Petty; b. September 1, 1953; Compton, California; 6'2", 251 lbs.) began wrestling in 1981. He wrestled under a mask as the Cheetah Kid from 1987, and held the UWA Light Heavyweight Title in New Jersey in 1992. He wrestled with Dean Malenko as the Kimoto Dragons in WWN in 1993. He also wrestled as Mario Savoldi. He wrestled with Johnny Grunge as Public Enemy in ECW from October of 1993, where they won the tag team belts in March of 1994. They lost the belts to Cactus Jack and Mikey Whipwreck in August of 1994, but reclaimed them in a rematch in November of 1994. They also held the ECW Tag Team Title for several months from April of 1995. Public Enemy entered WCW in late 1995, where they engaged in a feud with the Nasty Boys.

Rock, Man Mountain *see* Payne, Maxx

Rock 'n' Roll Express *see* Gibson, Robert & Morton, Rick

Rock 'n' Roll RPMs *see* Davis, Mike & Lane, Tommy

Rock 'n' Soul *see* Parsons, Iceman & Zumhofe, Buck

Rockers, The *see* Michaels, Shawn & Jannetty, Marty

Rockin' Robin (Robin Smith) is the daughter of wrestler Aurelian "Grizzly" Smith, and the sister of wrestlers Jack "the Snake" Roberts and Sam Houston. She captured the WWF Women's Title from Sherri Martel in Paris, France, on October 7, 1988. She vacated the title the following year. She was recognized as the Great Lakes Wrestling Association Women's Champion in 1992.

Rodriguez, Charles "Babe" (b. 1916, d. July 4, 1989) was born in San Marcos, Texas. He moved to St. Louis, Missouri, in 1921 and began wrestling professionally in 1935. He remained an active competitor in the ring until his retirement in 1962. Rodriquez died of cancer at a St. Louis hospital on July 4, 1989.

Rodriguez, Romeo, wrestling as Mephisto, teamed with Tommy Heggie, as Dante, to hold the USWA Tag Team Title in August of 1994.

Rodriguez, Tony wrestled as the Monster to hold the NWA Americas Title in Los Angeles in 1981.

Rodz, Johnny (New York; 5'10", 234 lbs.) began wrestling in 1974. Wrestling as Java Ruuk, he won the Los Angeles Battle Royal in 1976. He captured the NCW championship in Massachusetts in 1985, and retained the belt through the early 1990s. He also wrestled in the WWF.

Roeber, Ernest (b. 1861, d. 1943) was a leading wrestler in the early part of the century. He was defeated by Tom Jenkins for the American Title in July of 1901.

Roebuck, Tiny (d. 19??) was a Cherokee Indian from Oklahoma. He began wrestling in the early 1930s, and was a popular mat star for several decades.

Rogers, Big Bubba *see* Big Boss Man

Rogers, Buddy (Herman "Dutch" Rohde; b. 1921, d. June 26, 1992; Camden, New Jersey; 6', 227 lbs.) was born in Camden, New Jersey. He began wrestling as Dutch Rogers in July of 1939. He took the name Buddy Rogers in 1944 and held the NWA Texas Title several times in 1945 and 1946. He became known as "the Nature Boy" in California in 1947. He again held the NWA Texas belt in August of 1950. He captured the AWA Title in Montreal, Canada, in May of 1951. He held the Mid-American Title in 1957. He teamed with Ronnie Etchison to hold the NWA World Tag Team Title in San Francisco in October of 1958. Rogers teamed with Johnny Valentine to defeat the Fabulous Kangaroos for the WWWF U.S. Tag Team Title in November of 1960, but lost the belts in a rematch later in the month. Rogers defeated Pat O'Connor for the NWA Heavyweight Championship in Chicago on June 30, 1961. He also teamed with Johnny Barend to de-feat Valentine and Bob Ellis for the WWWF U.S. Tag Title in July of 1962. Rogers broke his ankle in a match against Killer Kowalski in November of 1962. He lost the NWA Championship to Lou Thesz in Toronto on January 24, 1963. He and Barend were defeated for the tag belts by Buddy Austin and Great Scott in March of 1963. Rogers suffered a heart attack shortly after the match, but soon recovered. He was recognized as the first heavyweight champion for the newly formed WWWF in April of 1963. He lost the title in a 47 second bout to Bruno Sammartino in New York on May 17, 1963. He subsequently retired, but returned to the ring as a manager and occasional wrestler in the late 1970s. He was defeated by the other "Nature Boy," Ric Flair, in a match in July of 1979. He also managed such mat stars as Jimmy Snuka, Big John Studd and Ken Patera in the NWA in the late 1970s. He died of a massive stroke in a Florida hospital on June 26, 1992.

Rogers, Jerry *see* Rougeau, Jacques, Jr.

Rogers, Rip (Atlanta, Georgia; 6', 238 lbs.) began wrestling in 1977. He teamed with Ricky Starr as the Convertible Blonds to capture the ICW U.S. Tag Team Title in 1981. He again captured the ICW tag belts with Pez Whatley in May of 1982. He teamed with Ted Oates as the Hollywood Blondes and captured the NWA National Tag Team Title in September of 1984. He held the Mid-America Title in May of 1986. He held the NWA Southeastern Title in November of 1986. He captured the NWA Central States TV Title in November of 1987. He teamed with Abbuda Dein to hold the WWC Tag Team Title in Puerto Rico several times in 1989. He also wrestled in Global and the WCW in the early 1990s.

Rogers, Rip *see* Graham, Eddie

Rogers, Tommy (b. May 14; St. Petersburg, Florida; 5'9", 222 lbs.) began wrestling in 1980. He held the U.S. Junior Heavyweight Title in Alabama in May of 1983. He teamed with Marty Jannetty as the Uptown Boys to capture the NWA Central States Tag Team Title several times in 1984. He formed the Fantastics with Bobby Fulton, and they held the World Class American Tag Team Title several times in 1984 and 1985. They held the Southern Tag Team Title in January of 1986. They also held the UWF Tag Team Title in Oklahoma several times in 1986, and held the World Class World Tag Team Title in 1987. They captured the PWA Tag Team Title in August of 1987, holding the belt until the following November. The duo twice held the WCW U.S. Tag Title in 1988. They feuded with Jim Cornette's Midnight Express during the late 1980s. They returned to the WCW in October of 1994.

Rogowski, Al *see* Anderson, Ole

Rohde, Herman "Dutch" *see* Rogers, Buddy

Roller, Dr. Benjamin F. (b. 1876, d. 1933) attended the University of Pennsylvania. He was a leading wrestler around the turn of the century. He claimed the World Light Heavyweight Title from 1893 until 1911. He also held the wrestling championship in 1914.

Roma, Paul (Paul Centopani; b. April 29, 1960; Kensington, Kentucky; 5'11", 235 lbs.) was born in Connecticut. He began wrestling in 1983 and entered the WWF 1986. He teamed with S.D. Jones early in his career and wrestled with Jim Powers as the Young Stallions. He teamed with Hercules as Power & Glory in the WWF in the early 1990s. He subsequently joined the WCW and joined the new Four Horsemen in June of 1993. He teamed with fellow Horseman Arn Anderson to capture the WCW Tag Team Championship on August 18, 1993. They were defeated for the belts the following month by the Nasty Boys on September 19, 1993. Roma formed the team of Pretty Wonderful with Paul Orndorff and won the tag title from Cactus Jack and Kevin Sullivan on July 17, 1994. They lost the belts to Marcus Alexander Bagwell and the Patriot on September 25, 1994, but regained the title in a rematch the following month on October 23, 1994. They were again defeated by Bagwell and the Patriot on November 16, 1994. Roma left the WCW in March of 1995.

Romano, Bruno *see* Sammartino, Bruno

Romero, Chris *see* Youngblood, Chris

Romero, Mark *see* Youngblood, Mark

Romero, Ricky teamed with

Pedro Morales to hold the WWA Tag Team Title in Los Angeles in February of 1967. He teamed with Eddie Gilbert to hold the NWA Central States Tag Team Title in January of 1982.

Romero, Rito held the NWA Texas Title several times in 1949 and 1950. He also held the NWA Texas tag belts in the late 1940s and early 1950s, teaming with Blackie Guzman and Carlos Moreno. He held the Pacific Coast Title in Los Angeles in 1952. He teamed with Sugi Sito to reclaim the tag title in May of 1954, and also held the belts with George Drake, Pepe Mendietta and Pepper Gomez.

Romero, Steve *see* Youngblood, Jay

Rood, Rick *see* Rude, Rick

Roop, Bob (Tampa, Florida; 6'1", 270 lbs.) was a leading amateur wrestler, and began wrestling professionally in 1968. He held the NWA Florida Title for several months in mid-1975. He teamed with Harley Race to hold the NWA Florida Tag Team Title in June of 1975. He teamed with Alexis Smirnoff to hold the NWA World Tag Team Title in San Francisco in March of 1977. Roop captured the NWA U.S. Title in San Francisco in September of 1977. He held the title until the following December, when he left the promotion. He again held the Florida championship in March of 1978. He held the ICW TV Title several times in 1980 and 1981, often feuding with Bob Orton, Jr. He held the Mid-South Louisiana Title in July of 1981. He held the MSWA

North American Title for several months from March of 1982. He also held the NWA TV Title several times in early 1985.

Rose, Bill (William Nason Rose; b. September 25, 1960) was born in West Memphis, Arkansas, and raised in Parkin, Arkansas. He attended Northwest Mississippi Junior College, where he played football. He was working as a bouncer at a Memphis nightclub when he was encouraged to enter professional wrestling by Steve Keirn and Bill Dundee. He wrestled with Larry Hoerr as the Destroyers in the Atlanta area in the mid-1980s. He also teamed with Don Bass in the Memphis area, wrestling as the Assassins and the A Team. Rose was also the Phantom of the Opera in Eddie Gilbert's army in the Mid-South area. Rose briefly wrestled in the WWF as one of the Shadows. He retired in 1990 after suffering a serious back injury as a result of an automobile accident.

Rose, Buddy (Paul Perschman; Minneapolis, Minnesota; 6', 312 lbs.) was born in Richfield, Minnesota. He trained at Verne Gagne's wrestling school and began wrestling in the AWA in 1973. He teamed with Jesse Ventura to hold the NWA Pacific Northwest Tag Team Title several times in 1976 and 1977. He held the Hawaiian Title in 1978. He captured the NWA U.S. Title in San Francisco several times in 1978 and 1979. He teamed with Ed Wiskoski to hold the NWA World Tag Team Title in San Francisco several times in 1978. He teamed with Chris Colt to hold the Canadian Tag Team Title in November of 1979. He held the NWA Pacific Northwest Title several times in 1979 and 1980. He teamed with Rip Oliver to hold the Canadian Tag Team Title in January of 1981. Rose wrestled in the WWF in the early 1980s. Billed as Playboy Buddy Rose he teamed with Doug Somers to win the AWA Tag Team Championship from Curt Hennig and Scott Hall in May of 1986. They lost the title to the Midnight Rockers in January of 1987. He returned to the Pacific Northwest to hold the tag belts several times in 1988 and 1989, teaming with Paul "Avalanche" Neu and Colonel DeBeers. He held the Oregon Professional Wrestling Federation Title in February of 1994.

Rose, Randy (6'1", 240 lbs.) began wrestling in 1974. Wrestling as Randy Alls, he held the NWA Central States Title in January of 1979. He teamed with Bryan St. John to hold the NWA Central States Tag Team Title in February of 1979. He teamed with Dennis Condrey as an original member of the Midnight Express in the early 1980s. They held the NWA Southeastern Tag Team Title numerous times from 1980 through 1983, with Norvell Austin and Ron Starr also competing as part of Midnight Express, Inc. The Midnight Express also held the Southern Tag Team Title several times in 1982. Rose was later replaced by Bobby Eaton. Rose and Condrey reteamed as the Original Midnight Express in the AWA in 1987. They defeated Jerry Lawler and Bill Dundee for the AWA Tag Team Title in October of 1987. They lost the belts to the Midnight Rockers in December of 1987. Rose sub-

sequently wrestled as a fan favorite in the Georgia All-Star area.

Roselli, Mike teamed with Randy Tyler as the Billionaire Boys Club to hold the WCCW International Tag Team Title in Vancouver, Canada, several times in 1993 and 1994.

Rosen, Benny (b. 1918; Texas; 6'3", 225 lbs.) was born in New York. He began wrestling in the late 1930s and remained a leading competitor through the 1950s.

Ross, Black Jack (d. 1954) was a leading wrestler in the 1930s and 1940s. His son, Jack Ross, Jr., also wrestled.

Ross, Chuck (b. 1916; Oklahoma City, Oklahoma; 6'8", 265 lbs.) was a football player in college. He began wrestling professionally in Topeka, Kansas, in 1940. He remained a popular mat star through the 1950s.

Ross, Jack, Jr. (Columbia, South Carolina; 215 lbs.) was the son of wrestler Black Jack Ross. He entered professional wrestling in the late 1940s and remained a popular competitor through the 1950s. He was also a football coach in Columbia, South Carolina.

Ross, Jim (b. January 3) worked as an announcer for WCW from 1988. He was WCW Vice-President from 1992 until early 1993, when he left to organization to announce in the WWF. He also worked as a booker for that promotion in the mid-1990s.

Rossi, Len held the Southern

Junior Heavyweight Title in December of 1960. He also held the World Tag Team Title in Tennessee, partnered with Tex Riley, in January of 1960. He often teamed with Mario Milano during the 1960s. They held the NWA Southern Tag Team Title in 1966. He held the World Tag Team Title in Tennessee several times from 1968 through 1971, teaming with Tamaya Soto, Johnny Walker, Don Carson and Bearcat Brown. He also reclaimed the Southern Junior Heavyweight Title in June of 1968 and in June of 1972. He teamed with Bearcat Brown to hold the Southern Tag Team Title in Tennessee in 1971. Rossi also held the Mid-American Title in July of 1971. He teamed with Tony Charles to hold the Mid-America Tag Team Title in April of 1972. He again held the Southern tag belts in 1972, teaming with Kevin Sullivan.

Roth, Ernie *see* Grand Wizard, The

Rotten, Axl (Brian Knighton; Philadelphia, Pennsylvania; 6'2", 301 lbs.) began wrestling in 1988. He was a major star in the UIW in 1990. He wrestled with his "brother," Ian Rotten, as Bad Breed in the 1990s, winning the Global World Tag Team Title in January of 1993. They also wrestled in ECW, and engaged in a bitter feud after splitting in 1994.

Rotten, Ian (John Williams; Philadelphia, Pennsylvania; 6', 281 lbs.) began wrestling in 1990. He was formerly known as Zak Blades. He teamed with his "brother," Axl Rotten, as Bad Breed in the 1990s.

They held the Global World Tag Team Title in January of 1993. They also wrestled in ECW, and engaged in a bitter feud after splitting in 1994.

Rotten, Johnny *see* Grunge, Johnny

Rotunda, Lawrence *see* Rotunda, Mike

Rotunda, Mike (Lawrence Rotunda; b. March 30, 1958; Syracuse, New York; 6'2 1/2", 245 lbs.) was an amateur wrestler at Syracuse University. He began wrestling professionally as Mike Rotundo in Georgia and Florida in 1981. He captured the NWA Canadian TV Title in Toronto in August of 1983. He was a two-time winner of the Southern Heavyweight belt in 1983, and held the NWA Southern Title in Florida several times in late 1983 and early 1984. He also held the U.S. Tag Team Title in Florida several times in 1983 and 1984, teaming with Mike Davis and Barry Windham. He subsequently moved to the WWF and was managed by Captain Lou Albano. He and Barry Windham defeated Adrian Adonis and Dick Murdoch for the WWF Tag Team belts in Hartford, Connecticut, on January 21, 1985. They lost the belts to Nikolai Volkoff and the Iron Sheik at Wrestlemania I on March 31, 1985. They regained the title on June 17, 1985, wrestling as the U.S. Express, but were defeated by Brutus Beefcake and Greg Valentine in Philadelphia, Pennsylvania, on August 24, 1985. Rotundo left the WWF soon after to return to Florida. He entered the NWA in 1988, wrestling with Rick Steiner in

Kevin Sullivan's Varsity Club. He and Steiner split in 1988 and Rotunda held the NWA TV Title several times in the late 1980s. Rotundo continued to wrestle in the Varsity Club with Steve Williams as his partner. They defeated the Road Warriors for the Tag Team belts in April 1989, but were stripped of the title a month later when they attacked special referee Nikita Koloff. He began wrestling as a single in 1990, wrestling as Michael Wall Street under the management of Alexandra York. Soon after he entered the WWF as Irwin R. Schyster and was managed by Ted DiBiase. He and DiBiase wrestled as Money, Incorporated. Under the management of Jimmy Hart, they defeated the Legion of Doom for the WWF Tag Team Title in Denver, Colorado, on February 7, 1992. They lost the belts to the Natural Disasters in July of 1992, but recaptured the title the following October. They ultimately lost the title to Rick and Scott Steiner in June of 1993. Rotunda returned to the WCW as VK Wallstreet in September of 1995.

Rougeau, Armand is a son of wrestler Jacques Rougeau, Sr. He teamed with Dan Kroffat to hold the Canadian International Tag Team Title in February of 1987.

Rougeau, Jacques, Jr. (b. December 30; Montreal, Quebec, Canada; 6'2", 232 lbs.) began wrestling in 1979. He held the NWA Southeastern Title in 1981. He teamed with his brother, Raymond, to hold the Canadian International Tag Team Title in Montreal several times in 1983. Wrestling as Jerry Roberts, he briefly held the Southern Heavyweight Title in November of 1982 and January of 1983. He held the Mid-America Title briefly in 1983 and again in November of 1984. He again wrestled with his brother, Raymond, to capture the Canadian International tag belts in June of 1985. They left the promotion to go to the WWF in January of 1986, where they were managed by Jimmy Hart. Jacques became known as the Mountie in the early 1990s, and he defeated Bret Hart for the Intercontinental Title in Springfield, Missouri, on January 17, 1992. He lost the belt to Roddy Piper at the Royal Rumble in New York the following day, on January 18, 1992. Jacques joined with Pierre as the Quebecers in July of 1993. They defeated the Steiners for the WWF Tag Team Title on September 13, 1993. They lost the title to Marty Jannetty and the 1-2-3 Kid on Monday Night Raw on January 10, 1994. They regained the title in a rematch the following week on January 17, 1994. They again lost the belts on March 29, 1994, in a match in London, England, to Men on a Mission. They regained the belts once more two days later in a rematch in Sheffield, England, on March 31, 1994. The Quebecers lost the belts again on April 26, 1994, in a match with the Head Shrinkers in Burlington, Vermont. Jacques Rougeau retired from the ring following a match in Montreal in October of 1994.

Rougeau, Jacques, Sr. was a leading Canadian wrestler in the 1960s. He is the father of wrestlers

Jacques, Phillipe, Raymond and Armand Rougeau.

Rougeau, Johnny (d. May 28, 1983) was the brother of wrestler Jacques Rougeau, Sr. He held the AWA Title in Montreal, Canada, several times in the late 1960s and early 1970s.

Rougeau, Raymond is a son of wrestler Jacques Rougeau, Sr. He teamed with his brother, Jacques, to capture the Canadian International Tag Team Title in Montreal several times in 1982. He and Jacques again captured the Canadian International tag belts in June of 1985. They left the promotion in January of 1986 to wrestle in the WWF, where they were managed by Jimmy Hart.

Rough Riders, The *see* Black Bart & Mantell, Johnny

Rover, Moondog *see* Moondog Rover

Royal, Gary (5'10", 220 lbs.) began wrestling in 1979. He held the NWA Central States TV Title in March of 1984. He defeated Denny Brown for the NWA World Junior Heavyweight Title on August 15, 1985. He lost the belt back to Brown the following month.

Royal, Nelson (5'8", 215 lbs.) began wrestling in 1955. He teamed with Black Hawk to hold the NWA Pacific Northwest Tag Team Title in May of 1958. Teaming with Paul Jones, he held the NWA Americas Tag Team Title in Los Angeles in January of 1969, and the NWA Atlantic Coast Tag Title in 1970. He again held the tag belts in 1973, teaming with Sandy Scott. He

teamed with Les Thatcher to hold the NWA Southeastern Tag Team Title in 1975. Royal defeated Ron Starr for the NWA World Junior Heavyweight Title on December 6, 1976. He held the title until his defeat by Al Madril on June 25, 1978. He reclaimed the belt on July 28, 1979, following Madril's inability to defend the title. Royal temporarily retired from the ring in December of 1979. He returned to the ring and again held the title from October of 1987 until the title was withdrawn in 1988.

Royal, Sean wrestled with Chris Champion as the New Breed. They held the Florida Tag Team Title several months in early 1987.

Royal Kangaroos *see* Boyd, Jonathan & Charles, Norman Frederich

Rubi, Bert (d. 1967) wrestled out of the Mid-West. He was a seven-time holder of the junior heavyweight championship. He was known for his flying scissors ring maneuver.

Rude, Rick (Rick Wood; b. December 7; Robbinsdale, Minnesota; 6'4", 246 lbs.) he began wrestling in 1983. He entered the Memphis area in mid-1984 with his valet, Angel and under the management of Jim Neidhart and, later, Jimmy Hart. He held the Southern Heavyweight Title for several months in mid-1984. He teamed with King Kong Bundy to capture the Southern Tag Team Title in October of 1984. He was managed by Percy Pringle in the NWA in Florida, where he held the Southern Title several times in 1985.

He held the U.S. Tag Team Title in Florida with Jesse Barr in April of 1985. He captured the World Class Title in Texas in November of 1985 and became the first WCWA champion when World Class broke with the NWA in February of 1986. Rude held the belt until his defeat by Chris Adams in July of 1986. He subsequently left the promotion. He teamed with Manny Fernandez to defeat the Rock 'n' Roll Express for the NWA World Tag Team Title in December of 1986. They relinquished the belts when Rude left the NWA for the WWF in May of 1987, where he feuded with Jake "the Snake" Roberts. Rude defeated the Ultimate Warrior of the WWF Intercontinental Title in April of 1989. He lost the belt in a rematch with the Ultimate Warrior in August of 1989. He returned to the WCW in 1991 and defeated Sting for the U.S. Title on November 19, 1991. He relinquished the belt due to an injury in December of 1992. Rude defeated Ric Flair for the WCW International World Title on September 19, 1993. He briefly lost the belt to Hiroshi Hase in Japan in March of 1994. He retained the belt until his defeat by Sting in April of 1994. Rude vacated the WCW International title and left the organization due to injuries in May of 1994.

Ruffen, Jackie (Gervaise Jones; b. 1959, d. June 19, 1982) began wrestling in the mid 1970s, competing in Ohio and Michigan. He entered the ICW in the early 1980s, wrestling in Kentucky in Tennessee. Ruffen was shot to death during a fight outside a Cincinnati bar on June 19, 1982.

Ruffin, Les (b. 1913, d. December 1990; Lawrence, Massachusetts; 6'1", 216 lbs.) was a middleweight boxer before he began wrestling in the early 1940s. A vicious competitor in the ring, he held the New England Junior Heavyweight Championship. He remained a leading wrestler through the 1950s.

Rumble, Tony (6'4", 250 lbs.) began wrestling in 1985. He managed Tony Atlas in the ICW in New England from the late 1980s.

Runnels, Dustin *see* Rhodes, Dustin

Runnels, Virgil Riley, Jr. *see* Rhodes, Dusty

Running Bear, Don teamed with Billy Two Eagles to hold the NWA Pacific Northwest Tag Team Title in January of 1985. He also wrestled as Relampago Leon.

Rush, Jack "Q-Ball" (William Rush; b. 1913, d. 1954; Tulsa, Oklahoma; 5'10", 210 lbs.) began wrestling in the mid-1930s. He held the Southern Junior Heavyweight Championship in the late 1930s, and claimed to have been the personal wrestler for the King of Arabia. Rush continued to compete through the 1950s.

Russell, Brother *see* Jares, Brother Frank

Russell, Lance began his career as a wrestling announcer in Jackson, Tennessee, in the early 1950s. He came to Memphis, Tennessee, in 1957, and remained with the local Mid-South promotion for over thirty years. He went to the WCW in 1989, where he worked as a commentator through the early 1990s. He returned to the USWA in Memphis in 1995, reuniting with his long time partner, Dave Brown.

Russell, Rebel Bob (b. 1904, d. 1984; Newport, Rhode Island; 5'11", 210 lbs.) wrestled as an amateur before turning pro in the early 1930s. He captured the AAU championship in 1931. He remained a leading competitor over the next several decades. He was the Southern States champion, and held the Pacific Coast Title in San Francisco in March of 1946.

Russian Brute, The (6'8", 330 lbs.) began wrestling in 1988. He wrestled in the AWA and was managed by Ox Baker, who taught him the heart punch.

Ruth, Glen *see* Headbanger Thrasher

Ruuk, Java *see* Rodz, Johnny

Ruvinski, Wolf was a leading Mexican wrestler in the 1940s and 1950s. He was also a popular Mexican actor, appearing in such films as *The Man Without a Face* (1950), *The Beautiful Dreamer* (1953) and *The Body Snatchers* (1956). He appeared in a series of Mexican films in the 1960, portraying the masked superhero Neutron in such movies as *Neutron vs. the Maniacs* (1961), *Neutron Against the Death Robots* (1961), *Neutron and the Black Mask* (1961), *Neutron Battles the Karate Assassins* (1962) and *Neutron vs. the Amazing Dr. Caronte* (1963). Ruvinski was also president of the Mexican Wrestler's Association.

Ryan, Mike "Red" (b. 1914; Philadelphia, Pennsylvania; 6', 238 lbs.) began his career wrestling in carnivals before turning pro in the late 1930s. He was sometimes called "the Smiling Villain" because of his ring antics. The red-headed Ryan was known for the stranglehold move called the Japanese head twist. He retired in the 1950s.

S & S Express *see* Savoldi, Joe & Simpson, Steve

Saad, Mohammad teamed with Chris Carter to hold the WWA Tag Team Title in 1986.

Sabaugh, Gary *see* Italian Stallion

Sabu (Terry Brunk; b. December 12, 1964; Bombay, India; 5'10", 220 lbs.) is from Michigan. He is the nephew of The Sheik and began wrestling in 1990, often teaming with his uncle. He wrestled in the Mid-South area in the early 1990s. Sabu defeated Shane Douglas for the ECW Title in October of 1993, but lost the belt to Terry Funk the following December. He teamed with Tasmaniac to capture the ECW Tag Team Title from Public Enemy on February 4, 1995. They lost the belts to Chris Benoit and Dean Malenko later in the month. He continued to competed often in ECW, and made occasional appearances in the WCW in 1995.

Sabu the Wildman *see* Samoa, Coco

Sagonivich, Jerome *see* Sags, Jerry

Saed, Mustafa *see* Mustafa Saed, Sheik Jamal

Sags, Jerry (Jerome Sagonivich; b. July 5, 1964; Allentown, Pennsylvania; 6'3", 290 lbs.) trained under Verne Gagne. He began wrestling in October of 1985 in the AWA, teaming with Brian Knobs. They were known as the Nasty Boys and won the Southern Tag Team Title in Memphis in September of 1987. They held the title several times over the following year. They subsequently wrestled in Florida until 1990 when they entered the WCW. They joined the WWF later in the year, where they were managed by Jimmy Hart. They defeated the Hart Foundation for the WWF tag belts at Wrestlemania VII on March 24, 1991, but lost the belts to the Legion of Doom at SummerSlam '91 on August 26, 1991. Sags was injured in a stabbing attack in January of 1992, but quickly recovered. The duo broke with Hart in October of 1992 and began a feud with Money, Inc. They subsequently wrestled in the WCW. They won the WCW Tag Team Championship in a match against Arn Anderson and Paul Roma on September 19, 1993. They lost the title the following month to Marcus Alexander Bagwell and Too Cold Scorpio on October 4, 1993. They regained the title from Bagwell and Scorpio several weeks later on October 24, 1993, and held the belts until their defeat by Cactus Jack and Kevin Sullivan on May 22, 1994. They defeated Harlem Heat for the WCW Tag Team Title at Slamboree '95 in St. Petersburg, Florida, on May 21, 1995. They lost the title in a rematch in the same month. They continued to compete in the WCW, feuding with the Road Warriors and Public Enemy in 1996.

St. John, Bryan teamed with Randy Rose to hold the NWA Central States Tag Team Title in February of 1979. He recaptured the title in May of 1979, teaming with Bill Irwin. He teamed with Stan Lane to hold the NWA Florida Tag Team Title several times in late 1979.

Saito, Akitoshi (b. August 8, 1965) began wrestling with WING in Japan in December of 1990. He entered New Japan in 1992.

Saito, Hiro (Hiroyuki Saito; b. May 25, 1961; Kanagawa, Japan; 5'9", 237 lbs.) began wrestling in Japan in August of 1978. He wrestled with New Japan during much of his career.

Saito, Masa (Masanori Saito; b. August 7, 1942; Tokyo, Japan; 5'11", 247 lbs.) began wrestling in September of 1965. He teamed with Kinji Shibuya to hold the NWA World Tag Team Title in San Francisco in July of 1968, and the NWA Americas Tag Team Title in Los Angeles in May of 1971. He and Shibuya again held the San Francisco belts in September of 1973. He teamed with Gene Kiniski to hold the Canadian Tag Team Title in November of 1974. He teamed with Ivan Koloff to hold the NWA Florida Tag Team Title several times in 1977. He also held the Florida tag belts several times with Mr. Sato over the next year. He teamed with Mr. Fuji to win the WWF Tag Team Title in October of 1981, defeating Tony Garea and Rick Martel. They lost the belts to Chief Jay and Jules Strongbow in June of 1982, but regained them the following month.

They were again defeated by the Strongbows in October of 1982. In April of 1984 Saito and Ken Patera were arrested for throwing a large rock through a window at a McDonald's in Waukesha, Wisconsin. They injured several police officers in a brawl at the Holiday Inn they were staying at. They were convicted of assault and battery and sentenced to two years in prison in June of 1985. The veteran Japanese star returned to the ring and defeated Larry Zbyszko for the AWA title in February of 1990. He lost the belt in a rematch in April of 1990.

Sakata, Harold (b. 1920, d. July 29, 1982; Kona, Hawaii) was a Hawaiian weightlifter who represented the United States at the London Olympics in 1948, where he won a silver medal. He began wrestling in 1949 as Tosh Togo. He teamed with Toi Yamamoto to hold the NWA Pacific Northwest Tag Team Title in November of 1952. He teamed with the Great Togo to hold the Canadian Open Tag Team Title in Toronto in July of 1954. He captured the Hawaiian Title in July of 1956, and held the NWA Texas Title in October of 1958. He teamed with Ike Eakins to hold the NWA Southern Tag Team Title in 1960. He teamed with King Curtis to capture the Hawaiian Tag Team Title in September of 1962. Sakata starred as Oddjob in the 1964 James Bond film *Goldfinger*. He continued appearing in films, often as an Oriental villain in such features as *Dimension 5* (1966), *The Poppy Is Also a Flower* (1966), *The Phynx* (1969), *Impulse* (1972), *The Wrestler* (1974), *The Jaws of Death* (1976), *Death Di-*

mension (1977), *Record City* (1977), *Goin' Coconuts* (1978) and the 1979 tele-film *The Billion Dollar Threat*. He also appeared on television regularly in the series *Sarge* in 1971 and *Highcliffe Manor* in 1979. He died of cancer in a Honolulu hospital on July 29, 1982.

Sakurada, Mr. held the Stampede North American Title in Calgary, Canada, in 1978. He teamed with Mr. Hito to hold the NWA Florida Tag Team Title in August of 1979. They also held the World Class American Tag Team Title in 1980. He teamed with Kasavubu to hold the Stampede International Tag Team Title in 1981.

Sakuro, Taro held the Southern Junior Heavyweight Title for several months in early 1962. He teamed with Yoshino Sato to hold the U.S. Tag Team Title in Tennessee in March of 1962.

Salazar, Oscar teamed with Ciclon Negro to hold the Texas World Tag Team Title in November of 1962.

Sallinger, Tex *see* Godwinn, Phinnius I.

Samantha (Donna Shepherd) was valet and manager for Bull Payne in the USWA from the late 1980s. She managed Bill Dundee in the USWA in 1996.

Samara, Seelie held the Pacific Coast Title in San Francisco from November of 1944 until March of the following year.

Sammartino, Bruno (Bruno Romano; b. October 6; Pittsburgh,

Pennsylvania; 5'10", 265 lbs.) was born in Abruzzi, Italy, where he trained as an amateur wrestler as a child. He came to the United States as a young man and boxed for a brief period before he began wrestling professionally in 1959. He teamed with Whipper Billy Watson to hold the International Tag Team Title in Toronto in May of 1962. He defeated Buddy Rogers for the WWWF Title in New York on May 17, 1963. He also briefly held the WWWF U.S. Tag Team Title with Spiros Arion in July of 1967. Sammartino remained WWWF champion for nearly eight years, until January 18, 1971, when he lost the belt to Ivan Koloff in New York. He won the Los Angeles Battle Royal in January of 1972. Sammartino briefly held the WWWF International Tag Team Title with Dominic Denucci during a series of bouts the Mongols. Sammartino was subsequently managed by Arnold Skoaland and reclaimed the WWWF Title in a match against Stan Stasiak in New York on December 10, 1973. He also held the WWA Tag Team Championship with Dick the Bruiser for several months in 1973. He suffered a broken neck in a match against Stan Hansen in April of 1976. His injured kept Sammartino out of the ring until near the end of the year. He retained the WWWF Title until his defeat by Billy Graham in Baltimore, Maryland, on April 30, 1977. He engaged in a bitter feud with his former protege, Larry Zbyszko in 1980. He was a ringside commentator for the WWWF in the late 1970s. Sammartino was known as the "Living Legend" for his exploits in the ring.

Sammartino, David (b. September 29; Pittsburgh, Pennsylvania; 5'10", 225 lbs.) began wrestling in 1980. He is the son of Bruno Sammartino. He became first champion of the NAW in Pittsburgh in September of 1986, holding the title for several years. He also held the Southern Championship Wrestling Title in Georgia in September of 1989.

Samoa, Coco (Samoa; 239 lbs.) wrestled as Sabu the Wildman to hold the Southern Heavyweight Title in 1981. Wrestling as Coco Samoa, he held the NWA Pacific Northwest Title in August of 1986. He held the Pacific Northwest tag belts several times in 1986 and 1987, teaming with Brady Boone and Ricky Santana. He wrestled as the Black Ninja to capture the tag title with Mike Miller in May of 1987.

Samoan Savage, The (6', 248 lbs.) began wrestling in 1983. He was known as the Tonga Kid and Tama earlier in his career. He later teamed with Fatu and Samu in the Samoan Swat Team. He is a cousin of wrestler Jimmy Snuka.

Samoans, The *see* Afa, Sika & Sionne

Samples, Mike (6'2", 252 lbs.) began wrestling in the USWA in 1991. He also wrestled as Leatherface in the USWA in 1993. Samples held the Tri-State Wrestling Title in Kentucky in 1993.

Sampson, Mike (6'1", 235 lbs.) began wrestling in 1987. He teamed with G.Q. Stratus as the Billion-Dollar Babies to win the IWCCW tag championship several times in 1990 and 1991. They were managed by Kevin Casey and often feuded with the Madison Brothers. He wrestled as the Mighty Destroyer in SMW in 1995.

Samu (Samula Anoia; b. January 29; Samoa; 6'4", 260 lbs.) began wrestling in 1981. He is the son of Afa. He held the Canadian International Title in Montreal in June of 1986. He teamed with Fatu to capture the WWC Caribbean Tag Team Title in Puerto Rico in November of 1987. He and Fatu formed the Samoan Swat Team and held the World Class World Tag Team Title in Texas several times in 1988. He teamed with Fatu as the Headshrinkers in the WWF. They were managed by Afa and Lou Albano, and captured the WWF Tag Title from the Quebecers on April 26, 1994. They lost the belts to Shawn Michaels and Diesel in August of 1994. Samu later left the WWF and was replaced by Sionne in the Headshrinkers.

Samurai, El *see* Matsuda, Osamu

Samurai, Guerrero (d. November 24, 1990) was a leading Mexican wrestler in the 1980s. He held the EMLL National Lightweight Title from 1984 until 1987, and again from February of 1988 until his death in an automobile accident in November of 1990.

Samurai Shiro *see* Koshinaka, Shiro

Sanchez, Alfonso wrestled in the Twin Devil tag team. He held the NWA Americas Title in Los An-

geles in October of 1978. He again captured the title in January of 1979.

Sanchez, Gilbert *see* Gilbert, Johnny

Sanchez, Pistol Pete wrestled in the 1960s and 1970s. He teamed with Manuel Soto as the Flying Tigers, and they engaged in a series of brutal matches with the Valiant Brothers in the 1970s. He subsequently retired to Brooklyn.

Sandman, The (Jim Fullington; Philadelphia; Pennsylvania; 6'3", 244 lbs.) began wrestling in 1989. He wrestled in the ECW and was managed by Woman. He won the ECW belt from Don Muraco in November of 1992. He lost the belt back to Muraco in a rematch in April of 1993. The chain-smoking grappler engaged in vicious feuds with Tommy Cairo and Tommy Dreamer. He again captured the ECW Title in April of 1995, defeating Shane Douglas. He held the title until October of 1995, when he was upset by Mikey Whipwreck. He regained the title the following December. He was accompanied to the ring by Missy Hyatt after Woman left the ECW in late 1995. He teamed with 2 Cold Scorpio to capture the ECW Tag Team Title from Public Enemy in October of 1995.

Sandor, Peter *see* Szabo, Sandor

Sano, Naoki (b. 1965; 5'9", 220 lbs.) began wrestling in 1983. He was a popular light heavyweight in Japan's Super World Sports federation.

Santana, Ricky (Orlando, Florida; 5'10", 235 lbs.) began wrestling in 1982. He teamed with Tony Torres as the Masked Hoods to hold the Texas All-Star Texas Tag Team Title in September of 1985. He teamed with Brady Boone to hold the NWA Pacific Northwest Tag Team in October of 1986, and held the tag belts with Coco Samoa in January of 1987. He held the NWA Pacific Northwest Title in March of 1987. He teamed with Curtis Thompson as U.S. Male to hold the Pacific Northwest tag belts in May of 1990. He and Al Madril wrestled as the Latin Connection to hold the tag team title in August of 1990 and Santana, wrestling as the Hood, teamed with Brad Anderson to recapture the tag belts in February of 1991. He teamed with Rex King to hold the WWC Tag Team Title in Puerto Rico several times in 1991 and 1992. He also held the WCW belts several times in 1993, teaming with Ray Gonzales. Santana also wrestled as the Iceman in Florida and Japan in the mid-1990s.

Santana, Tito (Merced Solis; b. May 10; Mission, Texas; 6'1", 245 lbs.) was born in Tocula, Mexico, and raised in Mission, Texas. He played college football at West Texas State University, and subsequently played professional football in the Canadian Football League. He began wrestling in Texas in 1975. He was soon wrestling in the AWA. The Latin-American star entered the WWF in the late 1970s and teamed with Ivan Putski to win the Tag Team Championship from Johnny and Jerry Valiant in New York on October 22, 1979. They lost the belts to the Samoans in Philadelphia on April 12, 1980. Santana returned

to the AWA, where he teamed with Mil Mascaras. He then returned to the WWF to defeat Don Muraco for the Intercontinental Title in Boston on February 11, 1984. He lost the title to Greg Valentine on September 24, 1984, in London, Ontario, Canada. Santana was sidelined with a knee injury, but soon returned to reclaim the belt from Valentine in Baltimore on July 6, 1985. He lost the belt to Randy Savage in Boston on February 8, 1986. Santana then teamed with Rick Martel as Strike Force. They defeated the Hart Foundation for the Tag Team belts in Syracuse, New York, on October 27, 1987. The duo lost the title to Demolition at Wrestlemania IV in Atlantic City, New Jersey, on March 27, 1988. Santana left the WWF in the early 1990s to return to Mexico. He reentered the WWF as the Matador in 1992. Santana also wrestled in the ECW, capturing the championship in August of 1993. He left the promotion the following month.

Santel, Ad (Adolph Ernst; d. November 1966) captured the World Light Heavyweight Title in 1912. He continued to claim the title for the next fourteen years.

Santiago, Manny *see* Head Hunter #1

Santiago, Victor *see* Head Hunter #2

Santo (Rudolfo Guzman Huerta; b. 1919, d. February 5, 1984) was born in Tulancingo, Hidalgo, Mexico. He began wrestling at the age of 16, and adopted his masked persona in 1942. He was known as El Santo (The Saint) or the Man in the Silver

Mask. He held the Mexican Welterweight Title several times in the early 1940s and the Middleweight Title in 1954. He teamed with Gory Guerrero as the Pareja Atomica (Atomic Couple) in numerous bouts in the 1950s and 1960s. He was also the Mexican Light Heavyweight Champion several times in the mid-1960s. He also held the Mexican Tag Team Title several times in the mid 1960s, teaming with Rayo de Jalisco. Santo was never unmasked in the ring and his true identity was a mystery to most of his fans. Santo was also a popular Mexican actor, appearing in over 60 films from the early 1960s through the early 1970s. His numerous film credits include *Santo vs. the Vampire Women* (1961), *Santo in the Hotel of the Dead* (1961), *Santo in the Wax Museum* (1963), *Santo vs. Baron Brakola* (1965), *Santo in the Revenge of the Vampire Women* (1968), *Santo and Blue Demon vs. the Monsters* (1968), *Santo vs. the Daughter of Frankenstein* (1971), *Santo and Blue Demon vs. Dracula and the Wolfman* (1972) and *The Mummies of Guanajuato* (1972). His son, El Higo Del Santo, was also a popular Mexican wrestler. Santo retired from the ring in 1983, but continued to perform in an action nightclub act. He died of a heart attack in his dressing room in Mexico City after performing on stage on February 5, 1984.

Santo, El Higo Del (Jorge Guzman; 5'6", 170 lbs.) began wrestling in 1982. The masked Mexican star is the son of legendary wrestler El Santo. He held the Mexican National Welterweight Title in late 1993. He wrestled with AAA Lucha Libra in 1994. El Higo del Santo also followed in his father's footsteps as an actor in such films as *El Santo el Enmascarado de Plata* in the early 1980s.

Santon, Charles *see* Dusek, Wally

Sapphire (Juanita Wright; b. 1935, d. September 10, 1996; St. Louis, Missouri) was a wrestling fan who began wrestling in the Missouri area in the mid–1970s as Princess Dark Cloud. She also became the first black female to hold a wrestling referee's license in Missouri and was the co-winner of a Battle Royal match against male wrestlers. She managed Dusty Rhodes in the WWF in the early 1990s, where she took the name Sapphire. She subsequently abandoned Rhodes for Ted DiBiase. She made a few appearances in the USWA in Memphis in 1993 before retiring to St. Louis. She died of a heart attack at her home there on September 10, 1996.

Sarpolis, Karl "Doc" (d. May 28, 1967) held the Southwestern Title in Texas in the 1930s. He was later a leading promoter in Amarillo, Texas, and served as president of the National Wrestling Alliance.

Sasaki, Haru "the Great" teamed with King Curtis to capture the NWA Pacific Northwest Tag Team Title in January of 1962. He reclaimed the tag belts with Stan Stasiak in June of 1965. He teamed with Kinji Shibuya to hold the NWA World Tag Team Title in San Francisco in May of 1968.

Sasaki, Kensuke (b. August 4, 1966; Tokyo, Japan; 5'10", 233 lbs.) began wrestling in 1987 with New

Japan. He wrestled with and against Hiroshi Hae in a series of bouts in 1990. He also made several appearances in the WCW. He broke his leg during a match in September of 1991 and was out of wrestling for nine months while recovering. Sasaki became Power Warrior and joined with Road Warrior Hawk to form the Hell Riders in 1992. They won the New Japan tag title in December of 1992. Sasaki defeated Sting for the WCW U.S. Heavyweight Title in Tokyo, Japan, on November 13, 1995. He relinquished the title to One Man Gang on December 27, 1995.

Sasuke, The Great (Masa Michinoku; b. 1969; 5'8", 190 lbs.) is a popular Japanese aerial artist in Mexico. He began wrestling in 1990.

Sato, Akio (b. February 13; 6', 238 lbs.) began wrestling in 1976. He teamed with Bob Geigel to hold the NWA Central States Tag Team Title in February of 1976. He teamed with Tarzan Goto to hold the CWA International Tag Team Title several times in 1986 and 1987. They were managed by Tojo Yamamoto. The Japanese star wrestled with Pat Tanaka as the Orient Express in the WWF in the late 1980s. He held the NWA Central States Title in March of 1989. He managed Hakushi in the WWF in early 1995.

Sato, Mr. *see* Kabuki, The Great

Sato, Yoshino teamed with Taro Sakura to hold the U.S. Tag Team Title in Tennessee in March of 1962.

Satullo, Perry *see* Eliminator Saturn

Saturn *see* Eliminator Saturn

Saunooke, Chief Osley (b. 1909, d. 197?; Cherokee, North Carolina; 6'4", 340) was a Cherokee Indian. He played football in the 1920s and began wrestling professionally in 1936. He was a leading wrestler until his retirement in the late 1950s. He died in the late 1970s.

Savage, Bill teamed with Buck Weaver to hold the NWA Pacific Northwest Tag Team Title in October of 1955. He held the NWA Pacific Northwest Title several times in the late 1950s. He also held the tag belts with Ed Francis, Tony Borne and Tito Kopa in the late 1950s and early 1960s.

Savage, Daniel Leo (b. 1905; Kentucky; 6'4", 255 lbs.) began wrestling in the 1930s. The heavily-bearded Savage often wrestled as Dan'l Boone. He was known in the ring for his great size and strength, and was a leading competitor in the South and West. He retired to Crestview, Florida, in the 1950s.

Savage, Dutch held the Canadian Tag Team Title several times in the late 1960s and early 1970s, teaming with Don Jardine, Stan Stasiak, John Tolos, Bob Brown and John Quinn. He held the NWA Pacific Northwest Title several times during the early and mid-1970s. He again held the Canadian tag belts in December of 1979, teaming with Stan Stasiak.

Savage, Randy "Macho Man" (Randy Poffo; b. November 15, 1952; Sarasota, Florida; 6'2", 237 lbs.) is the son of wrestler Angelo Poffo. He was a minor league baseball player when he made his wrestling debut under a mask as the Spider in November of 1973. He entered the WWWF in 1976, usually wrestling in preliminary matches. He teamed with his brother, Lanny Poffo, to hold the Gulf Coast Tag Team Title in February of 1976. They held the NWA Southeastern Tag Team Title the following year. As Savage's ring skills increased he became a leading contender in the Mid-South and ICW organizations. He held the Mid-America Title in early 1978. He exchanged the ICW World Title with his brother, Leaping Lanny Poffo, several times from 1979 through 1981. He captured the CWA International Title from Austin Idol in April of 1984. He held the WWC North American Title in Puerto Rico in late 1984. He defeated Jerry Lawler for the Southern Heavyweight Title in March of 1985. He held the belt several times until being forced to leave the area in a loser-leave-town match against Lawler in June of 1985. Savage returned to the WWF with his wife, Miss Elizabeth, acting as his valet and manager. He captured the WWF Intercontinental Title from Tito Santana in July of 1985. He lost the belt to Rick Steamboat at Wrestlemania II on March 29, 1987. Savage won the WWF Title in a tournament final over Ted DiBiase in Atlantic City, New Jersey, on March 27, 1988. He teamed with Hulk Hogan as the Mega Powers to defeat Ted DiBiase and Andre the Giant at Summerslam in August of 1988. He and Hogan subsequently broke their alliance in a dispute over Miss Elizabeth. He was defeated by Hogan for the WWF title at Wrestlemania V on April 2, 1989. Savage was managed by Sherry Martel when he defeated Jim Duggan in August of 1989 and became known as the Macho King. Savage beat Ric Flair for the WWF Title in Sarasota, Florida, on April 15, 1992. He lost the belt back to Ric Flair in Hershey, Pennsylvania, on September 1, 1992. Savage briefly held the USWA Unified Title in Memphis in October of 1993. Savage left the WWF to enter the WCW in November of 1994. He joined with Hulk Hogan in a feud against Ric Flair and Kevin Sullivan's Dungeon of Doom. Savage defeated the One Man Gang in a tournament to be crowned the WCW champion on November 26, 1995. He lost the belt to Ric Flair in Nashville, Tennessee, on December 27, 1995. Savage's feud with Flair escalated when his ex-wife, Miss Elizabeth, turned on him in the ring and joined with Flair.

Savannah Jack teamed with Ed Roberts as the Miami Vice Defenders to hold the PWA Tag Team Title for several months from April of 1985.

Savich, Danny teamed with Duke Keomuka to hold the NWA Texas Tag Team Title several times in 1950 and 1951. He also held the NWA Texas Title in early 1952. Savich held the Texas Brass Knucks Title in 1953. He again held the Texas tag belts with Keomuka in October of 1955.

Savoldi, Angelo (b. 1913; Hoboken, New Jersey; 5'9", 220 lbs.) was a popular wrestler from the 1940s through the 1960s. He was known in the ring as "Granite Chin," because of his ability to withstand hits to his jaw. He held the NWA World Junior Heavyweight Title on several occasions in 1958 and 1959. He is the father of Joe Savoldi.

Savoldi, Jumpin' Joe (b. 1908, d. January 25, 1974; South Bend, Indiana) was a fullback on Notre Dame's football team under Knute Rockne. He played professional football with the Chicago Bears in 1930, after being forced to leave Notre Dame when his marriage was revealed. He began wrestling professionally in the early 1930s. He defeated Jim Londos for the heavyweight title in 1933, holding the belt for two years before his defeat by Jim Browning. He served in the Army during World War II, and returned to competition after the war. He held the AWA Title in Montreal, Canada, in July of 1945. His brother, Angelo Savoldi, was also a popular wrestler. Joe Savoldi remained a leading competitor through the early 1950s. He retired to teach high school science in the 1960s. Savoldi died in Cadiz, Kentucky, after a long illness on January 25, 1974.

Savoldi, Jumpin' Joe (b. July 24; Parsippany, New Jersey; 6', 220 lbs.) is the son of Angelo Savoldi. He began wrestling in 1980. He teamed with Steve Simpson as the S&S Express to hold the NWA Pacific Northwest Tag Team Title in September of 1985. He held the IWCCW Title in New England four times from 1986 until February of 1989, defeating such wrestlers as Jonathan Boyd and Moondog Spike. He also held the IWCCW tag belts with Vic Steamboat several times in the late 1980s. Savoldi also held the

IWCCW Light Heavyweight Title several times in the early 1990s. Savoldi subsequently semi-retired from the ring, wrestling only occasionally during the mid-1990s.

Savoldi, Mario *see* Petty, Ted

Sawyer, Brett (St. Petersburg, Florida) wrestled as Brett Wayne in the NWA in the early 1980s. He held the NWA Pacific Northwest Title several times in 1982. He teamed with his brother, Buzz Sawyer, to hold the NWA Pacific Northwest Tag Team Title in April of 1981. He also held the tag belts with Rocky Johnson and Steve Pardee in 1982. He held the NWA National Title in September of 1983. He again teamed with Buzz Sawyer to hold the NWA National Tag Team Title several times in late 1983. He returned to the Pacific Northwest to reclaim the tag belts several times in 1984, teaming with Tom Prichard. He teamed with Chicky Starr to hold the Southwest Tag Team Title in September of 1984. He held the NWA Central States Title in December of 1985.

Sawyer, Buzz (Bruce Woyan; b. June 14, 1959, d. February 7, 1992; St. Petersburg, Florida; 5'11", 240 lbs.) began wrestling in 1979. He teamed with Matt Borne to hold the NWA Atlantic Coast Tag Team Title in 1980. He was known as the Mad Dog during his early 1980s feud with Tommy Rich in Atlanta. He teamed with his brother, Brett Sawyer, to capture the NWA Pacific Northwest Tag Team Title in April of 1981. He held the NWA National Title in May of 1982. He again teamed with his brother to hold the NWA National Tag Team Title several times in late 1983, until he left the promotion in early 1984. Sawyer was a popular wrestler in Japan, and he teamed with Matt Borne to win the World Class Tag Championship in the mid-1980s. He held the World Class Texas Title for several months in late 1987. He died of a drug overdose at his home in Sacramento, California, on February 7, 1992.

Sawyer, Steve "Bart" (Kansas City, Missouri; 6', 222 lbs.) began wrestling in 1990 in the Pacific Northwest. He teamed with Doug Masters to hold the USWA Tag Team Title in November of 1991.

Sayama, Satoru *see* Tiger Mask

Sbracchia, Eric (5'10", 240 lbs.) began wrestling in 1986. He held IWCCW light heavyweight championship in 1987, and teamed with Phil Apollo to hold the tag title in 1989.

Scaggs, Charles *see* 2 Cold Scorpio

Scarlet Pimpernel *see* Sherman, Ben

Scarpa, Frank (b. 1915, d. January 25, 1969) held the Big Time Wrestling Heavyweight Title from April of 1967 until his death on January 25, 1969.

Scarpa, Joe *see* Strongbow, Jay

Schiff, Herb *see* Freeman, Herb

Schmedley, Robert *see* Blaze, Bobby

Schnabel, Fritz (Bristol, Connecticut) began wrestling in the mid-1940s. He was known in the ring for his pile driver maneuver. He often teamed with his brother, Hans, in the late 1940s and early 1950s.

Schnabel, Hans (d. 19??; Bristol, Connecticut) began wrestling in the mid-1940s. He was known in the ring for his blockbuster move. He often teamed with his brother, Fritz, in the late 1940s and early 1950s. He teamed with the Zebra Kid to hold the Pacific Coast Tag Team Title in September of 1952. He held the Hawaiian Title in 1953.

Schoenberger, Bob *see* Shane, Bobby

Schoenlein, Gus *see* Americus

Schofro, Frank (b. 1919; Boston, Massachusetts; 5'11", 230 lbs.) played professional football with the Chicago Cardinals before becoming a pro wrestler. He was known in the ring as "Bosco," and was a leading competitor through the 1950s.

Schumann, Steve *see* Idol, Lance

Schwartz, Abe "Knuckleball" *see* Lombardi, Steve

Schwartz, Hans, Jr. (d. October, 1983) was the son of Hans Schwartz, Sr. He followed in his father's footsteps, capturing the World Greco-Roman Heavyweight Championship several times between 1934 and 1950.

Schwartz, Hans, Sr. (d. January 28, 1960) was a leading German wrestler in the early part of the century. He held the World Greco-Roman Heavyweight Championship numerous times from 1909 through 1930.

Schwartz, Ray *see* Becker, Bob

Schweigert, Johnny *see* Scott, George

Schyster, Irwin R *see* Rotunda, Mike

Scicluna, Baron Mikel (Malta; 265 lbs.) wrestled with Smasher Sloan to win the WWWF U.S. Tag Team Title from Antonio Pugliese and Johnny Valentine in September of 1966. They lost the belts to Pugliese and Spiros Arion in December of 1966. Scicluna was later managed by Lou Albano and teamed with King Curtis Iaukea to win the WWWF Tag Team Title in February of 1972. They lost the belts to Sonny King and Chief Jay Strongbow in May of 1972.

Scoggins, Doug *see* Mr. X.

Scorpion, The *see* Fontaine, Eric

Scott, George (Johnny "Dutch" Schweigert; b. 1919; Camden, New Jersey; 6'1", 225 lbs.) began wrestling in the mid-1940s. A former lifeguard, he was known in the ring as the Great Scott. He wore kilts and a plaid bathrobe to the ring and was accompanied by a bag-piping Scotsman. He teamed with Roy Shire to hold the NWA Texas Tag Team Title in October of 1954. He teamed with Buddy Austin to capture the WWWF U.S. Tag Team Title from Johnny Barend and Buddy Rogers in March of 1963. They lost the title to Skull Murphy and Brute Bernard the following May. He teamed with Tim Woods to hold the World Class American Tag Team Title in Texas in 1970. He held the World Class Texas Title in October of 1970.

Scott, Sandy teamed with George Becker to hold the NWA Southern Tag Team Title several times in 1961. He teamed with Jerry Brisco in 1972 to hold the NWA Atlantic Coast Tag Title, and partnered with Nelson Royal for a tag championship reign in 1973.

Scotty the Body *see* Anthony, Scott

Scotty the Body *see* Raven

Seitz, Michael *see* Hayes, Michael

Senerchia, Pete *see* Tazmaniac

Senior X *see* Dykes, J.C.

Sensational Sherry *see* Martel, Sherry

Sensationals *see* Snow, Al & Doyle, Mickey

Seone *see* Barbarian, The

Severn, Dan (b. June 9; Detroit, Michigan; 6'2", 265 lbs.) began wrestling in 1991. He won the Ultimate Fighting Championship IV and defeated Chris Candido for the NWA Heavyweight Title in February of 1995.

Sexton, Frank (b. 1912, d. 1967; Sedalia, Ohio; 6'3", 235 lbs.) played football and wrestled at Ohio State before becoming a professional wrestler in 1932. He was initially unsuccessful in the ring, until he captured the Pacific Coast Title in San Francisco as the Black Panther in April of 1941. He held the belt several more times during the year, competing against Bill Longson, Bobby Managoff and Jim Casey. He captured the AWA Title in Montreal, Canada, in July of 1944. He held the British Empire Title in Toronto, Canada, in September of 1944. He defeated Sandor Szabo for the AWA Heavyweight Title on May 21, 1945. He was defeated for the belt by Steve Casey on June 6, 1945, but recaptured the championship later in the month on June 27, 1945. Sexton continued to hold the belt during most of the late 1940s until his defeat by Don Eagle in Cleveland in 1950. He remained a leading competitor throughout the 1950s.

Sexton, Susan was a leading woman's wrestler from the 1980s. She held the Ladies Professional Wrestling Association Title in 1990. She retired in the early 1990s.

Shadow, The (Marv Westenberg; b. 1913; Tacoma, Washington; 6'2", 255 lbs.) defeated Steve Casey for the AWA Heavyweight Title in Boston, Massachusetts, on March 2, 1939. He lost the belt several weeks later to Gus Sonnenberg on March 16, 1939. He was also known as the Masked Black Spider.

Shamrock, Ken (b. 1962; 6', 220 lbs.) began wrestling in 1989. Wrestling as Vince Torelli, he held the NAWA/SAPW title in 1991. He was a leading wrestler in Japan before competing in the Ultimate Fighting Championship.

Shane, Bobby (Bob Schoenberger; b. 1935, d. February 20, 1975; 5'10") teamed with Mario Galento to hold the Southern Tag Team Title in 1966. He teamed with

Nick Bockwinkel to hold the Hawaiian Tag Team Title in March of 1969. He held the NWA Southern Title in Florida from November of 1971 until February of 1972. He teamed with Bearcat Wright to hold the NWA Florida Title for several months in the Spring of 1972. He also held the Florida tag belts with Chris Markoff in December of 1972, and with Gorgeous George, Jr., in February of 1973. He and Gorgeous George, Jr. also held the NWA Georgia Tag Team Title in December of 1973. Shane teamed with George Barnes to capture the Australasian Tag Team Title in Australia in April of 1974. He continued to wrestle in the Atlanta, Georgia, area until his death in a private airplane crash near Tampa, Florida, on February 20, 1975. Wrestlers Buddy Colt, Austin Idol and Gary Hart were also injured in the crash.

Shango, Papa *see* Soultaker, The

Shapiro, Morris (b. 1917; Brooklyn, New York) began wrestling in 1940. He became a leading wrestler in the Chicago area in the mid-1940s, and was known for his full nelson maneuver in the ring. He held the Eastern Light Heavyweight Title in 1947. He subsequently went to the Pacific Northwest where he wrestled as the Mighty Atlas. He held the NWA Texas Title in late 1951 and early 1952. He held the NWA Central States Title in 1956.

Shark, The *see* Earthquake

Sharkey, Ed (b. February 4, 1938) was born in Minneapolis, Minnesota. He was trained as a boxer before he began wrestling in carnivals in Fargo, North Dakota, in 1960. He wrestled for several years before he began training other wrestlers, including Bob Backlund and Jesse Ventura.

Sharpe, Ben (b. 1916; Hamilton, Canada; 6'7", 265 lbs.) began wrestling in the late 1940s. He held the Hawaiian Title in September of 1953. He teamed with his brother, Mike Sharpe, to hold the NWA World Tag Team Title in San Francisco over a dozen times during the 1950s. They also held NWA Texas Tag Team Title in April of 1959. He held the Pacific Coast Title in San Francisco in March of 1959.

Sharpe, Larry (6'3", 260 lbs.) began wrestling in 1974. He teamed with Ripper Collins to hold the Calgary Stampede International Title in 1976. He held the Hawaiian Title in November of 1978. He wrestled in the NAWF in Pennsylvania in 1983, holding their championship. He wrestled with the NCW promotion in Massachusetts, holding their title in the mid-1980s. He also held the NCW Title in Connecticut in 1988. He managed the Monster Factory, which trained wrestlers in the New Jersey and Ohio area.

Sharpe, Mike (b. October 28; 6'2", 271 lbs.) is the son of wrestler Iron Mike Sharpe. began wrestling in 1973. He teamed with the Black Avenger to hold the Canadian Tag Team Title in October of 1977. He also held the Canadian belts with Salvatore Bellomo in October of 1978. He teamed with Duke Myers to hold the Calgary Stampede International Tag Team Title in 1981. He

held the Mid-South Louisiana Title in September of 1982. He held the Mid-America Title in early 1985. He often wrestled in the WWF during the 1980s.

Sharpe, Mike, Sr. (b. 1913, d. 1988; Hamilton, Canada; 6'6", 260 lbs.) began wrestling in the late 1940s. He held the Pacific Coast Title in San Francisco several times in the early 1950s. He teamed with his brother, Ben Sharpe, to hold the NWA World Tag Team Title in San Francisco over a dozen times during the 1950s. They also held the NWA Texas Tag Team Title in April of 1959. He again held the Pacific Coast belt in 1960. His son, Mike Sharpe, Jr., also wrestled professionally.

Shaw, John R. (b. 1923, d. February 19, 1989) was a police officer in Dallas when he began competing in wrestling matches at carnivals. He achieved notoriety for wrestling bears in the Texas area. He became a full time wrestler after leaving the police force in the 1950s. He appeared in the ring as one of the Kowalski Brothers. He also wrestled as the villainous Ivan Bulba, the Mad Russian from Minsk, during the early days of televised wrestling. He retired from the ring to become a rancher in the 1960s. He also served as a trainer for younger wrestlers. Shaw died in Dallas after a long illness on February 19, 1989.

Shaw, Mike (b. May 9; Saginaw, Michigan; 6', 404 lbs.) was raised in Michigan. He was trained by Killer Kowalski and made his professional debut in Boston in 1980. He wrestled throughout New England before going to Canada to compete. He wrestled as Klondike Mike to capture the Canadian Tag Team Title several times in 1981, teaming with Danny O and Dean Ho. He held the Stampede North American Title several times from 1986 through 1988. He joined the WCW as Norman the Lunatic, where he remained for several years before joining Global as Makhan Singh. He joined WWF in 1993 as Friar Ferguson, but was soon wrestling as Bastien Booger. He left the WWF in 1995.

Sheik, The (Ed Farhat; Lebanon; 5'11", 247 lbs.) was born in 1924. He began wrestling in 1952 and became known for his legendary acts of brutality in the ring. He held the NWA Texas Title in October of 1954. The Sheik was often accompanied to the ring by his manager, Abdullah Farouk. He held the NWA U.S. Title over a dozen times between 1965 and 1980. He also held the NWA Americas Title in Los Angeles for several months in early 1969. He held the U.S. Title in Toronto several times from 1974 through July of 1977. He trained his nephew, Sabu, to be a professional wrestler in the late 1980s.

Sheik Hussein *see* Weingroff, George

Sheiks, The *see* Blackwell, Jerry & Patera, Ken

Sheldon, Dave *see* Angel of Death

Shepherd, Donna *see* Samantha

Shereef, El teamed with the Mad Russian to hold the NWA Pacific Northwest Tag Team Title in January of 1965. He teamed with Hard Boiled Haggerty to hold the WWA Tag Team Title in Los Angeles in October of 1966.

Sherman, Ben (Portland, Oregon) was born in Alaska and attended Yale University. He competed in the Olympic Games in 1928. He began wrestling as the Scarlet Pimpernel in the mid-1930s. He was the holder of the Hawaiian title until he was unmasked by Lee Grable. He remained a leading mat star through the 1950s.

Shibuya, Kenji teamed with Duke Keomuka to hold the NWA Texas Tag Team Title in February of 1956. He wrestled as Mr. Hito and teamed with Mr. Moto during the 1950s. They held the NWA Southern Tag Team Title in 1954. They again held the tag belts in 1957. He again teamed with Mitsu Arakawa to hold the NWA World Tag Team Title in Minneapolis in August of 1957. He again held the NWA tag belts, teaming with Hard Boiled Haggerty in April of 1958. He held the NWA Central States Title in 1960. He teamed with Arakawa to hold the NWA World Tag Team Title in San Francisco in late 1961 and 1962. He held the Canadian Tag Team Title several times in 1963 and 1964, teaming with Mitsu Arakawa, Sweet Daddy Siki and Don Leo Jonathan. He held the NWA U.S. Title in San Francisco several times from 1964 through 1968. He held the World Class Championship in Texas in 1968. He held the NWA World Tag Team Title in San Francisco several times in 1968, teaming with the Great Sasaki and Masa Saito. He captured the NWA Americas Title in Los Angeles in March of 1971. He teamed with Masa Saito to hold the NWA Americas Tag Team Title in Los Angeles in May of 1971. He held the Americas tag belts several more times in the early 1970s, teaming with Killer Kowalski and Saito. He again held the NWA World Tag Team Title in San Francisco in September of 1973, teaming with Masa Saito. He held the Calgary Stampede International Tag Team Title several times in 1975, teaming with John Quinn, Gil Hayes and Higo Hamaguchi. He teamed with Mr. Sakurada to hold the NWA Florida Tag Team Title in August of 1979 and the World Class American Tag Team Title in 1980. He also wrestled as Sato Keomuka. He retired in the early 1980s.

Shikat, Dick (d. 19??; 6'1", 220 lbs.) was recognized as the World Champion by the New York State Athletic Commission in 1929 and became NWA Heavyweight Champion following his defeat of Jim Londos in August of 1929. He relinquished the belt to Londos in June of 1930. Shikat held the World Heavyweight Championship from March of 1936 until his defeat by Ali Baba in Detroit, Michigan, on April 24, 1936.

Shikina, Oki (d. December 15, 1983) began wrestling in the United States in 1932. He held the Hawaiian Title in 1938 and 1939. He was largely inactive during the war years, but returned to the ring in the late 1940s. He teamed with Yasu Fuji to hold the NWA Central States Tag Team Title in March of 1975. He teamed with Sugar Bear Harris to hold the Tri-State U.S. Tag Team Title in Oklahoma in October of 1979.

Shinzaki, Kensuke *see* Hakushi

Shire, Roy (Roy Shires; b. 1921, d. October 1, 1992) teamed with George "the Great" Scott to hold the NWA Texas Tag Team Title in October of 1954. He teamed with Ray Stevens to hold the NWA Tag Team Title in Indiana several times in the late 1950s. He also teamed with Art Neilson to hold the belts briefly in May of 1961. Shire was a promoter with the NWA in San Francisco from the early 1960s through the 1980s.

Shires, Ray *see* Stevens, Ray

Shires, Roy *see* Shire, Roy

Shockmaster, The *see* Typhoon

Shreeve, Larry *see* Abdullah the Butcher

Shults, David "Dr. D." (6'5", 270 lbs.). was raised in Nashville, Tennessee. He was trained by wrestling promoter Herb Welsh and made his professional wrestling debut in Missouri in December of 1974. He teamed with Dutch Mantel to hold the Southern Tag Team Title in 1976. He teamed with Dennis Condrey to hold the NWA Southeastern Tag Team Title in November of 1979. He and Condrey also held the Southern tag belts in April of 1980. He teamed with Duke Myers to hold the Calgary Stampede International Tag Team Title in 1981. He held the NWA Southeastern Title in November of 1982. He also held the NCW Title in Massachusetts in the early 1980s. Shults entered the WWF in the mid-1980s. He was suspended and fined by the promotion in December of 1984 after an incident involving *20/20* investigative reporter John Stossel. While conducting an interview with Shults and in a corridor in the Madison Square Garden dressing room Stossel said that he felt wrestling was fake. Shults knocked him to the floor with two slaps to the head. Shults was subsequently fired by he promotion when the interview aired in February of 1985. Shults competed in Japan later in the year. He captured the Canadian International Title in Montreal in November of 1986. He subsequently retired from the ring, and worked as a bounty hunter.

Sicilians, The *see* Albano, Lou & Altimore, Tony

Sierra, David (6'1", 246 lbs.) began wrestling in 1979. Wrestling as the Assassin, he teamed with Rip Oliver to hold the NWA Pacific Northwest Tag Team Title several times in 1982 and 1983. He briefly held the NWA Florida Title in February of 1986. He teamed with Bob Brown to hold the NWA Central States Tag Team Title in February of 1988. Wrestling as Top Gun, he teamed with Scotty the Body to hold the Pacific Northwest tag belts in July of 1989. They split the team and Sierra relinquished the belts the following month. He teamed with Ron Starr as the Mercenaries to hold the WWC Tag Team Title in Puerto Rico in February of 1990. Wrestling

as Fidel Sierra he held the WWC TV Title in Puerto Rico in October of 1991. He held the ICWA championship in Florida several times in 1992 and 1993 as the Cuban Assassin. His brother, Bill Alfonso, is also a wrestler and referee.

Sierra, Fidel *see* Sierra, David

Sigel, Morris (d. December 26, 1966) was the first boxing and wrestling promoter licensed in Texas in 1933. He remained a leading promoter in the Southwest for several decades.

Sika (Sika Anoai; 6'2", 320 lbs.) wrestled with his brother Afa as the original Samoans. They held the Calgary Stampede International Tag Team Title several times in 1973. They held the NWA Florida Tag Team Title in June of 1973. They captured the Canadian Tag Team Title in November of 1973. They held the Southern Tag Team Title in 1977. Under the management of Lou Albano, they defeated Ivan Putski and Tito Santana for the WWF Tag Team Title in April of 1980. They lost the belts to Bob Backlund and Pedro Morales in August of 1980, but reclaimed them the following month in a tournament. They were defeated by Tony Garea and Rick Martel in November of 1980. Managed by Sonny King, the Samoans held the NWA National Tag Team Title in late 1982. They returned to the WWF championship in March of 1983, defeating Chief Jay and Jules Strongbow. They lost the title to Rocky Johnson and Tony Atlas in November of 1983. The Samoans left the WWF to wrestle in Louisiana, where they were managed by Ernie Ladd. They held the Mid-South belts before they turned on Ladd and joined Gen. Scandor Akbar's stable.

Siki, Sweet Daddy teamed with Bulldog Brower to hold the International Tag Team Title in Toronto in 1962. He held the NWA Texas Title in February of 1963. He teamed with Kinji Shibuya to hold the Canadian Tag Team Title in October of 1963. He held the Stampede North American Title in Calgary, Canada, in 1970. He teamed with Mad Dog Mayne to hold the Hawaiian Tag Team Title in October of 1971. He also held the North American Title in Honolulu in October of 1971. He held the WWC North American Title in Puerto Rico several times in 1983 and 1984.

Silencer *see* Storm, J.W.

Silverstein, Ralph "Ruffy" (b. 1918, d. April 5, 1980; Chicago, Illinois) was an amateur wrestling champion at the University of Chicago. He made his professional debut in the early 1940s. He served in the U.S. Army during World War II, seeing action on the Pacific front as a counterintelligence officer. He was a leading mat star through the 1950s.

Simmes, Misty Blue *see* Blue, Misty

Simmons, Ron (b. May 15, 1962; Warner Robins, Georgia; 6'2", 260 lbs.) played football at Florida State University in the late 1970s. He began wrestling in 1986. He briefly held the NWA Florida Title in late 1986. He teamed with Butch

Reed as Doom in the WCW in the early 1990s. Managed by Woman, the duo beat the Steiners for the WCW Tag Team title on May 19, 1990. They lost the belts to the Freebirds in February of 1991, and Simmons subsequently engaged in a bitter feud with his former partner Reed. Simmons teamed with Big Josh to captured the WCW U.S. Tag Team Title from the Young Pistols in January of 1992. They lost the belts the following month to Greg Valentine and Terry Taylor. Simmons won the WCW World Title in Baltimore, Maryland in August of 1992. He lost the belt to Big Van Vader in Baltimore in December of 1992.

Simms, Terry *see* Garvin, Terry

Simon, Dean *see* Malenko, Dean

Simon, Larry *see* Malenko, Boris

Simply Divine *see* King, Rex & Doll, Steve

Simpson, Miss *see* Adams, Toni

Simpson, Scott *see* Koloff, Nikita

Simpson, Shaun (Johannesburg, South Africa; 5'9", 200 lbs.) is the son of wrestler Sammy Cohen. He began wrestling in 1986. He often teamed with his brother Steve Simpson. They held the World Class World Tag Team Title in Texas in August of 1987. They held the World Class Texas Tag Team Title several times in 1988, often competing against John Tatum and Jack Victory. They again held the Texas tag belts in April of 1989.

Simpson, Steve (Johannesburg, South Africa; 6'2", 230 lbs.) is the son of wrestler Sammy Cohen. He began wrestling in 1984. He teamed with Joe Savoldi as the S&S Express to hold the NWA Pacific Northwest Tag Team Title in September of 1985. A South African native, he teamed with is brother, Shaun Simpson, to hold the World Class World Tag Team Title in Texas in August of 1987. They held the World Class Texas Tag Team Title several times in 1988, often competing against John Tatum and Jack Victory. They again held the Texas tag belts in April of 1989. He also teamed with Chris Walker to win Global's first World Tag Team Title in July of 1991.

Simunovich, Lucky teamed with Bobby Bruns to hold the Hawaiian Tag Team Title in 1952. They again held the belts in February of 1955. Simunovich also held the Hawaiian Title in February of 1955. He teamed with Al Lolotai to recapture the tag belts in 1957.

Singer, Jack (b. 1911; Savannah, Georgia; 5'11", 235 lbs.) was a native of Boston, Massachusetts. He was trained by Ed Don George and began wrestling in the mid-1930s. He was known in the ring as the Green Terror, and remained a leading contender through the 1950s.

Singh, Abudda *see* Bradley, Boo

Singh, Gama (5'11", 220 lbs.) began wrestling in the late 1970s. He teamed with Igor Volkoff to hold the Canadian Tag Team Title in December of 1977. The Pakistani native led the Karachi Vice organization in the Stampede area. He held the Stampede British Commonwealth Mid-Heavyweight Title several times in the late 1980s.

Singh, Makhan *see* Shaw, Mike

Singh, Nanjo (b. 1911; India; 5'9", 228 lbs.) began wrestling in the late 1930s. He held the British Empire Title in Toronto, Canada, in February of 1942. He again held the British Empire Title in May of 1948. He competed often in the United States in the late 1940s and early 1950s.

Singh, Rhonda *see* Monster Ripper

Singh, Tiger Jeet (6'4", 265 lbs.) began wrestling in 1964. The Pakistani native wrestled often in Japan. He held the U.S. Title in Toronto, Canada, in the late 1960s. He teamed with Dennis Stamp to hold the Canadian Tag Team Title in September of 1975. He is the son of Japanese wrestler Nanjo Singh.

Singh, Vokkan *see* Allbright, Gary

Sionne *see* Barbarian, The

Sister Sherry *see* Martel, Sherri

Sistrunk, Otis teamed with Michael Hayes to hold the NWA National Tag Team Title in September of 1981.

Sito, Sugi held the Mexican Middleweight Title several times in the early 1950s. He teamed with Rito Romero to hold the NWA Texas Tag Team Title in May of 1954. He teamed with Chin Lee to hold the Calgary Stampede International Tag Team Title several times in 1971 and 1972.

666 *see* Starr, Jim

Skip *see* Candido, Chris

Skoaland, Arnold (January 21, 1924; White Plains, New York; 5'11", 205 lbs.) served in the Marines during World War II. He was an amateur boxing champion before he entered wrestling in the late 1940s. Known as the Golden Boy, he held the Pacific Coast Championship during his years in the ring in the 1950s. He left active competition to manage Bruno Sammartino during his second title reign in the WWWF in the mid-1970s. He also served as the manager of WWF champion Bob Backlund in the early 1980s.

Sky, Bill teamed with Joe Sky to hold the World Tag Team Title in Tennessee in 1967. They also held the Southern Tag Team title several times between 1967 and 1969.

Sky, Joe teamed with Bill Sky to hold the World Tag Team Title in Tennessee in 1967. They also held the Southern Tag Team title several times between 1967 and 1969.

Sky Low Low was the midget world champion as the result of a tournament in 1949. He remained a popular midget wrestler through the 1960s.

Skyliners, The *see* Taylor, Chaz & Dane, Steve

Slammer, M.C. *see* Brown, Brickhouse

Slapowitz, Izzy managed Doug Vines and Jeff Sword as the Devil's Duo in the ICW in 1981.

Slater, Dick (Richard Van Slater; b. May 19; Tampa, Florida; 6'1", 235 lbs.) began wrestling in 1970. He was a leading mat star in the 1970s and 1980s. He teamed with Dusty Rhodes to hold the NWA Florida Tag Team Title in late 1973. He also held the Florida tag belts with Toru Tanaka and Johnny Weaver over the next two years. He teamed with Bob Orton, Jr. to hold the NWA Georgia Tag Team Title and U.S. Tag Title in 1975. He held the NWA Missouri Title for several months from August of 1977. He also held the NWA Georgia Title several times in 1976 and 1977, and held the NWA Southern Title in Florida several times from 1978 through 1980. Slater held the NWA TV Title in early 1983. He defeated Greg Valentine for the NWA U.S. Title in December of 1983. He was beaten for the belt by Rick Steamboat in April of 1984. Managed by his valet, Dark Journey, he captured the MSWA North American Title in January of 1986. He held the USWA Southern Title in September of 1990. He held the ICWA championship in Florida several times in the early 1990s. Slater teamed with the Barbarian to capture the WCW U.S. Tag Team Title in June of 1992, holding the belt for a month. He also teamed with Dick Murdoch as the Hardliners in the early 1990s. Teaming with Bunkhouse Buck as Colonel Parker's Stud Stable, he captured the WCW Tag Team Title from Harlem Heat on June 21, 1995. They lost the title in a rematch with Harlem Heat on September 17, 1995.

Slaughter, Sergeant (Bob Remus; b. August 27; Paris Island, South Carolina; 6'3", 310 lbs.)

began wrestling in 1977. He wrestled as Beautiful Bobby Remus in the Pacific Northwest before becoming Sergeant Slaughter in the Central States promotion. He held the NWA Central States Title several times in 1977. He captured the NWA U.S. Title in a tournament in October of 1981. He was defeated for the belt by Wahoo McDaniel in May of 1982, but reclaimed the title the following month. He again lost the belt to McDaniel in August of 1982. Slaughter teamed with Don Kernodle to become NWA World Tag Team Champions in a tournament in September of 1982. They held the title until March of 1983, when they were defeated by Rick Steamboat and Jay Youngblood. He held the NWA Canadian Title in Toronto in late 1983. Slaughter was a popular star in the WWF in the mid-1980s, and his ring persona was adapted into the G.I. Joe toy and cartoon line. Slaughter wrestled on the independent circuit in the late 1980s, capturing the NCW Title in Connecticut in 1989. Slaughter returned to the WWF in 1990, under the management of General Adnan and claiming allegiance with the Iraqis during the Gulf War. He defeated the Ultimate Warrior for the WWF Title in Miami, Florida, on January 19, 1991. He lost the belt to Hulk Hogan in Los Angeles on March 24, 1991. Slaughter subsequently broke with Adnan and reestablished himself as a fan favorite.

Slazenger, Tex *see* Godwinn, Phinnius

Sledge (Jamie Magnum) teamed with Hammer as the Punishers in the PWA. They teamed to hold the PWA Tag Team Title several times in 1990 and early 1991. Sledge also held the PWA singles title in February of 1992.

Slick (Kenneth Johnson) managed numerous villains in the WWF during the 1980s. He managed such stars as the Warlord, the Barbarian, Paul Roma, Hercules and Akeem. He left the WWF in the early 1990s to return to his calling as an evangelist as the pastor at a Fort Worth, Texas, Baptist Church.

Slinger, Richard (Richard Acelinger; b. September 16, 1971) made his wrestling debut in the Georgia area in 1988. The following year he began wrestling with All-Japan, where he became a leading contender.

Sloan, Smasher teamed with Baron Mikel Scicluna to win the WWWF U.S. Tag Team Title from Antonio Pugliese and Johnny Valentine in September of 1966. They lost the belts to Pugliese and Spiros Arion the following December. He wrestled with Don Jardine as the Spoilers to hold the World Class American Tag Team Title in 1968.

Smash (Barry Darsow; b. October 6, 1959; Dubuque, Iowa; 6'1", 282 lbs.) began wrestling as Krusher Khrushchev in the NWA in the early 1980s. He held the Mid-South TV Title in Louisiana in May of 1984. He teamed with Jim Neidhart to hold the U.S. Tag Team Title in Florida for several months in late 1984. He held the NWA Mid-Atlantic Title several times in late 1985. He teamed with Ivan and Nikita

Koloff as the Russians, defending the tag title as a rotating three-man team in 1985. He also held the NWA U.S. Tag Title with Koloff from September of 1986 until the following December. He entered the WWF as Smash and, with Ax, were the original members of Demolition and three-time winners of the WWF tag team title. They first won the title belts, under the management of Mr. Fuji, against Rick Martel and Tito Santana at Wrestlemania IV on March 27, 1988. They were defeated by Arn Anderson and Tully Blanchard in July of 1989, but regained the belts the following October. They lost the title to Andre the Giant and Haku in December of 1989, but recaptured the belts at Wrestlemania VI on April 1, 1990. They soon added Crush to Demolition, and he and Smash were defeated for the belts by the Hart Foundation in August of 1990. He subsequently wrestled as the Repoman in the WWF. He premiered as the Blacktop Bully in the WCW in September of 1994, where he feuded with Dustin Rhodes. He left the promotion in March of 1995.

Smirnoff, Alexi (Moscow, Russia; 254 lbs.) began his career as a popular scientific wrestler before becoming a rulebreaking villain. Wrestling as Michel Dubois, he held the AWA Title in Montreal, Canada, in 1973. He teamed with Bob Roop to hold the NWA World Tag Team Title in San Francisco in March of 1977. He held the NWA U.S. Title in San Francisco in April of 1977. He held the NWA Central States Title in January of 1978. He teamed with Bob Sweetan to hold the NWA

Central States Tag Team Title in April of 1978. He managed the Mongolian Stomper in Knoxville, Tennessee, in the late 1970s. He teamed with Ivan Koloff to capture the NWA Georgia Tag Team Title several times in early 1980. They were managed by Rock Hunter.

Smith, Aurelian, Jr. *see* Roberts, Jake

Smith, Aurelian, Sr. *see* Smith, Grizzly

Smith, Black *see* Peterson, Daryll

Smith, Curtis wrestled as the Executioner to hold the Mid-America Title in April of 1977. He regained the title in August of 1978, wrestling as the Blue Yankee.

Smith, Davey Boy (David Smith; November 27, 1962; Leeds, England; 5'9", 245 lbs.) began wrestling in 1978. He went to Calgary in 1981, where he feuded with the Dynamite Kid. He teamed with Bruce Hart to hold the Calgary Stampede International Tag Team Title several times in 1982 and 1983. He held the Stampede North American Title in Calgary in June of 1984. He teamed with the Dynamite Kid to recapture the Stampede International tag belts in March of 1984. They went to the WWF in 1985, where the became known as the British Bulldogs and were managed by Captain Lou Albano. They won the WWF tag team belts from Greg Valentine and Brutus Beefcake at Wrestlemania II on April 7, 1986. They lost the title to the Hart Foundation on January 26, 1987, in Tampa, Florida. He left the WWF late in 1988 and returned to Canada. He was injured in an automobile accident in July of 1989. The following year he broke with the Dynamite Kid. He returned to the WWF as the British Bulldog in 1990. He captured the WWF Intercontinental Title from Bret Hart in a match in London, England, on August 29, 1992. He lost the belt to Shawn Michaels the following October. Smith left the WWF soon afterwards and subsequently wrestled in WCW. He departed the WCW in December of 1993. He returned to the WWF, where he teamed with Lex Luger as the Allied Powers in early 1995. He broke with Luger later in the year and subsequently formed a tag team with is brother-in-law, Owen Hart. They were managed by Jim Cornette and wrestled as villains.

Smith, Don teamed with Doug Gilbert as the Super Infernos in the early 1970s. Managed by J.C. Dykes, they teamed to hold the NWA Georgia Tag Team Title several times in 1973.

Smith, Gary *see* Pit Bull #1

Smith, Grizzly (Aurelian Smith, Sr.) teamed with Luke Brown as the Kentuckians to hold the WWA Tag Team Title in Los Angeles in August of 1965. Wrestling as Ski Hi Jones, he teamed with Don Leo Jonathan to hold the Canadian Tag Team Title in March of 1968. He held the World Class Texas Title in June of 1968. He teamed with Fritz Von Erich to hold the World Class American Tag Team Title in July of 1968. He reunited with Brown as the Kentuckians to hold the U.S. Tag Team Title in Oklahoma in April of 1971. Smith is the father of wrestlers Jake "the Snake" Roberts, Sam Houston and Rockin' Robin.

Smith, J.T. (John T. Smith; Philadelphia, Pennsylvania; 6', 238 lbs.) began wrestling in June of 1990 and became Tri-State champion in Philadelphia in 1991. Smith wrestled in ECW in 1994, and held the TV title briefly in March.

Smith, Jimmy Dee *see* Smith, Pleasant

Smith, Johnny (b. August 7, 1965; Manchester, England; 6', 235 lbs.) began wrestling in 1982. He teamed with the Dynamite Kid as the New British Bulldogs in Canada and Japan in the early 1990s. He wrestled as the "brother" of Davey Boy Smith. He continued to wrestle with the Dynamite Kid as the British Bruisers with All-Japan from 1992.

Smith, Mark *see* King, Rex

Smith, Pleasant (b. 1885, d. March 12, 1969) was a leading wrestler in the early part of the century. He was also known as Tommy Lee Pleasant and Jimmy Dee Smith. He was also a screen actor in several silent films between 1913 and 1919. Smith died in Las Vegas, Nevada, on March 12, 1969.

Smith, Robin *see* Rockin' Robin

Smith, Rocky held the Southern Junior Heavyweight Title in late 1965. He wrestled with Frankie Cain as the Infernos. The duo captured the NWA World Tag Team Title in Florida in October of 1966. They held the belts several times over the next three years. They were often managed by J.C. Dykes. They also held the NWA Florida Tag Team Title in January of 1971 and again in January of 1972.

Smith, Roger wrestled as Roger Mason to capture the Mid-America Title in April of 1980. He teamed with Don Bass as the Assassins to hold the CWA Tag Team Title several times in 1983. Smith and Bass competed as the Interns to capture the Southern Tag Team Title in December of 1984. Smith wrestled as Dirty Rhodes to capture the Mid-America Title in February of 1986. Smith, wrestling as Flame, again held the tag belts with Bass, wrestling as Fire, in July of 1986. The duo again held the belts in September of 1986, with Smith again wrestling as Dirty Rhodes.

Smithson, Bill wrestled as Moondog Spike in the ICW and teamed with Moondog Spot to hold the tag belts in 1987. He also held the ICW Title in 1988. He teamed with Spot to hold the USWA Tag Team Title in November of 1991. He left the promotion the following April, but soon returned to form a three man team with Spot and Cujo. They held the tag title several times in 1992.

Smothers, Tracey (b. September 2; Atlanta, Georgia; 6'1", 227 lbs.) began wrestling in 1982. He held the Mid-America Title several times in late 1986. He teamed with Steve Armstrong as the Southern Boys to capture the Florida Tag Team Title in February of 1987. He teamed with John Paul to hold the

CWA Tag Team Title for several months from March of 1989. He and Armstrong entered the WCW as the Young Pistols in the early 1990s. They defeated the Patriots for the WCW U.S. Tag Team Title in November of 1991. They were defeated for the belts by Ron Simmons and Big Josh in January of 1992. Smothers wrestled in the Smoky Mountain area from 1993, where he held the championship for several months from April of 1993. He also wrestled occasionally in the USWA as a villain in 1995.

Snodgrass, Elvira (b. 1914, d. 19??; Smoky Mountains, Tennessee; 5'7", 150 lbs.) began wrestling in the late 1930s. She remained a top female competitor for several decades.

Snow, Al (Allen Sarven; Lima, Ohio; 6'1", 237 lbs.) began wrestling in 1982. He teamed with Rick Ciassio as the Fantastix to hold the Motor City Wrestling ICW U.S. Tag Title in November of 1986. They held the belts until April of the following year. He then formed the Sensationals with Mickey Doyle to capture the title in August of 1987. They were defeated for the belts three months later. He and Doyle subsequently competed in the WWA as the Motor City Hitmen, where the held the tag belts for several months in early 1989. Snow subsequently teamed with Mike Kelly as the Wild Bunch, holding the tag title four times in 1991 and 1992. He wrestled with Denny Kess as the New Fabulous Kangaroos in 1994, holding the Global Tag Team Title. Snow wrestled as Shinobi, the Oriental Assassin, later in 1994. He teamed with Unibomb in Smoky Mountain Wrestling in 1995. They captured the Smoky Mountain Tag Team Title from the Rock 'n' Roll Express in April of 1995. They lost the belts to Tony Anthony and Tracey Smothers the following July. He entered the WWF as Avatar in October of 1995. He wrestled as Leaf Cassidy in the WWF from the Spring of 1996, teaming with Marty Jannetty as the New Rockers.

Snow, Mitch wrestled in the AWA in the late 1980s. He retired from wrestling to become a radio commentator in Virginia.

Snowman, The (Eddie Crawford) held the Mid-South TV Title in Louisiana in May of 1985. He wrestled in the Memphis area in 1990. He defeated Jerry Lawler for the USWA Unified Title in June of 1990. He was stripped of the title several months later when he failed to defend the belt.

Snuka, Jimmy (James Reiher; Fiji Islands; b. May 18, 1943; 6', 250 lbs.) is a Fiji native who began wrestling in Hawaii in 1969. He sometimes competed under the name Jimmy Kealoha. He teamed with Frankie Laine and Dutch Savage to hold the NWA Pacific Northwest Tag Team Title several times in the early 1970s. He also held the NWA Pacific Northwest Title several times in 1973 and 1974. He teamed with Don Leo Jonathan to hold the Canadian Tag Team Title in April of 1976. He held the World Class Texas Title in May of 1977. Known as "Superfly," he was managed by Buddy Rogers when he won the NWA U.S. Title in a tournament in September of 1979. He teamed with Paul Orndorff to win the NWA World Tag Team Title in December of 1978. They retained the belts until the following April, when he also lost the U.S. Title. He teamed with Ray Stevens to again win the tag title in June of 1980, defeating Rick Steamboat and Jay Youngblood. They held the belts until November of 1980, when Paul Jones and the Masked Superstar won the title. Snuka teamed with Terry Gordy to hold the NWA National Tag Team Title in July of 1981. Snuka was a popular wrestler in the WWF in the 1980s. He fought a lengthy feud with Rowdy Roddy Piper. Snuka teamed with Ray Stevens to win the NWA Tag Team Title from Rick Steamboat and Jay Youngblood in Greensboro, North Carolina on June 22, 1980. He teamed with J.T. Southern to briefly hold the CWA International Tag Team Title in March of 1987. Snuka wrestled on independent cards in the early 1990s, capturing the All-Star Can-Am Title in 1992. Snuka won a tournament for the ECW championship in April of 1992. He was defeated by Johnny Hot Body later in the month, but recaptured the title in July of 1992. Snuka lost the belt to Don Muraco in September of 1992.

Snyder, Wilbur (b. 1929, d. December 25, 1991) played guard for the San Francisco 49ers football team for five years in the early 1950s. He subsequently began wrestling professionally. He teamed with Ray Gunkel to hold the NWA Texas Tag Team Title in October of 1955. He held the World Title in Nebraska from November of 1958 until August of the following year. He held the NWA U.S. Title in 1959 and 1961. He teamed with Leo Nomellini to defeat Hard Boiled Haggerty and Gene Kiniski for the AWA World Tag Team Title in May of 1961. They lost the belts in a rematch in July of 1961. He teamed with Nick Bockwinkel to hold the NWA World Tag Team Title in San Francisco in late 1962 and early 1963. He held the NWA U.S. Title in San Francisco in April of 1964. He teamed with Dick the Bruiser to hold the WWA Tag Team belts several times in 1964. Snyder also held the WWA tag title with Moose Cholak in 1965, Luis Martinez in 1966, Cholak again in 1970 and Paul Christy in 1971. Snyder again held the AWA tag championship when he teamed with Pat O'Connor to defeat Harley Race and Chris Markoff in November of 1967. They lost the belts the following month to Mitsu Arakawa and Dr. Moto. Snyder retired from the ring in the early 1970s. He died of lymphatic leukemia in a Pompano Beach, Florida, hospital on December 25, 1991.

Solid Gold *see* Estrada, Jose & Julio

Solie, Gordon began his career as a wrestling announcer in 1959. He was one of the best known commentators in the wrestling world, announcing for the NWA out of Atlanta, Georgia, during the 1980s. He retired from the WCW in June of 1995.

Solis, Merced *see* Santana, Tito

Solitario, El (d. April 6, 1986) was a leading Mexican mat star from the 1960s. He captured the EMLL Light Heavyweight Title from Rey Mendoza in November of 1970, holding the title until early 1972. He remained an active competitor through the next decade. He suffered a heart attack in the ring during a wrestling bout in March of 1986 and died two weeks later on April 6, 1986.

Somers, Doug (6'3", 245 lbs.) began wrestling in 1971. Managed by Scandor Akbar, he teamed with Ron McFarlane to hold the Tri-State Tag Team Title in Oklahoma several times in 1980. Known as "Pretty Boy," he teamed with Buddy Rose to capture the AWA Tag Team Title from Curt Hennig and Scott Hall in May of 1986. They lost the belts to the Midnight Rockers in January of 1987. Somers teamed with Soldat Ustinov to defend the tag title when Boris Zhukov left the promotion. Somers and Ustinov were defeated for the belts by Jerry Lawler and Bill Dundee in October of 1987.

Song Nam, Pak (d. 1982) held the NWA Americas Title in Los Angeles in November of 1973. He held the NWA Southern Title in Florida in 1974. He also held the NWA Florida Title in March of 1976. He teamed with Eric the Red to hold the NWA Florida Tag Team Title in October of 1978. He retained the title with Ciclon Negro after Eric's death the following month. He teamed with Takachiho (The Great Kabuki), with Scandor Akbar as their manager, to hold the NWA Central States Tag Team Title in April of 1980. He also held the World Class Texas Tag Team Title in 1980, teaming with Gino Hernandez.

Sonnenberg, Gus (d. September 11, 1944) attended Dartmouth College, where he excelled in athletics. He entered professional wrestling in the late 1920s, and defeated Ed "Strangler" Lewis for the World Heavyweight Title in Boston, Massachusetts, on January 4, 1929. He relinquished the belt to Ed Don George in December of 1930. Sonnenberg defeated the Shadow for the AWA Heavyweight Title in Boston on March 16, 1939. He lost the belt to Steve Casey several weeks later on March 29, 1939. Sonnenberg died of leukemia after a long stay at the Bethesda, Maryland, Naval Hospital on September 11, 1944.

Sopt, Monty *see* Gunn, Billy

Soto, Manny teamed with Porkchop Cash to hold the NWA Americas Tag Team Title in Los Angeles in July of 1974. He also teamed with Pete Sanchez as the Flying Tigers to engage in a series of brutal matches with the Valiant Brothers in the 1970s.

Soto, Roberto held the NWA Georgia Title in 1972. Wrestling as the Avenger, he captured the British Empire Title in New Zealand in 1982. He also held the Alabama Title in September of 1985.

Soto, Tamaya teamed with Len Rossi to hold the World Tag Team Title in Tennessee in December of 1967.

Soultaker (Charles Wright) (b. 1961; 6'6", 340 lbs.) began wrestling in September of 1989. He wrestled in GWF and USWA as Soultaker, where he briefly captured the USWA Unified Title from Jerry Lawler in October of 1989. He became voodoo priest Papa Shango in the WWF in the early 1990s, and engaged in a feud with the Ultimate Warrior. He returned to the USWA as Papa Shango to capture the Unified Title in May of 1993. He wrestled as Kama, the ultimate fighting machine, in the WWF from December of 1994. He was managed by Ted DiBiase and often competed against the Undertaker.

South, George (6'2", 234 lbs.) began wrestling in 1982. He wrestled in the WCW during the 1980s. He held the PWF Tag Team Title several times in the early 1990s, teaming with the Rising Sun, Terry Austin and the Italian Stallion. South held the Pro Wrestling Federation Heavyweight Title in the Fall of 1995.

Southern, J.T. teamed with Jimmy Snuka to briefly hold the CWA International Tag Team Title in March of 1987.

Southern Boys, The *see* Smothers, Tracy & Armstrong, Steve

Southern Rockers, The *see* King, Rex & Doll, Steve

Spellbinder, The (6'4", 273 lbs.) began wrestling in 1992. He entered the USWA as Del Rios in 1994. He also wrestled in the WWF as Fantasio.

Spencer, Clay *see* Mantell, Ken

Spicolli, Louie (Louis Mucciolo; b. 1970, d. February 15, 1998; 5'10", 248 lbs.) began wrestling in 1989. He held the IWF Title in Arizona in December of 1992. He wrestled with the AAA/IWC as Madonna's Boyfriend in 1994. He entered the WWF as grunge rocker Rad Radford in 1995, teaming with Skip of the Body Donnas. He broke with Skip later in the year. He entered the WCE in early 1998, but his career was cut short several weeks later when Spicolli was found dead in his Los Angeles apartment on February 15, 1998, of an apparent lethal combination of pain medication and alcohol.

Spike *see* Jeffers, Jim

Spike, Moondog *see* Smithson, Bill

Spivey, Dan (b. October 14, 1956; 6'8", 290 lbs.) began wrestling in 1983. He wrestled as Starship Eagle, with Scott Hall, in the American Starship tag team until 1985. He subsequently wrestled as Dan Spivey in WWF, WCW, Florida and Japan. He teamed with Sid Vicious, and later Mean Mark Callous, as The Skyscrapers in WCW in the early 1990s. He also wrestled frequently with All-Japan from 1992. Spivey entered the WWF as Waylon Mercy in June of 1995. He left the promotion later in the year.

Splat, Moondog *see* Moondog Splat

Spoiler, The *see* Jardine, Don

Spoiler, The *see* Morrell, Frank

Spoiler #2, The *see* Starr, Ron

Spoilers, The *see* Jardine, Don & Sloan, Smasher

Spoilers, The *see* Jardine, Don & Wolfe, Buddy

Spot, Moondog *see* Moondog Spot

Spunky, Hillbilly *see* Hillbilly Spunky

Stafford, Millie (b. 1926; Racine, Wisconsin; 5'3", 138 lbs.) was a former telephone operator before becoming a professional wrestler in the late 1940s. She was regarded as one of the leading challenger's to Mildred Burke's championship in the 1950s.

Stamp, Dennis teamed with Bull Bullinski to hold the U.S. Tag Team Title in Louisiana in February of 1973. Stamp again held the U.S. belts, partnered with Dewey Robertson, in May of 1973. He teamed with Tiger Jeet Singh to hold the Canadian Tag Team Title in September of 1975.

Stanke, Seigfried teamed with Bob Sweetan to hold the U.S. Tag Team Title in Louisiana in March of 1974. He held the Mid-South Louisiana Tag Team Title with Kurt Von Hess in 1978. He teamed with Steve Lawler to hold the Tri-State U.S. Tag Team Title in Oklahoma in December of 1979.

Stanlee, Bob wrestled with Steve Stanlee, who was billed as his brother, in the 1950s and 1960s. They held the International Tag Team Title for a New Jersey promotion in 1952. He teamed with Moose Evans as the Mighty Yankees to hold the International Tag Team Title in February of 1966.

Stanlee, Gene (Eugene Stanley Zygowski; b. 1921; Chicago, Illinois; 6'1", 225 lbs.) was a weight-lifter, boxer and amateur wrestler in his youth. He served in the Navy during World War II, where he captured the Navy wrestling title. After the war he achieved great popularity in professional wrestling. He wrestled as Mr. America and was one of the sport's leading competitors in the late 1940s and 1950s.

Stanlee, Steve (b. 1923; Chicago, Illinois; 6', 230 lbs.) began wrestling professionally in the late 1940s. He was known for his long blonde hair, his leopard-skin tights and long velvet cape. He wrestled with his "brothers," Gene and Bob Stanlee, in the 1950s and 1960s. He and Bob Stanlee held the International Tag Team Title for a New Jersey promotion in 1952.

Stanley, Ann (b. 1924; Cincinnati, Ohio; 5'9", 155 lbs.) began wrestling in the early 1950s. She was one of the tallest female wrestlers competing in the 1950s.

Star Rider *see* Evans, Ray

Stark, Mike was the first of several wrestlers to compete as Humongous in the Memphis area in the mid-1980s. He captured the Southern Heavyweight Title in April of 1984. Stark is a football coach at a Bartlett, Tennessee, high school.

Starr, Billy, wrestling as Fatback Festus, teamed with Cousin Grizzly as the Hillbillies to hold the Georgia All-Star Tag Team championship belts in June of 1990. He subsequently teamed with Jimmy Powell as the masked Ding Dongs to recapture the title in November of 1991.

Starr, Chicky held the Southwest Junior Heavyweight Title in August of 1984. He teamed with Brett Sawyer to hold the Southwest Tag Team Title in September of 1984. He teamed with Ron Starr to hold the WWC Tag Team Title in Puerto Rico in October of 1986. He also held the WWC Junior Heavyweight Title several times in 1986. Starr was the manager of Leo Burke in the WWC in the late 1980s.

Starr, Jim teamed with Billy Garrett as the Medics to hold the NWA Florida Tag Team Title several times in 1968 and 1969. The masked duo were managed by Dr. Ken Ramey. He wrestled in the NWA in Kansas City in the early 1980s as 666.

Starr, Mark (Mark Ashford-Smith; 5'11", 235 lbs.) began wrestling in 1986. He teamed with Steve Keirn to hold the CWA International Tag Team Title in April of 1987. He teamed with Billy Travis to hold the Southern Tag Team Title in June of 1987. He teamed with his brother, Chris Champion, as Wildside in the 1980s, gaining the CWA Tag Team Title in July of 1989. Starr wrestled with Chris Canyon as Men at Work in the WCW in the mid-1990s.

Starr, Ricki teamed with Ray Gunekl to hold the NWA Texas Tag Team Title in December of 1953. He remained a leading wrestler for the next three decades. He teamed with Rip Rogers as the Convertible Blonds in the ICW in the early 1980s. They held the ICW U.S. Tag Team Title for several months in 1981.

Starr, Ron (5'11", 235 lbs.) began wrestling in 1968. He defeated Pat Barrett for the NWA World Junior Heavyweight Title on December 2, 1976. He lost the title to Nelson Royal four days later. He teamed with Tom Andrews to hold the NWA Central States Tag Team Title in July of 1978. He held the NWA World Tag Team Title in San Francisco several times in 1978, teaming with Dean Ho and Enrique Vera. He held the NWA U.S. Title in San Francisco several times in 1979 and 1980. Starr again won the title on February 11, 1980, in a tournament, but relinquished the belt to Les Thornton the following month. Wrestling as Spoiler #2 he captured the NWA Americas Title in Los Angeles in April of 1980. He teamed with Steve Bolus to hold the Western States Tag Team Title in 1982. He wrestled with Randy Rose and Norvell Austin as part of Midnight Express, Inc. in 1983 and teamed with Wayne Farris as Devastation, Inc. to hold the NWA Southeastern Tag Team Title in November of 1983. He subsequently left the promotion to wrestle in Calgary, Canada. He teamed with Wayne Farris to hold the Calgary Stampede International Tag Team Title several times in 1985 and 1986. He teamed with Chicky Starr to hold the WWC Tag Team Title in Puerto Rico in October of 1986. He teamed with the Cuban Assassin as the Mercenaries to again capture the WWC tag belts in February of 1990. He teamed with Doug Masters to hold the WWC tag title several times in 1992.

Stars & Stripes *see* Bagwell, Marcus Alexander & The Patriot

Stasiak, Stan (Buzzard Creek, Oregon; 272 lbs.) was an amateur boxer and hockey player before becoming a professional wrestler in the late 1950s. He captured the NWA Pacific Northwest Title several times in 1965 and 1966. He also held the Pacific Northwest tag belts several times from the mid-1960s, teaming with Mighty Ursus, the Mad Russian, Haru Sasaki and Tony Marino. He teamed with Dutch Savage to hold the Canadian Tag Team Title in September of 1968. He also held the Stampede North American Title in Calgary, Canada, in 1968. He was managed by the Grand Wizard in the WWWF in the early 1970s. He was known for his rulebreaking tactics and crippling heart punch. He held the World Class Texas Title in June of 1972. He defeated Pedro Morales for the WWWF Title in Philadelphia on December 1, 1973. He lost the belt to Bruno Sammartino in a match the following week in New York on December 10, 1973. He teamed with Dutch Savage to hold the Canadian Tag Team Title in December of 1979. He teamed with Billy Jack Haynes to reclaim the NWA Pacific Northwest tag belts several times in 1983.

Steamboat, Rick (Richard Blood; b. February 28, 1953; Honolulu, Hawaii; 6'1", 238 lbs.) was born in Hawaii. His family moved to Florida in the late 1950s and Steamboat engaged in amateur wrestling. He studied under Verne Gagne before turning pro on February 15, 1976, in Minneapolis. He held the NWA U.S. Title in 1977, and teamed with Paul Jones to win the NWA tag championship in a tournament in April of 1978. The duo held the belts for several months. He again held the U.S. Title after defeating Ric Flair for the belt in December of 1978. He lost the belt back to Flair in April of 1979. Steamboat teamed with Jay Youngblood to capture the NWA World Tag Team Title from Baron Von Raschke and Paul Jones in October of 1979. They were defeated for the belts in April of 1980 by Ray Stevens and Greg Valentine. They recaptured the belts the following month on May 10, 1980, but lost them to Stevens and Jimmy Snuka in Greensboro, North Carolina, on June 22, 1980. He and Youngblood again captured the belts in a match against Sergeant Slaughter and Don Kernodle in March of 1983, losing them to Jack and Jerry Brisco the following June. They recaptured the belts from the Briscos in October of 1983, losing them in a rematch the following month. They again defeated the Briscos for the title in November of 1983. Steamboat relinquished the belts in late December of 1983 when he announced his retirement. He emerged from retirement and captured the NWA U.S. Title from Dick Slater in April of 1984. He relinquished the belt to Wahoo McDaniel in June of 1984, and entered the WWF in the Spring of 1985, adopting the name "the Dragon." He defeated Randy Savage for the Intercontinental Title at Wrestlemania III on March 29, 1987. He lost the title on June 2, 1987, to the Honky Tonk Man. He retired from the ring for several years. He returned to the WCW and defeated Ric Flair for the WCW World Title at the Chi-Town Rumble on February 20, 1989. He lost the belt to Flair in Nashville, Tennessee, at Wrestle War '89 on May 7, 1989. He left the WCW in July of 1989 and joined the newly formed North American Wrestling Association the following year. Steamboat reentered the WCW in March of 1991. He teamed with Dustin Rhodes to win the WCW Tag Team Title from Arn Anderson and Larry Zbyszko in November of 1991. They were defeated for the belts by Anderson and Bobby Eaton in January of 1992. He defeated Steve Austin for the WCW TV Title on September 2, 1992, though he lost the belt later in the month. Steamboat again shared the Tag Team Championship when he and Shane Douglas defeated Barry Windham and Dustin Rhodes on November 18, 1992. They were defeated for the title by Brian Pillman and Steve Austin in March of 1993. He again held the TV Title from August of 1993, until his defeat by Lord Steven Regal the following month. He teamed with Tom Zenk as Dos Hombres in the WCW in 1993. Steamboat captured the WCW U.S. Title from Steve Austin of August 24, 1994. He was forced to return to belt to Austin the following month when he was unable to defend the title. Steamboat subsequently retired from pro wrestling.

Steamboat, Sam teamed with Billy Varga to hold the Hawaiian Tag Team Title in August of 1956. He captured the Hawaiian Title in January of 1961. He teamed with Dick Hutton to hold the NWA Texas Tag Team Title in September of 1961. He teamed with Eddie Graham to hold the NWA World Tag

Team Title in Florida several times in 1964. He and Graham also held the World Tag Team Title in Tennessee in 1965. He also briefly held the tag belts with Ron Etchison in October of 1965 and with Jose Lothario in November of 1966. He teamed with Ciclon Negro to hold the NWA Florida Tag Team Title in September of 1969. He again held the Hawaiian Title in July of 1970. He teamed with Bearcat Wright to hold the Hawaiian tag belts in July of 1971. He held the North American Title in Honolulu several times in the early 1970s.

Steamboat, Vic (Honolulu, Hawaii; 6'1", 243 lbs.) began wrestling in December of 1986. He teamed with Joe Savoldi to hold the ICW tag title several times in the late 1980s. He also wrestled in the WCW and the CWA, where he held the title in 1993. He held the CWA Tag Title with Ray Odyssey in 1994. He is the younger brother of Rick Steamboat.

Stecher, Joe (b. April 5, 1896, d. March 29, 1974) was born in Dodge, Nebraska. He held the World Heavyweight Title from July of 1915 until losing the belt to Earl Caddock in Omaha, Nebraska, on April 9, 1917. Stecher again held the belt in 1920, until his defeat by Ed "Strangler" Lewis in December of 1920. He was again recognized as champion from May of 1925 until he lost the belt to Lewis in February of 1928. Stecher also defeated Ivan Padoubny for the Russian Graeco Roman championship in February of 1926.

Steele, Austin (6', 233 lbs.) began wrestling in 1991. Known as "Nature Boy," he teamed with Terry Austin to capture the PWF tag team belts in 1994.

Steele, George "the Animal" (Jim Meyers; Detroit, Michigan; 6'2", 280 lbs.) began wrestling in 1965. He was known for his maniacal ring antics and unpredictable behavior. He engaged in a series of brutal matches with WWF champion Bruno Sammartino in the late 1960. He was managed by Lou Albano when he returned to the WWF in the 1970s, where he continued to brutalize many wrestlers, including title holder Pedro Morales. He was unable to capture the title, so he again left the area. He again returned to the WWF in the mid-1980s, where he still displayed his maniacal ring persona, but soon became a fan favorite under the management of Captain Lou Albano. He engaged in feuds with such wrestlers as Nikolai Volkoff and Randy Savage. He retired from the ring in the late 1980s. Steele played wrestler Tor Johnson in the 1994 Tim Burton film *Ed Wood*. His son, Butch Meyers, also wrestled in the WWF.

Steele, Jack (b. 1920; East Orange, New Jersey; 6', 230 lbs.) served in the Navy during World War II. He began wrestling professionally in the late 1940s and remained a leading mat star through the 1950s.

Steele, Preston (6'2, 233 lbs.) began wrestling in 1987. He was trained by Domenic DeNucci and was the IWA U.S. champion in 1990.

Steele, T.D. (5'9", 210 lbs.) began wrestling in 1986. He often wrestled and refereed in the USWA through the mid-1990s.

Steele, Tom (b. 1920; Denver, Colorado; 5'11", 218 lbs.) attended the University of Southern California and served in the army during World War II. He entered professional wrestling after the war and remained a top competitor through the 1950s.

Stein, Abe (b. 1915; New York City; 5'9", 212 lbs.) began wrestling in the early 1930s. He appeared in several films in the 1940s and was Jimmy Cagney's coach for the film *Blood on the Sun* (1945). Stein also served as a bodyguard for Frank Sinatra and was Al Jolson's physical instructor. He remained a leading mat star through the 1950s.

Steinborn, Dick (b. 1932) was the son of wrestler Milo Steinborn. He began wrestling professionally in the early 1950s, sometimes known as Red Steinborn. He held the NWA Texas Title in July of 1958. He teamed with George Becker to hold the NWA Southern Tag Team Title in 1958. Wrestling as Dick Gunkel, he held the NWA Southern Title several times in 1959. Steinborn teamed with Doug Gilbert as Mr. High and Mr. Low to defeat Art and Stan Neilson for the AWA Tag Team Title in December of 1962. They lost the belts to Ivan and Karol Kalmikoff in January of 1963. He teamed with Hiro Matsuda to hold the NWA World Tag Team Title in Florida in November of 1965. He broke with Matsuda the following

month, then left the area. Steinborn, wrestling as Eric Von Brauner, teamed with Karl Von Brauner for several years in the mid-1960s, often competing in the Tennessee area. teamed with Bob Armstrong to hold the NWA Georgia Tag Team Title in August of 1972. He recaptured the title with Argentina Apollo in October of 1972. He left the promotion the following month to wrestle with Ann Gunkel's All South Championship Wrestling. He wrestled as the White Knight, teaming with Mark Lewin, to hold the World Class Texas Tag Team Title in October of 1978. He held the U.S. Junior Heavyweight Title in Alabama and the WWC Caribbean Title in Puerto Rico in 1980.

Steinborn, Milo (Milo Steinbeck; b. 1894, d. February 9, 1989) was a leading wrestling strongman during the 1920s and 1930s. He was also a manager and promoter, and operated several gyms through the 1970s. His son, Dick Steinborn, was also a professional wrestler. He died at his home in Orlando, Florida, on February 9, 1989.

Steiner, Hans *see* Dante

Steiner, Karl *see* Dellassera, Bob

Steiner, Rick (Robert Rechsteiner; b. March 9, 1961; Detroit, Michigan; 5'11", 248 lbs.) attended the University of Michigan. He was trained by Brad Rheingans and made his professional debut in 1983. He teamed with Sting in several matches in 1987, holding the UWF Tag Team Title in Oklahoma in April of 1987. He subsequently joined Kevin Sullivan's Varsity Club in the NWA. He teamed with Michael Rotundo and became known as the Dogfaced Gremlin. He subsequently broke with the Varsity Club and feuded with Rotundo and Sullivan. He defeated his former partner for the NWA TV Title in December of 1988. He lost the belt back to Rotundo in February of 1989. Steiner teamed with Eddie Gilbert as a member of the First Family before his brother, Scott, entered the WCW in April of 1989. The Steiner brothers defeated Jim Garvin and Michael Hayes for the WCW Tag Team Title on November 1, 1989. They lost the belts to Doom on May 19, 1990. They took the NWA's U.S. belts from the Midnight Express on August 24, 1990, and reclaimed the WCW Tag Title from the Freebirds on February 18, 1991. The Steiners were stripped of the belts in mid-July when Scott was temporarily side-lined by a shoulder injury. The team returned to defeat Arn Anderson and Bobby Eaton for the WCW tag belts on May 3, 1992. They lost the belts to Steve William and Terry Gordy in Atlanta, Georgia, on July 5, 1992, and left the promotion shortly thereafter. They debuted in the WWF in December of 1992 and defeated Ted DiBiase and Irwin R. Schyster for the WWF Tag Title on June 14, 1993. They lost the belts to Money, Inc., in Rockford, Illinois, on June 16, 1993, but again regained the title in St. Louis, Missouri, on June 19, 1993. Their title reign was ended by the Quebecers in September of 1993. The Steiners also competed in Japan and the ECW before returning to the WCW in 1996.

Steiner, Scott (Scott Rechsteiner; b. July 29, 1962; Bay City, Michigan; 6'1", 235 lbs.) attended the University of Michigan. He began wrestling professionally in 1986. He wrestled in the WWA and the CWA, often teaming with Dr. Jerry Graham, Jr. and Jed Grundy. He held the WWA championship from August of 1986 until May of 1987. He subsequently held the WWA Tag Team Title with Jerry Graham, Jr. in late 1987. He held the CWA Tag Team Title with Billy Travis in May and June of 1988. He again held the CWA tag belts in February of 1989, teaming with Jed Grundy. He joined his brother, Rick, in the NWA in April of 1989. The Steiner brothers defeated Jim Garvin and Michael Hayes for the NWA Tag Team Title on November 1, 1989. They lost the belts to Doom on May 19, 1990. They took the NWA's U.S. belts from the Midnight Express on August 24, 1990, and reclaimed the NWA Tag Title from the Freebirds on February 18, 1991. The Steiners were stripped of the belts in mid-July when Scott was temporarily side-lined by a shoulder injury. Scott returned to action in October of 1991 and the Steiners defeated Arn Anderson and Bobby Eaton for the WCW tag belts on May 3, 1992. They lost the belts to Steve Williams and Terry Gordy in Atlanta, Georgia, on July 5, 1992. Scott won the WCW TV Title in September of 1992. He left the promotion the following November. The Steiners debuted in the WWF in December of 1992 and defeated Ted DiBiase and Irwin R. Schyster for the WWF Tag Title on June 14,

1993, they lost the belts to Money, Inc. in Rockford, Illinois, on June 16, 1993, but again regained the title in St. Louis, Missouri, on June 19, 1993. They were defeated for the belts by the Quebecers in September of 1993. The Steiners also competed in Japan and the ECW before returning to the WCW in 1996.

Steinke, Hans (b. 1893, d. June 26, 1971; Chicago, Illinois; 6'3", 250 lbs.) was a native of Germany. He emigrated to the United States at an early age. He began wrestling in the late 1920s. He was recognized as the World Heavyweight Champion by the New York State Athletic Commission in 1928. He appeared as a beastman in the 1933 horror films *The Island of Lost Souls*. His other film credits include *Deception* (1933), *People Will Talk* (1935), *Once in a Blue Moon* (1936) and *The Buccaneer* (1938). Steinke died of lung cancer in Chicago, Illinois, on June 26, 1971.

Steinke, Seigfried held the Pacific Coast Title in Vancouver, Canada, in May of 1975. He also held the Canadian Tag Team Title several times in 1975 and 1976, teaming with Dale Lewis and Gene Kiniski. He held the World Class Texas Title several times in 1976.

Stern, Ray teamed with Ronnie Etchison to hold the NWA World Tag Team Title in San Francisco in October of 1955.

Stetson, Tony (Philadelphia, Pennsylvania; 5'10", 238 lbs.) teamed with Larry Winters to win the ECW Tag Team Title on April 2, 1993. They lost the belts to Johnny Hot Body and Chris Candido the following day. Stetson teamed with Hot Body to hold the tag title in October of 1993, but lost the belts the following month.

Stevens, Clyde (b. 1920; Somerville, Massachusetts; 6'2", 230 lbs.) served in the U.S. Navy, where he was the Pacific Fleet boxing champion. He was brought into professional wrestling by Jim Londos in the late 1940s, and made a leading mat star for the next several decades. Stevens wrestled as the Golden Terror when he teamed with Dick "the Destroyer" Beyer to hold the World Class World Tag Team Title in Texas in February of 1966.

Stevens, Don *see* Fargo, Don

Stevens, Ray "the Crippler" (b. 1936, d. May 3, 1996; San Francisco, California; 6'1", 248 lbs.) began wrestling in 1949. He held the Southern Junior Heavyweight Title in late 1957. Wrestling as Ray Shires, he teamed with Roy Shire to hold the NWA Tag Team Title in Indiana several times in the late 1950s. He held the NWA U.S. Title in San Francisco nearly a dozen times between 1960 and 1970. He also held the NWA World Tag Team Title in San Francisco several times from 1964 through 1969, teaming with Dan Manoukian, Pat Patterson, Pepper Gomez and Peter Maivia. He also held the U.S. Title in Honolulu in May of 1968. He teamed with Nick Bockwinkel to defeat Red Bastien and Crusher for the AWA Tag Team Title in January of 1972. They lost the belts to Verne Gagne and Billy Robinson in December of 1972, but reclaimed them the following month on January 6, 1973, with Bobby Heenan as their manager. They remained the champions for the next year and a half, before losing the title to Robinson and Crusher in July of 1974. They came back to reclaim the title in October of 1974. Their title reign came to an end in August of 1975, when they were defeated by Crusher and Dick the Bruiser. Stevens and Pat Patterson were awarded the AWA Tag Title in September of 1978. They retained the belts until their defeat by Verne Gagne and Mad Dog Vachon in June of 1979. He also held the NWA Eastern States Title briefly in 1979. He teamed with Mike Graham to hold the NWA Florida Tag Team Title in October of 1979. He won the NWA Tag Team championship with Greg Valentine from Rick Steamboat and Jay Youngblood in April of 1980. They held the belts for a month before losing the title in a rematch with Steamboat and Youngblood. Stevens teamed with Jimmy Snuka to recapture the belts in Greensboro, North Carolina, on June 22, 1980. They held the title until November of 1980, when they were defeated by Paul Jones and the Masked Superstar. Stevens returned to the championship, teaming with Ivan Koloff, in February of 1981. Jones and the Masked Superstar recaptured the title the following month. Stevens died of heart failure in San Francisco on May 3, 1996.

Stevens, Rock (6'4", 270 lbs.) was trained by Brad Rheingans and began wrestling in 1991. Known as the Punisher, he captured the Border City Wrestling Can-Am Title from Mickey Doyle in July of 1993.

Stevens, Shawn *see* Mussolini, Vito

Stevie Ray (Lane Huffman; b. August 22, 1958; Harlem, New York; 6'1", 244 lbs.) began wrestling in 1989. He wrestled with his brother, Booker T, as the Ebony Experience in Global in 1992. They held the Global World Tag Team Title in July of 1992. The duo entered WCW as Kane and Kole in Harlem Heat in July of 1993. They were managed by Sherri Martell and captured the WCW Tag Team Championship from Marcus Alexander Bagwell and the Patriot on December 8, 1994. They were defeated by the Nasty Boys for the title at Slamboree '95 in St. Petersburg, Florida, on May 21, 1995. They held the WCW tag belts several more times in 1995, defeating the Stud Stable and the American Males.

Stewart, Bobby *see* Golden Terror, The

Stewart, Jonnie (6'2", 242 lbs.) began wrestling in 1986. He is a former football player at Memphis State and UCLA. He was known as the Illustrious One in the AWA in the early 1990s.

Stewart, Nell (b. 1928; Birmingham, Alabama; 5'4", 140 lbs.) began wrestling in the early 1950s. She was known as the Alabama Assassin, and held the Texas Women's Title in 1952.

Sting (Steve Borden; b. March 20, 1959; Venice Beach, California; 6'2", 260) began wrestling in 1985. Wrestling as Steve "Flash" Borden, he teamed with Jim "the Ultimate Warrior" Hellwig as the Freedom Fighters in the Memphis area in 1985. He continued to team with Hellwig as the Blade Runners, Flash and Rock. He entered the UWF as Sting in 1986. He teamed with Eddie Gilbert to hold the UWF Tag Team Title in Oklahoma in July of 1986. He also held the UWF tag belts with Rick Steier in April of 1987. Sting defeated Ric Flair for the NWA Heavyweight Title in Baltimore, Maryland, on July 8, 1990. He lost the belt back to Flair on January 11, 1991, in East Rutherford, New Jersey. He won the NWA U.S. Title in a tournament on August 25, 1991, losing the belt to Rick Rude on November 19, 1991. He defeated Lex Luger of the WCW Heavyweight Title in Milwaukee, Wisconsin, on February 29, 1992. He lost the title to Big Van Vader in Atlanta, Georgia, on July 12, 1992. Sting recaptured the title from Vader in London, England, on March 11, 1993. He was again defeated by Vader for the title in Dublin, Ireland, the following week on March 17, 1993. Sting defeated Rick Rude for the WCW International Title in Japan on April 17, 1994. Sting lost that belt to Ric Flair in a unification bout at the Clash of Champions on June 23, 1994. He captured the WCW U.S. Heavyweight Title in a tournament on June 18, 1995. He was defeated for the belt by Kensuke Sasaki in Tokyo, Japan, on November 13, 1995. He and Lex Luger teamed to capture the WCW Tag Team Title in early 1996.

Stomper, The *see* Mongolian Stomper, The

Storm, Devon (Chris Ford; Rutherford, New Jersey; 6'3", 241 lbs.) began wrestling in March of 1993. He wrestled in the WCW in 1995.

Storm, J.W. (Jeff Warner; 6'3 1/2", 267 lbs.) began wrestling in 1988. He teamed with Tim Hunt as Maximum Overdrive to capture the PWA Tag Team Title in June of 1989. Wrestling as Big Juice Jeff Warner he teamed with Art "Beetlejuice" Barr as the Juice Patrol to hold the NWA Pacific Northwest Tag Team Title several times in early 1990. Storm lost a loser leave town match in Portland, Oregon, in June of 1990 and left the Pacific Northwest.

Storm, Lance (Lance Evers; Memphis, Tennessee; 231 lbs.) held the Canadian Rocky Mountain Wrestling Mid-Heavyweight Title in Calgary several times in 1992 and 1993. Storm captured the Catch Wrestling Association Junior Heavyweight Title in Europe in 1993. He wrestled with Chris Jericho as the Thrillseekers in Smoky Mountain Wrestling in 1994. He briefly held the TV Title in August of 1994.

Stratten, Todd *see* Morton, Todd

Strattus, G.Q. (6'3", 260 lbs.) began wrestling in 1988. He wrestled with Mike Sampson in the IWCCW, and they claimed the tag championship several times in 1990 and 1991. They often feuded with the Madison Brothers. He held the SSW Title in Tennessee for several months in early 1993.

Street, Adrian (b. December 5,

1941; Royal Forest of Dean, England; 5'7", 236 lbs.) began wrestling in 1961. A native of South Wales he was accompanied to the ring by his valet, Miss Linda. He held the NWA Americas Title in Los Angeles in March of 1982. He teamed with Timothy Flowers to hold the NWA Americas Tag Team Title in May of 1982. He briefly held the NWA Florida Title in April of 1983. He held the Mid-South TV Title in Louisiana in September of 1984. He held the NWA Southeastern Title several times from 1985 through 1987. Street held the PWI North American Title in Mississippi briefly in October of 1992. Street and Miss Linda appeared in the 1985 film *Grunt! The Wrestling Movie.*

Strike Force *see* Martel, Rick & Santana, Tito

Strimple, Shirley (b. 1929, d. 1989; Joplin, Missouri; 5'4", 130 lbs.) was a circus performer before she entered professional wrestling in the early 1950s. She was a top female grappler throughout the decade.

Strode, Woody (Woodrow Wilson Strode; b. 1913, d. December 31, 1994; California) was a football and track star at UCLA. He played professional football with the Canadian Football League before becoming a wrestling in the late 1930s. He was one of the best known black wrestlers in the 1940s, and was known in the ring as Goliath. He was also a popular character actor from the early 1940s, appearing in such films as *Sundown* (1941), *Star Spangled Rhythm* (1942), *The Lion Hunters* (1951), *Bride of the Gorilla* (1951), *Caribbean* (1952), *Bomba and the African Treasure* (1952), *City Beneath the Sea* (1953), *Demetrius and the Gladiators* (1954), *The Gambler from Natchez* (1954), *Jungle Gents* (1954) with the Bowery Boys, *Son of Sinbad* (1955), *The Ten Commandments* (1956), *Tarzan's Fight for Life* (1958), *The Buccaneer* (1958), *Pork Chop Hill* (1959) and *The Last Voyage* (1960). In 1960 Strode appeared in two of his best known roles, starring as the soldier on trial for rape and murder in *Sergeant Rutledge*, and the gladiator who befriends Kirk Douglas in *Spartacus*. He continued to appear in such films as *Two Rode Together* (1961), *The Sins of Rachel Cade* (1961), *The Man Who Shot Liberty Valance* (1962) with John Wayne, *Tarzan's Three Challenges* (1963), *Genghis Khan* (1965), *The Professionals* (1966) and *Seven Women* (1966). He became a popular star on the European screen following his performance in 1968's *Black Jesus*, and appeared in several other European films including *Once Upon a Time in the West* (1968), *Boot Hill* (1969), *Chuck Moll* (1970), *The Deserter* (1971), *The Last Rebel* (1971), *The Italian Connection* (1972), *Keoma* (1976) and *The Final Executioner* (1983). His other film credits include *Shalako* (1968), *Tarzan's Deadly Silence* (1970), *Winterhawk* (1975), *Loaded Guns* (1976), *Kingdom of the Spiders* (1977), *Ravagers* (1979), *Jaguar Lives!* (1979), *Key West Crossing* (1979), *Scream* (1979), *Vigilante* (1982), *The Black Stallion Returns* (1983), *Violent Breed* (1983), *Jungle Warriors* (1984), *The Cotton Club* (1984), *Lust in the Dust* (1985), *Storyville* (1992) and *Posse* (1993). He was also active on television, appearing in episodes of *Soldiers of Fortune, Thriller, Man from Blackhawk, Rawhide, The Lieutenant, The Farmer's Daughter, Tarzan, Batman, Daniel Boone, Buck Rogers in the 25th Century* and *Fantasy Island*. His final film performance was in the 1995 Western *The Quick and the Dead* with Sharon Stone. Strode died of lung cancer in Glendora, California, on December 31, 1994.

Strong, Billy *see* Long, Johnny

Strong, Billy Jack *see* DiSalvo, Steve

Strong, Steve *see* DiSalvo, Steve

Strongbow, Chief Jay (Joe Scarpa; Pawhuska, Oklahoma; 6'6", 325 lbs.) began his wrestling career under the guidance of Don Eagle in Los Angeles in the late 1940s. He served as Gorgeous George's campaign manager during the wrestler's presidential campaign in 1952. He wrestled in Memphis in the late 1950s and early 1960s. Wrestling as Joe Scarpa, he teamed with Lester Welch to hold the World Tag Team Title in Tennessee several times in 1961. He teamed with Jose Lothario to hold the NWA Southern Tag Team Title in Florida several times in 1968. He held the NWA Georgia Title in 1969. He teamed with Sonny King to capture the WWWF Tag Team Title from Baron Scicluna and King Curtis in May of 1972. They lost the belts the following month to Mr. Fuji and Toru Tanaka. Strongbow was again Tag Team Champion when he teamed with Billy White Wolf to win a tournament in December of 1976. They

vacated the title in August of 1977 when White Wolf was injured. He teamed with Jules Strongbow to regain the tag belts in a match against Mr. Fuji and Mr. Saito in June of 1982. They lost the belts in a rematch the following month, but recaptured them in October of 1982. Their title reign was ended by the Samoans in March of 1983.

Strongbow, Jay, Jr. (5'11", 233 lbs.) began wrestling in 1984. He wrestled as the son of Chief Jay Strongbow, and was active in the Pacific Coast area. He held the CPW Title in California for several months from December of 1988. He also wrestled as Don Giovanni.

Strongbow, Jules (Frank Hill; Shawno, Wisconsin; 6'3", 240 lbs.) began wrestling as Chief Frank Hill in 1974. He teamed with Terry Orndorff to hold the Tri-State Tag Team Title in Oklahoma in 1981. He teamed with his "brother," Chief Jay Strongbow, to capture the WWF Tag Team Title in a match against Mr. Fuji and Mr. Saito in June of 1982. They lost the belts in a rematch the following month, but recaptured them in October of 1982. Their title reign was ended by the Samoans in March of 1983. He wrestled in the IWA in the early 1990s as the Ghost Dancer.

Stubbs, Jerry (Pensacola, Florida; 235 lbs.) held the Mid-South Louisiana Title in December of 1978. Wrestling as the Matador, teamed with Dutch Mantell to hold the NWA Southeastern Tag Team Title in 1980. He also wrestled as the Olympian and Mr. Olympia, and held the NWA Southeastern Title several times in the early 1980s. He teamed with Junkyard Dog to hold the MSWA Tag Team Title in May of 1982. He held the MSWA tag belts again in April of 1983, teaming with Ted DiBiase. He teamed Arn Anderson, under the management of Sonny King, to hold the Southeastern Tag belts several times in 1984. He also held the Alabama Title several times in he early 1980s.

Stud Stable, The *see* Golden, Jimmy "Bunkhouse Buck" & Slater, Dick

Studd, Big John (John Minton; d. March 20, 1995; Los Angeles, California; 6'7", 364 lbs.) was trained by Charlie Moto and Killer Kowalski in 1972. He wrestled in various promotions under such names as Mighty Minton, Chuck O'Connor and the Big Machine before becoming Big John Studd in 1977. Wrestling as Chuck O'Connor, he teamed with Ox Baker to hold the WWA Tag Team Title for several months in early 1976. Studd wrestled with Kowalski as the Mad Executioners in the WWWF. Under the management of Lou Albano, they captured the Tag Team Title from Tony Parisi and Louis Cerdan in May of 1976. They were stripped of the title in October of 1976, and lost the belts to Chief Jay Strongbow and Billy White Wolf in a tournament the following December. Wrestling as Captain USA, Studd held the World Class Championship in Texas in July of 1977. He teamed with Bull Ramos to hold the World Class Texas Tag Team Title in 1977. He teamed with Ric Flair to hold the NWA Atlantic Coast Tag Title in 1978, and captured the belts again the following year partnered with Ken Patera. Studd wrestled in Texas in the late 1970s, where he was managed by Gary Hart. He teamed with Bill Eadie as the Masked Superstars to again hold the NWA Atlantic Coast Tag Title in 1980. He held the NWA Canadian Title in Toronto in September of 1981. He also held the NWA National Tag Team Title with the Super Destroyer from March until July of 1982. He subsequently wrestled in Florida, where he was managed by James J. Dillon. He was managed by Buddy Rogers in the Carolinas before entering the WWF in 1983, where he feuded with Andre the Giant. He wrestled with the Bobby Heenan family when he returned to the WWF. He won the Royal Rumble in Houston on January 15, 1989, outlasting 30 other wrestlers. He also appeared in several films including *Micki and Maude* (1984) with Dudley Moore, *Caged in Paradise* (1990) and *Harley Davidson and the Marlboro Man* (1991), and was featured in an episode of television's *Beauty and the Beast*. Studd died of Hodgkin's Disease on March 20, 1995.

Studd, Scott *see* Riggz, Scotty

Styles, Carl (6'3", 275 lbs.) began wrestling in 1985. Held the NWA Pacific Northwest Title several times in 1989. He has also wrestled in the USWA, sometimes under the name Dr. D.

Sullivan, Dave (Bill Dannenhauser; b. December 1, 1963; Boston, Massachusetts; 6'3", 250 lbs.) began wrestling in 1990. He wrestled as the Equalizer under war

paint in the Pacific Northwest territory. He teamed with Len "the
Grappler" Denton as the wrecking
crew to hold the NWA Pacific
Northwest Tag Team Title in December of 1990. He entered the
WCW in 1993 and wrestled as the
"brother" of Kevin Sullivan in the
WCW from 1994. He competed as
an ally of Hulk Hogan, and feuded
with Kevin Sullivan and Diamond
Dallas Page.

Sullivan, Eddie teamed with
Frank Morrell as the Mighty Yan-
kees to hold the World Tag Team
Title in Tennessee in July of 1968.
They also held Southern Tag Team
Title several times in 1969. He
teamed with Rip Tyler to hold the
U.S. Tag Team Title in Oklahoma in
1973.

Sullivan, Kevin (b. October 26,
1949; Boston, Massachusetts; 5'10",
252 lbs.) began wrestling in 1970.
He wrestled as Kevin Caldwell in the
South early in his career. He teamed
with Len Rossi to hold the Southern
Tag Team Title in 1972. He teamed
with Mike Graham to hold the
NWA Florida Tag Team Title several
times in 1973. He teamed with Ken
Lucas to hold the NWA Central
States Tag Team Title in April of
1978. They also briefly held the
NWA Southeastern Tag Team Title
in December of 1978. Sullivan
teamed with Tony Atlas to capture
the NWA Georgia Tag Team Title
in April of 1980. He also held the
NWA TV Title in November of
1980. Sullivan captured the NWA
Southern Title in Florida in November of 1982. He again held the
Florida title briefly in September of

1984. He wrestled and managed primarily in the NWA/WCW in the
1980s and 1990s. He managed the
Varsity Club, consisting of Mike
Rotunda, Rick Steiner and Steve
Williams. Sullivan and Williams
teamed to win the NWA U.S. Title
in December of 1988. They lost the
title to Eddie Gilbert and former
Varsity Clubber Rick Steiner in February of 1989. Sullivan led Rotunda
and Williams to the WCW tag
championship in April of 1989. In
December of 1993 Sullivan teamed
with the Tazmaniac to capture the
ECW Tag Team Title They held the
belts until March of 1994, when they
were defeated by Public Enemy. Sullivan teamed with Cactus Jack to
win the WCW Tag Team Title from
the Nasty Boys in Philadelphia on
May 22, 1994. They lost the belts to
Paul Roma and Paul Orndorff on
July 17, 1994. In 1995 Sullivan became known as the Taskmaster. As
leader of the Dungeon of Doom, he
waged a campaign against Hulk
Hogan and Randy Savage in the
mid-1990s.

Sullivan, Nancy *see* Woman

Sullivan, Patrick, 2nd (b.
1957, d. September 15, 1992) was
born in Charlestown, Massachusetts. He began wrestling professionally in the New England area in
the 1980s, where he was often
known as Irish Pat. He also frequently competed in exhibition
bouts in charity matches. Sullivan
died suddenly while returning to his
Charlestown home from work in
Chelsea, Massachusetts, on September 15, 1992.

Summers, Scott (6'1", 250 lbs.) began wrestling in 1990. Known as "Hot Body," he teamed with Johnny Paradise to form the Hot Paradise tag team. They held the Motor City Wrestling Midwest Tag Team belts in June of 1994.

Sun, Choi held the NWA Americas Title in Los Angeles in September of 1977.

Sunni War Cloud, Chief *see* Chorre, Sonny

Sunny *see* Fytch, Tammy

Sunshine (Valerie French) was Jimmy Garvin's valet in the World Class promotion in Texas in 1983. She turned on Garvin when she was replaced by Precious while Garvin held the World Class Title. She joined with Chris Adams and assisted him in his battles with Garvin through 1984.

Super Black Ninja *see* Muta, The Great

Super Destroyers, The *see* Irwin, Scott & Irwin, Bill

Super Infernos, The *see* Gilbert, Doug & Smith, Don

Super Mario (5', 400 lbs.) began wrestling in 1992. He was active in PWF in Florida and the USWA in Memphis. He also owns and operates a pizza parlor in Princeton, West Virginia.

Super Maxx (Sam Darrow) began wrestling in 1984. He wrestled with Mad Maxx as the World Warriors in the AWA. The duo was managed by Saul Creachman and Miss Maxine and held the WWA Tag Team Title in 1984. They also held the Pacific Tag Team Title in Honolulu several times in 1986.

Super Medics, The *see* Estrada, Jose & Julio

Super Ninja *see* Takano, Shunji

Super Swedish Angel, The *see* Johnson, Tor

Super Zodiac *see* Young, Gary

Superstar *see* Cook, Bob

Suzuki, Cutie (b. 1969; 5', 125 lbs.) made her wrestling debut in 1986. She was a leading Japanese mat star with All-Japan through the 1990s.

Swedish Angel, The *see* Johnson, Tor

Swedish Angel, The *see* Olafsson, Phil

Sweet Brown Sugar *see* Young, Skip

Sweet William *see* Bushwhacker Luke Williams

Sweetan, Bob (b. 1943; New Orleans, Louisiana; 6', 272 lbs.) began wrestling in 1966 in the Kansas City area. He was a leading mat villain for the next two decades, battling such mat stars Ron Starr, Ray Stevens and Dory Funk, Jr. Wrestling as K.O. Cox, he held the NWA Central States Tag Team Title with Dick Murdoch several times in 1969. He teamed with Seigfried Stanke to hold the U.S. Tag Team Title in Louisiana in March of 1974. He teamed with Killer Karl Kox to hold the U.S. Tag Team Title in Louisiana for several months from

May of 1976. He again held the tag belts with Tony Rocco in March of 1977. He held the NWA Central States Title in 1977. He teamed with Alexis Smirnoff to again capture the NWA Central States tag belts in April of 1978. He again held the belts in October of 1978, teaming with Bob Brown. He held the NWA U.S. Title in San Francisco several times in 1979 and 1980. Sweetan reclaimed the Central States tag belts in October of 1980, teaming with Mike George. He and Terry Gibbs also held the title in June of 1981.

Swenski, John began wrestling in the late 1920s. He remained active in the ring through the early 1950s.

Sword, Jeff teamed with Doug Vines as the Devil's Duo to hold the ICW U.S. Tag Team Title from April until June of 1981. They were managed by Izzy Slapowitz. They wrestled as the Barroom Brawlers in the USWA in the early 1990s. They captured the USWA Tag Team Title several times during 1991.

Sytch, Tamara *see* Fytch, Tammy

Szabo, Sandor (Peter Sandor; b. 1906, d. October 13, 1966; Monterey, California; 6'1", 225 lbs.) was born in Budapest, Hungary. He was an Olympic wrestling champion in the 1928 games. He made his professional debut in 1933 in a match against Dick Shikat. He held the Pacific Coast Title in San Francisco several times in the late 1930s, competing against Billy Hanson, Cy Williams and Bill Longson. He defeated Bronko Nagurski for the NWA World Heavyweight Title in St. Louis, Missouri, on June 5, 1941.

He retained the title until February 19, 1942, when he lost a match to Bill Longson in St. Louis. He held the AWA Title in Montreal, Canada, in March of 1944. Szabo defeated Steve Casey for the AWA Heavyweight Title on April 25, 1945, holding the belt until his defeat by Frank Sexton a month later on May 21, 1945. He again held the AWA belt in 1948 between two title reigns by Sexton. He also held the Pacific Coast Title several more times from the mid 1940s through 1951. He held the NWA World Tag Team Title in San Francisco in 1950, teaming with Primo Carnera. He teamed with Ron Etchison to hold the Pacific Coast Tag Team Title in late 1951.

Szatkowski, Rob *see* Van Dam, Rob

Szopinski, Terry *see* Warlord

T, Booker *see* T, Booker

T, Mr. (Lawrence Tero; b. May 21, 1952) was an amateur wrestler and football player before he gained fame portraying boxer Clubber Lang in the 1982 film *Rocky III* with Sylvester Stallone. Mr. T subsequently starred as B.A. Baracus in the television series *The A-Team* in the 1980s. He entered the world of professional wrestling in 1985, teaming with Hulk Hogan in a match against Paul Orndorff and Roddy Piper at Wrestlemania I on March 31, 1985. He subsequently made occasional forays in the ring. He fought against Piper in a boxing match at Wrestlemania II in April of 1986, and wrestled Kevin Sullivan at the WCW's Starrcade '94 on December 27, 1994.

Taboo, Bamba *see* Doganiero, Dominic W.

Tahitian Warrior *see* Anoia, Lloyd

Takachiho, Akihisa *see* Kabuki, The Great

Takada, Nobuhiko (Yokohama, Japan; 6'1", 230 lbs.) began wrestling in 1982. The Japanese star was trained by Lou Thesz.

Takaiwa, Tatsuhito (b. July 5, 1972) began wrestling with New Japan in July of 1992.

Takano, Shunji, wrestling as the Super Ninja, teamed with Rip Oliver to hold the NWA Pacific Northwest Tag Team Title in July of 1987.

Takanofuji *see* Yasuda, Tadao

Talaber, Frankie (b. 1912, d. September 7, 1994; Columbus, Ohio; 5'11", 200 lbs.) began wrestling in the late 1930s. He held the Ohio television title in the early 1950s.

Talun, Wladislaw (b. 1916, d. 1981; Poland; 6'6", 300 lbs.) was known in the ring as the Polish Angel. He began his career in the ring in the late 1930s. He continued to compete through the 1950s.

Tama the Islander teamed with Dan Kroffat to hold the WWC Tag Team Title in Puerto Rico in January of 1989.

Tamba, The Flying Elephant (5'8", 260 lbs.) began wrestling in 1974. He was a popular Mexican star, who continued to compete in the ring through the early 1990s.

Tanaka, Martin *see* Keomuka, Duke

Tanaka, Pat (b. August 5, 1961; Honolulu, Hawaii; 5'10", 226 lbs.) is the son of wrestler Duke Keomuka. He began wrestling in 1985. He teamed with Jeff Jarrett to hold the CWA International Tag Team Title in August of 1986, and the Southern Tag Team Title in February of 1987. He teamed with Paul Diamond to form Badd Company, capturing the Southern Tag Team Title in August of 1987. They subsequently went to the AWA, where they captured the Tag Team Title from the Midnight Rockers in March of 1988. They retained the title until their defeat by Ken Patera and Brad Rheingans in March of 1989. He was a member of the Orient Express, with Paul Diamond as Kato, in the WWF. He held the ICWA Light Heavyweight Title in Florida in November of 1991. He wrestled as Tanakasan in WCW in 1994. Tanaka wrestled in the USWA in 1995.

Tanaka, Prof. Toru was a leading Japanese-American wrestler from the mid-1960s. He held the North American Title in Honolulu in December of 1968. He wrestled with Mitsu Arakawa as the Rising Suns in the WWWF in the late 1960s. They held the WWWF International Tag Team Title from June of 1969 until their defeat in December of 1969. He held the World Class Championship in Texas several times in 1970 and 1971. He teamed with Thunderbolt Patterson to capture the World Class American Tag Team Title in Texas in July of 1971. Tanaka later teamed with Mr. Fuji in numerous tag bouts, winning the WWWF Tag Team Title from Sonny King and Chief Jay Strongbow in June of 1972. They were defeated by Tony Garea and Haystacks Calhoun in May of 1973, but recaptured the title the following September. They again lost the belts in November of 1973 to Garea and Dean Ho. Managed by Gary Hart, Tanaka teamed with Dick Slater to hold the NWA Florida Tag Team Title in October of 1973. Tanaka also held the NWA Georgia Title in September of 1975. Tanaka teamed with Assassin #2 to claim the NWA Georgia Tag Team Title in March of 1975. He reunited with Mr. Fuji to win the belts in a tournament in September of 1975. He held the NWA Americas Title in Los Angeles in February of 1977. He also held the NWA Americas Tag Team Title with Dr. Hiro Ota in February of 1977. He won the Los Angeles Battle Royal in 1977. Tanaka and Fuji again teamed to win the WWWF Tag Team Title in September of 1977, holding the belts until March of 1978, when they were defeated by Dominic Denucci and Dino Bravo. Tanaka held the Southern Heavyweight Title several times in early 1979. He and Fuji held the Southern Tag Team Title in May of 1979, and the NWA Southeastern Tag Team Title in July of 1979. He returned to Texas to recapture the World Class Title in April of 1980. He was managed during his career by Grand Wizard, Fred Blassie and Lou Albano. Tanaka wrestled on the independent circuit in the 1980s. He captured the NCW Title in Connecticut in 1988. He left wrestling to pursue an acting career full-time in the late 1980s. He appeared in such films as *An Eye for an Eye* (1981), *Revenge of the Ninja* (1983), *Chattanooga Choo Choo* (1984), *Pee-wee's Big Adventure* (1985), *The Running Man* (1987), *Dead Heat* (1988), *Darkman* (1990), *Alligator II: The Mutation* (1991) and *Last Action Hero* (1993). He also appeared on television in the tele-film *Deadly Game* (1991), and episodes of *Fantasy Island*, *Bring 'Em Back Alive*, *Modesty Blaise* and *The Wizard*.

Tangara, Joe *see* Brunetti, Joe

Tapu, Chief (Samoa; 228 lbs.) teamed with Tio to wrestle as the Manchurians. Managed by the Great Mephisto, they held the NWA Southeastern Tag Team Title several times in 1980. Wrestled as Tudui and Wakahi, the Maoris, Tapu and Tio held the Southwest Tag Team Title in January of 1985.

Tatanka (Chris Chavis; b. June 8, 1965; Pembroke, North Carolina; 6'1", 250) was trained by Larry Sharpe and began wrestling in 1989. The Native American wrestled as the War Eagle and Chris Chavis. He held the NAWA/SAPW Title in 1991. He joined the WWF as Tatanka in the early 1990s. He briefly held the USWA Unified Title in September of 1993. He initially wrestled as a fan favorite, but turned villain in 1994. He departed the federation the following year.

Tateno, Noriyo is a leading Japanese women's wrestler. She teamed with Itsuki Yamazaki as the Jumping Bomb Angels. They held the All-Japan WWWW Women's Tag Team Title in 1986. They won the WWF Women's Tag Team belts from Leilani Kai and Judy Martin in January of 1988. They lost the belts to Kai and Martin in a rematch in June of 1988.

Tattrie, Newton *see* Mongol, Geeto

Tatum, Hollywood John (Hollywood, California; 6'2", 236 lbs.) began wrestling in 1983. He introduced valets Missy Hyatt and Tessa to wrestling. He held the World Class TV Title in August of 1985. He teamed with Jack Victory to hold the UWF Tag Team Title in Oklahoma in October of 1986. He and Victory also held the World Class Texas Tag Team Title several times in 1988, often competing against Steve and Shaun Simpson. He teamed with Rod Price as the California Connection to hold the Global World Tag Team Title several times in 1991. He held the USWA Southern Title several times in mid-1990.

Taue, Akira (b. May 8, 1961; Tokyo, Japan; 6'5", 265 lbs.) began wrestling in January of 1988 with All-Japan. He was a former Japanese sumo wrestler who often teamed with Toshiaki Kawada.

Taurus *see* Hall, Dennis

Taylor, Chaz (b. 1971; Houston, Texas; 5'10", 223 lbs.) made his professional wrestling debut in Baytown, Texas, in April of 1988. Wrestling as Chaz, he soon entered Global, where he feuded with the Lightning Kid. He held the Global

Junior Heavyweight Title in September of 1991. He acknowledged veteran wrestler Tug Taylor as his father in October of 1991, and they teamed in numerous bouts. He teamed with Steve Dane as the Skyliners to hold the Global World Tag Team Title in September of 1993.

Taylor, Chris (b. 1950, d. June 30, 1979; Dowagiac, Michigan; 395 lbs.) was a leading amateur wrestler at Iowa State University and a two-time National Collegiate Athletic Association wrestling champion in the early 1970s. He won the bronze medal in wrestling at the 1972 Olympic Games in Munich. He began wrestling professionally in 1973. He retired from the ring for heath reasons in 1977. He died of a heart attack after a lengthy illness at his home in Story City, Iowa, on June 30, 1979.

Taylor, David (6'3", 285 lbs.) wrestled as Squire David Taylor in the WCW in 1996, teaming with Earl Robert Eaton as the Blue Bloods.

Taylor, Frankie (Pittsburgh, Pennsylvania) attended Toledo University in Ohio. He began wrestling in the mid-1930s and remained an active competitor through the 1950s.

Taylor, Lawrence (b. 1959; 6'3", 245 lbs.) was a prominent linebacker with the New York Giants, who led the team to two Super Bowl titles. He became involved in a dispute with Bam Bam Bigelow at a WWF event in early 1995. He accepted a challenge to wrestle Bigelow, and defeated him in the ring at Wrestlemania XI in April of 1995.

Taylor, Terry (Paul Taylor; b. August 12; Vero Beach, Florida; 6'2", 225 lbs.) began wrestling in 1980. He held the NWA Southeastern Title and the NWA TV Title in 1980. He teamed with Bob Brown to hold the NWA Central States Tag Team Title in April of 1981. He defeated Les Thornton for the NWA World Junior Heavyweight Title on June 7, 1982, but lost the belt back to Thornton two weeks later. He held the Southern Heavyweight Title several times in late 1982 and early 1983. He held the Mid-America Title in December of 1983. He captured the MSWA North American Title in March of 1985. He also held the CWA International Title several times in 1985. He teamed with Jim Duggan to hold the UWF Tag Team Title in Oklahoma in December of 1986. He also held the UWF tag belts with Chris Adams in February of 1987. He held the World Class Texas Title in February of 1988. He teamed with King Parsons to hold the World Class World Tag Team Title in 1988. He wrestled as the Red Rooster in the WWF during the late 1980s under the management of Bobby Heenan. He subsequently broke with Heenan and feuded with his stable of villains. He joined the York Foundation in the WCW in the early 1990s and teamed with Rick Morton and Tommy Rich to hold the WCW 6-Man Tag Team Title in late 1991. He later called himself the Taylor-Made Man and teamed with Greg Valentine to hold the WCW U.S. Tag Team Title from February until May of 1992. He remained in the WCW as a commentator through the mid-1990s, mak-

ing occasional appearances in the ring.

Taylor, Tio *see* Togo, The Great

Taylor, Tugboat (Houston, Texas; 6'1", 320 lbs.) began wrestling in 1983. He was a promoter for Texas All-Pro Wrestling in the early 1990s, holding the TAP title several times in 1991. He is the father of Chaz Taylor, who he often teamed with in the early 1990s.

Taylor-Made Man, The *see* Taylor, Terry

Taz (Pete Senerchia; b. October 11; Massapequa, New York; 5'11", 245 lbs.) began wrestling in June of 1987. He was managed by Tony Rumble in the IWCCW, where he was light heavyweight champion in 1991. He teamed with Kevin Sullivan to win the ECW Tag Team Title in December of 1993. They held the belts until March of 1994, when they were defeated by Public Enemy. He also briefly held the ECW TV Title in March of 1994. He remained with ECW in the mid-1990s, under the management of former referee Bill Alfonso.

Tazmaniac *see* Taz

Team America *see* Morgan, Heidi Lee & Blue Simmes, Misty

Tenant, O.L. "Dutch" (b. 1908, d. April 28, 1990) began wrestling professionally in 1925. He was known as the Flying Dutchman in the ring in matches throughout the southern United States. He retired from the ring in 1935 to become a machinist. Tenant occasionally wrestled benefit shows for servicemen during World War II. He died in a nursing home in Whitehorse, Texas, on April 28, 1990.

Tenario, Benny *see* Little Wolf, Chief

Tennessee Hillbilly, The *see* Dillon, Jack

Tenryu, Genichiro (b. February 2, 1950; Katsuyama, Japan; 6'1", 235 lbs.) began wrestling in 1976. He is a leading Japanese mat artist with experience in sumo wrestling. He teamed with Mr. Fuji to hold the NWA Atlantic Coast Tag Title in 1981. He held the All-Japan United National Title several times in the mid-1980s.

Tenta, John *see* Earthquake

Terminator (Marc Laurinaitis; 6'2", 270 lbs.) began wrestling in 1987. He originally wrestled in the UWF and was managed by Gen. Skandor Akbar. He teamed with Sonny Beach to hold the IWA Tag Team Title in August of 1990. The following month he teamed with Al Greene as the Dream Warriors to retain the title after Beach left the promotion. The duo held the ICWA Florida/U.S. Tag Team Title as the Terminators in 1991. Laurinatis joined the WCW as Fury in 1993 and teamed with Rage as the Wrecking Crew. He is the brother of wrestlers Road Warrior Animal and Johnny Ace.

Terminator Rigs (Dan Rignati) teamed with Terminator Wolf to hold the PWA Tag Team Title several times from 1985 through 1987. Rigs also held the PWA singles title in early 1991.

Terminator Wolf (Doug Fisher) teamed with Terminator Rigs to hold the PWA Tag Team Title several times from 1985 through 1987.

Tero, Lawrence *see* T, Mr.

Terry, Jack (b. 1908, d. 19??; Kitchener, Canada; 5'11", 200 lbs.) began wrestling in the late 1920s. He was known as Judo Jack Terry and the Ontario Hatchet Man. He remained an active competitor through the early 1950s.

Texan, The *see* Funk, Terry

Texan, The *see* Mulligan, Blackjack

Texas, Miss *see* Miss Texas

Texas Broncos *see* Windham, Kendall & Rhodes, Dustin

Texas Cowgirls *see* Grable, Joyce & Richter, Wendy

Texas Dirt *see* Mantel, Dutch

Texas Hangmen, The consisted of Killer & Psycho. They teamed to hold the WWC Tag Team Title in Puerto Rico several times in 1990 and 1991. They also held the USWA Tag Team Title from March until May of 1991.

Texas Mustangs, The *see* Duncum, Bobby, Jr. & Hawk, John

Texas Outlaw *see* Bass, Bobby

Texas Red *see* Bastien, Red

Thatcher, Les teamed with Nelson Royal to hold the NWA Southeastern Tag Team Title in 1975.

Theis, Therese (b. 1929; St.

Paul, Minnesota; 5'8", 140 lbs.) was trained by mat star Bronco Nagurski and began wrestling professionally in the early 1950s. She remained a leading female grappler throughout the decade.

Theophelos, Chris *see* Londos, Jim

Thesz, Lou (b. 1916; St. Louis, Missouri; 6'1", 225 lbs.) was the son of Hungarian light-heavyweight champion Martin Thesz. He was an amateur champion in St. Louis before he entered professional wrestling with the assistance of Warren Bockwinkel in 1936. He captured the MWA Heavyweight Title in December of 1937. He briefly held the AWA World Title in January of 1938. He defeated Evan Marshal for the NWA Heavyweight Title in St. Louis, Missouri, on February 23, 1939. He retained the belt until June 23, 1939, when he lost a title match to Bronko Nagurski in Minneapolis, Minnesota. He held the AWA Title in Montreal, Canada, in May of 1940. He held the NWA Texas Title in May of 1946. Thesz again captured the NWA Heavyweight Title in St. Louis, Missouri, on April 25, 1947, in a match against Whipper Billy Watson. He relinquished the belt to Bill Longson on November 21, 1947, but recaptured the belt from Longson in Indianapolis, Indiana, on July 20, 1948. He was recognized as champion by the combined National Wrestling Association and the National Wrestling Alliance in November of 1949. He unified the title with the AWA championship by defeating Gorgeous George in Chicago, Illinois, on July 27, 1950. He retained the belt until his defeat by Whipper Billy Watson in Toronto, Canada, on March 15, 1956. He regained the title from Watson in St. Louis, Missouri, on November 9, 1956. He retained the belt despite a loss to Edouard Carpentier in June of 1957 that split the NWA over recognition of Thesz as the champion. He remained NWA champion until November 14, 1957, when Dick Hutton captured the title in Toronto. Thesz teamed with Dory "the Outlaw" Funk to hold the Pacific Coast Tag Team Title in Vancouver, Canada, in 1961. Thesz was again the NWA champion following his defeat of Buddy Rogers in Toronto, Canada, on January 24, 1963. He defeated Jersey Joe Walcott in a wrestler vs. boxer match in April of 1963. He continued to hold the NWA title until his defeat by Gene Kiniski in St. Louis, Missouri, on January 7, 1966. He held the WWA Title in Los Angeles in October of 1966. Thesz briefly held the Southern Heavyweight Title in 1973. He continued to make occasional appearances in the ring while well into his 70s.

Thing, The *see* Jares, Brother Frank

Thomas, Baptiste *see* Thunderbird, Chief

Thomas, James "Shag" (d. July 25, 1982) teamed with Tony Borne to hold the NWA Pacific Northwest Tag Team Title several times in 1960. He also held the NWA Pacific Northwest Title in February of 1960. He held the Pacific Northwest tag belts several more times in the early 1960s, teaming with Luther Lindsay, Danny Hodge, Billy White Wolf, Bearcat Wright and Armand Hussein.

Thomas, Sailor Art was a merchant marine bodybuilder. He was a popular mat star from the early 1960s, holding the NWA Texas Title several times in 1962 and 1963. He retired from the ring in 1980, settling in Madison, Wisconsin.

Thompson, Curtis *see* Firebreaker Chip

Thompson, Freezer (6'3", 301 lbs.) began wrestling in 1987. He continued to compete in the ring, primarily wrestling in the USWA, through the mid-1990s.

Thompson, Scott *see* King Kong

Thor the Viking *see* Irwin, Scott

Thornton, Les (5'9", 238 lbs.) began wrestling in 1971. Known as the Man of 1,000 Holds, he held the Stampede North American Title in Calgary, Canada, in 1971. He also held the Calgary Stampede International Tag Team Title in 1975, teaming with Frankie Laine. He held the NWA Americas Title in Los Angeles in May of 1975. He teamed with Tony Charles to hold the NWA Georgia Tag Team Title in December of 1975. They also held the World Class Texas Tag Team Title in 1976. He claimed the NWA World Junior Heavyweight Title in March of 1980. He was defeated by Terry Taylor on June 7, 1981, but reclaimed the title on June 20, 1981. He lost the belt to Jerry Brisco on September 13, 1981, but again recaptured the title the following month. He was defeated by Tiger

Mask in a match in Japan in May of 1982. Thornton was again awarded the title in November of 1983, retaining the championship until he left the promotion in June of 1984.

Thunder (Clark Haines) wrestled in the WCW during 1994. He wrestled as Cobra from 1995.

Thunder Mountain, Chief (David Moser; d. August 1991) was a leading Indian wrestler in the 1960s.

Thunderbird, Chief (Baptiste Thomas; d. 19??) began wrestling in 1933. He was one of the first wrestlers to wear a full Indian headdress into the ring. He was a popular wrestling star and made several tours of Europe.

Thundercloud, Chief teamed with Chief White Cloud to hold the U.S. Tag Team Title in Louisiana in June of 1974. He teamed with Danny Little Beaver to hold the Southern Tag Team Title in November of 1976.

Thunderfoot #1 *see* Isley, David

Thunderfoot #2 *see* Ligon, Gene

Thunderfoots, The *see* Deaton, Dave & Joel

Tiger Jeet Singh *see* Singh, Tiger Jeet

Tiger Mask (Satoru Sayama) was a popular Japanese wrestler. He competed in Mexico in the late 1970s, holding the Mexican Middleweight Championship in 1979. He defeated Les Thornton for the NWA World Junior Heavyweight Title in May of 1982, but relinquished the title later in the year.

Tiger Mask *see* Misawa, Mitsuharu

Tiger Mask 3 *see* Kanemoto, Koji

Tillet, Louis teamed with Gypsy Joe to hold the NWA Southern Tag Team Title in 1960. He held the Texas Brass Knucks Title several times in 1963. He held the NWA Florida Title in March of 1967. He teamed with Tarzan Tyler to hold the NWA Southern Tag Team Title in Florida in late 1968. He teamed with John Tolos to capture the NWA Americas Tag Team Title in Los Angeles in February of 1975. He also held the NWA Americas Title in June of 1975. Tillet managed Wayne Farris and King Moondog in the Southeastern Championship promotion in the early 1980s.

Tillet, Maurice *see* French Angel, The

Timbs, Ken (5'11", 235 lbs.) began wrestling in 1979. He teamed with Eric Embry as the Fabulous Blonds to hold the Southwest Tag Team Title several times in 1983 and 1984. He teamed with Porkchop Cash to hold the NWA Central States Tag Team Title in April of 1987. He wrestled in Mexico as Fabuloso Blondie in the late 1980s and early 1990s, holding the EMLL Light Heavyweight Title several times.

Tinieblas was a popular Mexican wrestler in the 1970s and 1980s. He held the WWA Heavyweight Title in Mexico in 1987. He also appeared in numerous films during the 1970s from his debut in *Champions of Justice* (1971).

Tio, The Great teamed with Tapu to wrestle as the Manchurians. Managed by the Great Mephisto, they held the NWA Southeastern Tag Team Title several times in 1980. Tio held the ICW TV Title several times in 1981 and 1982. Wrestling as Tudui and Wakahi, the Maoris, Tio and Tapu held the Southwest Tag Team Title in January of 1985.

Togo, Great (Tio Taylor; b. 1915, d. December 17, 1973; California; 5'6", 218 lbs.) was a philosophy major at the University of Oregon. He began wrestling in the early 1930s. He was often accompanied to the ring by his valet, Hata, who burned incense before Togo would enter the ring. Togo had a lengthy feud with Argentina Rocca in the early 1950s. He teamed with Harold "Tosh Togo" Sakata to hold the Canadian Open Tag Team Title in Toronto in July of 1954. He teamed with Tokyo Joe to hold the NWA Central States Tag Title several times in 1973.

Togo, Great was managed by Tojo Yamamoto in the Tennessee promotion. Yamamoto and Togo teamed to hold the Mid-America Tag Team Title in July of 1979. Togo also held the Mid-America Title in May of 1980.

Togo, Tosh *see* Sakata, Harold

Toguchi, Tiger *see* Kim Duk

Tokyo Joe teamed with the Great Togo to hold the NWA Central States Tag Title several times in 1973. He remained a leading Japanese wrestler until the late 1970s, when he lost his leg in an automobile accident. While unable to continue competing in the ring, Tokyo Joe remained involved in wrestling as a talent coordinator for the International Wrestling Enterprise in Calgary, Canada, in the 1980s.

Tokyo Tom *see* Inoki, Antonio

Tolos, Chris teamed with his brother, John Tolos, to hold the AWA Tag Team belts in 1960. They defeated Killer Kowalski and Gorilla Monsoon for the WWWF U.S. Tag Team Title in December of 1963. They lost the title to Don McClarity and Argentina Apollo in February of 1964. They subsequently captured the NWA World Tag Team Title in Florida. He and his brother also held the Canadian Tag Team Title several times in 1967. Chris Tolos teamed with Stan Pulaski to hold the Mid-West Tag Team Title in Omaha in February of 1969.

Tolos, John was a leading mat star from the mid-1950s. He teamed with Duke Keomuka to hold the NWA Texas Tag Team Title in June of 1958. He teamed with his brother, Chris Tolos, to hold the AWA Tag Team belts in 1960. They defeated Killer Kowalski and Gorilla Monsoon for the WWWF U.S. Tag Team Title in December of 1963. They lost the title to Don McClarity and Argentina Apollo in February of 1964. They subsequently captured the NWA World Tag Team Title in Florida. He held the Canadian Tag Team Title several times in the late 1960s, teaming with the Black Terror, Tony Borne, Chris Tolos and Don Leo Jonathan. He held the NWA Americas Title in Los Ange-

les several times in the early 1970s. He also held the NWA Americas Tag Team Title in February of 1975, teaming with Louie Tillet. He held the World Class Texas Title in May of 1975. He again captured the NWA Americas Title in August of 1980. Tolos was known as the Coach when he briefly managed Curt Hennig and the Beverly Brothers in the WWF in 1991.

Tom Thumb (b. 1961, d. October 16, 1988) was a popular midget mat star who wrestled as Major Tom Thumb and Tiny Tom from 1978 until 1983. He was killed in an automobile accident in Manitoba, Canada, on October 16, 1988.

Tomah, Princess Tona was a Chippewa Indian from Naytahwaush, Minnesota. She was a leading female Indian mat star during the 1950s and 1960s.

Tomasso, Tiger Joe (Robert Tomasso; d. 1988) teamed with Guy Mitchell as the Assassins to hold the WWA Tag Team title three times in 1965 and 1966. He teamed with Earl Black to hold the Calgary Stampede International Tag Team Title several times in the early 1970s.

Tombes, Roderick *see* Piper, Roddy

Tomko, Al held the Canadian Tag Team Title several times in the early 1980s, teaming with Igor Volkoff and Bob Brown. He also held the Canadian Title in Vancouver, Canada, several times from 1983 through 1985. Tomko was also a promoter for professional wrestling in Vancouver.

Tonga, King *see* Haku

Tonga Kid teamed with Johnny Rich and Scott Armstrong as R.A.T. Patrol Inc. to hold the Southeastern Tag Team Title several times in 1984.

Top Gun *see* Sierra, David

Top Guns *see* Rice, Ricky & Dukes, Derrick

Torelli, Vince *see* Shamrock, Ken

Toro, El *see* McCoy, Robert "Bibber"

Torres, Alberto (d. June 17, 1971) was a popular Mexican wrestling star. He teamed with Enrique Torres to hold the NWA Texas Tag Team Title in March of 1958. He teamed with Ramon Torres to hold the WWA Tag Team Title in Los Angeles for several months from April of 1964. He teamed with Enrique Torres to hold the Hawaiian Tag Team Title in May of 1965. He again held the WWA tag belts in February of 1966, teaming with Thunderbolt Patterson. He reunited with Ramon Torres to hold the NWA Georgia Tag Team Title several times in 1968 and 1969. He teamed with Bob Ellis to capture the Midwest Tag Team Title in Omaha in May of 1971. Torres died in an Omaha, Nebraska, hospital on June 17, 1971, three days after being injured in a match against Ox Baker and the Claw.

Torres, Enrique "Miguel" (b. 1918; Mexico; 5'11", 230 lbs.) was a sheepherder in Mexico before becoming a professional wrestler in the late 1930s. His vicious tactics in the ring made him a leading mat villain for several decades. He held the World Title in Los Angeles in 1946. He held the NWA Central States Title in early 1952. He held the Pacific Coast Title in San Francisco several times in 1952 and 1953. He also held the Pacific Coast Tag Team Title several times in 1953 and 1954, teaming with Gino Garibaldi, Leo Nomellini, Ramon Torres, Ron Etchison and Jesse Ortega. He teamed with Leo Nomellini to hold the NWA World Tag Team Title in San Francisco in May of 1953. He held the title belts several more times in 1955 and 1956, teaming with Johnny Barend and Bobo Brazil. He teamed with Alberto Torres to hold the NWA Texas Tag Team Title in March of 1958. He recaptured the Pacific Coast belt in April of 1960. He again held the Central States belt for several months from December of 1963. He teamed with Bearcat Wright to hold the Canadian Tag Team Title in April of 1964. He captured the U.S. Title in Honolulu in December of 1964. He teamed with Alberto Torres to hold the Hawaiian Tag Team Title in May of 1965. He teamed with Ramon Torres to hold the World Tag Team Title in Atlanta several times in 1967. The duo also held the Southern Tag Team Title several times from 1967 until 1968.

Torres, Polo held the NWA Texas Title in late 1954 and early 1955.

Torres, Ramon (d. 19??) held the Pacific Coast Title in San Francisco several times in 1957 and 1958. He also held the NWA World Tag Team Title in San Francisco in September of 1957, teaming with Tex McKenzie. He again held the title belts several times in late 1957 and early 1958, teaming with Ciclon Anaya and Nick Bockwinkel. He held the Gulf Coast Title in Alabama in the early 1960s. He teamed with Enrique Torres to hold the WWA Tag Team Title in Los Angeles for several months from April of 1964. They also held the World Tag Team Title in Atlanta several times in 1967. The duo also held the Southern Tag Team Title several times from 1967 until 1968. He teamed with Alberto Torres to hold the NWA Georgia Tag Title several times in 1968 and 1969. Ramon Torres held the Mid-West Title in Omaha in August of 1971. He defeated Roger Kirby for the NWA World Junior Heavyweight Title in September of 1971. He lost the belt to Dr. X in December of 1971.

Torres, Tony teamed with Ricky Santana as the Masked Hoods to hold the Texas All-Star Texas Tag Team Title in September of 1985.

Tourtas, Ted (b. 1920; California; 5'10", 210 lbs.) was born in Greece and came to the United States as a young boy. He was an amateur wrestling champion before he became a pro in the late 1940s. He was known for his quickness in the ring and his rolling leg split maneuver. He remained a leading competitor through the 1950s.

Touville, Lauren *see* Tyler, Tarzan

Townsend, Frank, wrestling as Mr. X, teamed with Gene Kiniski to hold the Canadian Tag Team Title in February of 1963.

Train, Ice *see* Ice Train

Travis, Billy (Houston, Texas; 5'10", 218 lbs.) began wrestling in 1980. He wrestled often in the USWA during the 1980s. He held the CWA International Title for several months from March of 1986. He teamed with Jeff Jarrett to hold the Southern Tag Team Title several times in late 1986 and early 1987. He also held the Southern tag belts with Mark Starr in June of 1987. Travis teamed with Scott Steiner to hold the CWA Tag Team Title several times in mid-1988. He held the CWA tag belts with Perry Jackson in June of 1989. He teamed with El Gran Mendoza to hold the WWC Tag Team Title in Puerto Rico in May of 1991. During the 1990s he often wrestled as Billy Joe Travis, carrying a guitar to the ring which he often used against his opponents.

Travis, Steve (Charlottesville, Virginia; 245 lbs.) was the WWWF's Rookie of the Year in 1979. He held the NWA TV Title in January of 1980. He also held the Mid-America Title in April of 1980.

Travis, Ted (Boston, Massachusetts) held the Hawaiian Title in 1947. He held the Hawaiian Tag Team Title in November of 1961, teaming with Shoulders Newman.

Traylor, Ray *see* Big Boss Man

Tremaine, Andy (b. 1912; Tucson, Arizona; 5'11", 190 lbs.) began wrestling in the early 1930s. He held the NWA light-heavyweight belt in 1950. He teamed with Kurt Von Poppenheim to hold the Northwest

Tag Team Title in Vancouver, Canada, in September of 1952.

Tsuruta, Jumbo (Tonomi Tsuruta; b. March 25, 1951; Yamanashi, Japan; 6'4", 272 lbs.) began wrestling in March of 1973. He held the All-Japan United National Title several times from the mid-1970s through the early 1980s. The popular Japanese star defeated Nick Bockwinkel for the AWA Title in Tokyo, Japan, on February 22, 1984. He lost the title to Rick Martel the following May. He held the All-Japan Triple Crown Title several times in the late 1980s and early 1990s.

Tui Selinga, Superfly teamed with Super Samoan Sakalia to hold the Pacific Tag Team Title in Honolulu several times in 1984. He also held the Polynesian Pacific Title in Honolulu several times in 1986 and 1987.

Turkish Terror, The *see* Ali Bey

Turner, Ted (b. 1938) was a leading media magnate who purchased Jim Crockett Promotions in November of 1988, giving him controlling interest in the leading promotion in the NWA. He changed the name of Crockett's organization to World Championship Wrestling, becoming head of one of the two largest promotions in the country.

Twin Devil #1 *see* Sanchez, Alfonso

2 Cold Scorpio (Charles Scaggs; b. October 25; Denver, Colorado; 5'11", 222 lbs.) debuted with the Rocky Mountain Wrestling Association in Denver in April of 1990.

He wrestled in Mexico and Japan before entering the WCW in the early 1990s. He teamed with Marcus Alexander Bagwell in 1993. They defeated the Nasty Boys for the WCW Tag Team Championship on October 4, 1993, but were defeated for the belts in a rematch on October 24, 1993. Scorpio subsequently entered ECW, where he briefly held the TV Title in November of 1994. He teamed with the Sandman to capture the ECW Tag Team Title from Public Enemy in October of 1995. He also held the ECW TV Title in 1996.

Two Eagles, Billy teamed with Don Running Bear to hold the NWA Pacific Northwest Tag Team Title in January of 1984. He teamed with Joe Lightfoot to hold the NWA Central States Tag Team Title in July of 1986.

Two Rivers, Billy was a leading Mohawk Indian wrestler in the 1950s and 1960s. He teamed with George Becker to hold the NWA Southern Tag Team Title in 1959. He wrestled throughout the United States, Canada and England before his retirement in the late 1960s.

Tyler, Buzz (Rock Hill, South Carolina; 285 lbs.) teamed with Dutch Mantel to hold the Mid-America Tag Team Title in February of 1978. He held the NWA Central States Title in April of 1981 and late 1983. He teamed with James J. Dillon to hold the NWA Central States Tag Team Title in September of 1981. He and Bob Brown teamed to hold the Central States belts several times in 1983. He held the NWA Mid-Atlantic Title in 1985.

Tyler, R.T. teamed with Bobby Jaggers as the Cowboy Connection to hold the NWA Florida Tag Team Title several times in early 1981.

Tyler, Randy briefly held the Southern Heavyweight Title in June of 1979. He teamed with Mike Roselli as the Billionaire Boys Club to hold the WCCW International Tag Team Title in Vancouver, Canada, several times in 1993 and 1994.

Tyler, Rip teamed with Eddie Sullivan to hold the U.S. Tag Team Title in Oklahoma in 1973. He also held the MSWA North American Title in February of 1974.

Tyler, Tarzan (Lauren Touville; d. December 20, 1985) teamed with the Alaskan to hold the Texas World Tag Team Title in August of 1962. He teamed with Tim Tyler to hold the NWA World Tag Team Title in Florida in November of 1964. He held the NWA Southern Title in Florida from December of 1964 until he was stripped of the belt in April of 1965. He recaptured the belt for a month in February of 1966. He teamed with Louie Tillet to hold the NWA Southern Tag Team Title in Florida in late 1968. Tyler held the NWA Florida Title in December of 1970. He teamed with Luke Graham to capture the WWWF Tag Team Title in June of 1971. They won a unification match against the Mongols for the WWWF International Tag Team Title in November of 1971. They were defeated for the belts by Rene Goulet and Karl Gotch in December of 1971.

Tyler, Tim teamed with Tarzan Tyler to hold the NWA World Tag Team Title in Florida in November of 1964.

Typhoon (Fred Ottman; b. August 10; Tampa, Florida; 6'7", 384 lbs.) began wrestling in 1984. He has wrestled under the names Superstar Bubba, U.S. Steel, Big Steel Man and Tugboat before becoming Typhoon. He held the Florida Championship Wrestling Title for several months in late 1988. He teamed with Earthquake in the WWF as the Natural Disasters. They captured the WWF Tag Team Title from Money Inc. in July of 1992, but lost a rematch the following October. He began wrestling in the WCW as the Shockmaster in August of 1993.

U.S. Express, The *see* Rotunda, Mike & Windham, Barry

U.S. Male *see* Santana, Ricky & Thompson, Curtis

Ueda, Umanosuke *see* Ito, Mr.

UFO *see* Dellaserra, Bob

Uganda, Mr *see* Negro, Ciclon

Ultimate Dragon *see* Asai, Yoshihiro

Ultimate Warrior, The (Jim Hellwig; b. June 16; Queens, New York; 6'4", 280 lbs.) was trained by Red Bastien and began wrestling in the Mid-South as part of Powerteam USA in 1986. Wrestling as Rock, he teamed with Sting, then known as Flash, as the Blade Runners. He subsequently wrestled as the Dingo Warrior in World Class, where he teamed with Lance Von Erich to hold the World Class World Tag Team Title with Lance Von Erich in

November of 1986. He captured the World Class Texas Title in February of 1987, and held the belt until joining the WWF as the Ultimate Warrior in June of 1987. He won the WWF Intercontinental Title from Honky Tonk Man in August of 1988. He lost the belt to Rick Rude in April of 1989, but recaptured the title the following August. He gave up the Intercontinental belt after defeating Hulk Hogan for the WWF Title at Wrestlemania VI in Toronto, Canada, on April 1, 1990. He was defeated for the title in Miami, Florida, by Sergeant Slaughter on January 19, 1991. He left the WWF in the Fall of 1992. Hellwig appeared in the 1994 film *Firepower*. He returned to the ring in the Spring of 1996 to resume competition with the WWF.

Unabom *see* Jacobs, Glen

Undertaker, The (Mark Calloway; b. March 24, 1962; Dallas, Texas; 6'9", 328 lbs.) debuted in the USWA as the Master of Pain, briefly capturing the USWA Unified Title from Jerry Lawler in April of 1989. He later wrestled as Mean Mark Callous and the Punisher, capturing the USWA Texas Title in October of 1989. He wrestled as Punisher Dice Morgan in New Japan in 1990. He became the Undertaker when he entered the WWF in November of 1990, where he was managed by Paul Bearer. He captured the WWF Title from Hulk Hogan in Detroit, Michigan, on November 27, 1991. He lost the belt back to Hogan in a rematch a few days later in San Antonio, Texas, on December 3, 1991. He remained one of the leading stars in the WWF through the mid-1990s, often competing in "casket matches" against such wrestlers as Kimala, Yokozuna, Diesel and Goldust.

Undertaker II, The *see* Lee, Brian

Uptown Boys, The *see* Janetty, Marty & Rogers, Tommy

Uptown Posse, The *see* Brown, Brickhouse & Falcone, Sweet Daddy

Ustinov, Soldat (6'5", 265 lbs.) began wrestling in 1986. He teamed with Boris Zukhov to win the AWA tag championship in May of 1987. He remained champion with Doug Somers when Zhukov left the promotion in October of 1987. They lost the belts to Jerry Lawler and Bill Dundee later in the month. He subsequently wrestled in the WWF, where he again teamed with Zukhov.

Uyeda, Toyoki *see* Yamato, Tor

Vachon, Luna (Angelle Vachon; b. January 12; Montreal, Quebec, Canada; 5'5", 150 lbs.) is the daughter of Paul "Butcher" Vachon. She began wrestling as Angelle Vachon in North Dakota in the 1980s. She then joined Kevin Sullivan's organization in Florida, where she shaved part of her head and took the name Luna. She subsequently wrestled in Texas, Tennessee and Japan. She tag teamed with the Lock for awhile before managing Rock and Blade, the Star Riders, in Florida. She then went to Canada, where she began managing the Blackhearts. She managed Bam Bam Bigelow in the WWF and the Vampire Warrior in the USWA during 1993. She also held the USWA Women's Title in August of 1993. She married Dave Heath (A.K.A. Vampire Warrior) in October of 1994. They separated the following year.

Vachon, Maurice "Mad Dog" (Canada; 225 lbs.) represented Canada at the 1948 Olympic Games. He teamed with Pierre LaSalle to hold the NWA Texas Tag Team Title in early 1955. He teamed with his brother, Paul Vachon, to hold the NWA Texas Tag Team Title in November of 1960 and the NWA Southern Tag Team Title in 1961. He teamed with Fritz Von Goering to hold the NWA Pacific Northwest Tag Team Title in September of 1962. He also held the NWA Pacific Northwest Title several times in 1962 and 1963. He defeated Verne Gagne for the AWA Title in May of 1964. He held the title several more times during the mid-1960s, exchanging the belt with Gagne, the Mighty Igor, Crusher and Dick the Bruiser. His title reign was ended by Gagne in February of 1967. He held the AWA Title in Montreal, Canada, several times in 1967. He teamed with Paul "Butcher" Vachon to hold the Mid-West Tag Team Title in Omaha several times in 1968 and 1969. They captured the AWA Tag Team Title from Crusher and Dick the Bruiser in August of 1969. They were defeated for the belts by Red Bastien and Hercules Cortez in May of 1971. He teamed with Baron Von Raschke to hold the NWA Central States Tag Team Title in September of 1976. Vachon again teamed with Verne Gagne to win the tag championship in June of 1979, defeating

Pat Patterson and Ray Stevens. They relinquished the title to Adrian Adonis and Jesse Ventura in July of 1980.

Vachon, Paul "Butcher" wrestled as Nikita Zolotoff in the NWA in Texas in the late 1950s. He teamed with Ivan the Terrible to hold the NWA Texas Tag Team Title in September of 1957. He teamed with Hard Boiled Haggerty to hold the Hawaiian Tag Team Title in April of 1960. He teamed with Maurice "Mad Dog" Vachon to hold the NWA Texas Tag Team Title in November of 1960 and the NWA Southern Tag Team Title in 1961. He teamed with Stan Pulaski, wrestling as Stan Vachon, to hold the NWA Georgia Tag Team Title and the World Tag Team Title in Atlanta in 1968. He and Maurice Vachon also held the Mid-West Tag Team Title in Omaha several times in 1968 and 1969. They captured the AWA Tag Team Title from Crusher and Dick the Bruiser in August of 1969. They were defeated for the belts by Red Bastien and Hercules Cortez in May of 1971. He teamed with Chavo Guerrero to hold the NWA Americas Tag Team Title in Los Angeles in 1976. He is the father of wrestler Luna Vachon.

Vachon, Stan *see* Pulaski, Stan

Vachon, Vivian (b. 1951, d. August 25, 1991) entered wrestling in the late 1960s. She was the sister of Paul and Maurice Vachon. Vivian was killed, with her daughter Julie, in an automobile accident near Montreal, Canada, on August 25, 1991.

Vader, Big Van (Leon White; b.

May 14, 1956; Denver, Colorado; 6'5", 450 lbs.) was born in Lynwood, California. He played high school and college football at the University of Colorado. He played professional football with the Los Angeles Rams from 1977 until 1981. He trained to be a professional wrestler under Brad Rheingans and made his debut in the AWA as Leon "the Baby Bull" White in 1985. After a vicious feud with Bruiser Brody, he toured Europe and became the first American Catch Wrestling Association Heavyweight Champion when he defeated Otto Wanz in Denver, Colorado, in 1986. He again held the belt in 1989, following another victory over Wanz in Europe. He captured the vacant IWGP championship in Tokyo on April 24, 1989, in a match against Shinya Hashimoto. He also wrestled in Mexico, where he defeated El Canek for the UWA title on November 22, 1989. He held the three belts on several occasions before entering the WCW in January of 1992. He was managed by Harley Race and defeated Sting for the World Title at the Great American Bash in Atlanta, Georgia, on July 12, 1992. He lost the title to Ron Simmons the following month on August 2, 1992, but defeated Simmons for the title in Baltimore, Maryland, on December 30, 1992. Vader lost the title to Sting in London, England, on March 11, 1993, but reclaimed the belt from Sting in Dublin, Ireland, on March 17, 1993. He lost the title to Ric Flair at Starrcade '93 on December 27, 1993. He captured the WCW U.S. Championship from Hacksaw Duggan on December 27, 1994. He was

stripped of the belt in March of 1995. Vader left the WCW in 1995 following a locker room altercation with Paul Orndorff. He subsequently entered the WWF, where he was managed by Jim Cornette.

Vailahi, Sionne *see* Barbarian, The

Valen, Jim *see* Valiant, Jimmy

Valentine, Dale *see* Roberts, Buddy

Valentine, George *see* Fuller, Buddy

Valentine, Greg "the Hammer" (John Wisniski; b. September 10; Seattle, Washington; 6', 243 lbs.) is the son of wrestler Johnny Valentine. He began wrestling in 1971. He held the NWA Americas Title in Los Angeles several times in 1975. He teamed with Bill Watts to hold the U.S. Tag Team Title in Louisiana in January of 1976. He teamed with Ric Flair to twice capture the NWA World Tag Team Title in 1977. The duo were stripped of the title in November of 1977. Valentine teamed with Baron Von Raschke to again win the tag team belts in July of 1978. They retained the title until near the end of the year. He held the NWA Canadian Title in August of 1979. He and Ray Stevens defeated Rick Steamboat and Jay Youngblood for the tag team title in April of 1980, but lost the belts in a rematch on May 10, 1980. He was subsequently managed by Sir Oliver Humperdink. He defeated Ric Flair for the NWA U.S. Title in July of 1980, relinquishing the title back to Flair the following November. He entered the WWF in 1981 and was managed by the Grand Wizard. He soon returned to the NWA, where he again won the U.S. Title, defeating Wahoo McDaniel in November of 1982. He lost the belt to Roddy Piper in April of 1983, but recaptured the title the following month in a rematch. He was defeated for the belt by Dick Slater in December of 1983. He returned to the WWF and took on Captain Lou Albano as his manager in 1984. He captured the WWF Intercontinental Title from Tito Santana in September of 1984, retaining the title until his defeat by Santana in a rematch in July of 1985. Valentine and Brutus Beefcake, wrestling as the Dream Team, won the WWF Tag Team Title from Mike Rotundo and Barry Windham in Philadelphia, Pennsylvania, on August 24, 1985. They were defeated for the belts by the British Bulldogs at Wrestlemania II on April 7, 1986. He teamed with the Honky Tonk Man as Rhythm and Blues in the WWF in the late 1980s. He held the WWC Caribbean Title in Puerto Rico in December of 1991. Valentine entered the WCW in the early 1990s, and teamed with Terry Taylor to capture the U.S. Tag Team Title in February of 1992. They lost the belts to the Fabulous Freebirds in May of 1992. He held the WWC Universal Title in Puerto Rico in August of 1993.

Valentine, Johnny held the NWA Texas Title in August of 1954. He teamed with Chet Wallich as the Atomic Blonds to hold the NWA World Tag Team Title in Minneapolis in December of 1957. He teamed with Eddie Graham,

wrestling as Rip Rogers, to hold the NWA Texas Tag Team Title in April of 1958. He teamed with Jerry Graham to capture the WWWF U.S. Tag Team Title in November of 1959. He was replaced in the tag team by Eddie Graham. He teamed with Buddy Rogers to reclaim the tag title from the Fabulous Kangaroos in November of 1960, but lost the belts back to the Kangaroos later in the month. He then teamed with Bob Ellis to again win the belts in January of 1962. The duo remained champions until their defeat by Buddy Rogers and Johnny Barend in July of 1962. He teamed with Bulldog Brower to hold the International Tag Team Title in Toronto in February of 1963. Valentine held the IWA Title in Chicago in July of 1963 and was the NWA U.S. Champion in 1964. He again held the tag title from February of 1966 when he teamed with Antonio Pugliese to defeat Dr. Bill and Dan Miller. Valentine turned on Pugliese in a match against Baron Mikel Scicluna and Smasher Sloan in September of 1966 and relinquished the title. He held the NWA Florida Title several times in 1967 and 1968. He teamed with Boris Malenko to briefly hold the NWA Southern Tag Team Title in August of 1968. Valentine held the World Class Championship in Texas several times in the late 1960s, often wrestling against Fritz Von Erich. Wrestling as the Big O, Valentine also held the NWA Georgia Title several times in 1968. He held the World Class Texas Title several times in the late 1960s and early 1970s. He held the World Class American Tag Team Title in Texas several times in the early 1970s, teaming with Wahoo McDaniel and Thunderbolt Patterson. Valentine again held the NWA U.S. Title several times in 1973. He also held the NWA Missouri Title in January of 1973, and was the NWA Southern Champion in Florida in June of 1973. He teamed with Ripper Collins to hold the Hawaiian Tag Team Title in November of 1973. He also held the NWA Mid-Atlantic Title in 1974. He survived an airplane crash that injured Ric Flair and several other wrestlers in October 1975. He teamed with Killer Kowalski to hold the IWF Tag Team Title in Massachusetts in the early 1980s. He is the father of Greg "the Hammer" Valentine.

Valentine, Rick *see* Brown, Kerry.

Valentino, Eddie *see* Gorgeous George, Jr.

Valentino, Mike teamed with Gene Dubuque to hold the NWA World Tag Team Title in San Francisco in August of 1958.

Valiant, Jerry (Guy Mitchell) teamed with Joe Tomasso as the Assassins in the mid 1960s, holding the WWA Tag Team Title three times in 1965 and 1966. He wrestled as Mr. X to capture the Canadian Tag Team Title several times in 1973 and 1974, teaming with Buck Ramstead, Gene Kiniski and the Brute. Wrestling as Guy Mitchell, he held the Canadian tag belts with Ormand Malumba and Ricky Hunter in 1975. He wrestled as the Masked Strangler to capture the WWA Title in Indiana in 1976. He entered the WWWF in the late 1970s as Jerry, one of the Valiant

Brothers. He teamed with Johnny Valiant to capture the WWWF Tag Team Title from Tony Garea and Larry Zbyszko in March of 1979. They retained the title until October of 1979, when they were defeated by Tito Santana and Ivan Putski. He wrestled with Roger Kirby in the WWA to capture the Tag Team Title in April of 1980. They lost the belts the following August. He and Kirby also held the Southern Tag Team Title in November of 1980 and the NWA Central States Tag Team Title in March of 1982. Valiant teamed with Abdullah the Great to again hold the belts in 1983.

Valiant, Jimmy (Jim Valen; New York; 6'3", 251 lbs.) began wrestling in 1969. Known as "Handsome" Jimmy Valiant, the Boogie Woogie Man, he teamed with his "brother," Johnny, to briefly hold the WWA Tag Team Title in January of 1974. They went on to win the WWWF Tag Team Title from Tony Garea and Dean Ho in May of 1974. They lost the belts later in the month to Dominic Denucci and Victor Rivera. The duo also held the NWA Georgia Tag Team Title in July of 1976. Jimmy and Johnny Valiant teamed to capture the NWA World Tag Team Title in San Francisco in December of 1976. They also captured the WWA Tag Team Title in June of 1977. They retained the belts until March of the following year. They recaptured the title for several months late in 1978. Valiant held the Southern Heavyweight Title many times in the late 1970s and early 1980s, wrestling against Jerry Lawler, Tommy Rich, the Dream Machine, and many others. He teamed with Rocky Johnson to hold the Southern Tag Team Title in May of 1980. He held the NWA TV Title several times in 1982. He lost a loser leave town match to the Great Kabuki in 1983, but continued to wrestle in the area as Charlie Brown. He reclaimed the TV Title as Brown in November of 1983. Valiant captured the Mid-America Title in Memphis in March of 1984. He held the USWA Unified Title several times in the early 1990s and the USWA Southern Title in March of 1992.

Valiant, Johnny (6'4", 250 lbs.) began wrestling in 1969. Wrestling as "Luscious" Johnny Valiant, he often tagged with his "brother," Jimmy Valiant, holding the WWA Tag Team Championship briefly in January of 1974. Managed by Lou Albano, they defeated Tony Garea and Dean Ho for the WWWF Tag Team Title in May of 1975. They were defeated for the belts later in the month by the team of Dominic Denucci and Victor Rivera. He held the NWA U.S. Title in July of 1975 and teamed with his "brother" Jerry Valiant to capture the NWA Georgia Tag Team Title in July of 1976. The duo captured the NWA World Tag Team Title in San Francisco in December of 1976. They also held the WWA Tag Team Title in June of 1977. They retained the belts until March of the following year. They recaptured the title for several months late in 1978. They captured the WWWF Tag Team Title from Tony Garea and Larry Zbyszko. They lost the belts to Ivan Putski and Tito Santana in October of 1979. Valiant briefly held the WWA

Title in the Spring of 1981. He later managed such stars as Dino Bravo and Greg Valentine in the WWF and AWA from the mid-1980s. He managed Valentine and Brutus Beefcake during their WWF Tag Team Title reign in 1985 and 1986. Valiant returned to the ring in the NWA in the late 1980s.

Valois, Frank (b. 1915; Montreal, Canada; 6'2", 230 lbs.) captured the Canadian amateur wrestling title at the age of 15. He turned pro three years later and was a popular scientific star for the next three decades. He teamed with Andre Bollet to hold the NWA Texas Tag Team Title several times in early 1959.

Vampire Warrior (Dave Heath; 6'3", 256 lbs.) teamed with Tom Nash as the Black Harts to hold the Calgary Stampede International Tag Team Title in September of 1989. He debuted in the USWA as the Vampire Warrior in July 1993, managed by Bert Prentise. He also wrestled as the Warlock in the USWA in 1993. He married Luna Vachon in October of 1994, and they separated the following year.

Vampiro Americano *see* Bradshaw, Justin "Hawk"

Van Dam, Rob (Rob Szatkowski; b. 1970; Battle Creek, Michigan; 6', 215 lbs.) began wrestling as Rob Zakowski in 1990. He wrestled in Florida, the South Atlantic and All-Japan in the early 1990s as Robbie V and Rob Van Dam. He competed in the ECW in 1996.

Van Kamp, Jeff teamed with Dick the Bruiser to briefly hold the WWA Tag Team Title in January of 1984. Wresting as Lord Humongous, he held the Alabama Title several times in 1984 and 1985.

Varga, Count Billy (b. 1918; Hollywood, California; 5'11", 205 lbs.) began wrestling in the late 1930s. He was a master of the abdominal stretch and the step-over toe hold. Varga held the World Light Heavyweight Title in 1941 and 1942. He remained a leading wrestling star in the 1940s and 1950s. He held the Hawaiian Title for several months from March of 1956, and teamed with Sam Steamboat to hold the Hawaiian Tag Team Title in August of 1956. He also held the American Title in Texas in 1957. He retired to Los Angeles.

Varsity Club, The *see* Rotunda, Mike & Steiner, Rick

Varsity Club, The *see* Rotunda, Mike & Williams, Steve

Vasiri, Hossein Khosrow *see* Iron Sheik, The

Vaughn, Lance *see* Von Erich, Lance

Vaughn, Ricky teamed with Billy Jack Haynes to hold the NWA Pacific Northwest Tag Team Title in May of 1985.

Vaziri, Ali *see* Iron Sheik, The

Veazy, Dale *see* Earl, James

Vega, Savio (Juan Rivera; b. 1965; Vega Alta, Puerto Rico; 5'11", 250 lbs.) began wrestling in 1986. The Puerto Rican native wrestled as the masked Kwang in the WWF in 1994. He became Savio Vega in June of 1995, and teamed with Razor Ramon in several matches.

Vegas, Vinnie *see* Diesel

Vendetta, Tony (Tony Merro) wrestled as Tony Vincent in the WCW before becoming Tony Vendetta. He is the brother of Johnny B. Badd.

Ventura, Jesse "the Body" (James Janos; b. July 15, 1952; Minneapolis, Minnesota; 6'3", 280 lbs.) was born in Minneapolis, Minnesota. He served in the United States Navy from 1969 until 1973. He debuted in professional wrestling in Wichita, Kansas, in 1975 as Surfer Jesse Ventura. He held the NWA Pacific Northwest Title several times in 1976. He also held the Pacific Northwest tag belts several times from 1975 through 1978, teaming with Bull Ramos, Buddy Rose and Jerry Oates. He teamed with Adrian Adonis to form the East-West Connection and they received the AWA Tag Team Title in July of 1980. They retained the belts until June of 1981, when they were defeated by Jim Brunzell and Greg Gagne. He held the Southern Heavyweight Title several times in late 1983, where he was managed by Jimmy Hart. Ventura subsequently moved to the WWF. He suffered from a blood clot in his lungs while wrestling in the WWF. He retired from the ring in 1986, but remained with the WWF as a color commentator. He also began an acting career in the mid-1980s, appearing on television in an episode of *Hunter* and starring in the unsuccessful pilot film *Tag Team*, with

Roddy Piper, in 1991. He also appeared in the films *Predator* (1987), *The Running Man* (1987), *Abraxus, Guardian of the Universe* (1991) and *Demolition Man* (1993). Ventura was elected Mayor of Brooklyn Park, Michigan, in November of 1990. He left the WWF and joined the WCW as a color commentator in January of 1992. He did not run for reelection as mayor and completed his term in 1994.

Venura, Joe *see* Lightfoot, Joe

Vera, Enrique held the Mexican National Light Heavyweight Title in 1972. He teamed with Ron Starr to hold the NWA World Tag Team Title in San Francisco in November of 1978. He returned to Mexico to recapture the light heavyweight belt in 1979.

Verdi, Count Antonio (Alfred J. DeBenedetti; b. 1910, d. January 8, 1992) was born in Hamilton, Ontario, Canada, though he spent his youth in Italy with his family during World War I. He returned to Canada after the war, where he was employed by the Canadian Steel Co. DeBenedetti also served in the Canadian Army during World War II. He moved to Buffalo, New York, in 1953. He soon became known as a leading wrestler during the television era, competing in the ring as Count Antonio Verdi, the Madman from Milan. The villainous Verdi was known for his cape and monocle, handlebar mustache and long hair. He remained an active competitor until his retirement from the ring in 1960s. He occasionally made ring appearances as Tony Verdi in the 1970s and 1980s. He died after a long illness at a Buffalo, New York, hospital on January 8, 1992.

Verdu, Crusher (Rick Ferraro) held the NWA Americas Title in Los Angeles in June of 1976. He held the NWA Americas Tag Team Title several times in 1976, teaming with Roddy Piper and Frank Monte.

Vetoyanis, George *see* Zaharias, George

Vicious, Sid (Sid Eudy; West Memphis, Arkansas; b. July 4; 6'8", 318 lbs.) began wrestling in 1986 as Lord Humongous in the Memphis area. He held the NWA Southeastern Title in December of 1987. He held the CWA Title in December of 1988. He entered the WCW in 1989 and was managed by Teddy Long. He teamed with Dan Spivey as the Skyscrapers and subsequently joined the Four Horsemen. He left the WCW and entered the WWF as Sid Justice in the early 1990s. He walked out of the WWF in May of 1992. He wrestled in the WCW until he resigned following a fight and stabbing incident with Arn Anderson in a London hotel room in October of 1993. Vicious rejoined the USWA in July of 1994 and engaged in a lengthy feud with Jerry Lawler. He captured the USWA Unified Title in July of 1994. He relinquished the belt to Lawler on February 6, 1995. He returned to the WWF in 1995 as Psycho Sid. Physical problems plagued Vicious in the mid-1990s, and his appearances in the ring became more infrequent.

Victory, Jack (6'4", 230 lbs.) began wrestling in 1985. He teamed with John Tatum to hold the UWF

Tag Team Title in Oklahoma in October of 1986. He and Tatum also held the World Class Texas Tag Team Title several times in 1988, often competing against Steve and Shaun Simpson. He was a former flagbearer for the Sheepherders and was managed by Paul E. Dangerously in the WCW in 1989. He wrestled as Jacko Victory in the early 1990s and teamed with Rip Morgan as the Royal Family.

Victory, Ted *see* Zaharias, George

Viet Cong Express *see* Hase, Hiroshi & Niikura, Fumihiro

Vignault, Richard *see* Martel, Rick

Viking, The (Bob Morse; d. October 3, 1981) held the NWA Central States Title during the latter half of 1966. He teamed with Jack Donovan to hold the Central States Tag Team Title in July of 1966. He held the tag belts with Bob Ellis in October of 1967 and with Roger Kirby in July of 1968. He teamed with Bob Geigel to hold the Central State tag belts in December of 1968 and the Mid-West Tag Team Title in Omaha in March of 1969.

Viking, The *see* Nord, John

Villmer, Ray held the Pacific Coast Title in San Francisco from May of 1940 until he left the area several months later. He held the NWA Central States Title in 1954. He teamed with Jack Curtis to hold the NWA Southern Tag Team Title on several occasions in 1960.

Vincent, Tony *see* Vendetta, Tony

Vines, Doug teamed with Jeff Sword as the Devil's Duo in ICW in the early 1980s, where they were managed by Izzy Slapowitz. They held the ICW U.S. Tag Team Title for several months from April of 1981. He and Sword wrestled as the Barroom Brawlers in the USWA in the early 1990s. They held the USWA Tag Team Title several times in 1991. Vines wrestled as Deadhead in the USWA in 1993. He teamed with Mad Man Pondo as the Bar Room Brawlers in the USWA in 1994.

Virag, Ede (d. 1951; Wichita, Kansas) held the World Title in Kansas several times in the early 1940s.

Virgil (Mike Jones; b. June 13; Pittsburgh, Pennsylvania; 5'11", 230 lbs.) began wrestling in 1985. Wrestling as Soul Train Jones, he captured the CWA International Title in January of 1987. He teamed with Rocky Johnson to hold the Southern Tag Team Title in April of 1987. He was a valet for Ted DiBiase in the WWF in the late 1980s, before breaking with DiBiase.

Vodic, Igor *see* Mighty Igor, The

Volador (Remo Banda) held the Mexican National Tag Team Title several times in the early 1990s, teaming with Angel Azteca and Misterioso.

Volkoff, Igor held the Canadian Tag Team Title several times in 1977 and 1978, teaming with Gama Singh, Bob Dellaserra and the Mongol. He teamed with Roger Kirby to briefly hold the WWA Tag Team Title in April of 1979. He again held the Canadian tag belts in September of 1981, teaming with Al Tomko. He held the Canadian Title in Vancouver, Canada, in March of 1983.

Volkoff, Nikolai (Josip Peruzovic; b. October 14; Moscow, Russia; 6'7", 280 lbs.) began wrestling in 1968. He wrestled as Bepo, teaming with Geeto, as the Mongols in the WWWF in the early 1970s. They were originally managed by Tony Angelo before signing with Lou Albano. They captured the WWWF International Tag Team Title from Tony Marino and Victor Rivera in June of 1970. They exchanged the belts with Bruno Sammartino and Dominic Denucci in the Summer of 1971, and eventually lost the title to Luke Graham and Tarzan Tyler in November of 1971. Volkoff, with Killer Kowalski and Big John Studd, teamed as the Executioners under the management of Lou Albano in the WWWF in 1976. He teamed with Ivan Koloff to hold the NWA Florida Tag Team Title in August of 1980. He teamed with Chris Markoff to hold the NWA Atlantic Coast Tag Title in 1981. Volkoff teamed with the Iron Sheik under the management of Freddie Blassie to win the WWF Tag Title from Mike Rotunda and Barry Windham at Wrestlemania I on March 31, 1985. They were defeated for the belts in a return match with Rotundo and Windham on June 17, 1985. Volkoff wrestled for various independent promotions in the early 1990s. He held the NAW Title in Pittsburgh in 1992 and 1993. He returned to the WWF as part of Ted

DiBiase's stable for a brief period in 1995 before returning to the independent circuit.

Von Brauner, Eric *see* Steinborn, Dick

Von Brauner, Karl (272 lbs.) made his professional wrestling debut in 1960. He teamed with Kurt Von Brauner to hold the World Tag Team Title in Tennessee in March of 1960, and the NWA Southern Tag Team Title in 1961. They were managed by Gentleman Saul Weingeroff. They also held the AWA Tag Team Title in Indiana in late 1962. They captured the Texas World Tag Team Title in July of 1963. They again held the Tennessee World Tag Team Title several times in 1964. They also captured the WWA Tag Team belts in Memphis in October of 1964, holding the belts until their defeat by Nicolai Volkoff and Boris Volkoff the following May. He teamed with Eric Von Brauner when Kurt left the team for several years in the mid-1960s. He held the Southern Junior Heavyweight Title for several months in mid-1966. He also held the World Tag Team Title in Tennessee with Luke Graham in August of 1966. He teamed with Al Costello to hold the World Class World Tag Team Title in Texas in late 1966. He teamed with Waldo Von Erich to hold the U.S. Tag Team Title in Oklahoma in March of 1971. The Von Brauners held the Southern Tag Team Title and the Tennessee World belts several times in 1971 and 1972. The Von Brauners captured the NWA World Tag Team Title in San Francisco in March of 1974. Von Brauner teamed with Senior X to capture the NWA Americas Title in Los Angeles in February of 1976.

Von Brauner, Kurt held the NWA Southern Title several times in 1957. He teamed with Karl Von Brauner to hold the World Tag Team Title in Tennessee in March of 1960, and the NWA Southern Tag Team Title in 1961. They were managed by Gentleman Saul Weingeroff. They also held the AWA Tag Team Title in Indiana in late 1962. They captured the Texas World Tag Team Title in July of 1963. They also captured the WWA Tag Team belts in Memphis in October of 1964, holding the title until their defeat by Nioclai Volkoff and Boris Volkoff the following May. The Von Brauners held the Southern Tag Team Title and the Tennessee World Tag Team belts several times in 1972 and 1972. The Von Brauners captured the NWA World Tag Team Title in San Francisco in March of 1974.

Von Crush, Skull (Vito Lograsso) wrestled in the USWA in 1994.

Von Erich, Chris (Chris Adkisson; b. September 30, 1969, d. September 12, 1991; Denton, Texas; 5'3", 140 lbs.) was the youngest son of wrestler Fritz Von Erich. He began wrestling with his brothers on independent cards in Texas in the mid 1980s. He suffered from chronic asthma and his small size made a wrestling career difficult. He died in the yard of his family's farmhouse in Texas of a self-inflicted gunshot wound on September 12, 1991.

Von Erich, David (David Ad-

kisson; b. July 22, 1958, d. February 2, 1984; Denton, Texas; 6'4", 247 lbs.) was the son of wrestler Fritz Von Erich. He began wrestling in June of 1977. He captured the World Class Texas Title for the first of many times in September of 1978. He teamed with his brother, Kevin, to hold the World Class American Tag Team Title in late 1978, and the World Class World Tag Team Title in Texas in early 1981. Managed by J.J. Dillon, he held the NWA Southern Title in Florida from December of 1981 until July of 1982. He again captured the World Class Texas Belt in September of 1982, holding the title several more times in a series of matches against Jimmy Garvin. He held the NWA Missouri Title from September of 1983 until January of 1984. He died while on tour in Japan of severe enteritis, an acute inflammation of the intestines, on February 2, 1984.

Von Erich, Fritz (Jack Adkisson; Denton, Texas) was a leading wrestler in Texas from the 1950s. He teamed with Karl Von Schober to hold the Canadian Open Tag Team Title in Toronto several times in 1955. He again held the Canadian Open tag belts in October of 1957, teaming with Gene Kiniski. He held the Texas Brass Knucks Title in April of 1958. He teamed with Hans Hermann to hold the NWA World Tag Team Title in Minneapolis in July of 1958. Von Erich held the World Title in Omaha several times in 1962 and 1963. He also held the NWA U.S. Title three times in the early 1960s. He defeated Gagne for the AWA Title in July of 1963 in Omaha, Nebraska. He lost the belt back to Gagne the following month. He teamed with Killer Karl Kox to capture the World Class World Tag Team Title in Texas in June of 1965, and again held the tag belts the following year, teaming with Duke Keomuka. He held the World Class Championship numerous times from 1966 through 1977, wrestling against such stars as Johnny Valentine, Boris Malenko, Toru Tanaka, Blackjack Lanza, Blackjack Mulligan, Bruiser Brody and Ox Baker. He also held the World Class American Tag Team Title during the 1960s, teaming with Waldo Von Erich, Billy Red Lyons, Grizzly Smith, Dan Miller, Dean Ho and others. Von Erich reclaimed the World Class belt in a retirement match on June 14, 1982. He remained a promoter of the World Class organization until the late 1980s. Von Erich was the patriarch of a tragedy prone wrestling family. His seven-year-old son, Jack, Jr., died from an electric shock in 1959. His other sons Kevin, Kerry, David, Mike and Chris were all professional wrestlers. David died suddenly in Japan in 1984. Mike, Chris and Kerry were all suicides in the late 1980s and early 1990s.

Von Erich, Kerry (Kerry Adkisson; b. February 3, 1960, d. February 18, 1993; Denton, Texas; 6'2", 260 lbs.) was the son of wrestler Fritz Von Erich. He made his professional wrestling debut in Dallas, Texas, on May 7, 1978. He won the World Class Championship in Texas in December of 1980. He held the World Class Title several times through the mid-1980s. He teamed with Bruiser Brody to hold the

World Class American Tag Team Title in the early 1980s. He also held the World Class World Tag Team Title several times in 1981 and 1982, teaming with Terry Orndorff and Al Madrill. He held the NWA Missouri Title for several months from January of 1983. He defeated Ric Flair for the NWA World Title on May 6, 1984, at Texas Stadium in Dallas. He lost the title back to Flair in Yokosuka, Japan, on May 24, 1984. He teamed with his brother, Kevin, to hold the World Class American Tag Team Title in September of 1985. He was seriously injured in a motorcycle accident in Argyle, Texas, on June 4, 1986, which resulted in the amputation of his right foot. Von Erich secretly wrestled with a prosthetic foot for the rest of his career. He captured the WCWA World Title in October of 1986. He captured the title several more times before losing a unification match with AWA champion Jerry Lawler on December 13, 1988. He also held the World Class World Tag Team Title several times with Kevin Von Erich in 1988 and 1989, and held the tag belts with Jeff Jarrett in March of 1989. Von Erich held the USWA Texas Title several times in late 1989 and early 1990. He entered the WWF in 1990, where he was known as the Texas Tornado. He defeated Mr. Perfect for the WWF Intercontinental Title in August of 1990. He lost the belt back to Perfect in a rematch the following November. Von Erich was arrested on drug charges in Richardson, Texas, in February of 1992 and was dismissed from the WWF. Von Erich wrestled for various independent promotions later in

1992, winning the WWWA Title in Pennsylvania. He was facing a possible prison sentence for possession of illegal drugs when he died from a self-inflicted bullet wound at the family's ranch in Denton County, Texas, on February 18, 1993.

Von Erich, Kevin (Kevin Adkisson; b. May 15; Denton, Texas; 6'2", 235 lbs.) is the son of wrestler, Fritz Von Erich. He began wrestling in August of 1976. He teamed with his brother, David, to hold the World Class American Tag Team Title in late 1978. He held the World Class Championship in Texas for several months in early 1979. He held the NWA Missouri Title for several months from November of 1979. He held the World Class Title several more time in 1980. He again teamed with his brother, David, to capture the World Class World Tag Team Title in early 1981. He teamed with his brother, Kerry, to hold the World Class American Tag Team Title in September of 1985. They also held the World Class World Tag Team Title several times in 1988 and 1989. He was the last holder of the World Class Texas Title when the promotion closed in 1991. He is the older brother of Kerry, Chris, David and Michael Von Erich.

Von Erich, Lance (Lance Vaughn; Arlington, Texas; 6'2", 260 lbs.) began wrestling in 1984. He wrestled as a "cousin" of the Von Erich brothers in World Class from the mid-1980s. He held the World Class TV Title in March of 1986. He teamed with the Dingo Warrior to capture the WCWA World Tag Team Title in Texas in November of

1986. He was later known as Fabulous Lance and wrestled extensively in South Africa.

Von Erich, Mike (Mike Adkisson; b. March 2, 1964, d. April 11, 1987; Denton, Texas; 6'1", 200 lbs.) was the son of wrestler Fritz Von Erich. He began wrestling professionally in November of 1983. He captured the World Class Championship in Texas in August of 1984, when he substituted for his brother, Kevin, in a match against Gino Hernandez. Von Erich lost a rematch with Hernandez the following month. He suffered for a near fatal episode of toxic shock syndrome in 1985. He died of an overdose of tranquilizers on April 11, 1987.

Von Erich, Waldo held the NWA Texas Title in June of 1961. He teamed with Gene Kiniski to hold the WWWF U.S. Tag Team Title in 1964. He held the Texas Brass Knucks Title in August of 1966. He teamed with Fritz Von Erich to hold the World Class American Tag Team Title in 1967. He teamed with Karl Von Brauner to hold the U.S. Tag Team Title in Oklahoma in March of 1971. He held the NWF title in Cleveland in the early 1970s. He captured the Australasian Title in February of 1974. Wrestling as the Great Zimm, he held the MSWA North American Title in 1977.

Von Goering, Fritz teamed with Gene Dubuque to hold the NWA World Tag Team Title in November of 1958. He held the NWA Pacific Northwest Title in January of 1962. He teamed with Kurt Von Poppenheim to capture the Pacific

Northwest Tag Title in February of 1962. He again held the tag belts in September of 1962, teaming with Mad Dog Vachon.

Von Haig, Crusher *see* Hawk

Von Himmler, Kurt held the NWA Pacific Northwest Title in October of 1957. He also held the Pacific Northwest tag belts several times in the late 1950s, teaming with Juan Oinada and Kurt Von Poppeneim.

Von Krupp, Otto *see* Malenko, Boris

Von Poppenheim, Kurt teamed with Andy Tremaine and Johnny Cretorian to hold the Northwest Tag Team Title in Vancouver, Canada, in 1952. He held the NWA Pacific Northwest Tag Team Title several times from the early 1950s through the early 1960s, teaming with Leo Wallick, Henry Lenz, Jack O'Reilly, Kurt Von Himmler, Dan Manoukian, Fritz Von Brauner and Soldat Gorky. He held the Pacific Coast Junior Heavyweight Title several times in the mid-1950s. He also held the NWA Pacific Northwest Title in June of 1959.

Von Raschke, Baron (James Raschke; Berlin, Germany; 6'2 1/2", 271 lbs.) began wrestling in 1966. He was known as the master of the clawhold, and fought numerous bouts with Verne Gagne in the AWA during the 1960s and 1970s. He held the AWA Title in Montreal, Canada, in 1967. He held the World Class Championship in Texas in 1970. Von Raschke was managed by Bobby Heenan when he held the WWA Title several times between 1970 and 1972. He teamed with Ernie Ladd to hold the WWA Tag Team title for several months in 1973. He teamed with Mad Dog Vachon to hold the NWA Central States Tag Team Title in September of 1976. He held the NWA TV Title for several months in early 1978. He teamed with Greg Valentine to capture the NWA World Tag Team Title in July of 1978. They held the belts until the following December. Von Raschke then teamed with Paul Jones, defeating Jimmy Snuka and Paul Orndorff for the tag title in April of 1979. They were defeated by Ric Flair and Blackjack Mulligan for the belts in August of 1979, but recaptured the title the following month. They retained the belt until October of 1979, when they lost to Rick Steamboat and Jay Youngblood. Von Rashke held the NWA Georgia Title from June until August of 1980. He subsequently entered the AWA where he teamed with Crusher to take the AWA Tag Team Title from Jerry Blackwell and Ken Patera in May of 1984. They lost the belts to the Road Warriors in August of 1984. Von Raschke teamed with Ken Patera to hold the PWA Tag Team Title several times in late 1991 and early 1992.

Von Schacht, Frederick (b. 1912; Milwaukee, Wisconsin; 6'5", 260 lbs.) was a leading mat villain from the 1940s, known in the ring as Milwaukee's Murder Master. He held the Pacific Coast Title in San Francisco in June of 1950. He teamed with Tom Rice to hold the NWA World Tag Team Title in San Francisco in July of 1950.

Von Schober, Karl held the Hawaiian Title in August of 1954. He teamed with Fritz Von Erich to hold the Canadian Open Tag Team Title in Toronto several times in late 1955. He teamed with the Great Kato to hold the NWA World Tag Team Title in San Francisco in December of 1957. He also held the Pacific Coast Title in San Francisco in June of 1958.

Von Steiger, Karl teamed with Kurt Von Steiger to hold the NWA Pacific Northwest Tag Team Title several times in the late 1960s and early 1970s. They also held the Hawaiian Tag Team Title several times in 1969. They held NWA World Tag Team Title in San Francisco several times in 1977.

Von Steiger, Kurt teamed with Karl Von Steiger to hold the NWA Pacific Northwest Tag Team Title several times in the late 1960s and early 1970s. They also held the Hawaiian Tag Team Title several times in 1969. Kurt Von Steiger also held the NWA Pacific Northwest Title several times in 1970 and 1971. The Von Steigers held NWA World Tag Team Title in San Francisco several times in 1977.

Von Stroheim, Kurt (Willie Rutkowsky; b. 1923, d. February 17, 1993) teamed with Skull Von Stroheim to hold the Southern Tag Team Title in May of 1963. They held the WWA Tag Team Title in Los Angeles in early 1965. They captured the NWA World Tag Team Title in Florida in October of 1965. They again held the tag belts in September of 1967.

Von Stroheim, Skull teamed with Kurt Von Stroheim to hold the Southern Tag Team Title in May of 1963. They held the WWA Tag Team Title in Los Angeles in early 1965. They also captured the NWA World Tag Team Title in Florida in October of 1965. They again held the tag belts in September of 1967.

Wacholz, Kevin Patrick *see* Kelly, Kevin

Wagner, Bob (b. 1914; Oregon; 5'10", 235 lbs.) began wrestling in the mid-1930s. The rough competitor was known as the Strangler. He held the NWA Texas Title in May of 1949. He held the Northwest Tag Team Title in Vancouver, Canada, several times in 1955 and 1956, teaming with Don Kindred and Mighty Ursus.

Wagner, George *see* Gorgeous George

Walcott, Jersey Joe (Arnold Raymond Cream; b. 1914, d. February 25, 1994) was the World Heavyweight Boxing Champion from July of 1951 until his defeat by Rocky Marciano fourteen months later. Walcott engaged in several boxer versus wrestler matches, competing against Buddy Rogers in October of 1959 and losing a bout to Lou Thesz in April of 1963. Walcott died in Camden, New Jersey, on February 25, 1994.

Waldeck, Ella (b. 1922; Custer, Washington; 5'5", 148 lbs.) played basketball and softball before she began wrestling in the late 1940s. The athletic Waldeck was a leading female mat star during the 1950s.

Walge, Art (b. 1924; Philadelphia, Pennsylvania; 6'6", 248 lbs.) was a leading weightlifter before he entered professional wrestling in the late 1940s. He was a major grappler in the 1950s, known in the ring as "Dreamboat." He also appeared in several films in the early 1950s including *Meet Me After the Show* (1951) and *Quo Vadis* (1951) as Milo the Croton, a wrestler in ancient Rome.

Walker, Chris (Atlanta, Georgia; 6'2", 254 lbs.) began wrestling in 1989. Known as Conan, he teamed with Marcus Bagwell, as Fabian, to capture the Georgia All-Star Tag Team Title in May of 1991. He teamed with Steve Simpson to hold Global's first World Tag Team Title in July of 1991.

Walker, Hurricane (5'10", 223 lbs.) began wrestling in 1989. He was a popular wrestler in the Florida area and battled Jim Backlund in the PWF.

Walker, Johnny *see* Mr. Wrestling II

Walker, P.J *see* Montoya, Aldo

Wall Street, Michael *see* Rotunda, Mike

Wall Street, V.K *see* Rotunda, Mike

Wallich, Chet teamed with Johnny Valentine as the Atomic Blonds to hold the NWA World Tag Team Title in Minneapolis in December of 1957.

Waltman, Sean *see* Kid, The

Wanz, Otto (Graz, Austria; 6'2", 360 lbs.) began wrestling professionally in 1969. He won the European Heavyweight Tournament in 1978 and 1978. He held the Catch Wresting Association European Heavyweight Title several times from 1978 until his retirement in June of 1990. He also captured the AWA Title from Nick Bockwinkel in August of 1982. He lost the belt back to Bockwinkel in a match in Chicago on October 9, 1982. Wanz was a promoter for the CWA in Austria and Germany.

War Hawk, Joseph (d. 19??) was an Mohawk Indian wrestler from Canada. He wrestled in Canada and on the East Coast from the 1930s. He was the father of Chief Don Eagle.

Ward, Fred (b. 1916, d. May 8, 1992) was a wrestler during the 1940s. He became a wrestling promoter in Columbus, Georgia, in the early 1950s. He co-hosted Columbus Championship Wrestling on television with Jim Carlisle. He also served on the NWA Board of Governors. Ward died in his sleep at his home in Columbus, Georgia, on May 8, 1992.

Ware, Koko B. (James Ware; b. June 20; Union City, Tennessee; 5'9", 229 lbs.) began wrestling in the Mid-South in 1978. Wrestling as Sweet Brown Sugar, Ware teamed with Stan Lane to hold the Southern Tag Team Title in September of 1981. He formed a tag team with Bobby Eaton under the management of Jimmy Hart, and the duo captured the Southern Tag Team Title several times in 1982. He also teamed with Dutch Mantel to hold the tag belts in September of 1983. Ware also wrestled as Stagger Lee in the Memphis and Georgia area in 1983, winning the Georgia Superstars Title and the Mid-America Title. He teamed with Norvell Austin as the PYT (Pretty Young Things) Express, capturing the Southern Tag Team Title in February of 1984. They also held the U.S. Tag Team Title in Florida in February of 1985. They again held the Southern tag belts several times in 1985. He became known as the Birdman in the WWF in 1986, where he brought his parrot, Frankie, to the ring. He defeated Jerry Lawler for the USWA Unified Title in February of 1992. He lost the belt to Kamala the following month. He teamed with Rex Hargrove to briefly hold the USWA Tag Team Title in November of 1993.

Warlock, The *see* Vampire Warrior, The

Warlord (Terry Szopinski; b. March 28, 1962; Chicago, Illinois; 6'5", 360 lbs.) was encouraged to enter wrestling by the Road Warriors. He made his wrestling debut in the WCW in July of 1986 and was managed by Baby Doll. He was subsequently managed by Paul Jones, who teamed him with the Barbarian as the Powers of Pain. The duo feuded with the Road Warriors in the WCW before entering the WWF, where they competed against Demolition. The Warlord wrestled for various independent promotions in the early 1990s. He held the WWWA Title in Pennsylvania in 1992.

Warner, Jeff *see* Storm, J.W.

Warren, Dick *see* Bockwinkel, Nick

Warrington, Chaz *see* Headbanger Mosh

Washington, Reginald *see* Fine, Reggie B.

Watanabe, Harold *see* Yamamoto, Tojo

Watanabe, Tomoko (b. 1972, 5'6", 170 lbs.) made her wrestling debut in 1989. She was a leading star with the All-Japan Women's Promotion in the 1990s.

Watson, John *see* Whipwreck, Mikey

Watson, Whipper Billy (William Potts; b. 1915, d. February 4, 1990) was born in East Toronto, Canada. He went to England in 1936, where he became a leading wrestler. He was known for his Irish Whip and Canadian Avalanche maneuvers in the ring. He held the British Empire Title in Toronto, Canada, numerous times in the 1940s and 1950s. Watson defeated Bill Longson for the NWA Heavyweight Title on February 21, 1947, in St. Louis, Missouri. He lost the belt to Lou Thesz several months later on April 25, 1947. He held the Canadian Open Tag Team Title in Toronto several times in the early 1950s, teaming with Pat Flanagan, Yvon Robert, Hombre Montana, Tex McKenzie, Paul Baillargeon, Lord Athol Layton and others. He defeated Thesz for the title in Toronto, Canada, on March 15, 1956, but again lost the belt in a rematch in St. Louis, Missouri, on November 9, 1956. He held the

Pacific Coast Tag Team Title in Vancouver, Canada, several times in 1961 and 1962, teaming with Roy McClarty, Mr. Kleen and Bearcat Wright. He died at his home in Orlando, Florida, on February 4, 1990. His son, Phillip Watson, also wrestled professionally.

Watson, Whipper, Jr. (Phillip Watson) was the son of Whipper Billy Watson. He held the Mid-America Title in July of 1978. He held the Big Bear Promotions North American Title in Ontario, Canada, in 1982.

Watson, Winnett *see* Flanagan, Pat

Watts, Bill (b. May 5, 1939; Bixby, Oklahoma; 6'3", 278 lbs.) was a leading wrestler from the early 1960s. He held the NWA Texas Title in May of 1963. He teamed with Gorilla Monsoon to win the WWWF U.S. Tag Team Title in April of 1965. They lost the belts to Dr. Bill and Dan Miller the following July. He held the NWA U.S. Title in San Francisco in February of 1966. He teamed with Billy Red Lyons to hold the U.S. Tag Team Title in Oklahoma in January of 1971. He also held the MSWA North American Title in Louisiana several times from 1970 through 1972. Watts held the NWA Georgia Title several times in 1973. He briefly held the NWA Southern Title in Florida in 1974, and the NWA Florida Title in 1974 and 1975. Watts subsequently returned to the MSWA, where he again held the North American Title several times from 1975 through 1979. Watts subsequently headed the Universal

Wrestling Federation during the 1980s. He sold the promotion to Jim Crockett in April of 1987. Watts was director of operations for the WCW in the early 1990s. He briefly worked as a booker for the WWF in the fall of 1995. His son, Erik Watts, was also a popular wrestler.

Watts, Erik (b. 1970; Tulsa, Oklahoma; 6'5", 262 lbs.) is the son of Cowboy Bill Watts. He played football at the University of Louisville before making his professional wrestling debut in the WCW in Knoxville, Tennessee, in August of 1992. Watts, as Troy, wrestled with Chad Fortune in Tekno Team 2000 in the WWF from May of 1995.

Wayne, Brett *see* Sawyer, Brett

Wayne, Buddy (Dwayne Peal) began wrestling in 1953 as Dwayne Peal. He wrestled throughout the country during the 1950s and 1960s. He began wrestling as Buddy Wayne in the late 1960s, and continued to compete primarily in the Mid-South. He also worked as a promoter in the Memphis area in the 1970s and 1980s. He teamed with his son, Ken Wayne, in a feud against Tommy and Eddie Gilbert in Memphis in the late 1970s. Wayne appeared as Friday, Kamala's manager, in the USWA in the late 1980s. He retired from the ring in 1989.

Wayne, Ken (Memphis, Tennessee; 5'8", 208 lbs.) is the son of wrestler Buddy Wayne. He began wrestling in 1977. He teamed with Danny Davis as the Nightmares during the mid-1980s. They captured the Southern Tag Team Title in August of 1984. They held the

Southeastern Tag Team Title several times in 1985 and the Deep South Tag Team Title in Georgia in 1986. They subsequently broke and engaged in a feud, exchanging the U.S. Junior Heavyweight Title in Alabama several times in 1988 and 1989. Wayne held the USWA Junior Heavyweight Title from March until November of 1990. Wayne also wrestled as the Master of Terror in the USWA in 1993.

Weaver, Johnny held the NWA Southern Title in Florida in 1967. He teamed with George Becker to hold the NWA Southern Tag Team Title several times between 1965 and 1969. He teamed with Dewey Robertson to hold the NWA Atlantic Coast Tag Title in 1981. He subsequently teamed with Jay Youngblood to hold the tag belts the following year. He is married to female wrestler Penny Banner.

Weaver, Ralph "Buck" (b. 1906, d. July 28, 1956) was a leading amateur wrestler and football player at Indiana University in the late 1920s. He entered professional wrestling in the 1930s and remained a leading mat star for several decades. Weaver died in Toledo, Ohio, on July 28, 1956.

Webster, Mike teamed with the Professional to hold the NWA Florida Tag Team Title in May of 1972. He teamed with the Brute to hold the Canadian Tag Team Title in early 1973.

Weider, Chris *see* Evans, Chris

Weingeroff, Gentleman Saul (b. 1915, d. 1988) managed Kurt and

Karl Von Brauner in the Mid-South during the 1960s.

Weingeroff, George teamed with Leaping Lanny to hold the ICW U.S. Tag Team Title several times from 1979 through 1981. He wrestled as Sheik Hussein in the USWA and The Sheik in the WCW in the early 1990s. He held the MSWA Tennessee Title several times in mid-1993.

Welch, Herb held the World Junior Heavyweight Title in Nashville several times from 1942 through 1945. He teamed with Tex Riley to hold the Southern Tag Team Title in Tennessee in November of 1948. He held the Southern Junior Heavyweight Title in August of 1952, and in August of 1956. He teamed with Lester Welch to hold the World Tag Team Title in Tennessee in October of 1960. Welch teamed with Al Costello to again hold the tag belts for several months in mid-1966.

Welch, Lester teamed with Herb Welch to hold the World Tag Team Title in Tennessee in October of 1960. He also held the tag belts several times with Jay Strongbow in early 1961. He teamed with Jackie Fargo to hold the Southern Tag Team Title several times in 1962. He also teamed with Buddy Fuller to hold the tag belts in 1962. Welch also held the U.S. Tag Team Title in Nashville in May of 1962, partnered with Danny Hodge. Welch became the first NWA Florida champion in August of 1966, defeating Sputnik Monroe in a tournament. He held the belt until March of 1967. The following month he teamed with Buddy Fuller to capture the NWA

Southern Tag Team Title in Florida. They held the belts until the following November. Welch recaptured the tag title with Eddie Graham as his partner in February of 1968. He teamed with the Gladiator to capture the NWA Florida Tag Team Title in March of 1969.

Welch, Robert *see* Fuller, Robert

Welch, Roy (d. 1977) was a leading wrestling promoter in the Tennessee area. He is the father of wrestlers Buddy Fuller and Billy Golden.

Well, Timothy *see* King, Rex

WellDone *see* King, Rex & Doll, Steve

Wells, George teamed with Dean Ho to hold the Canadian Tag Team Title in January of 1976. He teamed with Jerry Morrow to hold the Calgary Stampede International Tag Team Title in 1978. He held the NWA U.S. Title in San Francisco in late 1979 and early 1980. He teamed with Dewey Robertson to hold the NWA Atlantic Coast Tag Title in 1980. He teamed with Ron Ritchie to hold the NWA Central States Tag Team Title in August of 1983.

Wendling, Francis Xavier (b. 1905, d. May 18, 1991) began wrestling professionally in the 1930s. He was known in the ring as the St. Louis Kid. He was also a practitioner of jujitsu. He retired from the ring in the 1940s to work as a machinist. He also worked as a wrestling coach in St. Louis. He died after a short illness at his home in south St. Louis, Missouri, on May 18, 1991.

Westenberg, Marv *see* Shadow, The

Weston, Mae (b. 1918; Leavenworth, Kansas; 5'3", 140 lbs.) was a carnival acrobat and boxer before she began wrestling professionally in the mid-1930s. She was one of the top female grapplers for the next several decades.

Wharton, Hogan teamed with Pepper Gomez to hold the NWA Texas Tag Team Title in January of 1961.

Whatley, Pistol Pez (b. January 10; El Paso, Texas; 5'10", 245 lbs.) began wrestling in the IWA in 1975. He teamed with Ray Candy to hold the Mid-America Tag Team Title in 1977. He teamed with Rip Rogers to hold the ICW U.S. Tag Team in May of 1982. He held the NWA Southern Title in Florida several times in 1984. He wrestled as Shaska Whatley in the World Championship promotion in the mid-1980s. He teamed with Tiger Conway as the Jive Tones in the late 1980s.

Whipwreck, Mikey (John Watson; b. June 4; New York City; 5'7", 187 lbs.) began wrestling in the ECW in 1994, and was television champion for several months. He also teamed with Cactus Jack to defeat Public Enemy for the tag team belts in August of 1994. They lost the belts in a rematch the following December. Whipwreck captured the ECW Heavyweight Title from the Sandman in October of 1995. He lost the belt in a rematch the following December.

Whistler, Larry *see* Zbyszko, Larry

White, Arthur "Tarzan" (Alabama) attended the University of Alabama, where he played football and majored in languages. He later taught Spanish there. White also played professional football with the New York Giants and Chicago Cardinals. He was a leading wrestler in the 1940s and 1950s.

White, Bubba *see* Moondog Splat

White, Jim teamed with Jerry Lawler in the Memphis area in the early 1970s. Managed by Sam Bass, the duo held the Southern Tag Team Title several times in 1973. They also held the U.S. Tag Team Title in Louisiana in September of 1974.

White, Leon *see* Vader, Big Van

White, Sailor wrestled as King in the Moondogs and, with Rex, captured the WWF Tag Team Title from Tony Garea and Rick Martel in March of 1981. King was refused entry in the United States from Canada and was replaced by Moondog Spot. He held the Canadian International Title in Montreal in 1982. He teamed with Rick Valentine to hold the Canadian International Tag Team Title in October of 1984.

White, Tarzan held the World Title in Colorado in July of 1947. He held the NWA Southern Title in 1952.

White Cloud, Chief teamed with Chief Thundercloud to hold the U.S. Tag Team Title in Louisiana in June of 1974.

White Knight, The *see* Steinborn, Dick

White   Ninja *see* Muta, The Great

White Wolf, Billy *see* Adnan al-Kaissie, Sheik

Whittler, Whitey (b. 1911; Roxanna, Illinois; 5'9", 200 lbs.) began wrestling in the mid-1930s. He was known in the ring for his step-over toe hold. He remained an active competitor through the 1950s.

Wicks,   Billy was a leading wrestler in the Mid-South area from the mid-1950s. He teamed with Yvon Robert to hold the World Tag Team Title in Tennessee in 1957. He held the Gulf Coast Title in Alabama in 1958. He exchanged the Tennessee State Title with Sputnik Monroe several times in 1959 and 1960.

Wiggins,   Stan *see* Martinelli, Angelo

Wight, Paul *see* Giant, The

Wiki Wiki, Oni was a leading Hawaiian mat star from the late 1950s. He teamed with Mike Clancy to hold the World Tag Team Title in Tennessee in May of 1960.

Wild Bunch, The *see* Irwin, Bill & Black Bart

Wild Bunch, The *see* Snow, Al & Kelly, Mike

Wildman,   The *see* McKigney, Dave

Wilkes, Del *see* Patriot, The

William, Sir *see* Dundee, Bill

Williams, Blackstud *see* Candy, Ray

Williams, Cy (d. 19??) captured the Pacific Coast Title from Sandor Szabo in December of 1937. He relinquished the title in a rematch the following February. He held the AWA Title in Montreal, Canada, in December of 1938.

Williams, Gary *see* Hart, Gary

Williams, James *see* Garvin, Jim

Williams, John *see* Rotten, Ian

Williams, Luke *see* Bushwhacker Luke

Williams, Patty *see* Precious

Williams, Rick *see* Renegade, The

Williams, Robert *see* Bushwhacker Butch

Williams, Steve "Dr. Death" (b. May 14, 1958; Norman, Oklahoma; 6'1", 265 lbs.) was a football star at the University of Oklahoma before he began wrestling professionally in 1982. He teamed with Ted DiBiase to hold the MSWA Tag Team Title in December of 1985. He held the UWF Title in Oklahoma in July of 1987. He joined Kevin Sullivan's Varsity Club and teamed with Sullivan to captured the WCW U.S. Tag Title in December of 1988. They lost the belts the following February. He remained with the Varsity Club and teamed with Mike Rotunda to win the NWA World Tag Team Title from the Road Warriors on April 2, 1989. They were stripped of the title the following month when they attacked special referee Nikita Koloff during a match. Known as Dr. Death, he was a popular wrestler in the U.S. and

Japan, where he often teamed with Terry "Bam Bam" Gordy. He and Gordy defeated Rick and Scott Steiner for the WCW Tag Team belts in Atlanta, Georgia, on July 5, 1992. They lost the belts to Barry Windham and Dustin Rhodes on September 21, 1992.

Williams, Steve *see* Austin, Steve

Williams, Tony (Memphis, Tennessee; 235 lbs.) wrestled in the USWA in 1989. He originally teamed with Brian Christopher as the New Kids. He and Christopher feuded briefly after splitting the team. He continued to compete in the USWA during the 1990s.

Williams, Vicki teamed with Joyce Grable to hold the women's tag team title in the early 1970s. She held the UWA Women's Title in Mexico several times in 1979 and 1980.

Wilson, Larry teamed with Carl Ben Patrick as the Flying Tigers in the mid-1980s. They held the Motor City Wrestling U.S. Team Title several times in 1986 and 1987.

Winchester, Kip *see* Gunn, Billy

Windham, Barry (b. July 4, 1960; Sweetwater, Texas; 6'5", 263 lbs.) is the son of wrestler Blackjack Mulligan. He attended West Texas State, where he wrestled and played football. He made his debut as a professional wrestler in Salt Lake City in 1980. He teamed with Scott McGhee and Mike Graham while wrestling in Florida in the early 1980s. He defeated Dory Funk, Jr. for the Florida State Title on January 12, 1981, but forfeited the belt several months later following an automobile accident. He wrestled with his father, Blackjack Mulligan, in the Mid-Atlantic and Georgia, and wrestled as Blackjack Mulligan, Jr. He broke with his father the following year and resumed wrestling as Barry Windham. He teamed with Ron Bass to defeat Big John Studd and Jim Garvin for the Global Tag Team Title on November 14, 1982. He briefly held the NWA Southern Title in Florida the following month. He held the NWA Florida Title several times in September of 1983. He teamed with Mike Rotundo in 1984 and both soon joined the WWF, where they wrestled in single and tag matches. Under the management of Lou Albano, they captured the WWF Tag Team Title from Adrian Adonis and Dick Murdoch in Hartford, Connecticut, on January 21, 1985. They lost the title to Nikolai Volkoff and the Iron Sheik at Wrestlemania on March 31, 1985. Wrestling as the U.S. Express, they regained the title on June 17, 1985, but were again defeated for the belts by Greg Valentine and Brutus Beefcake in Philadelphia, Pennsylvania, on August 24, 1985. Windham subsequently left the WWF to return to Florida, where he often teamed with his brother, Kendall Windham. He held the NWA Florida Title several times in 1986. He subsequently engaged in a series of unsuccessful challenges for Ric Flair's NWA championship. He teamed with Ron Garvin to win the NWA U.S. Tag Title in December of 1986. They held the belts until their defeat by Ivan Koloff and Dick Murdoch in March of 1987. Windham

teamed with Lex Luger to win the NWA Tag Title from Tully Blanchard and Arn Anderson on March 27, 1988. They lost the belts the following month when Windham turned on Luger and joined the Four Horsemen. Windham won the NWA U.S. Title, defeating Nikita Koloff in a tournament on May 13, 1988. He lost the belt to Luger on February 20, 1989. Windham then returned to the WWF, where he wrestled as the Widowmaker. He returned to the NWA in 1990 and became a fan favorite the following year. He defeated Steve Austin for the WCW TV Title in April of 1992, though lost the belt in a rematch the following month. He then teamed with Dustin Rhodes and captured the WCW tag belts from Steve Williams and Terry Gordy on September 21, 1992. The team split following the loss of the belts to Shane Douglas and Rick Steamboat on November 18, 1992. Windham subsequently engaged in a series of matches against his ex-partner, Rhodes. Windham defeated the Great Muta for the NWA Heavyweight Title in Asheville, North Carolina, on February 21, 1993. He lost the belt to Flair in Biloxi, Mississippi, on July 18, 1993.

Windham, Bob *see* Mulligan, Blackjack

Windham, Kendall (b. 1967; Sweetwater, Texas; 6'5", 220 lbs.) began wrestling in 1983. He is the son of Blackjack Mulligan and the younger brother of Barry Windham. He held the NWA Florida Title several times during 1986. He was briefly a member of the Four Horsemen in the NWA with Ric Flair, Butch Reed and Barry Windham. He also teamed with Dustin Rhodes as the Texas Broncos in Florida.

Winner, Mike (Virginia City, Virginia; 5'10", 234 lbs.) began wrestling in the Georgia All-Star area in 1990. He subsequently wrestled in the Pacific Northwest.

Winters, Larry (5'10", 243 lbs.) began wrestling in 1983. The Philadelphia native held the NWF belt in 1986 and teamed with Johnny Hot Body to win the Tri State Tag Team Title in 1990. Winters teamed with Tony Stetson to capture the ECW Tag Team Title in March of 1993, losing the belts the following day.

Wippleman, Harvey (David Lauer; b. October 27; Walls, Mississippi) began managing in the USWA as Downtown Bruno. He entered the WWF in the late 1980s as Harvey Wippleman. He also continued to manage, and sometimes referee in the USWA in the mid-1990s.

Wiskoski, Ed *see* DeBeers, Colonel

Wisniski, John *see* Valentine, Greg

Witzig, Jack teamed with George Becker to hold the NWA Southern Tag Team Title several times in 1956.

Wojokowski, Greg (6', 245 lbs.) began wrestling in 1981. He was a former amateur champion who wrestled in the WWA in the 1980s. Known as the Great Wojo, he held the WWA championship in 1984, 1985 and 1987.

Wolf, Jeanette (b. 1933, d. July, 1951) was the adopted daughter of leading female wrestler Mildred Burke. Wolf also began wrestling in the early 1950s. She died of a ruptured stomach and blood clot on the brain following a tag team match in Ohio in July of 1951. Her death was attributed to injuries she had suffered in a previous match.

Wolfe, Buddy (d. 19??) teamed with Don Jardine as the Spoilers to hold the U.S. Tag Team Title in Oklahoma in 1971. Wolfe held the World Class Texas Title in July of 1975. He held the NWA Florida Title for several months in early 1977.

Wolfe, Charles *see* Hernandez, Gino

Wolfe, Dusty (5'10", 230 lbs.) began wrestling in 1987. He wrestled in the WWF as Dale Wolfe. He teamed with Muhammad Hussein to hold the WWC Tag Team Title in Puerto Rico in June of 1993.

Wolfe, Kelly *see* Wolfie D.

Wolfie D. (Kelly Wolfe; 6'1", 250 lbs.) began wrestling in 1991. He wrestled with J.C. Ice as PG-13 in the USWA. They captured the USWA Tag Team Title in November of 1993. They held the tag belts numerous times in the mid-1990s, often feuding with Tommy Rich and Doug Gilbert. Wolfie D. also engaged in a feud with Bill Dundee in 1996. He and J.C. Ice competed under masks as the Cyberpunks after losing a loser-leave-town match in the Spring of 1996.

Wolser, Kim *see* Dirty White Girl

Woman (Nancy Daus Sullivan) was known as Fallen Angel in the late 1980s when she was valet to Kevin Sullivan. She entered the WCW as Robin Green to seduce Rick Steiner. She became known as Woman in the WCW and managed the tag team Doom. She managed the Sandman in ECW in 1994. She entered the WCW in late 1995, often accompanying Rick Flair to the ring. She is the wife of Kevin Sullivan.

Wood, Rick *see* Rude, Rick

Woods, Tim (Atlanta, Georgia; 235 lbs.) was a leading professional wrestler from the mid-1960s who usually competed under a mask as Mr. Wrestling. He held the NWA Georgia Title several times in 1967. He teamed with George Scott to hold the World Class American Tag Team Title in Texas in 1970. He held the NWA Southern Title in Florida several times in 1972, and held the NWA Florida Title in July of 1973. He teamed with Mr. Wrestling II to hold the NWA Georgia Tag Team Title in August of 1974. He survived an airplane crash that injured Ric Flair and several other wrestlers in October of 1975. He held the NWA World Tag Title with Dino Bravo in May of 1976. He also held the NWA TV Title in November of 1976. Woods again teamed with Mr. Wrestling II to reclaim the Georgia Tag Championship in January of 1977. He teamed with Thunderbolt Patterson to hold the title several months later.

World Warriors, The *see* Mad Maxx & Super Maxx

Woyan, Bruce *see* Sawyer, Buzz

Wrecking Crew, The *see* Denton, Len "the Grappler" & Sullivan, Dave "the Equalizer"

Wright, Alex (b. May 17; Berlin, Germany; 6'3", 220 lbs.) is the son of German wrestler Steve Wright. The young German competitor came to the WCW in October of 1994. He was known as "Das Wunderkind" and was a leading contender in the WCW, where he feuded with Jean-Paul LeVeque and Bobby Eaton.

Wright, Edward "Bearcat" (b. 1932, d. August 28, 1982) wrestled for Big Time Wrestling in Massachusetts in the early 1960s, holding that promotion's title for several months in 1961. He teamed with Whipper Billy Watson to hold the Pacific Coast Tag Team Title in Vancouver, Canada, in July of 1962. He held the WWA Title in Los Angeles for several months in late 1963. He teamed with Enrique Torres to hold the Canadian Tag Team Title in April of 1964. He teamed with Luther Lindsay to capture the Hawaiian Tag Team Title in July of 1965. He held the NWA Pacific Northwest Tag Team Title in October of 1965, teaming with Shag Thomas. He also held the belts in March of 1966, teaming with Billy White Wolf. He captured the NWA U.S. Title in San Francisco in December of 1967 and April of 1968. He held the Arizona Title in 1969. He teamed with Sam Steamboat to hold the Hawaiian Tag Team Title in July of 1971. He teamed with

Bobby Shane to hold the NWA Florida Title for several months in the Spring of 1972.

Wright, James Earl *see* Earl, James

Wright, Jim "Rube" (b. 1909, d. February 8, 1963; Los Angeles, California; 6'4", 250 lbs.) attended Arizona State and entered professional wrestling in the mid-1930s. He held the California Title in August of 1942. He wrestled throughout the United States and Western Europe and remained an active competitor through the early 1950s.

Wright, Steve was a leading German wrestler during the 1980s, holding the Catch Wrestling Association Middleweight Title several times during the decade. He is the father of wrestler Alex Wright.

Wykoff, Lee (d. 19??) held the MWA Title in Kansas City several times from 1941 through 1943, often feuding with Orville Brown.

Yachetti, John *see* Beast, The

Yakouchi, Chati *see* Yokouchi, Shinichi "Chatti"

Yamada, Fuji *see* Liger, Jushin

Yamada, Keiji *see* Liger, Jushin

Yamamoto, Hiroyoshi (b. March 23, 1971) began wrestling with New Japan in January of 1991. He held the Catch Wrestling Association Junior Heavyweight Title in Europe in 1993.

Yamamoto, Tojo (Harold Watanabe; b. 1927, d. February 19, 1992; 5'7", 230 lbs.) began wrestling in 1953. He teamed with Alex Perez to hold the Southern Tag Team Title several times in 1964. They also held the World Tag Team Title in Tennessee in August of 1964. He also held the Southern tag belts, teaming with Mitsu Hirai, Tor Kamata and the Great Higami from 1964 through 1966. He teamed with Professor Ito to hold the World Tag Team Title in Tennessee in October of 1966. He teamed with Johnny Long to again hold the belts in November of 1968. He also held the Southern Junior Heavyweight Title in 1968 and 1969. He teamed with Jerry Jarrett often in the early 1970s, holding the Southern Tag Team Title several times. Yamamoto teamed with George Gulas to hold the Mid-America Tag Team Title in late 1977. They again held the title from April of 1978 until the team broke up in August of 1978. Yamamoto also held the tag belts several times in 1979, wrestling with Gypsy Joe and the Great Togo. He held the Mid-America Title in March of 1980. He again teamed with Jerry Jarrett to hold the CWA Tag Team Title in July of 1980. He teamed with Wayne Farris to hold the Southern tag belts in 1981. During the 1980s Yamamoto primarily worked as a manager, overseeing such wrestlers as Phil Hickerson, Akio Sato and Tarzan Goto. He continued to wrestle and manage until late 1991, when he was forced to retire after developing kidney disease and diabetes. He died of a self-inflicted gunshot wound in his Hermitage, Tennessee, apartment on February 19, 1992.

Yamata, Tor (Toyoki Uyeda; d. December 11, 1960) held the Southern Junior Heavyweight Title several times in 1957. He held the Mid-America Title in February of 1959. He teamed with Mr. Moto to hold the World Tag Team Title in Tennessee several times in 1960.

Yamazaki, Itsuki is a leading Japanese female wrestler. She teamed with Noriyo Tateno as the Jumping Bomb Angels. They held the All-Japan WWWA Women's Tag Team Title in 1986. They won the WWF Women's Tag Team belts from Leilani Kai and Judy Martin in January of 1988. They lost the belts to Kai and Martin in a rematch in June of 1988.

Yamazaki, Kazuo (b. August 15, 1962; Tokyo, Japan; 5'10", 182 lbs.) began wrestling in 1982. He remained a leading Japanese mat star throughout the next decade.

Yandrisovitz, Brian *see* Knobs, Brian

Yankem, Dr. Isaac *see* Jacobs, Glen

Yasuda, Tadao (b. 1964) was a sumo wrestler known as Takanofuji in the early 1990s. He began wrestling professionally with New Japan in 1994.

Yatsu, Tola *see* Yatsu, Tola

Yatsu, Yoshiaki (b. July 19, 1956; Tokyo, Japan; 5'11", 235 lbs.) began wrestling in Japan in December of 1980. Wrestling as Tola Yatsu he held the World Class TV Title in Texas in February of 1983. He entered All-Japan in 1984, where he remained until the early 1990s. He returned to New Japan in 1994.

Yellow Dog *see* Pillman, Brian

Yellow Scorpion *see* Lawson, Buck

Yircov, Crusher *see* Bigelow, Bam Bam

Yokouchi, Shinichi "Chatti" (d. December 15, 1982) teamed with Mr. Ito to hold the NWA Georgia Tag Team Title in July of 1969. He teamed with Yasu Fuji to hold the Canadian Tag Team Title in October of 1970. He again teamed with Yasu Fuji to hold the NWA Central States Tag Team Title in February of 1972. He and Yasu Fuji also held the Calgary Stampede International Tag Team Title several times in 1973.

Yokozuna (Rodney Anoia; b. October 2, 1966; Samoa; 6'4", 340 lbs.) is a San Francisco native and the son of Sika. He began wrestling in 1985 as Kokina in the AWA. He teamed with Fatu and the Samoan Savage to hold the UWA Three-Man Title in Mexico in April of 1991. He joined the WWF in October of 1992 and was managed by Mr. Fuji. He won the 1993 Royal Rumble and defeated Bret Hart for the WWF Title in Las Vegas on April 4, 1993. He subsequently lost the belt to Hulk Hogan in a match immediately following his victory over Hart. Yokozuna pinned Hogan for the WWF Title at the King of the Ring Tournament in Dayton, Ohio, on June 13, 1993. He lost the championship to Bret Hart at Wrestlemania X on March 20, 1994. He teamed with Owen Hart to capture the WWF Tag Team Title from the Smoking Guns on April 2, 1995. They lost the title in a rematch against the Smoking Guns on September 25, 1995. Yokozuna later broke with Hart and engaged in a feud with Big Van Vader.

York, Alexandra (Terri Boatright) managed the York Foundation, consisting of Terry Taylor, Tommy Rich and Rick Morton, in the WCW in the early 1990s. She married Dustin Rhodes on July 25, 1993. She entered the WWF in January of 1996, accompanying Rhodes, as Goldust, to the ring as his director, Marlena.

York, Jay (d. 1995), wrestling as the Alaskan, teamed with Tarzan Tyler to hold the Texas World Tag Team Title in August of 1962. He also teamed with his brother Mike in the early 1960s. He teamed with Tony Borne to capture the NWA Pacific Northwest Tag Team Title in January of 1966. Wrestling as the Masked Terror, he teamed with Cyclon Negro to briefly hold the AWA Tag Team Title in December of 1963.

York, Mike, who was known as the Original Alaskan, teamed with his brother Jay in the early 1960s. He teamed with Frank Monte as the Alaskans to hold the NWA Florida Title in December of 1971. He teamed with Brute Bernard to hold the NWA Atlantic Coast Tag Title in 1973.

York Foundation, The *see* Rich, Tommy; Morton, Rick & Taylor, Terry

Yoshi Wan *see* Champion, Chris

Yoshida, Mitsuo *see* Chosyu, Riki

Young, Gary (Houston, Texas; 6', 240 lbs.) began wrestling in 1977. He teamed with Gino Hernandez to hold the World Class American Tag Team Title in October of 1980. Young wrestled in the Memphis area in the late 1980s. He teamed with Maxx Payne to hold the CWA Tag Team Title several times in early 1988. He also held the CWA tag belts with Don Bass in June of 1988 and with Cactus Jack in October of 1988. He held the World Class Texas Title several times in 1989, sometimes wrestling as Super Zodiac. He teamed with Steve Dane as the Goodfellows to hold the Global World Tag Team Title in May of 1992. He was managed by Skandor Akbar until becoming a fan favorite in Global in the early 1990s.

Young, Jerome *see* New Jack

Young, Mae (b. 1922; Sands Springs, Oklahoma; 5'6", 145 lbs.) began wrestling in the early 1940s. She was one of the toughest female grapplers for the next several decades.

Young, Skip (6'1", 230 lbs.) began wrestling in 1976. Known as Sweet Brown Sugar, he captured the NWA Southern Title in Florida in October of 1979. He captured the title again in February of 1981 and in July of 1982. He teamed with Tony Atlas to hold the World Class Texas Tag Team Title for several months from June of 1987. He has also wrestled in the USWA, UWF and Global.

Young Pistols, The *see* Smothers, Tracy & Armstrong, Steve

Youngblood, Chris (Chris Romero; b. 1967; 6', 235 lbs.) is the son of Ricky Romero. He began wrestling in 1986. He and his older brother, Mark Youngblood, formed the Renegade Warriors in the NWA in 1986. They held the WWC Tag Team Title in Puerto Rico several times in 1987 and 1988. He subsequently wrestled as Brave Sky with his brother in the Renegade Warriors with Global. He began wrestling with All-Japan in 1992.

Youngblood, Jay (Steve Romero; d. September 3, 1985) was the son of Ricky Romero and the brother of Mark and Chris Youngblood. He teamed with Rick Steamboat to win the NWA Tag Team Title from Baron Von Raschke and Paul Jones in October of 1979. They lost the belts to Ray Stevens and Greg Valentine in April of 1980, but recaptured them in a rematch on May 10, 1980. He and Steamboat lost the belts to Stevens and Jimmy Snuka in Greensboro, North Carolina, on June 22, 1980. He teamed with Joe Lightfoot to hold the Canadian Tag Team Title in November of 1980. He captured the NWA Pacific Northwest Title for the first of several times in December of 1980. He held the NWA Atlantic Coast Tag Title several times in the early 1980s, teamed with Jake Roberts, Johnny Weaver and Porkchop Cash. Youngblood and Steamboat returned to capture the title from Sergeant Slaughter and Don Kernodle in March of 1983. They exchanged the tag belts with Jack and Jerry Brisco several times in 1983, before giving up the title when Steamboat retired in late December of 1983. Youngblood teamed with his brother, Mark, to capture the U.S. Tag Team Title in Florida several times in early 1985. He suffered a ruptured spleen and several heart attacks before his death in New Zealand on September 3, 1985.

Youngblood, Mark (Mark Romero; b. 1963; 6', 249 lbs.) was the son of Ricky Romero. He began wrestling in 1981. He teamed with Mike George to hold the NWA Central States Tag Team Title in July of 1982. He captured the NWA World Tag Team Title with Wahoo McDaniel in March of 1984. The duo held the belts for several months. He also held the NWA TV Title in March of 1984. Teaming with his older brother, Jay, he captured the U.S. Tag Team Title in Florida several times in early 1985. He held the World Class TV Title in December of 1985. He teamed with his younger brother, Chris, as the Renegade Warriors in the NWA in 1986. They held the WWC Tag Team Title in Puerto Rico several times in 1987 and 1988. He subsequently wrestled as Nikona with his brother in Renegade Warriors in Global. Youngblood entered All-Japan in 1992.

Yousouff the Terrible Turk (Mamhoud Yousuf; b. 1918, d. 19??; Turkey; 6'4", 250 lbs.) was a leading wrestling villain during the 1940s.

Yuki, Blizzard *see* Hasegawa, Sakie

Yukon Eric (Eric Holmbeck; b. 1923, d. January 16, 1965; Fairbanks, Alaska; 6'1", 275 lbs.) was a leading competitor in the 1940s and 1950s. He was considered one of the strongest men in wrestling at the time. He held the AWA Title in Montreal, Canada, in February of 1950. He held the Canadian Open Tag Team Title in Toronto several times in the late 1950s, teaming with Whipper Billy Watson and Dara Singh. Yukon Eric died of a self-inflicted gunshot wound in a Cartersville, Georgia, church parking lot on January 16, 1965.

Yukon Lumberjacks, The *see* Pierre the Lumberjack & Irwin, Scott

Yuma, Cowboy Bob began his wrestling career in the Pacific Northwest in the early 1970s. He soon moved to the Arizona area, where he often teamed with Tito Montez. Yuma engaged in a vicious feud with ring villain Jimmy Kent. Known in the ring for his bulldog headlock and sleeper, he was a two-time holder of the Arizona State Championship. He and Montez held the Western States Tag Team Title for nearly three years in the mid-1970s.

Z-Man *see* Zenk, Tom

Zaharias, Babe (b. 1912; Cripple Creek, Colorado; 5'10", 250 lbs.) began wrestling in the 1930s. Known as the Crying Greeks, he and his brother, Chris, competed as one of the leading tag teams in the 1940s and 1950s.

Zaharias, Chris (b. 1911; Cripple Creek, Colorado; 5'7", 225 lbs.) began wrestling in the 1930s. Known as the Crying Greeks, he and his brother, Babe, competed as one of the leading tag teams in the 1940s and 1950s.

Zaharias, George (Theodore "George" Vetoyanis; b. February 27, 1908, d. May 22, 1984; 300 lbs.) was the son of Greek immigrants who settled in Pueblo, Colorado. He began his career as a professional wrestler in 1932, initially competing in the ring as Ted Victory. The huge grappler, who wore a size 56 suit, soon began competing as ring villain George Zaharias. He was known in the ring as "the Crying Greek." His "brothers," Babe, Chris and Tom, also competed in the ring. George Zaharias met and married champion athlete Mildred "Babe" Didrikson in 1938. Best known as a champion golfer, she was also a track and field medalist at the 1932 Olympics, and excelled in basketball, bowling, swimming, fencing, football and boxing. Zaharias retired from the wrestling arena to manage his wife's career. She died of cancer on September 27, 1956, at the age of 42. Their love story was the subject of a 1975 tele-film, with Alex Karras portraying the ex-wrestler. Zaharias suffered a stroke in 1974 and remained in poor health brought on by diabetes and uremia. He died in a Tampa, Florida, hospital after a long illness on May 22, 1984.

Zaharias, Tom (d. 19??) held the MWA Title in Kansas City for several months from March of 1942. He held the World Title in Colorado in July of 1947.

Zakowski, Rob *see* Van Dam, Rob

Zaman, Bholu *see* Big Bad John

Zambuie Express, The *see* Brown, Bad Leroy & Candy, Ray

Zane, Tony wrestled as Mr. Atlanta to capture the Peach State Wrestling U.S. Title several times in 1991.

Zangiev, Victor began wrestling in 1988. He was a former Russian amateur champion who wrestled primarily in Germany and Japan.

Zapata, Raul held the NWA Texas Junior Heavyweight Title in April of 1955. He teamed with Larry Chene to hold the NWA Texas Tag Team Title in May of 1955.

Zarna, Jack (John N. Zarna; b. 1905, d. August 27, 1992) was born in Youngstown, Ohio. He attended Ohio State University and Wittenberg College, where he wrestled and played football. He trained in wrestling with champion Jim Londos and began competing professionally in 1929. He wrestled throughout the world during the 1930s and early 1940. He retired from the ring to work as an inventory management specialist with the federal government. He died at his retirement home in Clearwater, Florida, on August 27, 1992.

Zavalza, Ray (b. 1916; Mexico; 6', 205 lbs.) was of Mexican-Indian parentage. He was a boxer before becoming a wrestler in the late 1930s. He was known in the ring as the Gentleman Grappler because of his strict adherence to the rules. He remained an active competitor through the 1950s.

Zbyszko, Larry (Larry Whistler; b. December 5; Pittsburgh, Pennsylvania; 5'11", 248 lbs.) began wrestling in 1973 as a protege of Bruno Sammartino. He teamed with Tony Garea to defeat the Yukon Lumberjacks for the WWWF Tag Team Title in November of 1978. They were defeated for the belts by Johnny and Jerry Valiant in March of 1979. Zbyszko turned on Sammartino in 1980 and the two men engaged in a series of vicious battles in the early 1980s. He bought the NWA National Title from Killer Brooks in March of 1983, but was subsequently stripped of the belt. He defeated Mr. Wrestling II for the title in a tournament in June of 1983, holding the title until the following September. He won the AWA Title in a tournament in February of 1989. He lost the belt to Mr. Saito in February of 1990. He reclaimed the belt several months later on March 4, 1990, and remained champion until he left the promotion for the WCW in December of 1990. Zbyszko teamed with Arn Anderson as the Enforcers and won the WCW World Tag Team Title in September of 1991. They were defeated for the belts by Rick Steamboat and Dustin Rhodes on November 19, 1991. Zbyszko captured the WCW TV Title from Lord Steven Regal in May of 1994. He lost the belt back to Regal in a rematch the following month. Zbyszko remained involved in the WCW as a television commentator. He is married to Cathy Gagne, the daughter of Verne Gagne.

Zbyszko, Stanislaus (Stan Cyganiewicz; b. 1879, d. September 22, 1967) attended the University of Vienna, where he studied music, philosophy and law. He made his debut in the United States in 1909, and won nearly a thousand matches before his defeat by Frank Gotch in 1910. He returned to Austria during World War I, and lost his considerable fortune during the war. He was forced to resume his wrestling career in 1918, and returned to the United States to compete. He defeated Ed "Strangler" Lewis for the World Heavyweight Title in May of 1921. He held the belt until losing a rematch with Lewis in March of 1922. He again held the belt briefly following his defeat of Wayne Munn in April of 1925. He was defeated for the title by Joe Stecher the following month. He subsequently retired from the ring. Zbyszko appeared in several films including *Madison Square Garden* (1932) and *Night and the City* (1950) where he co-starred as an aging professional wrestler with Richard Widmark. His brother, Wladek Zbyszko, was also a leading professional wrestler. He died at a St. Joseph, Missouri, hospital on September 22, 1967.

Zbyszko, Wladek (Wladek Cyganiewicz; b. 1893, d. June 10, 1968; 6', 220 lbs.) was born in Krakow, Poland. He received a law degree at the University of Vienna and spoke thirteen languages fluently. He followed in the footsteps of Stanislaus Zbyszko, his older brother, and was a leading professional wrestler in the 1920s and 1930s. Zybyszko served as an interpreter in the Pacific during World War II. He died at his home in Savannah, Missouri, on June 10, 1968.

Ze Gangsta *see* Lister, Tiny

Zebadiah, Uncle *see* Mantel, Dutch

Zebra Kid, The *see* Bollas, George

Zenk, Tom (b. November 30, 1960; Minneapolis, Minnesota; 6'2", 237 lbs.) began wrestling in 1984. He teamed with Scott Doring to hold the NWA Pacific Northwest Tag Team Title in December of 1985. He teamed with Dan Kroffat to hold the Canadian International Tag Team Title in Montreal in August of 1986. He wrestled as the Z-Man in the WCW in the early 1990s. He teamed with Brian Pillman to win a tournament for the WCW U.S. Tag Team Title in February of 1990. They were defeated for the title by the Midnight Express in May of 1990. Zenk captured the TV Title from Arn Anderson in December of 1990. He lost the belt back to Anderson in January of 1991. He teamed with Ricky Steamboat as Dos Hombres in the WCW in 1993. He wrestled with All-Japan the following year.

Zenni, Sheba (b. 1929; Cincinnati, Ohio; 5'7", 142 lbs.) began wrestling in the early 1950s. She had an exotic Arabic ring persona and remained a popular mat star during the 1950s.

Zeus *see* Lister, Tiny

Zhukov, Boris (Jim Darrell; Leningrad, Russia; 6'2", 254 lbs.) began wrestling in 1982. He wrestled as Private Jim Nelson to hold the NWA Atlantic Coast Tag Title with Don Kernodle several times in 1982. He held the NWA TV Title in

Toronto several times in 1982 and 1983. He subsequently joined the Mid-South promotion as Boris Zhukov. He won the AWA Tag Team Title with Soldat Ustinov in May of 1987. Zhukov vacated the title when he left the promotion to join the WWF in October of 1987. He teamed with Nikolai Volkoff in the late 1980s.

Zimbleman, Slim (Lodi, California; 278 lbs.) was a leading wrestling in the 1940s and 1950s.

Zimm, The Great *see* Von Erich, Waldo

Zip *see* Prichard, Tom

Zodiac, The *see* Beefcake, Brutus

Zodiac, The *see* Orton, Bob, Sr.

Zoko, Doc *see* Godoy, Pedro

Zolotoff, Nikita *see* Vachon, Paul

Zorro, Tarzan *see* Mortier, Hans

Zulu, The Magnificent *see* Magnificent Zulu, The

Zuma, The Amazing teamed with Ray Gunkel to hold the NWA Texas Tag Team Title in October of 1956. He again held the Texas tag belts in 1959, teaming with Johnny Walker.

Zumhofe, Buck (b. March 1955; 5'11", 222 lbs.) was born in Arlington, Minnesota. He wrestled as an amateur from high school and began wrestling professionally in 1976 in Minnesota. He was the original Rock 'n' Roll wrestler, and held the AWA Light Heavyweight belt from June of 1983 until his defeat by Steve Regal in March of 1984. He teamed with Iceman Parsons as Rock 'n' Soul to hold the World Class American Tag Team Title several times in 1984, often competing against Scott and Bill Irwin. He reclaimed the AWA Light Heavyweight Title in November of 1985. He was sent to prison on drug charges the following year. After his release he again won the AWA title in a tournament in August of 1990 and remained champion until the AWA closed the following year.

Zygowski, Eugene Stanley *see* Stanlee, Gene

Index